CompTIA Network+ Certification Guide (Exam N10-009)

Unleash your full potential as a network administrator

2nd Edition

Eithne Hogan

bpb

www.bpbonline.com

Second Revised and Updated Edition 2025

First Edition 2023

Copyright © BPB Publications, India

ISBN: 978-93-65892-673

LIMITS OF LIABILITY AND DISCLAIMER OF WARRANTY

To View Complete
BPB Publications Catalogue
Scan the QR Code:

www.bpbonline.com

Dedicated to

My beloved children:
Samantha, Patrick, Lesleyanne, Kathryn, Chelsea *and* **Dylan**
and
The best and most beautiful grandchildren:
Devin, Alannah, Frankie, Kara, Tyler *and* **Joshua**

About the Author

With just under 30 years of experience in education, **Eithne Hogan** has held a wide variety of roles. She currently coordinates the Datacenter Academy Program at her college, a program supported by Microsoft. Thanks to this partnership, the college boasts a fully functional three-rack mini datacenter lab, established in November 2019, to teach aspiring technicians about datacenter technologies, IT support, cybersecurity, network and server administration.

Eithne not only coordinates and instructs this program but also oversees the traineeship. Her college is an active member of the Microsoft Global Datacenter Academy Community, a community that is evolving and expanding across the globe. Eithne is a spokesperson and representative leader for her academy.

In addition to her primary role, Eithne is a part-time lecturer at other national higher education professional academies, where she teaches several CompTIA certification courses to include the A+, Network+, and Server+. She also manages the college's local Cisco Network Academy, holding certificates of recognition for Instructor Excellence and thirteen years of active service and participation. The CompTIA Academy partnership, which Eithne oversees, has been operational at the college for 25 years.

Eithne has developed nationally recognized curricula in IT, covering topics such as network infrastructure, network topologies, network administration, and switching, routing, and wireless technologies. As the digital lead for the community college, she collaborates with her colleagues to drive the transformation to digital teaching and learning practices.

About the Reviewer

Simone Bertulli is a cybersecurity professional, currently holding a senior position at the Cyber Defense Center of a leading Italian company.

He has over 15 years of experience in the IT field, with deep expertise in enterprise-class infrastructure technologies, holding certifications such as CompTIA Network+, CompTIA Security+, CompTIA Cloud+, CompTIA Storage+, CompTIA Linux+, and LPIC-3 Virtualization and High Availability.

A passionate advocate of open-source, he actively contributes to the community by writing for the Linux Professional Institute blog and delivering tech talks on FOSS-related topics, both from a technical perspective and in the field of professional training. Simone is also an official Linux Professional Institute Instructor, further strengthening his commitment to fostering open knowledge and supporting IT professionals in their career development.

Acknowledgement

I want to extend my heartfelt thanks to my family and friends for their unwavering support and encouragement throughout the writing of this book. A special mention goes to my children and grandchildren, who bring immense meaning to everything I do.

My gratitude also goes to BPB Publications for their invaluable guidance and expertise. The journey of reviewing and revising this book was long and challenging, but the collaboration with reviewers, technical experts, and editors made it a rewarding experience.

I am immensely grateful to my colleagues and the IT professionals I've had the privilege to work with over the years. Your collective wisdom, experiences, and rigorous training have been instrumental in guiding me through the rewards and challenges of this learning journey. A special mention goes to Janet Allen and Derek Haughton; your unparalleled skills and expertise in technology have been invaluable to me. Thank you.

Lastly, I want to thank all the readers who have shown interest in my book. Your support has been crucial in bringing this project to life. I hope you find the contents enriching and enjoy the learning journey as much as I have. Happy reading!

Preface

Network design and implementation are driven by organizational needs and changes. Network administrators possess a broad range of knowledge, including network planning and design, network infrastructure, network operations, security evaluation, and the ability to assess network capacity and performance. In a world where high availability and continuity of service are paramount, network administrators are the backbone of a company's assets.

The revamped Network+ exam addresses the evolving landscape of IT networking, focusing on the most sought-after skills to meet contemporary challenges, network optimization, hybrid infrastructures, and more. With Network+, candidates will gain the essential abilities needed to excel in their roles and attract potential employers. Network+ serves as the foundation for a rewarding career, making it the preferred choice for foundational networking skills across various job roles in the industry.

This book is designed to provide a comprehensive guide to the role and duties of a network administrator. While it prepares the reader for the CompTIA Network+ exam, it goes beyond that. This guide thoroughly equips readers with specific networking skills, setting them on a path toward a valuable career in technical support and IT operations. Readers will acquire the skills to install, configure, maintain, and monitor network hardware and software, and effectively use troubleshooting tools. The content also emphasizes the importance of security in network operations. This book is intended for anyone interested in pursuing a rewarding career in network administration. I hope you find it informative and helpful.

Second edition updates: The second edition includes new content reflecting changes in the exam, such as evolving use cases for modern networks, important factors of physical installations, and additional details on implementing IPv4 and IPv6 network services.

Chapter 1: OSI Model - The chapter emphasizes the importance of standards in the IT industry. It explores the origins and development of the OSI model, detailing how its seven layers decompose the essential concepts of networking functions and processes. Additionally, the chapter provides an overview and explanation of each individual layer, describing their roles in data transmission. It thoroughly explains the processes of encapsulation and decapsulation as data moves across networks. Through detailed descriptions and illustrations, the chapter guides the reader through the OSI model layers, enhancing their understanding of network fundamentals.

Chapter 2: Network Topologies - The chapter provides a comprehensive overview of network topologies, complete with illustrations for each type. It distinguishes between physical and logical topologies, explaining their differences. Additionally, the chapter delves into the functioning of virtual networks and highlights the crucial role of hypervisors. It emphasizes the importance of understanding virtualization in the modern networking landscape.

Furthermore, the chapter covers various network types, including PAN, LAN, CAN, MAN, WLAN, and WAN. This edition provides additional details on **software-defined networks (SDN)** and **software-defined wide area networks (SD-WAN)**, noting that these networks are application-aware, feature zero-touch provisioning, are transport agnostic, and have central policy management.

Chapter 3: Cables and Connectors - The chapter discusses the cables and connectors utilized in Ethernet, coax, and fiber networks. It illustrates the appropriate cable types and corresponding connectors for various network applications, specifying each cable's intended use. Readers learn the distinctions between wired and wireless networks and receive step-by-step guidance on constructing straight-through or crossover cables according to proper wiring standards. Additionally, the chapter covers best practices for effective cable management.

Chapter 4: IP Addressing and Subnetting - The chapter permits the reader to learn the fundamental concepts of IP addressing. The chapter covers IPv4 and IPv6 addressing structures, the transition to IPv6 and explains how the transition is taking place. Furthermore, the reader is shown how to subnet and apply best practices in creating network subnets. The chapter includes hands-on subnetting practice. IP addressing makes devices accessible for communication. As such, the chapter includes practical examples based on real scenarios. This chapter helps the reader to solve real addressing problems and provides an easy mechanism to identify addressing schemes in networks. The chapter and second edition extends understanding on how to implement IPv4 and IPv6 network services.

Chapter 5: Ports and Protocols - The chapter educates readers on the protocols within the TCP/IP suite. As the only routable protocol, TCP/IP is essential for data transmission across all network types, both locally and globally, wherever packets need to be sent and received. The chapter details port numbers and explains their relevance to understanding functionality and security practices. It also provides guidance on which protocols might be blocked by firewalls unless specifically required.

Chapter 6: Implementing and Troubleshooting Network Services - The chapter shows core concepts of networking services. The reader is walked through a typical installation of a role-based feature in Windows Server 2019. The reader is shown how to install and configure DHCP and DNS on a server operating system. This chapter also offers a detailed description of NTP as an important network service.

Chapter 7: Data Center Technologies - The chapter provides detailed explanations and numerous illustrations on the operation of datacenter technologies. It focuses on datacenter architecture, storage solutions, and RAID. Practical examples of RAID implementations for various scenarios are covered, demonstrating the best practices for specific use cases.

Chapter 8: Cloud Concepts - The chapter is aimed to give the reader more familiarity with cloud computing, deployment models and service models. This chapter covers real-world examples of cloud provision and allows the reader to comprehend the appropriate services suited to the needs of an organization. In essence, the chapter informs the reader and permits them to identify and make good choices, when discussing or selecting online services with colleagues or other stakeholders.

Chapter 9: Managing Network Devices - The chapter is a detailed description of network devices and how they are mapped to the layers of the OSI model. The chapter is intended to demonstrate the functionality and purpose of the device in order to enable the reader to identify which device is necessary for a specific job role on the network. Furthermore, the chapter describes how the device operates and shows the reader what to watch out for to ensure the device is optimally suited for its role. The chapter emphasizes how to ensure network performance, integrity and resilience to maintain the expected service levels and maximize bandwidth.

Chapter 10: Managing Switching Protocols - The chapter takes a deeper dive into switching technologies and protocols such as STP and ARP. The chapter focuses on how switches make decisions, and how they learn and build their MAC table. The chapter permits the reader to comprehend switching functionality in order to evaluate, diagnose and troubleshoot switches on a network. Additionally, the chapter introduces the concept of VLANs, explains switch segmentation and shows the reader how to make decisions about the presence of VLANs in their companies. The chapter also shows the reader how and when to implement port security.

Chapter 11: Managing Routing Protocols - The chapter takes a deeper dive into routing technologies and protocols such as OSPF, EIGRP, and BGP. The chapter focuses on how routers make decisions, and how they learn and build their routing table. The chapter permits the reader to comprehend routing functionality in order to evaluate, diagnose and troubleshoot routers on a network. Additionally, the chapter introduces the concept of subnets, explains router segmentation and shows the reader how to make decisions about the presence of subnets in their companies. The chapter also shows the reader how and when to implement static or dynamic routing and how to competently manage network bandwidth.

Chapter 12: Installing and Configuring Wireless Technologies - The chapter allows the reader to differentiate between IEEE 802.11 standards. The chapter provides detail on each of these standards, the frequency bands in use and configuration options per standard. Furthermore, the chapter also walks the reader through the steps to configure a SOHO router, adhering to best practices and optimum security measures.

Chapter 13: Managing and Monitoring a Network - The chapter outlines Windows integrated tools and free open source software, used to manage and monitor networks. The chapter's primary intention is to permit the reader to apply this knowledge in a practical way and show them how to use integrated or third-party tools to troubleshoot a system. The chapter offers examples of ways to assess network performance and provides mechanisms to narrow down relevant issues that negatively impact network operation.

Chapter 14: Policies and Procedures in Practice - The chapter emphasizes the practicalities of running a business or organization, focusing on required documentation and the negotiation needed for effective corporate network management. It highlights the importance of planning, designing, and reviewing policies and procedures as part of the organization's change management ethos. Additionally, it provides recommendations for being positive collaborators in IT and business operations.

The chapter also covers physical installations with guidance on the installation and maintenance of network equipment. It explains how to consider optimal locations (e.g., IDF, MDF), select the appropriate rack size, manage port-side exhaust/intake for cooling, organize cabling with patch and fiber distribution panels, ensure lockable components for security, and address power needs using UPS, PDU, power load, and voltage requirements. Furthermore, it details accounting for environmental factors such as temperature and humidity.

Chapter 15: Resilience, Fault Tolerance, and Recovery - The chapter offers a detailed description of backup and failover strategies and demonstrates where these strategies fit in with high availability planning and with a Disaster Recovery Plan. Furthermore, the chapter shows the reader how to implement RAID and explains which failover strategy suits a given scenario. This chapter covers practical examples of working with recovery strategies.

Chapter 16: Security Concepts - The chapter introduces the reader to common security concepts. The chapter lays the foundations for further topics covered in the upcoming chapters. Additionally, the chapter shows the user ways to safeguard users on a network and how to mitigate internal and external threats, thereby protecting the network users' privacy and data.

Chapter 17: Cybersecurity Attacks - The chapter extends on the concepts of the previous chapter and offers a detailed description of vulnerabilities, threats and attacks. This chapter shows the reader how to mitigate threats and demonstrates strategies for eliminating vulnerabilities and loopholes on the network. The chapter provides practical examples of real-world technology-based attacks and social engineering attacks and offers advice on how to counter these risks and threats.

Chapter 18: Network Hardening Techniques - The chapter covers practical techniques related to securing and hardening a network. Furthermore, the chapter also allows the reader learn and apply the strategies to manage workstations, monitor network devices, secure hardware and software, and educate users to ensure best practices while accessing the organization's network resources. The chapter covers network management policies and protocols such as password complexity, multi-factor authentication, SMNP and Syslog among others.

Chapter 19: Remote Management - The chapter shows core concepts of remote management procedures and provides practical examples and remote management connectivity options to the reader. The chapter includes practical examples and case use scenarios for diverse VPN configurations. The chapter covers remote desktop connectivity options and explains to the reader the context of their use, emphasising security implications. Additionally, this chapter provides the reader with a step-by-step guide to configuring an RDP gateway on a Windows server.

Chapter 20: Implementing Physical Security - The chapter focuses on the objectives of physical security controls and shows the reader effective security methods to be used, and how to implement these methods on networks. Furthermore, the chapter also instils in the reader the relevance of prevention measures and demonstrates proactive actions used by network administrators to optimize security procedures and protocols running on the network. These procedures includes perimeter security of the building itself and includes the concept of security zones.

Chapter 21: Network Troubleshooting - The chapter gives special attention to the network troubleshooting model. The chapter goes through the steps of the troubleshooting model and presents the reader with tips and tools for handing each step with proficiency. This chapter encourages the reader to follow this model and methodology and consequently become equipped with the cognitive awareness required for a job role in administering networks.

Chapter 22: Troubleshooting Cable Connectivity - The chapter covers the skills and competences required to troubleshoot cable connectivity. The chapter presents bounded media as the fundamental backbone of wired networks and shows the reader how to visually inspect cables and LEDs in Ethernet and fiber networks. Furthermore, the chapter shows the reader how to use hardware tools to diagnose and troubleshoot defective or incorrectly chosen cabling.

Chapter 23: Network Utilities - The chapter covers network software tools as used in command line interface and Cisco's IOS. The chapter offers real-world examples of problems that occur on networks where these tools are invaluable. Furthermore, the reader is shown how to use a wide variety of tools and is given practical case uses for each tool presented. The chapter demonstrates a range of third-party software tools and CLI commands, and explains how to use each tool and identify the correct purpose of its use.

Chapter 24: Troubleshooting Wireless Networks - The chapter presents a detailed overview of the infrastructure of wireless networks. Additionally, the chapter focuses on wireless deployments, standards and limitations, common issues and solutions and other common checks and tests. The chapter encourages the reader to follow troubleshooting methods to work through and resolve the issues that arise in wireless networks and at all times incorporate the learning of network models, such as the OSI model and the network troubleshooting model.

Chapter 25 Troubleshooting General Networking Issues - The chapter covers the common considerations applicable to general networking issues. The chapter provides the reader with comprehensive detail on common issues and shows the reader how to incorporate knowledge of the OSI model, when resolving network issues. Furthermore, the chapter also maps network problems to the relevant layer of the OSI model and offers the reader ways to manage problem-solving. This chapter brings the learning full cycle and permits the reader to apply the OSI model in a practical way, using it as a tool and guide in network repair.

Chapter 26: Network+ Practice Exams - The chapter provides the reader with practice multiple choice questions. The questions are aligned with the domains of the Network+, as outlined in CompTIA's official exam objectives.

Coloured Images

Please follow the link to download the
Coloured Images of the book:

https://rebrand.ly/kviekfn

We have code bundles from our rich catalogue of books and videos available at **https://github.com/bpbpublications**. Check them out!

Errata

We take immense pride in our work at BPB Publications and follow best practices to ensure the accuracy of our content to provide with an indulging reading experience to our subscribers. Our readers are our mirrors, and we use their inputs to reflect and improve upon human errors, if any, that may have occurred during the publishing processes involved. To let us maintain the quality and help us reach out to any readers who might be having difficulties due to any unforeseen errors, please write to us at :

errata@bpbonline.com

Your support, suggestions and feedbacks are highly appreciated by the BPB Publications' Family.

Did you know that BPB offers eBook versions of every book published, with PDF and ePub files available? You can upgrade to the eBook version at www.bpbonline. com and as a print book customer, you are entitled to a discount on the eBook copy. Get in touch with us at :

business@bpbonline.com for more details.

At **www.bpbonline.com**, you can also read a collection of free technical articles, sign up for a range of free newsletters, and receive exclusive discounts and offers on BPB books and eBooks.

Piracy

If you come across any illegal copies of our works in any form on the internet, we would be grateful if you would provide us with the location address or website name. Please contact us at **business@bpbonline.com** with a link to the material.

If you are interested in becoming an author

If there is a topic that you have expertise in, and you are interested in either writing or contributing to a book, please visit **www.bpbonline.com**. We have worked with thousands of developers and tech professionals, just like you, to help them share their insights with the global tech community. You can make a general application, apply for a specific hot topic that we are recruiting an author for, or submit your own idea.

Reviews

Please leave a review. Once you have read and used this book, why not leave a review on the site that you purchased it from? Potential readers can then see and use your unbiased opinion to make purchase decisions. We at BPB can understand what you think about our products, and our authors can see your feedback on their book. Thank you!

For more information about BPB, please visit **www.bpbonline.com**.

Join our book's Discord space

Join the book's Discord Workspace for Latest updates, Offers, Tech happenings around the world, New Release and Sessions with the Authors:

https://discord.bpbonline.com

Table of Contents

CHAPTER 1
OSI Model

Introduction

This chapter outlines the need for standards in the IT industry. The chapter describes the origins and evolution of the OSI model and how the seven layers of the OSI model break down the core concepts of networking functions and processes. Furthermore, the chapter also gives the reader an overview and explanation of each discrete layer and describes how the layer operates in data transmission. It explains in detail how encapsulation and decapsulation work as data traverses networks. The descriptions and illustrations walk the reader through the layers of the model and build their understanding of network fundamentals.

Structure

This chapter will cover the following topics:

- Need for standards
- Evolution of the OSI model
- Seven layers of the OSI model
- Data encapsulation and decapsulation

Objectives

After reading this chapter, you will be able to explain concepts related to the **Open Systems Interconnection** (**OSI**) reference model. You will also be able to understand protocol architectures and appreciate the need for standards and protocols, breaking down the overall functionality of data transmission into its constituent parts.

Need for standards

When new systems of communication emerge and evolve, the way they grow and develop is not necessarily evenly distributed. This occurs especially in the case of a global system, where changes are not limited to local or even regional factors. The way global systems spread, and scale is not geographically, logistically, or uniformly measured over time. Technology and networking are not immune to this *disruptive* but initially *fragmented* means of growth. When we go back to the inception, evolution, and proliferation of networks and observe how these networks and networking technologies have expanded throughout the world, especially from the early 80s, the need for organizational standards and guidelines is apparent. When you have technology as a diverse, globally distributed phenomenon, it is even more apparent that there must be guiding principles to keep everything intact, orderly, flowing smoothly, and operating in a somewhat cohesive, reliable fashion. Three words will stand you through the test of time in expressing the critical nature of having standards in place to fasten the growth and expansion of networking. These words are interoperability, compatibility, and scalability. Unless one considers all of these three areas and what they signify in physical or logical internetworking operations, what one manufactures, designs, innovates, or implements may not work in the landscape of a global operation or, indeed, within the network infrastructure itself. In real-world operations, organizing principles and standards are a must. When discussing networking, the OSI model (and other models such as TCP/IP) could be identified as the universal language for exchanging and discussing ideas about networking functionality and computer network operation and design.

Standards versus protocols

When one considers what is meant by standards, we usually qualify the word with *low, poor, high,* or *excellent* as a descriptor. In essence, standards are sought as a level of quality, achievement, and so on that is considered acceptable or desirable. In the narrative of networking, this is what occurred when multiple organizations were brought together to put shape and order to networks as they were expanding in the early decades of growth. Participants and experts hailed from many disciplines. Without proper growth management, this expansion of networking could have been an outright chaotic catastrophe. The gathering of minds and expertise met the challenges and problems posed. Regarding standards, one could ask, is there a difference between standards and protocols when discussing networking fundamentals? If there is, why is it good to mentally sharpen this distinction? As we move through the chapters, you will see why fine-tuning your definitions and spotting differences optimizes your understanding of networking concepts and practices.

Organizational standards mainly apply to people: what they create, manufacture, design, engineer, and build. Bodies that control these standards essentially seek uniformity in terms of quality in processes, methods, high quality, efficiency, and workability in tactical policies and procedures. But it would not be amiss to say that standards and the use of standards indicate or relate to the production and labor of people. Protocols, when one pursues networking, relate specifically to data. A network protocol is a set of rules for formatting and processing data. And there we have the difference. It is true to say that protocols are made and implemented by people, but when one speaks of protocols, one is directly considering what the function of the protocol is, the way the data is formatted or presented, why a given rule is required for data transmission, the impact of the protocol on data, and its role in networking as a practical thing. In short, when we think of standards, we associate organizational standards with people, but when we think about protocols, we associate protocols with data. As networking evolved over the decades, organizational standards helped to make worldwide networking a viable venture. Protocols make networking functions possible.

Evolution of the OSI model

The OSI model was developed in the 1970s by the **International Organization for Standardization (ISO)** and adopted as an international standard in 1984.

It was originally developed as a universal standard for creating networks. It provides us with a great teaching tool to understand networking fundamentals. The ISO model is a conceptual framework akin to a blueprint an architect may be given on a house or larger structure. It is a reference guide for all kinds of specialisms in networking practice. The OSI model is used to describe the functions of a networking system. When referred to as a guide, it assists us in understanding the flow of data as it travels across the network and between networks and explains what happens to the data along the way. The model is broken down into seven layers. Each layer handles the functions and tasks in hardware and software to promote error-free data transmission. Just as an architect who follows a blueprint aims to map out a structure accurately, professionals like network engineers, electricians, hardware manufacturers, and software developers strive for success by adhering to the OSI model's guidelines and rules. However, though absolute success is not guaranteed, successes are increased with careful adherence to these networking standards. Think of it like a *big-picture puzzle* or *jigsaw*. Although one piece is independent in its own right, it still holds integrity to the overall design and to the overall functionality in practice and in the interdependencies of the layers. The OSI model holds the pieces of the picture of networking functionality together. It does so by synthesizing and breaking down the overall picture and practice into seven layers that divide and distinguish the parts from the whole. If you ask yourself what a network needs to do to be fully operational, the OSI model will assist you with an answer.

This book focuses on explaining the OSI model, and describing how it is structured and used in networking. The book's intention is not to argue the legitimacy or relevance of the OSI model in modern networking. However, understanding the theory behind the OSI model offers several potential benefits for technicians and administrators. By exploring these theories and models, we can better grasp their practical applications and abstractions. Viewing these concepts from a problem-solving, solutions-focused perspective allows us to address questions like *if it works—then how? and apply what we learn to our daily tasks*. This approach enhances our ability to troubleshoot, design, and optimize network systems effectively. Consequently, our purpose in this chapter is to view the seven layers as IT practitioners and focus on the *actions* indicative of each layer.

We will focus on the following questions regarding the OSI model in this section:

- What is happening on this layer?
- How does it work?
- Moreover, how would you apply this understanding in practice in your day-to-day duties?
- Could knowing something about this specific area, assist you in your job role, perhaps as a network trouble-shooter or network administrator?

In summary, the OSI model presents us with a marvelous means of visualizing networking interactions and getting our teeth into the mechanics of what the model embraces.

The OSI model has seven layers, from layers 1–7: the physical layer, the data link layer, the network layer, the transport layer, the session layer, the presentation layer, and the application layer.

Note: Mnemonics are used to remember the seven layers. From layers 1–7, it is Please Do Not Tell Secret Passwords Anytime; from layers 7–1, it is All People Seem To Need Data Processing.

The model is usually presented in stack formation because this graphical representation demonstrates the concepts of data flow and protocols best as we *move up and down* through the stack.

Figure 1.1 outlines the seven layers and shows the protocol data units associated with each layer:

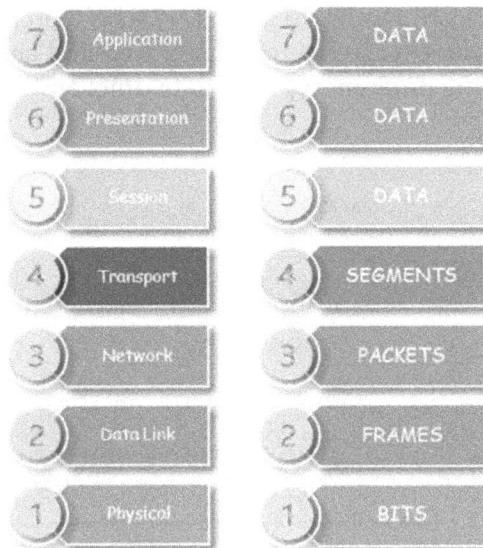

Figure 1.1: *OSI model layers*

In *Figure 1.2*, the primary functions of each layer are outlined. Note the focus is not on the protocols or mechanisms that implement the functions, just the functions themselves:

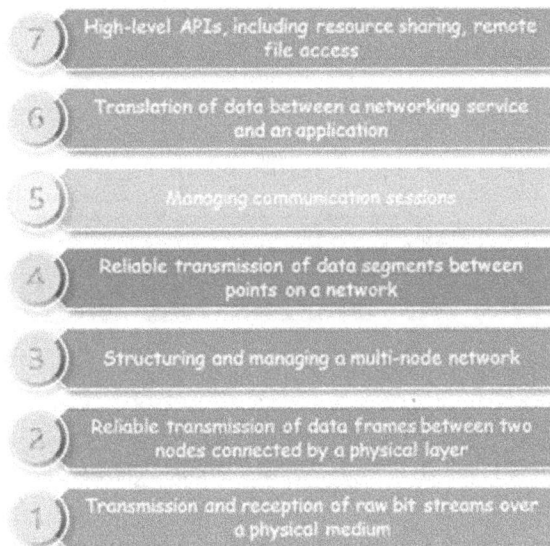

Figure 1.2: *The functionality at each layer*

Protocol data units

A protocol data unit is an OSI term that refers to a group of information added or removed by a layer of the OSI model. **Protocol data units** (PDU) is a significant term related to the initial four layers of the OSI model. In layer 1, PDU is a bit. In layer 2, it is a frame. In layer 3, it is a packet. In layer 4, it is a segment. In layer 5 and above, PDU is referred to as data. *Figure 1.3* illustrates the different types of data units and how they are structured in communications technology:

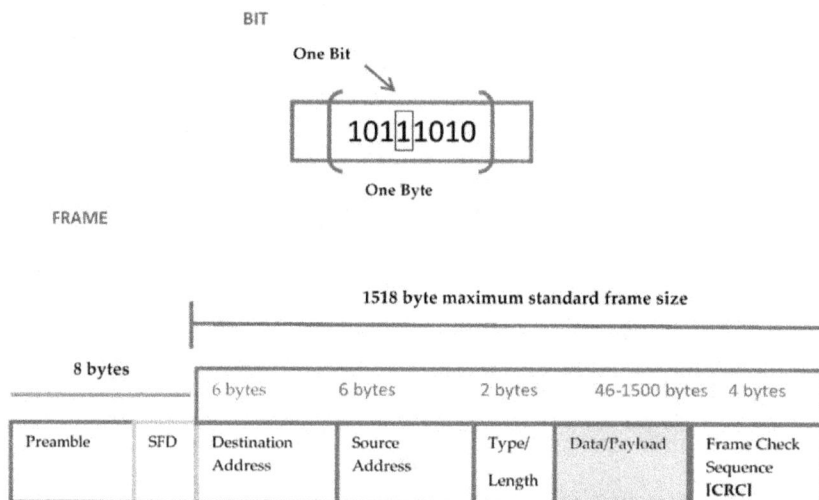

BIT

One Bit

101**1**1010

One Byte

FRAME

1518 byte maximum standard frame size

8 bytes

		6 bytes	6 bytes	2 bytes	46-1500 bytes	4 bytes
Preamble	SFD	Destination Address	Source Address	Type/ Length	Data/Payload	Frame Check Sequence [CRC]

An IEEE 802.3 Ethernet Frame

Composition 6 Segments

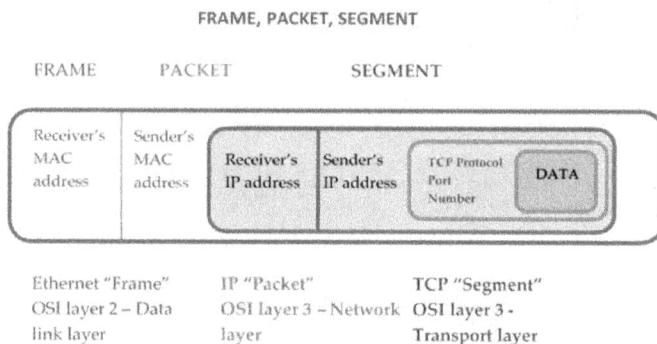

FRAME, PACKET, SEGMENT

FRAME   PACKET   SEGMENT

Receiver's MAC address	Sender's MAC address	Receiver's IP address	Sender's IP address	TCP Protocol Port Number	DATA

Ethernet "Frame"   IP "Packet"   TCP "Segment"
OSI layer 2 – Data   OSI layer 3 – Network   OSI layer 3 -
link layer   layer   Transport layer

Figure 1.3: Bit, frame, packet, and segment

Bit

A bit, short for binary digit, is defined as the most basic unit of data in telecommunications and computing. Each bit is represented by either a 1 or a 0 and this can be executed in various systems through a two-state device. A computer not only initiates multiple instructions that can manipulate and test bits but also performs these instructions and stores accumulated data in eight-bit parcels called **bytes**.

Table 1.1 shows the conversion from decimal to binary:

Decimal	Binary
0	000
1	001
2	010
3	011
4	100
5	101
6	110
7	111

Table 1.1: *Decimal versus binary*

Note: As a reminder, to quickly discover how many different values you can store in a binary number of a given length, you can use the number of bits as an exponent of two (that is, the power of two).

A three-bit binary number can hold 2^3 values thus 2^3 as a 3-bit number can hold eight different values, ranging from when the bits are all off to when the bits are all on. Example: an eight-bit binary number can hold 2^8 values. Since, 2^8 is 256, an 8-bit number can have any of 256 different values, which is why a byte, which is eight bits, can have 256 different values. Consequently, 2^9 is 512, 2^10 is 1,024, 2^11 is 2048, and so on. Notice when as we add an extra bit to the length, the answer doubles.

With the bit, the concept of positional value is also introduced, meaning that its position determines the numerical weight in the binary representation of data. This concept is essential for understanding base-2 numerical systems and for data processing in computing. For example, in the binary number 1101:

- The first bit (from right to left) has the value of $1 \times 2^0 = 1$
- The second bit has the value of $0 \times 2^1 = 0$
- The third bit has the value of $1 \times 2^2 = 4$
- The fourth bit has value of $1 \times 2^3 = 8$

Frame

In networking, a frame is a logical unit of data. Its function is to provide a structure for the transmission of data between two adjacent layers. It encapsulates data from the upper layers (layer 3 and above) and prepares it for transmission over the physical layer (layer 1). During the process of framing, extra bytes are added into a packet to give more information about how the data being transmitted is to be decoded and interpreted. A frame is the PDU at the data link layer of the OSI model.

Packet

In TCP/IP networks, a packet is the basic unit of communication in data transmission over IP networks. A packet is a smaller segment of a larger message. Packets are given a sequence number to identify which part of the message the packet is composed of, for example, packet 2/12. Data packets can traverse networks from a source to a destination over a given pathway, but the function of sequencing means that packets are able to travel across various routes to be recombined at the destination network. This division of data allows networks to use different bandwidths and multiple routes to optimize performance and timely delivery of data. Remember, a PDU is a generic term that can refer to data units at various layers of the OSI model. A packet is the PDU at the network layer of the OSI model.

Segment

A segment is a broken-down piece or smaller unit of a packet. Its function is to improve the performance of data transmission, by breaking down the packet into smaller transmission units. This process of segmentation takes place when the data packet is greater in size than the maximum transmission unit supported by the network and to improve reliability in data transmission. A segment is the PDU at the transport layer of the OSI model.

Analogy for data transmission

Before we investigate the layers of the OSI model in more detail, we will look at an analogy for the transmission of data. Please remember, no matter how difficult the terminology or concepts seem to be when considering networking, the fundamentals can be *simplified* to a working analogy. *Genius is making complex ideas simple, not making simple ideas complex* states *Albert Einstein*. Each one of us as humans has the ability to be ingenious, every time we use our creative power or natural ability to learn and articulate new things. We may not be *Einstein*, but we hold the capacity to solve many complex problems when we can state the problem in a simpler way.

What is happening in data transmission can be likened to the many ways you can send (or receive) a package, parcel, or even a suite of furniture. Let us take the biggest item as representative of bigger *data* to be transported, the various ways this suite of furniture can be delivered, and the stages of its journey from the warehouse or shop to your home. For this analogy to be extended visually, let us pretend you live on the fourth floor of an apartment block. Let us also factor into the equation, your purchase is not a flat pack product to be then assembled on arrival in the boxes in your home. We are purchasing the fully made-up suite: bulky, big, and apparently complex as a problem to deliver.

The suite is first packed into a truck with other products to be delivered. It needs to be carefully packaged so it does not get soiled, scratched, damaged, or scraped. The data needs to be intact at all times, no matter where it is, how it is maintained or monitored, or who is in control of the data as it *hits the wire* and travels the given roadways to its destination. Responsibility for the items (data) lies with the employees of the delivery firm as direct handlers and those who sold the goods and vouched for the safe arrival of the suite. Data flow needs to be signed off at certain points. Data integrity and safety in transit are validated and verified, and in some cases, depending upon the protocol for doing so, there will be more stringent tracking devices than a fast-track delivery with speed as its main driver.

Data is at the essence of networking and communications technology.

Just like transporting furniture involves stages with specific rules and protocols, data transmission follows similar principles. Trucks have a maximum capacity to ensure quality delivery, and similarly, data must be divided and transmitted in manageable sizes to maintain integrity. The OSI model helps guide this process, ensuring data is packaged and delivered correctly across different layers. By understanding the purpose and format of data at each stage, we can optimize transmission and achieve reliable results. This approach helps us navigate the complexities of networking and apply practical solutions effectively.

Seven layers of the OSI model

As a standard model, the layers in the OSI model are distinguished and differentiated from each other in terms of their services, interfaces, and protocols. This makes the model secure, flexible, and truly generic. As an open system, administration and maintenance tasks become easier than having to handle more complex ill-defined, or unregulated systems. If one only has an all-encompassing single layer to work with, one will need to perceive or visualize boundaries in design and operations, and this abstraction could lead to quite subjective and divergent computations and divisions. Consequently, when one breaks down a complex conceptual problem such as networking, layering, and compartmentalizing services, interfaces and protocols potentially make the problem easier. The subsequent sections take a closer look at the seven layers.

Physical layer

In *Figure 1.2*, we looked at the seven layers of the OSI model, outlining the services and functions at each layer. We saw that layer 1, the lowest layer of the OSI model is most closely associated with the physical connection between devices. This layer is responsible for the transmission and reception of raw bit streams over a physical medium. A bit stream, also known as a **binary sequence**, is a sequence of bits. Bitstreams may be composed of bits that represent data and bits that control the flow of data as the *data* travels. Control bits handle the transmission and reception of signals and are not concerned with what the bits signify or mean. The bits must be encoded into signals for transmission. The primary functions at this level are the representation of bits, synchronization between transmitter and receiver, the number of bits per second transmitted (rate of transmission}, the interface(s) used by the devices involved in the act of transmission, and the method of connectivity utilized in relation to network topologies. Other primary functions deal with baseband and broadband transmission or with the modes of operation and direction in which the bits are traveling, for example, whether the direction is simplex, Half-duplex, or Full-duplex. At this layer, we can have a point-to-point or multipoint configuration, depending upon the topology in place and the type of communication occurring. Hence, at this layer, these devices are connected to the medium. Some of its features are as follows:

- The main functionality of the physical layer is to transmit the individual bits from one node to another node.

- It is the lowest layer of the OSI model and closest to the medium.

- It activates, establishes, maintains, and deactivates the physical connection.

- It specifies the mechanical, electrical, and procedural network interface specifications.

The physical layer of the OSI model includes certain hardware and equipment.

This hardware and equipment include the cable, connectors, and radio frequency *link* (as found in a Wi-Fi network. The physical layer also relates to the format or layout of pins on devices or connectors, voltages used in deice or component operation, and other physical requirements utilized in computer networks.

Note: When a networking problem occurs, network administrators go right to the physical layer first to check that all cables are properly connected and that the power plug is correctly secured and power is on, for example.

This first (best) step in the troubleshooting process is relevant to all equipment cables and technologies. This first (best) step in the troubleshooting process is relevant to all equipment, cables, and technologies. A technician will check the integrity of the cables, verify that there are no loose connections, observe the status of LEDs to see if their blinking might be indicative, and ensure there are no sources of EMI nearby. After these initial checks, the technician will then move into the logical things and protocols further up the stack or model. In the troubleshooting model of CompTIA, a network technician is advised to move from the simpler things to the more complex ones. One of the top skills an administrator holds ties in directly with is the ability to frame a given strategy within the framework of OSI or TCP/IP and demonstrate comprehensive personal understanding.

Modes of communication

When we refer to transmission modes, we mean transferring data between two devices. There are three transmission modes: simplex, half-duplex, and full-duplex. A transmission mode is also known as a **communication mode** and can be uni-directional or bi-directional in terms of the flow of communication. The three modes are outlined as follows:

- **Simplex**: Simple and single, allowing telecommunication in one direction only.

- **Half-duplex**: A bi-directional mode of communication in which information can be sent in only one direction at a time.

- **Full-duplex**: A bi-directional mode of communication in which the characters sent to the computer from a remote terminal are echoed back to the terminal for display. This transmission may occur in both directions simultaneously.

Refer to *Figure 1.4*:

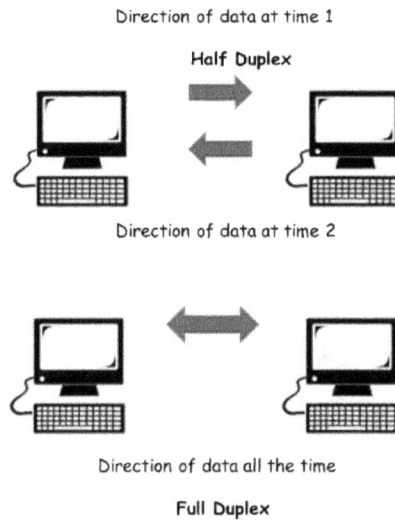

Figure 1.4: Communication modes

In *Figure 1.5*, we see the primary responsibility of the physical layer as it transmits and receives raw bit streams over a physical medium. The network medium can be wired or wireless, for example, the bits may travel via ethernet cable, fiber optics via light pulses, or through the air in radio waves on channels of different frequencies.

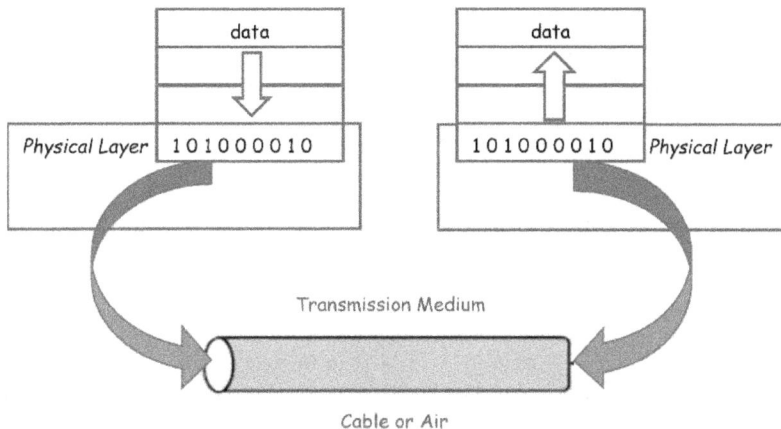

Figure 1.5: The physical layer

Data link layer

The primary function of the data link layer is to reliably transmit data frames between two nodes connected by a physical layer.

The data link layer is composed of two sublayers: the **Media Access Control** (**MAC**) layer and the **Logical Link Control** (**LLC**) layer. Layer 2 uses MAC addresses to connect devices. This layer performs the most reliable node-to-node delivery of data. The data link layer is responsible for multiplexing data streams, data frame detection, medium access, and error control. It ensures reliable point-to-point and point-to-multipoint connections in a communication network. The primary objective of the layer is to ensure a reliable, which is largely error-free transmission and to control access to the transmission medium. Typical hardware used at this level involves bridging and switching technologies.

The important thing to note about this layer is the operational local delivery of *frames* within **Local Area Networks** (**LANs**). When we consider the functions of the data link layer, we are not crossing the boundaries of a local area network. Traffic management and arbitration are happening at a local level. Protocols at this level focus on delivery, addressing, and media arbitration. Where contention exists regarding access to a medium, access methods such as **Carrier Sense Multiple Access Collision Detection** (**CSMA/CD**) or **Carrier Sense Multiple Access Collision Avoidance** (**CSMA/CA**) arbitrate and resolve the issues. Access methods relate to the proactive avoidance of collision (CSMA/CA) or the responsive (reactive) recovery strategies after a collision has inevitably occurred (CSMA/CD). Remember, frame collisions do occur so having a strategy to handle them is critical. CSMA/CA is mainly used in wireless networks (802.11 standard) while the CSMA/CD protocol is used in wired Ethernet networks (802.3 standard).

Figure 1.6 offers an example of how frames are transmitted and how the *framing* of the data is structured. As we can see from the illustration, with every other layer on the OSI model, the data remains intact and is never altered or changed. *How* the data is packaged or parceled is effectively what changes.

In *Figure 1.6*, a header is at the front of the frame, and a **cyclic redundancy check** (**CRC**) is at the end. CRC checks for errors in digital data. The sender injects the source and destination MAC addresses into the frame, and the switching device on the network segment handles the request. Each frame in the data link layer has checksum bits for error control. These bits are added by the layer and recalculated by the receiver. If the checksum bits differ, the frame is marked as corrupted, and the sender retransmits it. Note, the protocol in this example is HTTP, an application layer protocol at layer 7 of the OSI model, generated from web-based hypertext.

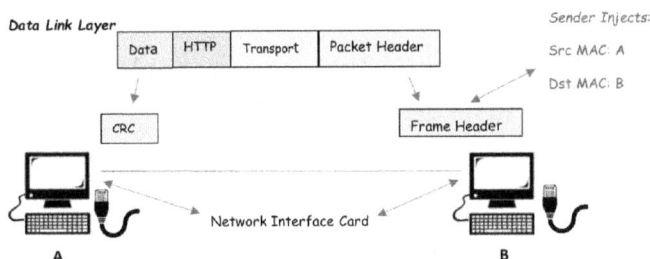

Figure 1.6: *The data link layer*

Switch segmentation also happens at the data link layer of the OSI model. Network administrators can divide users and workstations into separate virtual network segments using this strategy. These virtual or logical connections are called **virtual local area networks (VLANs)**.

As layer 2 devices, switches are segmented to assign ports (interfaces) to VLANs. Creating VLANs and switch segmentation improves network performance, significantly reduces broadcast traffic. When VLANs are implemented, a network administrator has more control over the network, especially where security is concerned. For example, an administrator might want tighter controls on a VLAN designed for the HR department, with less permission available to users, due to the nature of the data being accessed on storage devices in the VLAN. The network administrator can assess the security needs of the network easier, when users are divided by group, department and by VLAN. VLANs make upgrading hardware or software more streamlined, and the likelihood of unnecessary software installed or idle on devices is minimalized. These are just some factors related to implementing VLANs. When considered overall, VLANs make the job of the network administrator more efficient, organized, and easier in the long term. Effective VLAN design equally helps to support the objectives and purpose of an organization. Problem-solving becomes easier too, as when troubleshooting VLANs, an administrator can begin by checking and testing functionality at the physical layer of the OSI model and then move toward troubleshooting and verifying the protocols responsible for creating and activating the VLANs. They can do this by configuring or managing the switch (layer 2) or multilayer switch (layers 2 and 3).

In order to discuss internetworking or inter-VLAN routing, we need a layer 3 device and global addressing in situ. Note that a default gateway must exist to route traffic from one subnet or VLAN to another.

Network layer

The primary function of the network layer is the structuring and managing of a multi-node network. Consider the action words structuring and managing, these verbs imply constructing or shaping, organizing, and managing. But what exactly is being handled on this layer of the OSI model?

The network layer has essentially two functions given as follows:

- It breaks up data into network packets and reassembles data on the receiving end (that is, incoming packets at the destination).

- Using a layer 3 intermediary device, it routes packets from source to destination by discovering the *best* path from source to destination across the physical network.

When we speak about multi-nodes, we are referring to network devices. When we discuss multiple links, we are referring to networks. Links connect nodes on a network, and they can be wired, like Ethernet, or cable-free, like Wi-Fi. Links can either be point-to-point, where Node A is directly connected to Node B, or multipoint, where Node A is connected to Nodes B and C. Other terms we use for nodes are hosts, end devices, workstations, or clients when we allude to a client-server network.

To regulate and govern data transmission, an addressing system is essential. Data must reach the correct location, regardless of the node's position in the network, and especially when the destination node is on a remote network. Appropriate routing rules ensure this. The network layer provides connectivity and path selection between two host systems, even if they are on geographically separated networks. The network layer is responsible for translating logical addresses (i.e., IP addresses) to physical addresses (MAC addresses). TCP/IP is the only *routable* protocol, so when we speak about network addressing, IP addressing is ultimately relevant to our understanding. We will be covering MAC. Mechanisms to control the flow of data and error checking also take place at this layer.

The network layer of the OSI model includes certain hardware and equipment.

For example, routers and gateways operate at the network layer of the OSI model. Additionally, multilayer switches operate at the network layer as they hold the capacity to route as a marked feature of the abilities of the device.

The network layer manages QoS. These technologies or mechanisms control traffic and can improve performance, especially on networks with limited network capacity. Organizations that implement QoS can adjust and modify the network traffic in the organization by prioritizing types of traffic and ranking them in degrees of importance. Data ranked as highest will be on the top of the QoS queue above less mission-critical or business-led data.

Figure 1.7 illustrates data transfer through the public internet:

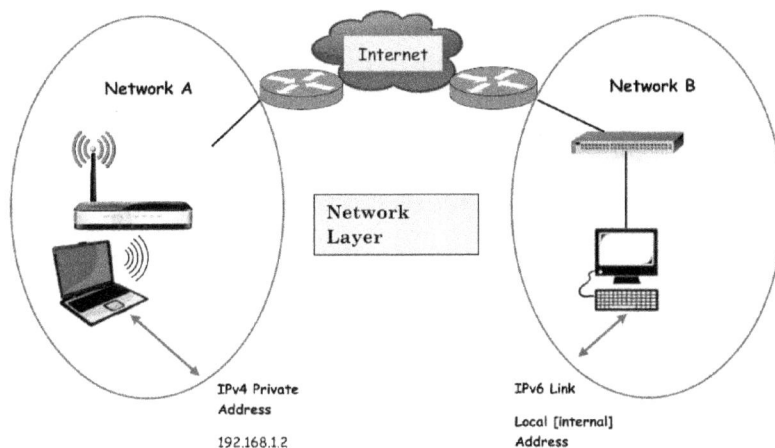

Figure 1.7: The network layer

The networks in the topology (**Network A** and **Network B**) are LANs. The data is traversing the internet using routing technologies. IP addressing mechanisms and network layer protocols help to make this communication viable. The networks between the routers (as typically there may be more than one) are **wide area networks** (**WANs**) and the interfaces on the routers linking to the cloud are characteristically external WAN links.

Transport layer

The primary function of the transport layer is the reliable transmission of data segments between points on a network.

The transport layer accepts data from the layer above, splits the data into smaller units, and then passes these units to the network layer. Part of the process is ensuring that all data units arrive correctly at the other end. The process of splitting the data up is called **segmentation**.

At this layer, connection control is either connection-oriented or connectionless. Flow control and error control are performed end to end. Error control identifies errors such as damaged packets, lost packets, and duplication of packets, and provides adequate error-correction techniques, where applicable.

Another function of the transport layer is to isolate the upper layers (user support layers) from the lower layers (network support layers).

Scenario

You have decided to purchase a favorite product online. You view and pay for the product. When you make this request, in terms of networking functionality, to begin with, your request descended through layers 7, 6, and 5 of the OSI layer, respectively, that is, the *application, presentation,* and *session* layers. When the process arrives at layer 4, the transport layer, data segmentation occurs. These data packets are then delivered to the lower layers, the network support layers, which are the network, data link, and physical layers. When the packets arrive at the *Web server* of the retailer, they are processed layer by layer upwards through the model: layers 1–7 in ascending order. Each layer handles the data in accordance with its rules and protocols. However, the top three layers handle functions supporting the user. The lower three functions handle hardware mechanisms and technological changes required by the functionality of the mechanism and its requirements. We will discuss the encapsulation and decapsulation process in a separate section.

In *Figure 1.8*, we can see data transmission across different layers of the OSI model. As we know, the transport layer is responsible for end-to-end communication over a physical network. In the illustration, we have two end devices as nodes or workstations on a network. The hosts are on two separate LANs and are remote from each other. We interpret that the end devices are on a LAN segment even though the networks at either end have not been fully populated with layer 2 switches. In this scenario, when data is traveling from source to destination, in either direction, it is transmitted across three intermediary devices, here, layer 3 routers. Note that there is no other pathway for the data to travel except to go through the networks linked to the three routers. The transport layer provides logical communication between application processes running on these different hosts within a layered architecture of protocols and other network components.

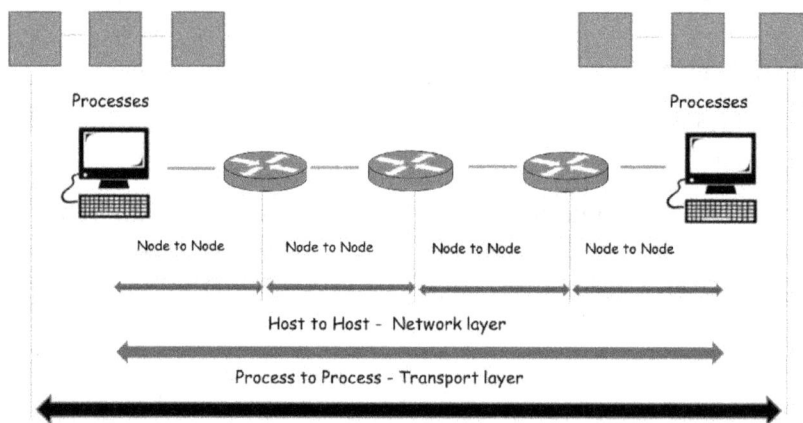

Figure 1.8: The transport layer

Session layer

The primary function of the session layer is managing communication sessions, which means managing and synchronizing conversations between two communicating systems.

In the session layer, file transfer, remote login, or other acts of communication are established and maintained. Essentially, these functions, as described, are that of a dialog controller. Throughout the session, timing is monitored and tracked, and synchronization points may be added at intervals into the stream of data being transmitted. This synchronization enables recovery strategies should crashes occur. Retransmission of data can then be assessed and transmitted where appropriate. Remember, when we looked at half-duplex and full-duplex operations earlier in the chapter, we saw that there are different modes of transporting the data regarding the direction of travel. A dialog controller, in accordance with the protocols used, will make decisions as to which direction of travel suits the purpose best. Sometimes, the session connections are full-duplex, but the upper layers sometimes communicate in half-duplex modes. In these cases, the session layer has to keep track of whose turn it is to talk. This is known as **dialog management**. Data tokens are used to implement dialog management in half-duplex transmissions. When the user of the data token is finished, they hand the token back for other users to employ. No token is required for Full-duplex operation. The session layer is designed to prevent two systems from conflicting when critical operations are needed to be communicated between systems, by implementing these strategies.

In summation, synchronization, dialog control, and token management are the three main functions of the session layer of the OSI model.

Figure 1.9 demonstrates synchronization as it occurs on the session layer:

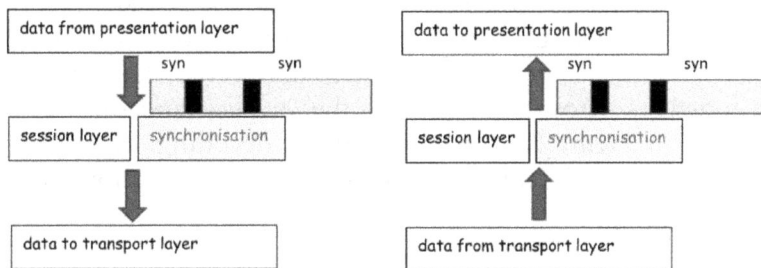

Figure 1.9: *The session layer*

Presentation layer

The primary function of the presentation layer is the translation of data between a networking service and an application.

The presentation layer *takes* the data from the application layer above it and changes the way the data is presented, for example, via encoding, compression, or encryption. The data itself remains unchanged. It executes the code changes, document compressions, and encrypts the data presented. This representation of the data is system-independent. Examples of data representation and data formats are the ASCII code or EBDIC, which relates to the functionality and workings of a keyboard. That is, ASCII is a character encoding standard for electronic communication.

Encryption formats are related to the secure transmission of data as opposed to sending data in plain text. One of the most popular encryption schemes that is usually associated with the presentation layer is the **Secure Sockets Layer** (**SSL**). SSL is succeeded by **Transport Layer Security** (**TLS**) as an authentication and more modern security mechanism. Encryption is implemented at this layer rather than at the link or even the physical layer to avoid having to encrypt the entire data flow, including all the information associated with the headers of the upper-layer protocols. Instead, it is sufficient to encrypt only the useful data coming from the application layer, thereby saving on the overall processing load.

Compression is concerned with making the transmission of larger data files more manageable as it reduces the size of files to be sent and received (files will subsequently be decompressed at the receiving end).

In the OSI model, the presentation layer guarantees that the information that one system's application layer sends out is comprehensible to the application layer of another system. In essence, the presentation layer acts as the translator between different data formats and sets out to ensure these data formats are understood by both ends in the act of communication between systems. Methods at each end are in mutual agreement before communication on a common scheme for transmission. Think of this the way you would do a translator of differing languages. Even when two people present their communication in distinct formats or with native tongues (for example, language systems), the translator needs to bring about mutual understanding and a common workable system. In this way, communication functions across systems once the *language* and the way it is presented is understood. Note in *Figure 1.10* how encoding, decoding, encryption, decryption, compression, and decompression are all occurring at the presentation layer:

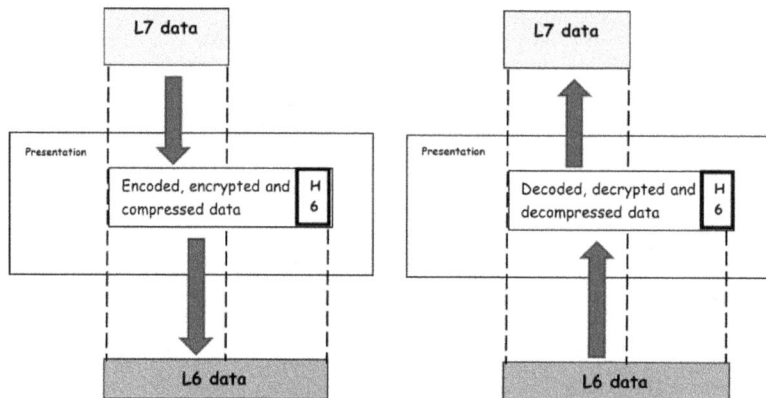

Figure 1.10: *The presentation layer*

Application layer

The primary function of this layer is the maintenance of high-level **application programming interface** (**APIs**), including resource sharing and remote file access.

The application layer is the seventh layer of the OSI model. When considering the application layer, its definition and delineation of functionality are narrower in scope than the application layer in the TCP/IP model. The application layer in TCP/IP comprises the functionalities of what are the top three layers of OSI when combined: application, presentation, and session. TCP/IP calls this combined composition of functionality its application layer. Thus, when we specify this layer in the OSI model, it is exclusively defined as the interface responsible for communicating with host-based and user-facing applications only. Ultimately, it describes the user interface as responsible for displaying received information to the user. Simply put, the application layer deals with application activities.

The application layer permits any software to send and receive information easily and present meaningful data to its users. Protocols associated with the application layer provide various functionalities across diverse applications. Remote access, e-mail, file transfer, addressing, network, and e-mail management are but a few. In brief, applications produce the data that must be sent across the network. The application layer also provides us with File Transfer Access and Management, Mail and Directory Services, and Virtual Terminal Emulation.

Note: Essentially, an API is an interface, or method or way, for two pieces of software to communicate. APIs have proliferated incredibly in recent years, especially with the Internet of Things (IoT) expansion. APIs are the interconnectors that provide the interface between the Internet and the Things. Devices connect to cloud-based services via APIs, so they are reckoned to be the driver of IoT, the solvent or glue, so to speak.

Figure 1.11 is an example of protocols at the application layer of the OSI model:

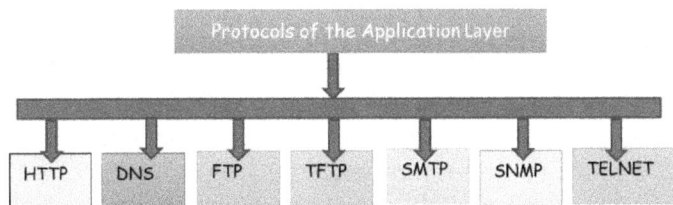

Figure 1.11: *The application layer*

Data encapsulation and decapsulation

If you have ever accidentally bitten down on a capsule holding medication, you will know that sometimes the taste of the powder inside the capsule may not be a nice or pleasant experience. The capsule holding the medication or drug does so to keep the powder inside intact and secure and hold integrity to the measurements and contents prescribed to make you well. In a way, the capsule protects the medication and ensures error-free delivery to your body or mind. Well, only error-free without you accidentally breaking the capsule and, unfortunately, tasting the powdery or, at times, bitter-tasting internals. In communications technology, when we speak of encapsulation, we are seeking out ways to carry the data (also known as **medication** in our analogy) through the layers of the models we employ. Different encapsulation strategies are used at each layer to let the layer know how the data is being packaged and what type of capsule we are currently using. Encapsulation describes the process of putting headers (and sometimes trailers) around some data. Notice the use of brackets in the previous sentence. These brackets encapsulated the words and sometimes trailers as a grammatical means of formatting data, as did the singular quotes in this current sentence. The brackets occurred in the middle of the sentence, whereas, in the OSI model, we encapsulate the frame or packet at the beginning or the end of the structure and the overall formation of a frame or packet. Encapsulation is an active process and moves through the OSI stack. We are aware of the seven-layer OSI stack so the process of encapsulation or augmentation of data can move from the higher layers down through the lower layers of the stack. There is a separate action moving from the lower layers upwards.

Defining data encapsulation

Data encapsulation refers to sending data where the data is augmented with successive layers of control information before transmission across a network. The term augmented simply means enhanced or additional, and successive, as we know, means one thing happens after another. The reverse of data encapsulation is decapsulation, which refers to the successive layers of data being removed (essentially unwrapped or stripped off) at the receiving end of a network.

The OSI model is also used to break up the complexity of how one computer (host) sends data to another computer (host). The process of encapsulation and decapsulation breaks down the complexity in the act of data transmission so that when the data is being sent from the source device/host to the destination or receiving host, as it arrives at each layer, the data is carried in a suitable, comprehensible capsule. What do we mean by suitable and comprehensible? Each layer considers the data and adds a header and footer containing addressing and error control information (encapsulation), protocol information, and the data format that matches or maps to the rules of the protocol in use at that specific layer. This method of matching and aligning the structures of data transmission makes the transmission viable and meaningful at each layer. Throughout the process of encapsulation and decapsulation, the data is always untouched and intact in its quantity and measure, just like the medication, which was described with the analogy of taking or swallowing a capsule. The actual message or date is inside the capsule.

Data flow and encapsulation

The OSI model provides a service that allows information to flow smoothly from one layer of the model to the next. When the information reaches the end device, it will be in a readable format. As previously discerned, at times, due to its size and the maximum capacity of the protocol to handle it, the data is too large to be sent as one piece. Files will need to be sent in several pieces and broken down accordingly.

Earlier in the chapter, we discussed the way that data can be encapsulated in order to protect it and keep it error-free. This wrapping up of data is a mechanism akin to a protective shield. On the inside of the shield, the data holds its integrity. *Protective shields* vary in terms of structure and format.

Encapsulation is a distinctive feature of the OSI model. Let us view this process visually in the subsequent section.

Stages of data flow

Let us take a look at the process and stages of data flow as the data moves down through the seven layers. We have discovered that the top layer focuses on the application protocols that are closest to the user. We will imagine that the application used in the example is web-generated over a secure browsing session (HTTPS) and that the data being transmitted is to be encrypted.

(Moving from layer 7 to layer 1, as illustrated in the following figures). The stages are as follows:

1. First, as users, we generate the application data. Refer to the following figure:

Figure 1.12: Data flow process, stage 1

2. The application adds encryption to the data. This occurs at the presentation layer, represented in *Figure 1.13*:

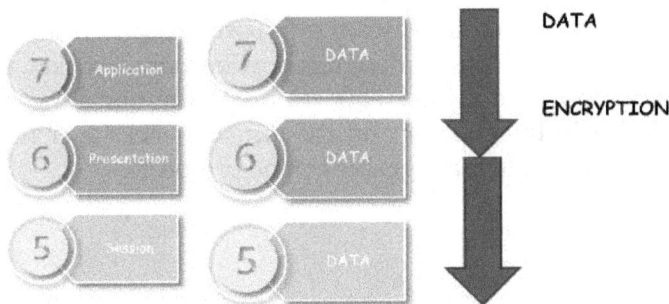

Figure 1.13: Data flow process, stage 2

3. The session ID is appended at the session layer, as shown in *Figure 1.14*. Note that the data is still a complete block of data and has not been subdivided.

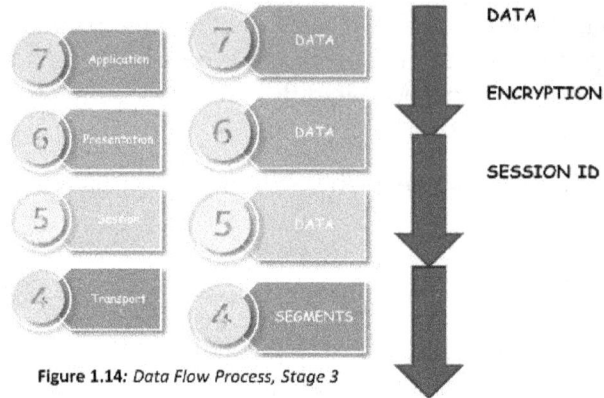

Figure 1.14: Data Flow Process, Stage 3

Figure 1.14: *Data flow process, stage 3*

4. Next, data goes down to the transport layer, as shown in *Figure 1.15*. The transport layer breaks the data into blocks of data which we call segments. The port number is added to every segment as an identifier. This number identifies which upper-layer application needs to receive the data on the destination device.

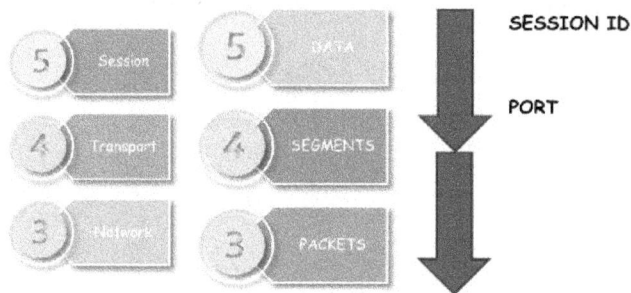

Figure 1.15: *Data flow process, stage 4*

5. The segment moves down to the network layer; see *Figure 1.16*. The network layer takes the segment, which includes the port number, and affixes the source and destination IP address. The segment has now become a packet. Note that the PDU differs for each of these layers. This relates to the parceling and packaging we discussed earlier in the chapter and the fact that each layer will have maximum transmission units made manageable by the protocols.

Note: You may come across the term datagram in your studies. Do not be confused by this networking term. Even though most people refer to a packet when discussing layer 3 PDU, a datagram is a true layer 3 PDU. A packet is a fragment of a datagram that was fragmented due to insufficient MTU at a particular network segment. However, unless a datagram is segmented, a packet and a datagram are considered identical.

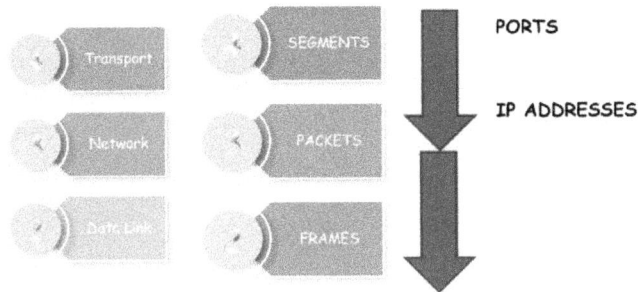

Figure 1.16: Data flow process, stage 5

6. The packet is then passed to the data link layer, see *Figure 1.17*. This is where the source and destination MAC address and the CRC are added. At this point, we have a frame. A network device we associate with sending and receiving frames is a layer 2 switch.

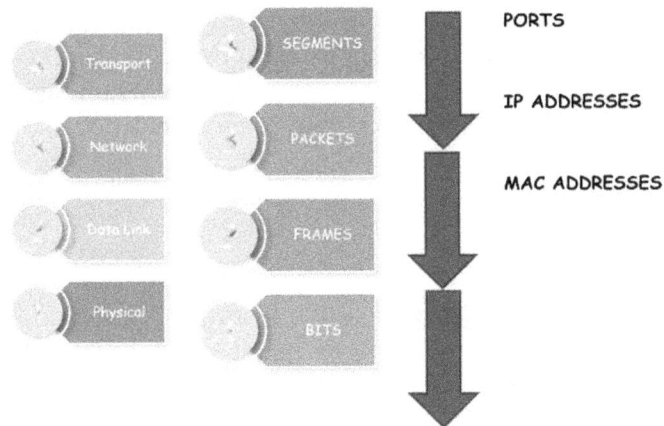

Figure 1.17: Data flow process, stage 6

7. The physical device translates the frame received into a signal. Signals may be electrical, radio waves, light (optical), or another type of other signal. This frame then becomes some kind of a signal that represents a series of zeros and ones. This is why at the physical layer we often call it Bits. The **Network Interface Card (NIC)** prepares those signals and sends them out on the transmission medium.

Decapsulation

Decapsulation is the process of opening up the capsule and stripping back the wrapped-up data as it moves from the physical layer and medium of transmission back up through the OSI stack. On the receiving device, the bits are converted back to frames, frames back to packets, and packets back into segments, and then the segments are reassembled into the original data at the application layer, which as we learned is the user interface closest to the user.

Note: CompTIA Network+ focusses on the OSI model in many of the course objectives and underpins topics addressed throughout the course. The content of this chapter is mapped to Domain 1: Networking Concepts, explaining concepts related to the OS reference model.

Conclusion

The OSI model is a significant starting point or reference guide for any person who participates in networking and wishes to understand its operations. It enables us to figure out and analyze how networks function, how components interact, and how protocols and mechanisms come together to bring about full functionality. Networks are made up of many parts, physically and logically. When you have a better comprehension of network operations, as a network administrator, you can fine-tune your networks, organize them more effectively and efficiently, and improve the performance of the implementations you undertake. With learning and practice, you will know what the best needs of the network are. Understanding network models puts you on the pathway to discover these needs and take mental ownership of them. Now that we have reviewed the OSI model, in the upcoming chapter, we shall be covering network topologies. We will learn about physical and logical network topologies and how the nodes and links are arranged on the network segment so that we can identify and comprehend the layout, connectivity, and specifications.

Points to remember

- The OSI model is a conceptual framework that enables those involved in networking to articulate and organize networking concepts and fundamentals. It operates like a blueprint, reference model, or a universal language.

- The OSI model is a guide to vendors, manufacturers, and software developers. These stakeholders can consult OSI as a guide when researching the functionality, interoperability, and rules of networking concepts and devices.

- The OSI model is a seven-layer model. It is not the only networking model in existence. TCP/IP is also a widely-used open standard. TCP/IP is a practical model and enables users to apply and implement the protocols in the TCP/IP protocol suite. It is a four-layer model and can be compared and contrasted with OSI. We will explore TCP/IP when we cover network protocols and network security. TCP and UDP will be extended in that section.

- If you know the OSI model or other networking models, it enables you to troubleshoot your network devices, and the connectivity and functionality of networks gain clarity. As a result of understanding this model, you can analyze different layers of communication and interoperability so you can systematically and accurately troubleshoot. These models form the backbone of computing.

Key terms

- **Interoperability**: It is the property that allows for the unrestricted sharing of resources between different systems. This can refer to the ability to share data between different components or machines, both via software and hardware, or it can be defined as the exchange of information and resources between different computers through LANs or WANs.

- **Compatibility**: It is designed to work with another device or system without modification.

- **Scalability**: It can be easily expanded or upgraded on demand.

- **Maximum Transmission Unit (MTU)**: It is the largest frame/packet that can be transmitted over frame/packet-based networks. Large packets can carry more information, but the processing time can take longer. Small packets are processed faster, but more need to be sent to transfer the same amount of data as a single large packet. MTU, therefore, is the optimal packet size for a given network.

- **Simplex**: Simple and single allowing telecommunication in one direction only.

- **Half-duplex**: A bi-directional mode of communication in which information can be sent in only one direction at a time.

- **Full-duplex**: A bi-directional mode of communication in which the characters sent to the computer from a remote terminal are echoed back to the terminal for display. This transmission may occur in both directions simultaneously.

- **CSMA/CD**: Carrier sense multiple access/collision detection is an access method that handles or responds to collisions on an ethernet network. It detects and responds to data collisions that have already occurred.

- **CSMA/CA**: Carrier sense multiple access/collision avoidance is an access method that works in 802.11 environments. The protocol was developed to minimize the potential of a collision occurring when two or more stations send their signals over a data link layer. It is a proactive avoidance method.

- **Multiplexing**: Multiplexing is a popular networking technique that integrates multiple analog and digital signals into a signal transmitted over a shared medium.

Multiplexers and de-multiplexers are used to convert multiple signals into one signal. This term is also known as **muxing**.

- **VLAN**: A VLAN is a logical group of workstations, servers, and network devices that appear to be on the same LAN despite their geographical distribution.

- **Node**: It is a point of intersection or connection within a data communication network. In an environment where all devices are accessible through the network, these devices are all considered nodes. The individual definition of each node depends on the type of network it refers to.

- **Connection-oriented**: In connection-oriented protocols, preliminary protocols are used to establish end-to-end connections. Connection-oriented protocols track conversations and are considered stateful protocols.

- **Connectionless**: In a connectionless protocol, no preliminary protocols establish a connection. A connectionless protocol is a form of data transmission in which an IT signal goes out automatically without determining whether the receiver is ready, or even whether a receiver exists. This is why connectionless protocols can be described as *best-effort* delivery.

Questions

1. What is the importance of the OSI model?
2. What is data encapsulation? Can you describe it?
3. How could a network administrator use the OSI model?
4. What are the differences between the OSI model and TCP/IP?
5. What is the difference between Half-duplex and Full-duplex?

Join our book's Discord space

Join the book's Discord Workspace for Latest updates, Offers, Tech happenings around the world, New Release and Sessions with the Authors:

https://discord.bpbonline.com

CHAPTER 2

Network Topologies

Introduction

So far, we have looked at the OSI model and observed how data is transmitted through the different layers of the model. We will now shift our focus from the OSI model and its layers to the networks that make this transmission possible. *Ted Williams*, an American author, stated that *Every major technological step forward has profoundly changed human society—that's how we know they're major, even if we don't always realize it at the time. Farming created cities. Writing, followed eventually by printing, vastly increased the preservation and transmission of cultural information across time and space.* True to say that the design and generation of computer networks heralded the most profound transformation to technology-based networks spanning the entire earth. However, even such a profound transformation breaks down to its component parts and elements. When the interrelatedness and interdependencies are broken down, network topologies and network types make these global communication networks possible.

Structure

This chapter will cover the following topics:

- Physical versus logical topologies
- Network types

- Virtual network concepts
- Hypervisors

Objectives

After reading this chapter, you will be able to compare and contrast network topologies, architectures, and types. You will differentiate between topologies, their connectivity, the cabling used, and the networking devices that manage the system, where applicable. You will identify topologies for given use cases and characterize their purpose, properties, advantages, and disadvantages. In relation to network types, you will be able to specify the design and understand the concepts and configuration of diverse network infrastructures, that is, wired and wireless.

Physical versus logical topologies

A **network topology** describes the arrangement of systems on a computer network. It defines how the computers, or nodes, within the network, are arranged and connected to each other. Some common network topologies include bus, star, ring, mesh, hybrid, and tree configurations.

The actual layout of a network and its media is its *physical topology*. The way in which the data accesses the medium and transmits packets is the *logical topology*.

When we consider physical things in networking, we look at the tangible and touchable hardware and cables that make up the infrastructure of the system. Examples of these tangible things are devices, connectors, cables, and modules such as external network adapters or add-on network-capable devices. This network infrastructure can be likened to the physical objects or hardware we see in the infrastructure of a national or even local roadway system. Think of all the hardware you see on a daily basis in the roadway system as it operates. A typical list would consist of signs, traffic lights, zebra or pedestrian crossings, roundabouts, junctions, traffic islands, ramps, and even *the more omniscient presence of cat's eyes* on the road itself, illuminating and guiding us through the dark nights as reflective road markings.

This is the physical infrastructure of the roadways system.

Consequently, the *actual* layout of the roadways system and its *media* is its physical topology.

But what happens when we drive, cycle, or walk about in these traffic systems? Do we not have to abide by the rules of the road to transport our *data*? Do we not have to follow traffic management protocols to organize, navigate, and guide ourselves safely through these multi-user and multi-faceted organized systems?

These protocols and rules of the road enable us to access the infrastructure and physical layout of the system we travel through. The protocols we use are the intelligence and logic of a functioning network of roads and pathways.

Accordingly, the *way in which* the data accesses the medium and transmits packets is the logical topology. It is the same in networking. Logical topology is the intelligence or access method of the system in use. Regarding collisions, this method may be proactive, as in wireless communication technologies (CSMA/CA), or reactive to collisions on an Ethernet segment (CSMA/CD).

Physical topologies

Prior to examining the types of physical topologies, we need to consider the relevant factors applicable to choosing an appropriate configuration. As a network administrator, your choice of logical topology will impact the physical topology, and vice versa.

Designing accurately saves time long-term and means that you are less likely to err midway through the installation and configuration of the network. Optimum planning should always be upheld in network administration practices.

Your choice in design will determine cable installation, network devices, network connections, and protocols. It may also be already influenced by the building or structure and the layout and positioning of walls, ceilings, offices, and the environment. When planning for WLANs, ensure to research the way antennae and access points installation and function and how coverage is reached and maintained. All the access points in a new or upgraded network need the sharpest attention to detail.

The factors impacting the choice of topology are as follows:

- Cost
- Scalability
- Bandwidth capacity
- Ease of installation and configuration
- Ease of troubleshooting and maintenance

Bus topology

You will discover when learning about technology; some learning could be perceived as *historical*. In this, we mean that some systems and implementations of networks are now legacy or obsolete and no longer in use in modern networking. So, why do we need to know about these technologies, and for what purpose?

When we know how networks evolved, and the types of installations and mechanisms that were used, the knowledge gleaned enhances our overall understanding of why some networks became obsolete, to begin with, and how the technology needed to be modified to work more efficiently. If we go into the past, our understanding of technology also deepens. At times, we need to pay a historical visit to observe what *was not* manageable long-term to fully appreciate and respect what *is* manageable and what works best for us now including the flaws and shortcomings of any technology currently applied. Let us have a look.

Observe the physical layout of *Figure 2.1*:

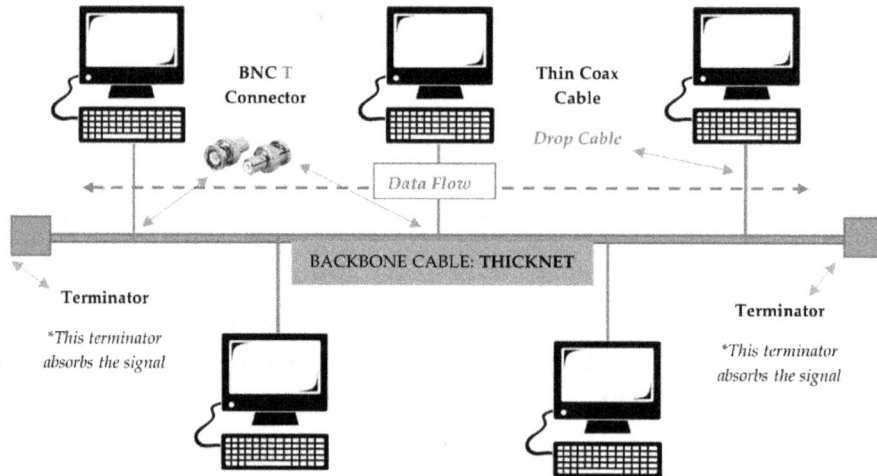

Figure 2.1: Bus topology

Note the following:

- The network is maintained by a single cable.

- The cable is referred to as a backbone cable.

- The backbone is a shared communication line. All workstations send and receive data via this backbone (this makes the backbone a busy *roadway,* needing an efficient traffic management system).

- It uses a thin coaxial cable, and the backbone uses thick coax (there are ThinNet and ThickNet configurations of this topology).

The cable segment must end with a terminator. The terminator absorbs the signal at either end, preventing signal bounce.

- **Signal bounce**: A signal that is placed on a bus that is unterminated or incorrectly terminated will continue to reflect from the end of the bus until that signal is attenuated (weakened in strength) by the impedance of the cable. A break in the cable, which essentially creates two unterminated ends for the two segments, is another cause of signal bounce. Thus, bounce is an effect that happens to signals on a bus topology network when the ends of the bus are improperly terminated or unterminated.

  Extra nodes/workstations can be added in a daisy chain manner.

Table 2.1 provides a summary of bus topology:

Features	Advantages	Disadvantages
Cost	Inexpensive to install	Legacy implementation
Scalability	Easy to add stations	A limited number of devices can be attached
Ease of installation and configuration	Uses less cable than other topologies	N/A
Bandwidth capacity	Works well for small networks	Sharing the same cable slows down response rates Each node added decreases the efficiency Data can only travel in one direction at any point in time (half-duplex) Collisions are detected and resolved via timing algorithms and retransmission of data (CSMA/CD)
Ease of troubleshooting and maintenance	N/A	If the backbone breaks, the whole network goes down, that is, a single point of failure Difficult to isolate problems Coaxial cable is quite rigid and not as malleable as twisted pair. Connectors are bulky and awkward at times to work with

Table 2.1: Bus topology

Bus topologies are often referred to as **line topology**. If there are two endpoints, the topology is then referred to as a **linear bus topology**. The relevant standard is IEEE 802.3. As noted, the two *flavors* are thin Ethernet (10Base2) and thick Ethernet (10Base5) with the thicker cable used for segment backbones.

In conclusion, we can see that the bus topology has a simple layout and is cheap to implement, particularly regarding the amount of cable required. However, the topology is susceptible to failure and is only suitable for low traffic volumes. Bus topologies are not used for office networks today, but the technology that was used to create the bus can still be observed in networking. We see that all nodes on the bus share the same cable. This concept of a shared cable can be observed in SCSI bus connectivity (that is, via the daisy chaining of devices) or in the internal electrical wiring of a hub or switch, which uses a backbone or shared link accessible by all devices that are connected to it. However, as a network administrator, you are unlikely to encounter a bus topology.

Star topology

A star topology is one of the most predominant network setups in modern networking. In this configuration, every node/workstation connects to a central network device. Central devices can be a hub, switch, or even another computer. The central network device acts as a server, and the peripheral devices act as clients. Refer to the following points:

- **Central devices**: A *Layer 1* device such as a hub or repeater, a *Layer 2* device such as a switch, multilayer switch, or bridge, or a *Layer 3* device such as a router or gateway.

- **Managing traffic**: For example, in *Layer 2* of the OSI model, a managed switch will handle incoming and outgoing data units and will filter, and forward frames allied to its decision-making capabilities. An Ethernet switch examines its MAC address table to make a forwarding decision for each frame, unlike legacy Ethernet hubs that repeat bits out all ports except the incoming port. Essentially, when speaking about data transmission, a hub can only broadcast, whereas a switch can **unicast, multicast,** and **broadcast** and make intelligent decisions about how it manages forwarding traffic. Switches can also perform **flooding** transmissions. The outcome of flooding is similar to the transmission of a broadcast frame, but the intention is starkly different. Flooding is a *one to all/everyone* transmission (with the exception of the device connected to the incoming or ingress port). Flooding occurs when a switch does not have a destination MAC address in its CAM table and is used to reach the intended destination. A broadcast frame differs in that the *intention* is to send the protocol data unit to everyone, using the broadcast address 255.255.255.255. These are some of the ways in which a switch manages traffic and controls the operations in the topology as a central device.

To summarize, the hub is a very limited repeater because it has no way of distinguishing which port a frame should be sent to; it forwards incoming data from any of its ports to all the others, making the process too inefficient. It should be noted that technologies such as hubs and bridges are now infrequently utilized, as they have largely become obsolete.

Let us examine star topology further.

Observe the physical layout of *Figure 2.2*:

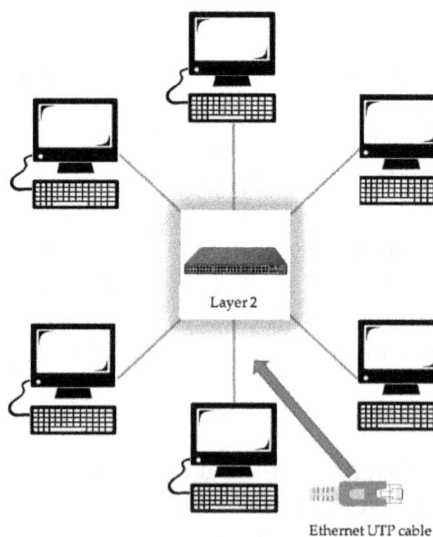

Ethernet UTP cable

Figure 2.2: *Star topology example*

Note the following:

- The center point is a hub/switch.

- Segments meet at the hub/switch.

- Each device needs its own cable to the hub/switch (that is, point-to-point connectivity).

- Due to the point-to-point connectivity in the design, any single local cable cut or NIC failure affects one node only in the topology. This leads to better generalized fault tolerance.

- More cables are required than the bus topology.

- There is no backbone cable taking the workload of data transmissions.

- The network is highly dependent upon the operations of the hub/switch as the central device in the network.

- The central device is taking the workload of data transmission.

- The reliance on one hub/switch needs to be considered in risk assessment strategies.

- If the central device slows down or stops working, or if components wear and tear, the network is negatively impacted.

Table 2.2 features a summary of a star topology:

Features	Advantages	Disadvantages
Cost	N/A	• A star network requires more cable than a ring or bus network • Costs are higher (installation and equipment) than for most bus networks. Extra hardware adds to costs
Scalability	• Can be upgraded to faster speeds • Easy to add devices as the network expands	N/A
Ease of installation and configuration	• Easy to install and robust in nature	N/A
Bandwidth capacity	• Switches can be daisy-chained to add more capacity and port density	• A finite number of switch ports limits the network's size

Features	Advantages	Disadvantages
Ease of troubleshooting and maintenance	• One cable failure does not bring down the entire network (resilience). • Hub/switch provides centralized management. • Lots of support as it is the most common topology used • Easy to find device and cable problems • No disruption to the network when adding or removing devices	• Failure of the central hub or switch can bring down the entire network • The network is reliant on the switch's and cable's capability and performance. The performance is predicated on the intermediary device as the star's concentrator • (All spokes connect to the hub) • As the central system, switches require monitoring and regular maintenance

Table 2.2: Star topology

A star topology is best suited for small and medium networks: a star topology can also be used in large networks, but traffic and performance management becomes a critical consideration: for very large networks, advanced switching technologies or the use of multiple interconnected hubs/switches are required, which can complicate the architecture. One has to ensure that the central device or intermediary device is always operational, and extra security features should be added to the device if it is the only device handling critical data or traffic. Port density and the number of available ports on a hub/switch are also serious considerations and might be a potential pitfall or limitation. Consequently, to expand on a star topology, you will need to add another hub or switch, go to a *star of stars* topology, and implement an extended star configuration. Most organizations you come across in real-world networking have an extended star network in operation as their network implementation. An extended star topology is a topology or star network that has been expanded to include an additional switch or switches.

As a network administrator, the likelihood of you managing and monitoring an extended star topology is very high.

Ring topology

In a ring network, each node/device is connected to two other devices. This forms a ring for the signals to travel around. Each packet of data on the network travels in one direction, and each device receives each packet in turn until the destination device receives it. Each computer serves as a repeater to amplify the signal and send it to the next computer. This serves to strengthen the signal on the network. Ring topologies make sure all the computers do not try to talk at the same time, and they also eradicate collisions.

IBM's Token Ring was the earliest implementation of a token ring topology. This implementation allowed for a single ring over copper. IEEE 802.5 was the standardized version that had similar speeds and a singular ring but did not officially define a medium required. Finally, FDDI was the higher-end solution with dual fiber rings. This permitted redundancy of the rings and allowed for longer distances due to the use of fiber cable instead of copper. The dual rings operated in different or opposing directions. This meant that if the primary ring went down or if there was a fault condition, the secondary data pathway took over, and redundancy was achieved. Dual ring topologies saw data travel in both directions making the overall topology full-duplex. On one ring, the data traveled clockwise, and on the second ring in the topology, the data traveled counter-clockwise to achieve this redundancy.

Observe the physical layout of *Figure 2.3*:

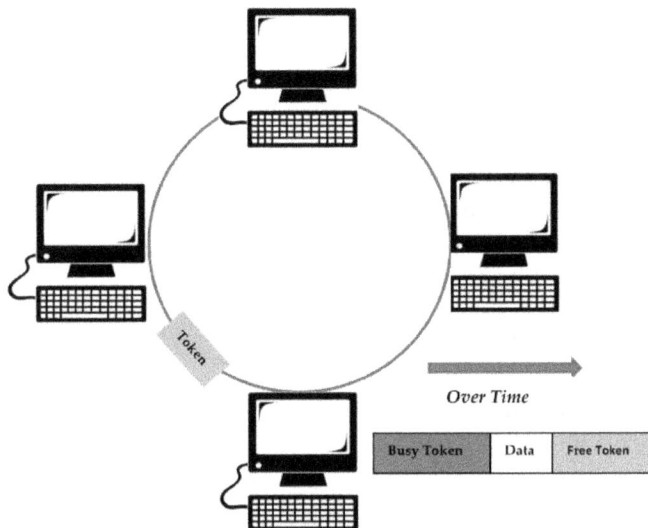

Figure 2.3: *Ring topology*

Note the following:

- The ring is a closed network, with no real starting or ending point, where the devices are all connected to form a continuous cycle. All devices share equal access to the media.

- This is a single ring; data travels in one direction only.

- Each device has to wait its turn to transmit, that is via accessing the token.

- This figure illustrates the most common type of ring topology: Token Ring (IEEE 802.5).

- The token contains the data and reaches the destination where the data is extracted. An acknowledgment of receipt is sent back to the transmitting device. The ack is removed and the empty token is passed on for another device to use.

Table 2.3 features a summary of a ring topology:

Features	Advantages	Disadvantages
Cost	N/A	• It is quite expensive to install due to the hardware required. Costlier than a star or bus topology but more affordable than a tree, hybrid, or mesh topology. • Building redundancies into the system may be proactive but more costly. • *Remember that the cost is totally dependent upon the needs of the company and the applications it desires to use.
Scalability	You can add more workstations without difficulty.	The more devices that are added to a network, the more communication delay the network experiences.
Ease of installation and configuration	N/A	Requires more cable than a bus.
Bandwidth capacity	• Bandwidth is higher than that of a bus, thus it performs better under heavy loads. • The risk of collisions is very low.	Bandwidth is shared on all links, therefore, when more hosts are added, performance is impacted.
Ease of troubleshooting and maintenance	• Easier to find a fault. • No terminators are required. • You can add redundancies to the topology to improve its performance.	• A break in the ring will bring it down. • The failure of one node can take the entire network out of operation. Thus, every connection in the ring is a point of failure. (There are methods that use one more backup ring—that is dual-ring topologies and redundancy solutions). • Not as common as the bus—less devices available.

Table 2.3: Ring topology

Ring topologies solve some issues that bus and star topologies were having at the early stages of networking, especially the issues of collisions and the use of bandwidth. Though they are historical and legacy implementations, we can see the benefits of this organized orderly transmission. The overhead of running such a design impedes its viability on a large scale, but in a very small operation, one can still see why it was implemented as an innovative solution in and of its time period.

Mesh topology

The mesh topology has a unique network design in which each node on the network connects to every other node, developing a **point-to-point** (**P2P**) connection between all the nodes or devices of the network.

Mesh network topologies create multiple pathways/routes for data transmission among the topology's connected nodes. This approach increases the resilience of the network, improves backup, and strengthens fault tolerance. Larger mesh networks may include multiple routers, switches, and other devices, which operate as connected nodes. A mesh network can equally include hundreds of wireless mesh nodes, which allows it to span a large geographical area and extend both the coverage and the reliability of the wireless mesh topology.

Due to the topology's generation of multiple pathways or routes, a mesh network topology sustains its viability if one of the nodes or links goes down. This is achieved with alternative pathways or routes in the case of a bad or unoperational node. This broken connection or link does not necessarily bring the entire network down. The network can heal itself around a bad node if other nodes can complete the mesh. In a full mesh topology, each node has two or more connections to other nodes depending on how many nodes are in the configuration. In a full mesh topology, every node or device is directly connected to each other. In a partial mesh topology, most of the devices are directly connected, but a small number of devices in the topology will not have the complete set of connections or links. These nodes may only have one or two connections. A partial mesh topology is usually found in peripheral networks connected to a fully meshed backbone.

Observe the physical layout of *Figure 2.4*:

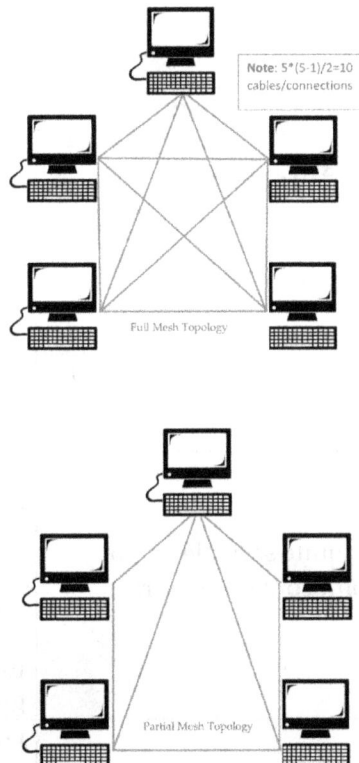

Figure 2.4: Full and partial mesh topology

Note the following:

- Each node is connected to every other node.
- This allows communication to continue in the event of a break in any one connection.
- It is fault tolerant.
- **In the full mesh topology**: There are five nodes in the topology depicted with a total of ten cables.
- **In the partial mesh topology**: There are five nodes in the topology depicted with a total of seven cables.

In order to calculate how many connections we require to make a network fully meshed; we can use the following formula. Required *connections = n * (n–1)/2*

Here, *n* is the number of end devices or locations.

n * (n - 1) / 2, with n equaling the number of hosts

Let us test that formula with our five-computer network. If we plug 5 in for *n*, we get the following:

$$5 * (5 - 1) / 2 = 10$$

This is a simple example, but you might agree that if we had nine or ten computers here, it would be easy to make a mistake by drawing all the lines and then trying to count them.

Table 2.4 features a summary of mesh topology:

Features	Advantages	Disadvantages
Cost	N/A	<ul><li>Expensive</li><li>Initial plan and build take a lot of time and effort when compared with other topologies</li><li>Utility costs per node need to be planned for</li></ul>
Scalability	Technically, quite scalable when point-to-point connections are considered	Expanding the mesh requires considering the number of connections needed and ongoing accurate planning. There is a high level of backup resources needed in a mesh infrastructure overall, as it grows, even more so
Ease of installation and configuration	N/A	Difficult to install and configure High maintenance

Features	Advantages	Disadvantages
Bandwidth capacity	• Multiple links = multiple pathways = greater speeds • Handles a high level of traffic and large volumes of data • More consistency in data transmission, that is high speed, reliability, and resilience	N/A
Ease of troubleshooting and maintenance	• Improves Fault Tolerance • Point-to-point connections make fault identification easier • Hugely difficult to take the entire mesh down due to its interconnectivity and backup	• Difficult to manage • Difficult to troubleshoot

Table 2.4: Mesh topology

When strategically implemented as a wired or wireless solution, a mesh topology is an excellent choice to make. If the main purpose of the interconnectivity is no downtime or the best coverage possible geographically, then a mesh topology is the perfect fit. Since data transmission is not disrupted by the failure of nodes or devices, data transmission is more consistent, can work at faster speeds, and can handle large volumes of data.

Hybrid topology

Simply put, a hybrid topology combines two or more physical topologies. Refer to *Figure 2.5:*

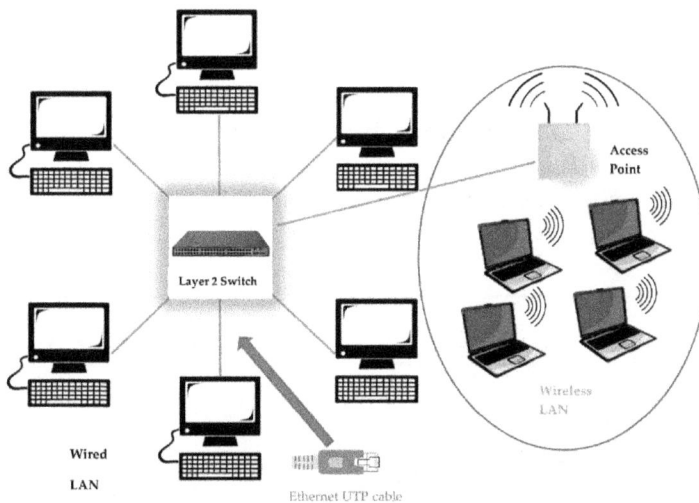

Figure 2.5: Hybrid topology

Observing *Figure 2.5*, one identifies a wired and wireless LAN combining. Initially, they resemble two-star configurations. Investigate further than a given snippet and if permissible, when you observe or suspect a topology, take a look at the way the cables are connected to each other and the network devices. In doing this, you will discover more about the physical look and feel of what you observe. Above all else, curiosity seeks to heighten learning. Curiosity and investigation also help us validate our initial speculations about cabling connectivity.

Remember, the wireless access points in this organization could well be configured in a meshed network! If that is the case, the mesh portal is the gateway between the wireless mesh network and the organization's wired LAN. Redundant mesh paths may be established between the wireless mesh network and the wired LAN if desired. An AP (mesh node) establishes an all-wireless path to the mesh portal by locating and associating with its nearest neighbor, thus finding the best path to the mesh portal. The mesh portal uses its wired interface to reach the controller and establish a link to the wired LAN, and there, we have a neat connection.

Another real-world experience occurs with old networks. Old networks may also be updated or upgraded. At times, this is where we spot some legacy or older technologies. We sometimes refer to these hybrids as **patchwork quilts**, and there is a strong similarity in differing shapes, sizes, and hardware implemented. There may even be gross or awkward mismatches in the technologies used.

Tree topology

A tree topology is a type of network topology that includes at least three specific levels in a topology hierarchy. Tree topologies are valued for their scalability and accessibility for troubleshooting. A tree topology is also a hybrid network topology whereby star networks are interconnected via bus networks. Therefore, tree networks are hierarchical, and each node can have a random or unfixed number of child nodes.

This hierarchical approach is also implemented in enterprise networks. For example, *Cisco* uses a three-layer hierarchical approach to promote better performance, more security, redundancy, improved scalability, and better solutions for managing, troubleshooting, and documenting its network infrastructures. As with other networking models, layering is also in use to act as a support in design and deployment; see *Figure 2.6*:

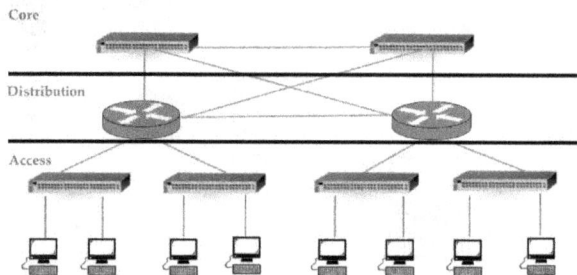

Figure 2.6: Three-layer hierarchy

Logical topologies

There are only two logical topologies (that is a bus or ring). A physical bus or ring is easy to conceptualize.

Note: A physical star could be either a bus or a ring in logical terms. The predominant type of network in operation is a star-bus topology.

Logical bus

The features of a logical bus are as follows:

- Modern Ethernet networks are star topologies (physically).

- The hub is at the center and defines a star topology.

- The hub itself uses a logical bus topology internally, to transmit data to all segments.

Refer to *Figure 2.7*:

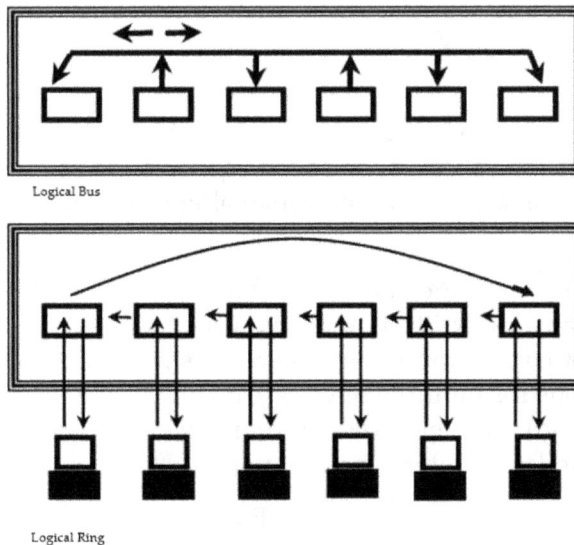

Figure 2.7: *Logical topologies*

Logical ring

The features of a logical ring are as follows:

- Data in a star topology can transmit data in a ring.

- The **Multistation Access Unit (MAU)** looks like an ordinary hub, but data is passed internally using a logical ring.

Network types

The size of a network can be conveyed by the geographic area they occupy and the number of computers that are part of the network. Networks can cover anything from a handful of devices within a single room to millions of devices spread across the entire globe. Examples of network types include:

- **Personal area network (PAN)**
- **Local area network (LAN)**
- **Campus area network (CAN)**
- **Metropolitan area network (MAN)**
- **Wide area network (WAN)**
- **Wireless local area network (WLAN)**

This section is an outline of these network types.

Personal area network

A PAN is a computer network arranged around an individual person within a single building. This could be inside a small office or home. A standard PAN would include one or more computers, telephones or smartphones, peripheral devices such as cameras or printers, video game consoles, and other personal entertainment systems, for example, sound bars or PDAs.

If several individuals use the same network within a residence, the network is sometimes referred to as a **home area network (HAN)**. In a very typical setup, a residence will have a single wired internet connection to a modem. This modem then provides both wired and wireless connections for multiple devices. The network is typically maintained by a single computer, although it can be accessed from any device, especially with remote log-in capabilities to the modem/router via a browser.

This type of network provides great flexibility. For example, it allows you to:

- Send a document to the printer in the office upstairs while you are in a different room.
- Upload a photo from your smartphone to your desktop computer.
- Synchronize devices.
- Watch movies from an online streaming service to your TV or screencast a favorite video from your phone or laptop to the TV.

In today's technology-based world, the likelihood is that we are in the presence of many PANs around us or a close approximation.

Local area network

A LAN is a computer network that interconnects computers within a limited area, such as a residence, school, library, or other small to medium organization. LANs are typically contained within a single building.

Simple LANs generally consist of cabling and one or more switches. A switch can be connected to a router, cable modem, or ADSL modem for internet access. A LAN can include a wide variety of other network devices, such as firewalls, load balancers, and network intrusion detection handling security measures. Advanced LANs are characterized by their use of redundant links with switches using the spanning tree protocol to prevent loops, their ability to manage differing traffic types via **quality of service** (**QoS**), and their ability to segregate traffic with VLANs.

Note: The creation of VLANs improves network performance, dramatically reduces broadcast traffic, hardens the network by securing who accesses what on the network, and, when considered overall, makes the job of the network administrator more streamlined, organized, and easier in the long term. An efficient VLAN design equally helps to support the goals of an organization. We referred to the benefits of VLANs in Chapter 1, OSI Model.

Campus area network

A CAN is a network of multiple interconnected LANs in a limited geographical area. A CAN is smaller than a WAN or MAN. CANs are typically found in universities, as the name suggests, or equally in hospitals or larger businesses. Any network that spans several buildings and maintains its integrity as an organizational network may be defined as a campus area network. Usually, a campus area network uses ethernet cabling on the inside and fiber connections to interlink the buildings, at times over *noisier* thresholds and spaces. As a technology, fiber is immune to electromagnetic interference and radio frequency interference. The integrity of signals is not affected by electrical noise in the environment.

A CAN is also known as a corporate area network.

Metropolitan area network

A MAN is a large computer network that usually spans a city or a large campus. A MAN network is optimized for a larger geographical area than a CAN, ranging from several blocks of buildings to entire cities—hence the word **metropolis**.

A MAN network is formed by connecting multiple LANs/CANs, but it is smaller than a WAN. In short, a MAN connects two or more local area networks together but does not extend beyond the boundaries of the immediate town, city, or metropolitan area.

Wide area networks

WANs are form of telecommunication networks that can connect devices from multiple locations and across the globe. WANs are the largest and most expansive forms of computer networks available to date.

As stated earlier in the chapter, these are the interconnected networks that span the globe. The internet is the biggest network of networks.

There are also different methods used in implementing WAN technologies. For example, now that virtualization has become even more pronounced in its uses in technology as a strong and viable solution, software-defined networking is also an approach in WAN operations, management and deployment.

Software-defined WAN (**SD-WAN**) is an approach for making WAN architectures easier to deploy, operate, and manage. It relies on virtualization, application-level policies, overlay networks, and onsite SD-WAN devices and software platforms.

SD-WAN increases data-transfer efficiencies across a WAN by moving traffic to lower-cost network links to do the work of more expensive leased or MPLS lines. This benefit is an attraction for many customers seeking cost-effective solutions.

An SD-WAN deployment can include existing routers and switches or **virtualized customer premises equipment** (**vCPE**), all running some version of the software that handles policy, security, networking functions, and other management tools, depending on the vendor and customer configuration. The ability to use existing hardware is a positive factor in deployment strategies and, again, is an attraction for customers seeking to lessen the costs of implementing WAN technologies.

One of SD-WAN's chief characteristics is the ability to manage multiple connections from MPLS to broadband to LTE. Another important piece is the ability to segment, partition, and secure the traffic traversing the WAN. This compatibility and interoperability are a great bargaining chip for potential customers.

WLAN

A WLAN is a LAN that uses radio technology instead of wiring to interconnect networked nodes. A WLAN allows users to move around the coverage area. A WLAN employs access points and clients, which are briefly explained as follows:

- **Access points** (**APs**): An AP is a networking hardware device that allows wireless devices to connect to a wired network using Wi-Fi or related standards. It typically connects to a router (via a wired network) as a standalone device. The primary function of an access point is to extend the wireless coverage of an existing network and to increase the number of users that can connect to it.

- Clients may include a variety of devices, such as desktop computers, workstations, laptop computers, IP phones, and other cell phones and smartphone devices. These devices may also be referred to as **end devices**.

There has also been some innovation toward peer-to-peer WLANs that work without a defined access point. These peer-to-peer WLANs challenge the traditional approach to WLAN infrastructure and technology.

Virtual network concepts

Now that we have looked at physical networks, we will begin to have a look at virtual networking concepts. Virtual networking and software-defined networking will additionally be addressed in fuller detail across other chapters but let us find a beginning point in this area of networking with a working definition of virtualization and an outline of important terms where virtualization is concerned.

In a physical network, physical machines are connected so that they can send data to and receive data from each other. In a virtual network, virtual machines are running on a physical machine. These virtual machines are connected logically to each other so that they can send data to and receive data from each other.

Some terms we need to understand include the following:

- **Virtual switch (vSwitch)**: A vSwitch is a software application that allows communication between virtual machines. A vSwitch does more than just forward data packets; it intelligently directs communication on a network by checking data packets before moving them to a destination. Virtual switches are usually embedded into installed software, but they may also be included in a server's hardware as part of its firmware. A vSwitch is completely virtual and can connect to a **network interface card** (**NIC**). The vSwitch merges physical switches into a single logical switch. This helps to increase bandwidth and create an active mesh between the server and switches. (Techopedia)

- **Virtual network interface card (vNIC)**: A vNIC represents the configuration of a VM connected to a network. A VM can be configured to have multiple vNICs. When a VM is provisioned, each of its associated vNICs can be attached to a virtual network bridge to gain connectivity to a specified network. You can manually create a vNIC anytime you want to give a VM access to a network configured on the VM host.

- **Network function virtualization (NFV)**: The primary logic of NFV is to use software functions in place of hardware so that network administrators do not need to configure and manage physical devices. NFV is a network architecture concept that uses IT virtualization technologies to virtualize entire classes of network node functions into building blocks that may connect or chain together to create and deliver communication services. Network functions that can be virtualized with

NFV include **domain name service (DNS)**, **network address translation (NAT)**, firewalls, caching, and intrusion detection. NFV decouples network functions or network services from proprietary hardware appliances so that they can be created in software simulations.

Hypervisors

A hypervisor is a program used to run and manage one or more virtual machines on a computer. The term hypervisor is a modification of the word supervisor, a traditional term for the kernel of an operating system: the hypervisor is the *supervisor of the supervisors*, with hyper used as a stronger variant of super.

There are two categories of hypervisors: type 1 and type 2:

- Type 1, also known as bare metal, includes solutions like VMware ESXi or **Red Hat Virtualization** (**RHEV**), which provide a direct platform for creating and managing **virtual machines** (**VMs**).

- Type 2, on the other hand, is application-based and requires installation on top of an existing operating system, such as Windows Hyper-V or VirtualBox.

In *Figure 2.8*, some steps are given to enable Hyper-V on a Windows 10 OS. By default, Hyper-V is disabled and must be enabled as a role in the operating system.

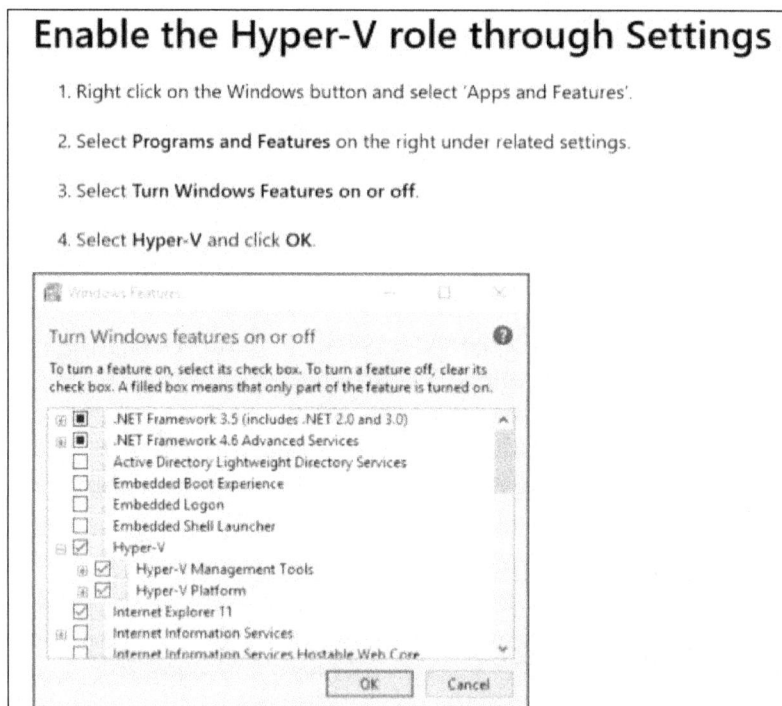

Figure 2.8: Enabling Hyper-V in Windows 10

Figure 2.9 illustrates how data centers can incorporate the virtualization of operating systems into their storage solutions:

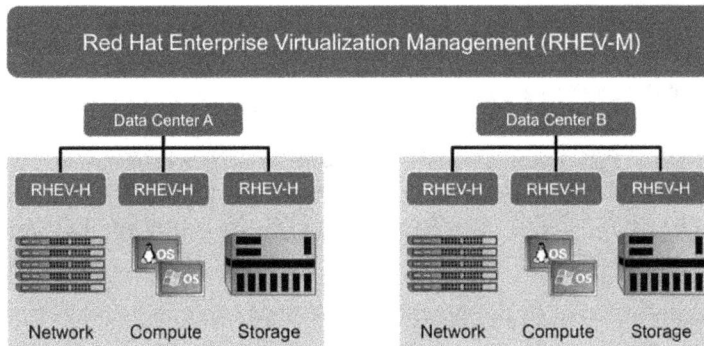

Figure 2.9: *RHEV*

Virtualization has many benefits in networking. These benefits and other practical considerations of virtualization will be specified in other networking concepts and practices. This section serves to offer a brief look at a hugely important technology; one that every budding or existing network administrator needs to know about.

> **Note: Provider links will be expanded on across other topics, for example, in cables and connectors, ports and protocols, and in switching and routing technologies. Applicable links to be further discussed include satellite, digital subscriber line (DSL), cable, leased line, and metro-optical.**

Conclusion

In this chapter, we learned how network topologies demonstrate the various applications and deployment of networking hardware and software to build network connectivity. Understanding network topologies, irrespective of whether they are now obsolete or the current trend, enables a technician to fully appreciate and acknowledge the many ways that one can build and manage a network. As network administrators, it allows us to understand what constitutes our networks and where and how they connect—identifying media, connectors, cables, devices, and other elements in the network design. Building the right structure for our organization is critical to the organization's operations. So, as administrators, we can use this knowledge to build and match our needs to the optimum structure in which our needs are met and proficiently resolved. Whether we work in a LAN, CAN, WLAN, or WAN environment, our technical abilities will be strengthened, and awareness deepened in accordance with our understanding of how networks are built and the technology underpinning their construction.

In the upcoming chapter, we are going to learn more about the cables and connectors used in the various types of networks. Additionally, we will discuss how, as a network administrator, you can make informed choices about cabling to meet the appropriate conditions for the network being built. The chapter demonstrates how to make twisted pair cabling and discusses how you can develop the skills required for handling network infrastructure.

Points to remember

- A network topology describes the arrangement of systems on a computer network. It defines how the computers, or nodes, within the network, are arranged and connected to each other. Some common network topologies include bus, star, ring, mesh, hybrid, and tree configurations.

- The actual layout of a network and its devices/objects is its physical topology.

- The way in which the data accesses the medium and transmits packets is the logical topology.

- The factors impacting the choice of topology are as follows:

    o Cost

    o Scalability

    o Bandwidth capacity

    o Ease of installation and configuration

    o Ease of troubleshooting and maintenance

- Understanding network topologies helps us:

    o To better understand networking concepts.

    o In determining the media type to be used to cable a network.

    o To troubleshoot or fault-find easier and more efficiently.

    o Effectively select and use resources and networking components.

    o Better understand that gathering all the requirements and needs should precede the building of any network design or topology.

- Virtualization is another means of implementing networks. Understanding the significance of virtual network concepts is a requisite in modern networking solutions.

- The content of this chapter is mapped to *Domain 1: Networking Concepts*. Compare and contrast network topologies, architectures, and types.

Key terms

- **Physical topology**: Physical topology refers to the actual layout of devices and cables in a network. It shows how different devices are physically connected to each other. Examples include star, bus, ring, and mesh topologies.

- **Logical topology**: Logical topology refers to the way data flows within a network, regardless of its physical layout. It shows the path that data takes between devices.

- **Network types:**

  - **PAN**: Covers a very small area, typically within a single room. Examples include Bluetooth-connected devices like a smartphone and a wireless headset.

  - **LAN**: Covers a small geographic area, such as a single building or campus. Commonly used in homes, schools, and offices to connect computers and devices.

  - **CAN**: A network that spans multiple buildings within a campus, such as a university or corporate campus. It is larger than a LAN but smaller than a MAN.

  - **MAN**: Spans a larger area than a LAN, such as a city or a large campus. It connects multiple LANs within a metropolitan area.

  - **WAN**: Covers a broad area, often a country or continent. The internet is the largest example of a WAN, connecting millions of devices worldwide.

- **Software-defined WAN**: An approach for making WAN architectures easier to deploy, operate, and manage. It relies on virtualization, application-level policies, overlay networks, and onsite SD-WAN devices and software platforms.

- **Multiprotocol label switching**: MPLS is a mechanism used within computer network infrastructures to speed up the time it takes a data packet to flow from one node to another. It enables computer networks to be faster and easier to manage by using short path labels instead of long network addresses for routing network packets.

Questions

1. What is a networking topology?

2. List the factors that impact choosing a network topology.

3. What topologies are now legacy or obsolete? Explain why this is the case. Give reasons for the topology's status as legacy, as it relates to practical networking.

4. What is the most predominant network topology in use today? Give reasons for this preference as it relates to practical networking.

5. List the various network types and the geographical locations they cover.

6. For what purpose is each network type used? Explain.

7. Do you see the benefits of including additional switches or backup techniques to star topology? Explain.

Join our book's Discord space

Join the book's Discord Workspace for Latest updates, Offers, Tech happenings around the world, New Release and Sessions with the Authors:

https://discord.bpbonline.com

CHAPTER 3

Cables and Connectors

Introduction

In this chapter, we get down to the bare bones of network connectivity to identify and observe the ways in which a network can be interlinked and cabled.

When handling network infrastructure or the accelerating evolution and growth of new technologies and applications, considering physical network cabling and compliance with present cabling standards and protocols is paramount. Cabling is the foundational backbone of all networks. Moreover, information and data transmission are currently moving at speeds considered impossible some decades ago. Yet, these same emerging technologies and applications drive and push the need for a network's infrastructure to be reliable, steadfast, and preferably forward-looking. Physical cabling implementations must keep up both strategically and structurally when scalable solutions are essentially the norm. Cabling design equally needs to demonstrate that the implementer is thinking ahead and predicting advances and modifications whilst planning for potential changes. Given the rapid pace of technological advancements, a network administrator plays a pivotal role in overseeing and enhancing the infrastructure to adapt to these ongoing changes.

Even if your business hires the services of other companies to look after the network cabling installation initially, once installed, as a network administrator, you will need to be aware of the connectivity and links between workstations, other end devices, and intermediary devices such as switches, routers, access points, and even more modern **Internet of Things (IoT)** devices. As a network administrator, you operate best when you know your network meticulously, and with this in mind, understanding the intricacy of how the network is cabled, how it is connected, and how cabling supports your network as it functions, enhances this IT awareness.

Structure

This chapter will focus on the following topics:

- Copper
- Coaxial cable
- Fiber
- Fiber optic cable types and distance
- Fiber connector types

Objectives

In this chapter, we will compare and contrast transmission media and transceivers. Upon completing this chapter, readers will be equipped to select the appropriate cables and connectors for network device interconnections. They will be able to distinguish between different cable and connector types and identify the network topologies in which they are used. Additionally, readers will understand Ethernet standards and other technical standards related to cables and connectors. They will be able to describe fiber-optic cabling and explain its main advantages over other media. Furthermore, readers will learn how to construct both straight-through and crossover Ethernet cables. Finally, they will appreciate the importance of cable management and be familiar with cable management procedures and practices.

Copper

Network cables and connectors come in many different types for different network configurations. When we discussed network topologies in *Chapter 1, OSI Model*, we saw that the most common type of network, especially in a LAN, is a star-bus configuration, that is, a physical star with a logical bus topology for accessing and managing the transmission of data.

In wired communication, connectivity in this topology is achieved using copper as most cabled LANs use copper as a medium in the transmission of data. The copper in use is primarily unshielded/shielded twisted pair. First, we will take a look at the structure of this copper cable.

Unshielded twisted pair

Unshielded twisted pair (**UTP**) cable is the most used cable in Ethernet LAN networking. Depending upon the specified category, there are two or more insulated copper conductors.

These wires/conductors are twisted around each other in pairs—thus the name twisted pair. In telephony, *Category 1* cable is used for telephone connections. In other networking implementations, such as Ethernet LANS, *Category 3* and above are typically used. The categories described in the following table address speed and bandwidth issues:

Type	Connector	Description
Phone cable	RJ-11	To establish a dial-up Internet connection, this cable is used to connect a modem to a phone jack in a wall outlet. There are two pairs of twisted cables in this product (a total of four wires). Old telephone cable.

Table 3.1: *Category 1 UTP*

Note: An RJ-11 telephone connector has six pins, and an RJ-45 connector has eight pins.

The categories listed in *Table 3.2* are UTP cable types that support slower/obsoleted topologies and slower transmission rates:

Type	Connector	Description
Cat 3	RJ-45	Designed for use with 10BASE-T, 10-megabit Ethernet, or 16-megabit token ring.
Cat 5	RJ-45	Supports 100 megabit and 1 gigabit Ethernet and ATM networking.

Table 3.2: *Older technologies*

We will look at the more modern cable types in use after an initial look at the structure of twisted pair cables and the various specifications in use.

Let us have a look at this UTP cable:

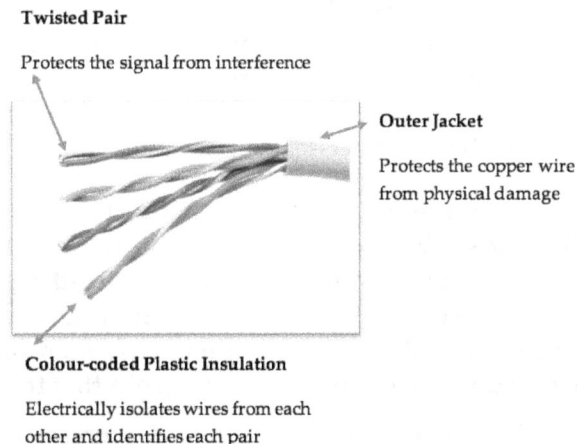

Twisted Pair

Protects the signal from interference

Outer Jacket

Protects the copper wire from physical damage

Colour-coded Plastic Insulation

Electrically isolates wires from each other and identifies each pair

Figure 3.1: *Unshielded twisted cable*

Observe the twisted pairs of cables. We can see eight wires/conductors that have been restructured or twisted into four pairs. These pairs are using balanced pair operation. The unbalanced transmission uses one signal wire that carries the voltage. The balanced transmission uses two signal wires that both carry the voltage—but the signal on one of them is phase-shifted by 180°, so it is exactly inverted. When we investigate the signals being carried over the wires, we identify that the signals are the same, with the exception that one of these signals will be a positive signal. The phase-shifted signal will be a negative signal. As the signal travels through the wires, the twist handles potential interference by continually moving away from it. Therefore, when the signals are calculated or revalued on the other end, we will determine the value that has passed through the pair.

A twisted pair decreases both internal and external electromagnetic radiation, as well as crosstalk between surrounding pairs, and enhances rejection of external electromagnetic interference. You may hear some IT technicians, long in the field, state triumphantly that the *secret is in the twist*. Consequently, when we, as technicians, make the cable, we too must pay attention to the twist and the rate of the twist in each of the pairs since this either *makes or breaks* a working cable. The differing rate of the twist is especially important in cables containing small numbers of pairs. When two conductors lie close to each other in a parallel formation, this could undo the benefits of the twist and engender crosstalk between the pairs. So, the rate of the twist is significant in the type of cables used in today's networks.

Therefore, you will notice that the pairs in *Figure 3.1* are twisted at different twist rates. This means that even if the interference impacted by the pairs is of the same strength, the end set of values from pair to pair will still differ. This is because the pairs have been twisted at different twist rates. The rate or pitch of the twist will combat crosstalk or interference, which occurs when cables are lying in parallel, and when signals interfere with each other. The other thing to heed in this figure is the absence of shielding. Nothing else, no other fabric or material, surrounds the pairs of conductors to protect them further or shield them from harmful interference. There is only the outer jacket. Due to the thinness of this outer jacket, the cable is quite susceptible to crosstalk. It can also be vulnerable to eavesdropping with potential unwanted threat actors listening in on the data transmissions. As you see, there is literally minimal protection coming from the outer jacket around the wires, thus the term unshielded. This cable would not perform well in a *noisy* environment with indicators of potential interference. Regarding the number of pairs available, pairs can range from 4 to 25 or even to 100 in larger-scale operations.

Tip: The polyvinyl chloride outer jacket protects the bundles of twisted pairs in ordinary UTP (PVC). When PVC is heated, it emits toxic gases. The majority of network cables run through the plenum space, which includes spaces in the ceiling, walls, and beneath the floor. Hazardous gases can swiftly spread through a structure if wires with PVC jackets fire in the plenum region. Only plenum-grade fire-resistant cabling should be installed in the plenum space to avoid this threat.

You may be questioned on your understanding of plenum grade cabling in the CompTIA Network+ examination.

In building construction, there are areas within a building that demand a specialized type or grade of cable. These areas are known as **plenum areas**. Effectively, there are separate spaces in a building where air circulation occurs. This area is also known as the heating, ventilation, and air conditioning or HVAC area. These *pathways for airflow* are required for heating, ventilation, and air-conditioning systems to operate efficiently. The plenum area or space is normally in a space between the structural ceiling and a drop-down ceiling or in the space underneath a raised floor. Plenum-rated cables are more expensive than regular cables, but they are also purpose-built as fire-resistant with low smoke emissions when aflame. The insulation used in manufacturing this cable, as well as being fire resistant, is non-toxic when burned. These low smoke and low flame features make plenum cable the appropriate cable for these plenum spaces. An example of the material used in the jacket of plenum cable is Teflon FEP. This type of cable, alongside other plenum grade types, goes through rigorous fire tests, which is why it must be strictly adhered to in construction practices. Twisted pair and coaxial cable are made in plenum versions for purchase and installation. Note that in order to comply with building codes and safety and health regulations or be knowledgeable about the same, a network administrator should know the types and standards of cable for varied usage, even when they are not directly involved in its installation. With a growing emphasis on data center technologies, a network administrator should also be familiar with the purpose and functions of the HVAC area.

Shielded twisted pair

Shielded twisted pair (**STP**) prevents interference better than UTP. The disadvantage of STP is that it is more expensive than UTP because of the extra shielding. It is bulkier than UTP and, therefore, more difficult to install due to the thickness of the cable and because it is less flexible than UTP.

The metallic shielding must be grounded at both ends. If not, the shield acts like an antenna picking up unwanted signals. These signals, when inadvertently captured, turn into interference. There are several different shield construction types. For example, shielded Cat5e, Cat6/6A, and Cat8/8.1 cables typically have F/UTP construction, whereas shielded Cat7/7A and Cat8.2 cables use S/FTP construction.

> **Note: The code before the slash designates the shielding for the cable itself, whereas the code after the slash determines the shielding for the individual pairs.**

Refer to the following:

- **U**: Unshielded
- **F**: Foil shielding
- **S**: Screened shielding (outer layer only)
- **TP**: Twisted pair
- **TQ**: Twisted pair, individual shielding in quads

When purchasing cable, it is good to know if the cable is solid or stranded. If you want to install cable and expect it may be used or moved around in the future, select stranded cables. Stranded cables are best for patch cords and increased mobility. Alternatively, solid cables are best used in semi-permanent and permanent installations. This is because they are not as flexible as stranded cables and may break easily when bent. On the positive side, solid cables (despite this susceptibility to poor handling or repeatedly being bent) are able to conduct signals better and carry the signals well.

Let us look at one example of STP cable:

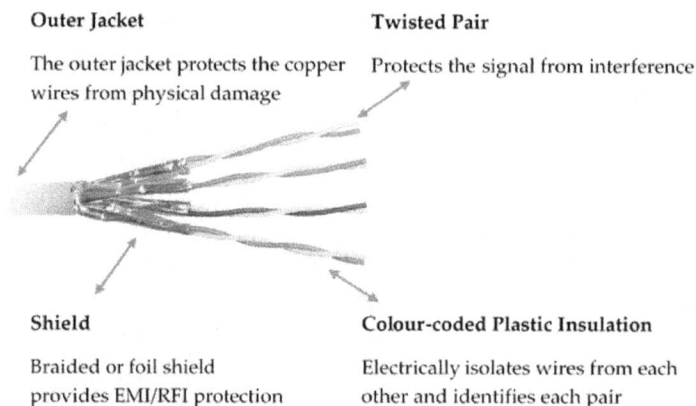

Outer Jacket

The outer jacket protects the copper wires from physical damage

Twisted Pair

Protects the signal from interference

Shield

Braided or foil shield provides EMI/RFI protection

Colour-coded Plastic Insulation

Electrically isolates wires from each other and identifies each pair

Figure 3.2: Shielded twisted pair cable

In *Figure 3.3*, we can see the use of a braided shield:

Figure 3.3[1]: Twisted pair cable shielding with braided shielding around all pairs

STP cables are used in noisy environments since they protect against EMF or other kinds of high interference. This type of high-level interference can come from power lines or close-by electromagnetic fields and even radar systems. STP cables can be found in network closets or communications (comm) rooms in business organizations. Another location where we find STP cables is in data centers. Data centers also use a very specific type of cable named **Pair in Metal Foil (PiMF)**. Unlike STP shielding, PiMF has shielding for individual pairs and is also shielded as an overall unit. This overall shield enables data transmission to run at frequencies up to 2,000 MHz with the latest specs in Ethernet cable. Transmissions of 25 or 40 gigabit Ethernet can be implemented. Viewing these stats, it is easy to see why accelerating the speed of transmission requires optimum cabling installations!

Having discussed the structure and makeup of twisted pair cabling, we will have a better perception of why the category of cable used is relevant to meeting standards and ensuring our networks perform optimally.

UTP cable types

Table 3.3 provides a detailed comparison of various categories of Ethernet cables, their corresponding connectors, and their specific characteristics. This information is crucial for understanding the capabilities and applications of each cable type, which is essential for selecting the appropriate cabling for different networking environments.

Type	Connector	Description
Cat 5	RJ-45	Supports 100 megabit transmission.
Cat 5e	RJ-45	*Category 5e* has more twists per foot than *Category 5* wiring. These extra twists further prevent interference from outside sources and the other wires within the cable.
Cat 6	RJ-45	Supports 10 gigabit for 55mt and 1 gigabit for 100mt.
Cat 6A	RJ-45	Supports up to 10 gigabits per second for a maximum length of 100mt shielded, frequency 500 MHz *Category 6* cable uses a plastic divider to separate and maintain the position of the pairs of wires relative to each other. This prevents interference. The pairs also have more twists than *Category 5e* cable.
Cat 7	GG45/TERA Non-RJ45	Supports 40gigabit for max 50mt and 10gigabit on 100mt.
Cat 8	GG45/TERA Class1: RJ45 Class 2: Non-RJ45	Supports up to 40 gigabits per second, shielded, frequency 2,000 MHz 25–40 gigabits Ethernet

Table 3.3: Newer technologies

Other considerations: When transmitting at 10 Gbps, Cat6 cable has a range of 37–55 m (depending on crosstalk). It can send signals at a frequency of up to 250 MHz, which shows how frequently the signal can pass through the cable. Furthermore, it uses the RJ-45 standard connector and is backward compatible with older Cat5 and Cat5e versions.

To accommodate 10 Gbps Ethernet, the Cat7 standard was ratified years before the Cat6a standard (10GBASE-T). Each twisted pair, as well as the entire cable, must be shielded. It also defines whether the connectors are GG45 or TERA. Cat6 cable has an expected life cycle of roughly 10 years, whereas Cat7 cable has an estimated life cycle of around 15 years.

Maximum lengths of cable

Signals degrade over a distance, so when using a cable, one must consider the maximum length advised for the cable being used.

Ethernet cables typically have a maximum cable length of 100 m (328 ft.). These maximum cable lengths are to counteract **attenuation** or **signal degradation**. If the reality for longer runs of cable is to be met accordingly, then a network administrator must know the technical specifications of the cable being installed as well as the rules for using a repeater or amplifier when required in the run. Do not let this 328 ft./100 m spec mislead you. Reaching further distances with cable is not as easy a calculation as simply purchasing a reel of Ethernet and just running it from source to *further* destination. Although the specifics of this calculation are beyond the scope of the CompTIA Network+ in terms of questions you may be asked, please note that in real-world networking, an administrator must consult the rules and methods of installation and whether the link is to be a permanent link. In short, your patch cables and keystone jacks need to be all the same categories, but you do have choice and variation in your approach/installation techniques and in adhering to calculating the end-to-end maximum length. This length encompasses all aspects of the installation—to include across cable/keystone jack usage. Moreover, maximum length can also be affected by EMI/RFI. Sometimes, you need to use shielded Ethernet cable, as seen in environments where shielded versus unshielded cable is used. You may need to reduce distances if your cable is subjected to heat above 68 °F as temperatures additionally have an effect on Ethernet cable length.

Attenuation or signal degradation essentially occurs when a signal loses its strength over distances. This is why adhering to the rules of maximum cable lengths is critical to maintaining signal quality and integrity. Attenuation happens with analog or digital signals and its potential must be addressed by network administrators whenever they plan to install network cable.

Repeaters are used in attenuating circuits to boost the signal through amplification (the opposite of attenuation). When using copper conductors, the higher the frequency signal, the more attenuation is caused along a cable length. According to *Techopedia,* modern communications use high frequencies, so other mediums that have a flat attenuation across all frequencies, such as fiber optics, are used instead of traditional copper circuits.

Repeaters operate at the physical layer of the OSI model. Essentially, their function is to amplify or regenerate a signal before transmission. They are normally used when a host machine or end device is outside the reach of the maximum length of Ethernet cable and where the signal would not reach that point accurately or with integrity without amplification. In this way, they can expand the coverage area of the network. We may also refer to these devices as **signal boosters**.

Another thing to be aware of is using the correct connector and the **twisted pair connector types**. Here is an outline of the connector types and their typical usage:

Connector	Description
RJ-11	• Has four connectors. • Supports up to two pairs of wires. • Uses a locking tab to keep the connector secure in the outlet and to prevent the cable from slipping or partially connecting, potentially causing performance issues. • Used primarily for telephone wiring. • You cannot plug an RJ45 cable connector into an RJ11 interface/port/slot; however, you can do the opposite (you should avoid doing so as it can damage the RJ45 port).
RJ-45	• Has eight connectors. • An 8-pin/8-position plug, or jack is commonly used to connect computers onto Ethernet-based LAN. • Supports up to four pairs of wires. • Uses a locking tab to keep the connector secure in the outlet *and* to prevent it from slipping out or becoming loose, potentially impacting network connectivity or link performance. • Used for Ethernet and some token ring connections.
GG45	• Has eight connectors. • Supports four pairs of wires. • GG45 or ARJ45 HD is the full connector with 12 contacts, providing a *Category 6* cable interface (100/250 MHz) for older devices as well as the new interface. • ARJ45 HS is the version without the Cat6-compatible contacts, for a total of eight contacts. • Four additional conductors in the corners of the connector that duplicate and replace the four inner pins on the RJ45.
TERA	• Has eight connectors. • Supports four pairs of wires. • Virtually immune to alien crosstalk and internal crosstalk, far exceeding 10GBASE-T requirements. • EMI/RFI protection for noisy environments and TEMPEST rated for high-security applications. • Incompatible with RJ45 and GG45. • Does not require special tools to install.
Field (Rugged) RJ45	• Heavy environmental shielding (IP-rated against dust, dirt, moisture, and so on). • Vibration shielding/screw-terminated shields.

Table 3.4: *Twisted pair connectors*

Ethernet cable color code standards

Network administrators should be aware of the cabling standards for Ethernet cables. The ability to make cable is a great skill to hold. It helps in troubleshooting and network configuration—plus, it can be cheaper to make *regular runs of cable* than purchase a manufactured cable with defined and exact measures. By *regular runs*, we mean the cable that runs from the wall jack to the end device or workstation. Many technicians will advise that homemade cable is perfect for these scenarios but equally recommend purchased, manufactured cables for patch panels or network intermediary devices like connections between switches and routers or other forms of equipment to be used in data transmission. When making cables, it is critical to comply with the standards and modify the cables properly. Improperly made cables can drop signals or cause disruptions or loss in network traffic and connectivity.

T-568a straight-through Ethernet cable

In terms of the functionality of Ethernet cable standards, there is no difference in the T-568A or T-568 cable. It is totally up to a network administrator which standard to choose. However, as with many other networking practices, it is best to ascertain what is already in place in an organization's network configuration and topology and adhere to the standard in use for continuity and best practice. The following two figures show the T-568A and T-568B cable configurations:

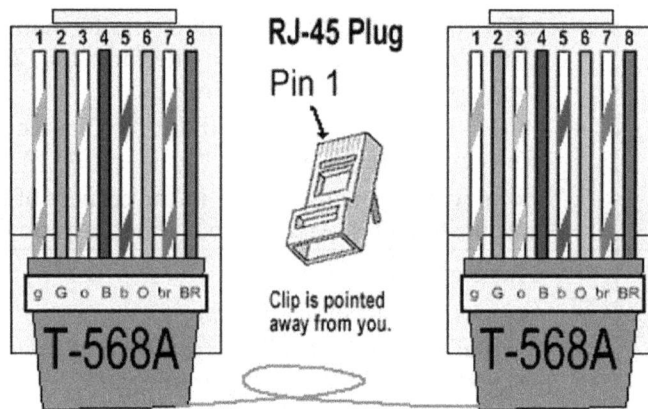

Figure 3.4: *Straight through Ethernet cable (T-568A)*

The following figure illustrates the color-coding standard for a straight through T-568B to T-568B connection:

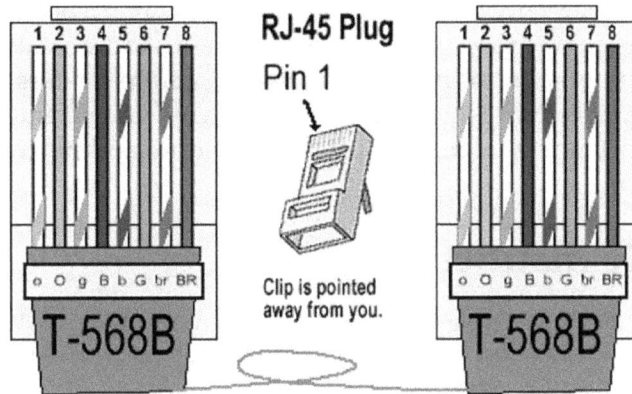

Figure 3.5: *Straight through Ethernet cable (T-568B)*

Straight-through cables can be either T-568A or T-568B. These cables are typically used as patch cords in patch panels. When connecting two devices that are *alike*, for example, a PC to a PC or a switch to a switch, a crossover cable is required. *Unalike* or dissimilar devices use straight-through cables for connectivity between them, for example, a PC to a switch or a switch to a router. One exception to this rule is when a PC is connected to a router without a switch in the middle. If the PC is directly connected to the router, even though they are *unalike* devices, a crossover cable is required. *Figure 3.7* illustrates a crossover cable configuration.

Rj-45 crossover Ethernet cable

The following figure shows the color-coding standard used for Ethernet crossover cable:

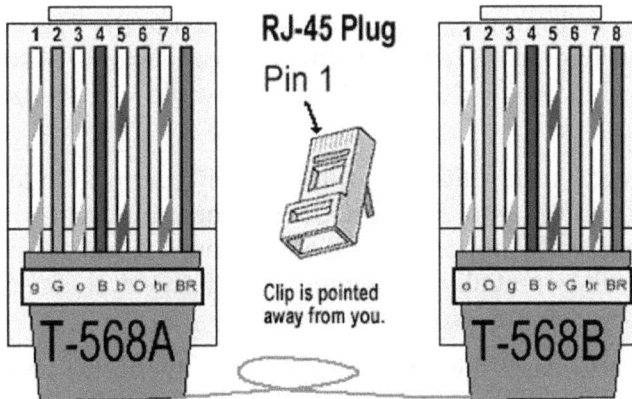

Figure 3.6: *Crossover Ethernet cable (T-568A to T-568B)*

The best way to make a crossover cable and the easiest procedure to remember and follow is to wire one end of the cable adhering to the T-568A standard and the other adhering to the T-568B standard. Administrators have different tips for recalling color codes, but one method is to switch the green set of wires with the orange set. To be more exact about this, we are switching the solid green with the solid orange. Additionally, we are switching green/white with the orange/white. Other network administrators use mnemonics or charts to assist them. These strategies are available to view online, but the best way to get to this stage of competence is to personalize the procedure and process for yourself with application and practice.

Ethernet cable instructions

Making a cable can seem quite daunting, but when you break it down into steps and follow the correct standards and rules, the process is not as overwhelming. The steps are as follows:

1. Remember to follow the standards and rules for the maximum length of Ethernet cable. If in doubt or if you want to double-check this, consult a relevant chart on Ethernet standards and maximum lengths. Ensure you have the correct tools and equipment to make the cable: a length of cable, RJ45 connectors, a cutting tool, a side cutter or scissors, a pair of crimpers, and an Ethernet cable tester so you can test the finished product when the process is complete, and cable made.

2. Now, you are ready to strip the cable ends. Remove the outer jacket about 1 to 2 inches from the end of the cable. Pay attention to the wires so that you do not accidentally damage them.

3. Looking at your chart for the desired cable standard, T-568A or T-568B, untwist the pairs and then align them in accordance with your needs. Trim off the extra wires and ensure that the length of the pairs is appropriate for fitting into the RJ45 connector. Please note that overly long cable ends may result in potential signaling issues and, when too short, will not correctly fit into the RJ45 connector. It is good to observe the inner length and breadth of the connector to observe the dimensions you need for the cable to fit correctly. Cut the cable lengths so that they are about 1.2 cm long.

4. Now, it is time to insert the wires into the RJ45 connector. Steer the cable so that the wires are guided into the connector, maintaining the correct color sequence. This part is especially important as the wires need to make a connection correctly or the cable will potentially fail when tested. Recheck that the wires are oriented correctly and match the color code standard.

5. Be careful not to bend the wires as you insert them. It is best to hold the RJ45 connector with the clip facing downward. Ensure that the wires are all the way up into the gold pins of the head of the connector.

6. Insert the cable into the crimpers and press down. Make sure the wires are flat against the connector and are fully seated and secure.

7. Test the cable with the relevant cable tester.

Basic theory

Figure 3.7 outlines the connectivity between a PC and a hub/switch and a PC to PC. On the left-hand side, we see the PC to hub configuration and the use of an Ethernet straight-through cable to form the connection. On the right-hand side of the illustration, we see a PC networked to another PC to form connectivity.

Since the internal wiring is different for dissimilar devices, we can identify that the **transmitter pins** (**TX**) on the PC are connected to the **receiver pins** (**RX**) on the hub. Additionally, the transmit-to-receive from the hub's perspective works and aligns perfectly with the PC's internal wiring. Now, observe the crossover connection between the devices that are similar or *alike*. The PCs transmit (TX) of 1 and 2 crossovers to 3 and 6, and connectivity is properly established. Likewise, Pins 1 and 2 of the PC to the right of the diagram crossover to Pins 3 and 6 of the PC on the left. This illustration demonstrates the internal operations of the cabling standards when used with hosts or devices. Pins 4, 5, 7, and 8 are not used in either standard but make the cabling easier to use when all the wires are grouped together into their respective pairs:

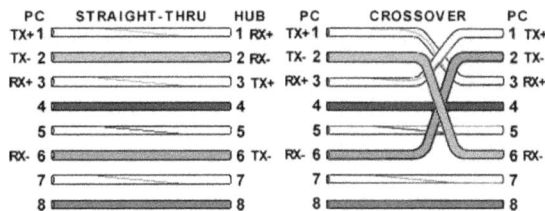

Figure 3.7: Color-coding and pins

UTP testing parameters

In *Figure 3.8*, we see an example of a wire mapping tester. These testers can test specific data such as the following:

- The length of the cable
- The amount of signal loss to signal degradation (attenuation)
- The presence of crosstalk
- The wire maps

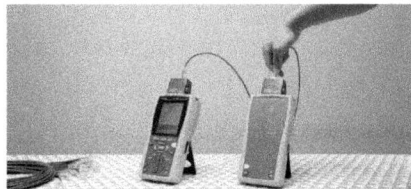

Figure 3.8: Testing copper cables with wire mapping tester

Image @community.fs.com

Coaxial cable

Coaxial cable is an older technology that is typically used in conjunction with an Ethernet IEEE 802.3 bus topology. Since the cable ends must be terminated, it is not suited for ring or star topologies. For LAN deployments within buildings, twisted-pair cabling has largely replaced coaxial cabling, whereas fiber-optic cabling has largely replaced coaxial cabling for high-speed network backbones.

A coaxial cable is a copper-cored cable surrounded by heavy shielding. There are several types of coaxial cable, including the following:

- **ThickNet or 10Base5**: Coax cable with a maximum length of 500 m that was used in networks and ran at 10 megabits per second

- **ThinNet or 10Base2**: Coax cable with a maximum length of 185 m that was used in networks and ran at 10 megabits per second

- **RG-59**: Most commonly used for cable television in the USA.

- **RG-6**: Higher quality cable than RG-59 with more bandwidth and less susceptibility to interference.

Coaxial cable types

The following table outlines the coaxial cable types:

Grade	Uses	Resistance rating
RG-58	10Base2 Ethernet networking (also called thinnet)	50 ohms
RG-59	Cable TV and cable networking	75 ohms
RG-6	Satellite TV	75 ohms
RG-8	10Base5 Ethernet networking (also called thicknet)	50 ohms

Table 3.5: Coaxial cable types

Cable structure

The cable structure consists of the following:

- Outer cable jacket to prevent minor physical damage.

- A woven copper braid/shield, or metallic foil, acts as the second wire in the circuit and as a shield for the inner conductor.

- A layer of flexible plastic insulation.

- A copper conductor is used to transmit the electronic signals.

The following figure outlines the typical cable structure of coaxial cable:

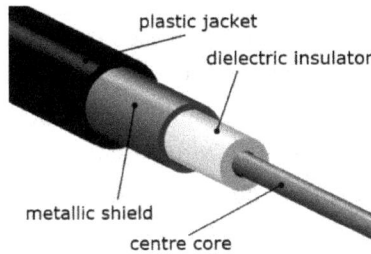

Figure 3.9: Coaxial cable

Coax connector types

Coaxial cable has distinct connector styles, male and female. Male connectors have a protruding metal pin in the center, whereas female connectors have a receptacle to receive that pin. Other connector types use mounted flush instead of mating mechanisms.

Table 3.6 illustrates connector types and typical uses:

Connector	Description
F-type	• This connector is used to connect a coaxial cable to a home broadband connection. This male connector is attached to the female counterpart via a screw. Coax is usually used to connect the cable modem to the wall outlet (more so in the US). An RJ-45 jack on the cable modem will be used to connect a computer or wireless access point. • Twisted onto the cable. • Used to create cable and satellite TV connections. • Used to hook a cable modem to a broadband cable connection.
Crimp on F connectors	• There are three types of F plug connectors. Screw On F Connectors, Crimp-on F Plugs, as seen in the illustration, and Compression F Plugs. Crimp-on F connectors are superior to screw-on plugs, but the optimum F-type plugs are Compression F plugs.
Weatherproof Compression F Plug	• A compression plug requires a specialist tool to terminate the F plug which can be quite expensive to purchase. • This is especially true with the tools that allow you to terminate onto the thicker diameter coax cables, like 1.25 mm or 1.65 mm center conductor coaxial cable. • Very secure connection.

Connector	Description
BNC (image of BNC connectors)	• A BNC connector is used in computer networks and with television equipment. • It was predominantly used in Bus topologies with Ethernet standards such as 10base2. • The central pin in the male connector is mated with the female connector, which has two bayonet lugs that make the connection when the coupling nut gets twisted.
AUI (image of AUI connector)	• The interface between the Ethernet/IEEE 802.3 controller and the baseband transceiver or broadband modem. • DB15 serial connector. • Used in 10Base5 Ethernet networks.

Table 3.6: Coaxial connectors

Fiber

It turns out that all Netflix streaming peak on Saturday night can fit inside a single fiber optic, which is the size of one human hair.

- Reed Hastings, CEO of Netflix

This single quote gives us a sense of just how much data fiber can handle in data transmission. However, alongside the transmission needs of *big data*, there are other huge benefits to fiber use in networking. Fiber is ideal for some networking scenarios, especially where distance, noisy environments, bandwidth needs, and reliable speed and continuity are factors. As it stands, fiber transmits data over longer distances at a higher bandwidth than any other networking media available. It is less susceptible to attenuation and completely immune to EMI/RFI. It is made of flexible, extremely thin strands of very pure glass and uses a laser or LED to encode bits as pulses of light to transmit data. The fiber-optic cable acts as a waveguide to transmit light between the two ends with minimal signal loss. This minimal signal loss is optimum for data transmission.

The use of fiber optic cabling has radically grown since networks have increased in speed and even still, faster speeds are sought after. Fiber cable used to be primarily used in WAN technology, but now we see it in broadband for home and enterprise installations and other LAN implementations. Examples of more recent usages are **Fiber to the Home (FTTH)** or Fiber to the Business.

In terms of operation, Ethernet cables use electrical pulses to transmit and receive signals/information, whereas Fiber uses light pulses. These light pulses are guided through the fiber cable by using glass or plastic in the cable due to glass or plastic's *transparent* properties. The two types of fiber-optic cabling are single-mode fiber and multimode, with single-mode fiber being able to handle faster speeds and further distances than multimode.

Types of fiber media

Single-mode fibers can only propagate one sort of light mode at a time, but multimode fibers can propagate numerous modes. Fiber core diameter, wavelength and light source, bandwidth, color sheath, distance, and cost are the primary distinctions between single-mode and multimode fiber optic cables. Let us look at the types of fiber media:

- **Multimode**: This cable uses a thicker code when compared with the core in single-mode. Multimode cable uses LEDs as its light source, whereas single-mode uses lasers. Due to the light source used, the distance of transmissions is short, that is, traveling a few km or less.

- **Single-mode**: Cable that has a very thin core. It is harder to make, uses lasers as a light source, and can transmit signals dozens of kilometers with ease.

An example of the difference in speeds between multimode and single-mode fiber is captured in the following statistic. SanSpot network design engineers estimate that 100G OS2 single-mode fiber cables are the highest-performing fiber optic cables available in 2022. These cables apparently outrun multimode specifications. Data can be transported with OS2 fiber with the following specifications:

- 100G for up to 10 km using a 1,310 nm transceiver

- Up to 40 km using a 1550 nm transceiver

The types of transceivers used are equally as important as the type of cable selected for use. In terms of compatibility, single-mode fiber and multimode fiber are incompatible. Fiber-optic cabling consists of a light conducting glass or plastic core surrounded by more glass, called **cladding**, and a tough outer shield. *Figure 3.10* illustrates this glass core:

Figure 3.10: Fiber-optic cable

Glass and plastic are the two types of material used for optical fiber cable construction. Plastic fiber is commonly used for consumer operations and in short-range implementations. Glass fiber tends to be used in short-range to medium transmission in multimode configurations, and in single-mode operations, it is used in telecommunications.

Regarding fiber optic cable structure, single-mode fiber:

- Has a very small core.
- Uses expensive lasers.
- Is suited to long-distance applications.

Whereas multimode fiber:

- Has a larger core.
- Uses less expensive LEDs.
- Uses LEDs that transmit at different angles.

In *Figure 3.11*, the structure of the cable is further outlined. In this figure, we can see the core, cladding, buffer, strengthening the material, and outer jacket:

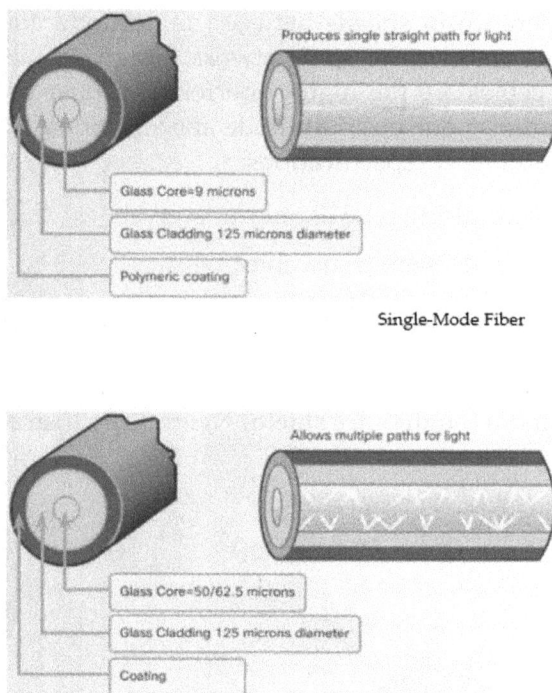

Produces single straight path for light

Glass Core=9 microns

Glass Cladding 125 microns diameter

Polymeric coating

Single-Mode Fiber

Allows multiple paths for light

Glass Core=50/62.5 microns

Glass Cladding 125 microns diameter

Coating

Figure 3.11: Single and multimode fiber

Light sources

The components of fiber optics are a transmitter, a receiver, and an optical fiber. As previously mentioned, the light sources include LEDs, lasers, and halogen. Testing fiber cables for fiber optic loss is very important when using fiber. Ethernet, as we know, uses cable testers. However, there are also special purpose testers available for fiber, just in case there is damage to a cable, or the cable is not transmitting data effectively.

The factors affecting the choice of the light source to be used are speed, transmission, distance, and cost.

Fiber optic cable types and distance

In terms of computer networking, fiber between computers in a single building or across nearby buildings becomes much faster using fiber optic cables. It is, therefore, ideal in many instances where there are LANs or CANs in an organization's infrastructure. As well as this use, Ethernet to fiber is implemented at the service provider or a data center facility that transmits local data over fiber connection to remote users. It is used in telephony, cable TV, and the Internet. In *Table 3.7*, we see implementations of fiber, the cable used, and the distances the fiber can reach:

Fiber optic cable type		Fiber distance						
		Fast Ethernet 100BA SE-FX	1 Gb Ethernet 1000BASE-SX	1Gb Ethernet 1000BA SE-LX	10Gb Base SE-SR	25Gb Base SR-S	40Gb Base SR4	100Gb Base SR10
Single mode fiber	OS2	200 m	5,000 m	5,000 m	10 km	/	/	/
Multimode fiber	OM1	200 m	275 m	550 m (mode conditioning patch cable required)	/	/	/	/
	OM2	200 m	550 m		/	/	/	/
	OM3	200 m	550 m		300 m	70 m	100 m	100 m
	OM4	200 m	550 m		400 m	100 m	150 m	150 m
	OM5	200 m	550 m		300 m	100 m	400 m	400 m

Table 3.7: Fiber speeds and cable types

The four main industries that use fiber are as follows:

- **Enterprise networks**: In these networks, fiber is used for backbone cabling applications and interconnecting infrastructure devices.

- **Fiber to the Home (FTTH)—Cable TV**: ISPs use fiber to provide always-on broadband services to homes and small businesses. Also called **Fiber to the Premises (FTTP)**, it involves the installation and use of optical fiber from a central point directly to individual buildings such as residences, apartment buildings, and businesses to provide high-speed internet access.

- **Long-haul networks**: Fiber is used by service providers to connect countries and cities.

- **Submarine cable networks**: As of late 2021, there are approximately 436 submarine cables in service around the world. In these installations, fiber is used to provide reliable high-speed, high-capacity solutions capable of surviving in harsh undersea environments at up to transoceanic distances.

Fiber connector types

In *Figure 3.12*, we see the different types of connectors used in fiber optics:

Connector	Description
ST Connector 	• They can be used with both short distance applications and long line systems. • Used with single and multi-mode cabling. • Keyed, bayonet-type connector. • Also called a push in and twist connector. • Each wire has a separate connector. • Nickel plated with a ceramic ferrule to ensure proper core alignment and prevent light ray deflection. • As part of the assembly process, it is necessary to polish the exposed fiber tip to ensure that light is passed on from one cable to the next with no dispersion. • They're spring-loaded, so users must make sure they are seated properly., but they are easily inserted and removed.
SC Connector 	• Used with single and multi-mode cabling. • Push on, pull off connector type that uses a locking tab to maintain connection. • Each wire has a separate connector. • Uses a ceramic ferrule to ensure proper core alignment and prevent light ray deflection. • As part of the assembly process, it is necessary to polish the exposed fiber tip.
LC Connector 	• The LC connector is just like a SC connector only it is half the size. Like SC connectors, LC connectors are half-duplex and can double fiber density in shelves and outlets. • Used with single and multi-mode cabling. • Composed of a plastic connector with a locking tab, similar to a RJ-45 connector. • A single connector with two ends keeps the two cables in place. • Uses a ceramic ferrule to ensure proper core alignment and prevent light ray deflection.
MT-RJ Connector 	• It has a small size, low cost, easy installation, and supports full-duplex. • Used with single and multi-mode cabling. • Composed of a plastic connector with a locking tab. • Uses metal guide pins to ensure it is properly aligned. • A single connector with one end holds both cables. • Uses a ceramic ferrule to safeguard proper core alignment and prevent light ray deflection. • With a size slightly smaller than a standard phone jack, it's easy to connect and disconnect.

Figure 3.12: Fiber optic connector types

Transceiver types

As previously stated, the type of transceivers is important in the implementation of fiber optics. The following is a list of transceivers in use:

- **Small form-factor pluggable (SFP)**: An SFP transceiver is a compact, hot-swappable input/output transceiver used in data communication and telecommunications networks. SFP interfaces between communication devices such as switches, routers, and fiber optic cables and performs conversions between optical and electrical signals. SFP transceivers support communications standards, including **synchronous optical networking (SONET)/synchronous digital hierarchy (SDH)**, gigabit ethernet, and fiber channel. They also allow the transport of fast Ethernet and gigabit Ethernet LAN packets over time-division-multiplexing-based WANs, as well as the transmission of E1/T1 streams over packet-switched networks (source: *Techopedia*).

- **Enhanced form-factor pluggable**: Enhanced **small form-factor pluggable (SFP+)** is an enhanced version of SFP. It supports data speeds of up to 16 Gbps. SFP+ introduces a direct attachment for connecting two SFP+ ports without dedicated transceivers.

- **Quad small form-factor pluggable**: This transceiver was introduced after the SFP transceiver. As the name suggests, instead of the single-channel SFP, it has four lanes for up to four wavelengths. Consequently, the bandwidth capacity is greater than that of the SFP. QSFP and QSFP+ are commonly used for 40G Ethernet (QSFP) and 100G Ethernet (QSFP+), and are designed for use in high-performance telecommunications networks or data centers.

- **Enhanced quad small form-factor pluggable**: The SFP+ (enhanced SFP) is an enhanced version of the SFP that supports data rates up to 16 Gbit/s. The SFP+ specification was first published on May 9, 2006, and version 4.1 was published on July 6, 2009. SFP+ supports 8 Gbit/s Fiber Channel, 10 Gigabit Ethernet, and Optical Transport Network standard OTU2.

Conclusion

When we explore network cables in-depth, we appreciate how critical network cables are to networking. Irrespective of whether we are speaking about Ethernet, coaxial, or fiber, these cables enable data transmission to take place and to do so in a reliable and consistent manner.

At times, to clarify this degree of importance, an analogy is drawn between network cabling and the infrastructure of our physical body and blood flow. Anatomists in *Visible Body* state that: *These arteries, veins, and capillaries make for a vast network of pipes. If you were to lay out all the blood vessels of the body in a line, they would stretch for nearly 60,000 miles. That's enough to circle the earth almost three times!* Now, that is a phenomenal network of connectivity, cabling, and network size through which *data* travels, is it not? It is also an amazing anatomical fact. In the upcoming chapter, we will be covering IP Addressing. And subnetting. In essence, while this chapter focused on physical cabling and the physical properties of cables, *Chapter 4, IP Addressing and Subnetting,* addresses the logical side by introducing addressing mechanisms and how these addressing strategies and systems enable us to send and receive data effectively and efficiently on and between networks.

Points to remember

- Ethernet is the most prevalent type of LAN, which is a set of standards and specifications that specify the network's wiring and communication. There are numerous standards and cable kinds to choose from.

- The main types of cabling in use in networking are copper, coax, and fiber.

- Copper cabling is the most common type of cabling used in networks today. It is inexpensive, easy to install, and has low resistance to electrical current flow.

- The data transmission capability of various cable types varies.

- Transmission speeds/bandwidth differ in accordance with the various cable types. Consequently, the purposes of use in networking scenarios and industries vary for each cable type.

- Coaxial cables like RG-58 and RG-59, which were once used in legacy Ethernet bus topologies, have found new applications. Although these topologies are now obsolete, these cables are commonly utilized for cable modem connectivity, broadband networking, and telecommunications. Fiber optic cabling, which was previously solely used for WAN connections, is now rapidly being used on LANs as well due to its potential for longer distances and higher speeds.

- There are distinctive connectors used with copper, coax, and fiber. Each connector has specific characteristics that support the speed of transmission, preferred bandwidth, network topology, network type, intended capacity, and network purpose.

- The content of this chapter is mapped to *Domain 1: Networking Concepts*. Compare and contrast transmission media and transceivers.

Key terms

- **Bandwidth**: A general phrase that refers to the bit-rate measurement of a network communication system's transmission capacity. The carrying capacity of a channel or the data transfer speed of that channel are additional terms used to characterize bandwidth. Broadly speaking, bandwidth refers to a network's capacity. Physical and wireless communication networks both have bandwidth.

- **Throughput**: The performance of tasks by a computing service or device over a given time period is referred to as throughput. It is a metric that compares the amount of work accomplished to the amount of time it takes to complete it, and it can be used to assess the performance of a processor, memory, and/or network communications.

- **Goodput**: The degree of application-level throughput of communication in a computer network, that is, the amount of data that is transmitted, is known as goodput (a combination of good and throughput). The number of bits of data delivered per second by the network to a specific destination. Goodput may be seen as actual data transmission.

The commonly used cables and connectors are:

- o **Coaxial cables (e.g., RG-58, RG-59)**: These cables have a central conductor, insulating layer, metallic shield, and outer insulating layer. They are used for cable TV, internet, and telecommunications.

- o **Twisted pair cables (e.g., Cat5e, Cat6, Cat7)**: Consist of pairs of insulated copper wires twisted together to reduce electromagnetic interference. Commonly used in Ethernet networks.

- o **Fiber optic cables**: Made of glass or plastic fibers that transmit data as light signals. They offer high-speed data transmission over long distances with minimal interference.

- o **F-type**: Used for cable TV and internet connections.

- o **BNC**: Utilized in professional video and radio frequency applications.

- o **N-type**: Suitable for high-frequency applications like wireless communication.

- o **RJ45**: The standard connector for Ethernet cables in networking.

- o **RJ11**: Used for telephone connections.

- o **Subscriber Connector (SC)**: Known for its push-pull latching mechanism, commonly used in telecommunications.

- o **Lucent Connector (LC)**: A small form factor connector, ideal for high-density connections.

- o **Straight Tip (ST)**: Uses a bayonet-style coupling, often found in network environments.

Questions

1. What are the main types of network media?
2. Summarize the types of copper cables and describe the cable uses.
3. Summarize the types of coax cable and describe the cable uses.
4. Summarize the types of fiber-optic cable and describe the cable uses.
5. List the connectors used in copper cabling.
6. List the connectors used in coax cabling.
7. List the connectors used in fiber cabling.
8. Give examples of networking implementations where the copper cable is used and the transmission rates achievable.
9. Give examples of networking implementations where coax cable is used and the transmission rates achievable.
10. Give examples of networking implementations where fiber cable is used and the transmission rates achievable.
11. Explain the differences between bandwidth, throughput, and goodput.
12. What is multiplexing?
13. Describe the types of multiplexing used in fiber installations.

Join our book's Discord space

Join the book's Discord Workspace for Latest updates, Offers, Tech happenings around the world, New Release and Sessions with the Authors:

https://discord.bpbonline.com

CHAPTER 4
IP Addressing and Subnetting

Introduction

In prior chapters, we studied the different layers of the OSI model, the functions and protocols at each layer, and how data is transmitted and encapsulated. In this chapter, we are focusing on the **internet protocol (IP)**. This protocol operates at the network layer, which is Layer 3 of the OSI model. We have previously stated that two main functions are attributed to the network layer of network operations. The first function is concerned with the breaking up of segments into smaller data units. At this layer, the smaller protocol data unit is called a **packet**. The segments are disassembled into these packets at the sending side of data transmission and subsequently, at the receiving side, the packets are reassembled. The second function occurring at the network layer involves network addressing (typically IP addresses) and the routing of these packets to their respective nodes and destinations.

IP is a protocol in the TCP/IP suite of protocols, operating at layer 2 of TCP/IP. Layer 2 is the internet/network layer of the protocol suite sharing functionality with layer 2 of OSI. We will learn about the TCP/IP protocol in more detail in later chapters. For now, IP layer-management protocols that belong to the network layer are as follows:

- Routing protocols
- Multicast group management
- Network-layer address assignment

IP layer address assignment is central to successful data transmission and to the appropriate routing of packets.

Structure

This chapter will cover the following topics:

- IP addressing
- IPv4 addressing
- Private vs. public addresses
- Variable Length Subnet Masking
- IPv6 addressing
- Subnetting with IPv6

Objectives

Upon completing this chapter, readers will be able to differentiate between the roles of a MAC address and an IP address, comprehending the purposes of physical and logical addresses. They will understand the necessity of a universal addressing scheme, such as IP addresses, for data transmission and global computer networking. Readers will identify the two parts of an IPv4 address—the network part and the host part (or the prefix and suffix)—and describe the significance of each portion. They will distinguish between private and public addressing, as well as between Class A, Class B, and Class C private addressing.

Additionally, readers will be able to describe the purpose of **network address translation (NAT)** and design a subnet addressing solution for an enterprise with a specific number of networks and hosts. They will express IP addresses in dotted-decimal notation and convert between binary and decimal formats. Readers will explain the role of a subnet mask and compute whether a host is on a specific network, given the subnet mask. They will understand the motivation for classless inter-domain routing (classless addressing) and write a subnet mask in CIDR notation.

Furthermore, readers will identify reserved addresses and special-purpose addresses, compare IPv4 and IPv6 in terms of address structure, addressing capacity, and benefits of usage, and explain the methods of transitioning from IPv4 to IPv6. Finally, given a scenario, readers will be able to implement and configure the appropriate addressing schema.

IP addressing

An IP address is a numerical label such as **192.0.2.1** connected to a computer network that uses the IP for communication. An IP address serves two main functions:

- Network interface identification
- Location addressing

Consequently, IP addressing is the global practice of assigning numerical labels to any device on a computer network.

The concept of this form of *numerical labeling* is best understood when one appreciates *why* it is needed and how networks would not function without some form of addressing.

Note: An IP address is a logical address. It is not a physical address or a MAC address. A physical address is hard coded on a network interface card (NIC) and used for finding hosts on a local network. MAC addresses operate on layer 2 of the OSI model. This involves switching and transmission of frames. IP addressing was designed to allow hosts (end devices) on one network to communicate with a host on a different network, irrespective of the type of local area networks the hosts are participating in. This means we are discussing routing and transmission of packets between networks. Transmission of packets and routing operates at layer 3 of the OSI model. Therefore, IP addressing is a layer 3 protocol.

In *Figure 4.1*, we see the output from an **ipconfig /all** command in the Microsoft Windows command prompt. The output displays the physical/MAC address on the wireless network adapter and the logical IP addressing configured on the system:

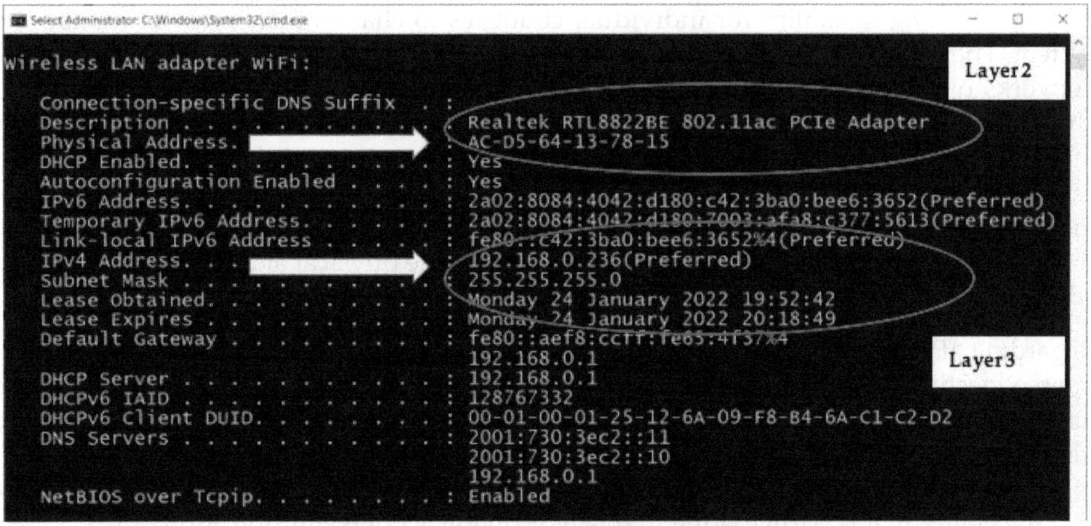

Figure 4.1: Layer 2 and layer 3 addressing

Understanding the significance of IP addressing through an analogy

We are all aware of the significance of telecommunications of our unique phone number. Many people now possess a smartphone or have a landline in their home or business. The number assigned to them by the phone provider is always unique. Nobody else in the world has this specific number. For if they did, how would transmission from a sender to receiver occur accordingly? Would communication work? Would conflicts and problems happen in the telephone system if duplicate numbers existed and ambiguity of device identity arose? Imagine, with duplication, you could be calling a friend or relative from your smartphone, and the call would be sent to a random unknown telephone subscriber; that is, if the transmission is able to work in the first place. So, in order to hold integrity and reliability, this act of communication requires a viable system for transmission.

Since this system of telephony is a global venture, the system needs to be tightly standardized with a reliable means of *number* allocation to providers across countries and regions to ensure the system functions. Thus, we see the breakdown of a landline number as defined by national conventions. National conventions vary across countries, but there are standards and rules adhered to by all countries and nations at an international level. Country codes are a component of the international telephone numbering plan and are necessary only when dialing a telephone number to establish a call to another country. Country codes are dialed before the national telephone number. Consequently, we have a numerical set of digits pertaining to a particular format or structure as defined by the implementation of geographical zones. Some examples of country codes are Argentina +54, Christmas Island +61, 89164, Ireland +353, India +91, UK +44, and USA +1. As you see from the examples, the codes vary in length. The codes are set by international standards while permitting flexibility for individual countries to change their internal numbering system. The existence of this standard enables users to reach telephone subscribers in the networks of the member countries or regions of the **International Telecommunication Union** (**ITU**). Notice that the term used to describe the member countries is networks. All these networks combine to create telecommunications as it operates in the world today. These networks have numbers as their identifiers. The numbers show us the location of the user, the user's unique *address* in the system, and the *network interface identification*; that is, the hardware or phone itself with its own unique physical and logical location and address.

Regarding IP addressing, what we see is a global network comprising a multitude of interconnecting networks spread across the world, with every device that exists in the network holding a logical address and a physical/MAC address. Every device is uniquely identified, much like the phone you use with its unique number. The device is recognized in a globally designed system where numerical labels tell us the location of the network and the device that is participating in this worldwide act of communication.

Figure 4.2 offers us a comparison of numerical values as they are used in telephony and in networking:

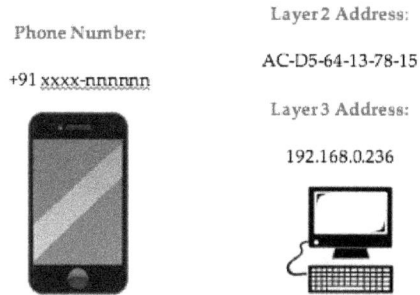

Figure 4.2: *Numbering conventions*

Functionally, telephone numbers and IP addresses do achieve broadly the same purpose. They do so in very different ways:

- The IP address is included in every packet of data; each router between source and destination decides packet-by-packet how it is routed toward the destination. Therefore, packets can follow multiple pathways.

Another difference in functionality is as follows:

- A telephone number is used to set up a fixed route through the network, and only when a complete circuit is established does communication begin. There is not the same *dynamic* flexibility as there is with layer 3 routing protocols. Routing protocols can combine dynamic routing with static routes, and network administrators may use their discretion and knowledge of their organization's network to manage and control their addressing system. With telephony, this element of control is not as emphatic.

- IP addresses have a non-hierarchical structure that is different from the structure of telephone numbers. That is, IP addresses do not show any geographical information about the host position, even though the network ID field in the address signifies which network a host belongs to.

Figure 4.3 illustrates this *network-to-network* transmission as data travels via the internet:

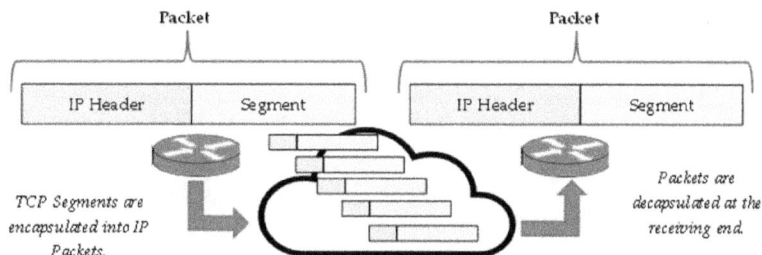

Figure 4.3: *Transmission of IP packets*

Structure of IP addresses

Please note that an IP address has 32 bits or 128 bits. We will discuss IPv6 further in this chapter. First, let us talk about why there are two versions of IP and who is in control of assigning these worldwide addresses. When the Internet and TCP/IP were first invented, it appeared that 32 bits were more than enough to satisfy any needs we might have for IP addresses because this standard, called **Internet Protocol version 4 (IPv4)**, created about *four billion potential IP addresses*. Today, we need way more than four billion IP addresses over the world.

The depletion of IPv4 addresses has been an ongoing concern in the IT industry and in technology in general. With the rapid acceleration of the **Internet of Things (IoT)**, devices requiring network connectivity have exponentially increased.

Consider a world of connected devices, 42 billion and counting: Devices we use daily are getting smart capabilities and gearing up to do more and generate more data than ever. The **International Data Corporation (IDC)** estimates we will have upwards of 42 billion connected devices by 2025, generating 79.4 zettabytes of data. To put things in perspective, one zettabyte is 1,000,000,000,000,000,000,000 bytes.

Now, do you get the picture of how many addresses will be in use when every one of these devices must carry an IP address in order to communicate?

Partly because of a shortage of 32-bit IP addresses, **Internet Protocol version 6 (IPv6)**, which uses an IP address with 128 bits, was developed. Currently, the internet uses a mix of 32-bit and 128-bit IP addresses. The **Internet Assigned Numbers Authority (IANA** at iana.org) is responsible for keeping track of assigned IP addresses and has already released all its available 32-bit IP addresses. IP addresses leased from IANA today are all 128-bit addresses. IANA delegates internet resources to the five **Regional Internet Registries (RIRs)** who, in turn, follow their regional policies to delegate resources to their customers.

Note: An IP address can be a dynamic IP address. (DHCP: The IP address is assigned by a server each time the computer or device connects to the network). Alternatively, the address is a static IP address. (The IP address is permanently assigned to the computer or device, manually assigned by a network administrator)

In *Figure 4.4*, we see the geographical location of the five regional internet registries:

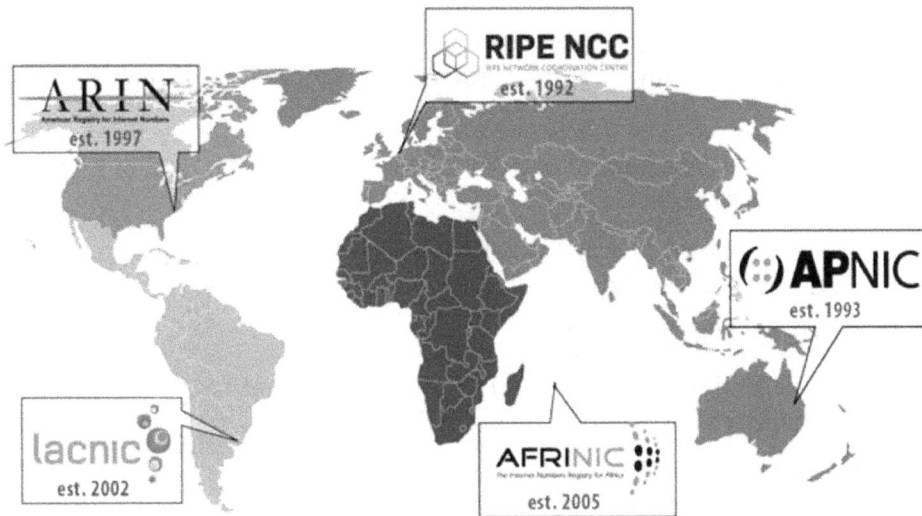

Figure 4.4: *Regional internet registries*

Figure 4.5 gives a further breakdown of the RIRs:

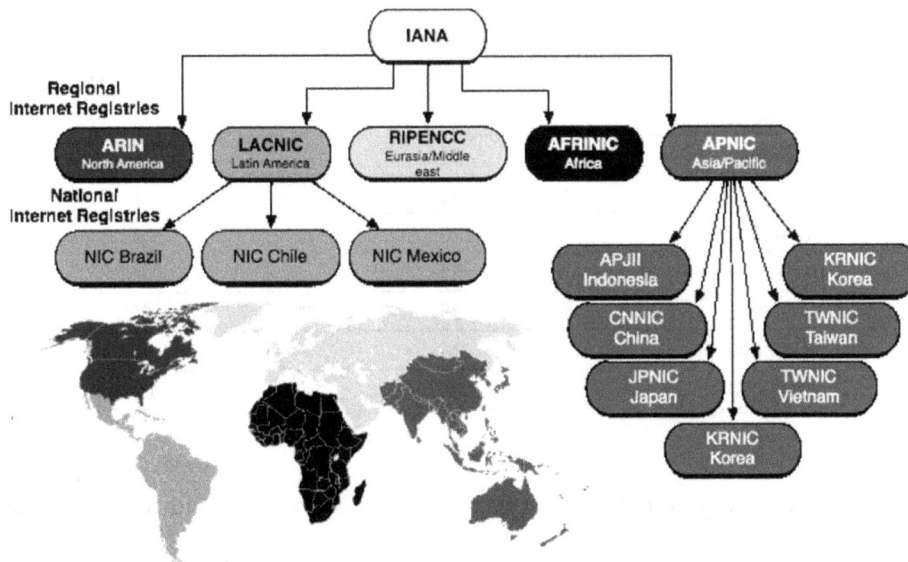

Figure 4.5: *Breakdown of regional internet registries*

The IANA is responsible for IP and coordinates global IP addressing, symbols, numbering, media type, and DNS root zone management.

Based at the **University of Southern California** (**USC**), IANA manages a centralized IP database and uses global DNS oversight to assign unique IP addresses to private or public organizations. IANA receives annual subscription fees for these services as per *Techopedia*.

IPv4 addressing

An IP address consists of 32 bits of information. These bits are divided into four sections.

These sections are referred to as **octets** or **bytes**. One also hears the sections referred to as **dotted quads** or with the breakdown of 8.8.8.8. As one detects, the total of this breakdown is the sum of 32 bits or 4 octets.

The lowest possible 8-bit number is 00000000, which is equal to 0 in decimal. The lowest IP address in decimal is 0.0.0.0, which in binary is:

00000000.00000000.00000000.00000000

The largest possible 8-bit number is 11111111, which is equal to 255 in decimal, so the largest possible IP address in decimal is 255.255.255.255, which in binary is as follows:

11111111.11111111.11111111.1111111

Binary bit position and value

To drill down more into this computation, let us take *one octet* and define what is known as the binary bit position and value. *Table 4.1* demonstrates how the binary bit position determines the value expressed in decimal:

Binary bit position	Exponent/to the power of	Value in decimal
00000001	2^0	0
00000010	21	2
00000100	22	4
00001000	23	8
00010000	24	16
00100000	25	32
01000000	26	64
10000000	27	128

Table 4.1: Binary bit position

For example, another way of expressing 24 is 2×2×2×2 (2 multiplied by itself four times), which equals 16.

Observe that 2^0 is 1. As a mathematical rule, any number raised to zero power is 1.

> **Note: The bit must be set to 1 (on) to hold a value, and the value grows as you move from the right to the left in the octet displayed. As well as this, spot the total sum of the values in the third column is 255. This infers that when all the bits are in the on position, the total value of an 8-bit binary value in decimal is 255. When set to 0 (off), the corresponding bit/s do not hold a value. For example, 11111111 = 255 while 01111111 = 127**

In *Table 4.2*, the decimal values of 1 to 16 are displayed. Note the binary bit positions and whether a bit is on or off. Can you calculate and verify the decimal value as, correct? Refer back to *Table 4.1* to assist you:

Binary	Decimal
00000001	1
00000010	2
00000011	3
00000100	4
00000101	5
00000110	6
00000111	7
00001000	8
00001001	9
00001010	10
00001011	11
00001100	12
00001101	13
00001110	14
00001111	15
00010000	16

Table 4.2: *Binary bit position*

Table 4.3 illustrates a worked example of binary-to-decimal conversion. Given the binary address:

11000000   10101000   00001010   00001010

We see it expressed as decimal:

192   .   168   .   10   .   10

In *Table 4.3*, the first octet is computed in more detail:

Radix	2	2	2	2	2	2	2	2
Exponent	7	6	5	4	3	2	1	0
Octet bit values	128	64	32	16	8	4	2	1
Binary address (Octet 1)	1	1	0	0	0	0	0	0
Binary bit values	128	64	0	0	0	0	0	0

*128 +64 = 192

Table 4.3: *Worked example of a binary number system*

As you can see, when you know the binary bit values, the calculations of 32-bit addressing become much easier.

Subnet mask

Now that we have an idea of binary and decimal representation, we need to identify the purpose of an IPv4 address and see how it functions when used with a subnet mask.

An IP address is split into two components: a network component and a node/host component. Remember, unicast packets of data are ultimately destined for a specific device or host on a network, and a router needs to know which network the packet is to be delivered to find the appropriate exit interface (link) to forward the packet. The number **192.168.0.10** on its own to the router means nothing if it has not received the intelligence or logic to inform the router which portion of the address stands for the network portion and which portion or component is delineating the host machine or number. The subnet mask provides the router with the logic to interpret the address and network correctly. With classful addressing, the rules are as follows. Where there is a 255 in the mask, this portion is the network portion, and where there is a 0, this signifies the host component.

If we use a capital **N** for network and a capital **H** for host, the subnet mask **255.0.0.0** becomes **N.H.H.H**. **255.255.0.0** becomes **N.N.H.H**. See what **I** mean?

Consequently, **192.168.0.10** with a subnet mask of **255.0.0.0** tells us that **192** is the network portion and **168.0.10** defines the host portion—that is, **N.H.H.H** – where the first octet bits (8 bits) are network bits, and the remaining three octets (24 bits) are host bits.

We could have a subnet of **192.168.0.10** with a subnet mask of **255.255.0.0** on the same routing table, and the router would hold the intelligence to differentiate between its routing entries and send the packets to the network defined as **192.168** with the host portion of **0.10** or **N.N.H.H**.

Here, we see two totally different networks using the same IP address, yet our key to understanding the difference between them lies in the value of the subnet mask. So, our packets will be routed correctly and grounded in the intelligence underlying the addressing system.

The need for knowing which network is critical to the proper functioning of a router as it manages and handles packets. This schema is no different from counteracting the potential confusion that can occur when there are two houses in an estate or residential area, where the numbers are the same on the houses, but the road (that is, network segment) is different. The courier delivering parcels knows the *packet* is intended for 101 Buttercup Walk and not 101 Buttercup Way because the address has a structure that is split into two parts—the house number followed by the road. This strategy is similar to the division in a subnet mask, where the network is then followed by the host address, informing us where the network is and how many host addresses it can hold and handle.

In early IPv4 networks, address classes were used to identify the number of bytes allocated to the network component.

The main classes were Classes A, B, and C. The allocation is shown in the following figure:

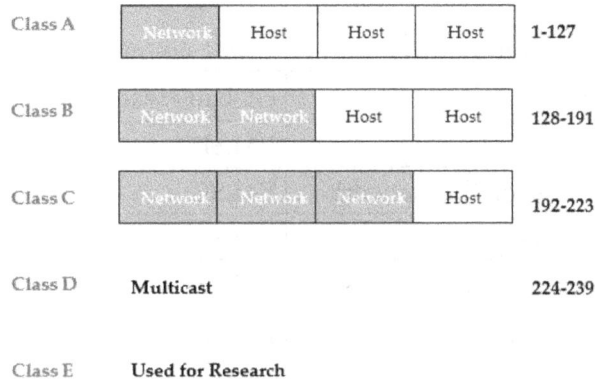

Figure 4.6: Classful address breakdown

In this figure, we can discern that the subnet mask is broken on the *boundary bit*. In other words, the full 8 bits of an octet either belong to the network portion or to the host portion.

In *Table 4.4*, we can determine this breakdown for Classes A, B, and C:

IP address class	Default subnet mask	Network and host portion
Class A	255.0.0.0	N.H.H.H
Class B	255.255.0.0	N.N.H.H.
Class C	255.255.255.0	N.N.N.H

Table 4.4: Default subnet masks

Note: There are currently three ways of showing the subnet masks for IPv4 addresses; you can show them in dotted decimal, binary, or classless inter-domain routing (CIDR). The dotted decimal is shown in Figure 4.6. The binary notation for a Class A default mask would look like 11111111.00000000.00000000.00000000, and finally, the CIDR notation uses a slash/then the number of bits that need to be turned on in the mask. For Class A, it would be /8; for Class B, it would be /16; and for Class C, it would be /24. This use of the slash is also referred to as a prefix, denoting how many bits of the address are network bits (*and implicitly host bits).

Private vs. public addresses

Not all IP addresses can be used by the general public, ISPs, manufacturers of software, or network administrators. IANA has a freely available IANA IPv4 **Special-Purpose**

Address Registry at the following link: **https://www.iana.org/assignments/iana-ipv4-special-registry/iana-ipv4-special-registry.xhtml**. We have extracted some of the data to present IPv4 addresses that are marked as reserved; see *Table 4.5*:

Address block	IANA IPv4 Special registry reserved addresses		
	Name	Globally reachable	Reserved-by-protocol
0.0.0.0/8	This network	FALSE	TRUE
0.0.0.0/32	This host on this network	FALSE	TRUE
127.0.0.0/8	Loopback	False [1]	TRUE
169.254.0.0/16	Link local	FALSE	TRUE
192.0.0.170/32, 192.0.0.171/32	NAT64/DNS64 discovery	FALSE	TRUE
240.0.0.0/4	Reserved	FALSE	TRUE

Table 4.5: IPv4 reserved addresses

As shown, IPv4 designates special usage or applications for various addresses or address blocks. The complete list may be accessed from the preceding link.

IPv4 reserved addresses

As shown in *Table 4.5*, IPv4 designates special usage or applications for various addresses or address blocks. The complete list may be accessed from the preceding link. We can determine that not all IPv4 addresses are available for use. An example of this is the value 255. When we see an IPv4 address ending in 255, we know that this address is a broadcast address. Other reserved addresses include **127.0.0.0.**, this address is known as the **loopback address**. This address cannot be used as an address on any device. As a matter of fact, the entire range of addresses with the first octet as 127 (from **127.0.0.0—127.255.255.255**) is unusable in device addressing due to the loopback address's special purpose in networking. The loopback address, when used in the command prompt with the PING command or when implemented via a physical loopback plug, checks to see if the host's NIC can send and receive data (thus, the term *loopback*) and whether the TCP/IP protocol is *bound* appropriately to the network card.

The mechanisms used in multicast routing require specific IP addresses to be used. The range of IP addresses reserved for these mechanisms is **224.0.0.0—239.255.255.255**. These address blocks are used for diverse multicast operations and serve various purposes in one-to-many data transmissions. Limited and directed broadcasts additionally use reserved addresses.

Having identified some of the reserved IP addresses, we will now differentiate between private and public IP addresses. *Table 4.6* outlines private address ranges typically used by network administrators:

Address block	Name	Globally reachable	Reserved-by-protocol
10.0.0.0/8	Private-use	FALSE	FALSE
172.16.0.0/12	Private-use	FALSE	FALSE
192.168.0.0/16	Private-use	FALSE	FALSE

Table 4.6: Private address ranges

All traffic using these addresses must remain local. As you can see in the *Globally reachable* column, these addresses are forwardable but not beyond a specified administrative domain. When used alongside **Variable Length Subnet Masks** (**VLSM**), these address ranges offer great flexibility to a network administrator when managing addressing issues and meeting network and host requirements.

Private address space

The IANA has reserved the following three blocks of the IP address space for private internet:

```
10.0.0.0 - 10.255.255.255 (10/8 prefix)
172.16.0.0 - 172.31.255.255 (172.16/12 prefix)
192.168.0.0 - 192.168.255.255 (192.168/16 prefix)
```

In RFC 1918, we can identify that public IPv4 addresses are globally routed between **internet service provider (ISP)** routers. These public addresses exclude reserved addresses and private IP address spaces. These address spaces are used *internally* in organizations and institutions, but it is critical to note that the addresses are not *externally* or globally routable. Private IPv4 addresses are not unique but can be used internally within any home/SOHO/business or large enterprise network. The three blocks of IP address space outlined preceding are, therefore, common blocks of addresses used by most organizations to assign IPv4 addresses to the organization's internal hosts. In networking practices, we will never be assigned any of these blocks or addresses for external routing.

As shown in *Figure 4.7*, the local addressing schema differs between the wired LAN and the WLAN:

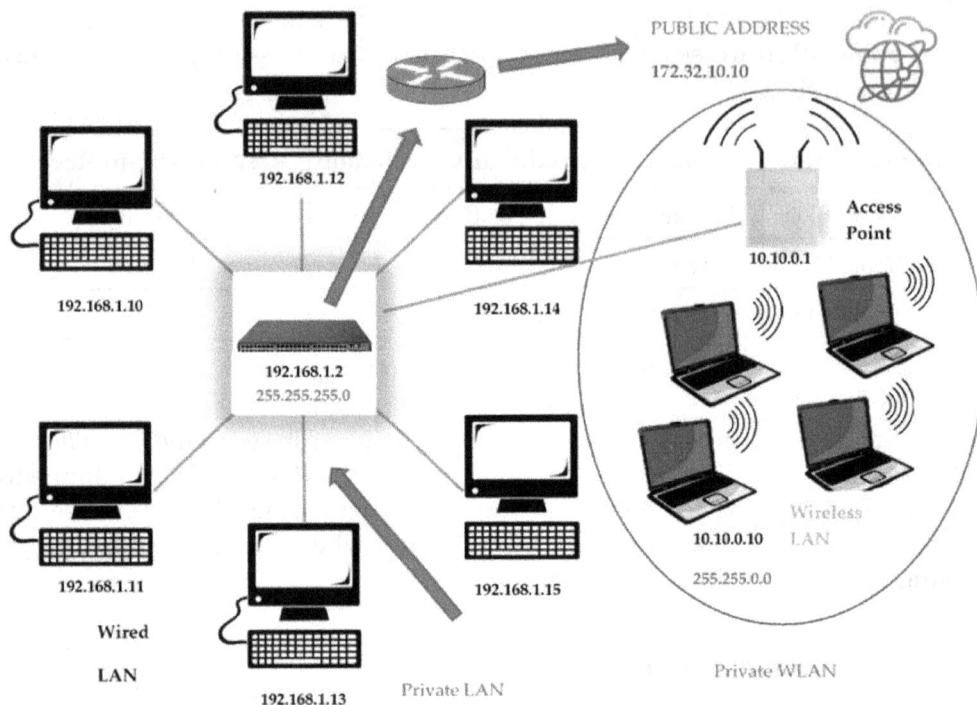

Figure 4.7: Private vs. public networks

The network administrator holds the flexibility to choose the private network address and range they deem as appropriate to the network's size and needs. The other option a network administrator has is the way they wish to use the subnet mask. A network administrator can use a *typical class A* address with a typical *Class B* subnet mask. Remember, the IP address on its own does not provide logic to the system. It is the mask's division between network and host that drives and underpins the addressing system and how it functions. Consequently, IP addresses are malleable and can be varied.

Note: In an IPv4 network, the hosts can communicate in one of three different ways: unicast, multicast, and broadcast. Broadcast addresses can be essentially broken down into two types. One type is what we call limited broadcasts. This address is defined as 255.255.255.255. The reason we define this broadcast as a limited broadcast is because of the way in which routers handle this broadcast. Routers will not forward a limited broadcast—as the packets involved in the transmission travel to the local network or subnet. This is why limited broadcasts are also called local broadcasts. In contrast to this type of broadcast, a directed broadcast may involve packets being transmitted from remote networks directed into a local network. These IP packets, as incoming packets and data transmission will then be broadcast to devices in the destination subnet as long as this ability is enabled on the receiving devices' interface.

Table 4.7 compares private and public addressing across a number of factors:

Factors	Private IP address	Public IP address
Scope	Private IP address scope is local to the private network—for example, a LAN inside a building with internal addresses aligned with the private IP address range as outlined below.	Public IP address scope is global and used over the public network—for example, a WAN. Public IP addresses can be routed on the Internet, unlike private addresses.
Communication	A private IP address is used to communicate within the network.	A public IP address is used to communicate outside the network, externally via the *default gateway*.
Format	Private IP Addresses differ in a uniform manner yet remain unique within the addressing system.	Public IP addresses differ in varying ranges yet remain unique with the addressing system.
Provider	The local network Administrator creates private IP addresses using a server operating system, normally implementing a mix of static addressing and DHCP.	ISP. The Internet Service Provider controls the public IP address. The address is assigned to ISPs by IANA via the RIRs.
Cost	Private IP Addresses are free of cost.	Public IP Addresses come with a cost, paid to the ISP.
Discovery	Private IP Addresses can be located using the ipconfig command. Additionally, regarding Public IP addresses, a **url/domain** can be discovered using the `nslookup` command.	The Public IP Address needs to be searched for on via a search engine/browser. (for example, what is my IP?)
Range	Private IP address range: 10.0.0.0—10.255.255.255, 172.16.0.0—172.31.255.255, 192.168.0.0—192.168.255.255	With the exception of private IP Addresses and special purpose reserved addresses, the remaining IP addresses are public addresses.

Table 4.7: *Private versus public addresses*

Five benefits of subnetting are listed as follows:

- Improved network security.
- Better network performance and speed.
- Administration of subnets easier (as long as the subnets are planned for and appropriately implemented).
- Easier to control the growth of the network.
- Less network congestion.

Classless inter-domain routing

Earlier, we discussed how subnet masks in classful addressing divide into the network and host portions of the address, divided *on the boundary bit*. The boundary bit denotes /8. /16 or /24, either one, two, or three octets into the 32-bit address where divisions are created. This system is a legacy system since, in real-world networking, network administrators implement varied lengths in their subnet masks and classless addressing. CIDR (pronounced as cider) is the standard way of referencing this form of addressing. When we explore classful addressing, we see that in the *Classes A, B,* or *C* network, the networks are divided on the boundary bit. An easier way to remember this is to note that when one views a classful address, no octet in the specified address has mixed bits or is made up of a mixture of network and host bits. For example, when you look at the subnet mask of a class A address, you observe this type of breakdown. The subnet mask for *Class A* is **255.0.0.0**. In each of the octets, the eight bits are either all network bits or host bits, denoted by the value of 255 or 0. This demonstrates a division generated on the boundary bit. With CIDR and alternative standards, internet service providers could allocate address spaces on any address bit boundary so that we can now detect mixed bits within the eight-bit group of a given octet. One of these arbitrary lengths is **255.255.255.252** as a specified subnet mask. This mask is a typical CIDR address with a prefix of /30. Its division into network and host bits can equally be expressed as N.N.N nnnnnnhh. The last octet holds the mixed bits, some network, and the remaining two bits as host. VLSM enables the network administrator and ISPs to manipulate and be flexible with address allocation. This ability counters what could have been a very rigid and fixed system if classful addressing were to be the only option available. VLSM permits the specification of arbitrary-length prefixes. Examples of the use of prefixes are as follows: 192.0.2.0/24 for IPv4 and 2001:db8::/32 for IPv6. As stated, VLSM makes network addressing adaptable, flexible, and certainly more viable as a tool to create networks of any size desired.

In *Table 4.8*, the list of classful (and classless) addresses is displayed. There are three classful addresses noted. All other prefixes are classless.

Classful addresses	Binary bits	Prefix	Subnet mask	Host addresses
Class A address	11111111.00000000.00000000.00000000	/8	255.0.0.0	16,777,214 host addresses
	11111111.10000000.00000000.00000000	/9	255.128.0.0	8,388,606 host addresses
	11111111.11000000.00000000.00000000	/10	255.192.0.0	4,194,302 host addresses
	11111111.11100000.00000000.00000000	/11	255.224.0.0	2,097,150 host addresses
	11111111.11110000.00000000.00000000	/12	255.240.0.0	1,048,574 host addresses

Classful addresses	Binary bits	Prefix	Subnet mask	Host addresses
	11111111.11111000.00000000.00000000	/13	255.248.0.0	524,286 host addresses
	11111111.11111100.00000000.00000000	/14	255.252.0.0	262,142 host addresses
	11111111.11111110.00000000.00000000	/15	255.254.0.0	131,070 host addresses
Class B address	11111111.11111111.00000000.00000000	/16	255.255.0.0	65,534 host addresses
	11111111.11111111.10000000.00000000	/17	255.255.128.0	32,766 host addresses
	11111111.11111111.11000000.00000000	/18	255.255.192.0	16,382 host addresses
	11111111.11111111.11100000.00000000	/19	255.255.224.0	8,190 host addresses
	11111111.11111111.11110000.00000000	/20	255.255.240.0	4,094 host addresses
	11111111.11111111.11111000.00000000	/21	255.255.248.0	2,046 host addresses
	11111111.11111111.11111100.00000000	/22	255.255.252.0	1,022 host addresses
	11111111.11111111.11111110.00000000	/23	255.255.254.0	510 host addresses
Class C address	11111111.11111111.11111111.00000000	/24	255.255.255.0	254 host addresses
	11111111.11111111.11111111.10000000	/25	255.255.255.128	126 host addresses
	11111111.11111111.11111111.11000000	/26	255.255.255.192	62 host addresses
	11111111.11111111.11111111.11100000	/27	255.255.255.224	30 host addresses
	11111111.11111111.11111111.11110000	/28	255.255.255.240	14 host addresses
	11111111.11111111.11111111.11111000	/29	255.255.255.248	6 host addresses
	11111111.11111111.11111111.11111100	/30	255.255.255.252	2 host addresses
	11111111.11111111.11111111.11111110	/31	255.255.255.254	0 host addresses
	11111111.11111111.11111111.11111111	/32	255.255.255.255	Host route

Table 4.8: *Classful and classless addressing*

Note the variety of hosts that can be accommodated and addressed by manipulating the subnet mask.

When examining the use of CIDR notation, we detect the layout of the IP address. An IP address is specified with the use of a decimal number followed by a slash character (/), and then a second decimal number. The number after the / character denotes the number of bits in the IP address belonging to the network portion of the IP address. We may also refer to this as the width, in bits, of the network prefix. A few examples of CIDR notation are as follows:

- `192.168.200.6/30`
- `10.10.0.0/23`

Variable Length Subnet Masking

When we speak about VLSM, we are talking about a *design strategy* for implementing subnets. The beauty of VLSM and manipulation of the subnet mask means that not all the subnets have to be the same size or have **Fixed Length Subnet Masks (FLSM)**. The subnets can be sized in accordance with the needs of the users and the amount of host addresses required on the network segment. An equivalent analogy occurs in the allocation and distribution of portion sizes in the serving of family meals. We would not give a young child the same size portion as a fully grown adult; therefore, if we were dividing a pizza, for example, the portion sizes for each person may differ in accordance with the needs of the individual. It is similar to networking and creating subnets. If we have departments in our organization and we want to implement subnets, the size of the subnets would be optimum if they met the needs of the users/hosts, plus some scope for scalability and growth of the network. This emphasis on the allocation of addresses in accordance with needs and requirements prevents IP address wastage and is hugely beneficial to an administrator who is managing the network. Be aware that VLSM computation is a skill that comes with practice. It is true that there are excellent online subnetting calculators and ready-to-print charts and mappings available online. However, it is recommended as best practice that a network administrator understands manual subnetting to make meaningful choices and adeptly problem-solve IP addressing issues. Consequently, though we are not going intricately through the stages and processes of CIDR and VLSM, it is recommended that you practice manual calculations. Again, there are plenty of books and videos available that enable you to hone this skill and address the topic in more detail. This chapter presents some worked examples.

Sample VLSM scenario

Subnetting allows you to take one larger network and break it into a bunch of smaller networks. Remember the pizza analogy? The main point is you are given a network space (original pizza size) and then required to divide the given space into smaller pieces or subnets. This tells us that we are limited to the size of the original network space, and how we divide the space will never go beyond the maximum host addresses of the original network allocation. That is a hugely important point to remember when planning the sizes of subnets.

Some important points to remember are given as follows:

- We create subnets by using one or more of the host bits as network bits.
- This is done by extending the mask to borrow some of the bits from the host portion of the address to create additional network bits.
- The more host bits used, the more subnets that can be defined.
- For each bit borrowed, we double the number of subnetworks available.

For example, if we borrow 1 bit, we can define 2 subnets. If we borrow 2 bits, we can have 4 subnets. However, with each bit we borrow, fewer host addresses are available per subnet.

Rules: Number of subnets: $2n$ (**n = the number of bits borrowed**)

Total number of addresses per subnet $2m$

The number of usable hosts $2m - 2$ (m = the number of host bits left)

Let us consider a specific network topology as illustrated in *Figure 4.8*:

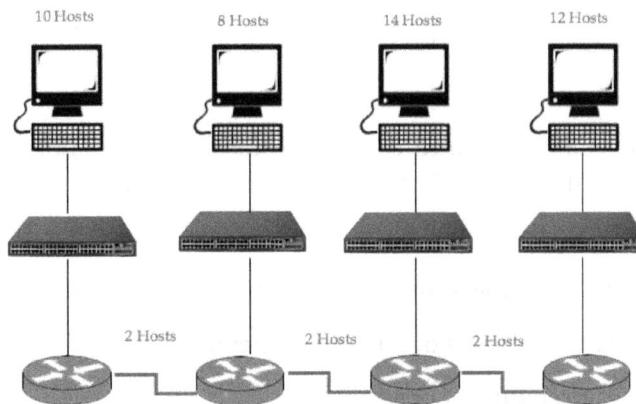

*A point-to-point-connection only requires 2 IP host addresses.

4 addresses are required in total to include the network ID and the broadcast ID for the WAN links.

Figure 4.8: Network topology

Note: The original address space is 172.31.1.0/24. Before being subnetted, this network can accommodate a total of 254 hosts (that is, 256 –2 since the prefix /24 tells us how many network bits there are. The last octet of the subnet mask is made up of all host bits: 255.255.255.0).

Rule: The network ID and the Broadcast Address cannot be assigned to a host device on a network, so we lose two host addresses for all networks/subnets. /24 means 8 hosts bits so 28 = 256 address, so we have 28 – 2 =254 hosts.

Network ID: **172.31.1.0**

Usable Addresses: **172.31.1.1 – 172.31.1.254**

Broadcast Address: **172.31.1.255**

Subnet the **172.31.1.0/24** network based on the maximum number of hosts required by the largest subnet.

Study the network topology, as shown in *Figure 4.8*. Consider the following questions:

Question: Based on the topology, how many subnets are needed?

Answer: 7. There are four LANs and three WANs in the topology.

Question: How many bits must be borrowed to support the number of subnets in the topology table?

Answer: 4

Number of subnets: 2^4 (n = the number of bits borrowed)

Question: How many subnets does this create?

Answer: 16

Question: How many usable host addresses does this create per subnet? Are there enough addresses? The host requirements are 14, 12, 10, 8, 2, 2, and 2.

Answer: 14. Yes. The largest network requires 14 host addresses.

The number of usable hosts $2^4 - 2$ (m = the number of host bits left)

Calculate the binary and decimal value of the new subnet mask.

We need to borrow 4 bits from the last octet.

11111111.11111111.111111111. 1   1   1   1   0   0   0   0

255 .   255 .   255 . 240

The prefix for all networks is /28

N.N.N.nnnnhhhh

Here is the resulting *Subnet* table that lists all the available subnets, the first and last usable host address, and the broadcast address:

Subnet number	Subnet IP	First usable Host IP	Last usable Host IP	Broadcast address
0	172.31.1.0	172.31.1.1	172.31.1.14	172.31.1.15
1	172.31.1.16	172.31.1.17	172.31.1.30	172.31.1.31
2	172.31.1.32	172.31.1.33	172.31.1.46	172.31.1.47
3	172.31.1.48	172.31.1.49	172.31.1.62	172.31.1.63
4	172.31.1.64	172.31.1.65	172.31.1.78	172.31.1.79
5	172.31.1.80	172.31.1.81	172.31.1.94	172.31.1.95
6	172.31.1.96	172.31.1.97	172.31.1.110	172.31.1.111
7	172.31.1.112	172.31.1.113	172.31.1.126	172.31.1.127
8	172.31.1.128	172.31.1.129	172.31.1.142	172.31.1.143
9	172.31.1.144	172.31.1.145	172.31.1.158	172.31.1.159
10	172.31.1.160	172.31.1.161	172.31.1.174	172.31.1.175
11	172.31.1.176	172.31.1.177	172.31.1.190	172.31.1.191
12	172.31.1.192	172.31.1.193	172.31.1.206	172.31.1.207
13	172.31.1.208	172.31.1.209	172.31.1.222	172.31.1.223
14	172.31.1.224	172.31.1.225	172.31.1.238	172.31.1.239
15	172.31.1.240	172.31.1.241	172.31.1.254	172.31.1.255

Table 4.9: Subnetting a Class C address

Note that the networks increment by 16: 0, 16, 32, 64, 80, 96, 112, 144, and so on. This shows us that the networks are of equal size and that this is an example of FLSM as opposed to VLSM. Looking at this network on a pie chart, you will see the equally divided portions. *Figure 4.9* illustrates how this FLSM looks graphed as a pie chart. As can be seen, the networks created are the same portion size. This is not a huge issue for the larger networks created when you factor in scalability as best practice from a network administrator's perspective, but consider the wasted addresses for the WAN links, which only needed two addresses as point-to-point connections. Look at the total of wasted addresses:

- 14 hosts required, 14 used, 0 waste addresses
- 12 hosts required, 14 used, 2 waste addresses
- 10 hosts required, 14 used, 4 waste addresses
- 8 hosts required, 14 used, 6 waste addresses
- 2 hosts required (× 3 networks), 14 used, 12 waste addresses per network = 36 total waste addresses on the WAN links

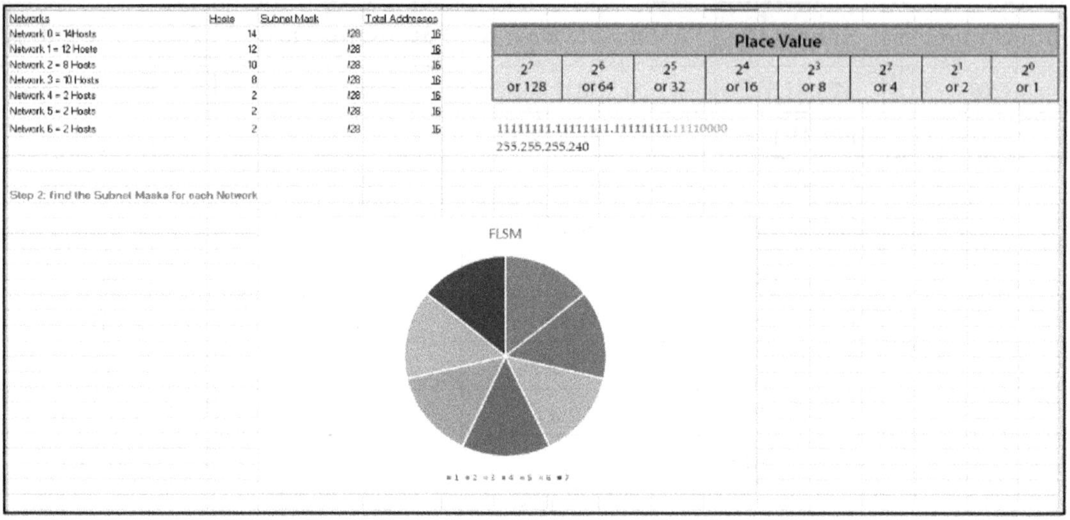

Networks	Hosts	Subnet Mask	Total Addresses
Network 0 = 14 Hosts	14	/28	16
Network 1 = 12 Hosts	12	/28	16
Network 2 = 8 Hosts	10	/28	16
Network 3 = 10 Hosts	8	/28	16
Network 4 = 2 Hosts	2	/28	16
Network 5 = 2 Hosts	2	/28	16
Network 6 = 2 Hosts	2	/28	16

Place Value							
2^7 or 128	2^6 or 64	2^5 or 32	2^4 or 16	2^3 or 8	2^2 or 4	2^1 or 2	2^0 or 1

11111111.11111111.11111111.11110000
255.255.255.240

Step 2: find the Subnet Masks for each Network

Figure 4.9: FLSM

In VLSM, we calculate *network-by-network* from the largest network down to the smallest, working out the subnet mask required for each *individual* subnet. Subnet masks will vary depending on how many bits have been borrowed for a particular subnet.

The network is first subnetted, and then the subnets are subnetted again. We can see this difference in size allocation in *Figure 4.10*:

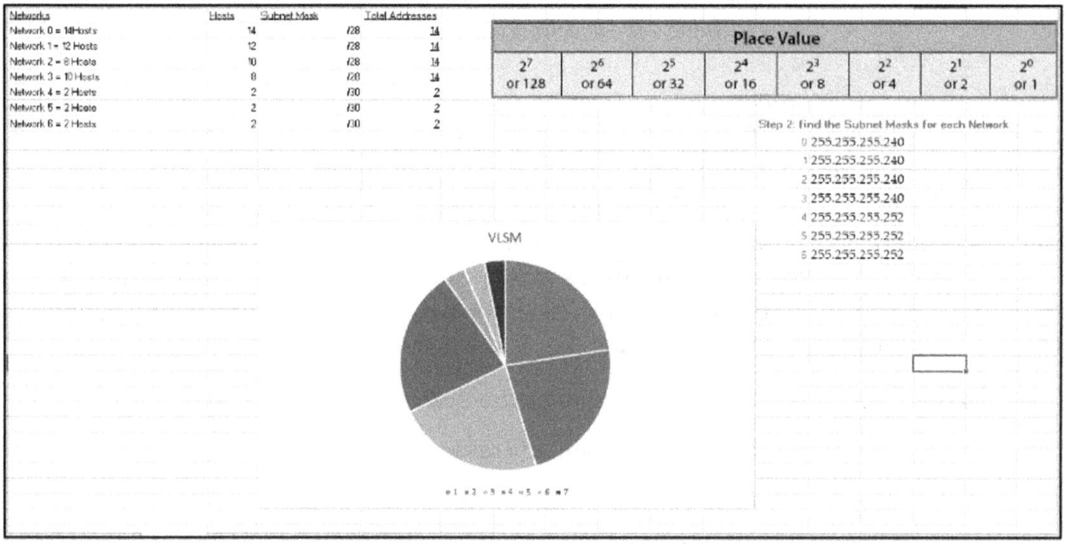

Networks	Hosts	Subnet Mask	Total Addresses
Network 0 = 14 Hosts	14	/28	14
Network 1 = 12 Hosts	12	/28	14
Network 2 = 8 Hosts	10	/28	14
Network 3 = 10 Hosts	8	/28	14
Network 4 = 2 Hosts	2	/30	2
Network 5 = 2 Hosts	2	/30	2
Network 6 = 2 Hosts	2	/30	2

Place Value							
2^7 or 128	2^6 or 64	2^5 or 32	2^4 or 16	2^3 or 8	2^2 or 4	2^1 or 2	2^0 or 1

Step 2: find the Subnet Masks for each Network
0 255.255.255.240
1 255.255.255.240
2 255.255.255.240
3 255.255.255.240
4 255.255.255.252
5 255.255.255.252
6 255.255.255.252

Figure 4.10: VLSM

Figure 4.11 shows the same calculation from **http://vlsmcalc.net/**, a free-to-use online calculator:

Subnetting Successful

Major Network: 172.31.1.0/24
Available IP addresses in major network: 254
Number of IP addresses needed: 50
Available IP addresses in allocated subnets: 62
About 30% of available major network address space is used
About 81% of subnetted network address space is used

Subnet Name	Needed Size	Allocated Size	Address	Mask	Dec Mask	Assignable Range	Broadcast
Network 0	14	14	172.31.1.0	/28	255.255.255.240	172.31.1.1 - 172.31.1.14	172.31.1.15
Network 1	12	14	172.31.1.16	/28	255.255.255.240	172.31.1.17 - 172.31.1.30	172.31.1.31
Network 2	10	14	172.31.1.32	/28	255.255.255.240	172.31.1.33 - 172.31.1.46	172.31.1.47
Network 3	8	14	172.31.1.48	/28	255.255.255.240	172.31.1.49 - 172.31.1.62	172.31.1.63
Network 4	2	2	172.31.1.64	/30	255.255.255.252	172.31.1.65 - 172.31.1.66	172.31.1.67
Network 5	2	2	172.31.1.68	/30	255.255.255.252	172.31.1.69 - 172.31.1.70	172.31.1.71
Network 6	2	2	172.31.1.72	/30	255.255.255.252	172.31.1.73 - 172.31.1.74	172.31.1.75

Back to form New calculation

If you have a question/suggestion/bug report, please use Feedback form.

Hosted at Novgorod State University

Figure 4.11: Online VLSM calculator

Benefits of VLSM

In VLSM, there are fewer wasted addresses. The key VLSM features include the following:

- A more real-world, manageable means of network configuration.
- The ability to manipulate IP addresses and resolve issues via empty subnet filling.
- The ability to be more efficient than when using FLSM.
- The ability to streamline routing practices via the use of prefixes.

VSLM is used in both private and public networks. However, the benefits of VLSM are evidenced more as a positive in addressing public networks. Since network administrator has more control over the way in which they use the allocated public address space, the address savings they make mean that they may not have to return to the regional IP address assignment authorities to be granted another IP network number. This saving of addresses is a huge plus to organizations and administrators alike. In private networks and with internal addressing, the network administrator does not meet these issues as negatives in the same manner because they can manipulate the subnet mask on the private class IP ranges and *dip into* any of the private ranges they wish to effectively meet subnetting or supernetting challenges.

However, one also has to consider the disadvantages or impact of using VLSM/subnetting on network administration and practice. In the case of a *single network*, only two IP addresses are wasted to represent the network ID and Broadcast address, but in the case of subnetting, two IP addresses are wasted for each subnet. Equipment costs may increase with the need for extra network intermediary devices, plus it takes a knowledgeable network administrator who understands subnetting proficiently to manage and monitor all the created subnets.

Discovering a network ID using the bitwise AND operation

The netmask can be applied to an IPv4 address by using the bitwise logical AND operator. This operation selects the network number and subnet number positions of the address. In this way, we can discover the subnet to which a host device belongs.

The rules of the bitwise AND operation are:

$$1 \text{ } AND \text{ } 1 = 1 \quad 1 \text{ } AND \text{ } 0 = 0 \quad 0 \text{ } AND \text{ } 1 = 0 \quad 0 \text{ } AND \text{ } 0 = 0$$

*The operation is carried out on the binary addresses of the IPv4 address and mask. The network ID *drops through* the mask.

Example: Given an IP address of **192.168.10.10** with a subnet mask of **255.255.255.0**. What is the network ID?

IPv4 Address in decimal: 192.168.10.10

IPv4 Address in binary: 11000000.10101000.00001010.00001010

Subnet Mask in decimal: 255.255.255.0

Subnet Mask in binary: 11111111.11111111.11111111.00000000

Network Address: 11000000.10101000.00001010.00000000

Network Address in decimal: 192.168.10.0

Here is another representation of the calculation:

11000000.10101000.00001010.00001010

11111111.11111111.11111111.00000000

11000000.10101000.00001010.00000000

Network ID = 192.168.10.0

Try the following VLSM/subnetting questions for your practice:

1. Given an IPv4 address of **172.16.41.101** with a subnet mask of **255.255.255.0**, what is the network ID?

2. Given a host **172.16.20.35/27**: What is its network address?

3. **172.31.1.69** is a host address on one of seven subnets. The netmask is /30. What is the network ID for this host? How many usable host addresses are on a /30 network?

The answers to these questions are at the end of this chapter.

Comparing IPv4 and IPv6 address structures

Basically, IPv6 dramatically increases the number of addresses available in IPv4. This is due to a major change in the addressing structure between the Internet protocols.

When working with IPv4, you have a 32-bit address format broken into byte-size units or octets. IPv4 allows for a total of 4.3 billion addresses (2^{32}). After you get rid of special address spaces such as loopback, multicast, and reserved blocks, you have only about 3.7 billion addresses to work with. This may sound like a lot of addresses, but in the global scheme of things, device addressing and the need for more address space have grown exponentially, especially with the expanding IoTs.

IPv6 increases that address space up to 128 bits, or 2^{128} addresses, or 3.4×10^{38} addresses. Observe *Table 4.10*, where it might make a little more sense:

IPv4 and IPv6 comparison		
	IPv4	IPv6
Bits	32	128
Octets	4	16
Binary address	10011101.10010001 .11111011.01101110	10011101.10000010.00010010.10010010. 00011101.0011 1011.10001101.11110001. 00111011.11000111.11000011. 10001110. 11001111.00001111.00111110. 00001110
Alternate address display	157.145.251.110	9D82:1292:1D3B:8DF1:3BC7:C38E:CF0F:3E0E
Total number of addresses	4.3×10^9	3.4×10^{38}

Table 4.10: IPv4 and IPv6 comparison

You may have noticed the alternate IPv6 address in the table, with its letters and numbers. This is called **hex-colon notation**, which takes 16 bits and converts them to four hexadecimal numbers rather than six decimal numbers in dotted-decimal notation. The purpose is to enable us to write the address in a more manageable format as opposed to writing a long stream of 128 binary bits. In other words, it is purely for shorthand or notation.

IPV6 addressing

IPv6 addresses are 128-bit addresses represented in the following:

- Eight 16-bit segments or hextets
- Hexadecimal (non-case sensitive) between 0000 and FFFF
- Separated by colons

Table 4.11 shows us the conversion from hexadecimal to binary and decimal:

Representing hexadecimal values		
Hexadecimal	Decimal	Binary
0	0	0000
1	1	0001
2	2	0010
3	3	0011
4	4	0100
5	5	0101
6	6	0110
7	7	0111
8	8	1000
9	9	1001
A	10	1010
B	11	1011
C	12	1100
D	13	1101
E	14	1110
F	15	1111

Table 4.11: Hexadecimal values

Figure 4.12 breaks down the IPv6 addressing structure into hexadecimal notation:

```
2001:0DB8:AAAA:1111:0000:0000:0000:0100/64
```

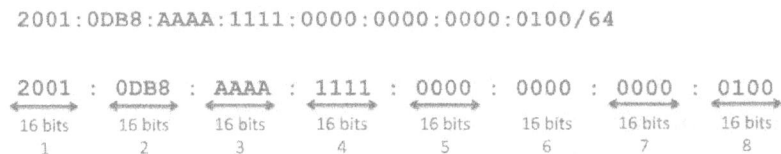

2001	:	0DB8	:	AAAA	:	1111	:	0000	:	0000	:	0000	:	0100
16 bits		16 bits		16 bits		16 bits		16 bits		16 bits		16 bits		16 bits
1		2		3		4		5		6		7		8

Figure 4.12: IPv6 address in hexadecimal notation

We can also use the *compressed notation* of IPv6 following two rules.

1st rule: Leading zeroes in any 16-bit segment do not have to be written.

2nd rule: Any single, contiguous string of one or more 16-bit segments consisting of all zeroes can be represented with a double colon.

Example 1:

2001 : 0DB8 : AAAA : 1111 : 0000 : 0000 : 0000 : 0100

2001 : 0DB8 : AAAA : 1111 : 0000 : 0000 : 0000 : **0**100

Rule 1

2001 : 0DB8 : AAAA : 1111 : ~~0000 : 0000 : 0000~~ : 0100

Rule 2

Compressed Format: 2001 : 0DB8 : AAAA : 1111 :: 100

Example 2:

2001:0db8:0000:000b:0000:0000:0000:001A

2001:**0**db8:**0000**:**000**b:**000**0:**000**0:**0000**:**00**1A. (Rule 1)

2001:db8:0:b:**0:0:0**:1A (Rule 2)

Compressed Format: 2001:db8:0:b::1A

> **Note: The case in Example 1 is uppercase and lowercase in Example 2. As explained, the hexadecimal notation of IPv6 is non-case sensitive.**

There are three types of IPv6 addresses, which are as follows:

- Unicast
- Multicast
- Anycast

In IPv4 and IPv6, unicast data transmission is normally referred to as aligned with a single sender or single receiver or as one-to-one transmission. Corresponding IPv6 unicast addresses are global unicast addresses and link-local addresses. The Link-local address range is as follows: **FE80::/10   1111 1110 1000 0000 ::   to   FEBF::/10   1111 1110 1011 1111 ::**

Every IPv6-enabled network interface is required to have a link-local address. Hosts use this address to communicate to the IPv6 network before it has a global unicast address. It is also utilized as the default gateway address by hosts on the network segment. Additionally, adjacent routers use this address to exchange routing updates. IPv6 also has a loopback address used for testing TCP/IP configurations or connectivity (via the ping command) on a local host. Multicast transmission is one-to-many/group, data transmission. Anycast(ing) is a process for routing network traffic where the sender delivers packets to a destination that is nearest to it in terms of a network topology in its proximity.

Assigning IPv6 addresses

The four methods of assigning IPv6 addresses are as follows:

- **Manual Interface ID Assignment**: An address is manually assigned to an interface.
- **EUI-64 Interface ID Assignment**: When this strategy is used, the administrator manually configures the network portion of the address. This will provide a part of the entire address when complete. The interface's MAC address auto-generates

and completes the IPv6 address. Earlier in the chapter, we discussed how MAC addresses are unique identifiers as 48-bit physical addresses. The designers of IPv6 extended this length in their design, and instead of the extended unique identifier of 48 bits, they implemented it as EUI-64. As a network administrator, using this strategy for allocation simplifies the entire process. Every device on a network segment will hold the same network ID and portion of the IPv6 address. The remainder of the address is auto generated from the interface's MAC address, which results in a globally unique identifier.

- **DHCPv6 (Stateful)**: This implementation is quite similar to the **Dynamic Host Configuration Protocol** (**DHCP**) allocation of addresses in IPv4. The DHCP server requires appropriate extensions to be installed pertaining to IPv6, but the terminology and technicalities share much in common with DHCP procedures and protocols in IPv4. DHCP employs leased temporary addresses given to hosts and taken from a pool of available IPv6 addresses. In stateful addressing, the network administrator can control the scope and the pool of addresses to be allocated, and they can also view currently assigned addresses.

- **Stateless Address Auto-Configuration (SLAAC)**: Of the four ways to configure IPv6 and address devices, this strategy and mechanism are quite straightforward. The mechanism allows for fully automatic configuration. Each network host/device on the network auto-configures its own unique IPv6 address. There is no monitoring or tracking in SLAAC utilization, so duplicate IP addresses are avoided. The host runs a process to detect whether the IPv6 address is currently in use and then generates another address to resolve the potential conflict if that is the case. After this, communicating with the router using **router solicitation** (**RS**), the router responds with a **router advertisement** (**RA**) and a 64-bit network ID prefix is then sent to the host machine. The host proceeds to configure its global unicast address and again completes the duplicate address detection process to ensure this address is also unique.

IPv4 and IPv6 coexistence and migration techniques

The migration techniques can be divided into three categories: Dual stack, Tunneling, and Translation, which are explained as follows:

- **Dual-stack**: In dual-stack networks (as the name implies), IPv4 and IPv6 are enabled on all the network nodes/hosts. On a router, enabling this dual means of operation is especially important since it operates as the gateway in and out of the local network or subnet. At least one of a router's ethernet interfaces will link to a local network segment—this aside from point-to-point connections between two routers via a serial link. Both IPv4 and IPv6 addresses, and configuration settings co-exist on the network segment, and the devices and hosts on the segment handle the protocol stacks at the same time.

- **Tunneling**: An IPv6 tunnel connects two endpoints over the Internet. These endpoints (routers) use a Virtual Tunnel Interface to provide termination at either end of the connection. Each router will be configured to carry out this termination. One example of this form of tunneling is known as **Teredo Tunneling**. This is a type of technology that permits transitioning from IPv4 to IPv6 as due to its implementation, IPv6-capable hosts resident on an IPv4 network communicate with IPv6-only networks. Essentially, tunneling encapsulates the IPv6 packet inside of the IPv4 packet. This mechanism resolves a situation where IPv6 is not *natively* connected to an IPv6 network, and the mechanism offers a solution to these devices to be able to exist on the IPv4 network but equally be able to communicate with other IPv6 devices and interfaces.

- **Translation**: NAT64 is a mechanism to handle translation between devices using IPv6 or IPv4. Like the operations of NAT in IPv4 translation techniques, NAT64 translates an IPv4 packet to an IPv6 packet and vice versa.

IPv6 translation technologies differ from IPv6 tunneling technologies; this is because the translation technologies enable IPv4-only devices to speak to IPv6-only devices, which is not possible with any of the tunneling methods. However, IPv4/IPv6 translation and IPv4-only translation entail a certain amount of complexity.

Subnetting with IPv6

In *Figure 4.13*, we can see the structure of a global unicast address:

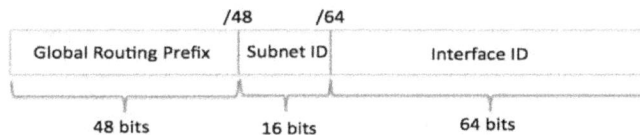

Figure 4.13: Global unicast address

Observe that the task of subnetting in IPv6, as compared with IPv4, is incredibly easier. This is how it is done; just increment by 1 in hexadecimal:

2001:0DB8:AAAA:**0000**::/64

2001:0DB8:AAAA:**0001**::/64

2001:0DB8:AAAA:**0002**::/64

2001:0DB8:AAAA:**000A**::/64

A valid abbreviation is to remove the three leading 0's from the first shown quartet. Consequently, we get the following:

`2001:0DB8:AAAA:1::/64`

With this, subnetting is completed, and the job is done.

Conclusion

IPv4 and IPv6, plus the types of transitioning practices to phase out IPv4 are essential to understanding practical networking. Being able to breakdown an IPv4 and IPv6 address into its component parts from its total structure while comprehending the purpose of addressing is an essential skill for a network administrator. Perceiving the rationale and need for a subnet mask, deciding whether to choose dynamic or static addressing, identifying and configuring a default gateway, and implementing DNS are critical to effective administration and problem-solving IP addressing issues. Now that we have explored IP addressing and subnetting, we are in a much stronger place to learn TCP/IP and common ports and protocols, their application, and encrypted alternatives. TCP/IP is the real-world implementation of practical networking. Unlike the OSI model, TCP/IP is not an abstract concept or theoretical framework. As a suite of protocols, it is implemented via the use and application of ports and protocols and is critical to an understanding of networking fundamentals.

In the upcoming chapter, we will be looking at Ports and Protocols in the TCP/IP suite of protocols. Understanding TCP/IP and how it works in real-world applications is extremely important for a network administrator.

Points to remember

- Comprehending the need for IP addressing.
- Implementing IPv4 and IPv6 addressing systems.
- Understanding notation systems, why they are needed, and their uses.
- Using VLSM and calculating subnets.
- Understanding how to interpret an IP address and figure out the network ID (IPv4).
- The content of this chapter is mapped to *Domain 1: Networking Concepts*. Given a scenario, use appropriate IPv4 network addressing. It also aligns with the objective: Summarize evolving use cases for modern network environments (regarding IPv6).

Key terms

- **APIPA address**: The APIPA address has been a feature of Microsoft Windows operating systems since Windows 98. Abbreviated as APIPA, Automatic Private IP Addressing is aligned with the workings and operations of DHCP. Basically, what occurs is that if a DHCP server has a problem, goes down or crashes, and cannot allocate addresses for whatever reason, this APIPA address *kicks in* as a temporary backup. In DHCP client configurations, the DHCP client boots up and consults the DHCP server to configure its settings, and if the DHCP server is not reachable, APIPA enables the client to self-configure an IP address and subnet mask automatically. The range used for APIPA is 169.254.0.1 - 169.254.255.254. The subnet mask is 255.255.0.0, which provides 65, 534 usable IP addresses. APIPA then checks for the presence of the DHCP server in specific periods of time (that is, every five minutes). APIPA allows for limited connectivity to the local network. It does not offer Internet access or access to external, public web-based services. When the DHCP issue is resolved, APIPA stops, and hands over functionality to the DHCP server, now active on the network again. When a network administrator runs ipconfig /all in the command prompt and detects the use of an APIPA address, they immediately know that there is a DHCP issue on the network and can investigate and troubleshoot this issue further.

- **Virtual IP**: These addresses are logical addresses. They do not relate to a physical network interface and are used for specific purposes. One of the protocols that use these addresses is **network address translation (NAT)**, most especially in multicast (one-to-many) communications. VIP addresses may also be implemented for fault tolerance providing fail-over options for machines. In terms of mobility, a VIP address can be moved to any place on the reachable network without the need to change the address to another subnet configuration. This is a huge benefit in the application of a VIP address.

- **Network address translation**: This is a translation mechanism for translating private IP addresses to public IP addresses—and vice versa. The LAN uses internal private addresses, and the NAT-enabled router provides a translation service to translate these internal addresses to external public ones. The NAT-enabled router handles translation for internal and external traffic. NAT allows a company optimally to use private/internal IP addresses. The company can form one single Internet connection and combine a number of connections. As an element of security, the use of NAT in a business or enterprise *hides* the internal addresses by providing a firewall between the inside and outside addressing configurations.

- **Port address translation (PAT)**: PAT refers to a form of dynamic NAT whereby all the private addresses used locally are translated to a single public IP address using different ports. When multiple private IP addresses are mapped to a single public IP address via PAT, IP addresses are conserved. Additionally, PAT is a cost-effective, efficient means of configuring and handling network traffic. It is the most typically used form of NAT in current networking practice.

Answers to VLSM/subnetting questions

1. 172.16.41.101 with a netmask of 255.255.255.0:

    10101100.00010000.00101001.01100101

    11111111.11111111.11111111.00000000

10101100.00010000.00101001.00000000

Network ID: 172.16.41.0

2. 172.16.20.35 with a netmask of 255.255.255.224 (/27):

10101100.00010000.00010100.00100011

11111111.11111111.11111111.11100000

10101100. 00010000.00010100.00100000

Network ID: 172.16.20.32

3. 172.31.1.69 with a netmask of 255.255.255.252 (/30):

10101100.00011111.00000001.01000101

11111111.11111111.11111111.11111100

10101100.00011111.00000001.01000100

Network ID: 172.31.1.68

*This network was one of the seven networks we looked at earlier in the chapter. See network 5 in *Figure 4.11*.

Questions

Ensure you can answer all the points as set out in the objectives, including the following:

1. Explain the need for a universal addressing scheme (IP addresses) in data transmission and in computer networking as a global phenomenon.

2. Differentiate between private and public addressing.

3. Describe the purpose of NAT.

4. Explore and design a subnet addressing solution for an enterprise with a specific number of networks and hosts.

5. Explain the role of a subnet mask.

6. Explain the motivation for classless inter-domain routing (classless addressing).

7. Compare IPv4 and IPv6 in terms of address structure, addressing capacity, and usage benefits.

8. Explain the methods of transitioning from IPv4 to IPv6.

Additionally, remember to seek out opportunities to practice the skills of subnetting.

CHAPTER 5
Ports and Protocols

Introduction

The purpose of this chapter is to outline the TCP/IP model and how this specific suite of protocols is used in the networking industry in everyday *practical* administration. While the OSI model is a conceptual framework or reference guide, the TCP/IP protocol suite handles practical applications in inter-network communication. Consequently, any discussion of TCP/IP will involve the area of *ports and protocols* and what is meant by a protocol stack. In *Chapter 1, OSI Model*, we discussed the OSI model. We identified the model as a *conceptual framework akin to a blueprint an architect may be given on a house or larger structure*. We explored it as a reference guide for all kinds of specialisms in the field of networking practice. The OSI model is additionally used to describe the functions of a networking system. When referred to as a guide, it assists us in understanding the flow of data as it travels across the network and between the networks and explains what happens to the data along the way. The model is broken down into seven layers, layers which were outlined in greater detail in that chapter.

The TCP/IP protocol stack is a system that implements protocol behavior using a series of layers. (Note that protocol stacks can be implemented either in hardware or software or in a combination of both hardware and software).

Typically, only the lower layers of networking models are implemented in hardware, and the higher layers are implemented in software. We will see this approach as we investigate TCP/IP layers in more detail.

In terms of similarities between the models, the OSI model and the TCP/IP model are both reference models used to describe the data communication process. The TCP/IP model is used specifically for the TCP/IP suite of protocols and the OSI model is used for the development of standard communication for equipment and applications from different vendors.

Regarding the breakdown of layers, the TCP/IP model performs the same process as the OSI model but uses four layers instead of seven. Due to similar functions and operations to OSI, for example, encapsulation, segmentation, data transmission methods, and encryption, in this chapter, we will focus primarily on ports and protocols in the TCP/IP suite and the logic and application of these protocols. Practically, every network-capable application in networking operations relies on TCP/IP to work accordingly. It is that fact and characteristic that makes TCP/IP's mechanisms; ones that should not be undervalued. That is the power and importance of TCP/IP.

Structure

In this chapter, we will discuss the following topics:

- TCP/IP protocol suite
- Ports and protocols
- Port assignment
- Charts of ports and protocols
- Internet layer protocols
- Transport layer protocols
- Application layer protocols

Objectives

On completion of this chapter, readers should be able to explain the primary difference between the OSI model and TCP/IP. They should understand what is meant by a protocol stack and comprehend the need for protocols and why they are assigned a port number. Additionally, the reader should be able to articulate the functions of specific protocols and match protocols with their relevant port numbers while mapping a protocol with the appropriate layer on the TCP/IP model. In brief, they should be able to explain common networking ports, protocols, services, and traffic types.

TCP/IP protocol suite

As with the OSI model, the TCP/IP model is usually presented in stack formation since this graphical representation demonstrates the concepts of data flow and protocols best as we *move up and down* through the stack. The four layers of TCP/IP are as follows:

- Layer 1—Application
- Layer 2—Transport
- Layer 3—Internet
- Layer 4—Network access

The following figure compares TCP/IP with the OSI model:

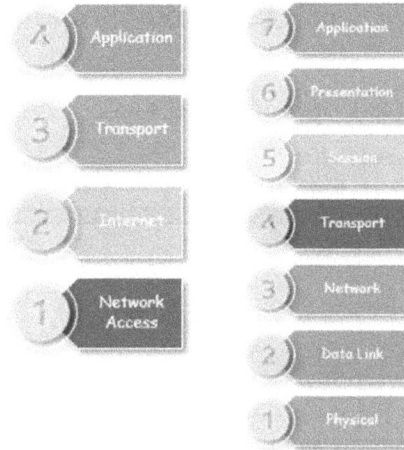

Figure 5.1: TCP/IP four-layer model vs. OSI seven-layer model

In the following figure, the primary functions at each layer are outlined:

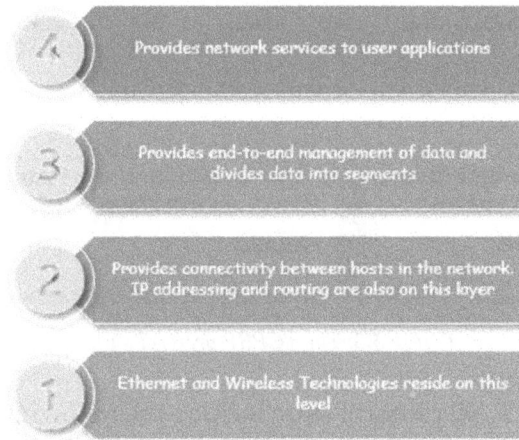

Figure 5.2: The functionality at each layer

TCP/IP did not begin as a fully finished model. In fact, it was developed over time in quite a piecemeal fashion. It began as a project for a couple of hundred devices on a network. These **400** devices were connected to the US Department of Defense's network named ARPAnet. ARPAnet was researching military and defense technologies and mechanisms.

Individuals made up of researchers, scientists, and computer engineers had been sharing applications for accessing files and improving collaboration in managing projects via shareware. ARPAnet saw the opportunity present and began to use the *TCP/IP* protocols these designers were collaborating on. That was back in 1983. Nowadays, it is hard to conceive that the global internet, with its billions of users, is using the protocols developed back then (plus more). However, TCP/IP is the only routable protocol. No other networking protocol handles internal-external communication like TCP/IP does. So, it became the *internet protocol*. Many of the commonly used protocols are listed in the following figure of the TCP/IP protocol suite:

TCP/IP Protocol Suite

TCP/IP protocols exist on Layers 2,3 and 4.
Layer 1 protocols relate to Ethernet, WLAN and other *physical* access technologies.

Application Layer	Name System	Host Config	Email	File Transfer	Web & Web Service
	DNS	DHCPv4	SMTP	FTP	HTTP
		DHCPv6	POP3	SFTP	HTTPS
		SLAAC	IMAP	TFTP	REST

Transport Layer	Connection-Oriented	Connectionless
	TCP	UDP

Internet Layer	Internet Protocol	Messaging	Routing Protocols	
	IPv4	ICMPV4	OSPF	
	IPv6	ICMPV6	EIGRP	BGP
	NAT	ICMPV6 ND	GRE	

Network Access Layer	Address Resolution	Datalink Protocols	
	ARP	ETHERNET	WLAN

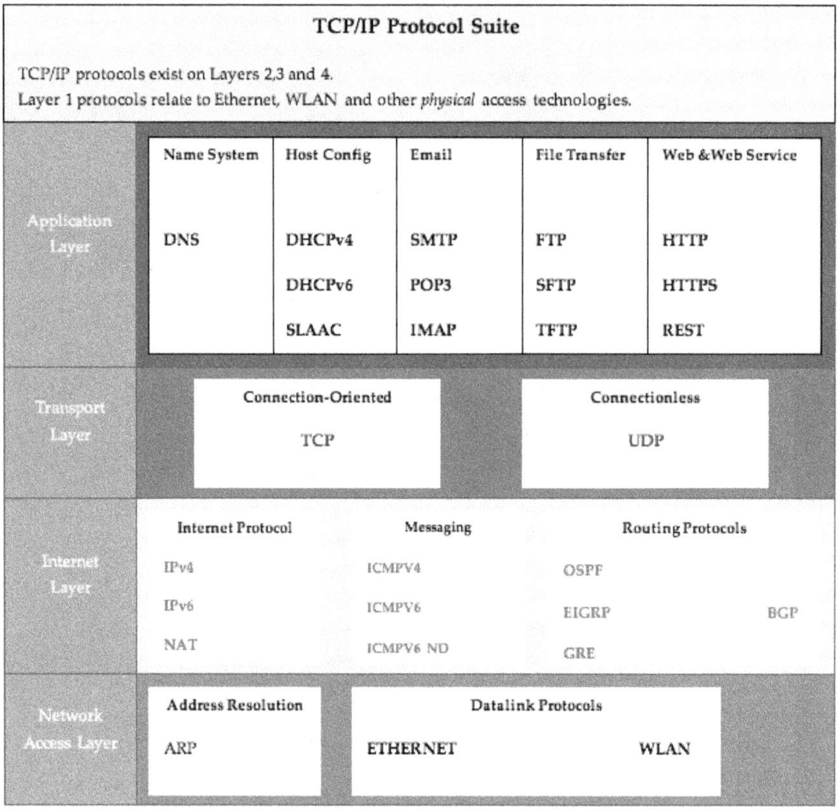

Figure 5.3: The TCP/IP protocol suite

Other protocols in the TCP/IP protocol suite include the following:

- **Application layer**: **Secure Shell (SSH)**, **Secure File Transfer Protocol (SFTP)**, Telnet, **Domain Name System (DNS)**, **Network Time Protocol (NTP)**, **Simple Network Management Protocol (SNMP)**, **Lightweight Directory Access Protocol (LDAP)**, **Server Message Block (SMB)**, and Syslog.

- **Security-related**: SMTP TLS, **Lightweight Directory Access Protocol** (over SSL) **(LDAPS)**, **Internet Message Access Protocol (IMAP)** over SSL, POP3 over

SSL, **Internet Protocol Security (IPsec)**, and **Authentication Header (AH)/ Encapsulating Security Payload (ESP)**.

- **Database management**: **Structured Query Language (SQL)** Server, SQLNet, and MySQL.

- **Remote access protocols**: **Remote Desktop Protocol (RDP)**, **Session Initiation Protocol (SIP)**.

Note: IPv4, IPv6, and NAT are discussed in detail in this chapter. They are included in this chapter to demonstrate their place in the TCP/IP model and show the layer on which they reside.

Ports and protocols

In *Chapter 1, OSI Model*, the difference between standards vs. protocols was delineated. Concluding on that section, a point was made that: as networking evolved over the decades, organizational standards helped to make worldwide networking a viable venture. Protocols make networking functions possible. As defined by *Techopedia*, a protocol is a set of rules and guidelines for communicating data. Rules are defined for each step and process during communication between two or more computers. Networks have to follow these rules to transmit data successfully. When we look at a protocol as a set of rules, this is how protocols make networking functions possible. In any act of communication, if we did not have rules, the potential is not only for chaotic transmission of data. With the absence of rules and orderly processes, the likelihood of not being able to transmit or receive data at all is quite palpable.

Imagine there is a group of people talking with each other, and the conversation, as we say, *gets out of hand*. Too many people are speaking at the same time. Some are speaking louder than others and interrupting other people's communications mid-sentence. Observing this disorder, we will detect crosstalk and much interference. No doubt, some messages or pieces of information will be lost or corrupted in transmission. Without rules and orderly agreement on protocols, the act of communication will be flawed and erroneous. In some cases, individuals may simply go mute and remove themselves from the act of communication completely because, as hosts, they have become overwhelmed with incoming data and have been inundated with mixed signals. The potential for devices in computer networking is to stop working optimally or to develop component burnout. In this, we find an example of communication without rules causing disruption to the flow of data and to the quality of the data sent and received.

In networking communication, rules and regulations exist to provide effective communication systems where the flow of data is seamless and efficient. Protocols handle many processes in networking. Some of these processes use a single protocol, whereas others may use multiple protocols to carry out the related tasks and functions successfully.

Port assignment

To define a port, we can consider what is meant by an endpoint. If we are speaking about a specific journey from A to B, the endpoint would be the source and destination, that is, A and B, in end-to-end communications. These endpoints can be reached using specific technologies such as the IP address or the MAC address of the host machine. Intermediary devices like switches or routers will use technologies aligned with their intelligence capabilities and mechanisms. Switches will forward frames using MAC addresses (Layer 2 of OSI), and routers will use IP addresses to identify and forward traffic to networks (Layer 3). The point is that there are physical and logical constructs embedded into the technologies that assist in locating the intended destination host for a protocol data unit to be delivered. Note the word *protocol*. It is a protocol data unit we are referring to being transmitted, so this implies that all data units are associated with specific protocols and that these protocols embody a set of rules or processes to enable them to operate correctly. It is also implied that protocols are logical systems with a set of rules and guidelines for communicating data. As explained in the definition by *Techopedia, Rules are defined for each step and process during communication between two or more computers.*

What about ports and port numbers? What is their purpose? Now, we can state that ports and port numbers are logical constructs integrated into the software of an operating system, which demarks a specific process or identifies a network service. Incoming and outgoing data, at the software level, will arrive at the host via a logical port, which has been assigned to the protocol in occurrence. Every protocol will hold its unique port number, and much like the function of MAC addresses and IP addresses, these port numbers will handle the flow of traffic by acting as endpoints in the act of communication. Think of it this way: if A and B are endpoints in hosts, *logical* ports have been set up to behave like gatekeepers, and every protocol will have its uniquely defined gatekeeper or port number.

> **Note: The difference between a port number and an IP address is this: an IP address identifies a host on a network or network segment. Port numbers pinpoint and align with a specific application or service on a system.**

In addition to IP addressing information, port numbers comprise the addressing information that helps identify senders and receivers in data transmission, informing us of the application or service in use. Since port numbers use 16 bits in total, there are a maximum of 65,535 port numbers available. The well-known port numbers in use range from 0 to 1,023. Other port numbers are reserved, as we saw with IP addresses. You can register a port number for an application or game, and for this type of use, the numbers 1,024 to 49,151 are used. Above that, individuals can use port numbers more freely as they are available to anyone in this manner.

Charts of ports and protocols

TCP/IP protocols operate on the internet, transport, and application layer. TCP/IP's network access layer combines the two bottom layers of the OSI model, the physical and data-link layer. In OSI, the physical layer handles the transmission and reception of raw bit streams over a physical medium. Functions at the data-link layer include ensuring reliable transmission of data frames between two nodes connected by a physical layer. Consequently, when we investigate the function of ARP or RARP, we will understand how the protocols operate to provide a service to the *logical* mechanisms required for data transmission and resolve the logical mechanisms with the physical network card's operations and the physical network. **Address Resolution Protocol** (**ARP**) maps or resolves the logical address or the Internet address of a host (that is, IP) to its physical address, which is pre-burned in the network interface card by the card's manufacturer. This unique address is the unique identifier of the NIC, synonymously, its physical address, MAC address, or **burned-in-address** (**BIA**), terms which can be used interchangeably. **Reverse Address Resolution Protocol** (**RARP**), as implied by the word *reverse*, finds the IP address of a host when its physical address or MAC address is known. Within an Ethernet or WLAN network, the physical address (MAC address) is necessary to provide intercommunication between devices. Therefore,

- It is not always possible for a source device to know the physical address of a destination device.

- ARP provides a service of matching or mapping an IP address to a MAC address.

- ARP broadcasts a request for the MAC address of a device with a particular IP address, and that device responds by sending back its MAC address.

- This allows the source device to send to a specific MAC address without having to broadcast all messages (and thus, offset slowing down the network).

Figures 5.4 to *5.6* and *Tables 5.1* to *5.3* focus on layers 1, 2, and 3 of TCP/IP. Protocols will be described, and the allocated ports will be included. The TCP/IP protocols have been divided into groupings that map to the layers of the TCP/IP model. Please remember that there are many more protocols in TCP/IP. For the purposes of the CompTIA Network+ exam, concentration will be placed on the protocols outlined in the Network+ exam objectives.

Internet layer protocols

Figure 5.4 shows the network layer in the TCP/IP protocol suite:

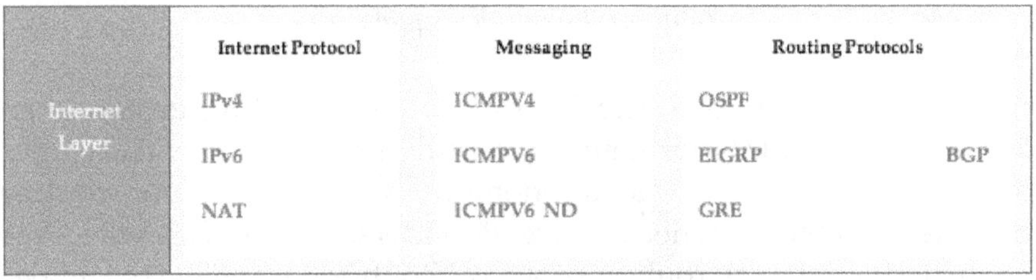

	Internet Protocol	Messaging	Routing Protocols	
Internet Layer	IPv4	ICMPV4	OSPF	
	IPv6	ICMPV6	EIGRP	BGP
	NAT	ICMPV6 ND	GRE	

Figure 5.4: Internet layer protocols

The following table outlines the protocols aligned at the internet layer of TCP/IP:

Protocol	Port number	Description
Internet protocol	The port number is added on or tagged to the IP address: for example, 192.168.1.44:80. IP addressing is a logical mechanism for locating and transmitting data across internetworks. The port number is associated with an application or service and is application or service-specific. The port number accompanies the IP address to enable the destination host to identify the type of data being transmitted.	IP is a connectionless protocol. It is classified as *unreliable, best-effort delivery*. IP addressing uses protocol data packets called datagrams that travel over different pathways across multiple routers. IP is also accompanied by the *Transport Control Protocol*, which is a connection-oriented protocol. Due to this complementary association between the two protocols, the entire suite became known as TCP/IP.
ICMP	N/A ICMP is a protocol used for sending messages between different hosts. It is used for testing connections and running diagnostics. It does not use port numbers. It does, however, use types and codes to differentiate between the types of messages being transmitted. For example, echo request messages use type 8, and echo reply messages use type 0.	ICMP determines if data is getting to its intended destination at appropriate times. It is also used to check if data is arriving in the right order and will send a message to the sending device if this is not the case. ICMP is an excellent error reporting tool for monitoring data transmission on networks and network performance. Two of the utilities that belong to ICMP are PING and TRACERT. Note that Ping and ICMP are not the same thing. ICMP is the protocol, and PING is a network utility used to test connectivity between devices on a network. A PING is generated using ICMP.
IGMP	N/A The purpose of IGMP is multicasting. In IPv4, the address range reserved for multicasting is 224.0.0.0 to 239.255.255.255. In IPv6, **Multicast Listener Discovery** (**MLD**) is used as a protocol instead of IGMP. However, the purpose remains the same in that it is used for one-to-many or one-to-a-group transmission.	IGMP is used to facilitate and allow multicasting messages to be transmitted between devices that are members of a multicast group. They do this by sharing one IP address as a network address. IGMP operates like a shared mail folder accessible by members of an e-mail group or security group. All members of the group who have the shared address can access and see the mail.

Table 5.1: Internet layer protocols

Routing protocols can be divided into interior gateway routing protocols and exterior gateway routing protocols. Interior gateway routing protocols essentially operate within organizational networks known as autonomous systems. Exterior routing gateway protocols operate between Internet Service Providers. Border Gateway Protocol is an example of an exterior gateway routing protocol. Routing technologies will be covered in a later chapter.

Note: ICMP is implemented on all TCP/IP networks, providing messaging that can help with troubleshooting, including Destination Unreachable, Time Exceeded, Redirect, Echo, Echo Reply, Information Request, Information Reply, and Address Mask Request.

Transport layer protocols

The following figure shows the transport layer in the TCP/IP protocol suite:

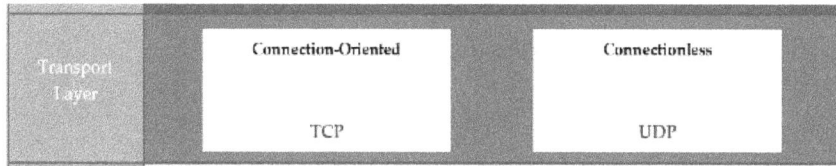

Figure 5.5: *Transport layer protocols*

Table 5.2 outlines the protocols aligned at the transport layer of TCP/IP. As shown, there are essentially two transport protocols. All other protocols will use TCP, **User Datagram Protocol** (**UDP**), or a combination of both protocols to transport the data applicable to the needs of the protocol being used. Both TCP and UDP have unique ways in which they handle the transmission of data.

Protocol	Port number	Description
TCP	N/A It is best to think of TCP as the handler of the data being sent. Much like a courier, TCP will handle the data in a specific manner. TCP controls the safe delivery of data and ensures the data is intact and in the right order. The application-specific port numbers accompany the IP address to provide the hosts with details about the relevant corresponding application or service.	TCP uses checksums that are added to data packets to aid error checking. TCP also uses sequence numbering to identify the order in which packets were sent. The destination devices acknowledge the correct receipt (via ACKs). Otherwise, data is re-transmitted). TCP is a reliable, guaranteed, connection-oriented delivery. The downside of this is the overhead on transmission.
UDP	N/A Again, like TCP, UDP defines how data is delivered, the processes used to deliver it, and the way in which it controls delivery. Some protocols are designed to use TCP or UDP, depending upon the purposes and requirements of the application or service. Ports are used to identify services.	UDP uses a connectionless transportation system. It does not use error checking or sequence numbering and assumes that other protocols will handle the error checking. UDP is only concerned with getting the data to the Transport Layer of the destination device. It does not re-transmit data. UDP requires fewer network resources and uses less bandwidth than TCP.

Table 5.2: *Transport layer protocols*

Application layer protocols

The following figure shows the application layer in the TCP/IP protocol suite:

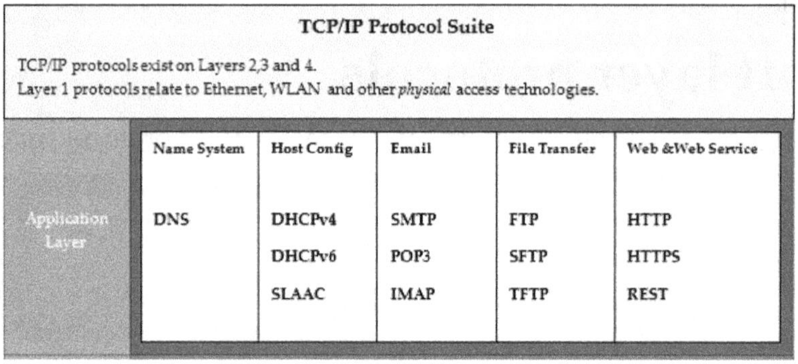

TCP/IP Protocol Suite

TCP/IP protocols exist on Layers 2,3 and 4.
Layer 1 protocols relate to Ethernet, WLAN and other *physical* access technologies.

Application Layer	Name System	Host Config	Email	File Transfer	Web &Web Service
	DNS	DHCPv4	SMTP	FTP	HTTP
		DHCPv6	POP3	SFTP	HTTPS
		SLAAC	IMAP	TFTP	REST

Figure 5.6: Application layer protocols

The following table outlines the protocols aligned at the application layer of TCP/IP: It is broken down into the name of the protocol, the port number, and a description of the protocol, with its usage and functions.

Protocol	Port number	Description
DNS	53 TCP, UDP	DNS resolves domain names to IP addresses. More specifically, DNS manages and centralizes domain names on the internet and matches a hostname to the IP address of a server where the host is located. DNS has been likened to a phone book. The analogy works well since DNS's resolver cache is consulted much like a person consults a phone book by searching for the telephone number via the person's name and then address. The address is mapped or matched to the number, and the query is completed. If the DNS resolver does not hold that specific record, the query is escalated to the top-level domain server or the authoritative nameserver until the client's query is resolved.
DHCP DHCPv4 DHCPv6	67, 68 UDP (TCP does not suit this protocol as two of the messages employed in DORA use broadcasting— that is, discover and request. TCP does not support broadcasting.)	DHCP dynamically provides IP addresses to devices on a network that do not have one implemented statically or manually. A network administrator has an option either way, to configure a manual permanent address or enable DHCP on the specified host(s). A DHCP server provides the address from a pool either for a limited time (lease) or the duration of the device's use of the network. DHCP has become very useful as the demand for IP addresses has substantially increased, most especially with IPv6 and IoT. DHCP uses a process called DORA for short. This process is a mechanism through which IP addresses get assigned their address from the DHCP server. It breaks down as discover, offer, request, and acknowledge. Messages are exchanged between the client and the server throughout this process.

Protocol	Port number	Description
FTP	20, 21 TCP Port 20 is used for the transfer of data. Port 21 is used for the management and control of data. This connection remains open while the client communicates with the server.	**File Transfer Protocol** (FTP) is a protocol, a service, and an application. It allows the transfer of files between devices. FTP was one of the first protocols to be developed and is a popular means of transferring files across networks—especially large ones. FTP is employed in server-client architecture. Due to its potential vulnerability as a protocol, network administrators must be aware of the port numbers in use and the strategies used to counteract this native vulnerability (for example, encryption methods). As well as being aware of OS configuration, administrators use third-party software as a countermeasure to FTP's susceptibility to eavesdropping and theft. Additionally, both ports 20 and 21 must remain open in the firewall for FTP to work correctly. Note that FTP uses TCP as its transport protocol. This ensures that the data is received in the right order, no packets are lost, and that the data reaches its destination.
TFTP	69 UDP	**Trivial File Transfer Protocol** (TFTP) works with UDP to transfer files across the Internet. It requires an acknowledgment of receipt of each packet before the next packet is transmitted. TFTP is not as robust as FTP but is certainly simpler in format. It is very useful for updating the firmware on network intermediary devices like switches and routers. Due to limitations in security and no mechanism for authentication before transmission, TFTP is also used to transmit data internally in a LAN or network segment.
SFTP	22 TCP	SFTP handles transferring large files over the internet. Building on FTP, SFTP consists of SSH security features. SSH is a component of internet security that utilizes encryption to offset the vulnerabilities of sending data in plain text. Prior to SSH, network and server administrators used telnet to access servers or other network devices remotely. Telnet's plain text was identified as a weakness, so SSH became the better solution. FTP commands are encrypted, so using this method alongside SSH alleviates password sniffing. Sensitive information is not exposed via plain text. Since authentication is implemented with the server and client during transactions, **man-in-the-middle** (**MiTM**) attacks are guarded against.
HTTP	80 TCP	**Hypertext Transfer Protocol** (HTTP) is used to access files on the Internet. It provides only two services (requests from the client and responses from the server). In this client-server model, the Web browser communicates with the Web server which is hosting the website. Since this transaction needs to be reliable and guaranteed, HTTP uses TCP to handle data transmission.

Protocol	Port number	Description
HTTPS	443 TCP	HTTPS is used primarily over the internet as a secure connection. When transmitting data in this way, the protocol is encrypted using TLS. TLS uses long-term keys to generate a short-term session key. These public and private keys, plus the generation of a session key, enable the data flow to be encrypted throughout transmission. This means that in contrast to HTTP, HTTPS is not as vulnerable to eavesdropping, malware, or man-in-the-middle attacks. However, regarding security practices and perceptions of protocols, a network administrator's best approach is to consider nothing as impenetrable; when HTTPS uses a deprecated version of Secure Sockets Layer, for example, security loopholes can be present or created. To copper fasten the security of a website, HTTPS should be used for the whole site and not partially implemented in some areas.
POP3	110 TCP Port 110 is the default port, which is not encrypted. Port 995 is used if the e-mail client wants a secure connection.	**Post Office Protocol** (POP3) is a protocol used for receiving e-mails. The act termed is when the client pulls in the mail from their inbox, mail residing on the e-mail server. POP3 is most frequently used in internet e-mail provision. POP3 implements a *store and forward* method. The e-mail client can also download e-mail from the remote server should they wish to store or view their e-mail offline. A network administrator needs to be aware of the address for the POP3 server when configuring e-mail accounts manually on hosts or smartphones, for the connection to work accordingly. The popularity of POP3 lies in its ease of configuration and the simplicity of the protocol to be monitored and maintained. POP3 over SSL. This provides the option of an encrypted connection and must be configured with the appropriate port to function.
IMAP	143 993 TCP An IMAP server listens on port 143. IMAP over SSL/TLS uses port 993.	Like POP3, IMAP is also a protocol for receiving incoming mail from a remote e-mail server. However, its popularity lies in its suitability for mobility. Users can receive and read their e-mail from multiple devices. When using IMAP, the e-mail remains stored on the e-mail server. Thus, the user can access their devices from work, home, or anywhere they use a device. IMAP over SSL/TLS (IMAPS) uses 993. This offers a secure connection to the e-mail server. TLS has been the preferred method for security since 2018. POP and IMAP are the most prevalent protocols utilized in e-mail services in client-server models.
SMTP	25 587 TCP Port 25 is used for plain text. SMTP TLS 587 Uses TLS encryption to ensure that e-mails are delivered safely and securely.	SMTP transfers e-mail between devices across the internet. SMTP transfers data between an e-mail server and the organization's e-mail server in server-to-server transmission and provides these intermediary services for the client to retrieve the mail delivered. Both delivery over plain text and secure connections are available with SMTP.

Protocol	Port number	Description
SNMP	161 162 UDP	SNMP allows the configuration, monitoring, and management of network resources and devices. Typical devices are switches, routers, cable modems, printers, servers, and client machines. Information is gathered from the device about the device's performance and behavior. The network administrator can act on this information and modify or adapt the components or device based on the results of the data gathered. SNMP is defined by the **Internet Engineering Task Force (IETF)**. SNMP has had several versions—currently at version 3.
SYSLOG	514 TCP, UDP	Syslog is used for system management and for logging security issues. Syslog gathers statistics, analyses statistics, and generates debugging messages. The server used is called a Syslog server. This centralized approach to auditing, monitoring, and reviewing data is advantageous to any organization using the service. System Logging Protocol is also used on Unix and Linux-based systems and is an effective auditing tool for assessing devices and equipment.
NTP	123 TCP, UDP	NTP is responsible for the handling of synchronization across networks. It is a hierarchical system that keeps devices attuned. It also provides timekeeping mechanisms for file servers. NTP servers have very precise atomic clocks and use efficient GPU clocks. The synchronization of devices is especially pertinent to real-time communications, so the accuracy of the servers is critical. Conflicts in time zones and server downtime must be continually counteracted due to the protocol's prominence and standing in effective information exchange.
LDAP	389 636 TCP, UDP	LDAP **Lightweight Directory Access Protocol** (over SSL) **(LDAPS)** LDAP handles the process of user access to the network's system and resources. Via authentication and authorization, users can access the resources if they meet the relevant criteria. Access is granted to networking equipment, files, and also to the servers themselves. Using SSL, connections are secure and encrypted. Another security implementation of LDAP is over TLS (STARTTLS). This option tends to be the preferred security option.
SMB	445 TCP, UDP UDP is used more for backward compatibility.	SMB provides shared access to files and printers across a network. It is a service used internally on LANs. Microsoft created this protocol for internal sharing purposes. They did move to a draft for internet usage, but this did not proceed to active fruition (CIFS). Interprocess communication is based on the SMB protocol. In IP networks, SMB uses TCP as its transport protocol. As the versions of SMB evolved, more security features were added to support authentication based on AES-128 encryption.

Protocol	Port number	Description
RDP	3389 TCP, UDP	RDP enables a person to access a host remotely. Providing the user with a graphical user interface, the user can interact with the PC/server remoted to and engage with the machine as if it were a local connection. RDP supports many different types of network topologies. Services included are keyboard and mouse data encryption, clipboard sharing, the running of desktop applications. Printer port and file redirection. These are some of the services RDP provides.
SIP	5060 5061 TCP, UDP	SIP combines with other application protocols to manage multimedia communication sessions over the Internet, for example, in VoIP. When a session is created between two endpoints, SIP is the signaling method that creates, modifies, and terminates the session. SIP is used for unicasting and multicast sessions. Typical applications that use the protocol are video conferencing, online games, instant messaging, file transfer, and streaming multimedia distribution.

Table 5.3: *Transport layer protocols*

Conclusion

As with the OSI model, understanding the TCP/IP suite of protocols is fundamental to appreciating how networks function and the processes and protocols that enable them to do so. As stated in *Chapter 1, OSI Model, when you hold better comprehension of network operations, as a network administrator,* you can *fine-tune* your networks, organize them more effectively and efficiently and improve the performance of implementations you undertake. With learning and practice, you will know what the best needs of the network are. Understanding network models puts you on the pathway to discover these needs and take mental ownership of them. In addition to this, knowing ports and protocols has so many benefits. It is a great support and toolkit to assist a network administrator in handling security issues and managing rules on a firewall or an operating system. Now that you can identify the ports and protocols, describe their functions, and gauge their relevance in networking operations, your practical skills will enable you to *fine-tune* the networks you work with.

In the upcoming chapter, we will explore implementing and troubleshooting network services. Network administrators need to know how to implement DHCP in their network. Even in small networks, manually assigning static addresses on devices is prone to err and if it does err, a network administrator must understand IP addressing thoroughly. The understanding of DHCP as a network management protocol ensures network devices are configured correctly and connected to the network.

Points to remember

- The TCP/IP model is a real-world implementation of networking technologies and processes.

- TCP/IP is a practical model and enables users to apply and implement the protocols in the TCP/IP protocol suite. It is a four-layer model that can be compared and contrasted with OSI.

- Standards define how devices communicate with each other and access media.

- Once a standard is implemented in software, it becomes a protocol.

- Protocols define how devices and applications communicate.

- The protocols on a network affect how it functions and its ability to interface with other networks.

- If you know networking models, ports, and protocols, it enables you to troubleshoot your network devices, and the connectivity and functionality of networks gain clarity. As a result of understanding this model(s), you can analyze different layers of communication and interoperability so you can systematically and accurately troubleshoot.

- These models form the backbone of computing.

- CompTIA Network+ concentrates on ports and protocols in its course objectives. The content of this chapter is mapped to *Domain 1: Networking Concepts*. Explain common networking ports, protocols, services, and traffic types.

Key terms

- **TCP/IP protocol suite:** A set of communication protocols used for inter-network data transmission, essential for internet functionality.

- **Protocol Stack:** A layered structure of protocols that work together to enable network communication.

- **Encapsulation:** The process of wrapping data with the necessary protocol headers as it moves through the layers of a network model.

- **Segmentation:** Dividing large data packets into smaller chunks for efficient transmission over a network.

- **Port number:** A unique identifier used to distinguish different network services on a device.

- **Common networking ports:** Predefined port numbers assigned to specific protocols, such as HTTP (80), HTTPS (443), and FTP (21).

- **Application layer protocols**: Protocols responsible for end-user services, including HTTP, FTP, and SMTP.

- **Transport layer protocols:** Provide communication reliability, with key examples being TCP and UDP.

- **Internet layer protocols:** Handle addressing and routing, including IP, ICMP, and ARP.

- **OSI model**: A conceptual framework used to understand network functionality across seven layers.

- **TCP/IP model:** A practical networking model with four layers that enables internet communication.

- **Data transmission methods:** Techniques like packet switching that allow efficient data transfer across networks.

- **Encryption:** A security method that transforms readable data into an encoded format to protect it from unauthorized access.

Questions

1. What is the importance of the TCP/IP model?
2. What is a protocol?
3. How could a network administrator use the knowledge of ports and protocols to assist them in their job role?

Join our book's Discord space

Join the book's Discord Workspace for Latest updates, Offers, Tech happenings around the world, New Release and Sessions with the Authors:

https://discord.bpbonline.com

CHAPTER 6

Implementing and Troubleshooting Network Services

Introduction

> *The good news about computers is that they do what you tell them to do.*
> *The bad news is that they do what you tell them to do.*

- Ted Nelson, Author

If any network is to function correctly and perform effectively, a network administrator must be cognizant of the importance of network services and how they operate to keep the network in an optimum condition. Network services include **Dynamic Host Configuration Protocol (DHCP)**, **Domain Name Service (DNS)**, and **Network Time Protocol (NTP)**. Network services can be low-level or high-level applications. Since they are network services, these services listed are typically installed, configured, and implemented on an organization's server(s), irrespective of whether the server is on-prem or residing in the cloud. Network services also include file and directory services, e-mail, printing, VoIP, the hosting of websites, and the facility of sharing hardware. For the purpose of covering the CompTIA Network+ course content and aligning with the course objectives, we will focus our attention on DHCP, DNS, and NTP.

Structure

This chapter covers the following topics:

- Dynamic Host Configuration Protocol
- Installing the DHCP server role
- Domain Name Service
- Network Time Protocol

Objectives

The learning outcomes of this chapter include the ability to understand DHCP, DNS, and NTP as sampled network services. On completion of the chapter, the reader should be able to install and configure DHCP on a server operating system, understand the operations and functionality of DHCP, DNS, and NTP, and practically engage with server software and the relevant consoles to manage, maintain, and troubleshoot network services, with a comprehension of how services should perform and how the client–server interaction should produce an efficient and effective pairing of protocols in a real-world working environment.

Dynamic Host Configuration Protocol

As explained in *Chapter 5, Ports and Protocols*, DHCP dynamically provides IP addresses to devices on a network that do not have one implemented statically or manually. A network administrator has the option to configure a manual permanent address or enable DHCP on the specified host(s). A DHCP Server provides the address from a pool either for a limited time (lease) or the duration of the device's use of the network. DHCP has become very useful as the demand for IP addresses has substantially increased, most especially with IPv6 and the **Internet of Things** (**IoT**). DHCP uses a process called DORA for short. This process is the mechanism through which IP addresses get assigned their address from the DHCP server. It breaks down as follows: discover, offer, request, and acknowledge. Messages are exchanged between the client and the server throughout this process. First, we will observe the DORA process in *Figure 6.1*. We will then look at a typical IPv4 configuration on NIC.

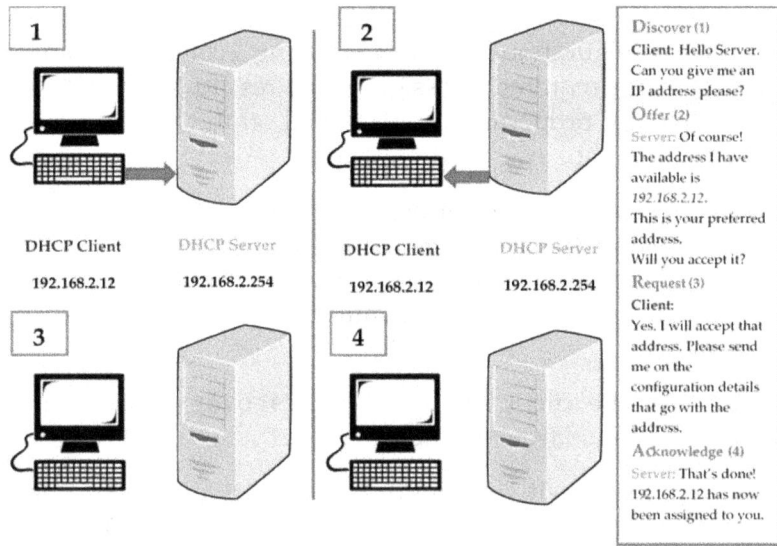

Figure 6.1: *Stages of the DORA process*

Figure 6.2 differentiates between static and dynamic addressing and shows the configuration settings on a typical Ethernet adapter:

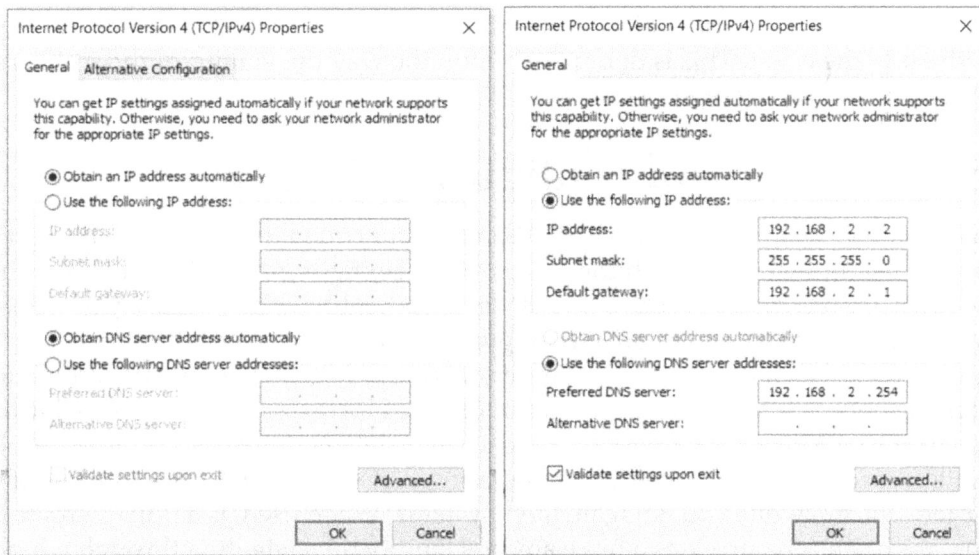

```
S1# config t
S1#(config)# interface vlan 1
S1(config-if)# ip address 192.168.1.2 255.255.255.0
S1(config-if)# no shut
S1(config-if)# exit
S1(config)#
```

Figure 6.2: *Static vs. dynamic addressing*

The intermediary device, specifically the switch, is assigned a manual static address as per best practice. This configuration is carried out using a command-line interface. Figure 6.2 presents the commands required to assign an address to the switch. At the top of the figure, dynamic addressing properties are displayed on the left, while static addressing properties appear on the right.

Regarding dynamic address configuration, *Figure 6.1* outlines the events that occur between the client and DHCP Server throughout the DORA process. To extend on this description, note that the communications sent from the client to the server are broadcast **protocol data units** (**PDUs**). The server's communications back to the client are sent in unicast transmission.

More specifically, when the client sends a **DHCPDiscover** message, it is a broadcast transmission in layer 2 and in layer 3 of the OSI model.

The DHCP server then replies with its **DHCPOffer**. This transmission is broadcast in layer 3, but it is a unicast transmission in layer 2. The client replies with a **DHCPRequest**. It is also a broadcast transmission in layers 2 and layer 3. Remember, the client does not have an IP address yet, so its ability to unicast is not viable.

The DHCP server sends its **DHCPAck**. It is a broadcast transmission in Layer 3 but is unicast in layer 2.

In short, due to the implementation of MAC addressing at layer 2, a server can unicast or broadcast to the client. This is dependent upon the way the vendor of the software has enabled functionality. However, the client will always broadcast.

Implementing and configuring DHCP

The best way to fully comprehend DHCP and its functionality is to implement it as a role on a server and work through the stages of the configuration. It is then that you will have a fuller appreciation of what a DHCP server is and how it operates. Consequently, the demonstration that comes next is a guided walk-through of implementing and configuring DHCP on a Windows 2019 Server operating system. For the purpose of clarity, some screenshots will have more notes than others. However, it is good to point out at this juncture that Microsoft Windows has excellent details on every window you open that explain exactly where you are in the operating system and what the functions of your specific location are while you navigate their systems. When used as a purposeful tool for learning, we can teach ourselves a huge amount simply by navigating through windows!

Network administrators need to know how to implement DHCP in their network. Even in small networks, manually assigning static addresses on devices is prone to err and if it does err, a network administrator must understand IP addressing thoroughly. The understanding of DHCP as a network management protocol ensures network devices are configured correctly and connected to the network.

First, we must assign the DHCP server role to the server designated as the DHCP server. Prior to this designation, the selected server must hold a static IP address. In this demonstration and example, the DHCP server's address is **192.168.2.254**. Second, you must have administrative privileges to designate DHCP or any roles to a server operating system.

Installing the DHCP server role

The following steps are required to install the DHCP server role to the designated server:

1. Log in as domain administrator. If **Server Manager** is not set to open automatically, launch it. When the **Server Manager** console is launched, click **Manage** on the top right of the dashboard. Refer to the following figure:

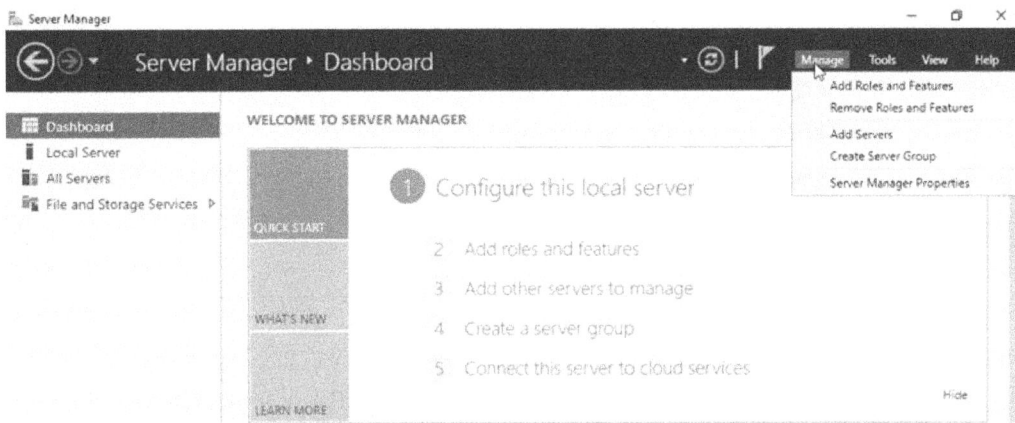

Figure 6.3: Installing DHCP role, step 1

2. Then, click on **Add Roles and Features**:

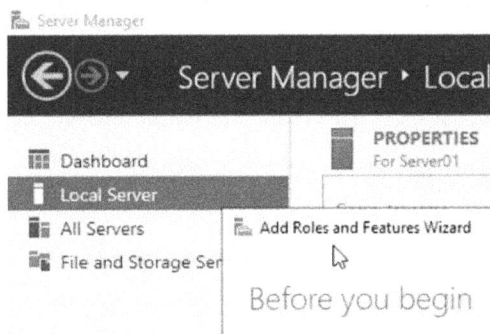

Figure 6.4: Installing DHCP role, step 2

3. Note the detail on the right panel of the screen. This information advises the administrator to verify certain tasks that have been handled before continuing with this installation, as shown in the following figure:

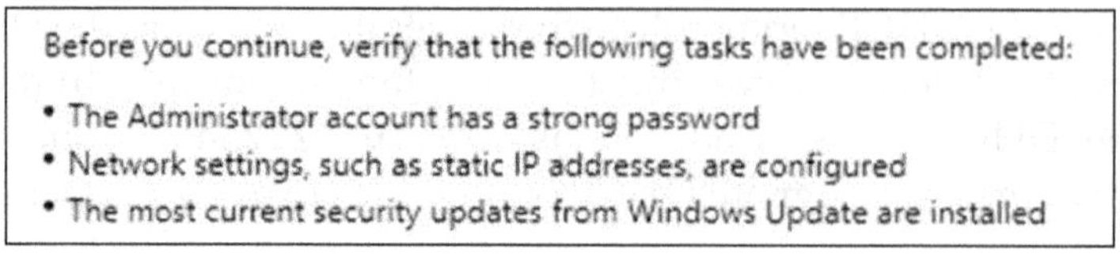

Before you continue, verify that the following tasks have been completed:

* The Administrator account has a strong password
* Network settings, such as static IP addresses, are configured
* The most current security updates from Windows Update are installed

Figure 6.5: *Installing DHCP role, step 3*

a.   Here is a zoom-in of the relevant details. After verification, click on the **Next** button to take us to the next step of setup, as shown in the following figure:

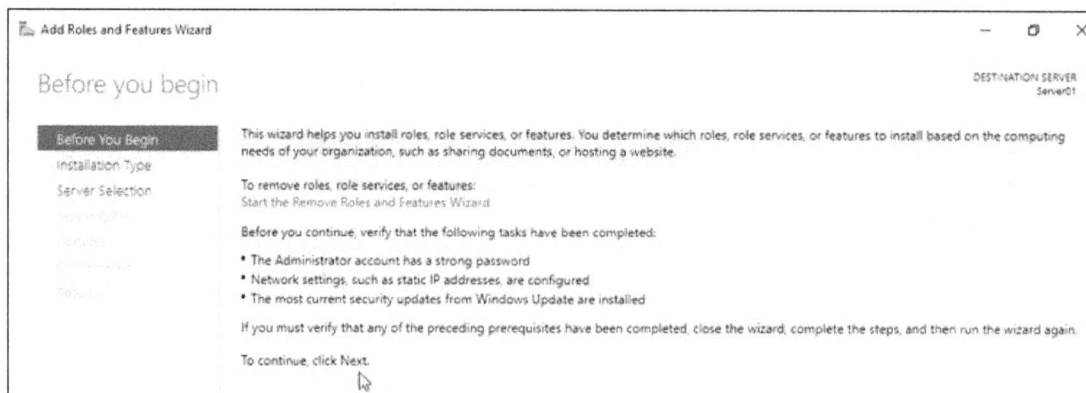

Figure 6.6: *Installing DHCP role, step 3a*

4.   We have now reached the selection pane for **Installation Type**. Choose **Role-based or feature-based installation**, as depicted in the following figure:

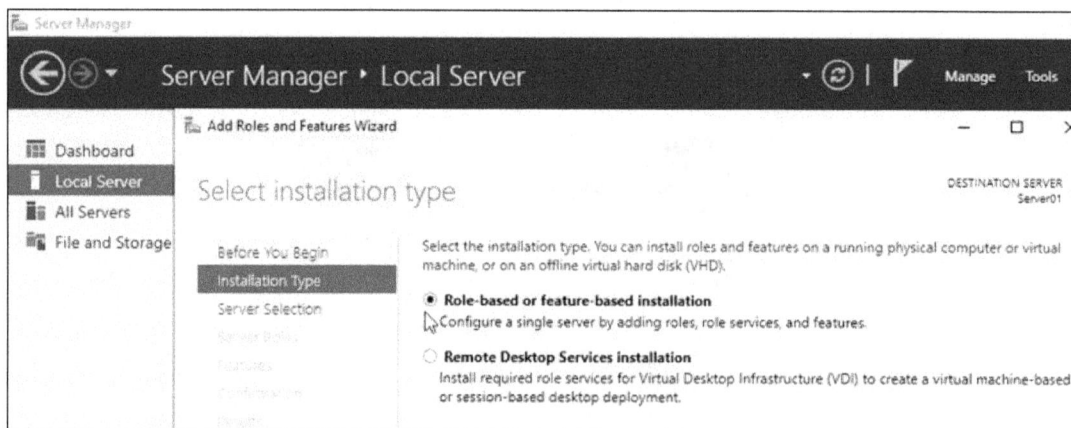

Figure 6.7: *Installing DHCP role, step 4*

5.   Click **Next** to continue the process. We are now asked to select a server in order to designate it as a DHCP server. Select the server from the server pool. In our example, the server is **Server01** on **Testlab.student.local**:

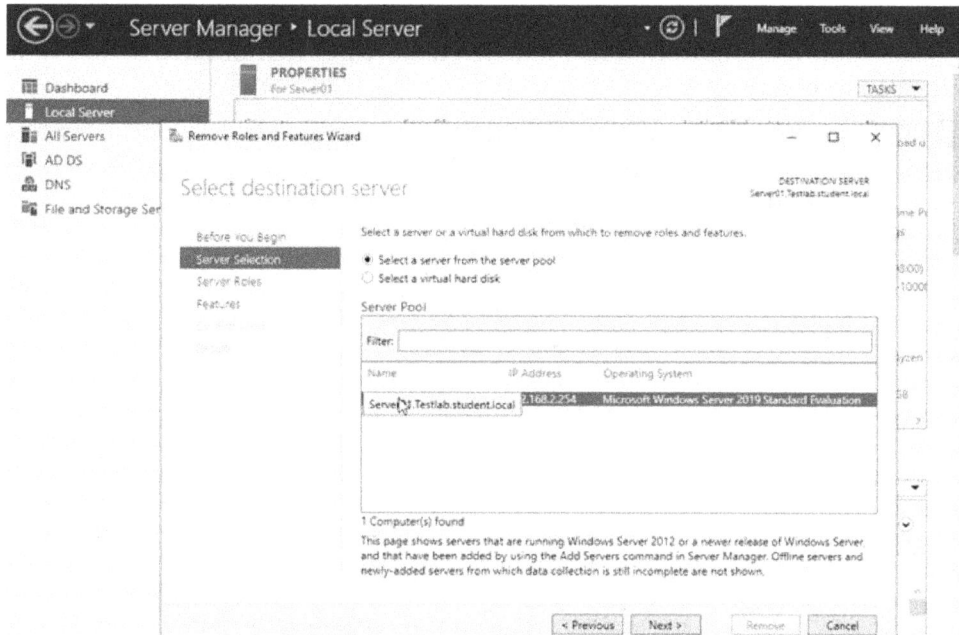

Figure 6.8: *Installing DHCP role, step 5*

6. Select the **DHCP Server** role. Notice the list of roles available on this screen. It is worth observing these roles at this point since the steps to install many role-based or feature-based installations will parallel these steps to this point:

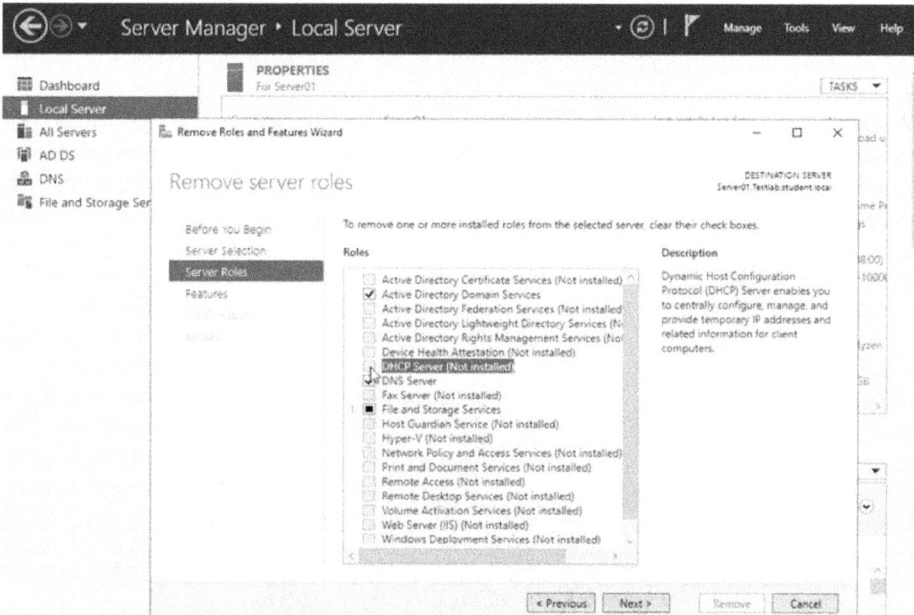

Figure 6.9: *Installing DHCP role, step 6*

7. We are now asked whether we wish to add features required for the DHCP role. These tools are required to manage this feature but do not have to be installed on the same server:

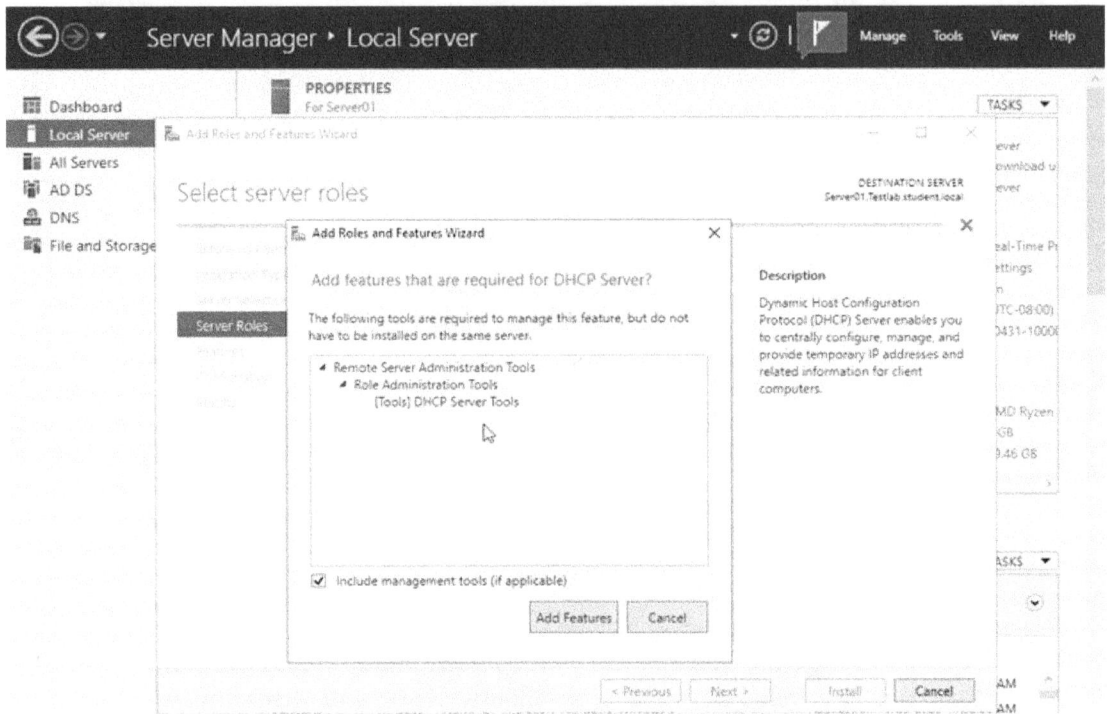

Figure 6.10: Installing DHCP role, step 7

8. On this screen, there is a brief description of the functions and operations of DHCP. In the Things to Note section, the administrator is offered some more advice for planning and implementing subnets, and so on. Verify the bulleted options and then click **Install** (the button is at the bottom of the fuller screen):

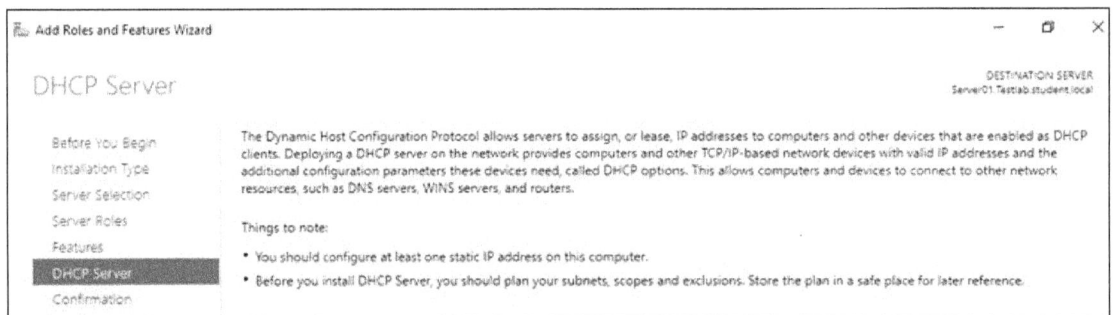

Figure 6.11: Installing DHCP role, step 8

9. The installation process begins. This process may take some time, especially with a restart of the server as part of the process, as shown in the following figure:

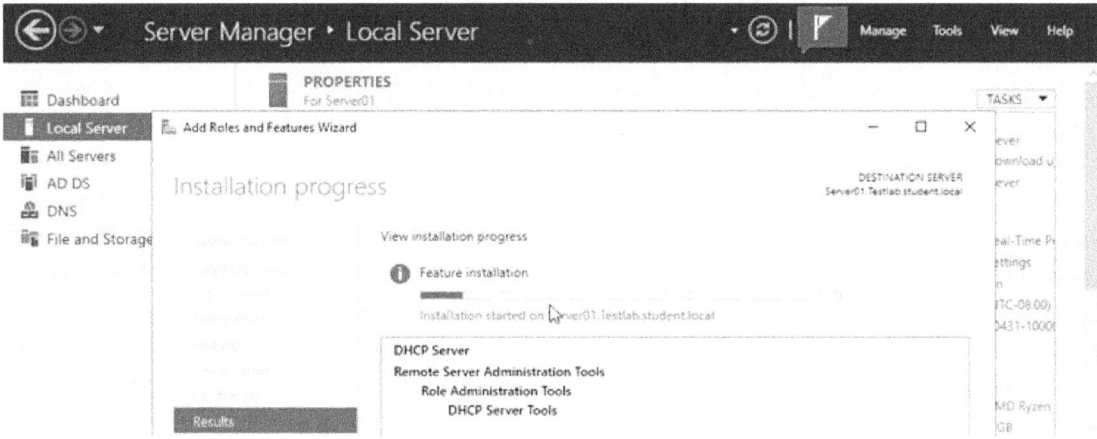

Figure 6.12: Installing DHCP role, step 9

10. When the installation is completed, click on the **Complete DHCP configuration link**. This is when the DHCP post-install wizard is initiated:

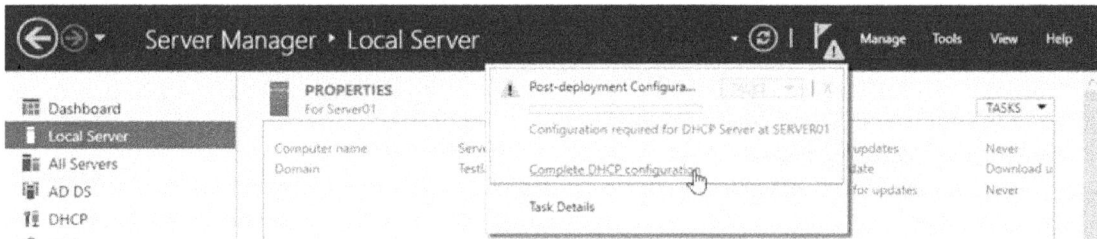

Figure 6.13: Installing DHCP role, step 10

11. We will now create security groups and delegate DHCP administration. Click **Next**:

Figure 6.14: Installing DHCP role, step 11

12. We have now reached the Authorization console. At this point, we need to specify the credentials to be used to authorize the DHCP server in **Active Directory Domain Services** (**AD DS**). Since the default is the current administrator log-on for **Server01**, we will run with that as the specified entry—**TESTLAB\Administrator**. Click on **Commit**:

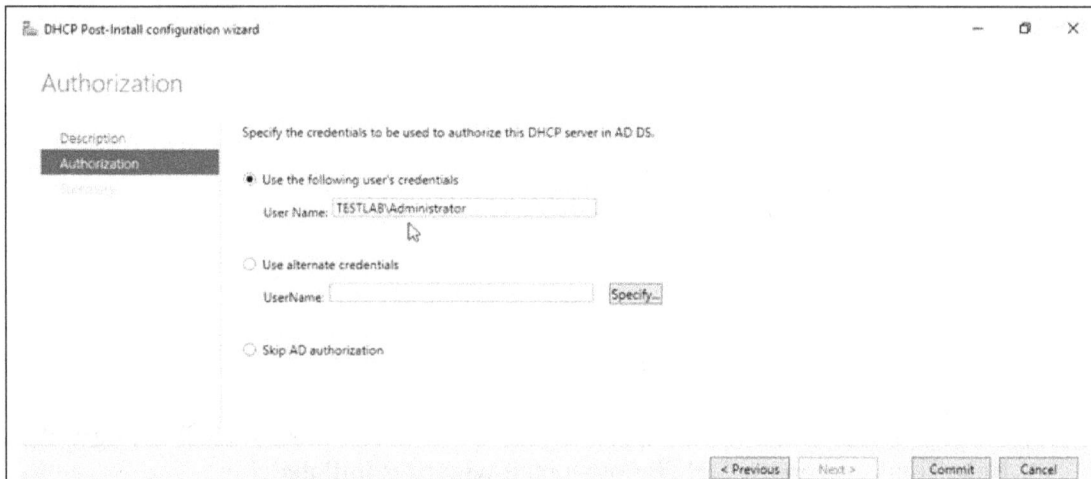

Figure 6.15: Installing DHCP role, step 12

13. In the final step of the DHCP Post-install configuration wizard, we are presented with a **Summary** and status of the steps previously taken. We can now press **Close** to complete the **Post-install process**:

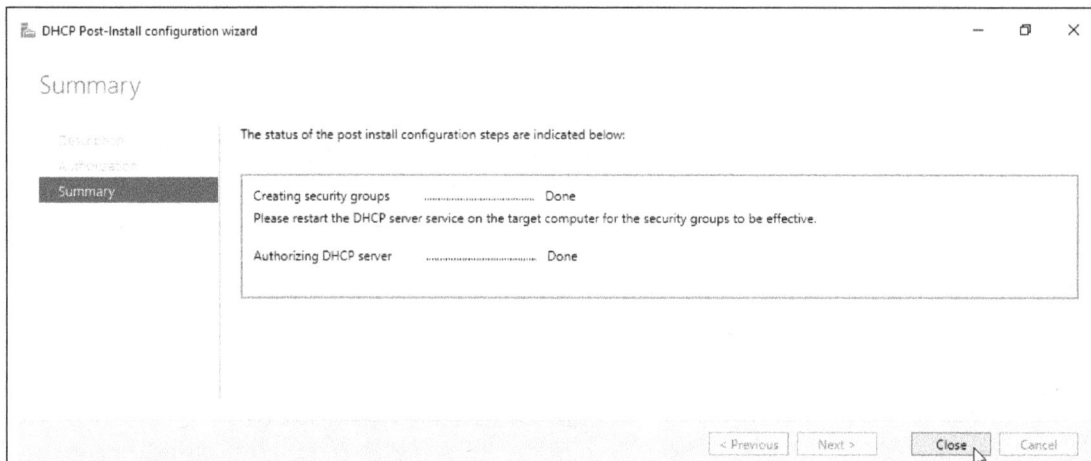

Figure 6.16: Installing DHCP role, step 13

Configuring DHCP

We will now configure our DHCP server. The first thing we need to do is create our DHCP scope. For the purpose of this demonstration, the configuration is based on the topology illustrated in *Figure 6.1* of this chapter. Follow the given steps:

1. On the **Server Manager** console, go to **Tools**. Select **DHCP**:

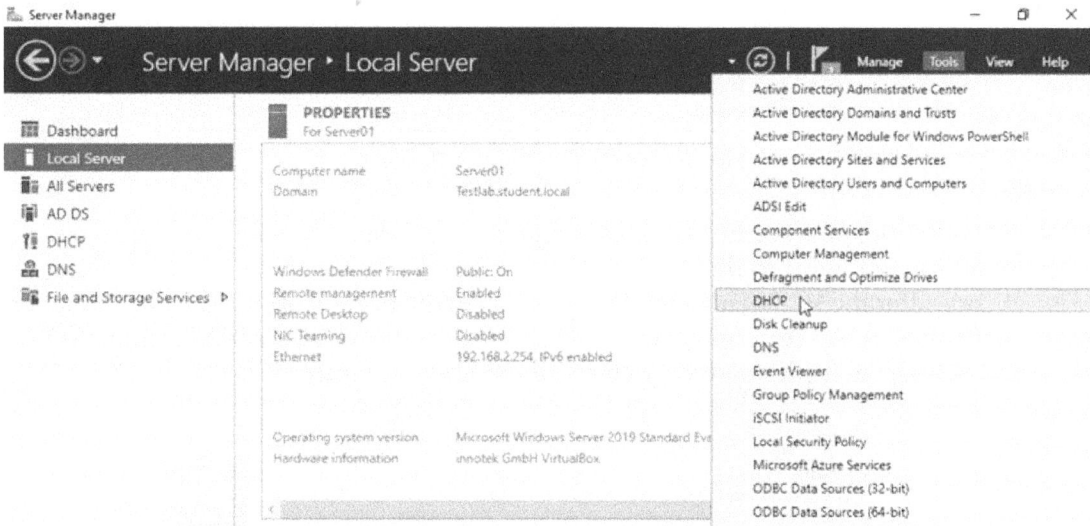

Figure 6.17: *Configuring DHCP, step 1*

2. This opens the DHCP management tool. Expand out the **DHCP Server Name**:

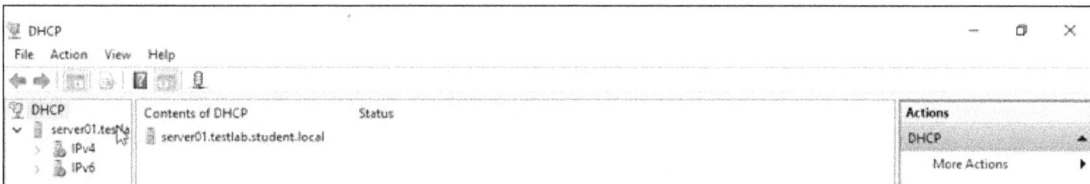

Figure 6.18: *Configuring DHCP, step 2*

3. On the left pane, select **IPv4** and expand it. Here, we see a brief definition of a Scope. Click on the **Actions** menu. Select **New Scope**. This runs a wizard to assist you with configuration, as shown in the following figure:

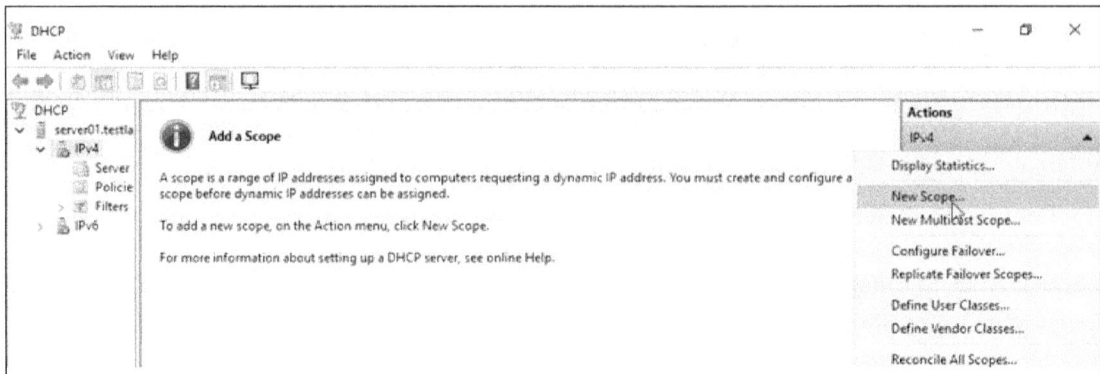

Figure 6.19: Configuring DHCP, step 3

4. Give the **Scope a Name** and a **Description**. Administrators should create a name that is meaningful to their network and topology. In this case, we are naming the Scope after the VLAN allocated to students in the organization. They are members of VLAN10. A scope may also be named to align with a specific subnet(s) the DHCP server is planned for. Refer to the following figure:

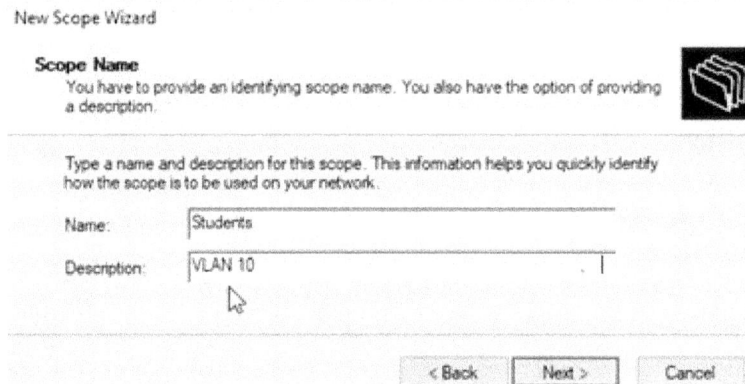

Figure 6.20: Configuring DHCP, step 4

5. Next, we define the scope address range by identifying a set of consecutive IP addresses. In the example, the scope address range begins at **192.168.2.10**, and the End IP address is **192.168.2.240**. This leaves a range of **192.168.2.1— 192.168.2.9** available for manual addresses on intermediary devices (or printers). At the end of our network range, addresses available for intermediary devices (or printers) are **192.168.2.241 – 192.168.2.253** because **192.168.2.254** is the address of **Server01**—our DHCP server. These selections are at our discretion and may be amended or modified if the need arises to shorten or lengthen the address range. This is shown in the following figure:

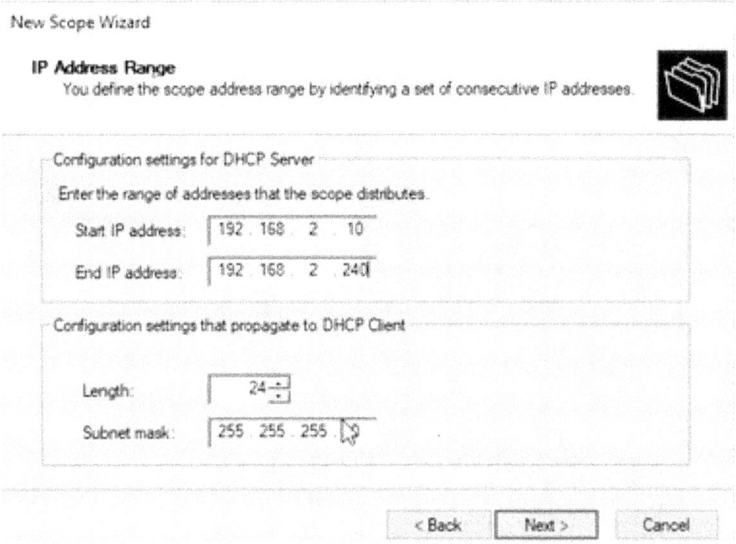

Figure 6.21: Configuring DHCP, step 5

6. The next step in configuration involves adding exclusions to the DHCP addresses available for distribution. Exclusions are IP addresses of host machines or devices that we do not want to be a part of DHCP address allocation. In this instance, we do not wish to have any excluded addresses, so we will click on **Next** to continue, as shown in the following figure:

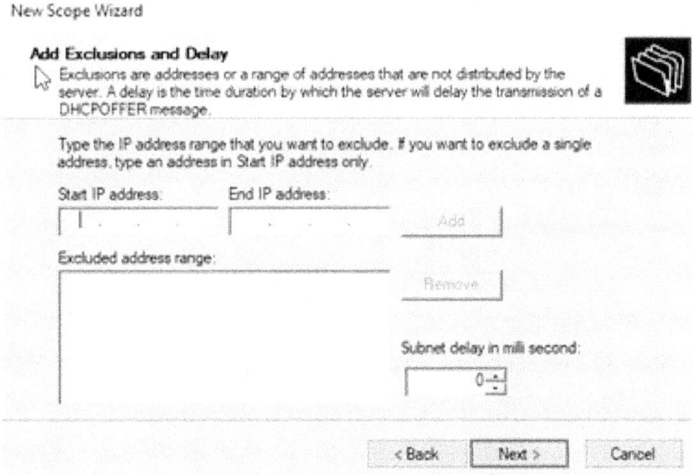

Figure 6.22: Configuring DHCP, step 6

7. The next step is to specify how long a client can use an IP address from this scope. The default for lease duration is eight days, but the administrator can customize the lease duration to suit the needs of the network and how many users will require

IP addresses versus address availability. Specify the lease duration and click **Next**, as depicted in the following figure:

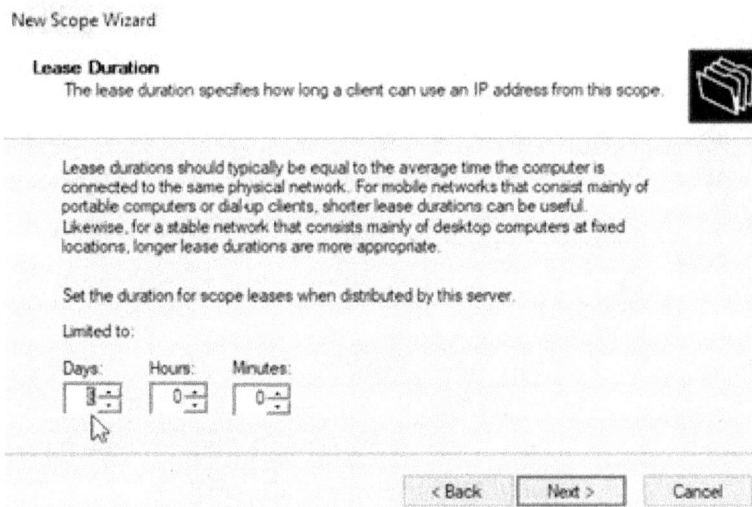

Figure 6.23: Configuring DHCP, step 7

8. Next, we are presented with the most common DHCP options as part of the configuration process. These options include DNS and WINS settings. Select **Yes** to agree, then click **Next** as shown in the following figure:

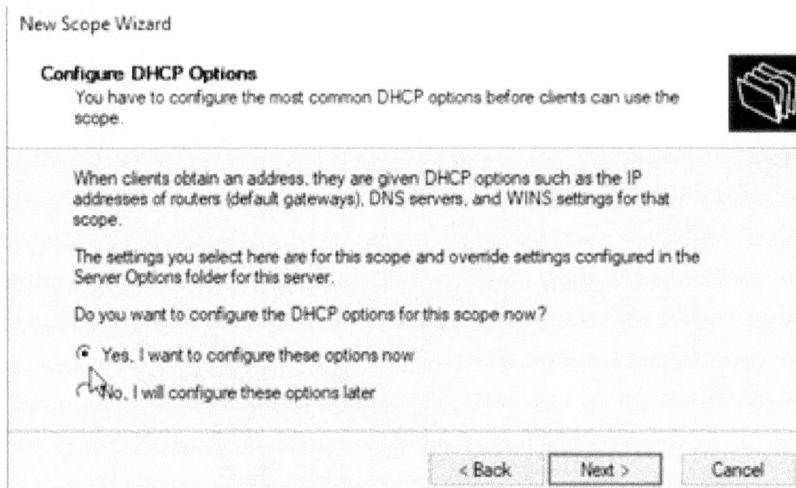

Figure 6.24: Configuring DHCP, step 8

9. Type in the IP address of the default gateway on the network. This is shown in the following figure:

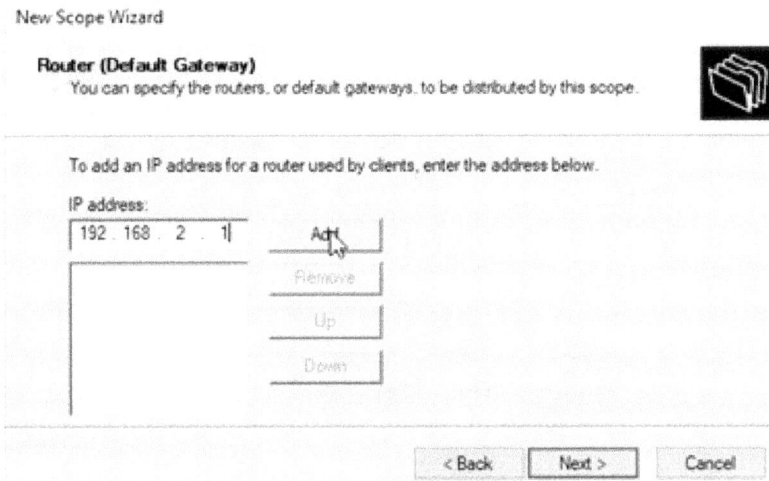

Figure 6.25: Configuring DHCP, step 9

Type in the IP address of the DNS server(s) on your network. Note that our DHCP Server is also designated as a local DNS server on the network.

10. Click **Next**, as shown in the following figure:

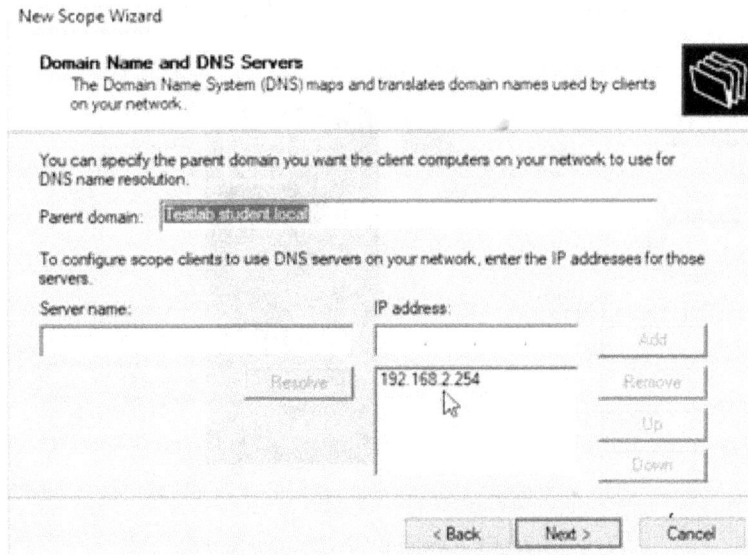

Figure 6.26: Configuring DHCP, step 10

11. Since we do not have to configure **WINS Servers**, click **Next**:

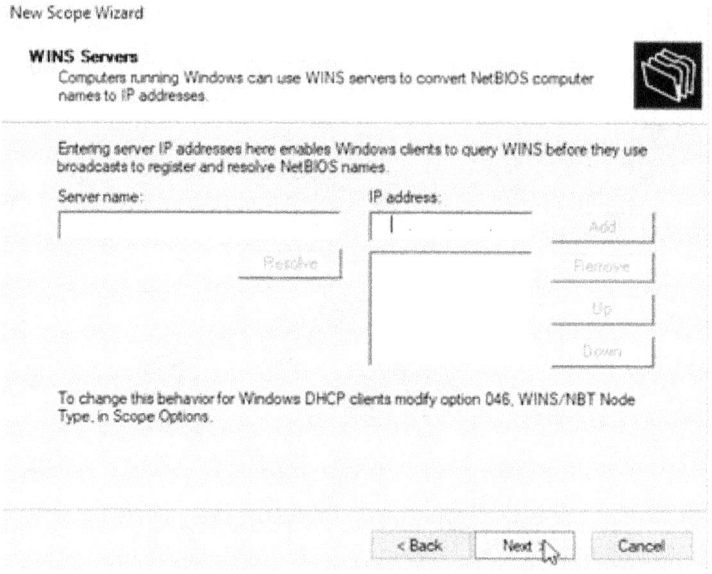

Figure 6.27: *Configuring DHCP, step 11*

12. At this point of setup, we are now ready to activate the scope. Select **Yes, I want to activate the scope now**. Then, click **Next**, select **Finish** to complete the configuration, and complete the **New Scope Wizard**:

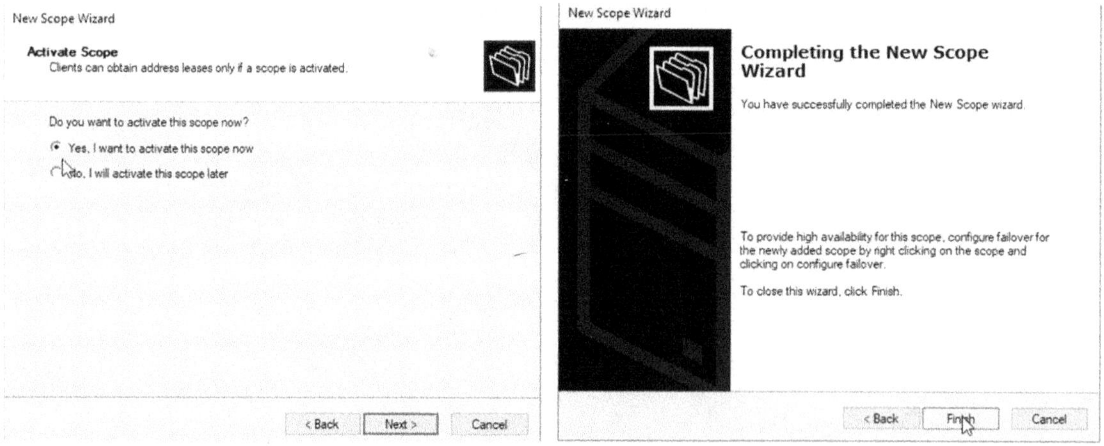

Figure 6.28: *Configuring DHCP, steps 12 and 13*

In *Figure 6.29*, we can now view the scope we created, our start and end IP addresses, exclusions selected, if applicable, the address leases and duration of the lease, and other scope options. This screen demonstrates the successful creation and implementation of a DHCP scope. It informs the chosen server to which network it assigns addresses and for how long these addresses will remain on the host machines and devices. As administrators, knowing and understanding our DHCP scope(s) is critical to managing IP addressing functionality across our network. This comprehension of DHCP additionally assists and supports us in troubleshooting practices, as shown in the following figure:

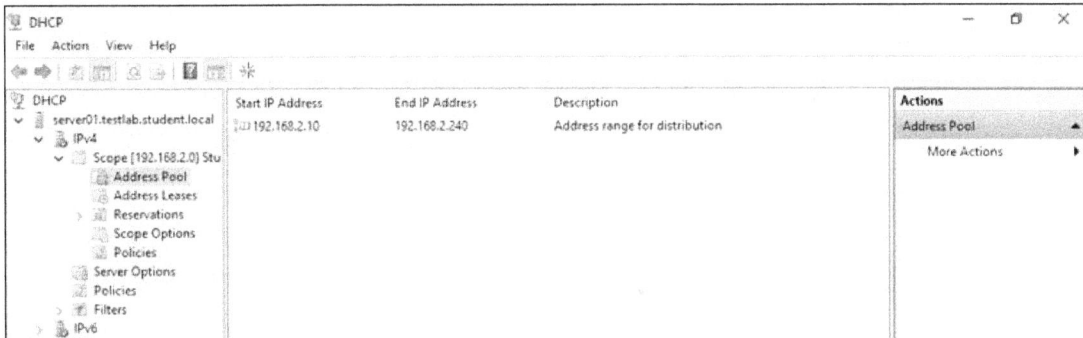

Figure 6.29: DHCP scope

Domain Name Service

DNS resolves domain names to IP addresses. More specifically, it manages and centralizes domain names on the internet and matches a hostname to the IP address of a server where the host is located. DNS has been likened to a phone book. The analogy works well since DNS's resolver cache is consulted much like a person consults a phone book by searching for the telephone number via the person's name and then locating the address. The address is then mapped or matched to the phone number, and the query is completed. In the case of DNS, if the DNS local resolver does not hold that specific record being searched for, the query is escalated to the top-level domain server or the authoritative nameserver until the client's query is resolved.

Working of DNS

Figure 6.30 illustrates how DNS operates and shows how the query is completed:

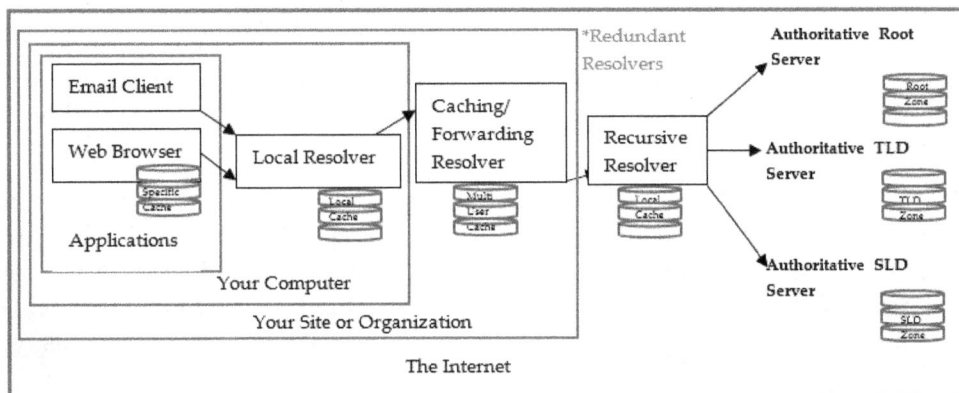

Figure 6.30: How DNS operates

To fully appreciate the operations of DNS and follow the illustration, we need to clarify several terms like Local Resolver, Caching/Forwarding Resolver, Recursive Resolver, Authoritative name servers, and **top-level domain (TLD)** servers. Other terms relating to DNS will be defined in the *Key terms* section at the end of this chapter. Some of the terms are given here:

- **Local DNS resolver**: The local DNS resolver is a piece of software/feature installed and running on the organization's dedicated DNS server. Local DNS servers need to have reference IP addresses since a function of the local DNS server forwards requests to the upstream DNS servers and subsequently caches the results. Queries may be forwarded to one of the external Google DNS servers by adding the IP addresses **8.8.8.8/8.8.4.4**. The IP address **127.0.0.1** on the DNS server references itself and the local database of records existing on the server. In other words, **127.0.0.1** points to the localhost, i.e., the server itself.

- **Caching/forwarding resolver**: This is a DNS resolver that stores previous records. If the domain/URL is not in the cache, the resolver will forward the query to the next level.

- **Recursive resolver**: This term is essentially the middleman between the client and a DNS server. This Resolver may pass queries on to authoritative name servers and TLD servers. The recursive resolver would respond to the client's query if the data requested is in its cache. If the data is not present in the cache, it will then send the request to root server, which is followed by another request. This request is sent to a TLD server. The TLD nameserver receives the request. The recursive resolver sends one last request to an authoritative nameserver. The authoritative nameserver sends a response to the recursive resolver. This reply contains the requested IP address for transmission to the client. As the *middleman*, the Recursive Resolver now responds with the IP address of the client. Any information received for authoritative nameservers is cached by the Recursive Resolver.

- **TLD**: A TLD nameserver retains information for all the domain names that share a common domain extension. Examples are **.com**, **.gov**, **.edu**, **.net**, and so forth. Since the DNS system works on a hierarchical model with a global hierarchy, TLD servers sit at the top of the model. In relation to the full-scale model, the DNS hierarchy consists of the root, the top-level domains, and the second-level and third-level domains.

As explained, DNS servers hold various types of records. These records relate to different activities and protocols that take place on the internet as data is transferred and as domain names and IP addresses are resolved. The record types include **Address (A vs. AAAA)**, **canonical name (CNAME)**, **mail exchange (MX)**, **start of authority (SOA)**, **pointer (PTR)**, **text (TXT)**, **service (SRV)**, and **name server (NS)**. *Figure 6.31* outlines the various types of DNS records, and explains what the function of each type is:

DNS Record Types

A (Address)—Most commonly used to map a fully qualified domain name to an IPv4 address and acts as a translator by converting domain names to IP addresses

SOA (Start of Authority) —Stores information about domains and is used to direct how a DNS zone propagates to secondary name servers.

SRV (Service)—Allows services such as instant messaging or VOIP to be directed to a separate host and port location.

AAAA (quad A) —Similar to A Records but maps to an IPv6 address.

NS (Name Server)—Specifies which name servers are authoritative foe a domain or subdomains (these records should not be pointed to a CNAME).

SPF (Sender Policy Framework)—Helps prevent email spoofing and limits spammers.

ANAME—This record type allows you to point the root of your domain to a hostname or FQDN.

PTR (Pointer)—A reverse of A and AAAA records, which maps IP addresses to domain names. These records require domain authority and cannot exist in the same zone as other DNS record types (put in reverse zones).

CNAME (Canonical Name) – An alias that points to another domain or subdomain, but never an IP address. Alias record mapping FQDN to FQDN, multiple hosts to a single location. The record is also good for when you want to change an IP address over time as it allows you to make changes without affecting user bookmarks, and so on.

MX (Mail Exchange—Uses mail servers to map where to deliver email for a domain (should point to a mail server name and not to an IP address).

TXT (Text)—Allows Administrators to add limited human and machine-readable notes and can be used for things such as email validation, site and ownership verification, framework policies, and so on, does not require specific formatting.

TIP: Always check for typos and mistakes when entering your DNS record information, especially your IPs. The Zone Config file is a good place to check your work and spot any mistyped information.

Data Courtesy of Google, DNS Management.

Figure 6.31: DNS record types

Note: The installation process for DNS is the same as the steps captured earlier in the chapter while installing DHCP on Windows Server 2019. The steps match exactly to the point where the network administrator adds and installs the features and tools necessary for the proper functioning of the protocol. After this point, the administrator configures the DNS zones applicable to the network and then adds specific records, if required.

Network Time Protocol

NTP is responsible for the handling of synchronization across networks. It is a hierarchical system that keeps devices attuned. It also provides timekeeping mechanisms for file servers. NTP servers have very precise atomic clocks and use efficient GPU clocks. The synchronization of devices is especially pertinent to real-time communications, so the accuracy of the servers is critical. Conflicts in time zones and server downtime must be continually counteracted due to the protocol's prominence and standing in effective information exchange.

According to *Techopedia*, NTP communicates between clients and servers using the User Datagram Protocol on port No.123. The NTP software package includes a background program known as a daemon or service, which synchronizes the computer's clock to a particular reference time, such as a radio clock or a certain device connected to a network.

NTP uses a systematic, hierarchical level of clock sources for its reference. Each level is called a **stratum** with a layer number that usually begins with zero. The stratum level serves as an indicator of the distance from the reference clock to avoid cyclic dependence in the hierarchy. However, the stratum does not represent the quality or reliability of time.

NTP is deployed across server technology. It is a low bandwidth service and not overly complex for an administrator to deploy. The beauty of NTP is that, as well as using minimal resources and being low in cost and CPU usage, it can handle hundreds of users in networks and enable the host machines to remain integral to the server and the server's time. Note that the integrity of the server remains critical to all devices on a network and if the organization's server is out of sync in real-time, then applications and services, especially those that call on real-time operations, can suffer and be problematic. Consequently, a network administrator must know their server's integrity and performance in real-time.

Stratum

To point to the expected accuracy of system clocks, NTP uses the concept of strata or the stratum model. In the Merriam-Webster dictionary, strata are defined as *one of a series of layers, levels, or gradations in an ordered system*. This implementation of strata suits NTP as a protocol because when we know the stratum level (0–15) of the NTP Server, we can determine the distance it is from the device with the most accuracy called the *reference clock* known as stratum 0. All devices, workstations, and servers synchronize their time with the reference clock. The reference clock uses a **Global Positioning System** (**GPS**), which has atomic clocks built into them. In total, NTP has a maximum limit of 16 strata layers or levels and as one moves further down the strata level, the devices on that layer may not hold the same accuracy to time as ones in closer proximity. A network administrator needs to be aware of how NTP integrates the Stratum Model into its operations and performance indicators.

Figure 6.32 is an illustration of NTP outlining what is referred to as the **Stratum Model**. The blue numbers indicate various *strata* or layers of operation in the model:

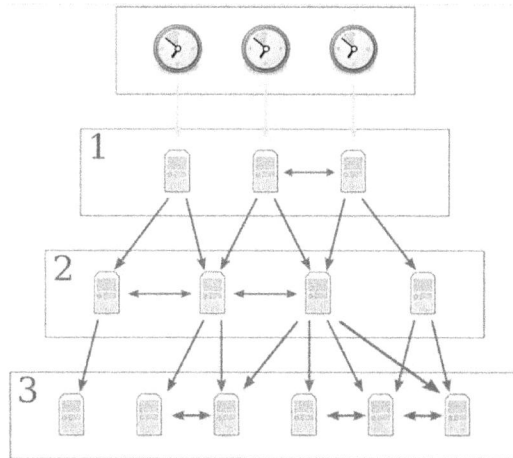

Figure 6.32: *Network time protocol servers and clients*

This figure outlines the relationship between the various levels of NTP servers. The blue numbers define the stratum numbers. The yellow arrows show a direct connection, such as RS-232 (serial connections). Finally, the red arrows indicate a network connection. NTP, as a *consistent, precise* element, is a required component for real-world activity and time-sensitive functionality. Activity such as network management and monitoring, VoIP, streaming, multicasting, routing protocol convergence, and many more time-sensitive applications must have synchronized procedures and controls to offset jitter and latency. Jitter in NTP refers to *the magnitude of variance, or dispersion, of the signal related to the timing reference across strata*. Therefore, it is crucial for network administrators to understand this concept.

Conclusion

Network services enable the network to perform optimally when configured and implemented correctly. It is good to remember that networks are everywhere, in every sector of life, whether it be social, educational, business-related, or otherwise. Consequently, network administrators hold an important position as they exist to ensure the integrity of the network they service and are expected to stand over the quality of how their network performs—whilst using the resources they are given to the best potential those resources hold. It is not always an easy or straightforward balance. However, as administrators, when we can drill deep into the function and features of server operating systems and what they offer us as management tools, we will appreciate the network services available and use them to our advantage and to the positive growth and stability of the network in our care. The world we live in is technology-based, and in that technology-based society, networks hold prominence in our lives and daily activities.

In this chapter, we focused on installing and configuring DHCP on Windows Server 2019. We explored the various role-based features and services that can be assigned to a server operating system. The installation steps for these features and protocols are similar until they diverge into the specifics of the protocol being installed. We covered numerous protocols and services relevant to network administration, management, and monitoring. Specifically, we described and demonstrated the purpose, functions, and operations of DHCP, DNS, and NTP. Additionally, we examined the use and purpose of network services. Troubleshooting network services will be further addressed in *Chapter 13, Managing and Monitoring a Network*.

In the upcoming chapter, we will investigate software-defined networking in more detail. Focusing on basic corporate and datacenter network architecture, we will explore how datacenters function and interact with worldwide network infrastructure. Datacenter network architecture and infrastructure have grown in prominence, especially in the last decade. An understanding of software-defined networking, virtualization, and datacenter operations is a must for a network administrator, no matter the level of comprehension they hold, since technology, as we know, is an evolving phenomenon and field.

Points to remember

Key points covered include:

- Installation and configuration of DHCP on Windows Server 2019.
- Role-based features and services for server operating systems.
- Installation steps for various protocols and services.
- Purpose, functions, and operations of DHCP, DNS, and NTP.
- Use and purpose of network services.
- Upcoming discussion on troubleshooting network services in *Chapter 13, Managing and Monitoring a Network*.
- The content of this chapter is mapped to *Domain 3: Network Operations*. Given a scenario, implement IPv4 and IPv6 network services.

Key terms

- **DHCP relay**: This is the process of forwarding DHCP packets between clients and servers. (This activity is akin to a baton being passed in a *relay* as part of a team sport, with DHCP packets as the baton. In the sport's relay, members of a team take turns completing parts of a racetrack or executing a certain action.) A router or host is known as a DHCP relay agent, and it is their role to forward the DHCP packets, that is, requests and replies, between clients and servers when the DHCP server is on a different network.
- **IP helper/UDP forwarding**: When a router is configured with an IP-helper address, it has the ability to accept a broadcast transmission and then forward it to a specific

IP address using unicast data transmission. If the DHCP server is not on the same network segment as the DHCP clients, the routers on the client side need an IP-helper address to help the DHCP server carry out its functions and provide the network service to its clients and scopes. To accomplish this, forwarding support is enabled on the UDP application port of the router.

- **Global hierarchy**: DNS is a global network system that collectively holds a database of domain names and IP addresses for the worldwide network. This system is structured as a global hierarchy that consists of DNS servers holding differing job roles and responsibilities in accordance with their position and level in the DNS hierarchy. The DNS hierarchy consists of the following elements: root level, top level domains, second level domains, sub-domain, and host.

- **Zone transfers**: When a DNS server passes on (transfers) part of its DNS database to another DNS server, this is called a zone transfer. The piece of the server's database that is duplicated is called a zone. The DNS query is known as type AXFR. There are five types of DNS zones: primary zone, secondary zone, active directory-integrated zone, stub zone, and reverse lookup zone.

- **Time to live (TTL)**: A mechanism used to limit the lifespan of data on a network. Data is discarded if the prescribed TTL elapses. The idea behind having a TTL is to prevent any data packet from circulating indefinitely. When forwarding IP packets, the router decreases the TTL value by at least 1. When the packet TTL value reaches 0, the router discards it and sends an **Internet Control Message Protocol** (**ICMP**) message back to the originating host (*Techopedia*).

Questions

1. What is DHCP?
2. What is the relevance of DHCP as a network service?
3. What is DNS?
4. What is the relevance of DNS as a network service?
5. What is NTP?
6. What is the relevance of NTP as a network service?

Join our book's Discord space

Join the book's Discord Workspace for Latest updates, Offers, Tech happenings around the world, New Release and Sessions with the Authors:

https://discord.bpbonline.com

CHAPTER 7
Data Center Technologies

Introduction

If we were to capture the global desire for data and data storage in the age of technology, it could be articulated with one word, insatiable. The appetite and desire for data and data storage are increasingly energized and fueled by many factors. However, what these factors consistently show is that as the amount of data grows, the urge and desire to have more data created, analyzed, or stored parallels the growth and in many cases, surpasses it. This thirst and drive for data fuels the expansion of data center technologies and the expansion of data centers as they proliferate across the globe. Key factors include (in no particular order of priority) global high-speed submarine cable projects, local and regional areas of tax incentives to stimulate investment and growth, the evolution of the **Internet of Things (IoTs)**, the use of cloud technologies, and interest in the sharing of applications and services via the cloud, the increasing demand for colocation and managed services and the correlated emergence of new skillsets and competences required in existing and newer job roles. It is frequently said that some jobs that will come into existence in the forthcoming decades have never even been heard of before, such as the nature of growth in technology and newer terrains. *Andrew McAfee*, a principal research scientist who studies and explores how digital data is changing the world in which we live, encapsulates the issue perfectly when he states, *The world is one big data problem*. This is the nature of the world; we are problem-solving. In this chapter, we will explore data center technologies and identify how businesses and corporations seek to create, store, and manage the data generated from their operations and the solutions offered in the field of computer networking.

Structure

The topics to be covered in the chapter are as follows:

- Data center network architecture
- Software-defined networking
- Storage area networks
- Fault tolerance and redundancy

Objectives

Upon completing this chapter, the reader can identify and explain what constitutes data center network architecture. They should understand software-defined networking and how this has become the norm in daily networking practices. The reader will be able to discern the type of storage solution for a given problem and networking scenario. By the end of this chapter, the reader will understand fault tolerance and redundancy as a critical aspect of data center operations—to include **Redundant Array of Independent Disks (RAID)** as a typical failover strategy.

Data center network architecture

As previously mentioned, the growth and expansion of data and the need for data centers have grown substantially over the last number of decades. As applications become more modernized, they require a modern data center infrastructure. Data center operations factor in the cost of hardware, the number of devices and networking devices required (for example, servers, layer 2 or layer 3 switches, routers, **Integrated Lights Out** (**ILOs**), cable, and so on), connectivity design, and the energy efficiency impact of the infrastructure chosen. Additionally, storage, processing, and power cooling technologies must equally be considered when a provider implements a solution for secure data storage and reliable uptime 24/7 accessibility. Consequently, data center network architecture is fine-tuned to yield the optimum solutions available for providers and enterprises alike.

A data center infrastructure may include the following:

- Host or access devices, for example, servers
- Standard computers
- Intermediary networking equipment, for example, routers and switches
- Security hardware, such as firewalls or biometric security systems
- Storage, for example, a **storage area network** (**SAN**) or backup/tape storage for archiving
- Data center monitoring or management software/applications

Data centers may also include devices such as:

- HVAC power and cooling devices, like air conditioners or power generators
- Physical server racks, cabinets, and server chassis
- Connectors and cables, for example, Ethernet and fiber
- An Internet core or backbone infrastructure

These components constitute the typical modern data center.

Tiered network architecture

Tiered architecture is a characteristic approach to organizing switches in a data center. This logical organization of switches incorporates the structure, technologies, and protocols in use while considering the physical layout and placement of the switches and other equipment in the building. A tiered approach to organization involves cabling, connectivity, throughput, scalability, and redundancy, and in terms of switching technologies that support complex mesh topologies, the implementation of Layer 2 protocols to prevent switching loops.

Three-tier designs consist of a core, distribution, and access layer of switches.

Simply put, the **access** layer switches connect the servers to the system. These access switches are referred to as the top-of-rack or top-of-row switches and are normally 24 or 48-port switches linked to the servers in the rack or chassis. Regarding speeds, 1 or 10 Gbps speeds with similarly sized uplinks suffice at this level of operation. On the other hand, the **distribution** (or aggregation) layer of switches handles the connectivity of the access switches. The focus on this mid-tier level is uplink speeds, in some cases, firewall applications, load balancing or switch aggregation, and, as suggested, *distribution* of services to the access switches. On the top and third layers of this infrastructure are the **core** switches. These core switches may be larger than the distribution or access switches and will usually have higher speed capacity and routing capabilities. In short, the access switches are connected to multiple distribution switches to provide redundancy. The distribution switches are then connected to the core, providing that top tier between the users and the services in the core. Services provided include Web servers or FTP servers, database servers (for example, SQL), DNS (name) servers, and even managed print servers.

Here is a sample illustration of a three-tiered data center infrastructure:

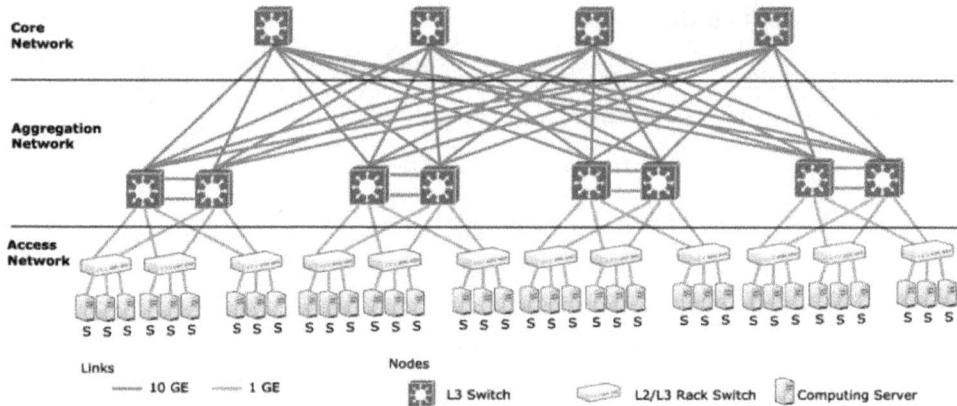

Figure 7.1: *Three-tier data center architecture*
Source: *https://www.researchgate.net/figure 221287793*

Note the need for the *Spanning Tree Protocol* between switches in the different tiers to counteract switching loops from occurring. Also, observe the number of connections and links between the switches in the aggregation network (distribution layer) and switches in the core network (core layer). These mesh topologies and aggregated links provide redundancy as well as the potential for load-balancing functions.

Three-tier high-speed data center architecture is also a strategy for handling higher speeds and network operations. Here is a sample illustration to demonstrate how switches may be interlinked to achieve higher speeds for users and enterprises who require this level of access and provision:

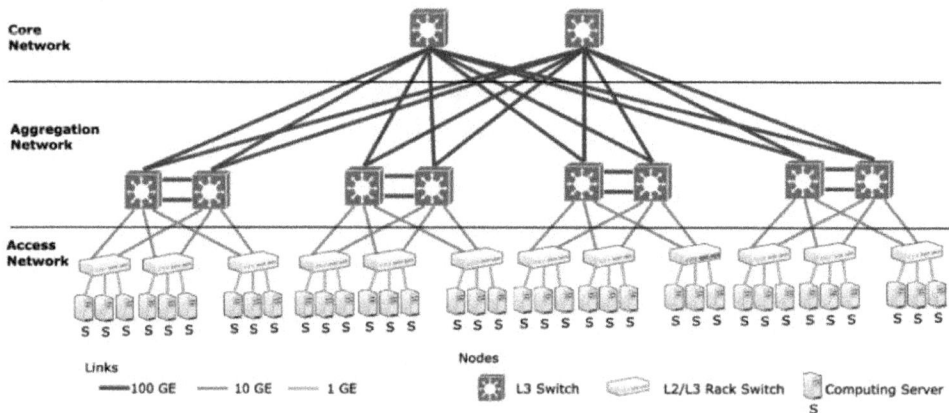

Figure 7.2: *Three-tier high-speed data center architecture*
Source: *https://www.researchgate.net/figure 221287793*

Note that the distribution tier or aggregation network manages communication between all the end users (via the servers) and the core of the network.

Software-defined networking

Over the last decade or so, there has been an emergence and emphasis on **software-defined networking** (**SDN**). When networking is *software-defined*, the process decouples the control from the networking hardware's firmware and puts it in the hands of the network administrator. Instead of the router's firmware telling the hardware where to forward the packet and send the packet to its destination, the network administrator can manipulate the transmission of data via software. The network administrator has a central control console and, by using this method, can control the traffic flow, set up firewall rules, and allow and block packets as they see fit. In brief, SDN decouples the control plane from the data plane in networking. Therefore, traditional technologies are somewhat atomized because control is disseminated across several devices. With SDN, the control of data transmission becomes centralized and, therefore, offers a more organized means of management. SDN is achieved by using smart applications, software programs, and virtualization setups. The data plane still handles the forwarding of packets, referred to as the muscle of the system. The decision-making process, regarded as the mind or brain of the system, is in the software, and the software is controlled by the administrator. These devices are managed through the application layer or management plane. Typical protocols used are **Secure Shell** (**SSH**) or **Simple Network Management Protocol** (**SNMP**). Other management strategies used are via programming and **application programming interface** (**API**) calls.

Spine and leaf

Like many aspects of computer networking, data centers are constantly evolving, and more traditional methods of three-tier network architecture have been replaced with two-tier architecture and models. The older three-tier model depicted is no longer perceived as the ideal setup. Some reasons for spine-leaf architecture to become more mainstream include the evolution of virtualization and application-intensive procedures, hyper-converged systems, and data center consolidation.

In the spine and leaf architecture, the leaf layer on the lower tier connects to the host devices, that is, the servers in the topology. The leaf layer uses access switches connecting to the servers, where the servers could host multiple **virtual machines** (**VMs**) and containers. The leaf layer is also connected to the spine layer in a full-mesh topology to provide redundancy and fault tolerance. This means that if one of the top-tier switches fails, pathways for data transmission are still open, and the overall performance of the network does not suffer from the failed device or a single point of failure. The spine layer is responsible for the interconnection of all the leaf switches and functions as the backbone of the spine and leaf configuration. One of the benefits of the spine and leaf architecture is scalability and the flexibility to include extra switches and devices at each layer. Another benefit is the implementation of an overlay network. An overlay network enables the separation and specialization of tasks and device functions across the network. Functions can be dedicated and allocated to specific devices. For example, an edge or leaf device can focus on the relevant protocols required, operating as a device directly connected to the servers, while a spine device focuses on uplink speeds and network convergence technologies. Due to the connectivity of devices in this architecture, latency is also minimized, as in typical infrastructures, there is a selective consistency in the pathways where data travels.

As shown in *Figure 7.3*, the leaf switches connect back to the spine switches, and the spine or backbone determines where the traffic is flowing. None of the leaf switches are connected to each other. Consequently, data transmission is orderly and controlled. Though this representation is quite simplified, when scaled up to accommodate data center devices, it offers an optimum solution for a scalable, low latency, fast, and effective data flow.

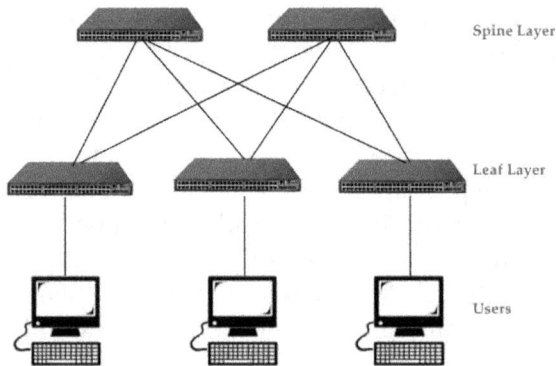

Figure 7.3: Two-tier spine and leaf architecture

Traffic flows

When we refer to the flow of traffic in a data center, we refer to it in directional terms. There are essentially two types of traffic flow in a data center: north-south and east-west traffic.

North-south traffic is defined as client-to-server traffic flowing between the data center and the remainder of the network outside the data center. East-west traffic denotes traffic within a data center—that is, server-to-server traffic, which goes between devices inside the data center. If traffic is coming into the data center via a perimeter device or firewall, for example, the traffic is referred to as southbound traffic. Alternatively, if the traffic is headed out of the physical boundaries of the data center beyond the perimeter, it is regarded as northbound. East-west traffic occurs when two or more devices communicate inside the boundaries of the data center. The devices communicating could be routers, switches, or even servers. An example of traffic is internal routers exchanging routing tables while running routing protocols. A second example occurs when a client engages with a data center server.

It is helpful to know the direction of traffic flow for many reasons, such as connectivity, differentiating between source and destination, decision-making strategies, monitoring and management of traffic, and security considerations of the devices, services, and protocols, depending upon their location and position in the data center and the role the device is playing in data transmission and directional flow. Network administrators need to know the *direction* of the devices they install and manage. Irrespective of the direction in which data flows, all data must be analyzed and effectively monitored.

Storage area networks

At its simplest, a storage area network is a dedicated network for data storage. A SAN presents storage devices to a host in such a way that the storage seems to be locally attached.

SANs can be implemented using various technologies. For example, **Fiber Channel (FC)**, **Fiber Channel over Ethernet (FCoE)**, **Internet Small Computing System Interface (iSCSI)**, and InfiniBand. iSCSI is typically used in small to medium businesses and organizations, but it costs less to implement than the costlier FC. InfiniBand is a technology that is used in computing environments that require high performance. Additionally, it is possible to use gateways that enable the transmission and transfer of data between various SANs.

Here is an illustration of a SAN. This SAN is an FC storage area network:

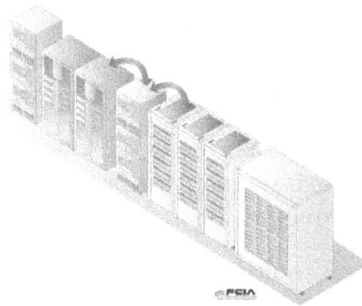

Figure 7.4: *Fiber channel storage area network*

This SAN connects the yellow storage devices with the orange servers via the purple Fiber Channel Switches.

The use of SANs provides enterprises with many benefits. Due to their makeup, SAN technology improves the availability of applications to users. With the support of virtualization, for example, multiple data paths mean multiple users can access the applications. Network administrators can take the stress of their local area networks by the provision of a SAN to carry out the functions of storage. Administrators can also handle the security of data in the SAN and improve the protection of sensitive or critical data. Resources can be organized more effectively, and the business can ensure that they have continuity and that users have reliable access to the data and applications they require in a seamless fashion. Although SANs can be more expensive than **network attached storage (NAS)** architectures, it is viewed that the initial cost of networking equipment and resources to configure a SAN is worth the value of the benefits gained when a SAN is fully functional. The devices used in a SAN include SAN servers, SAN switches, SAN host adapters, SAN-capable disk arrays, **Just a Bunch of Disks (JBODs)**, and tape drives.

Fault tolerance and redundancy

The ability to move beyond a single point of failure is a critical action in data center technologies. After all, the data center holds the precious data of an enterprise or organization, and this data is in the care and protection of the data center as the provider of its services to the client.

Fault tolerance is the ability of a system to respond gracefully to unexpected hardware or software failure. (RAID works the same with SCSI, iSCSI, or IDE drives). **Redundancy** is the ability of a system to continue service in a seamless manner.

The levels of RAID are as follows:

- **RAID 0**: Striped set (min two disks) w/o parity and no-fault tolerance. Any disk failure destroys the array.

- **RAID 1**: Mirrored set (min two disks) w/o parity. It provides fault tolerance from disk errors and single disk failure.

- **RAID 3 and RAID 4**: Striped set (min three disks) w/ dedicated parity. This mechanism provides an improved performance and fault tolerance similar to RAID 5, but with a dedicated parity disk rather than rotated parity stripes.

- **RAID 5**: Striped set (min three disks) w/ distributed parity. Distributed parity requires all but one drive to be present to operate; drive failure requires replacement, but the array is not destroyed by a single drive failure.

- **RAID 6**: Striped set (min four disks) w/ dual distributed parity. It provides fault tolerance from two drive failures; the array continues to operate with up to two failed drives.

Conclusion

In this chapter, we explored the importance of data centers and data center technologies. We saw how the importance of data centers has significantly grown over the last number of decades. Understanding data center technologies has become an important part of comprehending network administration and how computer networks encompass remote and off-site solutions in their networking solutions. As a reader, you now comprehend this. Businesses and organizations are using the services of data centers more frequently than previously. This is mainly because the cost of realizing this for themselves is too steep a cost to implement. By partnering with the data center as a subscriber, the enterprise cuts down on expenses, accesses state-of-the-art technology, is assured uptime and data security, and saves substantial costs on energy use, should it have implemented an on-premises network solution. In terms of scalability, the organization can scale up its network and not have to be concerned about holding the physical equipment in a comms room or on-site cabinet.

In the upcoming chapter, we will explore cloud concepts. We will differentiate between cloud deployment models, cloud service models, connection types, and the options available for payment. Each service model has its own financial models, but the primary consideration is the organization's needs and requirements and what works for them as customers.

Points to remember

- Understanding network architecture enhances your skillset as a network administrator.

- Comprehending the various approaches to data storage and where data is held is most important knowledge.

- Appreciating the different methods a data center can use to organize its equipment and resources for managing and monitoring client data enhances an administrator's understanding.

- This chapter aligns with CompTIA Network+, *Domain 1, Networking Concepts*. The chapter outlines basic corporate and data center network architecture and additionally explains evolving use cases for modern network environments.

Key terms

- **On-premises software**: On-premises software is a type of software delivery model that is installed and operated from a customer's in-house server and computing infrastructure. It uses an organization's native computing resources and requires only a licensed or purchased copy of the software from an independent software vendor. (*Techopedia*)

- **Colocation (Colo)**: When a person or enterprise rents space from a third-party data center to hold their organization's hardware and servers.

- **Branch offices (Branch networking)**: It refers to the manner in which data and information is distributed between branch offices, remote sites, and data centers and the elements that constitute this distribution.

Questions

1. What is the difference between three-tier data center network architecture and two-tier architecture?

2. What is fault tolerance, and why is it important in data center operations?

Join our book's Discord space

Join the book's Discord Workspace for Latest updates, Offers, Tech happenings around the world, New Release and Sessions with the Authors:

https://discord.bpbonline.com

CHAPTER 8

Cloud Concepts

The increasing presence of cloud computing and mobile smart phones is driving the digitization of everything across both consumer and enterprise domains. It is hard to imagine any area of human activity which is not being reengineered under this influence, either at present or in the very near future.

- Geoffrey Moore, Organizational Theorist, Management Consultant and Author

Introduction

As stated by *Geoffrey Moore*, we are witnessing the expansion of digitization across numerous activities in our daily lives via cloud computing. Cloud computing is essentially the provision, distribution, and dissemination of computing services to clientele requiring these services. The services provided include storage, servers, networking, software, Web hosting, infrastructure, security intelligence, and data analytics. Clients can comprise individuals, organizations, or enterprises that use the global internet. To take the mystery out of cloud computing and what it is, in earlier days of computer networking, network administrators regarded the cloud as merely *a hard drive(s)* residing on a remote server or shared mainframe in a comms room or data center, that is, a means of additional dedicated or shared storage. The simpler definition of cloud computing is *the practice of using a network of remote servers hosted on the internet to store, manage, and process data, rather than a local server or a personal computer*. This method of storing data and online provision of services saves costs on the procurement, acquisition, and maintenance of on-prem equipment or locally based resources. Using the cloud offers benefits in cost, security, and ease of access to data, especially when data is generated in greater volumes (big data). Over time since the 1950s, the added evolution of virtualization technologies radically changed cloud computing, with virtualization now being commonly implemented in data centers.

Virtualization and hypervisor technologies ultimately transformed how communications and computing mechanisms and systems operate. Instead of handling a host of separated out discrete hardware and software components, organizations and network administrators could now control and manage these components in a centralized single virtual resource, with multiple servers or operating systems running in the same location, even when in the physical world, the client software and applications may be geographically dispersed. Centralization of management is one of the key benefits of cloud computing. Organizations decide which roles they run on dedicated servers, whether they use multiple roles on servers, and whether they should keep server roles internal or outsourced to a cloud or hosting service, such is the importance of cloud computing in decision-making processes.

Structure

The topics to be covered in the chapter are as follows:

- Deployment models
- Service models
- Connectivity options
- Use cases for modern network environments

Objectives

By the end of this chapter, the reader will be familiar with cloud concepts and identify and differentiate between deployment models, service models, and connectivity options organizations can choose from to connect to the cloud and have a presence there. The reader should be able to research and map an organization's needs and requirements to the appropriate models and services. They should be aware of the purpose and function of **virtual private networks** (**VPNs**), understand how they operate and how they are secured, and evaluate the way VPNs use the cloud. Additionally, the user will be able to summarize evolving use cases for modern network environments.

Deployment models

When we speak about the act of deployment, we are concerned with the *process of setting up a new computer or system to the point where it is ready for productive work in a live environment.* Due to differing needs, there are various types of cloud deployment models. In the case of these models, the cloud provider consults with the business or enterprise requesting services and offers them an appropriate solution to the virtual environment required. The choices offered depend on the amount of data that is to be stored and who is to have access to the data and to the infrastructure employed. The four types of deployment models are public cloud, private cloud, hybrid cloud, and community cloud.

Public cloud

This type of cloud is used for **business to consumer** (**B2C**) type transactions. In B2C, the business deals directly with the customer, for example, *Amazon* or *eBay*. These businesses are primarily direct sellers or online retailers, some of whom also have physical store(s). The B2C model also includes community-based businesses, fee-based or subscription-based business models, businesses that act as an intermediary/middleman between the product or service provider and the customer, and models with businesses focusing exclusively on advertising.

In this public cloud deployment model, the computing resource is owned, governed, and operated by the government, an academic, or a business organization. Resources range from ready-to-use or on-the-fly software applications, to readily accessible VMs, to the fuller-scale infrastructures, development, and networking services required by enterprises. Resources may be free to access, or they may incur payment via a pay-per-usage pricing or subscription model.

The public cloud resembles a utility we use at home or in our business. For example, when we pay our electricity bill, we do not have responsibility for the task of managing or monitoring the suppliers' or providers' infrastructure (power grid). As customers, we pay for what we use plus a service charge, where applicable. The electricity provider builds, manages, and maintains the infrastructure to which we are connecting. Likewise, with the public cloud, the cloud provider assumes responsibility for the equipment, hardware, and software maintenance and connects us to a reliable, high-bandwidth, fast, and scalable networking solution to include the underlying virtualization software.

Private cloud

This type of cloud is typically **proprietary**. If the public cloud model is defined as generic, in that it is used by a wide range of individuals, businesses, and subscribers, then the private cloud is deployed for a particular enterprise or organization as proprietary. In a sense, it is *owned* by the organization and dedicated to the needs of the single business, with methods employed for intra-business interactions. Computing resources can be governed, owned, and operated by the same organization, where the physical infrastructure can be entirely localized with virtualized computing resources via physical components stored on-premises or accessible via a cloud provider's data center. Private cloud solutions offer enterprises a safe and secure set of options where they can carry out operations seamlessly and efficiently without necessarily having the concerns of needing to manage the entire operation. The organization ultimately has a high degree of control and can configure the environment to meet its requirements in a tailored way, totally customized to its needs, intentions, and purpose. Private cloud solutions are exclusive, adaptable, resilient, scalable, and secure, with options for a virtual solution or full provisioning of hardware and storage facilities. The business or enterprise has direct control over the infrastructure and only authorized and authenticated users can access the resources on the network.

Hybrid cloud

In a hybrid cloud, the two models, public and private, are bridged together with a layer of proprietary software. This type of cloud can be used for both types of business relations—**business to business (B2B)** or B2C. This cloud deployment technique is called a hybrid cloud, as the computing resources are bound together by different clouds. In other words, it is a mixed model. Vital or business-critical data can be stored in a secure on-site environment while the business simultaneously uses the advantages of a public cloud. The business can reduce its costs since it will only be paying for the computing power they are using as a business but is still availing of the high bandwidth, capacity, and speed of the public cloud. Businesses can handle some of their operations internally but as required, extend to the public cloud if they need more computing power or computational resources than what they have locally. Since some businesses may have certain times of the year when they require extra resources, the hybrid model suits many organizations. This model also appeals to start-up companies as a support for the company's development and growth. The model offers start-ups time to grow.

Community cloud

A community cloud model is essentially where computing resources are provided for a community and organizations. A community cloud is a hybrid form of a private cloud. In this deployment model, there are multi-tenant platforms that enable different organizations to work on a shared platform. Whenever we consider practices that require collaboration, for example, where government departments, though separate and distinctive in their mission and aim, still have some common goals, procedures, or protocols, we will understand the need for a shared space to collaborate in. This shared space for collaborative practices and data is where the community cloud comes in, as it is suited to business practices. A community cloud allows systems and services to be reachable by a group of several organizations to collaborate and share the information stored. A community cloud is typically owned, managed, and operated by one or more organizations in the community, a third party, or a combination of these elements.

An example of using a community cloud occurs when an organization wants to test-drive high-end security products or needs to test out some functionality and features of a public cloud environment. A second example of a useful community cloud is when numerous organizations may require a particular software application that resides on one set of cloud servers. Rather than giving each organization servers for the application (or service provision), the application is shared among the organizations via the community cloud. The hosting company allows multiple users to connect to the application in the shared context. This avoids replication and the cost of software deployment and distribution.

Service models

As previously stated, cloud computing is essentially the provision, distribution, and dissemination of computing services to clientele requiring these services. When referring to cloud services, they can be identified based on their business model used, their functionality and features, and the pricing and billing system implemented.

Think about it this way. As a company or organization, you could have your entire networking infrastructure and operations on-site, with all your hardware and software running from a local site. This means that the network administrator(s) have total control and responsibility over the network or domain. However, it also means that installing, configuring, upgrading, and troubleshooting hardware and software lies in the hands and minds of the owner of the business as well as the IT support team. On top of that is the cost of on-prem IT infrastructure, energy consumption, considerations of physical space, security implications, and access issues and permissions. It is a big responsibility; however, when you decide to use cloud computing services, some of that stress or responsibility is transferred to the service provider. The tasks of acquisition of components and maintenance of hardware and software can be delegated to the provider, in turn alleviating stress and taking some burden of responsibility off the organization's shoulders.

We will look at the main types of cloud-based services and explore their features and differences. You will note that each model includes the phrase *as a service*. This phrase shows us that each service model is delivered to the customer via a third party or provider. The main idea of provision *as a service* means that, in some way, an element of an organization's infrastructure, hardware, or software is provided by a third party with the aim of saving administrative time and energy, and as a cost-effective solution—saving the company money.

Software as a service

In this service model, the third-party provider hosts and maintains the application or set of software throughout the software's lifecycle. The entire application is managed by a **software as a service** (**SaaS**) provider via a Web browser. Maintaining applications involves upgrades, software updates, glitches and bug fixes, security checks, and other general software maintenance. This distribution model delivers applications to the users over the internet, so the users are at a remove to the job of maintaining the application since they are accessing the application through an API or dashboard. They do not have to install the software on individual machines locally. Individuals or groups can access the software through their internet connection. The owners of the application are entrusting the SaaS provider with the time and maintenance involved in ensuring their clients have a reliable experience with their software. Some examples of applications typically used in this model are Outlook, Gmail, Google Apps, or Dropbox.

SaaS offers the following advantages:

- **Mobility**: Clients can access the software from any computing device with an internet connection, including smartphones, fixed PCs, and laptops. They can use the software from multiple locations.

- **Software maintenance**: The software is updated, maintained, and patched by the SaaS provider. The client does not have to participate in this activity.

- **Cost**: The cost of SaaS (that is, access and storage) can be spread over time since the client can pay a subscription or pay-per-usage, depending on the SaaS provider's terms and pricing options.

- **Staffing**: Small businesses that may not have the required IT technical team or bandwidth to employ IT staff can use the SaaS service model.

The disadvantages of SaaS are as follows:

- **Control**: An ultimate reliance on a third-party SaaS provider to deliver quality and performance.

- **Awareness**: This loss of control means the company must then be alert to the cloud provider's integrity and cloud infrastructure. They should carry out their own pen tests and monitor cloud usage to ensure the reliability and safety of data.

- **Security risks**: Potential security issues in the cloud, for example, authentication issues if the SaaS provider does not supply or bundle in security controls automatically.

Infrastructure as a service

In this service model, the **infrastructure as a service** (**IaaS**) provider delivers a full computing stack. This includes storage, servers, operating software, and networking solutions. These computing resources are delivered as an abstract virtualized build or construct. Another term for IaaS is **hardware as a service** (**HaaS**). IaaS is a step away from on-premises infrastructure.

The client is responsible for the operating system and applications, data, runtimes, and middleware. The IaaS provider gives the organization access to, and management of, virtualization, network, storage, and servers.

IaaS offers the following advantages:

- **Reliability**: It refers to the availability of resources as required.

- **Scalability**: The ability to scale computing resources on the fly.

- **Cost**: An organization using this model can offload all its IT operations to a third party. This can be cost-effective as a solution.

- **Administration**: The business can focus on other business operations without needing to integrate IT support and administration into its local daily operations. IaaS providers also offer DevOps support.

- **Flexibility**: IaaS can be used by an organization as needed in a pay-per-usage model. For example, if a business requires the service for specialized workloads that occur at peak times in the year, or as temporary changes in the activity of the business. This use of IaaS may be running alongside a developing proprietary cloud infrastructure.

- **Security**: Most IaaS providers offer state-of-the-art security solutions.

- **Resilience**: IaaS is perfect for fault tolerance and backup solutions, replication, and disaster recovery options.

The disadvantages of IaaS are as follows:

- **Scalability**: If the organization's infrastructure scales, the price can become unsustainable.

- **Security risks**: Potential for security issues in the cloud environment.

- **Multi-tenancy**: Sharing infrastructure systems with other clients potentially impacts system performance or the reliability of the service.

Platform as a service

In this service model, the **platform as a service** (**PaaS**) provider rents or delivers a computing platform to an organization as an integrated solution, a solution stack, or *as a service* through an internet connection. Some examples of a solution stack include databases, Web applications that use operating systems, and even programming languages. The PaaS provider manages the data and application. The PaaS provider uses its own infrastructure, hosting its own hardware and software while delivering this platform to the user.

PaaS offers the following advantages:

- **Software development**: Developers use the platform and run code, build and run applications, and test, deploy, develop, and host applications. The developers do not have to worry about the environment since this environment is delivered by the PaaS provider. Developers can create their Web applications and customize their applications via this service model.

- **Cost**: Clients using PaaS do not take on board the expense of the infrastructure. They pay rent to the PaaS provider anytime they wish to use the services and do not have to be concerned about expenses during downtime.

- **Time**: The developer or programmer does not need to set up or maintain the core stack. This is carried out by the PaaS provider.

- **Efficiency**: Since the core stack and platform are in place, this quickens up the creation and production of apps, meaning the developer or programmer can market their products faster and more effectively.

- **Scalability**: The ability to scale up and down as needed.

- **Mobility and flexibility**: The ability to access the platform from multiple devices in multiple locations.

The disadvantages of PaaS are as follows:

- **Reliance and dependency**: Developers and programmers are ultimately dependent upon the PaaS provider.

- **Constraints**: Users of PaaS may be locked into a particular application or programming language.

- **Potential** Compatibility issues with software and development platforms.

- **Security risks**: The security of the applications built and developed resides with the developers. PaaS providers are solely responsible for the infrastructure or platform they distribute.

Desktop as a service

In this service model, **desktop as a service** (**DaaS**) is a cloud computing solution whereby the DaaS provider handles all the back-end responsibilities usually provided by application software. In DaaS, the virtual desktop infrastructure is outsourced by the DaaS provider. DaaS is also referred to as a **virtual desktop** or **hosted desktop** service. It is an efficient model since its functionality depends on the virtual desktop, a session that the user controls. DaaS enables the management of numerous types of computer resources. Resources include PCs, laptops, handheld units, and simple, low-performance computers known as **thin clients**. These thin clients have been optimized for establishing remote connections to a server-based computing environment. This is where DaaS comes in, as it uses distributed execution or remote execution, depending on the type of implementation.

DaaS offers the following advantages:

- Increased performance
- Reliability
- Cost reduction
- Simplified platform migration with minimum complexity
- Disaster recovery
- Continuity of connection
- Customization
- Security of data

The disadvantages of DaaS are as follows:

- **Licensing issues**: The inability to use on-prem licenses for the desktop in the cloud. (This may not apply to all DaaS providers).

- **Control**: No control over the DaaS infrastructure or resource allocation.

- **Data**: Confidential and sensitive data is not totally under the organization's control.

- **Internet connectivity**: DaaS requires a high-speed internet connection, which may be problematic in some remote or rural areas.

- **Decision-making**: Determining how to configure and provision virtual desktops can be cumbersome.

User-managed vs. provider-managed service models

In each of the service models, the control and responsibility for computing resources are split between the user and the service provider.

The following table illustrates the distribution of control and responsibility between the user and the provider:

User managed	Provider managed		
On Premises	**IaaS**	**PaaS**	**SaaS**
Application	Application	Application	Application
Data	Data	Data	Data
Runtime	Runtime	Runtime	Runtime
Middleware	Middleware	Middleware	Middleware
Operating system	Operating system	Operating system	Operating system
Virtualization	Virtualization	Virtualization	Virtualization
Networking	Networking	Networking	Networking
Storage	Storage	Storage	Storage
Servers	Servers	Servers	Servers

Table 8.1: Cloud computing service models

Throughout the chapter, we have discussed cloud services, cloud types, and explored some cloud characteristics. In the following figure, these concepts are graphically illustrated to summarize some of the concepts covered:

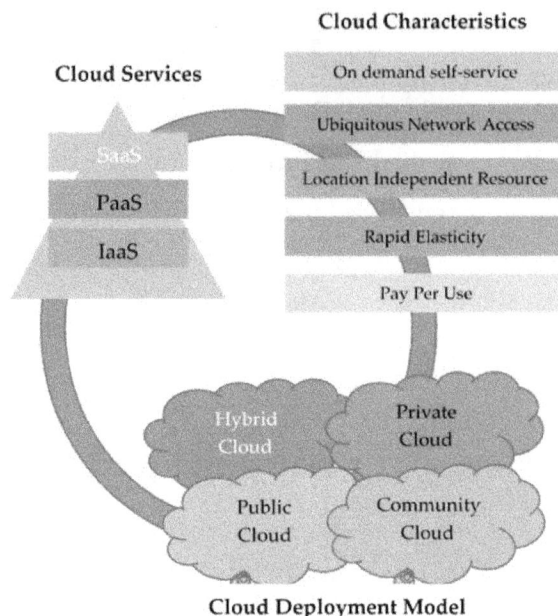

Figure 8.1: Cloud concepts

Connectivity options

There are multiple ways to connect to the cloud, and an aspect of cloud provision is to discuss these options with a business or enterprise. Essentially, the correct option will align with the business's applications or business requirements, in other words, the purpose and functions necessary for an appropriate connection. In cloud provision, solution architects will synchronize ongoing activities and translate the design concept to IT operations. Here are some options for cloud connectivity.

Virtual private network

One of the ways to connect to the cloud is via a private network connection. In a VPN, a user's computer accesses a server through the internet using an encrypted connection. A VPN is essentially a private network connection built over a public network infrastructure, for example, the Internet. VPNs use tunneling protocols and encryption to optimize security. These security mechanisms hide the user's IP address from public view. These mechanisms mean that the users of VPNs may access their corporate network remotely, in the knowledge that they are protecting personal data and are guarded and protected in more public settings, such as in public Wi-Fi settings or other public areas where they want to balance their ability to be mobile with security considerations and risk-taking.

On top of tunneling protocols and encryption of data transmitted, **multi-factor authentication** (**MFA**) is implemented. MFA uses context-aware security tactics and imposes on the user the use of strong (complex) passwords that randomize or are forced to change over time. In a VPN, the secure connection can be envisaged as a tunnel between your computer and a server run and provided by the VPN service/cloud provider in a remote destination.

The following figure illustrates how a tunnel functions:

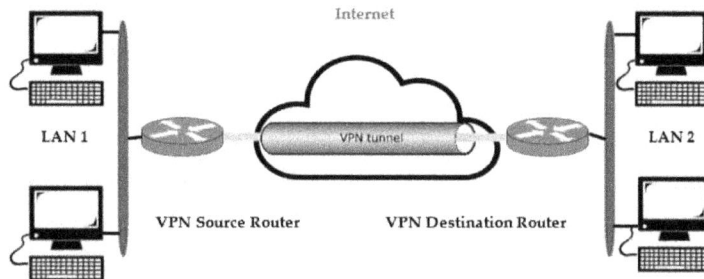

Figure 8.2: VPN tunnel

There are many benefits to using a VPN as a solution to accessing data. Due to encryption, the Internet connection is totally secure from end to end. There is also a high degree of connectivity and mobility with mobile devices. In terms of security, authorization and authentication of users can be tightly controlled.

The downside of using a VPN is speed. Due to the necessity of encryption and security overlays, speed is slow, and the connection's performance may be impacted as a result. VPNs are quite expensive to support and repair if problems exist since they are complex constructs. Consequently, specialized support is needed for a VPN connection and where initial manual installation is involved, time and labor are intensive.

Private-direct connection to the cloud provider

Organizations can have a private or dedicated connection to the cloud provider. For example, Google has an option named **dedicated interconnect**. Using this strategy, traffic designated to Google's VPC rides over the private link, and all other business traffic to other sites on the Internet travels via the regular internet connection. Private clouds are flexible and secure, scaling up and down capacity as the business requires. Cloud providers additionally offer metered connections or subscriptions as pricing options to make connection cost more viable and cost-effective. Using this model, businesses can provision, monitor and manage workloads, view apps, and monitor data, usage, and costs across the data center and clouds selected.

Multitenancy

A multitenant cloud architecture is a single cloud instance and infrastructure that is purpose-built to manage and support multiple tenants/customers. With this type of connectivity option, multiple systems, such as data or applications from different enterprises, are hosted on the same physical hardware in the cloud. This type of connection means that multiple users can share computing resources in a public or private cloud. *Tech Target* uses the analogy of an apartment building. Each resident in the building has authorized access to his or her own apartment, yet all residents share resources such as water, electricity, and common areas. This is similar to a multitenant cloud, whereby the provider sets all-encompassing rules and performance expectations for the tenants, but the individual tenants have private access to their information and are not aware of each other, as their data is kept totally separate.

Use cases for modern network environments

Modern network environments demand innovative solutions to address the increasing complexity and scale of network management. One such solution is the **software-defined wide area network** (**SD-WAN**), which offers enhanced flexibility, efficiency, and control over traditional WAN architectures.

Software-defined wide area network

In *Chapter 7, Data Center Technologies*, we discussed **software-defined networking** (**SDN**) and **storage area networks** (**SAN**). We discussed these concepts in the context of data center infrastructure and with typical implementations of their use.

You may recall that an SDN is achieved by using smart applications, software programs, and virtualization setups. You may also recall that when speaking of a **wide area network** (**WAN**) effectively, we describe it as a network of networks connected by long-distance links. When we consider a SD-WAN, we replace the hub-and-spoke-type designs, as discussed in *Chapter 7, Data Center Technologies*, with more efficient, but still secure, connectivity to corporate clouds, thereby handling some prior limitations and weaknesses of the original hub-and-spoke design, e.g., performance and reliability drawbacks, security weaknesses, and high operational costs. Cloud adoption has brought with it an extraordinary explosion of user data and WAN traffic.

This unprecedented growth in WAN traffic has heralded and driven the need for new ways of doing things. *Cisco Corporation* captures these changes perfectly as they appropriately refer to SD-WAN as **The new WAN**. As described by *Techopedia, By utilizing smart network functionality, an SD-WAN creates more functionality in the wide area network space. It in some ways automates some of the processes that used to be done by discrete hardware in a traditional circuit-switching environment*. Here, we discover that one of the key drivers of change and responding to change is *automation*. The second key driver and response is *orchestration*. Orchestration is essentially the arrangement, coordination (or synchronization), and administrative management of complex computer systems, middleware, and provision of services.

Software-defined wide area network in practice

An SD-WAN is an overlay network that provisions a corporate WAN across multiple locations and can facilitate secure access to the cloud directly from a branch office or other remote location. It uses automation and orchestration to provision links dynamically based on application requirements and network congestion, using **IP Secure** (**IPSec**) to ensure that traffic is effectively tunneled through the underlying transport networks in a secure manner. An SD-WAN network solution should also apply micro segmentation and zero trust security policies to ensure that all requests and responses are reliably authenticated and duly authorized.

> **Note: Zero Trust security policies and the principle of least privilege (PoLP) are covered in more detail in Chapter 16, Security Concepts.**

The SD-WAN is managed by a controller and management software. This software is located in a corporate data center or in the public cloud. Each site or branch has an SD-WAN capable router, a gateway, or a VPN app. The SDN controller *orchestrates* connections to networks and clouds that are enrolled in the SD-WAN. The controller uses any available IP underlay network, such as broadband Internet, 4G/5G cellular, or private **multiprotocol label switching** (**MPLS**) VPNs to provision the fastest or most reliable available transport to networks and clouds enrolled in the SD-WAN. This maintains it as a transport independent mechanism. The controller also ensures that each access request is authenticated and authorized. Therefore, the overall mechanism is agile, responsive, and secure, and it may be optimized for a variety of use cases due to its flexibility and agility, supporting an increasingly mobile and hybrid workforce.

In *Figure 8.3*, an SD-WAN is illustrated. We can determine the IP underlay network is utilizing a broadband connection, thus demonstrating the WAN technology as *transport agnostic*:

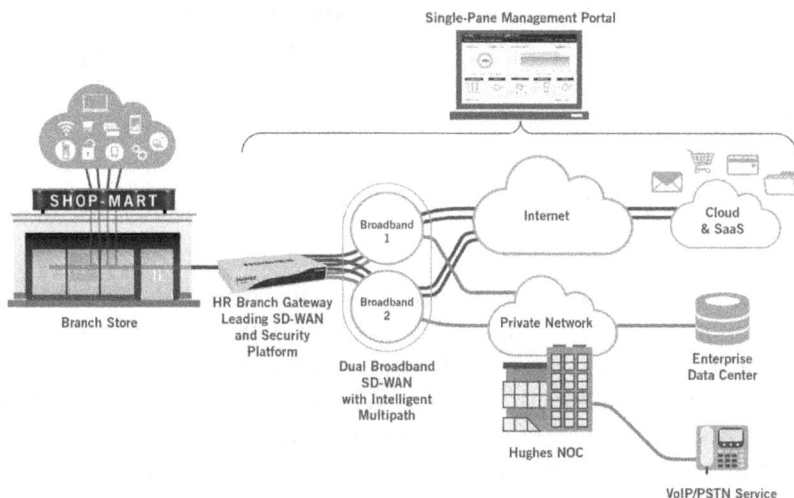

Figure 8.3: Example of an SD-WAN configuration

The system and connectivity are managed in this case through a single-pane management portal. Secure connections exist to the enterprise data center, and the HR Branch Gateway is leading an SD-WAN infrastructure and security platform. As previously stated, there are multiple implementations of SD-WANs; however, the commonalities between them are as follows:

- Transport independence (stemming from SD-WAN as transport agnostic)
- Central policy management
- Application awareness
- Zero-touch provisioning

In summation, SD-WANs are software-based solutions offering enhanced connectivity, central control, and easier deployments. They can be managed through virtualization, software apps, programming solutions, and scripting.

Infrastructure as code

Techopedia defines IaC as a type of IT abstraction where professionals provision and manage a technology stack with software, rather than setting up hardware systems. This focus on software encapsulates IaC in cloud deployments and provisioning.

One of the advantages of using IaC is that it mitigates against snowflakes or drifts. These specific terms describe configurations or builds that are inconsistent or differ from each other, therefore lacking a degree of consistency or standardization practices. IaC is not simply a matter of using scripts to perform repetitive tasks, nor is it a means of handling IT time more efficiently. Running scripts that have been written in an improvised manner is just as likely to cause environmental drift as manual configuration. Consequently, IaC means using carefully developed and tested scripts and orchestration playbooks to generate reliable and steady builds, in other words, to create a consistent and workable environment and practice. These playbooks aim to script as many aspects of the task as possible but leave intervention points required for manual handling of other areas or as a means of handling something that has failed and, therefore, calls for more manual, technical remediation.

Use case scenarios for IaC include the deployment of VMs and containers to cloud infrastructure.

Dynamic inventories ensure that your playbook runs reflect the existing state of your systems. The idea is that you do not need to carry manual updates to inventory data files. This is because access to external systems is occurring dynamically. Inventories can be sourced from external sources or cloud providers. Google Cloud, Microsoft Azure, or Amazon AWS are good examples of cloud providers with ready-to-use dynamic inventory scripts. Dynamic inventories are scalable, flexible, and accurate due to their ability to operate with real-world up-to-date data.

Upgrades, whether in hardware or software, call for critical attention to detail. The process of upgrading code holds the same challenges and focus since upgrading code may be a complex process from the beginning stages to the end results. Consequently, organizations must plan for upgrades diligently. There should be plans in place for a rollback in the case of failed or problematic upgrades. Testing needs to be in place at pertinent stages of the upgrade process. To carry out testing, organizations can utilize scripted test suites or use other testing tools and procedures to ascertain the given status of the upgrade process at particular points in time. Typically, network administrators will plan the upgrade and collaborate with other stakeholders and employees to ensure that all impacts and potential impacts are known to them as best as possible.

Branching strategies

Think of branching in IaC, like working on a group project in college. Imagine you and your friends are writing a report together. Instead of everyone writing on the same piece of paper, you each take a copy of the report to work on your sections separately. These copies are like *branches*.

In IaC, branching strategies are essential for managing changes and ensuring smooth deployments. Here are some common strategies:

- **Trunk-based development**: This strategy involves a single main branch (trunk) where all changes are integrated. Developers create short-lived feature branches, which are merged back into the trunk after passing tests. This approach is suitable for environments with frequent changes and rapid deployments.

- **Environment-based branching**: Different branches are created for each environment, such as development, staging, and production. Changes are promoted from one environment branch to the next, ensuring stability and consistency across environments. This strategy is useful for managing complex infrastructure with multiple configurations.

- **Feature branching**: Developers create separate branches for each feature or task. These branches are merged into a main branch (e.g., develop or master) once the feature is complete and tested. This approach allows for isolated development and testing of individual features.

- **Release branching**: Separate branches are created for each release. Once a release branch is created, only bug fixes and critical updates are merged into it. This strategy helps in maintaining stable releases while allowing ongoing development in other branches.

Selecting the appropriate branching strategy depends on factors such as the frequency of infrastructure changes, deployment timelines, and the need for synchronization with application code.

Returning to the analogy of collaboration and teamwork, when you finish your part, you bring your copy back and combine it with the main report. This process of combining is called **merging**. If everyone worked on the same paper simultaneously, it could get messy and confusing. Branching helps keep things organized and ensures that everyone can work on their tasks without interfering with each other. In IaC, branching allows different team members to work on different parts of the infrastructure code simultaneously. Once their changes are tested and verified, they merge their branches back into the main codebase, ensuring a smooth and coordinated update process. With IaC, branching strategies will depend on how often the infrastructure needs to change, the nature of the deployment, and how long it takes for the deployment to go into production. Other factors in choosing an IaC branching strategy include the coupling between infrastructure and application environments and whether they move tightly in tandem. However, it should be emphasized that the ability to deploy infrastructure without application changes is certainly advantageous, and in cases where this can be done, the necessity of having a separate branching strategy or repository for IaC might be essential. As we can see, use cases for IaC differ. Consequently, strategies to manage and handle IaC equally differ.

Conclusion

Cloud computing, as a rapidly developing information technology, has brought new change and amazingly creative innovation to computing. Cloud concepts are inspiring newer ways of handling infrastructure and data, bringing technologies and protocols to newer terrains and testing grounds. In terms of users of the cloud, cloud computing offers them increased performance, increased backup options, and fault tolerance. Additionally, it offers ease of access and constant availability and access from anywhere, in other words, increased mobility.

In the upcoming chapter, we will investigate network implementation. We will explore network devices and compare and contrast various devices, their features, and their appropriate placement on the network. This content will enable us to understand data transmission further as we observe how frames and packets travel through a network through layers 2 and 3 network devices, such as switches, routers, and APs—among other hardware covered.

Points to remember

- There are four types of cloud deployment models: public, private, hybrid, and community. These deployment models form the backbone of cloud computing.

- You now understand and will be able to differentiate between the following service models: SaaS, IaaS, PaaS, and DaaS.

- You can now distinguish between connectivity options to the cloud and compare and contrast these cloud connections.

- CompTIA Network+ concentrates on cloud concepts in its course objectives. The content of this chapter is mapped to *Domain 1: Networking Concepts*. Summarize cloud concepts and connectivity options.

Key terms

- **Elasticity**: In general terms, elasticity means the ability to change and adapt. When related to cloud computing, elasticity aligns with scalability. Elasticity and scalability refer to a system's capability to dynamically adjust to fluctuations in workload by autonomously allocating and deallocating resources, ensuring that the available resources consistently align with the current demand. Cloud providers incorporate this concept of elasticity and scalability in their service provision. The more adaptable a system is, the more customers will be drawn to and use the system being offered.

- **Infrastructure as code:** IaC involves the management and provisioning of data center resources using machine-readable configuration files, rather than relying on physical hardware setup or manual configuration tools.

- **Automation/orchestration**: When implementing automation, a single task is set up to run on its own automatically. An example of this is starting or stopping a service from running or directing an email to a very specific folder. Orchestration is where we combine these tasks, and the multiple tasks are orchestrated to manage a larger workflow or set of processes. The goal of orchestration is to streamline, manage, and control multiple processes to optimize data analytics or batch processing, for example.

- **Zero-touch provisioning (ZTP)**: ZTP is a strategy for setting up network devices so that the device is automatically configured. Due to this type of provisioning, the time and energy spent on manual configurations and setup is greatly reduced.

- **Zero Trust architecture (ZTA)**: This is a security model that assumes that all devices, users, and services are not inherently trusted, irrespective of whether they are inside or outside the corporate network's edge or perimeter. All users must be authenticated on each device that sits on the organization's network in accordance with policy-based authentication, threat scope reduction, and the principle of least privilege access. In other words, policy-driven authorization is strictly adhered to and complied with at all times.

- **Secure access secure edge**: This is a set of *access* technologies that negotiate access to cloud services and web applications. Zero Trust architecture is one instance of SSE technology. Another instance is the **cloud access security broker** (**CASB**). CASB is a point positioned between enterprise users and cloud service providers. It functions like a firewall that enables the organization or enterprise to extend their security control beyond the boundaries of their corporate network.

Questions

1. What are the four types of cloud deployment models?

2. Explain the following terms: SaaS, IaaS, PaaS, and DaaS.

3. Outline the connectivity options to the cloud as offered by a cloud provider.

4. What is an SD-WAN? Explain.

Join our book's Discord space

Join the book's Discord Workspace for Latest updates, Offers, Tech happenings around the world, New Release and Sessions with the Authors:

https://discord.bpbonline.com

CHAPTER 9

Managing
Network Devices

Introduction

In *Chapter 2, Network Topologies*, you learned the characteristics of network topologies and network types. You differentiated between topologies, their connectivity, the cabling used, and the networking devices that manage the network system. You also identified topologies for given use cases and characterized their purpose, properties, advantages, and disadvantages. In relation to network types, you also specified the design and learned to understand the concepts and configuration of diverse network infrastructures, that is, in wired and wireless communication systems.

In this chapter, we will explore how the networks are implemented and the network devices that are used in specific configurations. This chapter will take you one step further as a network administrator from prior chapters. Here, you will learn the different technologies used to transmit protocol data units and the hardware that must be installed and configured to build, construct, and support these protocols and technologies. These networking devices are often referred to as intermediary devices on a network(s) in that the devices are essentially in the middle of data transmission, mediating between other devices on a network. These core network components interconnect other network components on the computer network. A few examples of intermediary devices are hubs, switches, layer 3 switches, routers, firewalls, gateways, and wireless access points. Examples of end devices are PCs, laptops, VoIP phones, printers, tablets, smartphones, and **Internet of Things (IoT)** smart devices.

Structure

This chapter will explain the following topics:

- Networking devices
- Networked devices

Objectives

By the end of this chapter, the reader will be able to identify and explain what network devices are and how they are placed on a network. They should understand the device's main method of transmitting data and be able to recognize the intelligence of the specified devices. The reader will be able to distinguish between the devices and discern the type of device required for a given problem and networking scenario. After reading this chapter, the reader will use their knowledge of each component to compare and contrast networking appliances, applications, and functions.

Networking devices

Networking devices are deemed to hold different abilities, functions, and intelligence. The protocol data units differ across these devices in their purpose and the troubleshooting strategies used to resolve issues with them.

Table 9.1 outlines networking devices operating at each layer of the OSI and TCP/IP model:

Device	OSI layer	Purpose	TCP/IP layer	Protocol	Protocol Data Unit	Address	Troubleshooting methods (Examples)
-	Application	Interface (API)	Application	HTTP, SMTP, FTP, and so on	Message	–	Packet Sniffing Software for example, Wireshark
-	Presentation	Formatting, encryption, compression	Application	HTTP, SMTP, FTP, and so on	Message	–	Packet Sniffing Software for example, Wireshark
Gateway	Session	Authentication, Authorization	Application	HTTP, SMTP, FTP, and so on	Message	–	NSLOOKUP, NBTSTAT, Wireshark
Firewall	Transport	Reliability	Transport	TCP, UDP	Segment (TCP), Datagram (UDP)	Port	TELNET, SSH NETSTAT, PowerShell Wireshark

Router Multi-layer Switch	Net-work	Addressing, Routing	Internet	IP, ICMP	Packet	IP Address	IPCONFIG, PING, PATHPING, TRACERT, Wire-shark
Switch, Bridge, Access Point	Data Link	Logical Link Control, Media Access Control	Link	Ethernet, Wi-Fi, PPP, and so on	Frame	MAC Address	Status lights on device, ARP, Wire-shark
Repeater, Hub, NIC, Cable, Wireless	Physi-cal	Transmis-sion	Link	CAT 5, 6, 6a RJ-45, and so on	Bit	–	Status lights on device (LEDs)

Table 9.1: Networking devices

Network segments

There is no exact definition of a network segment. It typically refers to an area of a **local area network** (**LAN**), the cable connecting two devices, or *the area of the network bound by bridges or switches where collisions are propagated, or the area bound by a router to prevent the propagation of broadcasts. Techopedia defines a network segment as a physically connected segment of a network. This commonly consists of fiber-optic or Ethernet cable or a Wi-Fi connection.*

In networking practice, the more devices that are added to the network, the more traffic is generated. Consequently, the networking solution is to use a device to filter the traffic being propagated. Such a network device reduces congestion and improves the overall performance of the network as data is transmitted. Dividing a network into segments allows most of the traffic to remain local to the network.

Figure 9.1 illustrates the division of a local area network into segments:

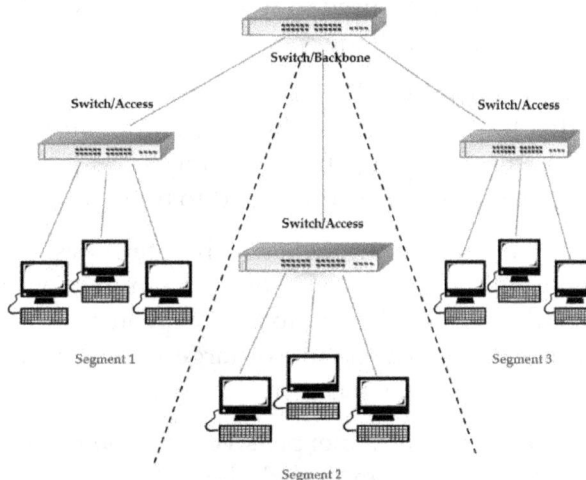

Figure 9.1: Network segments

Repeater

As seen in *Table 9.1*, a repeater is mapped to the physical layer of the OSI model and to the link layer of TCP/IP. A repeater permits the connection of network segments. It extends the network beyond the maximum length of a single segment or cable length. A repeater functions at the physical layer of the OSI model and the link layer of TCP/IP. A multi-port repeater is known as a hub that connects segments of the same network, even if they use different media.

A repeater has the following three basic functions:

- It receives a signal that it cleans up.
- It re-times the signal to avoid collisions.
- It transmits the signal to the next segment.

Hub

As seen in *Table 9.1*, a hub is mapped to the physical layer of the OSI model and to the link layer of TCP/IP. Hubs are now largely obsolete devices. Since 2011, connecting network segments by repeaters or hubs was deprecated by the communications standard IEEE 802.3. In earlier networking implementations, a hub was usually a central device or concentrator in a star topology. A hub allows multiple connections of end devices. At that time, it could be more than a basic hub, providing additional services to the network, for example, a managed hub, a switched hub, or an intelligent hub, but in reality, a hub is a repeater with multiple ports and functions in a similar manner to a repeater.

The hub passes data to all devices connected to it (except for the ingress port or *source* port), no matter which device, that is, the destination, the data is addressed to. This communication method is known as **broadcasting**. A broadcast is a signal sent by one device and read by all other devices on the network. It can be used to send a message to all users or may be used by the network to find the identity of all the computers on the network.

Broadcasting data consumes bandwidth. The problem quickly becomes more evident as more devices are added to the network. A broadcast domain defines the boundary of broadcasts. Some devices stop a message from passing through (the edge of a domain). Other devices pass the message on, an action related to hubs.

Therefore, a hub is merely a channel through which data flows. It has been referred to as a **dumb device**, acting without intelligence or decision-making capabilities, or it has been simply known as nothing more than a glorified repeater. This feature of exclusively broadcasting adds to congestion, and the use of large hubs (24 port), or stacking hubs exacerbated this negative feature in the past.

As an advantage, hubs were relatively inexpensive and could connect different media types. However, as explained, hubs extended the collision domain, could not filter information and passed data to all connected segments.

Regarding collision domains, collisions occur when two or more devices transmit at the same time. This causes the electrical charge of the signal to increase. That is, a collision occurs, and all data involved in the collision is destroyed.

Note: Network, broadcast, and collision domains are no longer the same since the introduction of switches.

Network interface card

As seen in *Table 9.1*, a **network interface card** (**NIC**) is mapped to the physical layer of the OSI model and to the link layer of TCP/IP.

At the source, the NIC:

1. Receives the data unit from the network layer.
2. Attaches its MAC address to the data unit.
3. Attaches the MAC address of the destination device to the data unit.
4. Converts data into suitable units for the particular network (for example, Ethernet, Token Ring, and FDDI)
5. Converts data into electrical, light, or radio signals.
6. Provides the physical connection to the media.

As a destination device, the NIC:

1. Provides physical connection to the media.
2. Translates the signal into data.
3. Reads the MAC address to see if it matches its own address.
4. If it does match, pass the data to the network layer (OSI).

Layer 2 switch

As seen in *Table 9.1*, a switch is mapped to the data link layer of the OSI model and to the link layer of TCP/IP. A switch is essentially a multiport bridge whereby each port of the bridge decides whether to forward data packets to the attached network. The key word in this description is the word *decides*. A switch has decision-making capabilities, unlike the hub as an amplifier and repeater. Remember, legacy Ethernet hubs repeated bits out of all ports except the incoming port. In contrast to this, a switch can unicast, multicast, or broadcast (flood) as required. The switch keeps track of the MAC addresses of all attached devices (just like a bridge) and holds these entries in its **Content Addressable Memory** (**CAM**) table or MAC address table. A switch is completely unaware of the data (protocol) being carried in the data portion of the Ethernet frame, for example, IPv4 packets, an **Address Resolution Protocol** (**ARP**) message, or even an IPv6 ND packet. It is oblivious to IP technologies. The switch makes its forwarding decisions based exclusively on the OSI Layer 2 Ethernet MAC addresses.

When a switch is turned on, the CAM/MAC address table is initially empty. The CAM table is populated via the following procedure and process. As a switch receives frames from different devices (dynamically), it can populate its CAM/MAC address table by inspecting the source MAC address of every frame. When the MAC address table of the switch contains the destination MAC address, the switch can filter the frame and forward out a single port in unicast transmission. A switch acts like a hub (when broadcasting) but filters like a bridge (when unicasting or multicasting). Each port on a switch is a collision domain.

A switch learns by examining the source MAC address. The switch consults its CAM table. If the source MAC address discovered does not exist, the MAC address is added to the table along with the incoming port number. If the MAC address is already in the CAM table, the timer is refreshed and updated for that particular entry. Recall that this table is built dynamically. Most layer 2 switches hold their entries in the table for approximately five minutes as entries are recorded and then held. If the MAC address is not an entry in the CAM table, the switch floods the frame to all connected devices (egress ports) apart from the incoming (ingress) port.

As well as learning, a switch can also *forward*. As we are aware, data transmission includes a source and destination address. To forward data to the destination address, the switch consults its MAC address table. If the address is in the table, the switch will unicast to the destination device. If the destination MAC address is not an entry in the table, the switch will then forward the frame out of all ports except for the incoming port. This method of learning and forwarding defines a switch as an intelligent networking device.

In the following figure, a CAM table is shown. Every switch has its unique CAM table, which changes dynamically as frames are transmitted around the network locally.

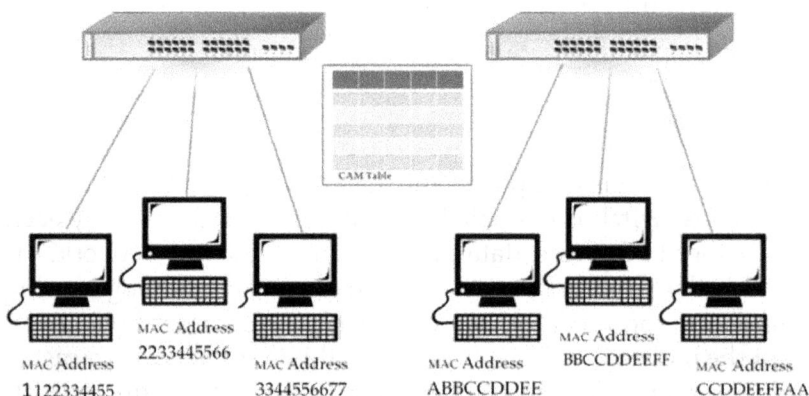

Figure 9.2: A switch

Note: A network administrator can manually configure entries in the MAC address table as required or as a security feature to offset MAC address spoofing. A static entry in a CAM table will always overrule dynamic entries.

Bridge

As seen in *Table 9.1*, a bridge is mapped to the data link layer of the OSI model and to the link layer of TCP/IP. A bridge builds a bridging table, monitors, and keeps track of devices on each segment of a network. The bridge filters packets but does not forward them if the destination device is on the local side of the bridge (as viewed from the perspective of the source device). A bridge makes decisions by examining the MAC address in the same way a switch does. It forwards packets whose destination address is on a different segment from its own (when the destination device is viewed as remote from the perspective of the source device). It divides a network into multiple collision domains, therefore, reducing the number of collisions on the network.

A bridge uses the **Spanning Tree Protocol (STP)** to decide whether to pass a packet on to a different network segment or not. In *Figure 9.3*, a bridge's operations and forwarding decisions are illustrated:

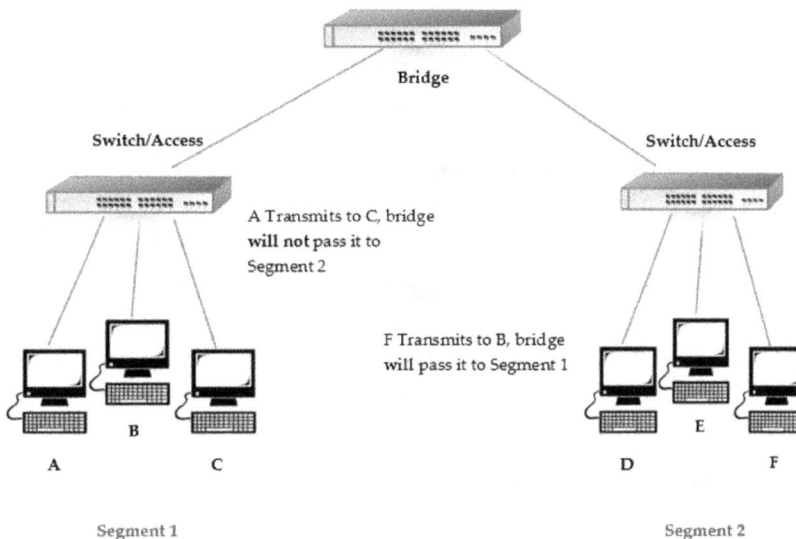

Figure 9.3: A bridge

Access point

As seen in *Table 9.1*, an access point is mapped to the data link layer of the OSI model and to the link layer of TCP/IP. Access points and wireless technologies will be covered in more detail in *Chapter 12, Installing and Configuring Wireless Technologies*. For this chapter, we will look at the basic functions of the device and where it is placed on a network. *Techopedia* defines an access point as *a hardware device or configured node on a local area network (LAN) that allows wireless capable devices and wired networks to connect through a wireless standard, including Wi-Fi or Bluetooth*. **Wireless Application Protocols (WAPs)** are comprised of radio transmitters and antennae, which facilitate connectivity between devices and the internet or between devices on a network or **wireless local area network (WLAN)**. An **access point (AP)** is also known as a **hotspot**.

Wireless clients use their wireless NIC (on mobile devices) to discover nearby APs and wireless networks or **Security Set Identifier (SSIDs)**. Clients then attempt to associate and authenticate with an AP to join the wireless network. After successful authentication, wireless users have access to network resources. APs can be categorized as either autonomous APs or controller-based APs. Autonomous APs are effectively standalone devices configured through a command line interface or **graphical user interface (GUI)**. Each autonomous AP acts self-sufficiently of the others and is configured and managed manually by a network administrator or network engineer. Controller-based APs are also known as **lightweight APs (LAPs)**. These APs use **Lightweight Access Point Protocol (LWAPP)** to communicate with an LWAN controller (WLC). Each LAP is automatically configured and managed by the WLC.

Router

As seen in *Table 9.1*, a router is mapped to the network layer of the OSI model and to the internet layer of TCP/IP. A router can connect different network segments if they are in the same building or even on the opposite side of the world. Routers are implemented in LAN, MAN, and WAN environments. A router allows access to resources by selecting the best path to move traffic around the network. It can interconnect different networks with different technologies in place, for example, Ethernet with (legacy) Token Ring.

A router has the ability to change the packet size and format to match the requirements of the destination network [that is, the **Maximum Transmission Unit (MTU)**. The two primary functions of a router are, firstly, to determine the best path and, secondly, to share the details of routes with other routers via a static or dynamic routing protocol.

A router holds a routing table just like the switch needs its CAM table to operate. This table is a database that keeps track of the routes to networks and the associated costs and metrics for data transmission.

In static routing, the routes are manually configured by a network administrator.

In dynamic routing, the routers involved in the chosen protocol converge, and the routes adjust automatically to changes in network topology and information routers receive from other routers in the routing configuration. Regarding collision domains, a router limits the collision domains. To summarize, a router can function in LAN or WAN implementations, connect differing media and architectures, determine the best pathway/route for data transmission, and filter broadcasts as deemed necessary. We will cover some routing protocols in *Chapter 11, Managing Routing Protocols,* in more detail.

In the following figure, a routing table is shown. Please remember that every router has its unique routing table that changes dynamically as packets are transmitted around the network to different subnets. Traffic is also managed via inter-VLAN routing or handled as packets traverse the internet through a router's serial interface.

Figure 9.4 shows two subnets with different network IDs and two network segments. The router in the middle of the topology acts as an intermediary device, forwarding packets to the specified subnets as required.

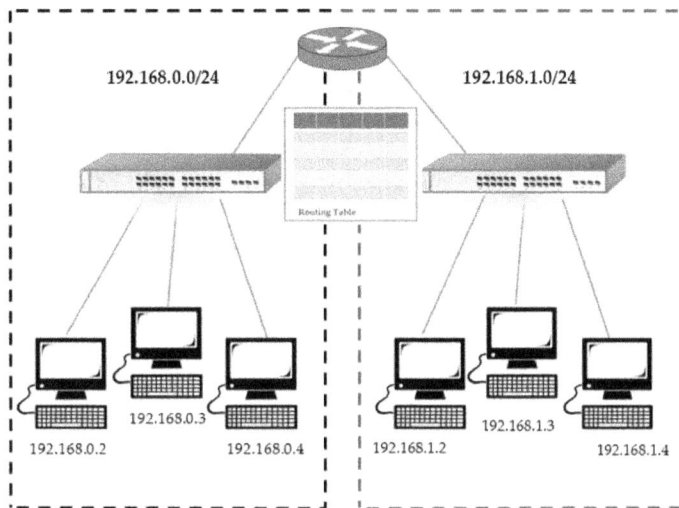

Figure 9.4: *A router*

Layer 3 capable switch/multilayer switch

As seen in *Table 9.1*, a layer 3 capable switch/multi-layer switch is mapped to the network layer of the OSI model and to the internet layer of TCP/IP. A multilayer switch has routing capabilities, unlike a layer 2 switch, which exclusively handles frames. A multilayer switch, therefore, switches and routes frames or packets, depending upon the specific port's configuration and how many ports have this routing feature available and enabled on the network device.

As explained earlier, a switch examines frames. In contrast to this examination, a multilayer switch examines *deeper* into the protocol description unit (at packet or even at segment level). Multilayer switches use an **application-specific integrated circuit** (**ASIC**) to perform routing functions. These hardware circuits can be customized for particular usage as opposed to general-purpose usage. This use of ASICs differs from typical router processes, which reside on a microprocessor and use applications running on the processor to achieve their routing operations. Though ASICs are relatively expensive devices to purchase, they provide significant benefits to an organization implementing multilayer switching technology. In short, multilayer switches route packets much faster than traditional routers. Multilayer switches can perform advanced routing protocols, for example, **Open Shortest Path First** (**OSPF**) or **Border Gateway Protocol** (**BGP**). In terms of security features, these switches can support more **access control lists** (**ACLs**) than a traditional router. Consequently, there are security advantages to having a multilayer switch on top of the advantages of greater speed and efficiency in network performance.

Firewall

As seen in *Table 9.1*, a firewall is mapped to the transport layer of the OSI model and to the transport layer of TCP/IP. Firewalls can either be a software application or a hardware appliance. As a piece of hardware, a firewall is set up, organized, and constructed using different methods and strategies. A firewall has at least two network connections: one to the internet, known as the **public side**, and one to the network, known as the **private side**. How a firewall is configured and where it is placed on the network is called the firewall architecture. There are four main firewall architectures: dual-homed, multi-homer, bastion host, and screened subnet. A dual-homed firewall architecture sits between the internal and external networks and operates as the chief line of defense. A multi-homed firewall architecture uses multiple firewalls and is placed in front of each network, making this architecture the most secure of the four types. A bastion host firewall architecture is where a specialized computer system has two network interfaces. In this specific setup, the firewall is placed between the internal and external networks. A screened subnet is also known as a **demilitarized zone** (**DMZ**). This firewall architecture uses a single firewall to protect multiple interfaces.

There are multiple technologies used in firewall implementation that a budding security analyst should know in depth. In contrast, a network administrator must have knowledge of firewall technologies in a more general way but should know what an ACL is and how firewall rules operate. ACLs enable rules that govern whether to allow or block (permit or deny) traffic. This is typically done via allowing or denying traffic via ports or protocols where a thorough understanding of ports and protocols is critical. Additionally, firewall rules may be established using source and destination IP addresses or services to allow or deny packet entry. In a firewall, rules enabled in ACLs are processed from the top down. Consequently, an administrator must know how to create firewall rules, as the order in which ACLs are listed makes a difference in the way the rules are enacted. The most significant and specific rules should always be placed at the top. The final rule in an ACL list is an *implicit* deny. This rule's purpose is to block traffic that does not match any other rule created in the list. As the word implicit suggests, you cannot always see this rule because it is built in as a default specification in the firewall's software. You can configure a firewall to filter packets based on rules that you (as a user) or the network administrator create and configure to strictly delimit the type of information allowed to flow in and out of the network's internet connection. This depends on whether you have the privileges to configure firewall settings or whether the company or organization prefer full control in the hands of the IT department. In essence, knowing the most appropriate firewall technologies and architectures for the company network is vital in keeping the network secure and the network users' data safe.

Voice gateway

A gateway allows different networks to communicate by offering a translation service from one protocol stack to another. Gateways work at all levels of the OSI model. This is due to the type of translation service they are providing. An address gateway connects networks using the same protocol but uses different directory spaces, such as Message Handling Service. A Protocol Gateway connects a network using different protocols. It translates source protocol so the destination can understand it.

An application gateway translates between applications, such as from an internet e-mail server to a messaging server. A **Voice over Internet Protocol** (**VoIP**) gateway is a network device that converts analog telephony signals to digital. After converting the signal, the VoIP gateway organizes it into data packets and then encrypts it for transmission. VoIP vendors use VoIP gateways for switched and network interfacing (*Techopedia*).

Load balancer

When you look at the term load balancer, the function of the device or action is strongly implied in the name of the device. In human activities and work projects, if we were to *balance the load* with others, we would be sharing the task with other colleagues or collaborators to reduce or alleviate *overload* or stress on any one specific individual or group. This distribution of tasks is essentially what a load balancer does in computer networking. Irrespective of whether it is hardware or software related, or what algorithm(s) it uses or strategies entailed in the means of distribution, a load balancer disburses traffic to different Web servers in the resource pool or server cluster to ensure that no single server becomes overworked, overwhelmed and subsequently undependable. It effectively minimizes server response time and maximizes data throughput.

A hardware load balancer is a hardware device configured with a specialized operating system. The OS distributes web application traffic across a cluster of application servers. To ensure ideal performance, the hardware load balancer distributes traffic according to custom-made rules so that the application servers are not overcome by data or traffic congestion.

There are four types of load balancers: application load balancers, network load balancers, classic load balancers, and gateway load balancers.

Media converter

In *Chapter 3, Cables and Connectors*, different types of cables, connectors, and technologies were introduced, for example, Ethernet, Coax, and Fiber Optics. The word convert means to change the format from one technology to another or to enable the translation of one technology or system to be understood via a different format/mechanism. As explained earlier, media is the channel through which we transmit data, in effect, the cable. Therefore, a media converter is a computer networking device or piece of hardware that transparently converts Ethernet or other communication protocols from one cable type to another cable type, usually copper CATx/UTP to fiber.

Wireless LAN controller

A WLAN controller manages wireless network access points. APs enable wireless devices to connect to the WLAN/network. The WLAN controller centralizes the operations of the APs and manages the APs using protocols like the LWAPP. The WLC handles the configuration of multiple APs and provides efficiency and better security options to an organization deploying wireless connectivity. WLANs will be discussed in more detail in *Chapter 12, Installing and Configuring Wireless Technologies*.

Cable modem

Cable modems are network hardware devices primarily used to deliver broadband internet access. The primary purpose of a modem is to provide us with access to the internet. The easiest way to think about what a modem does is to look at the structure of the word itself. The word modem is a construct of two words: modulate and demodulate. The first two letters of modulate are followed by the first three of demodulate.

This device modulates and demodulates an analog carrier signal to encode and decode digital information that is transmitted. In other words, it converts the signal from digital to analog and analog back to digital as required in data transmission.

In earlier days, when the term modem first emerged, the technology being used was transmitting digital data primarily over phone lines, the **Plain Old Telephone System (POTS)**. The modem was required to convert the signal from digital to analog so the signals could travel over the telephone wires and then come back into the PC in digital format. Now, access to the internet normally takes place using high-speed broadband cable modems and technologies such as ISDN are now defunct.

Digital subscriber line modem

Digital subscriber line (DSL) technology transports high-bandwidth data over a simple telephone line that is directly linked to a modem. DSL technology is still implemented in communications technology, especially in more rural areas and locations where broadband technology is not yet available.

Regarding internet access, popular services for home users and small offices include broadband cable, broadband DSL, wireless WANs, and mobile services. However, some organizations need faster connections to support VoIP phones, real-time video conferencing, and data center storage.

In some cases, business-class interconnections are usually provided by **internet service providers (ISPs)** and may include business DSL, leased lines, and Metro Ethernet as access options.

Other network devices

Larger networks have additional security requirements and therefore require security-related network devices and technologies, for example:

- Dedicated firewall systems
- Access control lists
- **Intrusion detection system (IDS)** or **intrusion prevention systems (IPS)**
- **Virtual private networks (VPN)**
- Proxy servers

These devices will be explored in *Chapter 16, Security Concepts*.

Networked devices

Other hardware devices used in networking include:

- VoIP phone
- Printer
- Physical access control devices
- Cameras

These devices will be explored in *Chapter 16, Security Concepts*.

Internet of Things

The IoT describes the network of physical objects, that is, things that use embedded software, technologies, and sensors with the intention of connecting and exchanging data with other devices and systems over the internet. These devices range from ordinary household objects to complex and more sophisticated industrial tools. Some examples of IoT devices include the following:

- Smart refrigerators
- Smart speakers
- Smart thermostats
- Smart doorbells
- Smart actuators, gadgets, or machines

Industrial control **systems/supervisory control and data acquisition (SCADA)**. SCADA systems are used for controlling, monitoring, and analyzing industrial devices and operation processes. The system is comprised of both software and hardware components and enables remote and on-site gathering of data from the industrial equipment. In that way, it allows companies to remotely manage their industrial sites, such as water management, oil and gas, renewable energy systems, wind farms, transportation, power distribution and control, and other industrial manufacturing processes. For example, in wind farm processes, SCADA is an optimum means of monitoring and management because the company can access the turbine data and control them without being on site.

Heating, ventilation, and air conditioning (**HVAC**) sensors are sensor networks that regulate heating, ventilation, and air conditioning. The most commonly used sensors for HVAC and building equipment applications are temperature, humidity, and pressure sensors.

Conclusion

In this chapter, you learned to identify and explain what network devices are and how they are placed on a network. You understood how to comprehend the device's main method of transmitting data and recognize the intelligence of the specified devices from *Table 9.1*. You should be able to distinguish between the devices and discern the type of device required for a given problem and networking scenario. You also learned to use this knowledge of each component to compare and contrast various devices used in computer networking and, as a network administrator, identify these devices.

In the upcoming chapter, we will explore the concept of switching protocols and go deeper into the operations of layer 2 switching technologies.

Points to remember

- The types and functions of network devices can be mapped against the OSI model and TCP/IP. Approaching learning about network devices against the framework of these models enhances understanding and comprehension. The purpose, protocols, PDUs, and troubleshooting strategies and approaches regarding the devices are delineated and aligned with a very specific set of intelligence (and multiple intelligences) assigned to each device.

- Devices operating at each layer of the networking models are contextualized, illuminated, and clarified with this particular mapping.

- A network administrator must know the intermediary devices in data transmission as well as the newer IoT sensors, software and smart devices and technologies. This chapter introduces the functionality of these devices, their know-how and their particular set of mechanisms and protocols.

- The content of this chapter is mapped to *Domain 1: Networking Concepts*. Compare and contrast networking appliances, applications, and functions.

Key terms

- **Sensor**: A sensor is a device that changes a physical parameter to an electrical output. It is situated at the input port of a device, as in *sensing* data.

- **Actuator**: As against a sensor, an actuator is a device that converts an electrical signal to a physical output. The sensor is situated at the input port to take the input, whereas an actuator is placed at the output port.

Note: An IoT device is made up of a physical object (a thing), a controller (a brain), sensors, actuators, and networks (that is, the internet). An actuator is a machine component or system that moves or controls the mechanism, or the system being controlled.

Questions

1. What devices are mapped to the physical layer of the OSI model? Why?
2. What devices are mapped to the data link layer of the OSI model? Why?
3. What devices are mapped to the network layer of the OSI model? Why?
4. What devices are mapped to the transport layer of the OSI model? Why?
5. Name some other networked devices.

Join our book's Discord space

Join the book's Discord Workspace for Latest updates, Offers, Tech happenings around the world, New Release and Sessions with the Authors:

https://discord.bpbonline.com

CHAPTER 10
Managing Switching Protocols

Introduction

In *Chapter 9, Managing Network Devices,* a switch was defined and described as a layer 2 device. In this chapter, switching features and protocols will be outlined and explained to build on the understanding of switching technologies. Comprehending the reasons why **virtual local area networks** (**VLANs**) are implemented, their purpose, and how they enhance and boost performance on a network is a brilliant addition to a network administrator's conceptual and practical *toolkit*. Additionally, with the critical nature of security and hardening networking devices becoming even more pronounced, understanding switch and port security is a must. The operation of link aggregation in a switched **local area network** (**LAN**) environment is now commonly practiced, especially in larger networks seeking to improve performance on high-traffic Ethernet switch links. **Spanning Tree Protocol** (**STP**) is now natively integrated into switch functionality as a necessary protocol to alleviate or eliminate broadcast storms, switching loops or MAC Table instability. STP can be customized and configured to suit the needs of any topology and switch infrastructure, ranging from small organizations to larger, more complex topologies.

In switching technologies and data transmission, we see that the sending device/host needs a way to find the MAC address of the destination for a given Ethernet link. To achieve this purpose, **Address Resolution Protocol** (**ARP**) is used. This protocol is not without its issues. Too many broadcasts via ARP can cause excessive overhead on the network. ARP operations should be understood by a network administrator, as hackers or threat actors can use this protocol to discover security loopholes in a network and use this knowledge to carry out security breaches and attacks. By understanding switching features and how Ethernet protocols fit together to make a network (like the internet or your local LAN) work, you can troubleshoot any network far more efficiently.

Structure

This chapter will explain the following topics:

- Operations and functions of a switch
- Virtual local area networks
- Port security
- Other protocols
- Spanning tree protocol

Objectives

Upon completing this chapter, the reader will be able to understand the purpose and functionality of VLANs. They will understand the basic operations of a switch as it learns about filters and forwards traffic. They will be able to distinguish between different switching protocols. The reader will use their knowledge of each feature and protocol to make optimum practical decisions regarding creating VLANs while understanding how they are based on logical instead of physical connections. Readers will appreciate that switch segmentation can be based on function, team, or application and be able to identify and distinguish between the different types of VLAN traffic. Other protocols, such as STP, ARP, and Port Security, should equally be understood upon the completion of this chapter.

Operations and functions of a switch

In *Chapter 9, Managing Network Devices*, a switch was described as having decision-making capabilities and could both learn and forward as it explored the entries held in its CAM table to make its determinations. The process of how a switch learns and forwards is also described in detail in *Chapter 9, Managing Network Devices*. Here is a brief synopsis of the process. As the switch receives frames from different devices, it populates its MAC address/ CAM table. After examining the MAC addresses of the source and destination device, the switch has the ability to unicast, multicast, or broadcast (that is, flood the network). Here is an example of unicasting. In *Figure 10.1*, the desired conditions for **unicast** transmission have been met since the MAC address table holds both source and destination addresses in its current entries. Thus, in this scenario, the switch can filter the frame and forward out a single port.

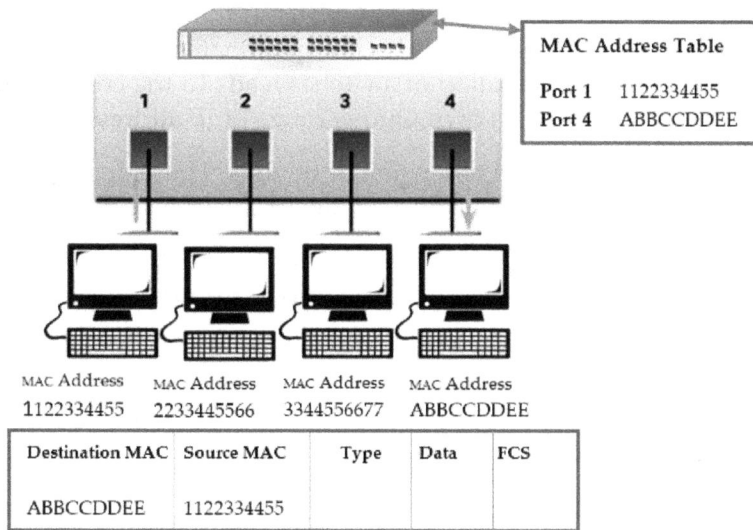

Figure 10.1: Unicast transmission

In contrast to this unicasting scenario, if the destination MAC address is not an entry in the table, the switch will then forward the frame out of all ports with the exception of the incoming port in a process named flooding. To summarize, when a device is forwarding a message to an Ethernet network, the Ethernet header includes the source and destination MAC addresses. In Ethernet networks, different MAC addresses are used for layer 2 unicast, broadcast, and multicast communications. A layer 2 switch can:

- Flood if the message is intended as a broadcast message or the unicast destination is unknown.

- Forward traffic is when the unicast destination is in the table, and the source is also known.

- Filter traffic when the switch receives a frame where the source and destination are on the same port.

Note: A switch will never permit traffic to be forwarded out of the ingress port (that is, the interface through which it receives the traffic).

Virtual local area networks

In a LAN design, all devices connected to the switch will belong to the same LAN. LANs typically exist inside a single building. Network devices such as switches, hubs, bridges, workstations, and servers in LAN designs connect to each other in the building internally. Externally, the LAN will typically be linked to a **wide area network (WAN)**. Additionally, the LAN may be subnetted into multiple smaller networks by segmenting the allocated IP address space. Creating logical subnets is a mechanism of LAN segmentation occurring at layer 3 IP addressing (as demonstrated in *Chapter 4, IP Addressing and Subnetting*). In contrast to this, layer 2 segmentation of LANs is implemented on switches in the network infrastructure. The logical segmentation of switches leads to the creation and generation of VLANs. Each VLAN will have its own unique range of IP addressing.

VLANs are logical connections with other similar devices. These devices may be common to a group of users, applications, or a company department. Placing devices into various VLANs have the following characteristics:

- VLANs provide segmentation of the various groups of devices on the same switches.

- They make the organization's networking and allocation of resources more manageable.

- Unicast, multicast, and broadcast traffic are isolated inside the individual VLAN.

- Smaller broadcast domains exist as a result of implementing VLANs.

An apt definition of a VLAN is a logical group of workstations, servers, and network devices that appear to be on the same LAN despite their geographical distribution. (*Techopedia*)

The keyword in this definition is *appear* because although the devices on the VLAN are dispersed across the actual network, the devices operate and perform as if they are on the same physical LAN.

In *Figure 10.2* three VLANs are depicted. Note that these switches may be in completely different locations in the physical building. Yet, users on VLAN 10 will be able to communicate with other users in VLAN 10, irrespective of the device's geographical location. This is made viable due to inter-VLAN routing. Unicasts, multicasts, and broadcasts will remain internal to the specific VLAN and IT operations, such as the deployment of software, access permissions, and privileges of the group, and security policies can be tied into the requirements and needs of users in VLAN 10. The same applies to VLAN 20 and 30.

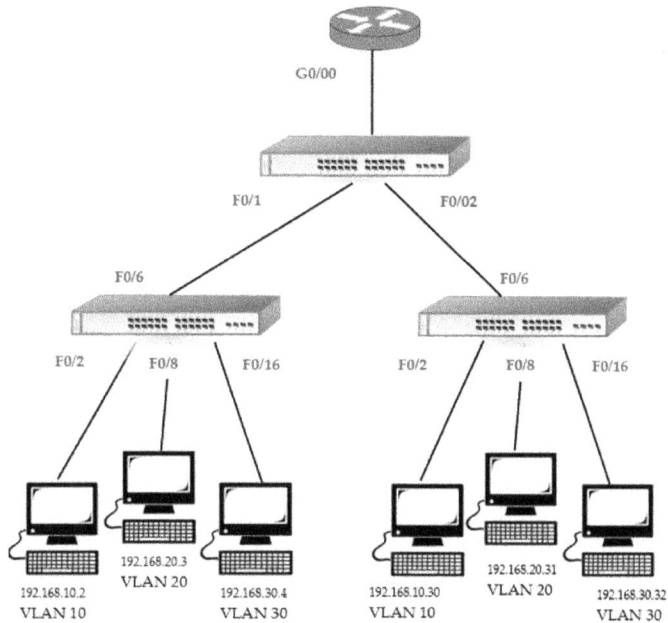

Figure 10.2: *VLANs*

Figure 10.3 illustrates how VLANs may be distributed across a building as a network design and solution. Note how even if employees/users are dispersed across the different floors of the building, they maintain their access and privileges to the VLAN they are members of. In this way, the IT department can access IT-specific tools and resources as they repair and configure workstations, and no member of a department or VLAN is enforced to be in a specific area of the building since the network design is secure while remaining adaptable and flexible.

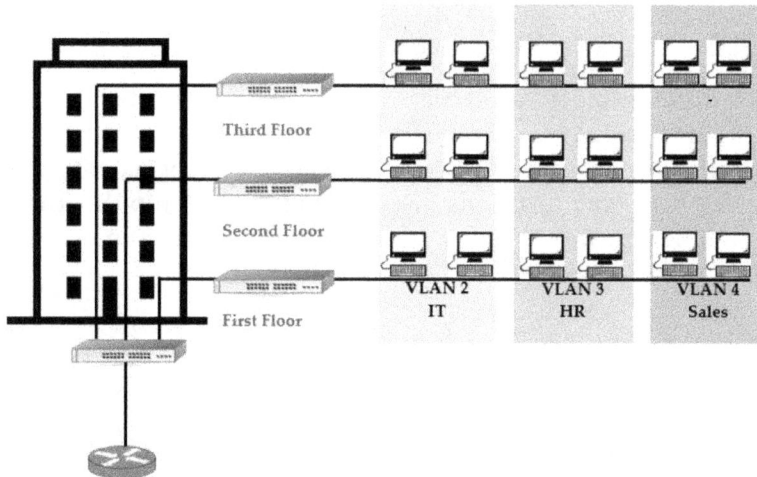

Figure 10.3: *VLAN-based office network overview*

In relation to switch functionality, the ability to assign different switch ports to different VLANs permits you to reuse a single physical switch for multiple purposes.

Access ports and trunk ports

Organizations may wish to extend a VLAN to multiple switches. By extending the configuration, VLANs can be expanded across many floors, departments, and locations in a building.

A port on a switch has two modes of operation. These modes are called **access ports** and **trunk ports**. Access ports are the connections to the devices and hosts. Trunk ports are the connections and links between the switches. It is critical to be aware of these modes of operation because if the links are incorrectly configured, the transmission of data will fail.

Note: An access port is a switch port that is a member of only one VLAN. A trunk is a switch port that carries traffic for multiple VLANs.

The standard and protocol for supporting VLANs and trunking on Ethernet networks is IEEE 802.1Q. It is often referred to as Dot1q. On Cisco switches, the proprietary protocol used is known as **Dynamic Trunking Protocol (DTP)**.

To summarize:

- A trunk is a *point-to-point* link between two intermediary network devices, for example, switch to switch or switch to the router.

- A trunk carries the traffic of multiple VLANs.

- A network administrator configures the trunk link to allow **permissible** VLAN traffic, which improves performance, streamlines traffic, and enhances security across the network.

- A trunk link extends the VLAN across the entire network.

In *Figure 10.4*, the difference between access ports and trunk ports is illustrated. You can observe the trunk links between the switches and between the switch and the router's ability to carry traffic from multiple VLANs. To appropriately identify and differentiate between traffic, *VLAN tagging* functions insert the VLAN ID into the frame that is being transmitted. Consequently, the network device receiving the frame is aware of which VLAN the frame is destined for:

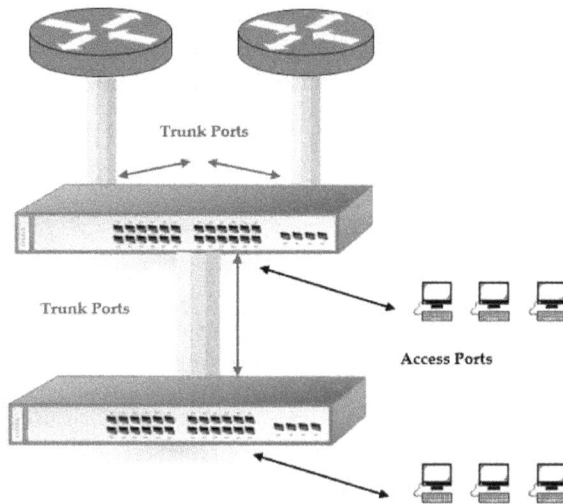

Figure 10.4: *Access ports and trunk ports*

In *Table 10.1*, access ports are compared with trunk ports:

Switchport Mode Access vs. Switchport ModeTrunk	
Access Mode Port	**Trunk Mode Port**
In this mode, the port functions as a non-trunking untagged single VLAN Layer 2 interface.	In this mode, the port functions as a trunk allowing multiple VLANs to cross it using VLAN tags. (VLAN IDs)
Belongs to a single VLAN	A member of all VLANs by default for transmission purposes. This setting can be limited by configuring/customizing memberships on switches which support VLAN features.
These ports are used to connect end-point hosts	These ports are used to connect switches together
Does not carry VLAN tags	The port carries VLAN tags and uses 802.1Q encapsulation

Table 10.1: *Comparison table of access vs. trunk ports*

Voice VLANs

In telephony and communications technology, voice and data are separated from each other. We see this separation happening in the **Digital Subscriber Line (DSL)** configuration in terms of the need for filtering traffic. In DSL, filters separate the voice and data signals sent through the phone lines, safeguarding that neither signal interferes with the other signal. In Voice VLANs, voice and data traffic are also separated for optimal functionality.

Voice data requires additional features when compared with data traffic with a different set of considerations and additionally, these VLANs need to be prioritized as real-time data. In Voice VLANs, a separate VLAN is necessary because voice traffic:

- Cannot afford traffic congestion and needs to avoid it.
- Requires guaranteed bandwidth to function optimally.
- Needs QoS priority set as high in the QoS stack.
- Needs minimal latency in transmission.

In terms of the configuration of Voice VLANs, the entire network must be designed to support voice. Therefore, a network administrator needs to be cognizant of the network infrastructure when planning for Voice VLANs is taking place.

Voice VLANs permit access ports to transmit voice traffic from an IP phone on the network. *Figure 10.5* demonstrates how Voice VLANs are members of a VLAN separated from other VLANs on the network:

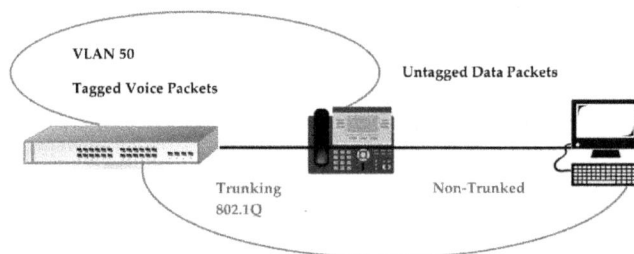

Figure 10.5: Voice VLAN

Voice VLANs allow IP phones to run (voice) along with regular desktop or laptop computers (data) over your access switch ports.

The benefits of using VLANs are listed as follows:

- Due to switch segmentation, one switch can be used to create and manage multiple VLANs.
- The use of equipment resources and network devices is cost-effective since a smaller number of switches are required to support multiple VLANs, network users, and specific groups of employees.
- Since users in the same VLAN can only communicate with each other, security is enhanced.
- Broadcast traffic is minimized in VLAN configurations since dividing the LAN reduces broadcast traffic. This, in turn, increases the bandwidth on the network and improves network performance.
- Collision domains are significantly reduced.

- Simpler management in IT administration.

- Sharing of sensitive data, deployment, configuration, and distribution of software and other applications is streamlined per VLAN.

- Firewall rules can be created per VLAN and traffic on the network can be prioritized to reach target groups and network segments as needs arise (via QoS).

- Network administrators can monitor and manage VLAN traffic proficiently, such as when group policies are aligned to Active Directory in Windows Server operating systems.

Port security

On a switch, all ports are enabled by default. This means that any port, especially unused ports, can be a potential security risk. What happens if an unauthorized user manages to access a company switch and, using the correct software, gains access to the organization's network and domain? The answer is anything from a minor breach to a more sophisticated security threat can occur. As soon as the threat actor plugs the device into the switch's port, the interface comes up immediately, and access to the network is achieved. Passwords, sensitive data, and company records can be eavesdropped on or, worse still, accessed and stolen. Essentially, this is a very basic risk common to all switches and switch ports. Under usual circumstances, there are no restrictions on the devices that can be attached to a port. However, with switch port security enabled, the devices that can connect to a switch through the port are restricted.

Port security uses the MAC address to identify allowed and denied devices. This is similar to MAC address filtering on a router or WAP. Using the configuration settings of the switch, a network administrator can disable all unused ports and configure the ones enabled to align with authorized user devices. By default, port security allows only a single device to connect through a switch port. You can, however, modify the maximum number of allowed devices. (On Cisco devices, this is known as MAC address sticky in the operating system). This security feature offers the ability to configure a switch port so that traffic can be limited to only a specific configured MAC address or a specified list of MAC addresses.

As previously stated, MAC addresses are stored in the CAM table in RAM memory and are identified with the port and by a MAC address type.

Secure MAC address types

There are three different types of secure MAC addresses, which are explained as follows:

- **Static secure MAC addresses**: This type of secure MAC address is statically configured on a switch port and is stored in an address table and in the running configuration of the device's IOS. It has been manually identified as an allowed address.

- **Dynamic secure MAC addresses**: This type is learned dynamically from the traffic that is sent through the port. These types of addresses are kept only in an address table and not in the running configuration file of the switch. These addresses will dynamically *be held and passed through* the address table.

    o When a device connects to the switch port, its MAC address is identified.

    o If the maximum number of allowed devices has not been reached, the device's MAC address is added to the table, and the port is allowed to be used.

- **Sticky secure MAC addresses**: This type of secure address can be manually configured or, alternatively, be dynamically learned. These types of secure addresses are held in an address table and in the running configuration.

Port violation

A port violation happens when the maximum number of MAC addresses has been reached on the port, and an unknown MAC address is seen. Administrators can configure the switch to take one of the following actions when a violation takes place:

- Shut down the port (shutdown). This is the default setting on a switch.

- Drop all frames from unauthorized MAC addresses (protect). No notifications are sent to the administrator with this particular action.

- Drop all frames and generate a **Simple Network Management Protocol (SNMP)** trap (restrict). An SNMP trap is sent via Syslog, and a violation counter is incremented whenever traffic is dropped by the switch.

Port security offers a network administrator a way of managing and securing switches locally on the LAN or across VLANs. Disabling all unused ports is best practice while simultaneously utilizing switch port security types where applicable.

Other protocols

Other protocols play a crucial role in enhancing network performance and reliability. One such protocol is link aggregation, which is essential for optimizing bandwidth and ensuring redundancy in network connections.

Link aggregation

A good analogy for expanding on the capacity and bandwidth of a network is the road infrastructure. On a regular dual carriageway, there is an ability to send traffic bi-directionally at the same time. Cars and vehicles travel up and down the roadway, and traffic flow is maximized with no bottlenecks. However, at times in certain locations, especially when coming closer to cities, there is a requirement for a wider channel through which traffic can flow, and vehicles can travel in larger quantities. A perfect solution to this problem is the motorway or highway, a roadway where there are multiple lanes in both directions, enabling more traffic to pass through these wider channels and conduits. This solution is similar to the concept of link aggregation on switches. Link aggregation is used for extending the bandwidth on switches and enabling larger quantities of data to pass through the switches. Link aggregation also facilitates load balancing and redundancy on networks.

In Ethernet networks, link aggregation allows the creation of logical links. These logical links (or groups) are made up of several physical links (that is, cables). *EtherChannel* is a method of link aggregation that is used in switched networks.

In *Figure 10.6*, EtherChannel has been implemented across the switches:

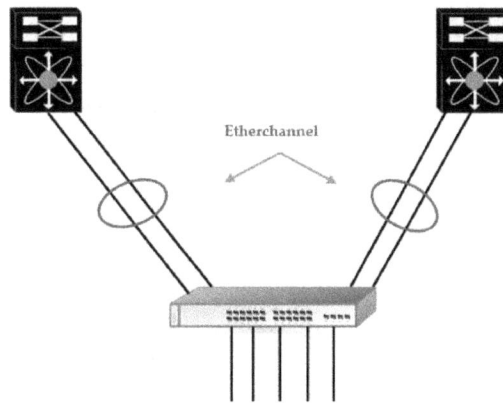

Figure 10.6: EtherChannel

Note that the links are created to provide redundancy since if one physical link breaks or goes down, the second link will take over and keep the transmission of data active. The links provide the opportunity for load balancing and sharing a load of traffic across the switches. Load balancing takes place between the links on the same EtherChannel.

EtherChannel combines multiple ports on a Cisco switch into a single logical link between two switches. With EtherChannel:

- You can combine 2–8 ports into a single aggregated link. This is sometimes referred to as **grouping** or **bundling**.
- All links in the channel group are used for communication between the switches.
- The bandwidth between the connected switches is amplified. (This is similar to the analogy of the road system, where extra lanes of traffic are added to the existing infrastructure to increase traffic.) Ethernet provides full-duplex bandwidth.
- Fault tolerance: Automatic redundant paths between switches are established. If one link fails, communication will still occur over the other links in the EtherChannel group.

- STP: Spanning tree convergence times are reduced and readiness to transmit is enhanced. This occurs because the overall link (group) is viewed as one logical connection. If one physical link within the group channel goes down, this does not bring about a change in the overall topology and, consequently, does not require an STP recalculation.

The two main protocols for link aggregation are: **Port Aggregation Protocol (PAgP)** and **Link Aggregation Control Protocol (LACP)**. PAgP is a Cisco Systems proprietary protocol for link aggregation. LACP is based on the IEEE 802.3ad standard and is used to link Cisco devices with non-Cisco devices. Both protocols have their own unique commands and configuration settings, though the purposes, functions, and outcomes share commonalities.

Spanning tree protocol

At this point, we have discussed two of the main functions of a switch. These functions are learning and forwarding. Essentially, a switch in a network has the following three main functions:

- Address learning
- Forwarding decisions
- Loop avoidance

The third function brings us to the concept and application of the STP.

Note: Multilayer switches, operating at layers 2 and 3 of the OSI model have many more functions than a layer 2 switch.

STP's origins began when bridges were the primary means of data transmission at layer 2. Please note that the terminology in configuration commands and terms used in STP still include the word bridge or bridging, even though it is known that we are now working with layer 2 switches. Consequently, bridging loops refer to a loop in switching. A bridging loop is a process of forwarding a single frame around and between switches. Bridging loops form because parallel bridges are unconscious of each other. Bridging loops have a negative effect in that valuable bandwidth in the network is consumed as Ethernet frames do not have a **Time to Live** (**TTL**) field in the frame.

In routing technologies, TTL in data transmission occurs when a data packet at layer 3 routing expires after a specified time in transmission. As the packet traverses the routers, TTL values decrease in value by one. This mechanism of subtraction limits the lifespan or lifetime of the data packet in a computer or across a network or WAN. It prevents the data packet from circulating indefinitely around the network and limits potential issues with traffic congestion and other issues arising from circulating loops. Network administrators can manually set the value of TTL between 1 and 255 on devices, though it is worth noting that different operating systems and network processes have their preferred settings. When a packet is received by a router, the router subtracts 1 from the TTL count, and the TTL value continues to decrement at each HOP until the TTL expires, and the packet is then discarded. A common setting of TTL in networks is 128. However, as stated, operations at layer 2 and the mechanism of switch frames do not hold this ability. Thus, the potential of loops and the need for loop avoidance in switching.

STP was developed to mitigate bridging/switching loops in a network. To prevent switching loops, the IEEE 802.1d committee defined the STP originally developed by DEC. Various versions of STP have been developed. These include the following:

- IEEE 802.1D
- IEEE 802.1w
- IEEE 802.1s

With STP, one switch for each route is assigned as the designated bridge (via an election process). Only the designated bridge can forward packets. Redundant switches are assigned as backups.

With STP, the key is to elect a common reference point. This reference point is what is known as the root bridge. All other decisions are made from the perspective of the root bridge, such as decisions relating to determining root ports, designated ports, and blocking ports. The switch with the lowest **bridge ID** (**BID**) is elected the root bridge (or MAC address). The root bridge is determined by the switch with the lowest bridge ID:

- The bridge ID is composed of two parts: a bridge priority number and the MAC address allocated to the switch.

- The default priority number for all switches is 32,768. This means the switch with the lowest MAC address becomes the root bridge unless you customize the priority values.

- You can manually configure the priority number to force a specific switch to become the root switch.

A designated bridge is any other device that participates in forwarding packets through the network. All redundant devices are classified as backup bridges. Ports on the switches in an STP configuration have different port states and roles. These port states are listening, learning, forwarding, blocking, or disabled.

In *Figure 10.7*, a looped topology is contrasted with a loop-free configuration. The process is achieved by blocking specific ports. The ports marked in orange on the left side of the figure have been blocked to achieve the loop-free topology, which is displayed on the right side.

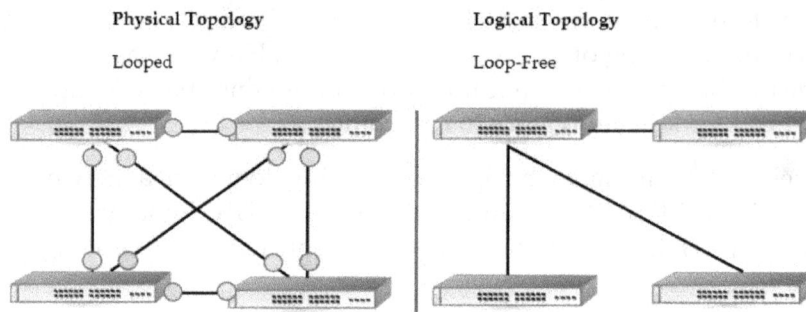

Figure 10.7: Looped vs. loop-free topology

In brief:

- STP is enabled by default on all Cisco switches.

- Ports in a forwarding state send and receive frames and act as normal switch interfaces. In *Figure 10.7*, these ports are circled in green. Ports in the blocking state do not process any frames except for STP messages and do not learn MAC addresses. In *Figure 10.7*, these ports are shown circled in orange.

- As the number of switches scales up in number, the number of ports needing to be blocked will also grow, but the fundamentals of the procedure and protocol remain the same. Therefore, scaling networks are handled more efficiently, and networks can expand to more complex designs than the design and topology depicted in *Figure 10.7*.

Other STP considerations

STP left to itself works fine but may converge to an unanticipated topology. This is why STP optimization features, such as Root Guard, BPDU Guard, and UDLD were developed to protect the integrity of the switched network further.

When topology changes occur, the reconvergence times for STP are undesirable. This is why optimization features such as UplinkFast, Portfast, and BackboneFast were developed as Cisco proprietary extensions to accelerate convergence and reconvergence processes.

Address resolution protocol

In Ethernet networks, ARP caches are kept on all operating systems. Every time a device requests a MAC address to send data to another device connected to the LAN, the device looks and verifies its ARP cache to see if the IP-to-MAC-address connection has already been established and entered into the cache. If the MAC address being sought exists, then a new request becomes unnecessary. However, if the translation/mapping has not yet been carried out, then the request for network addresses is sent, and the ARP process is performed.

ARP is covered in more detail in *Chapter 5, Ports and Protocols*. In terms of switching protocols, ARP functions at layer 2 of the OSI model and supports switches in their ability to learn and forward frames. To align ARP with switching functionality and handling frame transmission, we know that:

- It is not always possible for a source device to know the physical address of a destination device.

- ARP provides a service of matching or mapping an IP address to a MAC address.

- ARP broadcasts a request for the MAC address of a device with a particular IP address, and that device responds by sending back its MAC address.

- This allows the source device to send to a specific MAC address without having to broadcast all messages (and thus, offset slowing down the network).

This process is illustrated in *Figure 10.8*. In this example, the sending host broadcasts a request for the MAC address corresponding with a specific IP address **192.168.2.13**. Every device on the network segment attached to the switch will see the frame. The host device **192.168.2.13** responds by sending back its MAC address.

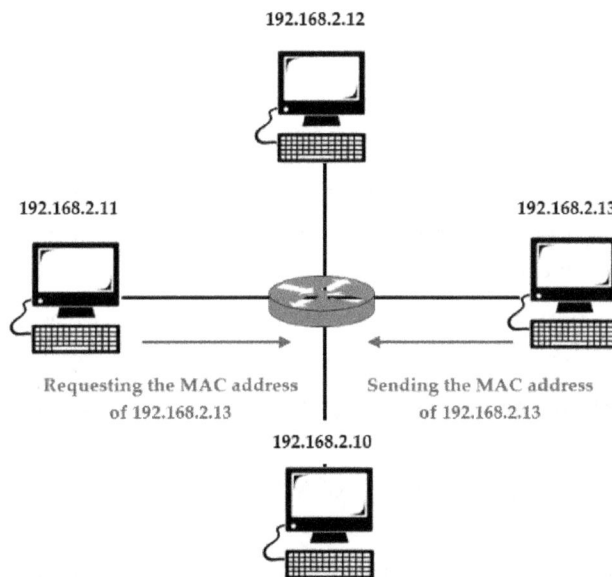

Figure 10.8: The ARP process

ARP is necessary because the layer 3 address (IP address) of the host or computer connected to the network needs to be translated to a hardware address (MAC address) for effective data transmission. Without this protocol, a host or end device would not be able to figure out the hardware address of another host on the network segment. The LAN keeps a table or directory that maps IP addresses to MAC addresses of the different devices in the LAN, including both endpoints and routers on that network.

Conclusion

In this chapter, you learned to identify and explain switching protocols and how they are implemented on a network. You learned to comprehend the purpose of VLANs and how they function to streamline traffic. You understood how they improve a network's performance and appreciate how segmenting networks enhances security. You should now be able to comprehend port security, link aggregation, STP, and ARP. After reading this chapter, you should be able to apply this knowledge when working on network design and configuring devices at layer 2 of the OSI model.

In the upcoming chapter, we will explore routing protocols and go deeper into the operations of layer 3 routing technologies. It will expand on layer 2 functionality and transmission of frames and move us into the process of routing and the subsequent transmission of data packets.

Points to remember

These points are crucial for understanding the fundamental operations and protocols involved in layer 2 switching.

- **Ethernet**: The primary layer 2 protocol, ensuring reliable data transmission within LANs.

- **MAC address**: A unique identifier for network interfaces, facilitating communication on the physical network segment.

- **VLANs**: Enable network segmentation within a switch, enhancing security and reducing broadcast domains.

- **STP**: Prevents network loops by establishing a loop-free logical topology for Ethernet networks.

- **Link aggregation**: Combines multiple network connections to boost throughput and provide redundancy.

- **Port security**: Restricts the number of MAC addresses on a switch port to improve security.

- **QoS**: Manages network traffic to prioritize critical applications and ensure their performance.

- **FDB**: Maintains a table of MAC addresses and their associated switch ports for efficient data forwarding.

- **Frame types**: Includes unicast, multicast, and broadcast frames, each serving different communication purposes within the network.

- **Error detection and correction**: Ensures data integrity by identifying and correcting errors in transmitted frames.

- The content of this chapter is mapped to *Domain 2: Network Implementations*. Given a scenario, configure switching technologies and features.

Key terms

- **Flow control**: Part of TCP is to ensure the receiver is not inundated with or overwhelmed by the speed and transmission of data. An aspect of the protocol is to regulate and synchronize transmission so that two workstations or hosts of varying speeds work more beneficially in a communication session with each other. It ensures that a fast sender does not overwhelm a slower receiver.

- **Jumbo frames**: The Ethernet standard IEEE 802.3d sets the frame size as 1,500 bytes. Anything more than this limit is called a jumbo frame.

- **Port mirroring**: This is configured on a network switch to reserve a port and then sends a mirrored copy of anything passing through the reserved switch port (or an entire VLAN) to a network monitoring connection on another switch port.

- **Neighbor Discovery Protocol (NDP)**: NDP is a protocol and method for gathering data and statistics from connected devices. The information gathered includes IPv6-related DNS, gateway configurations, the configuration of local devices, and connections on the network.

- **Link Layer Discovery Protocol (LLDP)**: A vendor-neutral protocol for network device discovery and management.

- **Cisco Discovery Protocol (CDP)**: A Cisco-specific protocol for discovering and sharing information between directly connected Cisco devices.

Questions

1. What is the purpose of a VLAN?

2. What are the benefits of implementing VLANs?

3. Describe the following switching features: Port security, STP, link aggregation, and ARP.

Join our book's Discord space

Join the book's Discord Workspace for Latest updates, Offers, Tech happenings around the world, New Release and Sessions with the Authors:

https://discord.bpbonline.com

CHAPTER 11
Managing Routing Protocols

Introduction

In *Chapter 10, Managing Switching Protocols,* we discussed the functions, features, and protocols of switching at layer 2 of the OSI model. In this chapter, we examine layer 3 functionality and investigate data transmission and protocols associated with routing. In switching, we learned that the primary function of a switch is the learning and forwarding of traffic around a network. In the case of routing, the primary responsibility of a router is the routing of traffic between networks. These networks can be inside an organization, between cities, or across wide area networks and the internet. Think of this transmission process as if you were a traveler leaving your immediate location geographically. There are many ways to travel to destinations further afield than where you are situated currently, and you have the ability to cross over longer distances. You make choices as to how you will travel, which type of transport you will use to do so, and which pathway you will take to reach your destination optimally and cost-effectively. You do so because you are aware that there may be multiple pathways available to you. These decisions will provide you with your ultimate plan of action. With this analogy in mind, when we explore the functions and features of a router, we will identify similar decisions to be made by a router as it identifies the destination of data packets and subsequently, upon consultation with its routing table, decides the optimum way to reach these destinations.

The following figure illustrates a router with multiple pathways, highlighting its role in directing data packets efficiently across different network segments:

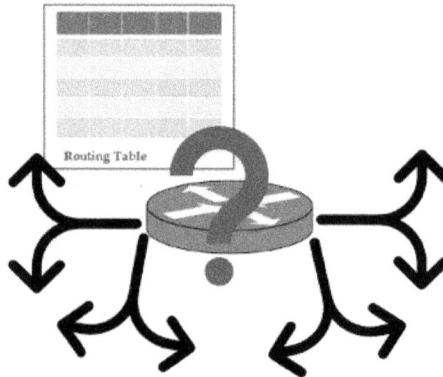

Figure 11.1: *Multiple pathways*

Structure

This chapter will explain the following topics:

- Primary functions and features of a router
- Static and dynamic routing
- Bandwidth management

Objectives

After reading this chapter, the reader will be able to understand the purpose and functionality of routing. They will appreciate the basic operations of a router as it consults its routing table and forwards traffic. The reader will be able to compare and contrast different routing protocols. They will be able to identify and distinguish between internal and external routing protocols, understand static and dynamic routing, and know the concepts of bandwidth management.

Primary functions and features of a router

The main purpose of a router is to connect multiple networks and forward packets from one network to the next. Routers make their primary forwarding decision at layer 3 of the OSI model, identified as the network layer. Remember that the network layer of the OSI model aligns with the internet layer of the TCP/IP model. However, router interfaces equally participate in layers 1, 2, and 3 of OSI. This occurs because layer 3 IP packets are encapsulated into a layer 2 data link frame and encoded into bits at layer 1. If you wish to revisit the process of encapsulation and decapsulation, it is detailed in *Chapter 1, OSI Model*.

Router interfaces may also participate in layer 2 protocols, such as with ARP, when an Ethernet interface on a router, connected to a LAN takes part in address resolution.

Router interfaces

A router can have serial interfaces to connect with other routers on a WAN link as well as Ethernet or Gigabit interfaces. This means that a router characteristically has multiple interfaces. Each interface on a router is a member or host on a different IPv4 and/or IPv6 network. The simplest way to consider this connectivity is that every router interface is (creates) a network.

The main interfaces on a router are as follows:

- **Ethernet interfaces (one or more)**: An Ethernet interface typically connects to a LAN.

- **Serial interfaces (one or more)**: A serial interface is used to connect the router to another router on a **point-to-point (P2P)** link, to a leased line, or to another WAN service or ISP.

- **An ISDN interface**: This interface connects routers to the ISDN network.

- **A console port (via a USB and/or serial connector)**: This port is used for administrative management purposes.

- AUX port.

In *Figure 11.2*, a Cisco router backplane is illustrated. This figure depicts some of the common interfaces to be found on a router. The router belongs to the Cisco 1941 series of routers.

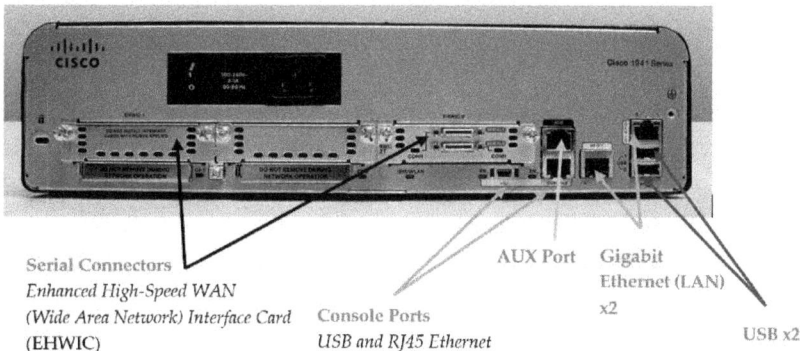

Figure 11.2: Router backplane

Additionally:

- The built-in USB ports support eToken devices and USB flash memory. The USB eToken device feature provides device authentication and secure configuration of Cisco routers.

- The USB flash feature offers discretionary secondary storage capability and an extra boot device.

- There are two CompactFlash memory slots available on this model, CF0 and CF1. These slots are used for high-speed storage.

- EHWIC 1 (on the left) supports a double-wide expansion card.

- EHWIC can natively support HWIC cards and **WAN interface cards** (**WICs**). Regarding voice technologies, EHWIC supports **voice interface cards** (**VICs**) as well as **voice/WAN interface cards** (**VWICs**).

- The AUX port is used for connecting to an external modem, providing dial-in access to a router.

Note: Router models and interfaces are quite varied in number and type. A network administrator needs to know the purpose of the router, what functions are expected from it, and how it is to fit into the organization's network in terms of network infrastructure and role before procurement of equipment or its deployment. Planning and research of all network devices is essential. Decisions to be made include budgeting and cost/cost-effectiveness.

Routing table

The routing table is a list of networks known by the router. A routing table is like a map. The router's decision-making capability will be based on its table/map. This section brings us back to the earlier analogy of a person traveling before they set off on their journey and the function of routing. If a person wishes to make good decisions about their impending journey and how best to reach their destination(s), they will or ought to go by the best map to be found with sharp and considered plotted out detail. After all, decisions made will be heavily influenced by the quality and detail of the map the individual is working from.

A router consults its routing table to make forwarding decisions in a similar way the switch consults its MAC address/CAM table. To visualize the idea of a routing table, here are the relevant codes for various types of network connections and the protocols associated with routing, as depicted on a Cisco router:

```
R3#show ip route
Codes: L - local, C - connected, S - static, R - RIP, M - mobile, B - BGP
       D - EIGRP, EX - EIGRP external, O - OSPF, IA - OSPF inter area
       N1 - OSPF NSSA external type 1, N2 - OSPF NSSA external type 2
       E1 - OSPF external type 1, E2 - OSPF external type 2, E - EGP
       i - IS-IS, L1 - IS-IS level-1, L2 - IS-IS level-2, ia - IS-IS inter area
       * - candidate default, U - per-user static route, o - ODR
       P - periodic downloaded static route
```

Figure 11.3: Routing table of codes

In *Figure 11.3*, **codes** are designated to local or connected routes. These networks are typically sitting at the other end of an Ethernet or serial connection **belonging** to the router itself, in other words, a directly connected LAN or WAN network with one side on the router's interface as a **local** network. Other networks are **remote** to the router, in that the distance is longer to reach these networks, or more importantly, the networks listed in the table are one or more **hand-off points** (**HOPs**) away as viewed from the router's perspective. In other words, the specified router in question does **not** have an interface *directly connected* to the LAN or WAN it intends to send a data packet to. From the viewpoint of a router, networks are either local or remote.

- **Local route interfaces** are added to the routing table when an interface is configured.

- **Directly connected interfaces** are added to the routing table when an interface is configured and active.

    Note: Interfaces can be up or down or administratively up or administratively down when manually configured. Interfaces can also be physically up and logically down if there is an error or problem in the logical protocol or if there are problems in the administrator's manual configuration of the router. They can also be physically down when a link/cable is broken or shut down for security reasons. By default, on a Cisco router, all interfaces are down until they are brought up by the administrator.

- **Static routes** are added when a route is manually configured by a network administrator and the exit interface is *up* and active.

- **Dynamic routing protocols** are added when protocols such as RIPv2, EIGRP, or OSPF are implemented, and networks are identified.

Figure 11.4 outlines dynamic routing protocols and distinguishes between **Interior Gateway Protocols (IGPs)** and **Exterior Gateway Protocols (EGPs)**:

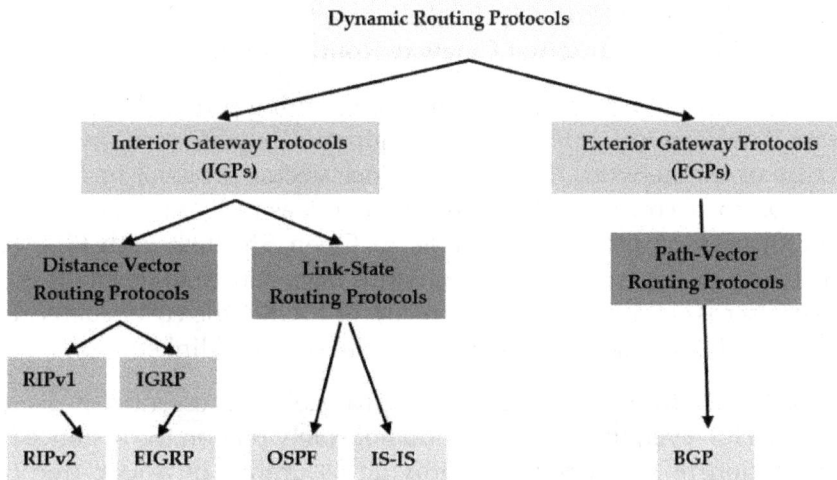

Figure 11.4: *Dynamic routing protocols*

The terms in *Figure 11.4* are defined as follows:

- **Interior gateway protocols**: Protocols used for transferring routing information between gateways, which typically belong to an **autonomous system (AS)**. When we refer to an AS, we are discussing the gateways on routers in a LAN, CAN, or MAN. The distinguishing aspect of an autonomous system is that the network is owned by a company or organization. The size of the network may vary from a small to medium corporate local area network to a network that spans buildings or campuses to those that traverse a city (IES). It is important to note that geographically dispersed networks may need to connect to each other through the cloud, but once you enter the interior of any network of the organization, that specific network is part of the AS.

- **Exterior gateway protocols**: These protocols transfer and exchange routing information between autonomous systems. These protocols are typically implemented by ISPs, who sit at the boundaries and borders of autonomous systems and interior protocols and handle traffic and routing information through routers in and around the cloud.

- **Distance vector routing protocols**: These protocols measure the distance from the router to all other routers configured as part of the protocol. The best path to any given destination is based on the distance. Each individual router keeps a distance vector table. This table holds the distance between itself and all possible destination devices. Distances are constructed on a chosen metric. The most common metric used is HOPs and the distance with the shortest HOP to the destination will be the chosen pathway. The algorithms used in the protocol are computed using information from the neighbors' distance vector tables and a map is built of routes and distances. The distance vector calculation is based on minimizing the cost to each destination in the topology. Some examples of Distance Vector Routing Protocols are Routing Information Protocol (v1 or v2), Cisco's **Internet Gateway Routing Protocol (IGRP)**, and Cisco's **Enhanced Internet Gateway Routing Protocol (EIGRP)**.

- **Link-state routing protocols**: The link-state routing protocols generate a complete picture of the network topology. Consequently, they are more aware of the entire structure of the network than any distance vector protocol is. *Link state* implies that the protocol considers the status of the link as well as its capacity or perceived quality of performance. For example, in **Open Shortest Path First (OSPF)**, the cost is based on the cumulative bandwidth from source to destination (that is, the total sum across all links to be traversed). In EIGRP, the cost is determined by the bandwidth, delay, load, and reliability of the specified links.

- **Path vector routing protocols**: These protocols are essentially distance vector protocols. However, these protocols do not solely rely on the distance from source to destination of given paths to provide assurance of a loop-free path. These protocols analyze the path itself to make forwarding decisions subsequently. **Border Gateway Protocol (BGP)** is an example of a Path Vector Routing Protocol.

Note: A metric is a value used to measure the distance to a given network. The best path to a network is the path with the lowest metric. Cost refers to the arbitrary metric values that are assigned to links and/or manually configured or tweaked by the network administrator to impact a router's decisions on the best path.

Interconnecting networks

When we consider the interconnection of networks, we are discussing the interrelationship between anything from a home network with a router to the internet as the largest WAN there is, the network of all networks. Routers connect and interconnect networks. To clarify the concept of internal links and infrastructure and compare these with the external links, we will explore a simple LAN.

In *Figure 11.5*, a LAN in the building is illustrated. The Ethernet interface G0/0 is the default gateway for the local area network. The router links to the company switch, providing access to host devices in the network. The serial interface S0/0 is the company's external link to the cloud. In other words, at the other side of the S0/0's interface, there is an interface or router belonging to the company's ISP.

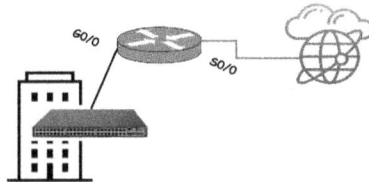

Figure 11.5: LAN to WAN connection

Now, let us scale up the model. In *Figure 11.6*, the network topology and infrastructure are more complex. We are shown two autonomous systems—networks owned by a larger organization. Interior Gateway Protocols are configured to handle and exchange router information inside each AS. Externally, there are two routers interlinked through the cloud, typically through an ISP. Most likely, the EGP is Border Gateway Protocol:

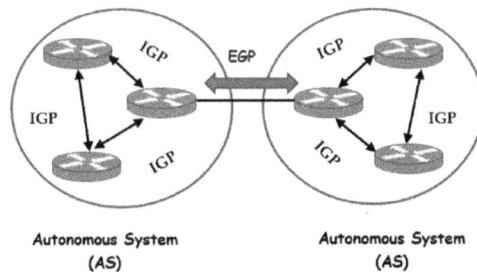

Figure 11.6: IGP vs. EGP

This AS on the left is connected to only one other AS. Internet routing occurs across autonomous systems, routing information between autonomous systems.

In *Table 11.1*, the attributes and factors associated with routing are outlined:

Attribute	Description
Bandwidth	Network bandwidth measures the capacity of a link. If bandwidth is an aspect of the cost, a link with a lower capacity link will have a higher cost than a link with a high bandwidth link. For example, Ethernet Gigabit would have a lower cost than Fast Ethernet due to its higher bandwidth and ability to handle packets at greater speeds.
Throughput	Bandwidth is one thing and determines the link's capacity. But other factors affect how much data actually gets through routers in a given amount of time. This actuality is known as throughput. Although the advertised bandwidth is the maximum capacity of a link, its actual throughput will be less due to latency and other network overhead. If used in the cost calculation, larger throughput will contribute to a lower cost.
Goodput	On top of the term throughput, some technicians refer to Goodput. Goodput relates to the quality of the data transmitted. It is the number of useful information bits delivered by the network to a specific destination per unit of time. Though it is not a means of measuring cost, it is a term worth being aware of, as it relates to data transmission.
Hop count	The distance between networks can be measured in hop counts. The hop count is the total number of network intermediary devices such as routers through which data packets must pass as they are transmitted between the source and destination networks. It can also be the number of times a router forwards an IP packet from one network to another network. For a directly connected link, the hop count will be zero since the network is owned by the router and the gateway exists on the router's interface.
Link utilization	Link utilization is the percentage of a network's bandwidth that is currently being consumed by network traffic. If utilization is used as a factor of routing, the cost will be less for links with low utilization and not suffering from traffic congestion.
Load	Load refers to the amount of computational work or calculations a router performs and processes. If the load is a factor in the cost, links for routers that are performing under a heavy load will have a higher cost. We sometimes relate this term to overhead.
Reliability	Reliability is measured by how often the path is down. If it is used in cost calculations, a highly reliable path will have a lower cost simply because the path will be deemed to be more guaranteed to function in a dependable manner than one that is less reliable.
MTU	The **maximum transmission unit** (**MTU**) setting on a router governs the maximum payload size for a frame. This attribute is not usually included in a metric. However, it is sometimes used in computations when two links or paths have equal costs. It is called in and operates as a tiebreaker.
Packet loss	At times, packets transmitted fail to reach their intended destination. Packet loss happens when IP data packets do not arrive since routers may drop packets for numerous reasons, such as traffic congestion, a failed link or simply aging or failing hardware components. If packet loss is used in calculating cost, a link that experiences greater packet loss will have a higher cost than one that is handling the transmission of packets better.
Latency	Latency is another word for delay or a wait state. Latency is the delay in transmissions over the path. If latency is used in the cost, a path with higher latency will have a higher cost, essentially because you are waiting longer for successful packet transmission.

Table 11.1: Routing attributes and features

Static and dynamic routing

Local route interfaces and directly connected interfaces are added to the routing table when an interface is configured and active. Simply put, the router **knows** these networks as they *belong* to the router via the router's interfaces. Essentially a router knows or **learns** networks. To put it another way, a routing table consists of what the router **knows** and what it **learns**.

A router can learn about remote networks in one of the following two ways:

- **Manually**: Network administrators manually add remote networks into the routing table using static routes.

- **Dynamically**: Remote routes are automatically learned using a dynamic routing protocol.

Static routes

With static routing, you are basically telling your router to send traffic with a destination IP address to a router with an IP address of X.X.X.X. When a packet comes into the router and is ready to be routed, the destination IP address is looked up in the routing table, and the data packets are forwarded to the specified network via the relevant interface.

Static routes are often used:

- To support a small network with less than five routers that do not intend to scale or expand on its existing topology.

- In a network where all routers link back to a single router (that is, in a hub-and-spoke topology).

- Under certain time constraints. For example, when you need to create a route from one router to another device quickly.

- To link and connect to a particular network.

- To provide a gateway of last resort for a stub network.

- To reduce the number of routes advertised by summarizing several contiguous networks as one static route.

- To create a backup route in case a primary route link fails.

Static routes break down into standard static routes, default static routes, summary static routes, and floating static routes.

Benefits of static routing

If you have a small network, configuring static routes can be a once-off, relatively easy process. Static routes are not advertised over the network, resulting in better security.

In dynamic routing protocols, the routers will continually send messages to each other to keep the table and map of the network current. This means data transmitted (for example, via keep-alive messages) includes information about network routes, which is advertised frequently. Moreover, the router does not learn inaccurate or insecure routes and inadvertently adds this vulnerability to the routing table.

Static routes use less bandwidth than dynamic routing protocols. In terms of processing power, no CPU cycles are used to calculate and communicate routes or implement algorithms since the static network is a constant entry in the routing table. In this way, there is no overhead when using static routes. Compared with dynamic routing protocols, static routes do not require the same significant resources, such as router hardware and components.

The path a static route uses to send data is known. A router will not need to determine the best path continually.

Drawbacks and limitations of static routing

Unfortunately, static routes do not scale well as your network grows. A common feature of a network is scalability and room for growth, and most networks tend to grow organically over time. The network administrator must be aware of the importance of configuring error-free routes. If initial errors are made in the entries manually input into the table, these errors cause negative impacts and barriers in data packet transmission. When changes occur in the network infrastructure, manual administration is required. This requirement can complicate the flexibility of network design and maintenance. The administrator must know the company's network in its entirety. There is no scope here for misinterpretation of connections, devices, and links. In summary, static routing can be, at times, overwhelming and cumbersome for the network administrator and be more time-consuming than implementing a dynamic routing protocol.

Here is an example of a static and default route:

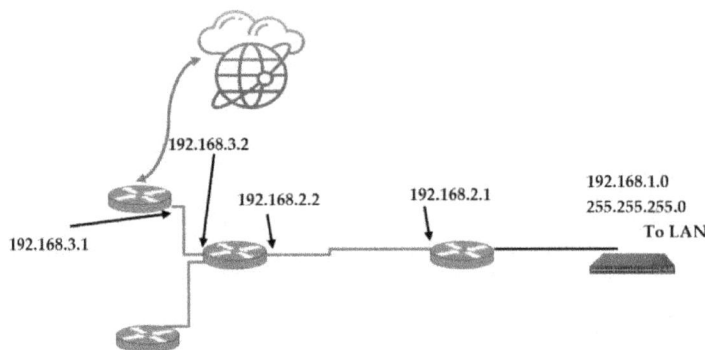

```
ip route 192.168.1.0 255.255.255.0 192.168.2.1 – STATIC
ip route 0.0.0.0 0.0.0.0 192.168.3.1 - DEFAULT
```

Figure 11.7: Static/default route example

Here are the steps to show how data travels across this network.

1. To reach the destination network 192.168.1.0 with a subnet mask of 255.255.255.0, packets should be sent to the next hop address, 192.168.1.0.

2. This entry is static and logical because there is only one pathway to this network, which is via the serial link between 192.168.2.1 and 192.168.2.2.

3. To reach any destination network via the Internet, packets should be sent through the exit interface 192.158.3.1. The address that matches all networks is the "any any" address, which is 0.0.0.0/0.

4. This entry is a default static route and is logical because it will capture all potential routes and destinations via the link and default gateway to the cloud. The router has an interface connected to the cloud.

Dynamic routes

Dynamic routing protocols are used by routers to automatically learn about remote networks from other routers. Their purpose includes the discovery of remote networks, maintaining up-to-date routing information and routing tables, and choosing the best path to destination networks. These protocols hold the ability to find a new best path if the current path is no longer available and if there are any topology changes or errors on the network.

Routing Information Protocol

As defined by *Techopedia*, **Routing Information Protocol** (**RIP**) is a dynamic protocol used to find the best route or path from end-to-end (source to destination) over a network by using a routing metric/hop count algorithm. This algorithm determines the shortest path from the source to the destination, which allows the data to be delivered at high speed in the shortest time. RIP is a dynamic routing protocol that suits very simple topologies and network infrastructures. There are three versions of RIP: RIPv1, RIPv2, and RIPng, which is designed for IPv6 applications. *Table 11.2* compares the versions of RIP and some of the features of this protocol:

RIPv1	RIPv2	RIPng
Sends update as broadcast	Sends update as multicast	Sends update as multicast
Broadcast at 255.255.255.255	Multicast at 224.0.0.9	Multicast at FF02::9 (RIPng can only run on IPv6 networks)
Does not support the authentication of updated messages	Supports authentication of RIPv2 update messages	–
Classful routing protocol	Classless protocol updated supports classful	Classless updates are sent

Table 11.2: Routing information protocol

> Note: RIPv1 does not send information about subnet masks in its routing table. It typically uses the structures of classful addressing as Classes A, B, and C, for example, so the subnet masks are implicit. It is referred to as Classful Routing Protocol. RIPv2 sends information about subnet masks and exchanges routing information to other routers in its routing updates. It is referred to as Classless Routing Protocol.

RIPv1 is the first-generation legacy protocol. RIPv2 is a simple distance vector routing protocol. RIPv1 and IGRP were created when network addresses were allocated based on classes (Classes A, B, or C). As such, they do not support **Variable Length Subnet Masking** (**VLSM**) or classless addressing (CIDR), rendering the protocols unusable in modern networking designs.

Interior Gateway Routing Protocol

IGRP is a Cisco proprietary protocol. It is a distance vector routing protocol and is used to exchange routing information within a host network. The host network may be a corporate LAN or organizational network. This protocol handles the flow of routing information within the connected routers in the autonomous system or corporate network. The protocol guarantees that every router has routing tables updated with the best available path for potential destinations. IGRP also mitigates against routing loops by constantly updating itself with the changes occurring over the network, should a path change, or a link go down, for example. In this way, the protocol has strategies for managing errors.

EIGRP advances and enhances the principles and mechanisms of IGRP. IGRP is a first-generation Cisco proprietary protocol, which is now obsolete.

EIGRP is the advanced version of distance vector routing and maintains its viability in routing. EIGRP is a hybrid routing protocol developed by Cisco for routing within an AS. EIGRP uses a composite number for the metric, which indicates bandwidth and delay for a link. The higher the bandwidth, the lower the metric.

IGRP and EIGRP use the **Diffusing Update Algorithm** (**DUAL**) routing algorithm, as created and developed by Cisco.

Open Shortest Pathway First

OSPF is a link-state protocol. An OSPF link is an interface on a router. Information about the state of the links is known as link states. OSPF uses the **Shortest Path First** (**SPF**) network communication algorithm (Dijkstra's algorithm) to calculate the shortest connection path between the known devices in the OSPF topology. By using Dijkstra's algorithm, routers can calculate the best path route to given destinations. The algorithm uses the accumulated costs along each path, from source to destination, to determine the total cost of a given route.

OSPFv2 is the version of OSPF for IPv4 networks. OSPFv3 is the version of OSPF for IPv6 networks. In OSPF, the pieces of information shared are known as **link state advertisements**

(**LSAs**). By exchanging their LSAs with each other, all routers in the OSPF topology can build their link state databases and a real-time map of the entire network. Think of this map like your typical GPS or navigation system. Your GPS reads the current state of all routes to your intended destination. If there is an accident on a route, roadworks, or traffic congestion, your GPS will interpret the status of the links and routes and reroute you to the shortest pathway and best pathway to your destination. This is the primary advantage of a link-state routing protocol, as it maintains its map in accordance with real-time events. In OSPF, we can have single-area OSPF or multi-area OSPF. Larger networks can be divided to reduce router processing and RAM overhead. Consequently, in multi-area OSPF, a large OSPF area is divided into smaller areas. This saves wear and tear on hardware components and time in processing complex calculations with potential replication of router information or LSAs. OSPF uses relative link cost for the metric. As explained, OSPF divides a large network into areas. Each AS requires an area 0 that identifies the network backbone. All areas are connected to area 0, either directly or indirectly through another area. In multi-area OSPF, routes between areas must pass through area 0. Here is an example of an OSPF topology:

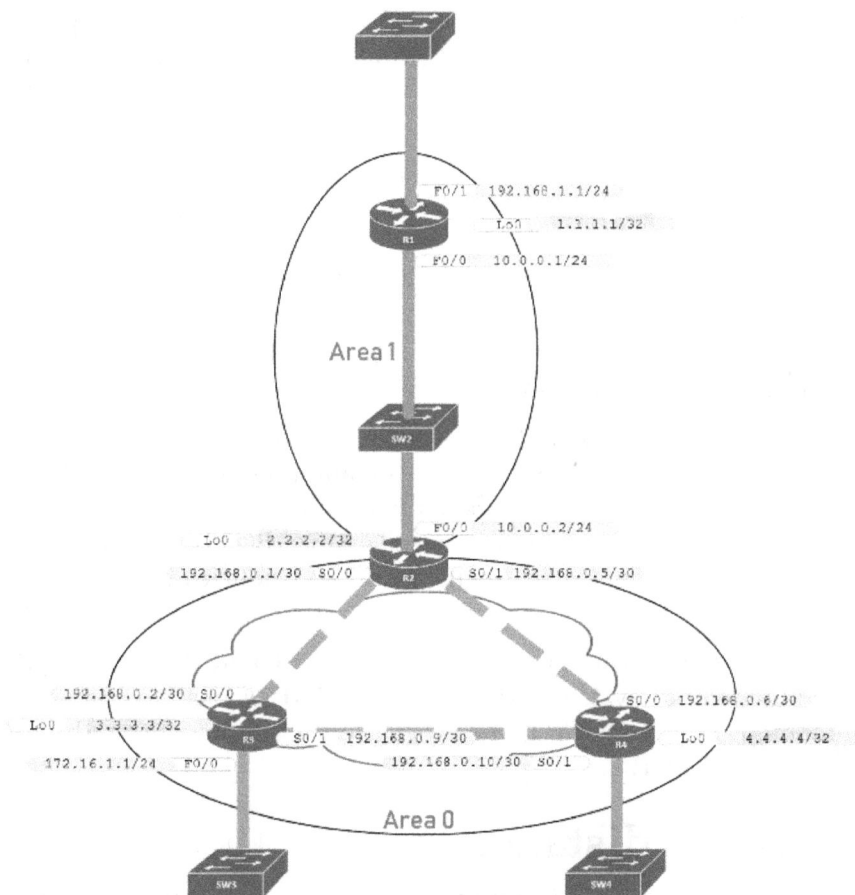

Figure 11.8: OSPF topology

Internal routers share routes within an area; *area border routers* share routes between areas; *autonomous system boundary routers* share routes outside of the AS. This system manages and controls the flow of traffic inside and outside the AS.

A router is the boundary between one area and another area.

By using this structure and network design to designate specific roles and responsibilities for participating routers, the network administrator controls and manages the OSPF topology. This makes the overall system design and routing protocol streamlined, centralized (to area 0), and efficient.

Note: In link-state routing protocols, to eliminate looping, each router forwards the packet to every neighbor except the one it received the packet from. A smart flooding algorithm prevents looping when there are circular routing paths.

Intermediate System to Intermediate System

Intermediate System to Intermediate System (IS-IS) is a dynamic routing protocol intended to exchange routing information efficiently within a computer network configuration. This protocol, like other routing protocols, accomplishes this by determining the best route for data as it travels through a packet-switching network. IS-IS uses relative link cost for the metric.

IS-IS is a classless protocol supporting VLSM and CIDR. The original IS-IS protocol was not used for routing IP packets, but IP routing support is now integrated into the protocol. Like OSPF, IS-IS divides a large network into areas. However, there is no area 0 requirement in the protocol and IS-IS offers greater flexibility for creating and connecting areas than OSPF offers.

Border Gateway Protocol

As defined by *Techopedia*, BGP is a routing protocol used to transfer data and information between different host gateways, the Internet, or autonomous systems. BGP is a **Path Vector Protocol (PVP)**, which maintains paths to different hosts, networks, and gateway routers and determines the routing decision based on that. BGP is an EGP used for routing between autonomous systems. It uses paths, rules, and policies instead of a metric for making routing decisions.

BGP is also a classless protocol supporting VLSM and CIDR. **Internal BGP (iBGP)** is used within an autonomous system. **External BGP (eBGP)** is used to manage traffic flow between autonomous systems. BGP is the official routing protocol used by the internet, extending and replacing EGP.

Administrative distance

In *Figure 11.3*, we explored the codes used in a routing table. It is important to remember that routers may be using more than one type of routing protocol. Therefore, when more than one protocol is enabled on a router, each protocol is given an **administrative distance** (**AD**). Each dynamic routing protocol has a unique administrative value. The same goes for static routes and directly connected networks. The lower AD is the preferred route. AD is the first criterion that a router uses in its discovery of the best path. When the best path is determined, protocols with a lower AD are chosen over those with a higher AD. Most routers have a default AD assigned to each routing protocol. *Table 11.3* outlines the administrative values allocated to each routing protocol:

Source of the route	Default administrative distance
Connected interface or static route to an interface	0
Static route to an IP address	1
EIGRP summary	5
BGP external	20
EIGRP internal	90
IGRP	100
OSPF	110
IS-IS	115
RIP	120
EIGRP external	170
BGP internal	200
Unknown source	255

Table 11.3: Administrative distance values

Benefits of dynamic routing

Maintaining static-only routing in a large network with multiple routers would be very tough and complex, especially when there are multiple network paths that an IP packet can take to get to its destination. With dynamic routing, routers can dynamically learn about networks by sharing routing information with other routers and exchanging network changes as they occur.

Compared with static routing, dynamic routing is scalable. Dynamic routing protocols have the ability to automatically adapt to topology changes or errors on the network. In this way, they offer flexibility and potentially a smooth flow in the transmission of data packets with optimal configuration.

Drawbacks and limitations of dynamic routing

Dynamic routing protocols are heavy on CPU and memory, and they require additional resources in terms of link bandwidth. Remember that the router is constantly learning about routes and best paths, so holding this changing data in RAM while processing algorithms requires quality router hardware components combined with an administrator's vigilant observation of their lifespan. With static routing and directly connected interfaces, the router knows the networks and does not have to process the status of the networks continually.

As the current topology changes, so does the best path; a network administrator needs to be extremely aware of the configurations they make and any changes occurring on the network or between autonomous systems. True to say, the company is in control of the AS, and this brings with it advantages. The company or organization owns and controls the routers and determines where the routers are located.

The administrator needs to understand the logical and the physical topology, the network devices and interfaces that connect the routers to the network, and which interior routing protocols are enabled. However, this advantage brings responsibility over what is controlled. It necessitates vigilance and acute awareness, especially if the protocol(s) in use is complex and the exchange of router information occurs across different autonomous systems. This adds the weight of security issues and implications of what happens to data as it is transferred across routers and over links to other networks.

Bandwidth management

Bandwidth management measures, monitors, and controls the amount of data packets traveling on a link. The objective is to optimize the network in terms of data flow and network performance. There are many third-party providers of this type of management software, for example, SolarWinds, ManageEngine, and NetFlow Analyzer (and other packet sniffing software).

A few examples of concepts relating to ensuring bandwidth management are congestion avoidance, bandwidth reservation protocols, algorithm scheduling, and categorization or classification of traffic.

Conclusion

In this chapter, we explored the functions and features of a router, how the router interconnects networks, and how it uses routing protocols to send and receive data packets. The reader should now be able to describe the functions of a router and articulate how a router operates at layer 3 of the OSI model. The difference between IGP and EGP was established and explained. You should be able to list all the common protocols used in routing and differentiate between them. Static and dynamic routing protocols were described and clarified. You should be able to consider and evaluate when static or dynamic routing is most fitted for a given networking scenario and infrastructure. This understanding underpins an ability to apply knowledge and configure protocols on a layer 3 device.

In the upcoming chapter, we will cover the concept of *Installing and Configuring Wireless Technologies*. Wireless networks are now commonplace in many organizations and social and public spaces. Knowing how to install and configure a wireless device with appropriate settings with awareness of security is fundamental to network administration.

Points to remember

The reader should now understand:

- Static routing
- Dynamic routing
  - o Border Gateway Protocol
  - o Enhanced Interior Gateway Routing Protocol
  - o Open Shortest Path First
- Route selection
  - o Administrative distance
  - o Prefix length
  - o Metric
- Address translation
  - o **Network address translation (NAT)**
  - o **Port address translation (PAT)**
- **First Hop Redundancy Protocol (FHRP)**
- **Virtual IP (VIP)**
- Subinterfaces
- The content of this chapter is mapped to *Domain 2: Network Implementations. Explain characteristics of routing technologies.*

Key terms

- **Contiguous networks**: The word contiguous is defined as *sharing a common border; touching*. Therefore, when we speak of contiguous networks, we are referring to networks that can be logically grouped and share a similar classful IP addressing scheme. Here is a list of contiguous networks. These networks can be summarized in a routing table and presented as a single entry:
  - o 192.168.0.0/26
  - o 192.168.0.64/26
  - o 192.168.0.128/26
  - o 192.168.0.192/26

The networks listed as contiguous networks *share a common border,* so when data packets are transmitted, they do not pass through networks of a different class or subnet to reach each other.

- **Discontiguous network**: A discontiguous network occurs when packets sent between at least one subnet must pass through subnets of a completely different network.

- **Stub network**: A stub network is a LAN that does not interconnect to outside, external networks and where data packets transmit internally, or they are dead-end LANs that know of only one network exit or exit interface.

- **Standard static routes**: These routes are made up of a destination network address or host, a subnet mask, and the IP address of the next-hop IP address.

- **Default static routes**: These routes match all packets. They use the *any any* IP address. A default static route is simply a static route with 0.0.0.0/0 as the destination IPv4 address.

- **Summary static routes**: These routes use a single summary route to represent multiple networks. The networks can be summarized in the routing table.

- **Floating static routes**: These routes are used for redundancy and backup. They provide a backup path to a primary static or dynamic route, should a link go down or fail.

Questions

1. What are the primary functions and features of a router?
2. Describe static routing. Give examples.
3. Describe dynamic routing. Give examples.
4. Outline what is meant by metrics and cost.

Join our book's Discord space

Join the book's Discord Workspace for Latest updates, Offers, Tech happenings around the world, New Release and Sessions with the Authors:

https://discord.bpbonline.com

CHAPTER 12

Installing and Configuring Wireless Technologies

Introduction

*In many parts of the world, being able to download information
on a smartphone, tablet, or laptop in a few seconds is the norm. In Silicon Valley,
wireless high-speed Internet connections are more ubiquitous than Starbucks.*

- Tae Yoo, Silicon Valley Senior VP

Corporate Affairs, Cisco

Over the past few decades, the nature of work has transformed significantly. Business and productivity are no longer confined to fixed locations or specific time periods. We now work and learn in various spaces, both offline and online, often moving seamlessly across the globe. In this technological age, individuals and organizations expect constant connectivity, whether at the office, airport, library, restaurant, or home. Users of computer networks expect to roam wirelessly and participate in various online communication systems without losing connection. Wireless technologies are pervasive, offering connectivity in different ranges and environments.

Wireless technologies are classified by size and geographical coverage:

- **Wireless personal area network (WPAN):** Bluetooth operates within approximately 30 feet (10 meters).

- **Wireless LAN (WLAN)**: Functions up to 150 feet (46 meters) indoors and 300 feet (92 meters) outdoors.

- **Wi-Fi**: An IEEE 802.11 standard providing network access up to 0.18 miles (300 meters).

- **WiMAX**: Based on IEEE 802.16, delivering high-speed Internet up to 50 kilometers (30 miles).

- **Wireless wide area network (WWAN)**: Spans miles, depending on the media or fiber used.

- **Satellite broadband**: Uses LEO or geostationary satellites for remote network access.

- **Cellular broadband**: Provides mobile broadband connectivity through standardized, licensed transmissions.

The suitability of any wireless technology solution depends on its purpose and required functions.

Structure

This chapter will explain the following topics:

- Benefits of wireless technologies
- Wireless standards
- Channels and frequency bands
- Configuring a SOHO router

Objectives

By the end of this chapter, the reader will be able to identify and differentiate between the different IEEE 802.11 wireless standards. They should be able to estimate and match a specific wireless configuration to the requirements of an individual or enterprise. The reader will be able to compare and contrast different means and mechanisms of using antennas for the best signaling and quality connections. They should be able to apply this knowledge in a practical way and navigate a router to configure the optimum settings for effective connections to the router and AP. They will be able to understand the setup procedures for a SOHO router and recognize the commonalities between all routers and access points.

Benefits of wireless technologies

There are many benefits of wireless technologies. Some of the attractions and benefits include the following:

- **Enhanced connectivity**: As the name *wireless* states, we do not need to carry cables or bulky adapters with us when in our office networks. This ability provides us with ease of movement and adaptability in spaces where we wish to work and connect. This means as mobile users we are rarely *out of touch*.

- **Enhanced efficiency**: These fast and higher-speed connections increase efficiency. Data transmission can be fast and effective. Wireless communications technology is a robust, practicable voice, and data transport mechanism.

- **Roaming profiles**: Our unique login to networks supports mobility (via roaming profiles). No longer do we need to be tied to a specific workstation or PC with the advancements made with both hardware and application software. Technology travels with us as we roam.

- **Cost effectiveness**: Wireless technologies can be cost-effective in terms of installation and maintenance as costs can be reduced with wireless over wired implementations.

Wireless standards

To get a firm mental grasp on wireless concepts and standards, it is beneficial to see the timeline of the standards to be covered. Then we can make our own personal or historical associations of what was happening in technology at that time, irrespective of whether we lived through the particular time period personally or heard about it from others. In this way, we gain the perspective of change.

Table 12.1 outlines the year-specific **Institute of Electrical and Electronics Engineers** (**IEEE**) standards were released:

IEEE 802.11 Standards timeline	
1997	802.11
1999	802.11b
1999	802.11a
2003	802.11g
2009	802.11n
2013	802.11ac
2018	802.11ad
2019	802.11ax

Table 12.1: IEEE 802.11 Standards Timeline

The following table describes the various wireless standards and their specifications:

Specifica-tion	IEEE 802.11 Standards and characteristics						
	802.11a	802.11b	802.11g	802.11n	802.11ac	802.11ad	802.11.ax
Frequency	5 GHz (U-NII)	2.4 GHz (ISM)	2.4 GHz (ISM)	2.4 GHz (ISM) or 5 GHz (U-NII)	5 GHz (U-NII)	2.4 GHz, 5 GHz and 60GHz	2.4 GHz and 5 GHz
Maximum speed	54 Mbps	11 Mbps	54 Mbps	600 Mbps	1.3 Gbps	7 Gbps	1.2Gbps Single stream 9.6Gbps (theoretical)
Maximum distance	100 ft.	150 ft.	150 ft.	300 ft.	150 ft.	35 m/115 ft—indoors	Better than AC
Channels (Non-over-lapped)	23 (12)	11 (3)	11 (3)	2.4 GHz: 11 (3 or 1) 5 GHz: 23 (12 or 6)	Depends on configuration	20 MHz channels, 40 MHz channels, 80 MHz channels, and has optional support for 160 MHz channels	20, 40, 80, 80+80, 160 MHz
Modulation technique	OFDM	DSSS, CCK, DQPSK, DBPSK	DSSS (and others) at lower data rates OFDM, QPSK, BPSK at higher data rates	OFDM (and others depending on implementation)	OFDM	Multi-user MIMO	(OFDM) (OFD-MA)
Backwards compatibility	N/A	None	802.11b	802.11a/b/g, depending on the implementation	802.11b/g/n	802.11b /g/n/ac	802.11b /g/n/ac

Table 12.2: *IEE 802.11 standards*

Throughout the chapter, these wireless characteristics will be further explained.

Channels and frequency bands

To understand channels and frequency bands currently in use in wireless communication, it is helpful to hold even a basic understanding of wireless technologies as determined in their historical setting. The various specifications of standards, for example, 802.11a/b/

g/n/ad/ac/ax, are technically known as a wireless/Wi-Fi spectrum or spectra and are established by the IEEE. Knowing the terms in use will enhance your ability to comprehend and apply your understanding of wireless technologies.

Historical context

Frequency bands are specified ranges of radio wave frequencies used for data transmission in the wireless spectrum. These bands can further be broken down into Wi-Fi channels. The guiding principle to differentiate between the properties of frequencies is *the higher the frequency, the faster the data transmission. The higher the frequency, the shorter the signal range.*

Fundamentally, there are two frequency bands used for Wi-Fi technology: 2.4 GHz and 5 GHz. 2.4 GHz has been around for a longer period of time than 5 GHz. However, as you can see from *Table 12.1*, both 803.11a and 802.11b were released at the same time, that is, in 1999. However, the 2.4 GHz range ultimately became the frequency band of choice and most commonly used compared to the 5 GHz range. Since the 2.4 GHz band was unregulated and more freely available to providers and manufacturer design, IEEE 802.11b became the standard and frequency more used. Both frequency bands are unlicensed. However, manufacturers could design their products, and vendors could manufacture 2.4 GHz devices less expensively than they could with the stricter, more regulated 5 GHz frequency band. This difference between regulated and unregulated *air space* could be said to be one of the primary drivers behind the evolution of wireless technology and the growing and *overly accessed* use of 2.4 GHz space. Everything from microwaves to cordless phones, baby monitors, car alarms, garage door openers, and a multitude of Bluetooth devices were being manufactured and sold in this expanding consumer-driven market.

In *Table 12.2*, you can identify that the better coverage and ranges align with the 2.4 GHz frequency. For example, when comparing 802.11a with 803.11b, we note that 802.11b has a maximum distance of 150 ft. In contrast to this, 802.11a's maximum distance is 100 ft. So, we see the guiding principle in action. However, with the 5 GHz frequency band, faster speed is achieved than what can be accomplished with the 2.4 GHz frequency band. There is a significant difference in speed between 54mbps (802.11a) and 11mbps (802.11b). Note the speeds of 802.11n/ac and ad. Again, we see the principle cited above in operation.

Historical context is relevant in technology. This is why understanding the procedural, legal, economic, and financial context of what was happening in the late 90s onward is important in fully comprehending the evolution of wireless technology and why the 2.4 GHz frequency band became the frequency of choice. Simply put, there is always a combination of factors that impact the evolution of technology and how it is accessed and used globally.

We say this because some individuals inadvertently assume that 5 G and the use of the 5 GHz range is innovative and emerging technology; when the fact remains, it has been there and existed for quite some time now as a regulated space but is being called on as a new space for disruptive technologies requiring higher speed and broader technical scope. In brief, the 2.4 GHz frequency over time has become an excessively used and crowded networking space, susceptible to interference. However, we should not forget that the 5 GHz space remains a regulated space, and just because something is classified as unlicensed does not mean it can be used without knowledge of the rules and obligations attached to using it.

The **Unlicensed National Information Infrastructure** (**U-NII**) radio band, as defined by the United States Federal Communications Commission, is part of the radio frequency spectrum used by WLAN devices and by many wireless ISPs.

In total, there are four bands in the unlicensed spectrum that Wi-Fi can function in. To explain these bands and regulations further, here is a table outlining the 5 GHz frequency band and how it is regulated and managed:

Band	Channel	Frequency in MHz	Usage
U-NII-1	34	5,170	Indoor use only
	36	5,180	
	38	5,190	
	40	5,200	
	42	5,210	
	44	5,220	
	46	5,230	
	48	5,240	
U-NII-2	52	5,260	Do not use
	56	5,280	
	60	5,300	
	64	5,320	
U-NII-2e	100	5,500	Indoor use only
	104	5,520	
	108	5,540	
	112	5,560	
	116	5,580	
	120	5,600	
	124	5,620	
	128	5,640	
	132	5,660	
	136	5,680	
	140	5,700	
U-NII-3	149	5,745	Indoor and outdoor use
	153	5,765	
	157	5,785	
	161	5,805	
	165	5,825	

Table 12.3: 5 GHz frequency bands

Note the following:

- U-NII-2 is not to be used at all as it is reserved for radar.

- More Wi-Fi bands are under consideration by the FCC to add even more bandwidth for Wi-Fi use.

- A rule change effectively opened up the U-NII 1 band for general use, removing the indoor-only stricture.

- Channel 165, previously in the 5.8 GHz ISM band, is now available as part of the U-NII 3 frequency band.

- There are ongoing proposals and considerations to expand on the space and extend the use of this frequency band.

Now that we understand what U-NII is, we can take a look at the channels in both the 2.4 GHz frequency band and the 5 GHz bands:

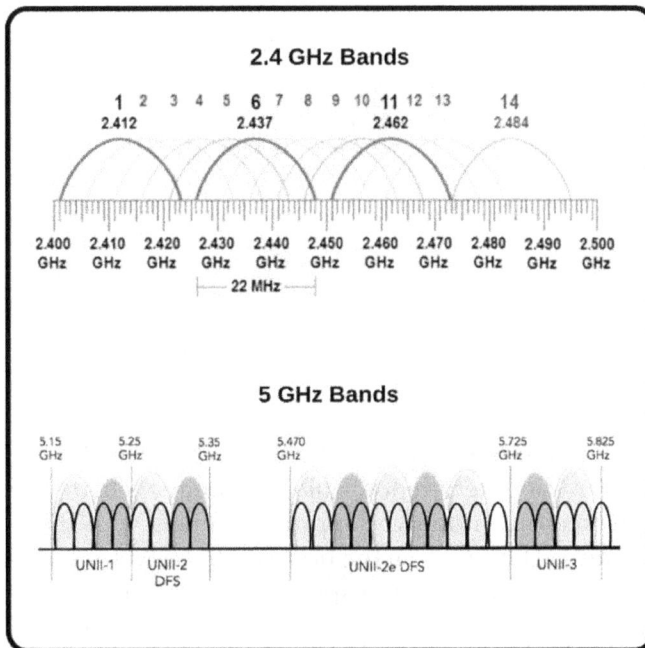

Figure 12.1: 2.4 GHz and 5 GHz frequency bands

2.4 GHz frequency band

As explained, the 2.4 GHz frequency band is more predisposed to interference because of the number of devices that use this frequency band. The solution to this interference (that is, RFI) in this frequency band is to use non-overlapping channels 1, 6, and 11, as seen on the diagram. Since these channels are five channels apart, they are called **non-overlapping** channels.

There are a total of fourteen channels defined for use by Wi-Fi installations and devices in the 2.4 GHz ISM band. However, not all channels are allowed in all countries: 11 are allowed by the FCC and used in the North American domain, and 13 are allowed in Europe, where channels have been defined by the organization ETSI.

The Wi-Fi channels (or WLAN) are spaced 5MHz apart. The exception to this measurement occurs in the spacing between the last two channels. The length of this spacing is 12 MHz.

The 2.4 GHz band uses longer waves, which makes it better suited for longer ranges or transmission through obstacles such as walls and other solid objects. Preferably, you should use the 2.4 GHz band to connect devices for low bandwidth activities like regular browsing of the Internet and less taxing applications or services.

The 2.4 GHz band supports a larger coverage area but achieves lower data rates.

Figure 12.2 outlines the difference between the waveform and lengths of the 2.4 GHz and 5 GHz bands:

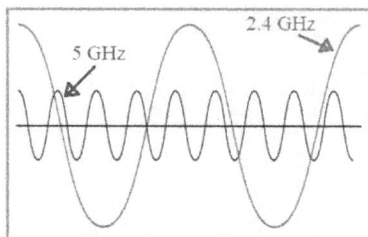

Figure 12.2: 2.4 GHz and 5 GHz waveform comparison

5 GHz frequency band

The 5 GHz functions over a larger number of unique channels. Less overlap across these channels means far less radio interference. This factor equals better performance. The 2.4 GHz frequency range has three non-overlapping channels, and the 5 GHz range has 24 non-overlapping channels. The 5 GHz is the best-suited band for high-bandwidth devices or Internet activities that call on real-time speed with QoS priority, such as multi-media gaming and streaming HDTV.

In terms of attenuation (signal degradation), these higher frequencies of waves attenuate stronger, and the signal is more sensitive to numerous obstacles. Obstacles such as walls, the ceiling, the floor, thicker doors, and other obstacles obstruct the signal relatively easily.

The reduction of the coverage area in the 5 GHz range is particularly noticeable when the router is used in infrastructures like apartment blocks or in corporate offices with multiple rooms instead of architecture with an open plan design. Open plan designs with cubicles and fewer doors and walls are much more conducive to wireless technologies when combined with the positioning of antennae and APs. A solid wood door decreases the signal level by about one and a half times stronger in the 5 GHz frequency range than it does in the 2.4 GHz range. To achieve the best connection to a 5 GHz access point, it is recommended to remain within the sight line (that is, within one room), with minimal obstacles in the signal path and coverage area.

As can be seen, faster data transmission in this range is possible than at low frequencies. However, it is additionally 5G's big plus and benefit (due to the extended 80 MHz band).

Channel bonding

Channel bonding combines two 20-MHz channels into one 40-MHz channel. This improves the bandwidth to increase by slightly more than double the bandwidth.

As discussed, the 2.4 GHz range has a total of 11 channels, with three of them accessible as non-overlapping. This number allows for a maximum of *one* non-overlapping bonded channel. Understandably, the application of channel bonding is deemed to be impractical for the 2.4 GHz range. In contrast to this limitation, the 5 GHz range has a total of 23 channels, with 12 non-overlapping channels. This characteristic allows for a maximum of *six* non-overlapping bonded (combined) channels.

Channel bonding is a complex configuration and should not be seen as a simple matter of combining channels without trade-offs. A network administrator should check where and when this technique is best used and should not be used. The downside of channel bonding is the potential for collisions, the transceiver's inability to distinguish between signals, and co-channel interference or adjacent-channel interference in overlapping channels. Bearing in mind our understanding of the impact of retransmissions and collisions on a network segment, we observe that the overall performance and effectiveness of data transmission may be negatively compromised with this potential. Channel bonding and adding more access points to a network is not always the best solution to quality Wi-Fi. Research and consultation with experts are necessary in the planning stage of wireless installation.

Modulation techniques

Digital modulation techniques minimize frequency channel saturation. There are several signaling methods used in wireless technologies. These methods include the following:

- **Orthogonal frequency-division multiplexing** (OFDM): This is primarily used by IEEE 802.11g/a/n and ac wireless networks to achieve higher transfer speeds. OFDM is a subset of frequency division multiplexing whereby a single channel uses multiple subchannels on adjacent frequencies. With OFDM, there can be a large number of small data streams in a single frequency. Consequently, it minimizes signal interference that is caused by walls or buildings.

  o **Mechanism**: OFDM breaks data into very small data streams to send the information across long distances where environmental obstacles may be an issue. As defined by *Techopedia, Orthogonal frequency division multiplexing (OFDM) is a technique, method or scheme for digital multi-carrier modulation* *using many closely spaced subcarriers—a previously modulated signal modulated into another signal of higher frequency and bandwidth.* Since OFDM uses subchannels, channel usage is very efficient. OFDM modulates adjacent radio signals *orthogonally*, meaning a linear transfer that conserves length and distance. *Orthogonal* refers to a line or object meeting at right angles or something that is intersecting at right angles.

- o **Uses**: OFDM is used for some mobile and digital TV systems, digital radio systems, power line communication, home networking solutions, and specific types of broadband access through phone lines, that is, POTS.

- **Frequency hopping spread spectrum (FHSS)**: FHSS is used by the original 802.11 standard. It uses a narrow frequency band and depends on spread-spectrum methods to communicate. As defined by *Techopedia, Frequency-hopping spread spectrum (FHSS) is a method of transmitting radio signals by shifting carriers across numerous channels with a pseudorandom sequence which is already known to the sender and receiver.* Using pseudo randomness in mathematics means that though the numbers generated in the system are random, they are selected by a definite computational process. This allows statistical randomness to occur under a defined set of outcomes. The prefix *pseudo* infers something that is apparently real as opposed to actuality, thus the mathematical process of pseudo-randomness.

  - o **Uses of FHSS**: The active system numbers used are higher than those used in the **direct sequence spread spectrum** (**DSSS**). This means that FHSS is suited well for installations designed to cover large geographical areas where there are several co-located systems required. In mobile communications, it suits deployment situations where direct sequence spread spectrum cannot be used and where fixed broadband wireless access is in place.

  - o **Mechanism**: FHSS transmits radio signals by rapidly switching a carrier signal among many frequency channels. This is known as **frequency hopping**. Via this frequency hopping technique, a predictable sequence hops from frequency to frequency over a wide band of frequencies. In this way, FHSS can avoid interference that may be on a single frequency. Moreover, this channel-hopping process permits efficient usage of the channels and consequently decreases channel congestion and channel saturation.

Regarding security, the process of hopping between multiple frequencies increases transmission security by making it harder for threat actors to eavesdrop on data packets as they are transmitted, and as a result, interception and data capture become more difficult for prospective hackers.

- **DSSS**: This was initially used by the IEEE 802.11b standard and protocol. It is designed to spread a signal over a larger frequency band to make it more resistant to and offset interference. As defined by *Techopedia* with DSSS, the transmitter breaks data into pieces and sends the pieces across multiple frequencies in a defined range.

- o **Uses of DSSS**: DSSS was originally established for military use. It used wideband signals as a means of resisting jamming attempts. It is known to have high immunity to noise, this immunity becoming more so with well-selected mathematics. Mathematical calculations and patterns are used, such as *The Gold Sequence*, named after its inventor, or the Barker codes. It is also used for various business and commercial purposes in WLANs, Wi-Fi, and Zigbee.

- o **Mechanism**: The stream of information in DSSS is divided into small pieces, each associated with a frequency channel across spectrums. Data signals at transmission points are combined with a higher data rate bit sequence, which divides data based on a spreading ratio. The chipping code in a DSSS is a redundant bit pattern associated with each bit transmitted. This helps to increase the signal's resistance to interference. If any bits are damaged during transmission, the original data can be recovered due to the redundancy of transmission (description by *Techopedia*). Some benefits of DSSS include the time stamping of incoming messages (along with secrecy), improved immunity, and a means of communication for multiple simultaneous users.

Examples of wireless deployments

There are many deployments of wireless technologies available. These deployments break down into home and business usage. *Figure 12.3* shows the components used in a wireless local area network in the home. A home user generally uses a router that operates as an Ethernet switch (with usually four ports available for wired connections), a router and gateway, and an access point to serve wireless clients on the network.

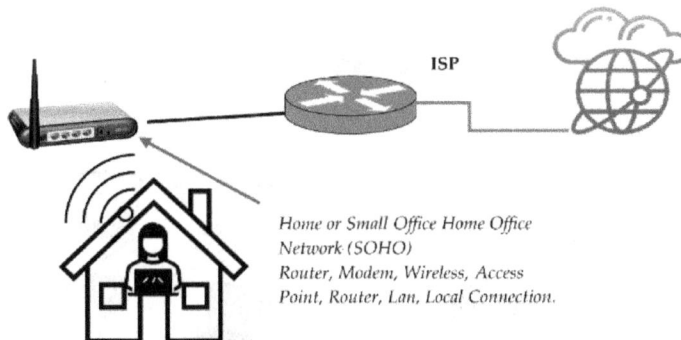

ISP

Home or Small Office Home Office Network (SOHO) Router, Modem, Wireless, Access Point, Router, Lan, Local Connection.

Figure 12.3: Home network, typical wireless components

The benefits of home networking include the following:

- Practically *cable-free* networks with freedom from unsightly or bulky wires.

- Mobility with the freedom to move around the house or apartment and work in personal spaces.

- Increased access to **Internet of Things (IoT)** and smart devices.
- Accessible bandwidth for streaming video, real-time voice, gaming, online chats, and other forums.
- Sharing of files, printers, and other peripherals in the network.

In *Figure 12.4*, a WLAN is illustrated with an autonomous **access point (AP)** configuration:

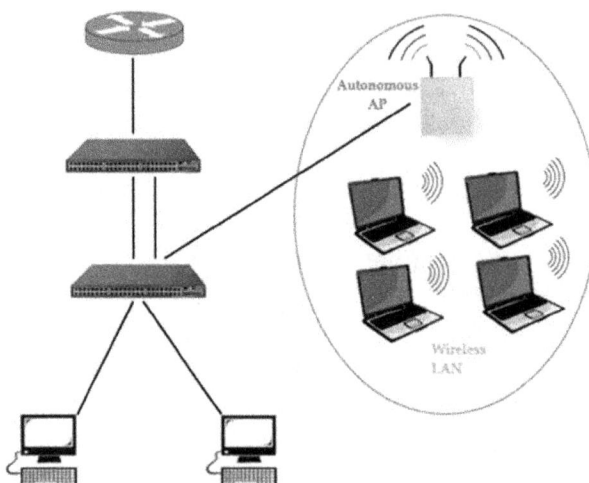

Figure 12.4: WLAN with an autonomous AP

Figure 12.5 shows a WLAN deployment implementing central switching technology:

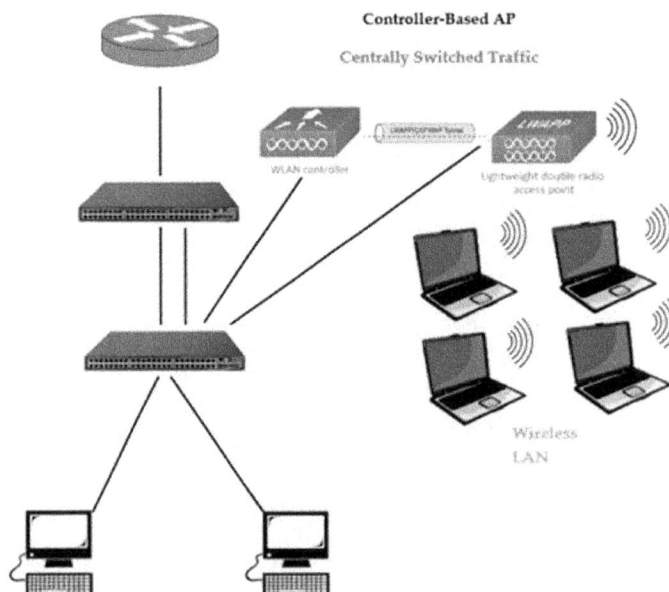

Figure 12.5: WLAN with a controller-based AP

Autonomous AP vs. central switching

Autonomous APs work as independent, standalone devices with no knowledge of other APs on the network. Each AP must be configured independently of the others. This can become a problem when several APs are required. This mode of configuration suits small networks but as the network scales, this mode becomes cumbersome and unviable. Due to the need for several APs in many businesses, educational, and social spaces, many technicians will *cluster* the APs to minimalize configuration and any upgrades. Clustering occurs when a group of independent APs (up to 16) are configured to function as a unified group or cluster. This means a network administrator configures a single AP, and the remaining Aps in the same cluster will copy the configuration details from the first one. As you can imagine, this makes network administration and management of the network and APs much easier to handle and work with. It is analogous to the minimizing of replication in a word processing application with the simple action of a copy and paste. All other APs are replicated and duplicated to align with the single configured AP. The network administrator no longer needs to worry about multiple configurations or configuring separate devices as such, or interference coming from individual APs between the APs. Regarding manual input of data, administrators do not have to be vigilant *as often* when deploying multiple APs. Still, they must be very attentive to data input when accessing a single AP running the system. This implementation suits small businesses, educational facilities, organizations that may not wish to subscribe to cloud-based services, or companies that do not require technical support outside their own IT department.

Central switching solutions are more complex configurations with additional hardware in the mix. Some APs support the clustering of APs without the use of a wireless controller. In *Figure 12.5*, there are extra wireless networking devices in situ. *Figure 12.6* zooms in on these devices so that we can identify them and observe the configuration more closely:

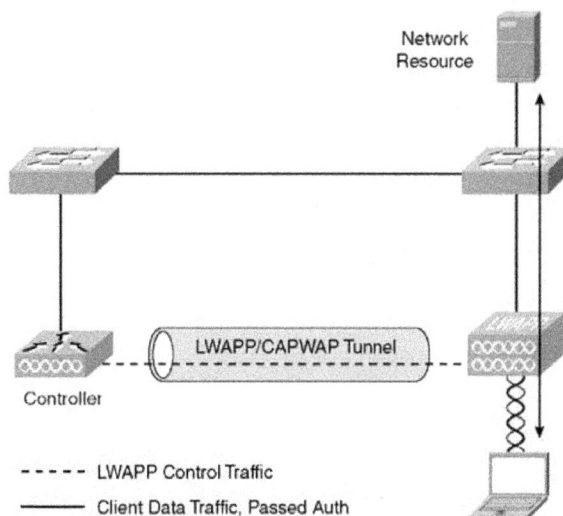

Figure 12.6: *WLAN with a controller-based AP*

- **Physical links**: In the topology, there are two network switches. The **wireless LAN controller** (**WLC**) is physically connected to the switch on the left. The AP is physically connected to the switch on the right. From the client-side, the laptop, as an end device/host, is connected via wireless (unbounded) media to the AP. The network resource, resident on the physical server, is physically cabled to the switch on the right.

- **Protocols**: The AP runs a wireless protocol (LWAPP) designed for a central switching management system. **Lightweight Access Point Protocol** (**LWAPP**) is the name of a Cisco proprietary protocol that can control multiple Wi-Fi wireless Aps at once. **Configuration and Provisioning of Wireless AP** (**CAPWAP**) is the generic equivalent of LWAPP. CAPWAP superseded LWAPP as an international protocol and standard accessible to all wireless LAN controllers.

- **Data transmission**: When the user on the laptop needs to access the network resource, they are authenticated against the access point in their vicinity and coverage area. This client data traffic is sent and received seamlessly for all authenticated users and traffic. However, there is another set of actions and processes occurring between the access point and the wireless controller. This LWAPP or CAPWAP control traffic is part of the management system. There are far more intricacies of detail in these operations, but for the purposes and scope of the network plus exam, we must understand how the devices interlink and their basic operations.

Figure 12.7 depicts a zoom-in on *Figures 12.5* and *12.6* regarding the interoperability between an AP in the system and the WLC (please remember that there may be multiple APs in a network topology, positioned around the building. The illustrations here are designed to simplify the relationship between devices and highlight network devices and prescribed roles.).

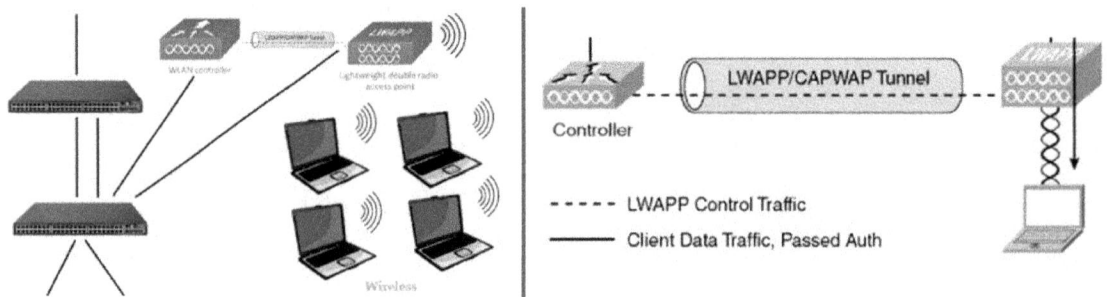

Figure 12.7: *Controller-based AP to AP connection*

The benefits of a WLC are listed as follows:

- **Scalability**: This infrastructure allows for multiple APs.

- **Security**: The WLC can authenticate users in the system and prevent rogue Aps from being on the network.

- RF information can be shared among the APs.

- Roaming profiles and clients are made more manageable with this centralized management system.

- A network administrator has centralized management and system monitoring via a browser and terminal emulation software or SSH.

Some drawbacks and considerations of using a WLC include pricing, limitations on some Web browser interfaces, terminal access issues with protocols such as **Secure Shell** (**SSH**), and strict licensing and subsequent access or ability to procure products.

Wireless topology modes

An **ad hoc network** is commonly used as a temporary connection and topology, frequently used in Bluetooth technology. With this topology, devices are paired in a *peer-to-peer* network, like the way you would pair your phone with your car to access your phone's music or data. Wireless tethering of devices, such as connecting a smartphone with a laptop and creating a hotspot, is a variation of an ad hoc network and mode of wireless operation. These peer-to-peer topologies do not require an access point since the phone functions as a hot spot to provide Wi-Fi accessibility. The devices interconnect without the use of an AP or a router.

Infrastructure networks tend to be more permanent in design. In infrastructure mode, an access point is typically in use. The AP can be physically connected to the wired network and devices interconnect using the services provided by the AP or router. Scaling an infrastructure topology is relatively easy. A network administrator can easily add hosts without increasing administrative efforts. When building infrastructure-based networks, planning a wireless network design is essential to the creation of a robust and viable network. One of the primary considerations in any plan is to gather the network requirements and select the network equipment most suited to the expected design and purpose.

> Note: APs can be implemented as independent standalone devices, in small clusters, or in a larger controller-based network.

Antenna types

The wireless antenna is a key component of any Wi-Fi network. Essentially, it fulfills two key roles. First, as a *receiver*, it absorbs incoming radio signals from other devices, and second, as a *transmitter*, it radiates outgoing radio signals to other devices. Antennas are critical components in any Wi-Fi network, WLAN, or other wireless topology that calls on the use of an AP. They facilitate our internet connectivity to enable all online activities we participate in and provide us with signal strength and range to permit a connection.

There are three main types of antennas used in wireless configurations: Omnidirectional, Directional, and Yagi:

- **Omnidirectional Wi-Fi antennas**: Factory Wi-Fi gear often uses basic dipole antennas. These are also referred to as **rubber duck** designs. This design is like those used on walkie-talkie radios. Omnidirectional antennas provide 360-degree coverage.

- **Directional Wi-Fi antennas**: These antennas focus the radio signal on a given direction. This enhances the signal to and from the AP in the direction the antenna is pointing.

- **Yagi antennas**: This type of directional radio antenna can be utilized for long-distance Wi-Fi networking.

Table 12.4 outlines the basic properties of these antennas and their usage:

Antenna type	Description	Recommended deployment(s)
Omnidirectional	Creates a 360-degree coverage pattern. The circular pattern covers wide areas. Ceiling or mast pole mounted.	Open office areas, conference rooms, warehouses, manufacturing floors, and outdoor seating areas. Indoor/outdoor retail environments.
Dipole	Creates a 360-degree coverage pattern. Can be bent at different angles to modify the coverage for wall and ceiling mounted as needed. Available in colors for aesthetic preferences.	Office areas, classrooms, hallways, conference rooms, and shared (multi-tenant) environments.
Directional (including Patch and Yagi)	Focuses the signal to direct energy in certain directions. Patch and Yagi antennas are typically mounted to a wall or mast and provide coverage in a limited-angle pattern.	Down a hallway in a hospital or office corridor. In a warehouse or manufacturing facility with high steel shelving. In mining shafts and drifts.

Table 12.4: *Antenna types*

Some considerations to be made regarding selecting the correct antenna include the power or gain of the antenna, that is, whether it is low gain or high gain in terms of the signal's reach and strength. The antenna's radiation pattern is also important as that will be one of the determining factors in our choice as we observe how the antenna spreads its gain, for example, whether it is a directional or omnidirectional antenna. As laid out in *Table 12.4*, the purpose and location of the antenna also need to be weighed and measured. The power range, gain, and designated location are all factors in choosing the correct antenna type to ensure appropriate coverage and signal strength for any given networking scenario.

Wireless identification

A **service set identifier** (**SSID**) is primarily designed to differentiate a wireless local area network in specific locations where other WLANs might also be broadcasting simultaneously. It is similar to a network identifier in that it distinguishes between wireless networks that are broadcasting and appear on a scan for local networks. A service set identifier works in accordance with a **basic service set** (**BSS**), a combination of APs and connected clients, and an **extended service set** (**ESS**). An SSID should not be confused with a BSSID. The BSSID is a 48-bit MAC address associated with an AP's radio card.

An SSID is generated to cluster and identify the ESS so that a new host or device connecting to this network can easily recognize and connect to it. An example of this occurs when all APs and host stations must specify the correct SSID of their ESS. This is done to authenticate and gain access to a specific wireless network correctly. SSIDs are typically used in collaboration with a security passphrase as long as the network is not an open network functioning without any security parameters. Encryption standards are designed to protect the data on your wireless network. These encryption standards will be discussed further in *Chapter 16, Security Concepts,* as wireless authentication methods. Encryption standards include **Wired Equivalent Privacy** (**WEP**), **Wi-Fi Protected Access** (**WPA-TKIP**), and **Wi-Fi Protected Access Version 2** (**WPA2- AES**).

Cellular technologies

Cellular technologies are used in mobile communications technology. In terms of wireless technologies, most mobile devices come with support for internet connectivity. Laptops, notebooks, netbooks, and smartphones, among others, are built with the capacity to go online and connect to the internet. Cellular technologies include 4G, 5G, LTE, CDMA, Wi-Max, Dual-band, and multi-band technologies. Cellular networking uses cellular phone infrastructure for internet access.

There are various ways in which mobile devices can access the Internet. A user can:

- Tether their smartphone to their laptop or another device using a USB cable and gain internet access.

- Create a mobile hotspot with mobile hotspot functionality and support on their phone.

- Use integrated wireless antennas or adapters such as internet dongles.

The speeds at which the cellular network functions are contingent on the network connection (that is, whether it is 3G, 4G, 4G LTE, or 5G). Cellular devices will achieve faster data, upload, and download speeds; the better the network connection is, the closer they are to the cellular tower. General Internet browsing, email, streaming video, and accessing other multimedia content are the typical practices and activities of cellular users. The most important aspect of cellular Internet access is users of this technology require a data plan and a paid subscription to a mobile phone provider to successfully get access to the Internet.

Multiple-Input and Multiple-Output

Multiple-Input and Multiple-Output (**MIMO**) exploit multipath propagation of signals to multiply link capacity, boost performance, and extend the bandwidth of a wireless network. With this mechanism, multiple transmission and receiving antennas participate in the process.

In *Figure 12.8*, a simplified version of this propagation is shown:

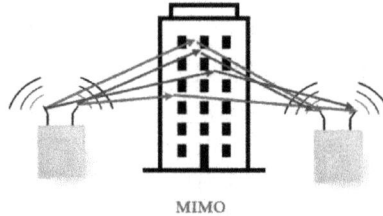

MIMO

Figure 12.8: Multiple-Input and Multiple-Output

MIMO uses multiplexing techniques, primarily precoding, spatial multiplexing, and diversity coding. MIMO technology is implemented in a great variety of wireless standards such as LTE and LTE-Advanced, WLAN, and WiMAX. Due to the way MIMO functions, it leads to better coverage for the users in a cell. The signal processing algorithm used by MIMO is pretty advanced. This, in turn, means the Bit Rate Error is reduced. Better uplink and downlink rates are achievable due to the multiplexing technique in use. In terms of drawbacks, MIMO technology calls for complex equipment and additional RF units. Additionally, running the algorithms can cause the batteries to drain faster than normal, increasing the power requirements. The overall cost of implementing MIMO is higher than the cost of implementing single antenna systems.

Configuring a SOHO router

This demonstration uses TP-Link online emulation software, which offers an ideal means of learning about home/business router navigation and making decisions pre-purchasing. TP-Link alongside other router manufacturers, provide excellent emulating software, hugely beneficial to learning about wireless technologies and router/modem/APs functionality. As technical tools, they are a positive addition to educational provision and a recommended tool for teaching and learning. Emulating software is available at **www.tplink.com.**

The model used for the demo is an AC750 Wireless Dual Band Router, Model No. Archer C20. The purpose of the demo is a walkthrough of a basic configuration and setup.

> **Note: The beauty of using these emulators and routers is you learn as you navigate. There are detailed explanations on every step and stage of a router's interface, so the best practice is to read as you go and learn.**

Let us look at the steps:

1. Open the router in a new browser tab. Open your browser and navigate to **http://192.168.0.1**, the default IP address of the TP-Link router:

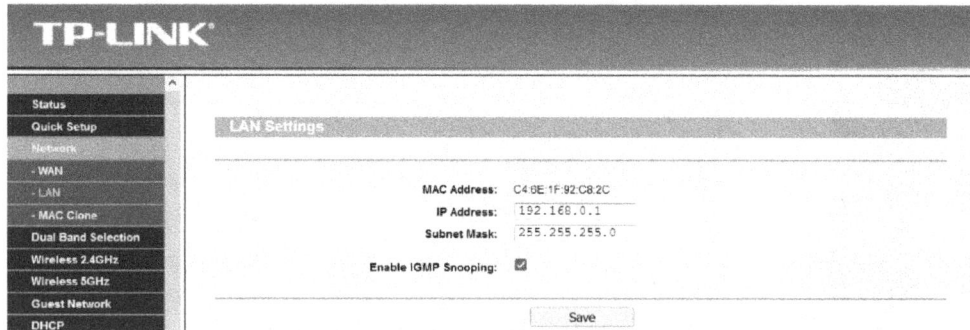

Figure 12.9: *SOHO router setup, step 1*

The default router password of a TP-Link Archer C20 router is **admin**. The default username is **admin**. After you are logged in, you can use the Quick Setup Wizard (on the top left menu). If you do not want to avail the setup wizard, you can proceed with setup manually.

2. Log in.

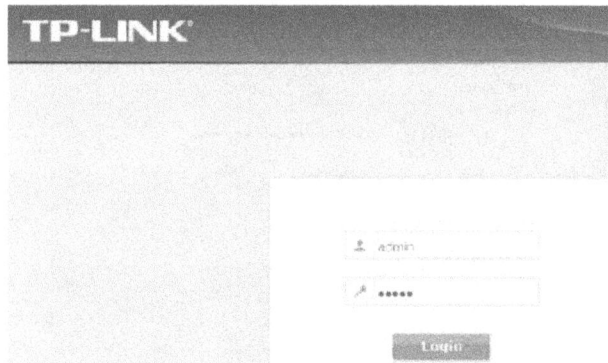

Figure 12.10: *SOHO router setup, step 2*

All wireless routers and network intermediary devices are shipped with a default username and password. This default login information is readily available on the internet. This presents a potential hacker with an instant opportunity to infiltrate your network, so the advice is to change this password before you do anything else. Always use a strong password, as advised on this interface.

It is strongly recommended that you change the factory default username and password of the router. All users who try to access the router's web-based utility will be prompted for the router's username and password.

3. Change the default username and password. Navigate to **System Tools** | **Password**:

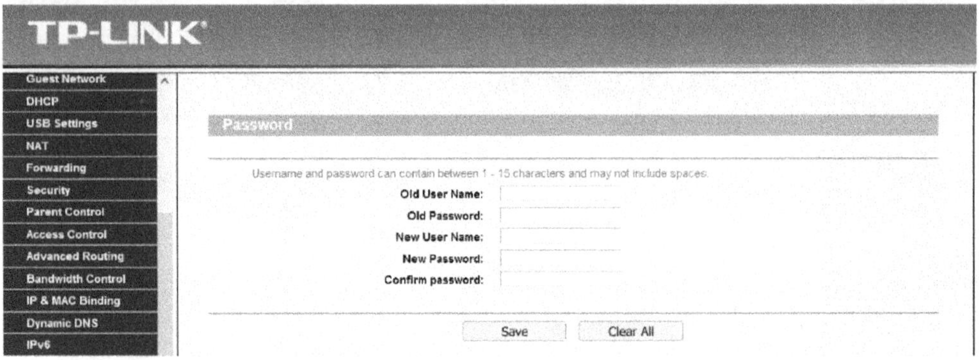

Figure 12.11: SOHO router setup, step 3

4. Set up your **Time Settings**:

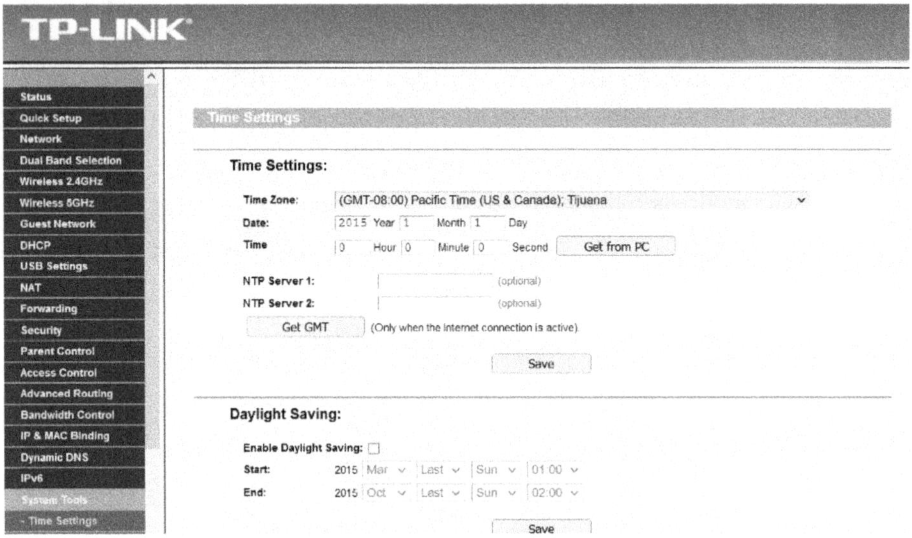

Figure 12.12: SOHO router setup, step 4

This setting will be used for some time-based functions such as firewall functions. These time-dependent functions will not work if time is not set. Therefore, it is important to specify time settings as soon as you successfully log in to the router.

- The time will be lost if the router is turned off.

- The router will automatically obtain GMT from the internet if it is configured accordingly.

- In daylight saving configuration, the start time and end time shall be within one year, and the start time shall be earlier than the end time.

- • After you enable the daylight-saving function, it will take action in one minute.

5. Configure the internet connection:

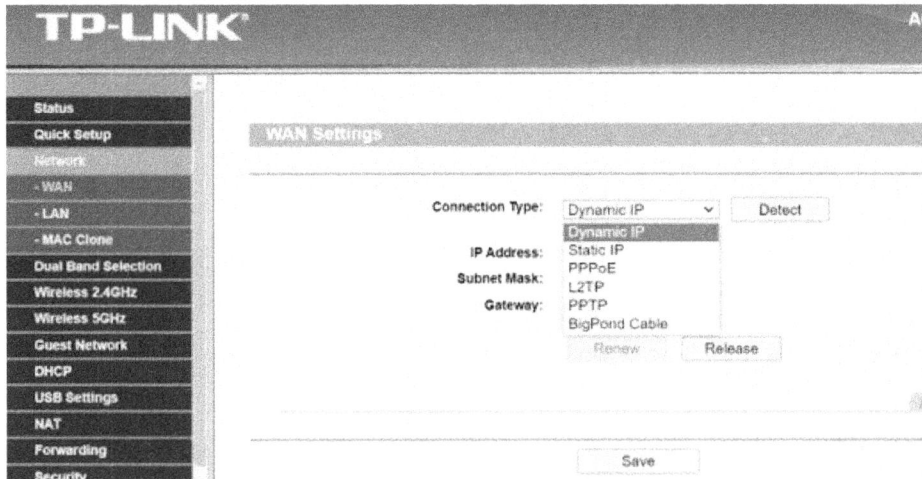

Figure 12.13: SOHO router setup, step 5

Use the **Dynamic IP** (DHCP), where you have a modem from your ISP. Just select **Dynamic IP** and follow the setup.

Use the **Static IP** if your ISP provides a static or fixed IP address, subnet mask, gateway, and DNS setting. Select the **Static IP** option.

Other options are provided on this interface, dependent upon the desired outcome and configuration.

Now that our router is connected to the internet, we will carry out further security measures and other configurations. There are many ways in which we can customize our SOHO router and tweak the settings. The purpose of this demonstration is to identify the primary features and security mechanisms.

6. Select the desired frequency bands:

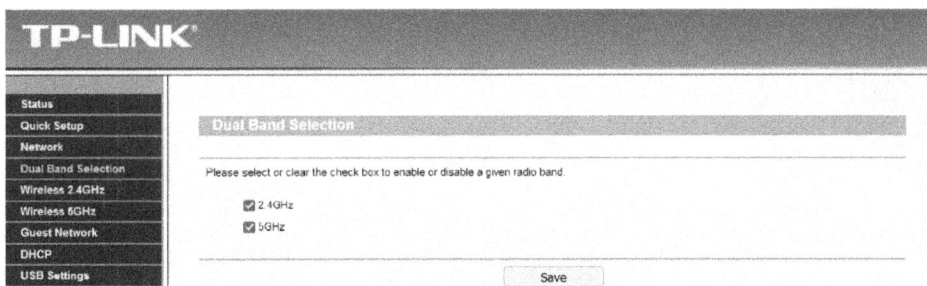

Figure 12.14: SOHO router setup, step 6

Since this model is a dual-band radio, to change the SSID, you need to select the wireless 2.4 GHz band, make changes, and then enter the 5 GHz band to implement amendments to details there further.

7. Change the SSID and select the **Region**, **Mode**, **Channel**, and **Channel Width**. Enable/Disable SSID broadcast. Enable/Disable WDS:

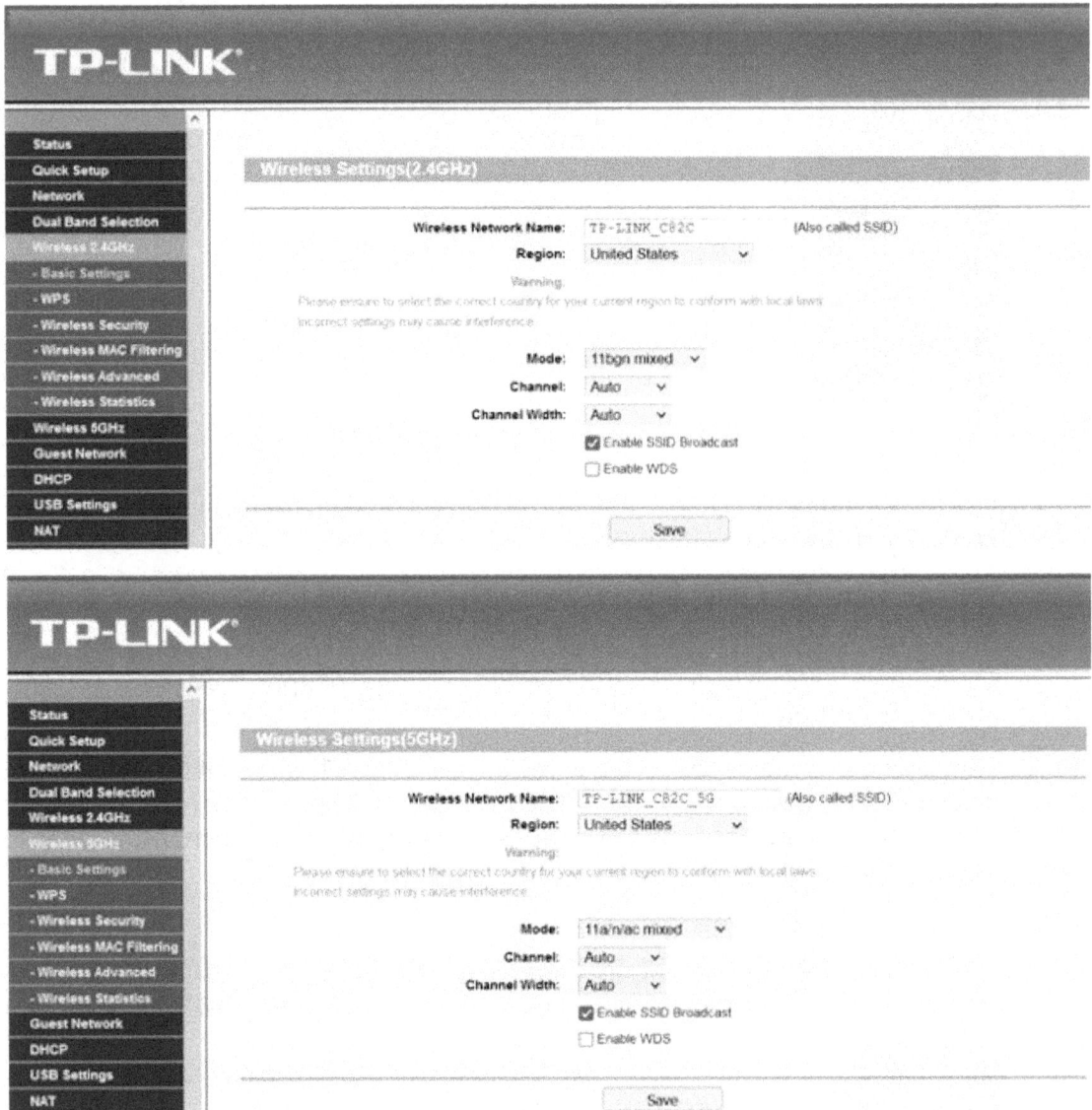

Figure 12.15: SOHO router setup, step 7

Note: Apply your understanding of overlapping and non-overlapping channels. Your ISP may advise you of a certain channel to use.

As per instructions, you can select one of the following security options:

- **Disable wireless security**: The wireless security function can be enabled or disabled. If disabled, the wireless stations will be able to connect to the Router without encryption. It is strongly recommended that you choose one of the following options to enable security.

- **WPA/WPA2—Personal**: Select WPA based on the pre-shared passphrase.

- **WPA/WPA2—Enterprise**: Select WPA based on RADIUS server.

- **WEP—Select 802.11 WEP security**: Each security option has its own settings.

    Note: A Remote Authentication Dial-In User Service (RADIUS) Server/ Terminal Access Controller Access-Control System TACACS Server is used for authentication in a VPN setting.

8. Authentication and encryption:

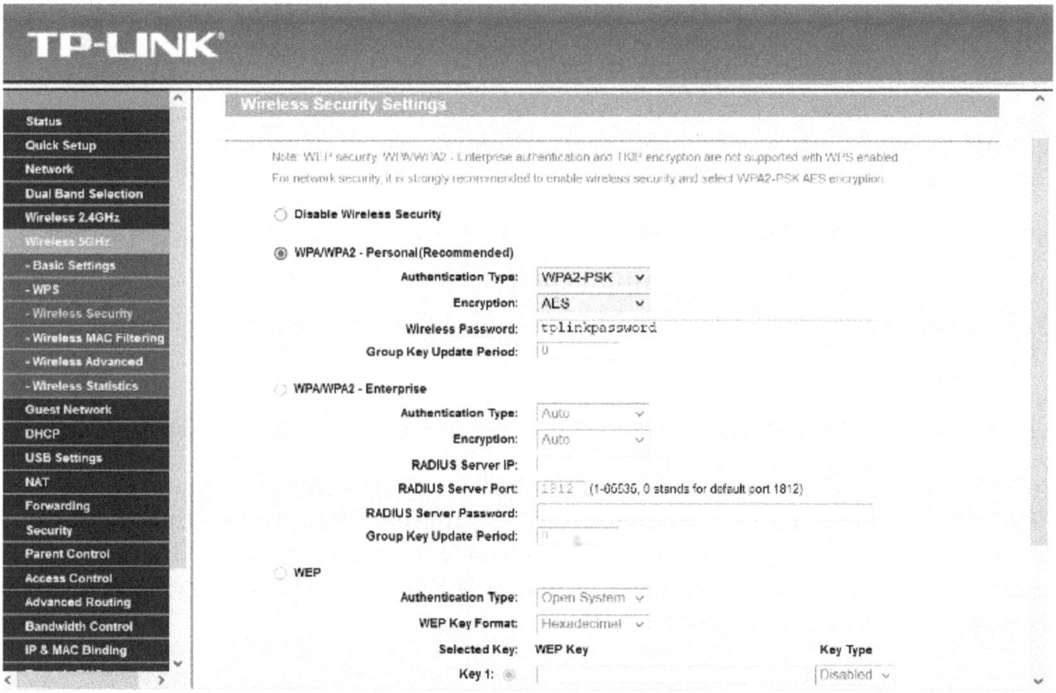

Figure 12.16: *SOHO router setup, step 8*

Read the wireless security help section carefully. Wireless security will be covered in more detail in *Chapter 16, Security Concepts*. For network security, it is strongly recommended to enable wireless security and select WPA2-PSK AES encryption.

Other security settings include implementing a firewall, disabling the guest account, content filtering, IP filtering, MAC address filtering, WPS, and UPnP.

Additionally, NAT and QoS settings can be customized to suit the purpose of the network.

9. Example: MAC address filtering:

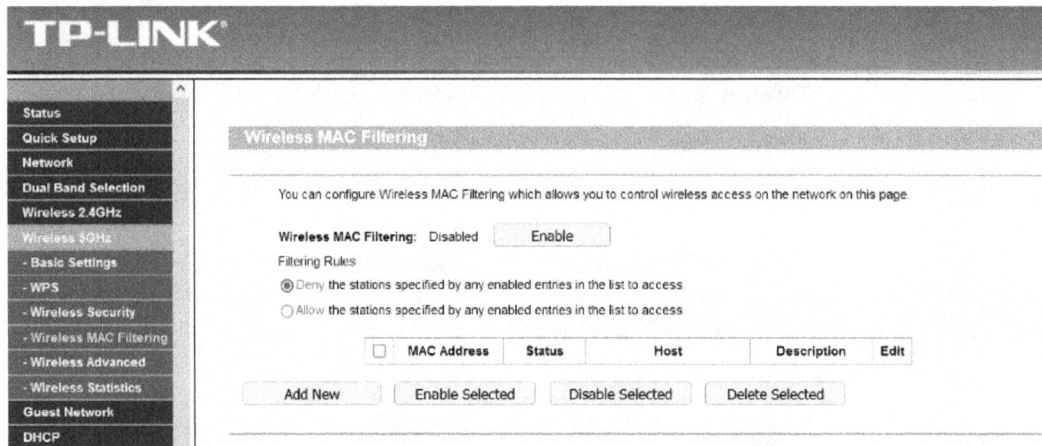

Figure 12.17: *SOHO router setup, step 9*

The Wireless MAC Address Filtering feature allows you to control the wireless stations accessing the AP, which depends on the station's MAC addresses.

- **MAC Address**: The wireless station's MAC address that you want to access.

- **Description**: A simple description of the wireless station.

- **Status**: The status of this entry is either Enabled or Disabled.

- **Host**: The wireless name.

To disable the **Wireless MAC Address Filters** feature, keep the default setting **Disable**.

As a best practice, you can then back up the configuration. This action creates a configuration bin file that you use if a restore is required. Though updating the firmware is recommended as a beginning point, an internet connection is required to achieve this. The most important point regarding this action is that before you update the firmware, always make a backup of the configuration.

Conclusion

In this chapter, we learned about wireless technologies. We explored the evolution of the IEEE 802.11 standards and protocols and the key concepts and workings of each standard. The reader should now be able to identify and differentiate between the different IEEE 802.11 wireless standards. The main considerations for differentiation are maximum speed and maximum distance, channels in use, modulation techniques, and backward compatibility and interoperability.

They should be able to apply this knowledge in a practical way and navigate a router to configure the optimum settings for effective connections to the router and AP. They should be able to understand the setup procedures for a SOHO router and recognize the commonalities between all routers and access points. Concepts should include security features such as securing the router's log-in, disabling SSID broadcast (if applicable to the scenario), MAC address filtering, and setting up a DMZ. Other settings understood include time settings, dual-band radio, QoS, managing updates, and applying the techniques for maximizing the router's performance.

In the upcoming chapter, we will explore network operations, learn about methods for gathering statistics, and the use of sensors to ensure network availability.

Points to remember

Key points for wireless configuration:

- Each wireless configuration should meet the requirements of an individual, business, or enterprise.

- The plan for installation and configuration of equipment and software is critical.

- Consider the type of antenna suited to the purpose and location of the network:

  o **Omnidirectional antennas**: Provide 360-degree coverage, suitable for general use.

  o **Directional antennas**: Focus the signal on a specific direction, ideal for long-distance connections.

  o **Dipole antennas**: Commonly used for short to medium-range coverage.

- Compare and contrast different means and mechanisms of using antennas for optimal signaling and quality connections.

- Apply practical knowledge to navigate and configure routers for effective connections to the router and access points.

- Follow setup procedures for a SOHO router and recognize commonalities between all routers and access points.

- Understand that while routers differ in interfaces and software appearance, they share fundamental similarities in functions and mechanisms.

- Building knowledge of these common features enables a network administrator to navigate and work with any wireless network device effectively.

- The content of this chapter is mapped to *Domain 2: Network Implementations*, given a scenario, select and configure wireless devices and technologies.

Key terms

- **Basic Service Set**: This term is used to describe the group of stations that may communicate together within an 802.11 network. The BSS may or may not include an access point. In some topologies, an AP provides a connection to a fixed distribution system, such as in the case of an Ethernet wired network.

- **Extended Service Set**: An ESS is composed of one or more interconnected BSSs and their related local area networks. These interconnected WLANs integrate into LANs and appear as a single BSS to the logical link control sublayer of the OSI model.

- **Independent Basic Service Set**: As the name suggests, an IBSS constitutes an ad hoc, self-governing, and self-contained network. All traffic flows are handled internally, and station-to-station traffic is filtered based on the MAC address of the receiver and intended destination.

Questions

1. List the IEEE 802.11 standards.
2. Define the following terms: Channels, frequency bands, modulation techniques, and channel bonding.
3. Give examples of wireless deployments.
4. Name the types of antennas used in wireless technologies.
5. Match the appropriate antenna to recommended deployment scenarios.

Join our book's Discord space

Join the book's Discord Workspace for Latest updates, Offers, Tech happenings around the world, New Release and Sessions with the Authors:

https://discord.bpbonline.com

CHAPTER 13

Managing and Monitoring a Network

Introduction

At the heart of every company lies its network. The company network is part of the basic infrastructure of any business. It is also an essential component, for it enables teamwork and provides access to the Internet. It also allows for all members of staff (including management) to share a company's hardware, printers, servers, and services, and thus communicate and exchange data with one another.

- Courtesy of Paessler, Network Monitoring Experts

As creators and builders of networks, it is apparent that the work and production of networking do not end with completing a network's initial configuration. No house nor road nor any other business or social infrastructure remains integral to its purpose and design unless it is successfully managed and monitored throughout its term of existence. In computer networks, there is so much hardware and software combined to keep the network properly functioning. As network administrators, we not only desire to have a functioning network but also equally aspire to have a network with solid and robust performance, one that is running a smooth engine in all its constituent parts and as a whole. This management and monitoring of networks is an integral part of network policy, procedure, and practice.

Structure

This chapter will explain the following topics:

- Performance metrics and sensors
- Open-source network monitoring tools
- System logs

Other operating system monitoring tools will also be addressed.

Objectives

After completing this chapter, the reader will be able to recognize the appropriate statistics and sensors to ensure network availability. They should differentiate between a variety of network management tools and monitoring techniques. They should be able to apply this knowledge in a practical way and use integrated or third-party tools to troubleshoot a system and/or network performance and narrow down relevant issues that negatively impact network operation. Interpreting event logs and system logs is imperative to troubleshooting and diagnosing software and hardware issues on a device or the system. A network administrator must be adept at reading the details of logs and acting on the details of device component functionality and system logs gathered. By spotting abnormal statistics, an administrator can classify the component that is overloaded or not responding correctly.

Performance metrics and sensors

Network infrastructure is comprised of multiple physical and logical components. Maintaining and monitoring these devices and keeping them up and running as smoothly as possible involves a few basic conditions. Organizations and enterprises need to determine how data is exchanged between these network hosts and intermediary devices and invest in clear-cut and precise network device management. When optimally achieved, these conditions make diagnosing, troubleshooting, and remedying problems effective and efficient. With the correct tools on hand, businesses can save time, money, labor, and costs while counteracting the headache and heartache involved in living with degraded and underperforming devices and systems.

Network performance and resource monitoring range in scale and coverage. An administrator can carry out monitoring on a single PC, laptop, switch, router, or interconnected devices on a network segment to the entire network as a single entity. Each component will have its mechanism for logging performance or resource monitoring. To give an example of performance monitoring on a micro-level, we will look at the integrated monitoring tool in a Windows operating system. Despite the multitude of free or paid-for third-party tools on offer, they all share a degree of common features, and the resources observed on devices are typically similar, most fundamentally at a hardware level of operation.

The components/resources to be monitored include the following:

- Device/chassis
- Temperature
- **Central processing unit (CPU)** usage
- Memory
- Storage

Network metrics include the following:

- Bandwidth
- Latency
- Jitter

Some common tools for computer monitoring and management in Windows include Task Manager, Resource Monitor, Performance Monitor, and Event Viewer. It is helpful to establish a **baseline** when starting a system to use as a comparison as more software and hardware are added to the system over time (and the device is viewed as a networked device). Being proactive and frequently monitoring system performance as preventative maintenance can help you eliminate components during diagnostics or troubleshooting steps, plus enable you to problem-solve more easily and narrow down issues as they arise.

Note: A baseline is a starting point or minimum used for comparisons. Benchmarking is establishing or evaluating a component's performance using a comparison with a component of a similar status or standard. A benchmark test typically takes components of similar functionality and tests their performance while simultaneously comparing the statistics and outcomes of the tests carried out. These tests occur in an offline or online environment. Benchmarking uses metrics to carry out comparative testing.

Performance Monitor on a Windows 10 System

Performance Monitor is a utility program in the Windows operating system used for collecting data. To access **Performance Monitor**, right-click on the start menu, select **Run**, and then type **perfmon** into the **Run** box OR open Windows search and type in the tool's name. You can also press the *Windows* key + *R* keyboard shortcut to open the **Run** command or use the *Windows* key + *X* keyboard shortcut. This opens the **Power User** menu, where you select **Computer Management** and then click on **Performance**. As with other tools or utilities, there are various ways to navigate Windows to access them.

Once assessed, the tool opens with an **Overview of Performance Monitor**. Note the overview of the **Performance Monitor** described in *Figure 13.1* and the functions it offers:

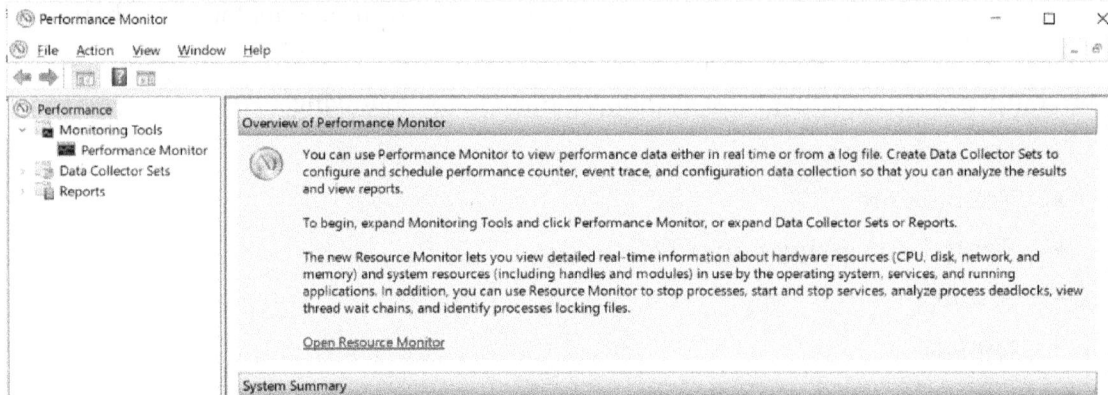

Figure 13.1: *Overview of Performance Monitor*

On opening the Resource Monitor, you can examine the performance of common components. The following are some typical components that may be examined:

- Processor (CPU)
- Hard disk
- Memory
- Network

A single device on a network can encounter different problems. For example, when your computer suddenly is not as fast as usual, and things have slowed down, or the system keeps freezing up or *hanging*, you are likely to deal with performance issues that could be caused by a number of reasons. The issue could be a result of problems with specific hardware, apps, or drivers that were inadequately designed or are incorrect versions of the specified system. The operating system may be using excessive system resources (that is, a bottleneck), or there may even be a virus or malware that has infected your device or corrupted system files. These issues are all indicators of a problematic system. Moreover, they all point to the need for further investigation. Consequently, you will need to gather the relevant statistics from one of the system utilities integrated with the edition of Windows.

Windows recognizes system performance statistics using the following terminology:

- A **counter** is a specific statistic you can monitor (such as the amount of free memory or the number of bytes sent on a network card).

- An **object** is a statistic group, often corresponding to a specific type of hardware device or software process (such as the processor or memory). In *Figure 13.2*, we can see the Data Collector Sets accessible for viewing and analyzing:

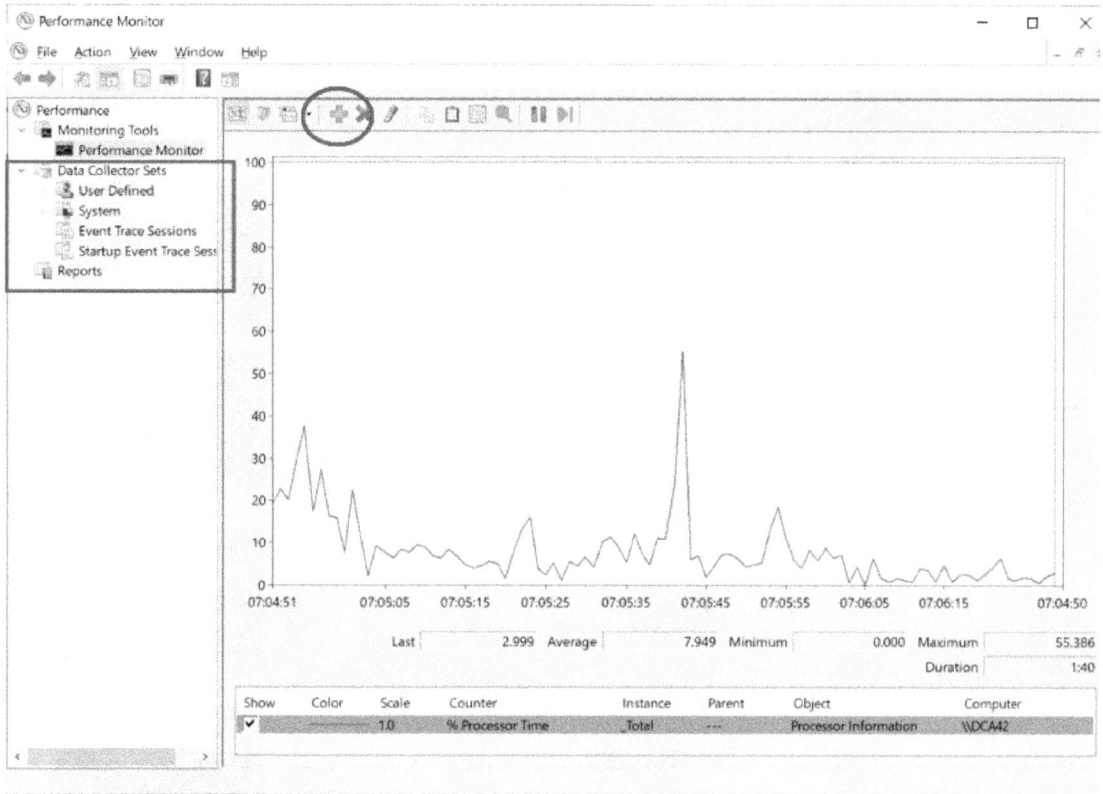

Figure 13.2: Data counters

On the left panel, you will find the navigation pane with access to Performance Monitor, Data Collector Sets, and Reports.

Selecting **Performance Monitor**, you will see a screen with a single counter. This is the **Processor Time** counter. This counter displays the processor load in the last 100 seconds. However, you can add or customize other counters to monitor practically anything on the system being monitored or investigated. Note that the green plus button, which is above the graph, is displayed on the screen. This button enables you to add more counters that are available on the system.

Selecting **Resource Monitor** on the initial dialog box takes you to the screen shown in *Figure 13.3*:

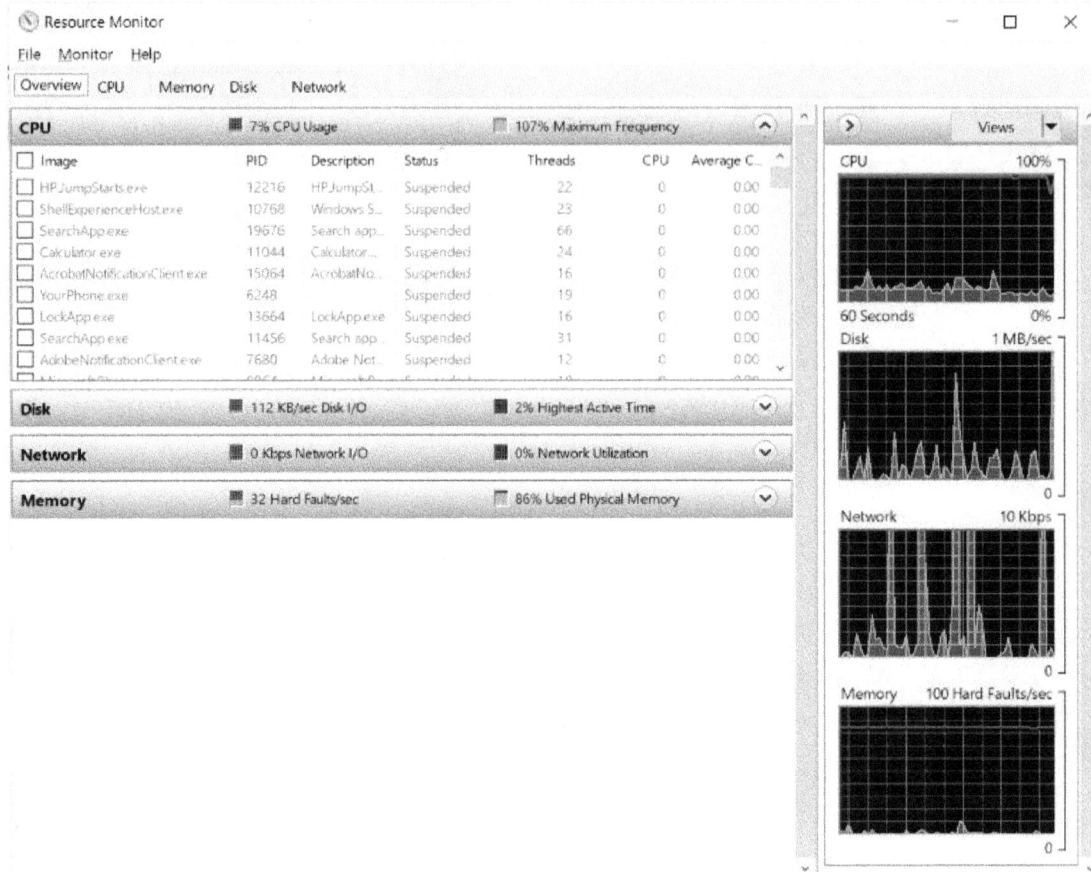

Figure 13.3: Resource Monitor

Here, you can view graphs for the CPU, Disk (storage), Network, and Memory. Again, you can monitor applications and hardware performance, drilling down deeper into specific areas to be monitored or measured.

Windows performance counters include the following:

- % Processor time (processor utilization)
- % Disk time (highest active time)
- Average disk queue length
- Available, used, and free physical memory
- Memory committed bytes (commit charge)
- Page file usage
- Memory pages per second
- Network utilization

As you can see, these statistics are invaluable to diagnose or problem-solve a device on a company or organization's network. In terms of *network utilization*, it identifies the amount of traffic sent and received by a network connection. Here, you can determine how much bandwidth your wireless or Ethernet adapter is using. If the user on this device's job role requires downloading large files or if they must stream high-resolution videos or video-conference frequently and the bandwidth is consistently hitting 85%. For example, you may want to look at the components, such as RAM or the CPU to resolve bandwidth issues. Alternatively, the bandwidth issue may be problematic across the network segment as opposed to this single device, and other courses of action may need consideration. The point is that the ability to view performance and gather statistics from a single networked device is both rewarding and opens the gateway to the further resolution of network issues. Remember, the device being investigated can be a PC, laptop, smart device, printer, server, switch, router, or any device attached to the company network.

If the internet connection here is not an issue, but you still see high network activity on the device monitored, it could indicate a problematic **network interface card** (**NIC**) or another component, or it could also be a virus or malware, such as a rootkit, hidden on the device being investigated. Again, when you know the baseline for the network and expected statistics of bandwidth and internet properties, all devices monitored can be ultimately addressed.

Note: Network utilization is listed as a percentage of the total available theoretical bandwidth (such as 100 Mbps for a Fast Ethernet connection or higher for Gigabit Ethernet). System performance that has low CPU, disk, and memory statistics but suffers high network utilization could indicate a bottleneck at the network adapter causing degraded performance. Bottlenecks may be problematic at a micro or macro level. *In this scenario, as indicated by the other resource statistics, the resources are deemed as operating normally.

Network availability monitoring

It would be very difficult for a network administrator to log on to many devices and monitor them individually. Moving from device to device and accessing separate screens and interfaces would be an arduous task. However, there are many third-party utilities that provide software to manage and monitor devices on a network via a single interface. One of these network performance monitoring tools is available from SolarWinds and is an excellent example. **Network performance monitor** (**NPM**) is a proven, tried, and tested tool. It is a multi-vendor network monitoring system specially designed for scalability on business networks. NPM offers a wide range of tools for monitoring and analyzing network performance, gathering statistics, supporting advanced alerts, log reporting, and working with diagnostics. It offers an administrator a centralized location to view network devices and observe network traffic as it passes through the network. NPM's interface is called LUCID. This stands for logical, useable, customizable, interactive, and drill-down. This vantage point offers an administrator a bird's eye view of the company network and operations.

The key features of NPM are as follows:

- Multi-vendor network monitoring
- Network Insights for deeper visibility
- Intelligent maps
- NetPath and PerfStack for easy troubleshooting
- Smarter scalability for large environments
- Advanced alerting

The following figure depicts a screenshot of the NPM interface:

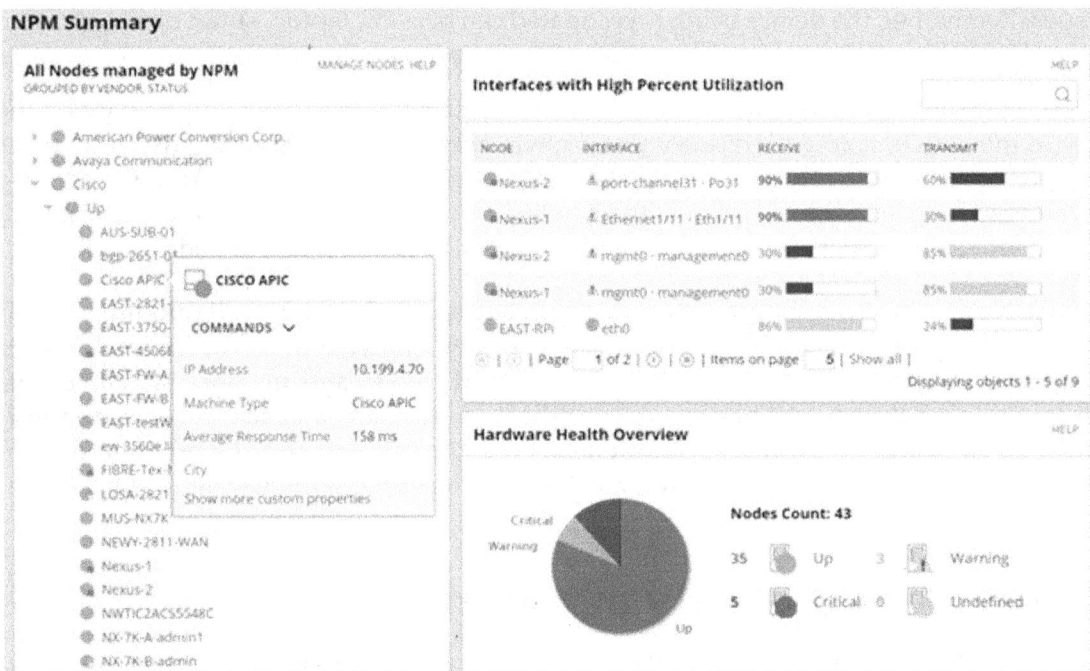

Figure 13.4: Network performance monitor, @SolarWinds

Open-source network monitoring tools

Other third-party open-source software available for network performance monitoring include Cacti, Checkmk Raw Edition, EventSentry Light, Icinga, LibreNMS, LogRhythm NetMon Freemium, Nagios Core, NetXMS, ntopng, and Observium Community. Please note that this list of tools can alter over time. On top of this, the list of **free open-source software** (**FOSS**) seems limitless, plus administrators may prefer paid subscriptions that provide additional support. The list aims to demonstrate how network performance monitoring and network availability monitoring are a significant part of an administrator's responsibility and duty and that there is no shortage of tools available for use.

Simple network management protocol

In *Chapter 5, Ports and Protocols*, the purpose of **Simple Network Management Protocol** (**SNMP**) was explained. SNMP allows the configuration, monitoring, and management of network resources and devices. Typical devices are switches, routers, cable modems, printers, servers, and client machines. Information about the device's performance and behavior is gathered from the device. The network administrator can act on this information and modify or adapt the components or devices based on the results of the data gathered. SNMP is defined by the **Internet Engineering Task Force** (**IETF**). SNMP has had several versions and is currently at version 3. SNMP uses UDP ports 161 and 162.

SNMP has a very rich set of data records and data trees for both sets and gets information from networking devices.

According to *Techopedia*, the traffic statistics from network traffic analysis help in the following:

- Understanding and evaluating the network utilization
- Download/upload speeds
- Type, size, origin and destination, and content/data of packets

It can be used by network administrators, security professionals, as well as attackers or intruders. One can then understand the evolution of SNMP as it aims to add and enhance security features such as authentication and encryption to its functionality.

There are several versions of SNMP, including the following:

- **SNMPv1**: The SNMP is a Full Internet Standard defined in RFC 1157.

- **SNMPv2c**: This version was defined in RFCs 1901–1908 and uses a community-string-based Administrative Framework. SNMPv2 has different message formats and protocol operations. Both SNMPv1 and SNMPv2 are now deemed to be obsolete.

- **SNMPv3**: In this newer version, the concept of authentication is expanded. V3 is an interoperable standards-based protocol originally defined in RFCs 2273 to 2275. It provides secure access to devices by **authenticating** and **encrypting** packets over the network. SNMPv3 includes these security features: *message integrity* to ensure that a packet was not tampered with in transit; *authentication* to determine that the message is from a valid and reliable source; and *encryption* to prevent the contents of a message from being read by an unauthorized source by ensuring the data is securely packaged, replacing simple password sharing as clear text.

You can install SNMP on a Windows Server operating system using the **Add Roles** and **Features** Wizard. The following figure displays a list of roles that can be added to the server:

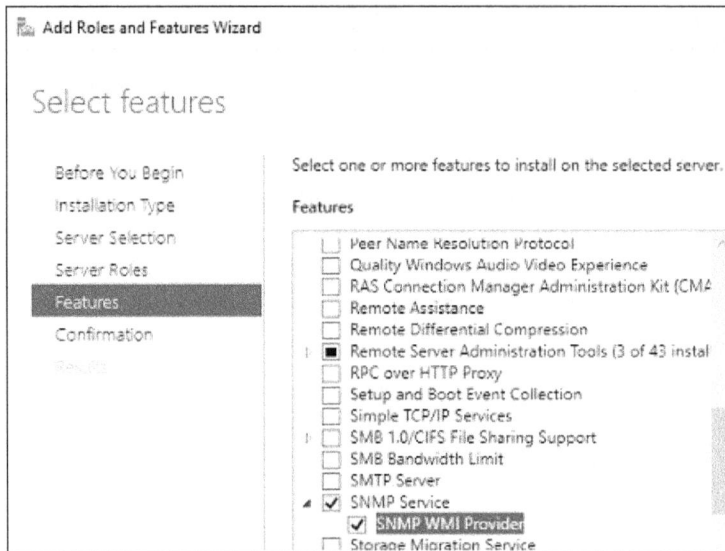

Figure 13.5: Add roles and features: Windows Server 2019

Alternatively, you can use Windows PowerShell or the Windows Admin Center Web interface on Windows Server Core. *Figure 13.6* demonstrates this interface:

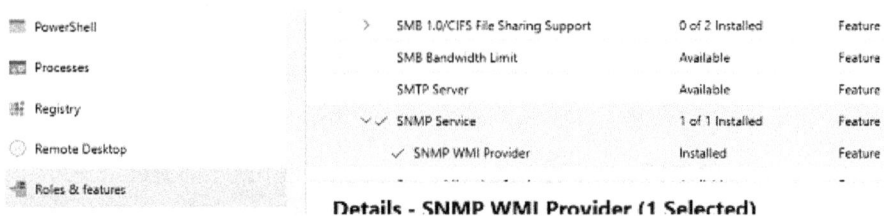

Figure 13.6: SNMP service: Windows Server Core

SNMP is also enabled on Cisco devices like switches or routers. The settings are configured in the device's IOS. A setting configures the community string and access level (read-only or read-write) with the `snmp-server community string ro | rw` command. An administrator then has the option to document the device's location and the contact person's name and details, `snmp-server contact` text command. The main point is that many devices on a network can be enabled as SNMP agents or traps.

The basic components of SNMP are managed devices, SNMP agents, SNMP managers, and MIBs or Management Information Databases, also known as **Management Information Base (MIB)**.

A MIB enables the management of network elements. The MIBs are composed of managed objects known by the name **Object Identifier** (**Object ID** or **OID**). An SNMP-compliant MIB comprises definitions and information about the properties of managed resources and the services that the SNMP agents support.

The manageable features of resources, as defined in an SNMP-compliant MIB, are referred to as managed objects or management variables (or just objects or variables).

Each Identifier is unique and represents specific features of a managed device. When queried, the return value of each identifier could be different. For example, the return value can be *text, number, counter*, and so on.

Network device logs

As observed, there are many ways to install and configure a Network Management Appliance. Network management and monitoring at a *scalable* level usually occur in an appliance dedicated to the task of gathering statistics and data, which may then be analyzed and interpreted. Here, *Figure 13.7* shows the basic functionality, where system messages transfer (in this case) from a router and a switch on a network to a **network management system** (**NMS**).

The NMS displays the performance data collected from each network component, thereby enabling network administrators and engineers to make changes as required.

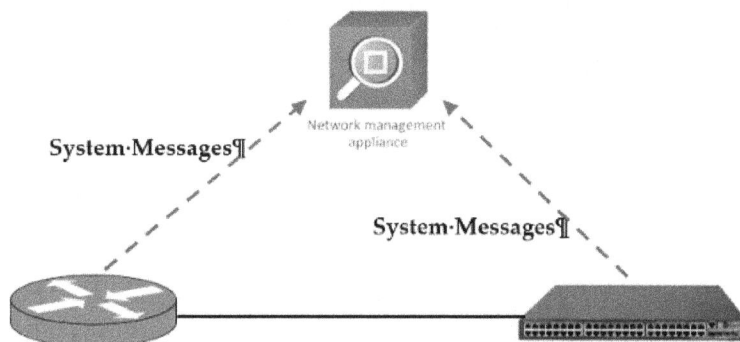

Figure 13.7: *Network management appliance*

In *Figure 13.8*, the SNMP process is outlined. Note the managed devices, SNMP Agents, SNMP Manager, and MIB on both devices being managed:

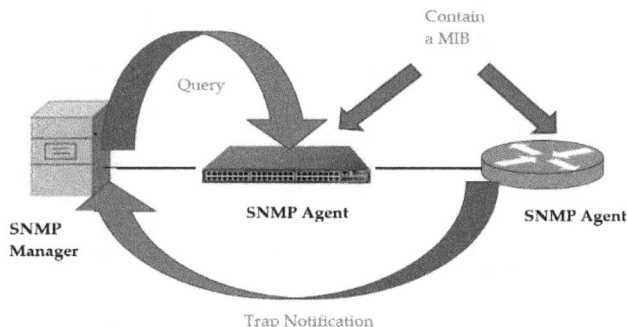

Figure 13.8: *SNMP process*

Figure 13.8 shows the SNMP architecture. The SNMP manager is our NMS server. In the example, there are two managed devices: a switch and a router. The two devices are running SNMP agent software. The switch and router both have an MIB, which includes variables relevant to that particular type of device.

The SNMP manager shares an understanding of the MIB, plus the SNMP manager can send queries to the managed devices to gather information from them, where necessary. The devices can also send trap notifications to notify the SNMP manager that something has occurred with the device that needs attention or further investigation. Additionally, as an administrator, you have a third option where the SNMP manager may push and change information on the devices; however, this function is not commonly implemented in applications.

System logs

A log is a record of events that have occurred on a system. Earlier, we briefly looked at Performance Monitor on a Windows 10/11 system. In Windows, there are other system utilities that generate logs and where logs may be customized. One of these utilities is Event Viewer, which is an excellent integrated tool in Windows for logging system activity. In essence, logging capabilities are built into operating systems, services, and applications. Log entries are generated in response to changes in configuration, system state, or network conditions.

Every program that starts on your PC posts a notification in an Event Log, and every functioning program posts a notification before the application stops. Every system access, security change, operating system glitch or tweak, hardware failure or component hiccup, and other driver hiccups and malfunctions all end up in one or another type of Event Log or system notification. Event Viewer holds an incredible repository of centralized data and statistics about a single device to incorporate the functionality, features, and performance of its hardware and software operations. When it comes to networking, this viewpoint would be interpreted at a micro level, occurring on a single host or device. As a network admin, we need both the micro and macro view of our network.

The Event Viewer scans those text log files gathered, collates them, and presents them in an easy-to-read and interpret format. Underlying this presentation are a multitude of flat text files, accumulating data in a database that is easier to handle and view.

Figure 13.9 presents the items under which logging entries are generated: **Application**, **Security**, **Setup**, **System**, and **Forwarded Events**.

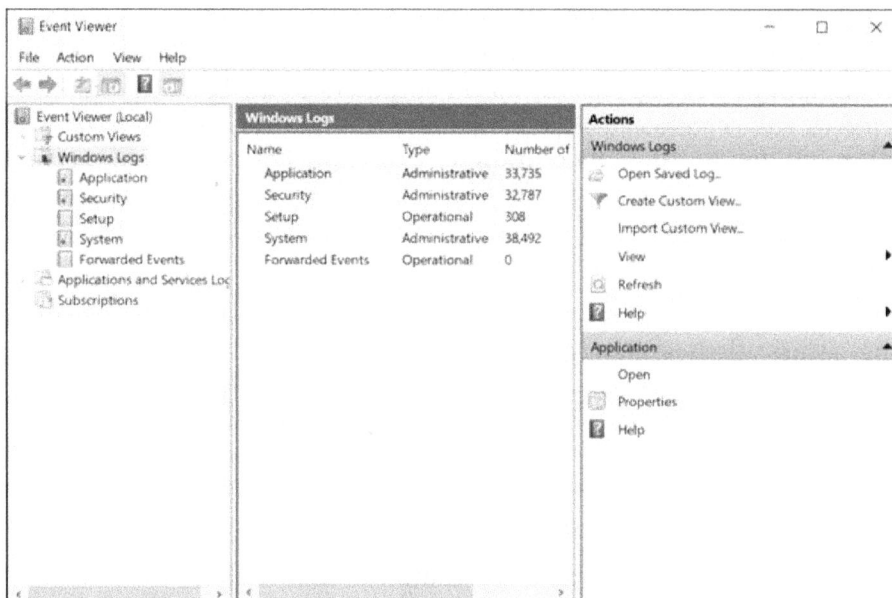

Figure 13.9: Event Viewer, Logs

Applications and Service logs are also available to view as saved logs or with the ability to create a custom view. Events are categorized in terms of their severity and type. *Table 13.1* categorizes these events:

Event	What caused the event
Error	Significant problems, possibly including loss of data or functionality
Warning	Not necessarily significant, but might indicate that there is a problem presenting in the future
Information	Regular data about an application, like an FYI

Table 13.1: Event breakdown

Remember, these logging capabilities are built into operating systems, services, and applications. If required, you can customize logs or enable extensive logging but please take note that the logging activity does consume system resources such as RAM, Disk, and CPU. A dedicated server or network monitoring appliance is far more suited to make logging and interpreting logs more practical at a macro level to include the most significant devices on your entire network.

Syslog

SNMP and Syslog are both used for logging. NMS servers will generally support both SNMP and Syslog.

A variety of devices are needed to build a computer network and make up the network's infrastructure. Intermediary devices and media such as switches, hubs, cables, wireless APs, antennas, and power supplies connect computers to the LAN internally. IoTs, VoIP phones, printers, and servers also link to the organization's router (and point to the LAN), as do all other end devices (directly or indirectly). In terms of external connectivity from a LAN, the router connects the company's local network (LAN/WLAN) to WAN and to the outside world. Many of these listed devices can be configured to generate personal activity logs and forward these logs to a dedicated server.

As described in *Chapter 5, Ports and Protocols*, Syslog is used for system management and logging security issues. Syslog gathers statistics, analyzes statistics, and generates debugging messages. The server used is called a Syslog server. It is usually a paid-for third-party appliance and software. This centralized approach to auditing, monitoring, and reviewing data is advantageous to any organization using the service provided. System Logging Protocol is also used on Unix and Linux-based systems and is an effective auditing tool for assessing devices and equipment. Syslog uses TCP and UDP port **514**.

The Syslog server provides a (moderately complex) user-friendly interface for viewing the Syslog output. Remember that logs are only ever useful if they are analyzed and interpreted.

In computing, **parsing** means analyzing (a string or text) into logical syntactic components. The Syslog server parses the syslog output and places the messages into pre-defined columns for easier interpretation. If timestamps are configured on the networking device that is sourcing the Syslog messages, the date and time of each message subsequently display in the Syslog server output.

Network administrators can (easily) navigate the large amount of data compiled on a Syslog server. As with all tasks, practice and continuity of practice makes perfect. As explained, this data can be levied for time-critical information, system monitoring, network maintenance, diagnostics, and troubleshooting.

Open-source Syslog Servers

As with the availability of open-source network monitoring tools, there are a lot of open-source Syslog server software available for an administrator to choose from. Some Syslog servers need client-based software to install and manage, but many developers also provide Web-based solutions. This web-based approach can ease network management remotely and/or bring together data from different systems running on a different network environment.

Open-source solutions include Kiwi Syslog Server, PRTG, SNMP Soft Sys-log Watcher, Splunk Light, The Dude, TFTPD32, Icinga Open-Source Monitoring, Visual Syslog Server, and 3cDaemon. As specified with the open-source *network monitoring tools*, these server softwares can alter over time. On top of this, the list of FOSS seems limitless, plus administrators may prefer paid-for subscriptions that provide additional support.

In *Figure 13.10*, you can see that the options to install the Kiwi Syslog Server are as a service or as an application. By selecting to install the software as a service, the user does not need to be logged on to the system for the processing of data to take place.

Figure 13.10: *Kiwi Syslog Server (SolarWinds)*

You can then choose a **LocalSystem** account or a network administrator to continue installation. The remainder of the installation is relatively straightforward. As with other tools, you can add filters, select actions, and customize the type of data queried. *Figure 13.11* displays the service install options:

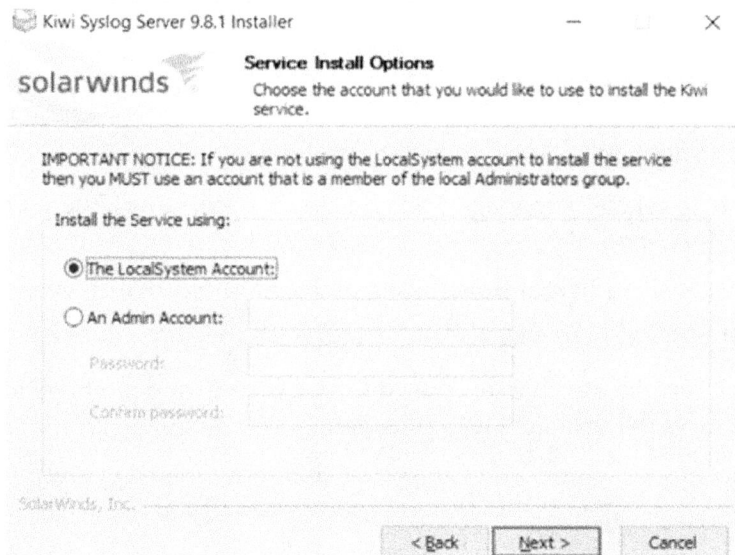

Figure 13.11: *Kiwi Syslog Server install*

You can do many things with this Syslog utility. You can alter how the messages are displayed by going to display, and you can set alarms when certain conditions are met, or events are triggered. You can also receive traps. SNMP traps are similar to syslog in that they are real-time notifications that notify you when you have a network problem.

You can set the utility to listen for SNMP traps by going to **SNMP** under **Inputs**. In *Figure 13.12*, the creation of a trap is demonstrated from the Syslog service manager:

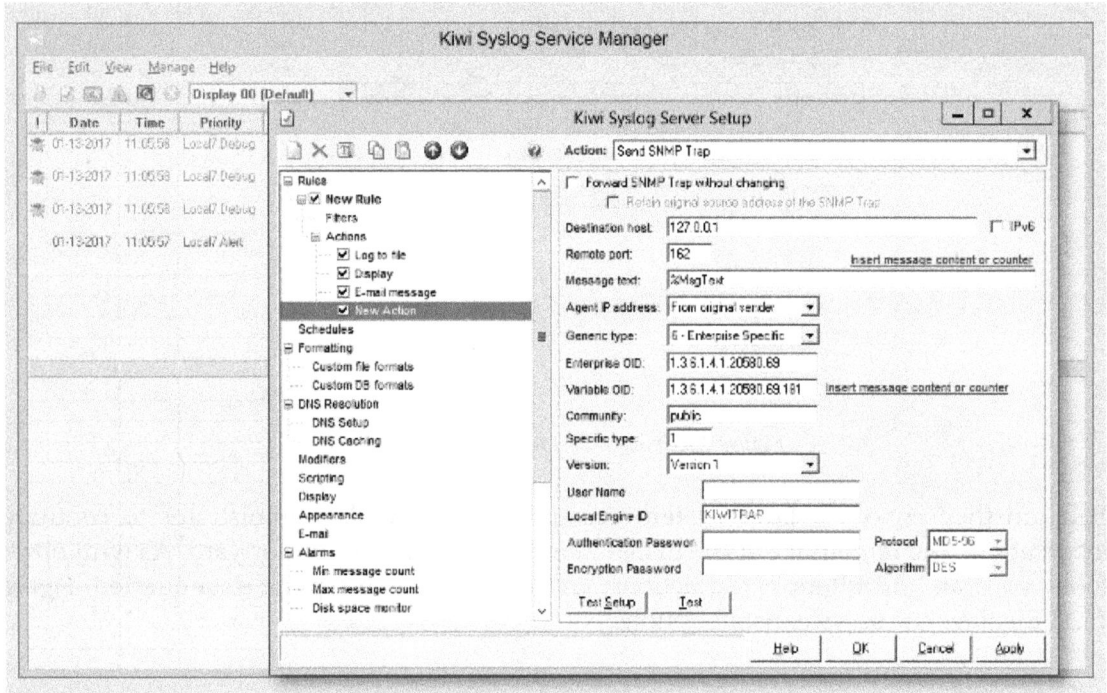

Figure 13.12: Kiwi Syslog Server, SNMP traps

The key features of the Kiwi Syslog Server are as follows:

- The ability to centrally manage Syslog messages, Windows Event Logs, and SNMP traps.

- Alerts are received in real-time (based on highlighted critical events).

- The ability to automatically handle syslog messages.

- A central repository, that is, the ability to store and archive logs to support compliance with regulatory compliance.

- The option to view and analyze syslog data anywhere securely—with safe web access.

Syslog is also configured on routers and switches to include Cisco devices. Syslog provides an elementary tool for collecting and displaying messages as they appear on a Cisco device console display. An administrator can view logging information or related configuration information via the device's console.

The router in *Figure 13.13* is named R1. When an interface goes up, the Cisco IOS formats the log message:

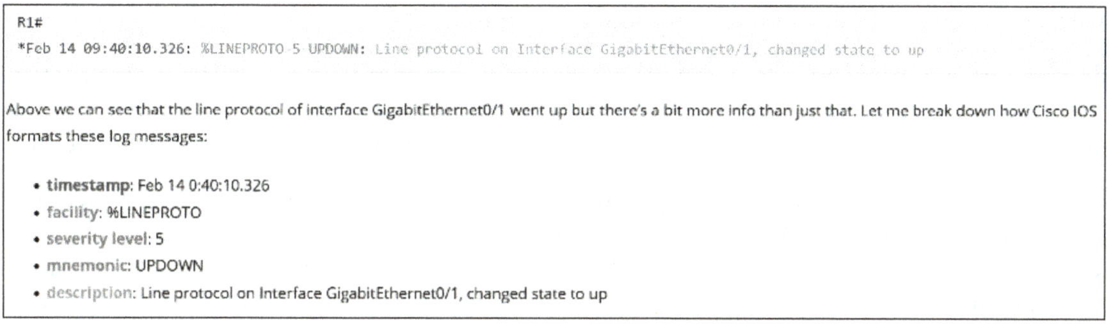

```
R1#
*Feb 14 09:40:10.326: %LINEPROTO-5-UPDOWN: Line protocol on Interface GigabitEthernet0/1, changed state to up


Above we can see that the line protocol of interface GigabitEthernet0/1 went up but there's a bit more info than just that. Let me break down how Cisco IOS
formats these log messages:

   • timestamp: Feb 14 0:40:10.326
   • facility: %LINEPROTO
   • severity level: 5
   • mnemonic: UPDOWN
   • description: Line protocol on Interface GigabitEthernet0/1, changed state to up
```

Figure 13.13: Kiwi Syslog message on a Cisco router

As demonstrated, Syslog is supported by a variety of devices. The Syslog protocol provides a wide range of system info, thus making syslog monitoring an important part of network monitoring.

Syslog messages will capture many events. These include the following:

- Interface statistics/status
- Interface errors or alerts (CRC errors, Jumbo frames, Runts, encapsulation issues, and so on)

If an interface goes down, the administrator must know immediately to proceed with an investigation. Thus, there are different severity levels on Cisco devices. The severity levels range from 0 to 7, with the lower number being the more serious in terms of priority. Levels are as follows: 0—Emergency, 1—Alert, 2—Critical, 3—Error, 4—Warning, 5—Notice, 6—Informational, and 7—Debug. Note the similarity across all logging systems, whereby we have a strategy for handling information gleaned from logs and addressing the needs of the network in accordance with this information.

Network administrators can change the severity levels shown for the console or the terminal lines (telnet or SSH) and those to be sent to the external Syslog server.

Environmental factors and sensors

Sensor nodes in computer networks capture sensitive and valuable information. These sensors can send data to a gateway node to be processed by a central management system as in a wireless sensor network. Wireless sensor networks are gaining popularity. In these networks, there needs to be a secure and reliable way of gathering information at a central point, plus the data gathered should be reliable.

Embedded systems and Industrial Control Systems use sensors to react and make changes to their operations in real time. **Real-time operating systems** (**RTOS**) handle processing in a *deterministic* manner. Tasks must be carried out with almost no latency so sensors will play an important part in the proper functioning and accuracy of embedded systems. Some examples of embedded devices are gaming consoles, mobile phones, household appliances, and industrial machinery and equipment.

Regarding industrial control systems, these control systems are used in critical infrastructure such as water treatment facilities, transportation industries, oil and gas units, power plants, manufacturing, hospitals, telecom systems, food production systems, and other systems.

Supervisory control and data acquisition (**SCADA**) controllers monitor and control **programmable logic controller** (**PLC**) systems. These SCADA controllers gather data and adjust the system based on the data acquired from sensors. Users are provided with a **human-machine interface** (**HMI**) to analyze and process data based on data and measurements. **Remote terminal units** (**RTUs**) gather data from the sensors and devices in a company or plant. This gathered data can be used for automated responses such as reducing pressure in a system when it gets too high, identifying humidity, changing temperature, or even predicting flooding, and so on. Sensors offer intelligent insights into the production process. They are part of the process required to trigger alarms when there is a failure and enable the problem-solving of events and issues in industrial systems and in production.

Regarding time constraints, these systems help to optimize time and energy on top of mitigating downtime. As noted, SCADA systems are used in water treatment plants, power grids, HVAC systems, and many other manufacturing and industrial processes.

In essence, making smart decisions calls for smart logging *and* smart investigation.

NetFlow data

NetFlow is a Cisco networking protocol for gathering and analyzing network data. According to *Techopedia*, NetFlow is primarily designed for network administrators and managers to help them with detailed information, statistics, and overall network operation data. NetFlow is integrated within the proprietary Cisco IOS installed on the supporting routers and switches by default and works by registering all the IP traffic that flows in and out of the network through these devices.

Most organizations use NetFlow for some or all the following key data collection purposes:

- To measure who is using what network resources for what purpose and do so proficiently.
- To account for resource usage and then charge back according to the resource utilization level.
- To use statistics gathered to do more effective network planning so that resource allocation and deployment are well-aligned with customer needs and requirements.

- To use the information to better structure and customize the set of available applications and services to meet user needs and customer service requirements.

Figure 13.14 shows the NetFlow architecture and demonstrates the processes used in NetFlow design:

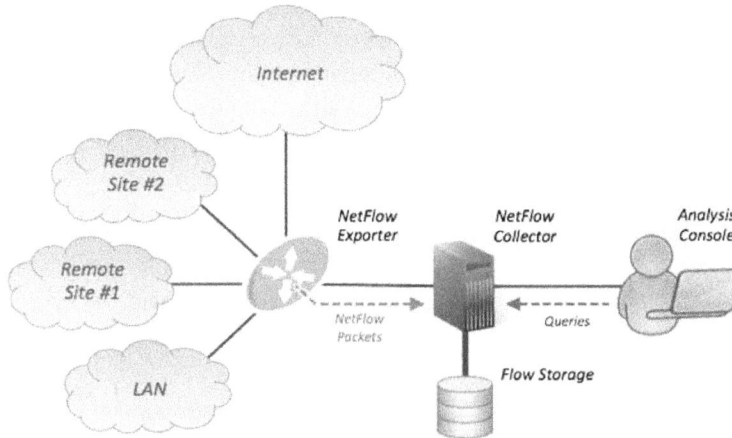

Figure 13.14: *NetFlow architecture*
Source: Amp 32, CC BY-SA 3.0 via Wikimedia Commons

NetFlow has a newer iteration called Flexible NetFlow. This release also provides a means of collecting IP operational data from IP networks, but in terms of scalability of flow data, it moves beyond traditional NetFlow functionality. Flexible NetFlow uses **deep packet inspection (DPI)** to achieve these enhancements.

NetFlow provides data to enable network and security monitoring, network planning, traffic analysis, and IP accounting. Cisco IOS Flexible NetFlow is the next-generation in-flow technology. Enhanced tools and filtering techniques make this iteration appealing to device administrators, especially in the field of security and the use of network security detection.

In summation, all NetFlow collectors provide sophisticated analysis options for NetFlow data. Flexible NetFlow pushes the sophistication and specificity of data collection further.

Other methods and tools for monitoring and testing networks and/or viewing logs generated via load testers, throughput testers, packet sniffers, and protocol analyzers.

Conclusion

In this chapter, we explored the tools and technologies used to manage and monitor networks. The reader should now be able to identify and differentiate between these tools and technologies. The reader should recognize the appropriate statistics and sensors to ensure network availability and understand embedded systems, industrial control systems and SCADA. They also learned to differentiate between a variety of network management tools and monitoring techniques. All systems generally have a means of generating logs and reports. With the support of external software, these systems can be configured to provide a series of logs and reports that can be assessed and diagnosed.

As previously stated, a network administrator must be adept at reading the details of logs and acting on the details of device component functionality and system logs gathered. By spotting abnormal statistics, an administrator can classify the component that is overloaded or not responding correctly. The reader should use logging software to keep track of network conditions, recognize situations that might signal potential problems or critical events, pinpoint the sources of problems and problem-solve them, and locate areas of the company network that might need to be replaced, upgraded, or modified.

In the upcoming chapter, we will discuss the critical purpose and functions of plans, procedures, and policies in an organization. We will identify and describe how a business uses these plans and how documentation is a crucial part of network and business operations.

Points to remember

- There are many methods for logging on systems and networks to gather data, interpret data, and use the information gathered for decision-making and problem-solving networks.

- Monitoring tools can either be integrated into the system or run as software on a separate system configured to send and receive data to the monitored devices. There are many third-party tools available for ensuring network availability and optimum performance of hosts, intermediary devices, interfaces, and any other element essential to the running of a computer network.

- Monitoring a network is ideal for tracking network conditions to identify situations that might signal potential problems. These strategies and statistics pinpoint the sources of problems and help you, as an administrator, to locate areas of your network that might need to be tweaked, replaced, upgraded, or revised.

- Performance Monitor, Task Manager, Event Viewer, Syslog, SNMP, and NetFlow are some of the tools a network administrator uses in a modern network to manage and monitor the collection, display, and analysis of events related to the functioning of networking devices.

- The content of this chapter is mapped to *Domain 3: Network Operations*, given a scenario, use network monitoring technologies.

Key terms

- **Uptime/downtime**: This term is used in the computer industry for when a computer is operational. Downtime is the time when it is not operational. Uptime is frequently measured in terms of a percentage/percentile. For example, one standard for uptime that is sometimes discussed is a goal called five 9s—that is, a computer that is operational 99.999% of the time.

- **Top talkers**: The ability to view pairs of computers or devices using the most bandwidth can be viewed on some system logging software. These devices are referred to as top talkers. This ability may lead to the discovery of a trojan horse or to an abusive use of torrent software. These hosts send the most data, either from the organization's network or into the organization's network.

- **Top listeners**: These hosts or devices receive most of the data in the network. They can be constantly streaming or downloading large amounts of data from the internet (or an unwanted server). These computers generate heavy traffic and lower the performance of the network because of consuming high bandwidth.

Questions

1. Give examples of network monitoring tools and techniques.
2. Define and describe sensors as used in computer networking.
3. Explain the reasons why networking management and monitoring are critical to network availability and performance.
4. Give some examples of network management software.

Join our book's Discord space

Join the book's Discord Workspace for Latest updates, Offers, Tech happenings around the world, New Release and Sessions with the Authors:

https://discord.bpbonline.com

CHAPTER 14
Policies and Procedures in Practice

Introduction

In the previous chapter, we explored how the management and monitoring of networks is an integral part of network policy, procedure, and practice. We viewed this activity from the perspective and viewpoint of a network administrator and/or the IT department and technical team as a whole. We discussed the tools and techniques for enabling and securing a functional, viable network. Now, we will take that viewpoint and look at the policies and procedures that necessitate a viable and efficient *organization*, one that is aimed at the creation of consistency and standards within the organization, one that is focused on the management and monitoring of internal company practices (to include the effective training of staff and handling of staffing issues). The key terms connected with this area of discussion are continuity of practice, communication, consistency, the controlling of risks, and *planned-for* compliance with regional, national, or international rules and expected standards of operation. Drafting policies and procedures and documenting or amending existing ones takes both an individual and collaborative approach. The process of these activities involves making checks, running tests, and undertaking thorough documentation reviews.

Structure

This chapter explains the following topics:

- Plans and procedures
- Change management
- Incident response plan
- Disaster recovery plan
- Business continuity plan
- Standard operating procedures
- Policy compliance
- Common documentation
- Important factors of physical installations
- Hot Aisle/Cold Aisle layout
- Main distribution frame vs. intermediate distribution frame
- Sensors

Objectives

After completing this chapter, the reader should recognize the plans and procedures organizations participate in. They will be able to explain the purpose of these procedures and policies and interpret them as a critical aspect of the viable functioning of a company and organization. The reader will also identify the competencies and skills a network administrator holds and how *defined* procedures, policies, and practices in the IT department feed into the company's functionality as a whole. Designing, developing, defining, and reviewing these policies must be clear, unambiguous, and easily discernible and demonstrate a keen eye for the company's nature, ethos, and mission going about its daily practice. A network administrator should understand their role within the overall system.

Plans and procedures

First, let us differentiate between a plan and a procedure. At its most basic level, a **plan** may be a drawing or diagram. It may encapsulate an objective or a method for achieving an end goal. It may detail or formulate a plan of action, be very specific or more general in nature—depending upon the scope of the operation or the expected outcomes. In other words, a plan can also be composed of smaller, more detailed plans or sets of plans. The purpose of the plan is to achieve a goal or reach targets. Plans have specified intentions. A **procedure** or procedures outline specific methods that express policies in action or delineate activities that align with achieving a plan of action. Procedures may be flexible or adaptable to meet change or new industry requirements. To analogize, a plan is a thing, a map, a sketch, and an illustration of moving from source to destination as a marked-out engendered journey. Procedures are the means to get there, the actions to be taken along the way, plus the strategies necessary to enable the plan to succeed. Note that in this analogy, the plan is visualized as a noun, and procedures are seen as the actions and verbs as they pertain to the noun.

Business plans include action plans like **Business Continuity Plans (BCP)**, and **Disaster Recovery Plans (DRP)** to respond to incidents and restore critical functionality to company operations.

Figure 14.1 illustrates a business process action plan with a hierarchical process aiming toward success:

Figure 14.1: *Business process action plan, designed by Stories/Freepik*

Change management

The most important factor in an IT environment regarding change is that changes should never impede or negatively impact the delivery of IT services—wherever this delivery is achievable. Changes in IT are unavoidable. Changes may range from the need for a new set of mobile devices to a new printer, switch, router, or **access point (AP)** to a fully-fleshed need for a more major change in the infrastructure of the organization's network. For example, the entire network may need an upgrade to the latest version of an operating system, or the hardware on a network segment may be nearing its end-of-life and require replacement. The one fact remains: change is inevitable, and consequently, change must be handled accordingly.

There is no shortage of business templates or companies that assist other companies in handling and managing change, *but* a majority of larger enterprises and organizations have change management procedures in place *internally* to ensure that software or hardware installations and upgrades go smoothly and do not interfere with the continuity of business or provision of services to the users on their network. The key focus in this area is for the company to be *causative* over change, to be in *control* of change, and to be able to *plan and execute* change while controlling network operations. Sustaining connectivity and access to the network while ensuring access to files and resources contributes to the smooth flow of business operations.

Effective change management processes can avert business functions from being negatively impacted by necessary installations, hardware or software updates, equipment upgrades, component replacements, and application reconfigurations that are an expected or anticipated normal part of IT operations. In short, change control policies minimize or eliminate *chaos* and disorder.

Most change management processes include the following elements:

- **Identification of the change**: Typically dealing with what, when, and why questions.

- **Assessment**: Auditing areas impacted, costs, risks, and so on of changes to be undergone. Uptime/downtime. Frequency of change.

- **Planning**: The period of time when change is happening. *For how long will the change last?* Fall-back procedures should change, fail, or partially work.

- **Endorsement**: *Who sanctions the change?* Rationale and logic for change.

- **Execution**: Re-delegation and distribution of tasks. *Who does what?*

- **Acceptance**: Who ratifies the changes made? Who tests it?

- **Documentation**: For example, system logs, results of tests, and narrative of change.

Incident response plan

Security in IT is at the forefront of every organization's thinking. Cybersecurity attacks and security breaches are *inevitably* in our everyday world. All organizations and enterprises must consider the nature and types of attacks that can occur on their network or with the data transmitted to and from their company's devices. Consider the sheer amount of personal, sensitive, and company data traveling around a company domain or LAN, internally and via the cloud. True to say, even one device can generate significant amounts of private/sensitive data. Then consider the magnitude of data on CANs, MANs, and WANs!

Take the data illustrated in *Figure 14.2*. Imagine the volume of traffic and pathways created by even a single user on a network and the routes through which these data frames or packets may travel. Multiply this data generated by a hundred, several hundred, or even a thousand employees and you just about get the scope and depth of data we are at times considering.

Figure 14.2: All the data concepts, designed by Stories/Freepik

All the data and the devices need to be secured. Therefore, security policies outline all aspects of information technology. These policies and plans include security incident response methods. An **Incident Response Plan** (when optimally actioned) prevents data and monetary loss and enables the organization to resume its operations with minimum disruption.

Proactive planning helps people know what to do when a security incident occurs. Incident response plans should define what is considered to be a security incident, identify first responders and other strategic personnel in the chain of command, outline the processes and steps to be followed when an incident occurs, outline reporting strategies and mechanisms, and ensure proper communication and incident handling happens at all stages of the response. All relevant staff and management should be notified throughout the incident response, and all outcomes should be documented and addressed after the incident ends for (digital) forensic analysis and re-evaluation moving forward.

In many areas of life, education is the key. It is no different in organizations as they handle and manage incidents. Training of key personnel should be thorough, and all employees should be aware of the role they play and the responsibilities they hold before, during, and after an incident is declared. As noted, proficient handling of incidents and security incidents ensures business continuity in the event of a security breach or attack.

Competent documentation of the incident and implementation of countermeasures and processes to reduce the likelihood of a future attack form part of the response in its review stages. All incidents should be investigated as a reflective exercise, and the response itself should be critically analyzed to eliminate loopholes and tighten security practices.

In *Chapter 13, Managing and Monitoring a Network*, we stated that a network administrator must be adept at reading the details of logs and acting on the details of device component functionality and system logs gathered. By spotting abnormal statistics, an administrator can classify the component that is overloaded or not responding correctly. In addition to identifying malfunctioning components, an administrator must remain up to date with security logs from devices and be able to call upon these documents or logs when required to locate or interpret a security attack or data breach. Forensic tools, archived log files, or data in backups can assist in investigating a security incident. A network administrator should know their role in the event of a security incident and respond in accordance with the incident response plan.

The incident response plan can be a distinct document or be included as part of a larger disaster recovery and BCP.

One organization that assists professionals and businesses in cybersecurity measures is the SANS Institute. SANS offers solutions and training to cybersecurity leadership. Its mission is to combat adversaries and enable organizations to establish a critical line of defense against hackers and threat actors. Regarding constructing a plan, the SANS Institute recommends that every incident response plan should comprise the following six components:

1. Staff training
2. Incident identification
3. Breach containment
4. Problem eradication
5. Data recovery
6. Lessons learned

There are many cybersecurity firms whose mission is to provide advice and training to staff and business leaders. There are also many tools available to research and investigate attacks and evidence gathered from incidents that have occurred. Some examples of utilities include SANS Investigative Forensics Toolkit, Autopsy, the Sleuth Kit, EnCase, Image creation: FTK imager, The Coroner's Toolkit, COFEE, and packet sniffing software such as Wireshark.

Disaster recovery plan

There is one thing about disasters that we can immediately agree on. Disasters are relative to the person or group who is experiencing one. In other words, disasters do not have to be *catastrophic* such as tornadoes or tsunamis, when speaking about natural disasters. A disaster for one company could be a minor setback for another. It all depends upon the nature and scale of the disaster and the degree to which the organization has the personnel or technical know-how and tools to handle it when it happens. A disaster can include anything from natural disasters that affect the network structure, like storms or flooding leading to electrical power outages, to malicious attacks on the network itself. There is a gradient scale and range of disasters applicable to a specific company, and these disasters are relative. We are aware that the impact of data loss or data corruption from unplanned outages caused by hardware failure, human error, hacking, or malware can be substantial and costly in labor and lost profit. Therefore, a company's plan to recover from a disaster will be unique and distinctive.

A **disaster recovery plan** is a comprehensive document that describes how to restore business and network operations quickly and will address strategies to keep critical IT functions running during or after a disaster occurs. DRPs are typically constructed as a subset of a BCP. IT-related recovery and continuity are addressed by the DRP. The DRP planning group needs to have a clear understanding of the business processes, applications, and technology required to keep the business running. This enables the planning group to devise a plan to differentiate between the severity of disasters—for example, mission-critical, critical, essential, and non-critical. The key people from each business department should be members of the planning group. This representation ensures all areas of the business are overviewed and analyzed. A risk and business impact analysis should be prepared by each representative in advance of drawing up the plan. From this analysis, priority levels can be assigned, and the impacts understood cohesively. The evaluating group will comprehend how departments interact and engage with each other and the way in which IT functions to support communication within the organization. The nature of the data that is transmitted and received will be addressed. In short, the flow and type of data in transmission will be weighed and measured. On recovery, systems will be secured, and critical pieces of equipment will be locked down if necessary. *Figure 14.3* shows the importance of having a secure server:

Figure 14.3: Secure server concept, designed by Stories/Freepik

The server in any domain is a critical focal point of security hardening practice.

Business continuity plan

A BCP enables the organization to continue operations during a disaster. This includes all IT operations, but nowadays, the plan encapsulates every other aspect of the business *holistically*, extending beyond IT. The vital functions of the business will be outlined and broken down into component parts in accordance with its systems and processes. BCP commonly covers risks, threats, IT hacks and cyberattacks, and any other event threatening business operations. In terms of things at the IT front, a network engineer or administrator sometimes creates a plan for their department to cover network and technology operations. In brief, BCPs should be a solutions-focused response to disasters. To be effective, the company should be capable of running throughout the duration of a disruptive incident or in the event of a disaster. The BCP is typically comprised of resources, actions, procedures, and information as a preparation and explanatory guide to the business and may outline typical events causing disruption or minor to major disasters that require responses.

A BCP contains certain steps to hold a strong and resilient plan of action. The steps to be followed can include a business impact analysis, continue and recover business operations, staff training, and the names/roles of an organizational team to handle and manage the implementation of continuity. Checklists, resources required, location of relevant backup data, and risk scenarios may be features of the business continuity plan specific to the company. As observed, the BCP is comprised of significant detailed documentation. However, the main consideration is this: the better the plan of action is, the more solid and reliable the details are, and the better the outcomes. The BCP is, after all, an organization's battle plan in the event of a disaster.

Figure 14.4 describes the stages of the business continuity planning lifecycle:

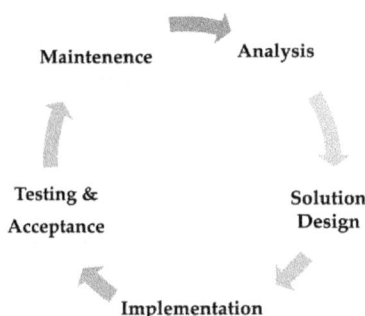

Figure 14.4: *Business continuity planning lifecycle*

A **business impact analysis** (**BIA**) emphasizes the impact losses will have on the organization. It is depicted as a stage in the BCP lifecycle. A BIA:

- Recognizes risks and threats affecting the system or production processes and assets.

- Determines the crucial nature of business activities and related resource requirements.

- Quantifies the impacts of disruption to the business or consequences of a disaster.

- Qualifies the recovery point aims and objectives.

- Measures the maximum downtime the business can survive without each process and asset (operating as functional entities).

- Approximates concrete impacts (such as financial loss) and intangible impacts (such as loss of customer trust) on the organization.

The solution design extends on this analysis. Implementation of the plan is further outlined and described. All stakeholders are included in the analysis, so recovery is optimized. A recovery timeframe can subsequently be derived from the analysis and a maintenance program put in place, so the BIA remains relevant.

System lifecycle

One of the critical aspects of managing network devices is asset management. It supports the life cycle management of both hardware and software.

Asset management may include the following:

- Holding an inventory or audit of stock and equipment
- Contracts and service plans
- The financial aspects of assets owned
- An asset management database
- A procedure that follows assets from their acquisition through to their disposal, such as servers, laptops, desktops, mobile devices/smartphones, tablets, and notebooks
- Legal issues
- Licensing requirements/Service level agreements
- Equipment location
- Offsite storage—if applicable

Assets may also be labeled with **radio frequency identification (RFID)** tags, serial numbers, bar codes, and/or numbered stickers. These forms of labeling will also be collated and presented in documentation as part of a systems logging *trail*.

The IT department must be aware of *warranty* issues as well as legal processes and procedures. The equipment might be under warranty for a specific period of time, and this timeframe may vary according to the manufacturer, service, or cloud provider. Remember, one of the main tasks a technician or administrator has to undertake with systems is related to managing and repairing problematic devices. A network administrator will be required to decide whether to repair or replace an asset and at what stage these checks on functionality and performance are to be made. There is nothing worse for an administrator regarding asset management than to discover a device is just out of warranty when a discovery or problem is found to exist with the device. If the repair of the asset occurs through warranty, this is a more cost-effective solution should the device worsen or continue to fail. In this regard, timing is crucial.

A typical **system lifecycle** entails procurement, deployment, use and support, maintenance, retirement or redeployment, and (safe and secure) asset disposal, as depicted in the following figure:

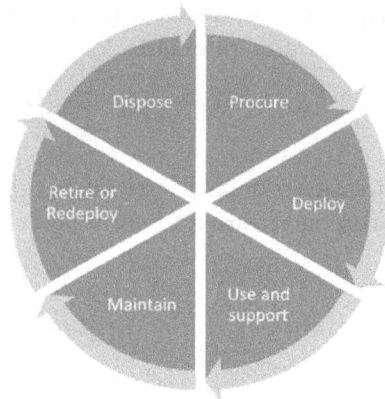

Figure 14.5: Systems life cycle

As you can see, the system lifecycle is quite comprehensive. Consequently, it will comprise various types of documentation and perhaps be managed via third-party software built for this very purpose.

Standard operating procedures

Each organization will commonly have its unique set of routine procedures. These procedures are captured in a document(s) outlining the standard operating procedures of the organization. Typically designed with the purpose of supporting staff to carry out their daily tasks and routines, a **Standard Operating Procedure** (**SOP**) focuses on clarity, effective communication of roles and responsibilities, and what to do as an employee should equipment go down (downtime) or if there is an issue with any of the company facilities. The primary purpose of an SOP is to maintain consistency and ensure the quality of performance during *regular* business operations. The SOP might be written as a step-by-step guide or could be a detailed document broken down into explicit sections and processes.

The SOP might be a checklist, a step-by-step to-do list, or a bulleted list. This type of checklist works for relatively easy tasks. If the tasks are more difficult or involve steps and stages rising through the management structure, the document may be a hierarchical list. Flowcharts such as process flowcharts equally work well for more comprehensive or complex tasks. Needless to say, there are plenty of templates and third-party software or support to design and develop any of the documents outlined in this chapter.

Communication is key in business. With a detailed, well-written, and presented SOP, employees will comprehend tasks better, understand personal responsibility and accountability, have a go-to place for clarification and queries, and essentially be able to use the document as a helping hand and guide to day-to-day practice. Initially, an SOP may be time-consuming or difficult to write, but once done, it aids the organization in its purpose to be an effective smooth-running engine.

Policy compliance

Policies are *principles, rules, and guidelines formulated or adopted by an organization to reach its long-term goals* (**www.BusinessDictionary.com**). Policies are guiding principles about how business should be conducted, and they commonly outline standards of conduct and expected conformity with internal and external legal responsibilities and guidelines. They also exemplify consistent ways of handling situations. In brief, policies should reflect the organization's mission, ethos, work ethics, and intrinsic values. Policies cut across all areas of business operations.

Hardening and security policies

Effective security is underpinned by solid business plans and strategic planning. There are many types of security policies that incorporate the daily practice of an organization and how the business views and handles security issues. Some policies included in a business's documentation include the following:

- Password policy
- Acceptable use policy
- Human resource policies
- Code of ethics
- Bring your own device policy
- Security policy
- Data loss prevention
- Remote access policy
- Onboarding and Offboarding Policy
- Authorized access policy documents
- A change and configuration management policy
- Privileged user account policy
- Account management
- Data ownership

You can see that the preceding list outlines a comprehensive collection of security policies. The main point of observation here is that these policies cover the ethics, behavior, and actions of people as much as they cover the way in which hardware and software are accessed and used by all staff. They are most certainly guiding principles about how business should be conducted and how security needs to be planned, maintained, and appropriately used so that compliance is attained. Network administrators must be familiar with all security documentation since, inevitably, documents are consulted as part of problem-solving and handling actual and potential security breaches.

In addition to security policies, **security frameworks** help establish consistency and provide a baseline for an organization's policy compliance. Security frameworks list company objectives and actions to counteract or mitigate a security threat or potential attack. Frameworks might be prescriptive, quite rigid, and hold strict controls or they can allow for flexibility and some degree of discretionary action. The security framework is a bit like scaffolding around the business. This scaffolding ensures that the structure of the business is held secure and intact. *Figure 14.6* shows four individuals painting a building. The building is supported by scaffolding. This scaffolding supports the workers by keeping them safe and secure while carrying out their work. It is akin to the way the security framework ensures that all members of the organization are safe and secure, plus all business operations are held within the framework of security operations. In this way, the business can operate effectively.

Figure 14.6: Scaffolding supports

Common documentation

All organizations hold common documentation as part of the structure and running of their business. These documents include the following:

- A physical network diagram (Topology)
- A logical network diagram (Topology)
- The organization's floor plan
- Wiring and cabling diagrams
    - o Rack diagram (s)
    - o Intermediate distribution
    - o Frame (IDF)/Main distribution
    - o Frame (MDF) documentation
- Site survey report
    - o Proposed construction

- o Locality
- o Surroundings
- o Property lines or boundary markers
- Audit and assessment report
  - o Examination of results
  - o Judgments and recommendations
- Baseline configurations (that is, a description of a system at a given point in time)

Important factors of physical installations

Now is an appropriate time to explain the important installation implications related to hardware and devices and how physical installations call for accurate and reliable documents. The documents listed in this section are not purely conceptual. Documents provide the organization with a critical means of ensuring that hardware and devices are located in the correct areas of the building, that they are secure, and that they are installed in the correct environment with the correct sanitary requirements and temperature.

The location of where the networking equipment is installed is very important. First and foremost, network equipment and hardware should always be located in a secure area of the building. This area can be a dedicated telecommunications room (comms room), server room, or closet. The documents listed previously will operate as reference points for the location of physical equipment and the mapping of the organization's infrastructure. For example, the physical network diagram should pinpoint the exact location of the equipment on the premises. This diagram should align with the floor plan of the building, and it should be updated whenever the layout of the building or condition of the building changes. Policies outlining physical access controls will also play an important role in the equipment's location and in the supervision and monitoring of employee access to the hardware. Remember, these policies and procedures are intended to be implemented and enforced. Other security measures for installing network appliances are discussed in *Chapter 20, Implementing Physical Security*.

The network hardware can be stored in a rack or mounted on a wall in the comms room. Alternatively, it can be stored in a cabinet. A server rack is a compact and secure installation option for servers and other networking devices and appliances. Manufacturers are aware that rack systems have specific dimensions, so most networking equipment will comply with the standards of width, height, and depth and align with the rack measurement system of units. Being aware of the varied options for mounting requirements assists a network administrator in making an educated purchase. Remember that there are always choices. Regarding rack systems, the standard height is 48U (i.e., 7-foot rack) or, on some occasions, 42U, where U stands for the term Unit. U spaces equal 1.75 inches. In terms of rack width, the most common standard rack width measures 19 inches. In terms of rack solutions, an administrator can consider the overall setup for installation and decide on the plans for equipment installation. There are many consultants out there who offer advice and walk a person or team through the solution that is best for the business.

In brief, racks are sold in heights from 8U to 48U. As stated, rack-compatible equipment is designed with a vertical height quoted in U, so you can plan exactly how much vertical space you require. In *Figure 14.7*, two rack dimensions are compared with each other. Careful attention to detail illustrates the important factors involved in selecting the appropriate spaces and locations in which our network devices are stored in.

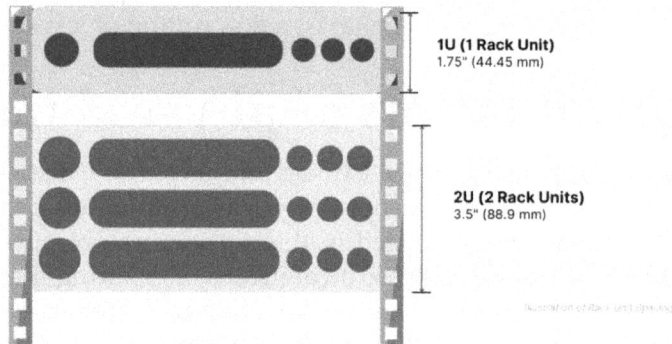

Figure 14.7: 19 inch vs. 10 inch rack dimensions

Hot Aisle/Cold Aisle layout

Originated by IBM in 1992, a Hot Aisle/Cold Aisle layout is one of the oldest ways to save energy in the data center. Rack-mounted appliances are usually designed with intake fans to draw in cool air from the front. At the back of the equipment are the exhaust fans. These fans are designed to expel warm air. Some models of switches can be configured between, where hot air is expelled on the same side as the port interfaces and port-side intake. Port-side intake permits a switch to be installed with ports facing the front of the rack, which supports some cable management solutions better. Some data centers implement raised floors. This design delivers cold air from the computer room air conditioner system.

Main distribution frame vs. intermediate distribution frame

Companies may choose between a **main distribution frame** (**MDF**) or an **intermediate distribution frame** (**IDF**). The MDF is a cable rack that interconnects and manages the telecommunications wiring between itself and any number of IDFs. An IDF connects internal lines to the MDF. The MDF connects private or public lines coming into the building with the internal network. Placement of these distribution frames must be planned for and executed with precision, in accordance with building design. MDF and IDF are key factors and components in a network design.

Regarding physical installations, we can see that no matter the solution chosen, choices call for site surveys and thorough investigation and planning. Cooling, humidity, temperature, airflow, fire suppression strategies, and considerations of potential electrical hazards must be carefully well-thought-out before and throughout the placement and installation of network devices and appliances.

Sensors

In data centers, a **heating, ventilation and air conditioning** (**HVAC**) system uses temperature sensors and moisture detection sensors. These moisture sensor detectors measure humidity. Sensors can be installed near racks or closets to gauge ambient environmental conditions for an organization's network rack or server enclosure. Sensors can equally be placed within a server room or within the equipment closet. Some of the environmental factors that need monitoring in data centers or where company equipment is housed include temperature, humidity, electrical power, local flood risks, or even other man-made or natural phenomena. These potential occurrences or risk factors will influence the design and contents of the organization's **disaster recovery plan** or its **business continuity plan**. Essentially, policies should align with company practice.

Common agreements

In the business world, it is common practice for one organization to work directly with another organization. This *integration* or merger agreement may be with a cloud provider or with a supplier/vendor in a partner relationship. The information systems in both organizations might, therefore, need to connect, collaborate, and securely integrate with each other. A merger clause or an entire agreement may be drawn up between the related partners so that the potentiality of risk or IT vulnerabilities is identified, analyzed, and mitigated against.

Each organization's network, strategies, and resources must be clearly defined and evaluated. The *onboarding* phase occurs when the relationship originates, and the *off-boarding* phase happens when the relationship is finalized or completely terminated.

Non-disclosure agreement

A **non-disclosure agreement** (**NDA**) is a legally binding, enforceable contract by law. An NDA creates a confidential relationship between an organization and staff/employee to protect the company's assets from being *disclosed* to competitors and the general public. In this way, it establishes confidentiality.

An NDA is an important framework that has two main functions. First, it is to protect sensitive and confidential information. By signing an NDA, employees promise not to give, or release data or information shared with them by the company or to which they have access. If the data is leaked or there is a data breach, the company can claim a breach of contract. A person who breaches an NDA can be sued. Those who are potentially in breach may be given a court order or be subjected to an injunction so they are prevented from disclosing the information in question.

Second, an NDA's function is to delineate private information (such as PII) and what is okay to share with others. The NDA is a document that classifies exclusive and confidential information. It is hugely important for a company to draft up and execute an NDA correctly. Otherwise, it may not hold up in court, and the company will not be able to make those in breach of it fully accountable.

The best practice incorporates computer forensics procedures into the organization's approach to documenting computer and network security to ensure compliance with the rules and safeguard the integrity of the data. These policies and procedures help the business to capture necessary data in the event of a network or data breach. Ensuring the viability and integrity of the captured data allows the organization to prosecute the intruder and/or employee.

Service-level agreement

A **service-level agreement** (**SLA**) defines which services will be performed by the third party and the level of service to be expected. An SLA may also clarify how disputes will be handled, declare the minimum term for services to be provided, outline delivery of warranties, summarize disaster recovery procedures, and specify when the agreement will be terminated. SLAs are generally used between customers and service providers. They may include an uptime requirement, a response requirement, the metrics by which the service is measured, and agreed-upon penalties or remediation actions should any problems arise. Metrics might include security mechanisms, technical performance indicators, errors or defect rates and counters, service availability (uptime) and business impacts, and charting of outcomes and results. SLAs should be reviewed periodically or as the business changes over the term of the contract. They should never be viewed as static documents and should be regarded in the same light as one observes change and change management procedures.

Memorandum of understanding

A **memorandum of understanding** (**MOU**) is a crucial document between two or more parties. An MOU provides a brief summary of which party in the business relationship is accountable for carrying out specific tasks and actions. Essentially, the MOU specifies who will do what and when each party will accomplish their tasks, taking note of each party's responsibilities and requirements. An MOU is not the same as a legally binding contract, but it is a non-binding agreement similar to what in earlier days was regarded as a *gentleman's agreement*. At times, it is the starting point of negotiations, defining the scope and purpose of further talks. It remains, however, a formal expression of willingness and commitment to act.

Conclusion

This chapter explained the need for an organization to design, develop, and comply with policies and procedures for optimum operations to be attainable. The main plans and procedures relevant to the company's optimum performance were outlined and detailed.

Additionally, the purposes of various types of documentation were covered and highlighted.

Standardizing procedures and practices are conducive to healthy business practices as they can be repeated accurately in the future. Ensuring that the correct information is available to all concerned means that documentation needs to be properly planned for, created, reviewed periodically, and updated as required. In terms of IT, documents must be kept up to date as changes are inevitable. Policy documents, operation and planning documents, project documents, and user documentation regarding hardware and software are components of an IT department's written repository of documents. A network administrator must comprehend the importance of these diverse documents.

In the upcoming chapter, we will explore concepts of high availability and disaster recovery. We will investigate backup procedures, fault tolerance, and **high availability (HA)** options and solutions. It will then be noticeable how documentation links in with HA and recovery.

Points to remember

- Recognize the plans and procedures organizations participate in.

- Explain the purpose of these procedures and policies and interpret them as critical to the viable functioning of a company and organization.

- Be aware of the competencies and skills a network administrator holds and how defined procedures, policies, and practices in the IT department contribute to the company's overall functionality.

- Differentiate between plans, policies, and standard operating procedures and practices.

- Understand how an IT professional must follow these procedures and maintain their own documentation.

- Identify the various forms of IT documentation and follow due practices.

- Understand the legal and ethical issues inherent in the IT industry and related businesses.

- Consider privacy and confidentiality concerns.

- Interact effectively with users and others in the organization and the IT field.

- The content of this chapter is mapped to *Domain 3: Network Operations*, explain the purpose of organizational processes and procedures. The content is additionally mapped to *Domain 2, Network Implementation*. Explain important factors of physical installations.

Key terms

- **Acceptable use policy (AUP)**: This policy defines how users should engage with information and network resources (that is, hardware and software) in the organization. It lays down the boundaries and rules for the use of internet access while on the company network, what may or may not be saved and stored on computer equipment, and what rules are in place for the personal use of company resources.

- **Bring your own device policy**: This a policy that permits employees in an organization to use their personally owned devices to carry out work-related activities. The purpose of the policy is to balance fairness of use and access with the safety and security of company information and resources.

Questions

1. Differentiate between a plan, a procedure, and a policy.
2. Give examples of commonly used documents as they relate to technology.

Join our book's Discord space

Join the book's Discord Workspace for Latest updates, Offers, Tech happenings around the world, New Release and Sessions with the Authors:

https://discord.bpbonline.com

CHAPTER 15

Resilience, Fault Tolerance, and Recovery

Introduction

For our systems to be online and available, we should implement strategies for **high availability** (**HA**) and redundancy. Consequently, a network administrator needs to be able to identify and understand these important concepts. As an organization, when you want your network to be as close to 100% operational and consistent as possible, there are three areas of system design that the organization must address and aim for. These areas and principles are essential:

- The elimination of *single points of failure* (via fault tolerance/redundancy)
- A reliable crossover or failover point (as in backup strategies)
- Failure detection capabilities (with a means to respond to and control the errors detected)

Thus, we observe that HA is achieved via existing redundancy and backup strategies. If our infrastructure has built-in capabilities of moving beyond a single point of failure and can manage this *failover* seamlessly and without latency, our organization's network and the services it provides to users and clients will be accessible, reliable, and ensure an agreed level of continuity of business and operational performance. If a system is not accessible to a user, it is deemed to be unavailable. This characteristic is classified as the system being down or downtime. No company *worth its salt* desires downtime (outside of planned maintenance or known events, of course). Every effective organization desires its business to be available to customers and users. At the same time, they promote that the higher the availability achievable by them, the better the status of the services provided.

True to say, successful businesses operate with the least number of technological disruptions. Effective configuration of IT systems, appropriate equipment, successful training, and detailed guidance of staff, plus standardized implementation of cybersecurity measures and preparation of IT systems for any given emergency (expected or unexpected), guarantees your business its maximum amount of productive uptime. That is what users of a network's resources need and that is what they want.

Structure

This chapter explains the following topics:

- Redundancy of hardware and software strategies
- Implementations of RAID
- Redundancy and high availability concepts

Objectives

After completing this chapter, you will learn about backup and failover strategies and where these strategies fit in with HA planning and a disaster recovery plan. Note that these plans were described in *Chapter 14, Plans, Procedures, and Policies in Practice.*

In this chapter, you will study the meaning of fault tolerance and how to move beyond a **Single Point of Failure** (**SPoF**). RAID and other technologies that provide resilience and backup will be discussed and demoed throughout the chapter.

The primary objective of this chapter is to enhance your understanding of these concepts so that you can assess and evaluate the strategies and mechanisms suited to specific networking designs and find appropriate solutions to match the infrastructure and topology of a given network.

Redundancy of hardware and software strategies

Before considering HA as an outcome or product of redundancy, let us examine some strategies for implementing fault tolerance in the infrastructure and design of a network. The main point to make about these strategies is that redundancy can be implemented at different layers of the OSI model, and that backup and failover strategies can be configured and applied to network devices and application software. In other words, a network administrator can implement these strategies on host devices, switches, routers, and servers and run them across the physical, data-link, and transport layers all the way up to the application layer of the OSI model.

Load balancing

According to *Techopedia*, load balancing is an even division of processing work between two or more computers and/or CPUs, network links, storage devices, or other devices, ultimately delivering faster service with higher efficiency. To put it simply, balancing the load in networking is sharing or dividing up tasks or processes to lessen the burden on one device or application. It is a little bit like **delegation** in a business or company, where a number of people collaborate or work in a team so that the physical or mental (logical) stress of the project or tasks to be accomplished does not land on the shoulders of a single employee. Distribution and entrusting tasks to other employees lessen the load and is an indicator of strong management leadership. Effectively, the load or burden is shared to generate the best outcomes and results for the business.

Figure 15.1 illustrates the delegation process, where two individuals are allocating roles and building the infrastructure for planned operations. This generation of roles and loads may be established per project, or they may be constructing the default hierarchy of the organization.

Figure 15.1: *Delegation process*

Figure 15.2 illustrates the way load balancing operates across servers:

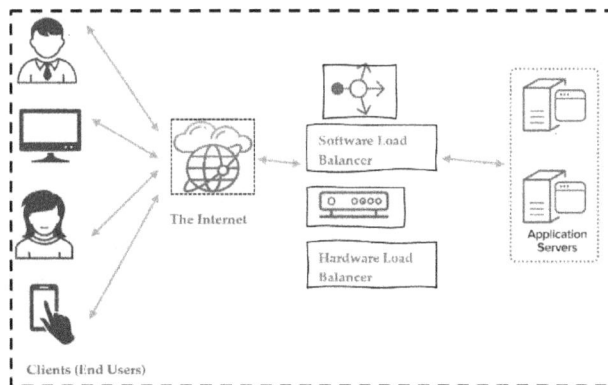

Figure 15.2: *Load balancing*

As explained in *Chapter 9, Managing Network Devices*, irrespective of whether it is hardware or software-related, or what algorithm(s) or strategies are involved in the means of distribution, a **load balancer** disburses traffic to different Web servers in the resource pool or server cluster, to ensure that no single server becomes overworked, overwhelmed, and, subsequently, undependable. Load balancing effectively minimizes server response time and maximizes data throughput.

> **Note: When we examined switching technologies in** *Chapter 10, Managing Switching Protocols***, one technology explored was link aggregation. Link aggregation is used for extending the bandwidth on switches and enabling larger quantities of data to pass through the switches. Remember, link aggregation and EtherChannel facilitate load balancing and redundancy on networks.**

In **routing** technologies, the typical router sends incoming packets to their designated correlative IP address on the domain or network, but a load balancer can send incoming packets to multiple machines hidden behind one IP address. This provides an impressive advantage to routing performance. Modern load-balancing routers follow various rules to determine specifically how they will route network traffic. In accordance with the organization's needs, an administrator can set rules based on the fastest response times and the least load or fault tolerance. An administrator can divide up (delegate/balance) outbound requests for smoother and more flowing network operations. Large networking environments and e-commerce, which depend on scalability and uptime, gain great benefits using load balancers in their network design and operations.

In server technology, implementing load balancers:

- Spread server tasks over multiple servers configured in a cluster.
- Can decrease the chance of a server failing, resulting in the inability to process requests.
- Can redirect requests to a different server if there is a server or component failure.
- Can help with fault tolerance and HA.
- Can distribute IP traffic in a *round-robin* fashion by rotating connection requests among servers.

Multipathing

Servers require a physical path or pathway to store data on drives or on storage devices. The multipathing technique, as it implies, creates more than one physical pathway between the server and its storage devices. This technique is used in **Internet Small Computer Systems Interface (iSCSI)** or **Fibre Channel (FC)** SAN environments. By establishing these multiple physical routes between the server and its storage devices, a SPoF is eliminated should a single physical pathway fail, where only one pathway exists. This multipathing facility establishes a failover technique, allows load balancing, and reduces latency while transferring I/O data across the network.

Figure 15.3 shows multiple paths running from a server with access to a RAID array configuration. This simplified image demonstrates the use of DM-Multipath technology.

For further understanding of acronyms, **Host Bus Adapter (HBA)**, and **Storage Area Network (SAN)**.

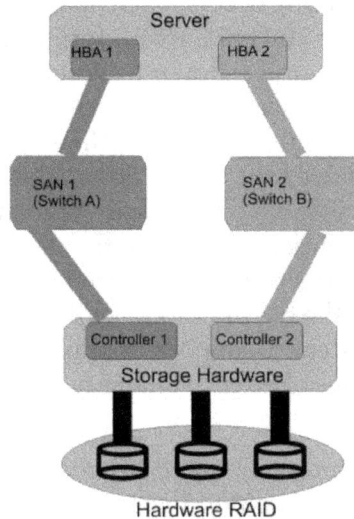

Figure 15.3: Multipathing configuration

In the configuration outlined, there are two HBAs on the server, two SAN switches, and two RAID controllers. Possible failure in this configuration can take place with the following components:

- HBA failure
- FC cable failure
- A SAN switch failure
- (RAID) Array controller/port failure

In the event of a failure, DM-Multipath will switch to an alternate I/O path as a failover strategy. Configurations of multipathing techniques include Active/Passive multipath with a single RAID device, Active/Passive multipathing with two RAID devices and two RAID controllers, and Active/Active multipathing with one RAID device. Irrespective of how many paths and links are configured, in terms of Active/Passive links, only one link is operational at any given time. In contrast to this and with the advent of more advanced handling and virtualization technologies, data traveling in parallel became a reality in multipathing and Active/Active or Dual Active techniques became viable. Note that the terminology used in multipathing is also used in other technologies, such as server clustering. These same concepts are applicable outside the field of data storage and I/O transmission. Many server clustering systems use the same terminology in relation to CPU processing and workloads.

In terms of operating systems, Red Hat Enterprise Linux distros use the Device Mapper multipath feature to configure and manage multipathing implementations.

Network interface card teaming

Network interface card (**NIC**) teaming occurs when network physical adapters are grouped together to improve fault tolerance and enhance performance. With this mechanism, traffic can be distributed over networks, and failover techniques can be used. Consequently, if system hardware fails, having multiple network cards plugged into the server becomes a failover strategy. Using NIC, teaming increases uptime in a business and helps maintain continuity of service. Should a cable break or go down, the host/server will automatically transfer the traffic to another active NIC. In the case of load balancing, traffic is balanced equally between the NICs. It is important to note that switches are the devices handling physical NICs and how they are operating. The servers do not handle the physical NICs. Regarding switch management, the two modes of switch management of NICs are Switch Dependent and Switch Independent. Using NIC teaming increases bandwidth, optimizes network resources, and guarantees better availability of servers. These benefits serve to enhance the network's uptime.

In Microsoft Windows, there is a protocol called **Microsoft Network Adapter Multiplexor Protocol**. If this protocol is enabled in Windows, Network Interface Bonding can occur. Consequently, a network administrator can combine two network adapters (ethernet cards) to form one physical device. This is done to increase bandwidth and comes with a special set of configurations that must be carried out for the technology to function appropriately.

In *Figure 15.4*, the Ethernet properties of a Windows Server edition are displayed. If multiplexor protocol is enabled manually, an error message may be displayed. This happens when the option is selected while other items are running. When an administrator creates a NIC team connection, servers will automatically enable this protocol. In other words, servers are aware of the need to do this.

Figure 15.4: Microsoft NIC teaming

Implementations of RAID

RAID is a technology that is used to increase the performance and/or reliability of data storage. The abbreviation RAID stands for **Redundant Array of Inexpensive/Independent Disks**. A RAID system consists of two or more disks working in parallel. These disks can be hard disks but there is a tendency to also use the technology for solid-state drives.

The software to perform RAID functionality and to manage and control the hard disks can either be located on a separate controller card (that is, a hardware RAID controller) or it can basically be a software driver. Many versions of Windows include integrated software RAID functionality. It is worth noting that hardware RAID controllers cost more than pure software, *but* they also offer superior performance and additional functionality. Software RAID tends to offer duplication or mirroring of data, whereas hardware RAID offers parity-based protection.

In this situation, parity in computing is where the parity bit is set for error detection across the disks. The results of the computation are stored on the parity disk/block. Parity *equals* failover strategies and *achieves* redundancy.

In *Chapter 7, Datacenter Technologies,* RAID is described as a strategy for moving beyond an SPoF while using storage devices. RAID works the same with SCSI, iSCSI, or IDE drives and has several configurations and implementations. Some of these implementations of RAID are outlined in the following tables. The tables do not show how to implement RAID. They operate as a guide to understand how the disks are configured and the manner in which the specific array of disks aligns with the concept and application of fault tolerance.

Table 15.1 compares RAID levels in terms of requirements and impacts:

RAID levels comparison chart								
	RAID 0	RAID 1	RAID 1E	RAID 10	RAID 5	RAID 50	RAID 6	RAID 60
Minimum number of disks	2	2	3	4	3	6	4	8
Fault tolerance	None	1 disk	1 disk	1 disk	1 disk	1 disk	2 disks	2 disks
Disk space overhead	None	50%	50%	50%	1 disk	2 disks	2 disks	4 disks
Read speed	Fast	Fast	Fast	Fast	Slow			
Write speed	Fast	Fair	Fair	Fair	Slow			
Hardware cost	Cheap	High (disks)	High (disks)	High (disks)	High	Very high	Very high	Very high

Table 15.1: *RAID levels comparison chart*

As observed, there are different RAID levels, each suiting a specific situation. As technology evolved, these RAID levels were not standardized by an industry group. This means that server administrators in organizations were sometimes creative and produced their own designs and unique implementations. It also explains why multiple forms of RAID exist now. However, most organizations nowadays will tend toward the most commonly used configurations and RAID levels.

In a **RAID 0** system, the technique of striping is used. With this method, data is split up into blocks and written across all the drives in the array *contiguously*. When we use the term contiguous or contiguously in technology, we allude to an unbroken sequence, as is observed in a terraced row of houses, connected and unbroken (un-detached). This method explains why the term *striping* is an accurate depiction of the strategy in the process.

By using multiple disks (at least two) at the same time, RAID 0 offers superior I/O performance. This performance can be enhanced further by using multiple controllers, ideally one controller per disk.

Table 15.2 shows the arrangement of disks in a RAID 0 array:

RAID 0

Disk 1	Disk 2	Disk 3
1	2	3
4	5	6
7	8	9

Table 15.2: RAID 0

RAID level 0 improves read and write performance by spreading operations across multiple disks so that operations can be performed independently. RAID 0 is ideal for non-critical storage of data that has to be read or written at a high speed. It is used optimally on a Photoshop image retouching station.

RAID 1E is a mirror configuration. This duplication of data is made over an odd number of disks. There are three disks in the example. With RAID 1E, you still get 50% overhead because each data block is stored on two mirror copies. As an advantage, we still achieve the increased read speed as is achieved in **RAID 0**. *Table 15.3* demonstrates a RAID IE array:

RAID 1E

Disk 1	Disk 2	Disk 3
1	1	2
2	3	3
4	4	5
5	6	6

Table 15.3: RAID 1E

The most important point regarding fault tolerance in this specific implementation is that in RAID 1E, if any of the drives fail, the read/write operations are subsequently assigned to other operational hard drives within the RAID array. In short, RAID 1E provides improved drive performance and better redundancy when compared with RAID level 1.

RAID 1 does provide fault tolerance. This level is also known as **disk mirroring** because it uses a disk file system called a mirror set. With disk mirroring, a redundant and identical copy of a selected disk is provided. All data written to the primary disk is written to the (secondary) mirror disk. RAID 1 generally improves read performance. However, it may degrade write performance. RAID 1 mirroring can also be achieved with a set of data disks and a mirrored set of data disks.

In *Table 15.4*, a simple mirror copy of a single disk is shown. If a disk fails, the RAID controller uses either the data drive or the mirror drives for data recovery and continues operation. You need a minimum of two disks to create a RAID 1 array.

RAID 1

Disk 1	Disk 2
1	1
2	2
3	3

Table 15.4: RAID 1

RAID 1 is used for mission-critical storage. Due to its excellent read speed, it is also suited to technical processes, such as video production and video editing, image editing, pre-press applications, or any other application requiring high bandwidth. The write speed of RAID 1 is comparable with a single disk. The primary disadvantage of RAID 1 is that the effective storage capacity is only half the total disk capacity available because all data gets written twice. If you combine two 1TB drives in RAID 1, you will only get 1 TB of *usable* disk space. This further makes sense because the reason why it is ideally suited for mission-critical data is that an organization or enterprise cannot afford to lose data, so taking the hit on storage capacity becomes acceptable.

Regarding the components required to run this array, since the software RAID 1 solution does not always allow a hot swap of a failed disk (that is, failed disks cannot be replaced while the server remains running), if possible, a hardware controller ought to be used in RAID 1 configurations. In terms of backup solutions, RAID 1 is not advisable. The reason is that if corrupted data stems from the operating system or damaged system files are negatively impacted and modified, this same error will transfer to the mirror disk or mirrored set of disks. Consequently, in this scenario, RAID 1 is not a great solution.

Table 15.5 illustrates a **RAID 5**, three-disk array running striping with parity:

RAID 5

Disk 1	Disk 2	Disk 3
1	2	P
3	P	4
P	5	6
7	8	P

Table 15.5: RAID 5

Note that parity blocks as they are spread across each disk in the array. Parity is distributed across all the disks in the array. RAID 5 is the most commonly used and is the most popular RAID level. The data redundancy in RAID 5 is provided by the parity information. The data and parity information are arranged so that the two are always stored on different disks. In general, RAID level 5 has better performance than RAID level 1 and provides notable fault tolerance. RAID 5 combines effective storage, security, and failover strategies. It can tolerate a single disk failure.

Some hardware manufacturers support hybrid versions of RAID 5 as well as other RAID levels, and so on. There are a variety of different applications of RAID 5 in use. Typical uses for RAID 5 include storage for files and application provision and services.

If you are using a large number of disks and want to have several disks as hot spares, **RAID 50** can be implemented as an option. RAID 50 combines parity RAID techniques with data striping as a solution. *Table 15.6* shows how parity is striped across six disks:

RAID 50

RAID 0 made over two RAID 5 sets						
Disk 1	Disk 2	Disk 3		Disk 4	Disk 5	Disk 6
1	2	P		3	4	P
5	P	6		7	P	8
P	9	10		P	11	12

Table 15.6: RAID 50

As shown, a minimum of six disks are required for RAID 50 to be fully operational.

Now, we come to **RAID 6**. RAID 6 is a complex, expensive, robust, highly reliable storage and fault-tolerant system. Note in *Table 15.7* that the two different parity functions are in operation. These parity configurations strive to derive two different parity blocks per row. You can see this in the yellow and green combinations in the table as they are generated on every row. The entire configuration demonstrates a RAID 6 implementation:

RAID 6

Disk 1	Disk 2	Disk 3	Disk 4
1	2	P1	P2
3	P1	P2	4
P1	P2	5	6
P2	7	8	P1

Table 15.7: RAID 6

In RAID 6, there are significant demands on processing greater demands than exist with RAID 5. RAID 6 can withstand the failure of two hard disks. Consequently, the capacity of two disk drives is used to provide fault tolerance.

To implement **RAID 60** successfully, you need a minimum of at least eight disks distributed equally over two RAID 6 sets or groups. In *Table 15.8*, there are eight disks in the array. Again, as with RAID 6, parity is striped across each row as double parity. Then, the set is mirrored across to the other four disks, as with RAID 0. In terms of fault tolerance, RAID 60 can withstand the failure of two disks. The best practice is to have several hot spares available to optimize this configuration.

RAID 60

RAID 0 made over two RAID 6 sets							
Disk 1	Disk 2	Disk 3	Disk 4	Disk 5	Disk 6	Disk 7	Disk 8
1	2	P1	P2	3	4	P1	P2
5	P1	P2	6	7	P1	P2	8
P1	P2	9	10	P1	P2	11	12
P2	13	14	P1	P2	15	16	P1

Table 15.8: RAID 60

RAID 10 combines RAID 0 and RAID 1. *Table 15.9* shows how striping is used across each set of disks to speed up data transfers. The set of disks (Disks 1 and 2 in the table) is mirrored to Disks 3 and 4.

RAID 10

Disk 1	Disk 2	Disk 3	Disk 4
1	2	1	2
3	4	3	4
5	6	5	6
7	8	7	8

Table 15.9: RAID 10

RAID 10 brings together the advantages and disadvantages of RAID 0 and RAID 1 into this combined array. RAID level 10 is otherwise known as mirroring with striping. As shown in the preceding table, this RAID configuration implements a striped array of disks mirrored to another identical set of striped disks. Remember that with mirroring, we will lose half of the storage capacity of the total disk space used.

Redundant hardware/clusters

When we looked at load balancing (or even link aggregation in switching), we were discussing redundant hardware and the process of clustering. Redundant switches/routers in a network permit traffic to be routed over less congested available paths. Switching and routing protocols such as **Open Shortest Pathway First** (**OSPF**), Enhanced Interior Gateway Routing Protocol, or **Rapid Spanning Tree Protocol** (**RSTP**) in switching provide redundancy and incorporate multiple pathways through the network.

When one host/node fails in a cluster, the operations of that node are swapped over to another node or piece of hardware that is a member of that cluster. This *failover* ensures uptime in operations. For example, servers can be clustered together to provide a service to an end user. The user does not see the cluster and interacts with the interface and software as if they were engaging with a single machine or piece of hardware.

Redundant hardware can be implemented on switches, routers, firewalls, and wireless access points to provide continuous services to end users. In SAN, for example, RAID storage systems, managed switches, routers, firewalls, servers, backup devices, interface cards, and cabling all coalesce to form a reliable storage system and provisioning of services and resources that facilitate the policies, procedures, and practices of an IT organization and enterprise. High-availability clusters harness the power of multiple devices to generate a solid and reliable mechanism, where failover strategies deliver continuous access to the resources required. Again, the hardware available to achieve this result exists across all the layers of the OSI model in physical and logical technologies.

Facilities and infrastructure support

Facilities and infrastructure support comprise a variety of components. Some of these components are on-site, providing failover and backup to servers and systems in organizations, or alternatively are part of the infrastructure of a data center:

- An **uninterruptible power supply** (**UPS**) is an enhanced battery system that will self-activate in the event of power disruption and function as the primary power source until electronic devices can safely be shut down or an emergency generator takes over operations. The purpose is to provide electrical and mechanical equipment with interim power, typically in the event of a power outage from the primary power source.

- **Power distribution units** (**PDUs**) are typically large power strips used for controlling electrical power in a data center. Power strips can be duplicated to provide primary and secondary-based power and backup.

- **Heating, ventilation, and air conditioning** (**HVAC**) units are responsible for heating and cooling a building. They also provide a source of proper ventilation, allowing for any moisture to escape that is not conducive to the equipment or devices being managed and protected. In terms of cooling and ventilation, **data centers** (**DC**) primarily focus on keeping their equipment at the right temperature and humidity. The primary role of DCs is to gather and manage those vast quantities of data. To do this effectively, these facilities must operate 24/7 with HA and be consistent and reliable. Servers in large numbers, alongside supporting devices and network infrastructure, consume huge amounts of energy and generate huge quantities of heat. Removing or dissipating this heat is crucial because proper cooling prevents electrical components from overheating and failing or potentially catching fire. The presence of HVACs in data centers guarantees the reliability of a data center and the continuity of operations it proposes.

- Data center fire suppression is a critical aspect of safeguarding equipment and data. However, fire suppression strategies and procedures are a part of every organization. Having an efficient fire suppression system in place protects people's lives, minimizes site and equipment damage, and decreases downtime.

Redundancy and high availability concepts

Most HA solutions rely on traditional hardware and software solutions. However, the rise in the need for HA over the last decade or more also drove innovative techniques and HA strategies and helped to push these newer approaches to the forefront of cloud computing and virtualization. Newer approaches upended and disrupted the customary approaches. These newer approaches include off-site cloud hosting as part of a high availability IT solution, additional software-oriented solutions, and clustering and purpose-built management and monitoring software.

In earlier decades, manufacturers achieved HA by designing mainframe systems that used more than one physical processor (multi-processing), several stacks of physical memory, multiple storage adapters, and, again, multiple physical network adapters. The primary objective was to monitor the system firmware, assess and check the health of discrete components, and predict and manage ways to move the workloads required to surviving components in the event of a failed component. If a component failed to respond or entered an error state, recovery strategies were also included in the response mechanism. Generally speaking, HA clusters use a *heartbeat* private network connection, which is used to monitor the health and status of each device/node in the cluster.

In *Figure 15.5*, we see a two-node HA cluster with redundancy featured in the solution. Note that there can be more than two nodes in HA configurations but having two is common and less expensive to implement. In specific circumstances, HA solutions can be comprised of dozens of nodes.

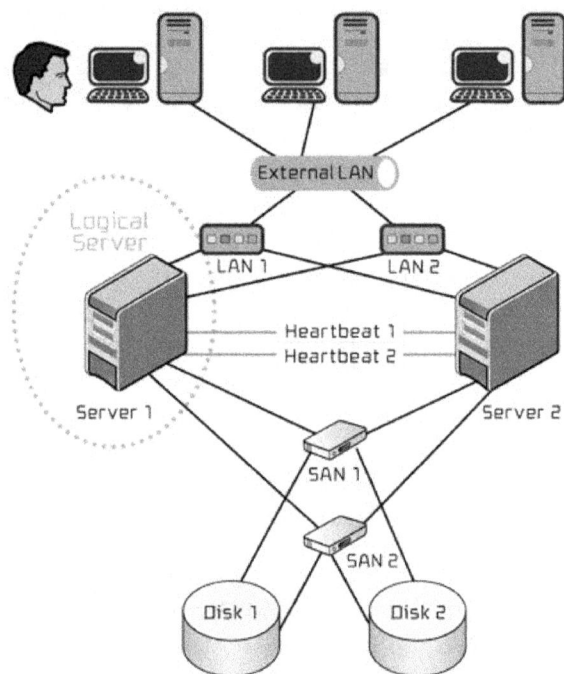

Figure 15.5: A two-node high-availability cluster

Network device backup/restore

With the considerable growth of data in recent years, much focus has been directed upon backing up and restoring data. From network intermediary devices, such as switches, routers, and other access points or firewalls, to servers, sensors, and automation mechanisms to network-wide management and monitoring, network configuration management software is designed exclusively with network administrators in mind. There is a huge range of third-party (and native) management software available for administrators to choose from. When we consider how long it takes to back up a single server or redo the configuration settings on a single switch or router, it makes perfect sense that administrators will opt to seek support and help in managing their network via management software.

There are a few golden rules an administrator should adhere to when handling backup and restore issues. Whenever you make a change to the settings of a device, you should ensure these configurations are backed up. At times, you may need to roll back to prior states in your network devices and hardware and software in general (for example, driver changes, updates to operating systems, new batch files, or modified scripting). Any change to the *state* of hardware or software should be duly noted and recorded. Automated systems are typically better at handling this monitoring, but that does not mean they should go unwatched. When changes occur, unauthorized changes should always be reverted back to the authorized settings with automated processes, and this change ought to be observed and verified by the administrator. Scrutiny is an effective security practice.

Automation of processes is advantageous for routine tasks because it cuts down the workload and time required for these types of procedures. Generally, standard procedures are best handled this way as, again, time is always a consideration in technical administration. So, finding ways to be error-free is inevitably the best practice since all humans (even accidentally or inadvertently) are prone to err. Time taken for new deployments and roll-out of hardware and software is minimized, and tasks can be accomplished much faster and easier with this type of support. Regarding security practices, whenever unexpected changes are discovered on a network device, the system can be kept secure by reloading stored configurations from an earlier time. This automated feature counteracts potential acts of security breaches or hacking. Some of these management tools additionally include features for policy enforcement and compliance.

Having strategies for the backup and restoration of business-critical data is an integral part of any network administrator's disaster recovery plan. It is essential to business operations as it should ensure the security of the network, the protection of business assets, and compliance with organizational policies, procedures, and practices. Alongside third-party management software procured by administrators, cloud providers also offer solutions and services to organizations for handling storage, backup, and recovery of data on top of their many other networking solutions.

Conclusion

This chapter explored HA and disaster recovery concepts. We investigated backup procedures, fault tolerance, and HA options and solutions. We noted that backup procedures and the creation of backups are critical steps in network and computer maintenance. We identified that in order to protect your data in the event of a system or network outage or failure, you need to understand proper backup procedures. Equally so, the practical undertaking of these strategies applies to recovering from cases of data and file corruption.

In today's digital world, there is a constant threat of data risk and threatened security breaches. Ransomware, hackers, phishing and spear phishing, malware, viruses, spyware, and physical disasters are all daily reminders that, above all else, our data needs protecting. This, in turn, implies that our networks do, too. The reader of this chapter should now understand the importance of securing data as much as securing a network.

In the upcoming chapter, we will investigate security concepts in more detail, focusing on how to explain, compare, and contrast common security attacks. We will learn that a solid network security system helps reduce the risk of data loss, theft, and sabotage. Topics to be covered include CIA, AAA, and risk assessment.

Points to remember

- In this chapter, we explored backup and failover strategies and where these strategies fit in with high-availability planning and with a disaster recovery plan.

- There are many different strategies and mechanisms that provide failover and recovery at all levels of the OSI model, applicable to both hardware and software, from the physical cables all the way up to application software.

- As a network administrator, you can assess and evaluate these strategies and mechanisms suited to specific networking designs and find appropriate solutions to match the infrastructure and topology of a given network.

- The content of *Chapter 15* is mapped to *Domain 3, Network Operations*. Explain **disaster recovery (DR)** concepts.

Key terms

- **Cold site**: A cold site is a disaster recovery site where a backup location or facility has in place the essential electrical and physical components of a computer network or environment. It provides sufficient space and infrastructure. However, this facility does not have computer equipment in place, for example, PCs, telephones, or copiers. It is a stripped-back version of a hot site.

- **Warm site**: A warm site is where a backup location or facility has in place the essential electrical and physical components of a computer network or environment, providing sufficient space and infrastructure. A warm site is partially fitted with the hardware necessary pre-installed. A warm site is deemed the middle-ground option for disaster recovery but does not have the same operational capacity as the company's primary site.

- **Hot site**: A hot site replicates the company's network and operations. It is essentially a duplicate of the company's primary operations center and, therefore, can be brought into operation instantly, thus the inference from the word *hot*. Failover to this site can happen in minutes or hours, minimizing downtime and ensuring high availability.

- **Cloud site**: A Cloud site is where a company's infrastructure, software, platform, or services are managed or hosted via a cloud provider.

- By using multiple **internet service providers (ISPs)**/diverse paths as a redundancy solution, fast, reliable internet connections are more achievable. Companies are provided with local redundancy and diversity options.

- **Virtual Router Redundancy Protocol (VRRP)**/First Hop is an open standard protocol. Its purpose is to provide redundancy in a network. The protocol operates at the network layer, whereby virtual routers are members of a group. If the primary virtual router goes down, one of the other virtual routers takes its place and makes forwarding decisions in data transmission.

- **First Hop Redundancy Protocols (FHRP)** are mechanisms that provide alternate default gateways in switched networks where two or more routers are connected to the same VLANs. Their purpose is to prevent network failure at a default gateway by creating a single virtual router.

- **Mean time to repair (MTTR)** is a metric that is computed on the time it takes to repair a component.

- **Mean time between failure (MTBF)** is the predicted time that occurs on a device between anticipated or inherent failures.

- **Recovery time objective (RTO)** is essentially the aimed time or target that a company holds as an objective before a process or service is fully restored.

Questions

1. What is high availability, fault tolerance, and redundancy?

2. Give examples of strategies and methods used in organizations to achieve HA and fault tolerance.

Join our book's Discord space

Join the book's Discord Workspace for Latest updates, Offers, Tech happenings around the world, New Release and Sessions with the Authors:

https://discord.bpbonline.com

CHAPTER 16
Security Concepts

Just as drivers who share the road must also share responsibility for safety,
we all now share the same global network, and thus must regard computer security
as a necessary social responsibility. To me, anyone unwilling to take simple
security precautions is a major, active part of the problem.

- Fred Langa, professional writer, and author

Introduction

The comparison of computer users to drivers on a road demonstrates an especially strong viewpoint about the critical nature of security while living and working in a digital age. Moreover, the social responsibility the author suggests implies an active awareness of responsibility, akin to international citizenship, where the onus of accessing networks and *networking* belongs to each one of us as users of this global structure and internetwork. As users who are continually making online and virtual connections, we are frequently *driving*, which incorporates an understanding of safety. To further the analogy, the potential prospect of danger on this *roadway* can be easily visualized. Damage and threats to both hardware and software, the negligible or inadvertent loss of data, intentional data theft, and the degree of criminal and negligent activity by users are just some dangers to be identified, just as there are dangers on the roadways. These dangers to safety advocate that the responsibility of practical engagement ought to be incorporated into our mindset, with a shared approach to networking and the use of internet applications and services.

The origin of the word security derives from the Old French word *securite* or Latin *securitas*, from *securus*, which means *free from care*. Merriam-Webster defines security in its fullest meaning as *the state of being free from danger or threat*. This definition aligns with Langa's viewpoint and perspective. Networks and the internet, to be wholly safe places and *free from care*, must be secured in such a way that mechanisms, technologies, policies, procedures, and practices embed security into their design and makeup. To make the roadways safe, we must protect the system's infrastructure and safeguard data transmission at every point and junction of its journey and in its connections.

Structure

The chapter explains the following topics:

- Confidentiality, integrity, and availability
- Threats
- Principle of least privilege
- Zero Trust model
- Defense in depth
- Authentication methods
- Risk management
- Security information and event management

Objectives

After completing this chapter, you will be able to comprehend common security concepts and identify and explain common security threats and their countermeasures. The reader will also be able to describe the purpose and use of security procedures in protecting network infrastructure and how this relates to managing the use of physical equipment in networks.

Finally, you will also understand the importance of safeguarding users (that is, identity/data) as they participate in networking activities.

Confidentiality, integrity, and availability

The **confidentiality, integrity, and availability** (**CIA**) of Security outlines three of the most fundamental principles and needs in cybersecurity. The acronym refers to confidentiality, integrity, and availability. These principles are often acknowledged as three main elements and goals of cybersecurity.

Confidentiality safeguards data from being disclosed to unintended or unauthorized persons. The mechanisms and strategies chosen aim to prevent confidential or sensitive data from falling into the wrong hands. Examples of methods used include encryption, which converts the data into a form, making it more likely to be of no value if received by an unintended recipient. Other strategies include user education, knowledge of complex passwords and password usage, an understanding and identification of social engineering exploits, the benefits of multi-factor authentication, and the options to use biometric verification.

Integrity ensures that data is not modified or tampered with. This principle should not be confused with keeping the data secure or preventing it from getting corrupted or damaged, as data security handles this aspect of data transmission. The integrity of data is more about keeping the information intact and correct for the entirety of its *journey in transmission*, plus its overall existence or lifecycle. Data security and data quality are two facets of data integrity. However, when we discuss data integrity, what we are saying is that if data is ever retrieved at a later stage of the data's lifecycle, it has held its *integrity* when nothing about the data has been changed or modified. Changes to data can occur from unauthorized access, human error, hardware or software issues, bugs, viruses, malware or hacking, malicious or negligent intent, or the absence of data security or poor data security. Data security is the act of protecting data. Data integrity is the accuracy and validity of the data itself and could be said to be one of the targets of effective data security. Approaches and strategies to maintain data integrity include strict access controls (that is, the setting of permissions and privileges), data back-ups, removing duplicates, and documented audit trails.

Availability ensures the *uptime* of the system so that data is readily available as required. This principle was discussed in detail in *Chapter 15, Resilience, Fault Tolerance, and Recovery*. In HA systems, we saw that high availability is achieved via existing redundancy and backup strategies. Newer approaches to HA include off-site cloud hosting as part of a high-availability IT solution, additional software-oriented solutions, clustering, and purpose-built management and monitoring software.

Figure 16.1 illustrates the composition of the CIA triad:

Figure 16.1: CIA triad

Threats

When discussing security, we define an **asset** as anything a person or company regards as valuable. Assets such as confidential data, sensitive information in a database, personal data in files, hardware such as servers or networking equipment, mission-critical software or applications, and other support systems all need safeguarding and protection from damage, loss, or theft.

Potential danger to these assets is regarded as a **threat**. Weaknesses or loopholes are regarded as **vulnerabilities**.

Attempts to attack, compromise, take advantage of, or play on vulnerabilities are defined as **exploits**. Exploits refer to the hardware and software used, procedures, or actions taken while an attack or incident is taking place or being carried out.

Individuals involved in cybersecurity incidents are referred to as **threat actors** or **threat agents**. Note that even if the breach or damage is the outcome or product of human error or accidental actions on behalf of the person or people involved, the causative individuals concerned in the breach are still referred to as threat agents. Many types of threats exist that directly impact computer systems and networks. These threats can be insider threats (internal threats) or originate from outside an organization or company (that is, external threats).

Examples of **internal threats** include the following:

- Employees (for example, discontented employees/past employees with a grudge or who are disgruntled with management decisions regarding firing, promotions, task allocations, and so on. Bribery or intimidation of an employee can also feature as an internal threat)
- Poor access control management
- Privilege accumulations (for instance, when an employee moves department or is promoted, they build up permissions and privileges that remain unchecked or are not revised or aligned with the new role)
- Failed hardware
- Human error
- Malicious downloading of internet content
- Poor access control management
- Disclosure of data

Examples of **external threats** include the following:

- Malware attacks
- Social engineering attacks
- Phishing, spear phishing, whaling, vishing, and smishing (SMS phishing)
- Ransomware
- Password attacks (for example, Brute Force Attacks)
- Software supply chain attacks
- **Advanced persistent threats** (APT)
- Denial of service and distributed denial of service
- **Man-in-the-Middle** (MitM) attack
- Password attacks

Note: An unpatched device or application does not count as an internal threat. This is an example of vulnerability. Software must be updated and upgraded appropriately. Otherwise, it can be high risk and potentially be the origin of a security breach or incident. Malware wears a million masks and hides in many covert ways.

Social engineering originates from inside an organization or outside. It is also overt or covert and underpinned by impersonation and pretense.

Common vulnerabilities and exposures

According to the MITRE organization, *The mission of the CVE® Program is to identify, define, and catalog publicly disclosed cybersecurity vulnerabilities.* The **common vulnerabilities and exposures** (CVE) program is operated by MITRE and funded by the US government and multiple partners in research and IT around the world. US funding primarily comes from The National Cyber Security Division of the United States Department of Homeland Security. All Partners involved are self-identifying. Since its inception in 1999, past partners include **CVE Numbering Authorities** (**CNA**), whose role is to assign CVE IDs to vulnerabilities and publish these records to the public. A vulnerability has a unique CVE ID (tracking number). Organizations such as Android, Apache Software Foundation, Canonical Ltd., TeamViewer, and Zyxel Corporation are CNAs but note that CNAs number in the 100s and are spread around the world geographically. Most CNAs deal with their own organization's product issues exclusively, while other CNAs have a broader scope and coverage.

Essentially, there are six stages of the CE process, beginning when a vulnerability is discovered in an application or product and ending with publication and release to the public:

1. Discover
2. Report
3. Request
4. Reserve
5. Submit
6. Publish

The growth and proliferation of **software-driven industrial** (**SCADA**) equipment and accelerated expansion on the **Internet of Things** (**IoT**) devices have led to an increase in the number of vulnerabilities reported to the CVE program. The **Common Vulnerability Scoring System** (**CVSS**) is a free and open industry standard for measuring the severity of security vulnerabilities in computer systems. This scoring system assesses, ranks, and prioritizes vulnerabilities. Calculations are based on metrics and metric values. Examples of metrics are CIA Requirements, Target Distribution, and Collateral Damage Potential with values of low, medium, medium to high, and high, attributed to each metric as quantified. Organizations utilizing this measurement system include CERT Coordination Center, the **Open-Source Vulnerability Database (OSVDB)**, and the **National Vulnerability Database (NVD)**.

Principle of least privilege

We are all aware that to carry out our jobs optimally, we need to have access to the right resources and equipment. Otherwise, our productivity will diminish, and morale will decrease. Organizations, including network administrators, should ensure that all employees have access to the required tools to do their work well. However, an administrator's best practice regarding security measures and compliance with the policy is to assign access with minimum privilege in mind. In other words, give the employees what they need to do their job and no more. Remember, it is much harder for an administrator to decrease or pull back privileges retrospectively than to assess and assign them in a proactive and planned approach.

The **Principle of Least Privilege (PoLP)** or **Principle of Minimum Privilege** states that users or groups are given *only* the access they need to do their job role and granted nothing more. The other thing an administrator needs to remember when assigning privileges is to be aware that it is often easier to give a user more access when they need it, in a discretionary manner, than to take away privileges already granted. So, although it appears to be a strict approach, it is operating on fairness balanced with security.

The PoLP assists with the classification of data. It helps alleviate or (optimally) prevent the spread of malware and, therefore, decreases the chances of a security attack. The productivity of users in the organization may be improved or enhanced with the added focus on using essential tools aligned with their job role. PoLP counteracts *privilege creep* or the continuing accumulation of unnecessary privileges. When used effectively, a network administrator may make PoLP the default model in their organization, elevate privileges on a situational basis only, and only elevate privileges with logic, rationale, and evidence to support the need for escalation. This is known as a **just-in-time** approach. This allows the administrator to monitor and track permissions and privileges proficiently and document changes on a timely basis. Using this model also means the administrator has control when auditing identities and systems in use and can be flexible while remaining integral to the framework.

Figure 16.2 encapsulates the role of a network administrator or an IT support technician. In terms of computer security and access control, they operate like the arm of the *law* in that they impose and enforce access control.

Figure 16.2: Access denied

Zero Trust model

The main idea underpinning the Zero Trust model and approach to network security stems from the proverb, *never trust, always verify*. This proverb implies that everything, that is, all elements involved in the act of communication across networks, must be verified and validated. Trust nothing, and always verify. This strictest validation relates as much to devices and applications as it does to people and processes as they interact with these devices, applications, systems, and networks.

When an organization implements this framework and approach, all users, whether inside or outside of the organization, are checked and verified as authorized and authenticated users. They are checked to ensure that they hold permission to access data, applications, and devices. The approach to this security model perceives the network as *borderless*, that is, with no traditional network edge or boundary, and interprets that basically, we are living in a perimeter-less environment and digital world with no simplistic distinctions or dividing lines in the network operations. In today's modern world, the nature of work has become more fluid and potentially hazier with the digital transformation into a newer hybrid workforce and the rise in remote workers. These workers still need to be authenticated and authorized on company networks. There are several Zero Trust frameworks available to organizations to employ and although diverse, they all share some commonalities. These shared elements include strong user identity authentication procedures, PoLP practices, rigorous access control procedures, and device and software baselines and compliance.

All Zero Trust models should handle and address three levels of access. These levels are application access, intra-application access, and network access. The models used should address the devices used on the network as well as the overall network infrastructure, plus how the LAN interconnects with cloud-based operations and WAN functionality. This is why the model interprets digital security operations as perimeter-less security. Zero Trust architecture incorporates identities, devices, data, applications, networks, and infrastructure, all of which must be addressed and verified.

Zero Trust through network segmentation

Network segmentation is the practice of breaking down a network into smaller networks, VLANs, or subnets. Regarding security, this practice permits network administrators the ability to control the flow of traffic more proficiently and take a finer granular approach to policy-making and decision-making. Now that there has been a move away from *assumed trust* models, the segmentation of networks can create and enforce microperimeters within the organization's network. **Data, application, asset, or services (DAAS)** are thereby protected within the microperimeter, and DAAS becomes harder to move between these micro entities. A typical use of this segmentation is a guest wireless network, separated from the wired LAN. The administrator can create a microsegment that allows the guests access to the internet and no other access rights. Segmentation can be physical (using hardware and firewalls) or logical (via switching or network addressing and routing technologies). In switch segmentation (VLANs), only users in the same VLAN can communicate together. User group access can be set up, and if an employee attempts to access data from another VLAN or carries out a security breach, an alarm or alert can be triggered and sent to the administrator to notify them of the breach. Logical segmentation through subnetting means an administrator needs a solid understanding of addressing schemes.

When creating zones, the strictest security zone can be created for confidential or sensitive data. Security in this zone can be rigorous. An administrator can configure firewalls or security devices in accordance with the zero-trust model, remembering that anyone inside the perimeter of the network can be an internal threat or threat agent.

Zero-day

In cybersecurity, a zero-day refers to vulnerabilities that are unknown to the software vendor and have not yet been patched. These vulnerabilities can be exploited by attackers to gain unauthorized access or cause damage before the vendor becomes aware and issues a fix:

- **Zero-day**: It is also referred to as zero-day attacks, zero-day threats, or zero-day exploits. Hackers use the vulnerability to turn it into an attack. This is the day that an unknown vulnerability has been discovered by the vendor. The term is a reference to the amount of time that a vendor or developer has had to address the vulnerability and fix it.

- **Zero-day vulnerability**: This is a security software flaw that is unknown to someone interested in mitigating that flaw. Vulnerabilities include weak passwords, bugs, unencrypted data, or flaws or weaknesses in the software.

- **Zero-hour**: This is the time when the exploit is discovered.

The software can be exploited until a patch that addresses the vulnerability is made available.

The black market for selling digital exploits is a very lucrative market. Zero-day exploits are virtual products and can be easily sold without mediators over the internet because accessible technologies are strong enough to provide anonymity at a low cost. If intermediaries are required, unsuspecting or naïve *data mules* can be used to circumvent proof of criminality or wrongdoing.

Examples of the impact of zero-day exploits are as follows:

- Data/identity theft.
- Remote access/hackers/hacktivists taking remote control of devices.
- Files or systems damaged or corrupted.

- Contact list of personnel accessed and spam messages circulated to the list.

- Spyware is installed to steal sensitive information; for example, spyware from corporate espionage spies to carry out the theft.

- Other malware installed; for example, trojans or worms.

Bug Bounty Programs offer incentives and rewards to researchers and developers to locate vulnerabilities and report them. There are programs and communities of developers involved in this venture.

Defense in depth

An approach to **defense in depth** (**DiD**) occurs where there is *layering* in security practices and where an administrator applies the right technologies in each chosen layer of defense. **Layering** involves using various security measures to protect the same asset. DiD or security in depth is the principle that no single layer is completely effective in securing assets *on its own*. The most secure system or network has many layers of security, and this act of layering eliminates single points of failure and further hardens the network. The redundancies in place are intentional redundancies. These redundancies not only improve uptime and availability, but their inclusion also tightens security. A very effective metaphor for DiD is the *castle approach*. This analogy captures the defense strategy perfectly. When we consider the security features of a medieval castle, we will identify a moat, a drawbridge, portcullis, building up high (or layering deep), ramparts, battlements, tall towers, and so on. Simply put, multiple layers add security at each point of entry or advancement. This security model made medieval castles mostly impregnable unless the attack was a sustained attack or siege over time when the castle's layered approach was broken down.

Figure 16.3 illustrates the topology and architecture of a **screened subnet**. Network equipment comprises a screened router separating the external network (internet) from the *bastion* hosts in the **demilitarized zone** (**DMZ**). The bastion hosts are special-purpose *fortified* servers. A separate screened router outlines the internal network.

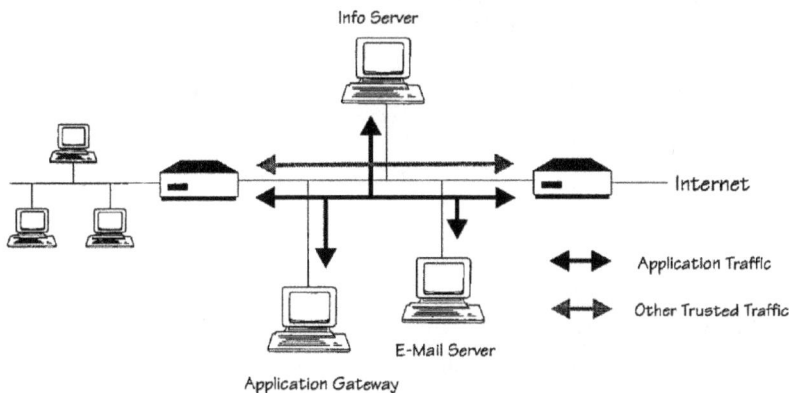

Figure 16.3: Screened subnet

In short, defensive layers should be varied and diverse. Executing multiple layers of the exact same defense does not provide sufficient strength against network attacks or breaches. A security breach occurs when system defenses are penetrated. From the perpetrator's perspective, the *know-how* is typically achieved through information gathered by *reconnaissance* to penetrate the system defenses and then gain unauthorized access.

James Scott, an expert in cybersecurity and a Senior Fellow at the **Institute for Critical Infrastructure Technology** (**ICIT**), expresses that there is no winning in cybersecurity, only a marathon of defense; and you do not only expect to be hacked, assume you already are.

Earlier in the chapter, we saw that malware wearing many masks can come in many forms.

In *Figure 16.4*, the same quote by *Scott* is presented as a meme. It is displayed this way to demonstrate that even an *innocuous* photograph or meme can contain hidden malware (though this one does not), and even if it did, the question is, how do regular viewers detect it?

Steganography is the practice of concealing information or messages with other visible data, image, or text. With photographs, they function as somewhat of a Trojan horse. Malicious code can be incorporated and hidden in images, audio files, and other normal-looking media to evade detection cunningly.

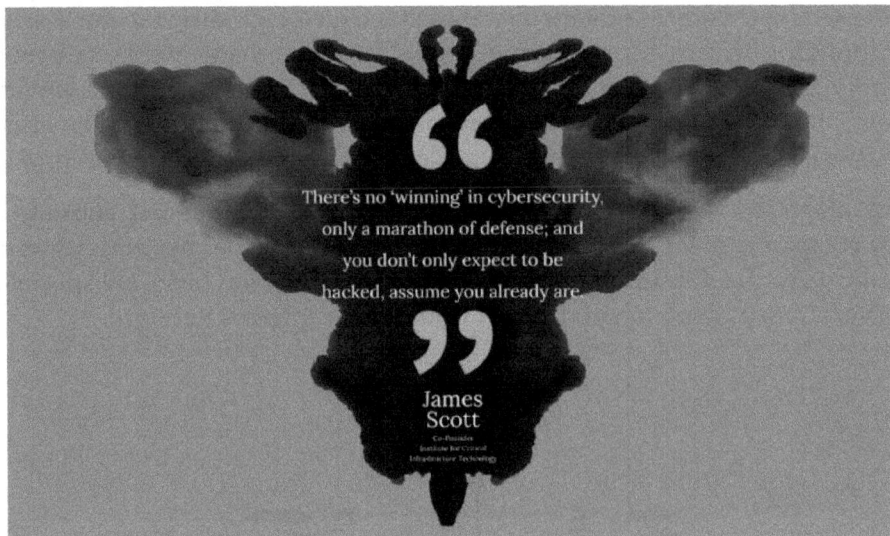

Figure 16.4: *A marathon of defense*

For example, a threat agent might attempt to deliver a PNG filled with bad code to a browser with a known vulnerability in how it loads PNGs. A hacker or threat actor might break into an organization's network and then use malicious PNGs to slip past security features and deliver even more viruses, malware, or encrypted messages or data. The point is, although this type of attack is time-consuming and more complex than others if it can be done, it will be done, and security professionals need to be ready to counteract it if and when they spot it.

Authentication methods

Every time we use the Internet, we come across authentication methods. We are prompted to respond to computer-recognition CAPCHAS, passwords, two-factor authentication, **Single sign-on** (**SSO**), and various other techniques for identity validation and verification.

Remember, the utmost responsibility of a secure system is to guarantee that only authorized users have access to the network. In short, network and security protocols need to allow legitimate users in while simultaneously keeping hackers and cybercriminals out. Ensuring users are legitimate users of a network and its resources is a critical aspect of network security.

There are three main principles or **factors** of authentication. These three factors are as follows:

- Something you *know* (Knowledge factor)
- Something you *have* (Possession factor)
- Something you *are* (Inherence factor/Biometrics)

Security is strengthened when two or more factors are combined in security mechanisms. Other factors used in security strategies are as follows:

- Somewhere you *are* (such as your location, using geolocation technologies)
- Something you *do* (such as gestures on a touch screen, using patterns or shapes)

Two-factor (2FA)/multifactor authentication

An example of 2FA occurs in Internet/online banking. When the user inputs a pin or password, the bank can send a code number to the user's phone. This means that two of the factors of authentication have been incorporated into the authentication method: something you know (that is, password or pin) and something you have (that is, your phone).

Some organizations use security methods comprising of the three factors by additionally using biometrics (that is, fingerprints, voice recognition, palm scan, facial scanners, iris, or retina scanning).

Multifactor authentication provides a more robust and resilient solution for logging on to systems and for verification and validation.

SSO is an authentication or log-on method that permits users to securely authenticate with multiple applications and websites by using just one set of credentials. SSO is not the same as password management or password vaulting. Password vaulting methods require you to enter the same credentials as you move through different applications or websites. Credentials are stored in the system's management repository as you move through the separate actions. In SSO, there is a trust relationship in place, and the company implementing the SSO solution approves all the applications and websites without requiring you to log in again. **Active Directory Directory Services (ADDS)**, **Lightweight Directory Access Protocol (LDAP)**, and **Active Directory Federation Services (ADFS)** use forms of SSO solutions.

Risk management

In a world that is experiencing rapid growth of digital technologies, risk management has become more and more critical. Business operations have been radically disrupted and further driven and transformed by digital innovation, and the acceleration of hybrid employment models. New risks are continually being observed and recognized by analysts, especially with the impact of Covid-19 and the threat of climate change (for example, attacks on digital systems and supply markets). These disruptors in the modern-day use of technology have brought positive risks as much as negative ones. Opportunities from changes can transform productivity for the better as much as risks can threaten or destruct production models. Organizations are now taking a fresh look at networks and digital mechanisms to newly assess technology and exposure to risk, as they meet and are challenged by ongoing change. Irrespective of whether the organization is in finance, health, governance, education, or any other sector, the management of risks, policies, and procedures for risks needs addressing and monitoring. Continuity of practice is the key. Futures-Thinking or strategizing is the ability to spot signals, imagine possibilities, and then use these creative visualizations to inform practice. This form of assessment holds a harness and strength as a prospective enabler of change. Co-constructing reality is at our fingertips, particularly in this digital landscape we inhabit. We are all responsible agents of change.

There are many forms of risk assessments that organizations can carry out. Some assessments undertaken are as follows:

- Security risk assessments
- Threat assessment
- Vulnerability assessment
- Penetration testing
- Posture assessment
- Business risk assessments
- Process assessment
- Vendor assessment

This list is not exhaustive.

Security information and event management

Security information and event management (**SIEM**) is a field within the sphere of computer security. It is a security solution that facilitates organizations to detect, analyze, and respond to security threats before they harm business operations. Software products and services bring together **security information management** (**SIM**) and **security event management** (**SEM**) in their design. This software provides the ability to analyze security alerts generated by software applications, networking devices, and hardware in real time. Suppliers produce SIEM as monitoring or management software, as hardware or appliances, or as managed services.

These products can log security events as they happen, thus enabling an administrator to generate viable and timely reports on incidents and threats. Data is collected from a range of sources, giving organizations and administrators visibility into the network and activities as they occur. SIEM tools and technologies have advanced over time and now include technologies stemming from AI. With this advancement, organizations can detect and respond to security threats faster and more proficiently. Anomalies can be detected and dealt with effectively and instantaneously.

In *Figure 16.5*, the graphic illustrates that security involves local devices in LAN and cloud-based security practices. Organizations need to focus on all elements and entities in their network, whether these devices are on the LAN, WLAN, or residing in the cloud.

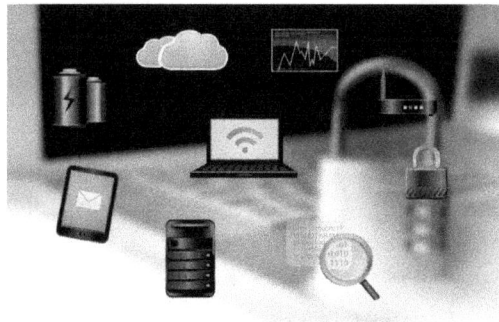

Figure 16.5: *Securing devices*

Conclusion

This chapter explored security concepts and security strategies. We focused on how to explain, compare, and contrast common security attacks. We learned that a solid network security system helps reduce the risk of data loss, theft, and sabotage. The topics covered include CIA, AAA, and risk assessment.

In the upcoming chapter, we will study security loopholes, threat agents, and how they operate. Learners will use critical thinking to observe use-case scenarios and gauge the risk and vulnerability present in these scenarios.

Points to remember

- Comprehend and explain common security concepts.
- Identify key terms and concepts in common security threats and their countermeasures.
- Describe the purpose and use of security procedures in protecting network infrastructure.
- Manage the use of physical equipment in networks.
- Safeguard users' identity and data during networking activities.
- Protect equipment, infrastructure, applications, and information as it is transmitted across networks and through the cloud in a perimeter-less network.
- The content of *Chapter 16, Security Concepts,* is mapped to *Domain 4, Network Security.* Explain the importance of basic network security concepts.

Key terms

- **AAA**: Authentication, authorization, and accounting.
    - **Authentication** provides the identity, such as with a password or pin. Authentication verifies the user as a legitimate user and validates them against an ACL or other list of users and groups.
    - **Authorization** grants users the authority to access resources based on their proven identity.
    - **Accounting** methods and strategies manage, monitor, and track user activity and record the activity in log files.
- **Terminal Access Controller Access-Control System Plus (TACACS+)**: TACACS+ is a Cisco proprietary authentication protocol similar to RADIUS. It has an added benefit. TACACS+ encrypts the entire authentication process, whereas RADIUS encrypts only the password.
- **Remote Authentication Dial-in User Service (RADIUS)**: RADIUS provides a centralized method of authentication for multiple remote access servers. RADIUS encrypts the password packets, but not the entire authentication process.
- **Lightweight Directory Access Protocol (LDAP)**: This protocol is used to communicate with directories such as Microsoft Active Directory. It identifies objects with query strings using codes such as CN=Users and DC= comptialabs. learnondemand. DC is short for domain component. The **CN** normally refers to the **Common Name** of an Active Directory object.

- **Lightweight Directory Access Protocol Secure (LDAPS)**: LDAPS is a protocol to encrypt LDAP traffic with **Transport Layer Security** (**TLS**). The TLS runs in the presentation layer of the OSI model. This protocol aims principally to provide security, including CIA—that is, confidentiality, integrity, and authenticity through cryptography. Methods include the use of certificates between two or more communicating computer applications.

- **Kerberos**: This is a network authentication method used with Windows Active Directory domains and with some Unix environments called realms. It uses a **Key Distribution Center** (**KDC**) to issue tickets. The KDC is a third-party trusted server whose main purpose is to act as a **Ticket Granting Service** (**TGS**) and an **Authentication Service** (**AS**).

- **Local authentication**: An alternative to using an external login service such as, *Do you wish to login with Google/join with Google or Login by Facebook,* you get the users to create accounts on the stack using their e-mail address and a password of their choice. This is done without sending the users out for external logging into another site or domain.

- **802.1X**: 802.1x defines certificate-based authentication (IEEE 802.1x). IEEE 802.1x is a port-based authentication protocol. An 802.1x server provides port-based authentication and can thereby authenticate clients. Clients unable to authenticate to the server (for example, individuals with guest accounts) can be redirected to the guest network. This permits them to access the Internet, but they cannot gain access to the internal network (WLAN or wired LAN).

- **Extensible Authentication Protocol (EAP)**: EAP is an authentication framework that supports general guidance for authentication methods. EAP is not an authentication method. It allows vendors to design, develop, and implement new EAP methods. The variations of EAP include PEAP, EAP-TLS, EAP-TTLS, and EAP-FAST.

- **Security risk assessments**: Any processes that identify, assess, evaluate, and prioritize security risks. Risk assessments may be qualitative or quantitative in nature.

- **Threat assessment**: A threat assessment is an estimate or evaluation of potential threats. Some general types of threat assessments are internal and external, environmental, manmade, or natural disasters. A threat assessment also tries to identify the potential impact of specific threats.

- **Vulnerability assessment**: A vulnerability assessment evaluates vulnerabilities (such as flaws, loopholes, or weaknesses), not potential dangers.

- **Penetration testing**: Security analysts/testers typically execute a penetration test to actively demonstrate the actual (factual) security vulnerabilities within a system. The purpose is to discover weaknesses and test the strength of the security mechanisms in place on a network or system. Normally, security issues discovered are presented to the company, together with an assessment of their impact and the recommended remedial actions or solutions. The objective of the penetration test is to determine the likelihood of an attack from outside the network and the business impact and implications of a successful exploit to the company. It is good to remember that (perfect) security policies written on paper may not necessarily be translated into practice.

- **Posture assessment**: It focuses on building the baseline perspective of an organization's security capabilities from end to end. Essentially, it is an overall view of the company's resilience or health in terms of its security measures.

- **Vendor assessment**: It occurs when a company is monitoring and managing its list of active suppliers. The firm checks the risk level of the third parties with whom they wish to do business. Products and services are evaluated to ensure they are defect-free, and vendors are further assessed to ensure they have safe and secure practices when handling business with others.

Questions

1. What is meant by CIA? Give examples.

2. Outline the benefits of a defense in depth model.

3. Give some examples of risk management procedures.

Join our book's Discord space

Join the book's Discord Workspace for Latest updates, Offers, Tech happenings around the world, New Release and Sessions with the Authors:

https://discord.bpbonline.com

CHAPTER 17
Cybersecurity Attacks

Introduction

In *Chapter 16, Security Concepts*, we explored assets, vulnerabilities, threats, and attacks. We learned that when speaking about assets:

- Any potential danger to these assets is regarded as a **threat**.
- Weaknesses or loopholes are regarded as **vulnerabilities**.

Attempts to **attack**, compromise, take advantage of, or play on vulnerabilities are defined as **exploits**. Additionally, we learned that exploits refer to the hardware and software used, procedure, or actions taken while an attack or incident is taking place or being carried out.

In this chapter, we will study security loopholes, threat agents, and how they operate. Learners will use critical thinking to observe scenarios and gauge the risk and vulnerability related to these scenarios. We will also differentiate between various types of attacks and compare and contrast common types of attacks and exploits.

Structure

The chapter explains the following topics:

- Technology-based attacks
- Social engineering
- Case studies

Objectives

After reading this chapter, you will be able to compare and contrast common types of cybersecurity attacks, identify and explain specific technology-based attacks, and give examples of human and environmental attacks. You will also be able to understand the concept of social engineering and give specific examples of attacks that use impersonation as a strategy.

Technology-based attacks

Digital innovation, tech solutions, and digital transformation have grown and accelerated in the last decade, especially in the past few years. Now, with an evolving hybrid workforce, technology is a critical component in making companies more secure. However, technology and the tools used to secure networks, network endpoints, and equipment, may also be used for malicious and intentional attacks. Remote working opportunities are expanding globally, but this new focus on how we work and how we use our networks comes with its inherent dangers. We are in a world where every industry uses technology. This technology and the data it transfers, stores, and archives, need safeguarding unquestionably.

Jeffrey Deaver, in his acclaimed fictional novel *The Blue Nowhere,* wittily captures the volatility of security systems when pitted against hackers who hold the confidence and know-how to compromise them. In the narrative, one of his characters, when asked about an IT system, states: *As a matter of fact, yeah, they were fool-proof. The problem is that you do not have to protect yourself against fools. You have to protect yourself against people like me*. In reality, threat actors and those with the technical know-how can build or design a *fool-proof* system or just as easily take this system down!

An individual's place in this *battle*, figuratively, depends upon the color of the hat they wear and whether they are a white hat hacker intended to do positive service to security systems or a black hat hacker with the intention to attack and destroy. In many areas of life, technology in the wrong hands is a dangerous liability instead of a positive or progressive asset. In the world of technology, as with other ventures, we all hold the ability to create or destroy things.

OSI model and cyber-attack examples

A good way to visualize threats and attacks is to map these attacks against the layers of the OSI model. In the previous chapters, we broke down the OSI model into functionality, technologies, and protocols.

Let us briefly review the functions and purpose of the OSI model. The OSI model is a conceptual reference model to demonstrate how computer networks operate and provide standard methods of data transmission and communication. About security concepts, businesses and organizations can understand where network vulnerabilities may exist within their infrastructure using this ISO framework. Consequently, they can implement security controls. The model is a hierarchical model, which demonstrates and frames how **Power Distribution Units** (**PDUs**) move throughout a network and how attacks can happen at any level.

In *Figure 17.1*, threats (exploits) are aligned to the seven layers of the OSI model. The protocols and corresponding network vulnerabilities associated with these functions and protocols are listed in the last column.

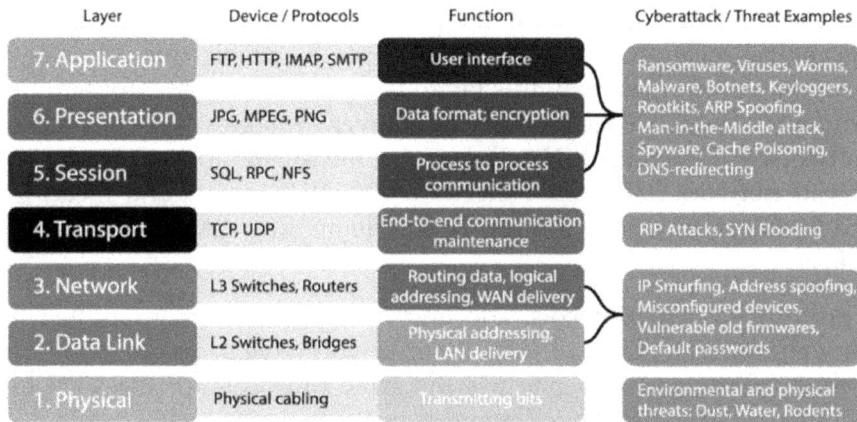

Layer	Device / Protocols	Function	Cyberattack / Threat Examples
7. Application	FTP, HTTP, IMAP, SMTP	User interface	Ransomware, Viruses, Worms, Malware, Botnets, Keyloggers, Rootkits, ARP Spoofing, Man-in-the-Middle attack, Spyware, Cache Poisoning, DNS-redirecting
6. Presentation	JPG, MPEG, PNG	Data format; encryption	
5. Session	SQL, RPC, NFS	Process to process communication	
4. Transport	TCP, UDP	End-to-end communication maintenance	RIP Attacks, SYN Flooding
3. Network	L3 Switches, Routers	Routing data, logical addressing, WAN delivery	IP Smurfing, Address spoofing, Misconfigured devices, Vulnerable old firmwares, Default passwords
2. Data Link	L2 Switches, Bridges	Physical addressing, LAN delivery	
1. Physical	Physical cabling	Transmitting bits	Environmental and physical threats: Dust, Water, Rodents

Figure 17.1: The OSI model and cyber-attack examples

By aligning these attacks, the figure clarifies why we need to implement security at *every* layer of the model. Remember that this list includes examples of exploits and a few attacks in existence. The list is by no means exhaustive.

Beginning from the first layer upwards, we will explore examples of cybersecurity issues relevant to the specific layer of the OSI and some of the core elements and functions that can be exploited at the layer. More details on these cyber-attacks are defined in the *Key terms* section of this chapter.

Layer 1: The physical layer

The physical layer in the OSI model can include anything from wires to pins, connectors, sockets and conductors, *endpoints*, cables, wireless connections, routers, and anything tangible that can be damaged, degraded, or sabotaged. Internal threats such as disgruntled, malicious employees, unintentional errors, or even hacktivists can do some damage with cable cutters or other tools to damage or degrade the equipment and devices at the physical layer. Network administrators should be astutely aware of any menace to the physical layer, as this layer is neglected at times. Threats also include environmental or natural disasters.

The threats listed in the illustration are dust, water, and rodents. Additionally, damage may happen to cables, equipment, and network infrastructure through fire, problems with temperature or humidity, and even through the wear and tear or degradation of physical links and other hardware components.

Note that *endpoints* are hosts, which commonly consist of desktops, servers, laptops, and VoIP phones, as well as employee-owned (BYOD) devices. Endpoints are particularly vulnerable to malware-related attacks that originate through phishing attacks or Web browsing threats or loopholes. To counter this threat, an organization can implement e-mail or Web security appliances, firewalls at the perimeter of the network, and **Host-based Intrusion Prevention Systems** (**HIPSs**). Additionally, organizations should assess the access to their infrastructure, know the physical location of endpoints, and be aware of the geographical location of all hardware to hold a viable plan to safeguard them. The organization will need to view this layer as a part of business operations regarding potential downtime and means of recovery or failover strategies. Network security devices include a **network access control** (**NAC**) device, a **next-generation firewall** (**NGFW**), and a **virtual private network** (**VPN**) enabled router. RADIUS servers and Tacacs+ servers are also selected by organizations as a means of implementing AAA when using a VPN for remote workers.

Tunneling protocols, AAA protocols, and encryption levels, when applied to the VPN connections, determine the level of VPN security you have access to. VPN functionality requires both the client and server to use the same protocols for the VPN to be viable. Essentially, VPNs can provide the following security capabilities:

- Secure authentication
- Data encryption
- Data integrity (this ensures that the data is not amended or modified in transmission)
- Nonrepudiation (this assures that the packets came from the claimed source at a specific time, that is, time-stamped with proof of the sender's ID)

A VPN uses the concept of tunneling to establish and maintain a logical network connection. Tunneling strengthens the security of data transmission and remote work.

Layer 2: The datalink layer

This layer consists of switches using protocols such as **Spanning Tree Protocol** (**STP**) and **Dynamic Host Configuration Protocol** (**DHCP**). Switch functionality provides **local area network** (**LAN**) connectivity and access to the network to host devices. Other protocols implemented are address resolution protocols such as **Address Resolution Protocol** (**ARP**) and **Reverse ARP** (**RARP**).

Network administrators routinely implement security solutions to protect the protocols, features, and elements in layer 3 of the OSI model up through to the applications layer at layer 7. This necessary course of action is critical to security controls. However, administrators must also know that exploits and threat actors do not always *directly* attack layer 7 functionality or protocols. Some *preliminary* attacks can occur on switches, compromising Ethernet frames or switching protocols and targeting MAC table operations. These layer 2 attacks can subsequently be used as the entry routes or foothold to engage attacks at higher layers of operations. Initial attacks can permit the hacker to gain access to passwords and data, thus having no need to go directly to other higher-layer functions. Ultimately, network users may not even be aware that their application-layer information has been compromised.

Attacks at layer 2 include the following:

- MAC address flooding via MAC table attacks
- STP Attacks via the manipulation of Spanning Tree Protocol
- DHCP (server) spoofing, DHCP starvation
- **Man-in-the-Middle (MitM)** attacks using gratuitous ARP
- IP host spoofing
- VLAN hopping, VLAN double-tagging via Ethernet Frame manipulation
- Misconfigured devices, vulnerable old firmware, and default passwords

To mitigate against these attacks, the following strategies are implemented on networks: **IP Source Guard (IPSG)**, which is a proprietary Cisco security feature; **Dynamic ARP Inspection (DAI)**, **DHCP Snooping**; and switch **Port Security**. DAI mitigates against ARP spoofing and ARP poisoning attacks, whereas DHCP Snooping counters DHCP starvation and DHCP spoofing attacks.

Other techniques used to secure the data link layer are enabling MAC address filtering, disabling unused ports, and ensuring that VLAN implementation is configured correctly. Regarding encryption and device management protocols such as TFTP, Syslog, or SNMP, the best practice is to always use secure variations of these protocols such as SSH, **Secure Copy Protocol (SCP)**, **Secure FTP (SFTP)**, and **Secure Socket Layer/Transport Layer Security (SSL/TLS)** for privacy as well as security.

Layer 3: The network layer

In *Chapter 1, OSI Model*, the network layer was described as essentially having two functions:

- It breaks up data into network packets and reassembles data on the receiving end (that is, incoming packets at the destination).
- Using a layer 3 intermediary device, it routes packets from source to destination by discovering the *best* path from source to destination across the physical network.

This layer consists of routers and multilayer switches (with routing capability). Cyber-security attacks at this layer are listed in *Figure 17.1* as IP Smurfing, address spoofing, misconfigured devices, vulnerable old firmware, and default passwords. Threat actors can attack this layer by IP/port sniffing or IP spoofing or by overloading a network (with *ping* packets, for example). Using **Internet Control Message Protocol (ICMP)**, the attacker can bring about a *ping flood* or a **denial of service (DoS)** to a targeted or unsuspecting device.

These attacks can impact a part or all of a network and, at worst, bring the entire network down.

Denial of service and distributed denial of service

Network attacks today are varied and diverse in terms of severity and impact. Attacks can stem from a single individual or group and even be coordinated attacks on equipment or endpoints that originate from a single device or person. *Figure 17.2* shows a single attacker with an arrow pointed at a very specific target:

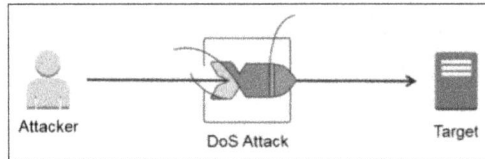

Figure 17.2: DOS attack

Note that the attacker is using a single computer with a single connection to a single target. This defines a DOS scenario and context.

The intention of this DOS attack is to flood a network server with more packets than the server can handle. The onslaught of data overloads and overwhelms the server, so much so that the server is unable to handle legitimate requests and traffic. This cyber-attack can slow down or shut down a machine, making it inaccessible to users and other hosts who are attempting to connect to it for information or services. In DOS attacks, the requests sent to the server are made to look like legitimate traffic. Since the server is now trying to assess the validity of this large number of requests, it becomes caught up with verifying and responding to the legitimate and invalid types of requests received and may even be brought down or offline.

In a **distributed denial of service (DDOS)** attack, the attacker has the ability to create and implement a **collaborated** attack by using the *services* of other devices. *Figure 17.3* illustrates an attack where the threat actor (hacker) uses a controller to *gather an army* of devices against the target. This attack is more common than a DOS attack.

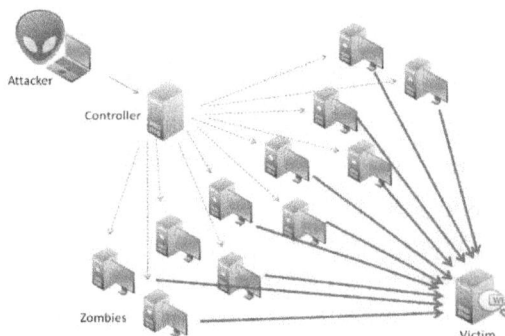

Figure 17.3: DDOS attack

In DDOS attacks, numerous computers and internet connections across the world are used to burden and overload targeted servers or systems.

These attacks are usually executed through a network of *zombie* devices that are controlled by the attacker. The zombie devices have been previously compromised (usually through a user inadvertently downloading malware).

Note: Botnet/command and control. The compromised zombie devices are recruited to cooperative/collaborative teams called botnets. This becomes an army of attackers with more force and impact than an individual device. The botnets work in a coordinated attack on the specified target. Typically, this attack occurs on a particular day and time.

Layer 4: The transport layer

We will now explore the upper layers of OSI, regarded as the *host* layers of the OSI model. The transport layer accepts data from the previous layer, splits the data up into smaller units, and then passes these units to the network layer. Part of the process is ensuring that all the data units arrive correctly at the other end. The process of splitting the data up is called **segmentation**.

At this layer, connection control is either connection-oriented or connectionless. Protocols implemented on this layer are **Transport Control Protocol** (**TCP**) and **User Datagram Protocol** (**UDP**). A quick differentiation between TCP and UDP is that TCP prioritizes data quality over speed. UDP is essentially *quick-fire* transmission.

Cyber-security attacks at this layer are listed in *Figure 17.1* as RIP attacks and SYN flooding. In an SYN flood, an attacker initiates numerous connections to a server using a spoofed IP address. The attacker does not wait for a connection to conclude. Smurf attacks use malware to overload the network's resources. The attacker will broadcast Internet Control Message Protocol (ping) echoes, thus, causing an infinite loop of requests. In an RIP attack, the attacker forges RIP routing updates and sends them to a router to cause the router to forward packets toward the attacker.

Using packet sniffing software and other reconnaissance methods, an attacker can learn about your network and study it for further engagement.

Firewall configuration should focus on locking down this layer as much as possible. Only allow what is needed and nothing more.

A network administrator should know firewall methodologies such as packet filtering, NAT endpoint filtering (NAT filtering), and creating an **application-level gateway** (**ALG**)/circuit-level gateway. Understanding ACLs and how to apply and understand them is a must.

Security devices such as firewalls, IPSs, and IDSs are the main defense for an organization's networks, whether they are LANs, WANs, intranets, or extranets.

Layers 5, 6, and 7: The session, presentation, and application layers

Let us now look at these next three layers:

- **Session layer**:
  - o **Primary function**: Managing communication sessions.
  - o The primary purpose of the session layer is to manage and synchronize the conversation between two communicating systems.
  - o In the session layer, file transfer, remote login, or other acts of communication are established and maintained.

- **Presentation layer**:
  - o **Primary function**: Translation of data between a networking service and an application.
  - o The presentation layer *takes* the data from the application layer above it and changes the data.

- **Application layer**:
  - o **Primary function**: High-level APIs, including resource sharing and remote file access.

Cyber-attacks

In *Figure 17.1*, the list of cyber-attacks on the top right is aligned with these upper three layers of the OSI model. The list consists of the following attacks: ransomware, viruses, worms, malware, botnets, keyloggers, rootkits, ARP Spoofing, MitM attacks, spyware, cache poisoning, and DNS re-directing.

Additionally, an attacker can *hijack* the session layer of data transmission. Session hijacking can occur on a network using different methods. These methods include **cross-site scripting** (**XSS**), session side jacking/sniffing, session fixation, cookie theft, predictable session IDs, and other brute force attempts.

At the presentation layer, threat actors or attackers look for exploits in encryption flaws. One of the most common strategies is **secure socket layer** (**SSL**) hijacking or sniffing.

It probably goes without saying that the application layer of the OSI model is where attacks are widest and far-ranging. Consequently, those involved in cybersecurity are extremely busy with ongoing challenges, threats, and attacks. Putting aside all the myriad technical-based attacks, the security worker must also be prepared and knowledgeable about social engineering tactics to be able to provide services to organizations and teach them how to educate the users on a network.

Mitigation against these technical attacks (at all three layers) demands high-quality coding, effective management (and prevention) of cookies, and the use of encryption, such as HTTPS.

Man-in-the-Middle attack

According to *Techopedia*, A MiTM attack is a form of eavesdropping where communication between two users is monitored and modified by an unauthorized party. Generally, the attacker actively eavesdrops by intercepting a public key message exchange and retransmits the message while replacing the requested key with his own.

In almost all cases of this attack, the attacker is on the same broadcast domain as the victim of the attack (sender). The sender of the message is totally oblivious to this interception and carries on transmitting regardless. This allows the attacker to control the entire act of communication between the sender and the receiver. The attack places the attacker between two victim devices, forcing data transmission to pass through the devices by duping each victim into believing that they are communicating with the other. In doing so, the attacker is rewarded with access to all data exchanges, encrypted or not, meaning it is easy for an attacker to extract information or even amend the data to their benefit.

In *Figure 17.4*, the reoriented traffic is captured by the attacker. We can observe that the original communication link is broken.

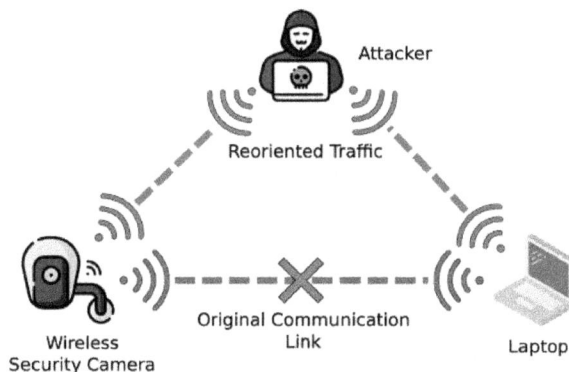

Figure 17.4: *MitM attack*

Note: MitM attacks can be on any endpoint device.

Malware

Malware is typically installed on a computer without user awareness. Once a device is infected, the malware can take the following steps:

1. Change the computer configuration.

2. Cause equipment to become locked or unusable.

3. Delete, encrypt, steal files, or corrupt hard drives.

4. Collect information stored on the computer or take remote control of the device without the user's agreement.

5. Open extra windows on the computer or redirect the browser.

6. Compromise the device to become a zombie as part of a botnet.

7. Access credentials that allow access to your organization's systems or services that you use.

8. Enable the *mining* of cryptocurrency.

These are some of the impacts of malware. Other types of malwares are worms, Trojans, rootkits, adware, spyware, and ransomware. These types further break down into various sub-types and formats.

Network administrators need to ensure that users are educated on security attacks to prevent malware in an organization optimally. Administrators should use anti-malware software with integrated anti-ransomware features. Proper backup of data is also recommended. Password managers support security monitoring and maintenance and are an effective means of ensuring the best use. Company software should be regularly patched and updated. AAA and PoLP should be part of the organization's policy, procedures, and practice, regarded as the norm in business operations and planning. In short, all organizations should aim for a positive cybersecurity culture where staff training and education are ongoing and continuous.

Network administrators can also arm themselves with knowledge about the software and tools attackers use to target and exploit a network, for example, SuperScan, Nmap, Nipper, Metasploit, Invicti, and Nessus, to name a few.

Social engineering

Social engineering covers a wide range of malicious activities accomplished through human behavior and interactions. The core element of this type of attack is that it involves impersonation, deception, or pretense on behalf of the attacker. Attackers use psychological manipulation to fool users into making security mistakes or into inadvertently giving away sensitive or confidential information. Some of these cybercriminals are master manipulators, but others are not so masterful, and so, there is a broad range of caliber and quality in the makeup and category of these attacks. Social engineering is also ever-evolving as cyber-criminals find innovative techniques to carry out scams or data theft. Once social engineers gain access to the network, they can exploit information, data, and others' identities or cause disruptions to business operations or services. Attackers often depend on human nature and people's behaviors, such as their willingness to be supportive and helpful, or, in some situations, avoid confrontation with *alleged* outcomes of their work practices, such as a fear that their boss will identify weaknesses or lack of awareness of technical know-how. Social engineering is often combined with other network attacks.

Some examples of social engineering include e-mail hacking, phishing, spear phishing, scareware, tailgating, baiting, pretexting, watering hole attacks, quid pro quo, physical breaches, shoulder surfing, something for something, spam, and dumpster diving. This list is a partial list of attacks that are prevalent in networking activities.

In *Figure 17.5*, the main stages of a social engineer's strategy are outlined as follows:

1. Preparing the ground for the attack.

2. Deceiving the victims to gain a foothold.

3. Obtaining the information over a period of time.

4. Closing the interaction, ideally without arousing suspicion.

If a social engineer plans well, the impact of the attack can be greater and potentially more damaging.

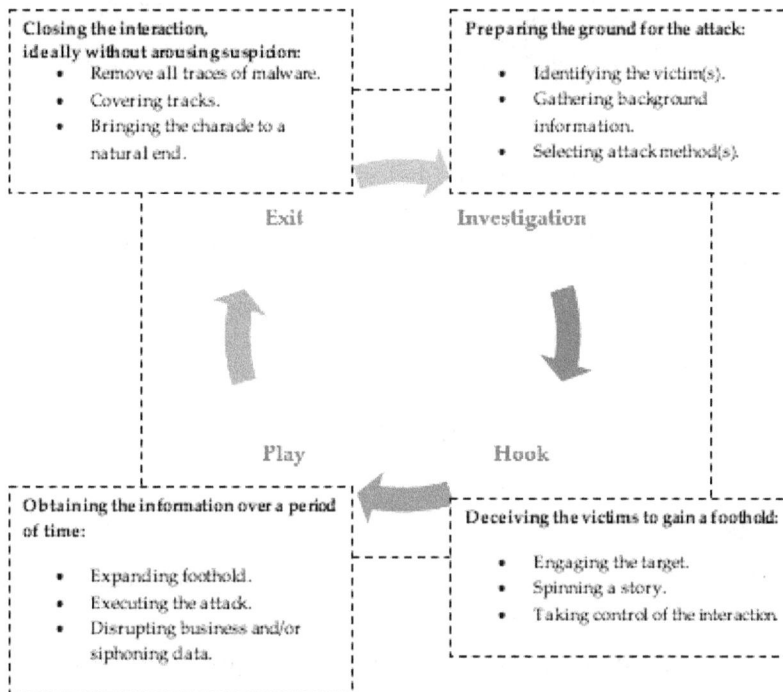

Figure 17.5: Social engineering attack lifecycle

Figure 17.6 offers examples of educational material for building staff awareness of social engineering. Many anti-malware sites, organizations, and educational institutions provide free resources that can be printed and displayed around the company or staff areas.

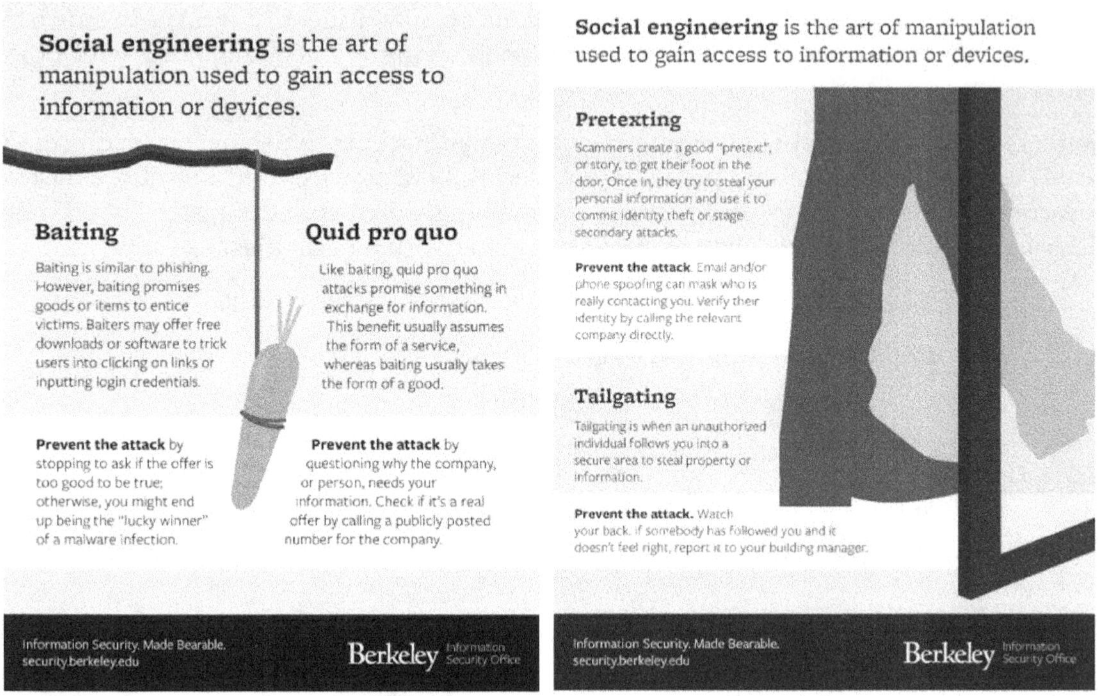

Social engineering is the art of manipulation used to gain access to information or devices.

Baiting

Baiting is similar to phishing. However, baiting promises goods or items to entice victims. Baiters may offer free downloads or software to trick users into clicking on links or inputting login credentials.

Prevent the attack by stopping to ask if the offer is too good to be true; otherwise, you might end up being the "lucky winner" of a malware infection.

Quid pro quo

Like baiting, quid pro quo attacks promise something in exchange for information. This benefit usually assumes the form of a service, whereas baiting usually takes the form of a good.

Prevent the attack by questioning why the company, or person, needs your information. Check if it's a real offer by calling a publicly posted number for the company.

Social engineering is the art of manipulation used to gain access to information or devices.

Pretexting

Scammers create a good "pretext", or story, to get their foot in the door. Once in, they try to steal your personal information and use it to commit identity theft or stage secondary attacks.

Prevent the attack. Email and/or phone spoofing can mask who is really contacting you. Verify their identity by calling the relevant company directly.

Tailgating

Tailgating is when an unauthorized individual follows you into a secure area to steal property or information.

Prevent the attack. Watch your back. If somebody has followed you and it doesn't feel right, report it to your building manager.

Information Security. Made Bearable.
security.berkeley.edu
Berkeley Information Security Office

Information Security. Made Bearable.
security.berkeley.edu
Berkeley Information Security Office

Figure 17.6: Social engineering, educating the user

Security awareness programs and training help staff and users understand how criminals use tactics such as tailgating or other impersonation techniques. Well-informed and educated users are less likely to be deceived, even by a friendly smile or engaging conversation from a friendly or helpful individual.

Case studies

Let us look at some case studies in this section:

- **LoanDepot ransomware incident:**
  - **Date**: January 2024
  - **Impact**: Data breach affecting 16.9 million customers and $27 million in response and recovery costs.
  - **Summary**: LoanDepot, a prominent mortgage lender, suffered a ransomware attack that compromised sensitive data, including social security numbers, account numbers, names, and addresses. The company had to take systems offline and faced substantial recovery costs.

- **Schneider Electric ransomware incident**:
  - **Date**: January 2024

- o **Impact**: 1.5 terabytes of data stolen.
- o **Summary**: The ransomware-as-a-service group known as Cactus successfully infiltrated Schneider Electric's networks, stealing a vast amount of data from its Sustainability Business Division.

- **Equifax data breach**:
  - o **Date**: 2017
  - o **Impact**: Personal information of 147 million individuals exposed.
  - o **Summary**: Equifax, a major credit reporting agency, experienced a massive data breach due to an unpatched vulnerability in the Apache Struts web application framework. This breach underscored the importance of timely software updates and transparent incident communication.

- **Target data breach**:
  - o **Date**: 2013
  - o **Impact**: Credit card information of over 40 million customers compromised.
  - o **Summary**: Attackers gained access to Target's network through a third-party HVAC contractor, leading to a breach of customer credit card information. This incident highlighted the risks associated with third-party vendors and the necessity for advanced threat detection systems.

Note: More details can be found about these specific attacks online since they are used as examples of cybersecurity breaches. The general and technical questions and answers expand on the summaries of the case study scenarios.

Questions

Here are some general questions based on the case studies:

1. What was the primary cause of the Equifax data breach?

   Answer: The primary cause was a known vulnerability in the Apache Struts web application framework that Equifax failed to patch promptly.

2. How did hackers gain access to Target's network in the 2013 data breach?

   Answer: Hackers gained access through a third-party HVAC contractor.

3. What was the financial impact of the LoanDepot ransomware attack?

   Answer: The attack resulted in $27 million in response and recovery costs.

4. Which ransomware group was responsible for the Schneider Electric attack?

   Answer: The ransomware-as-a-service group Cactus.

Here are some technical questions based on the case studies:

1. What vulnerability did the attackers exploit in the Equifax data breach?

2. How did the Cactus ransomware group gain initial access to Schneider Electric's network?

3. What type of malware was used in the LoanDepot ransomware attack?

4. What specific technique did the hackers use to escalate their privileges within Target's network?

5. Which security controls failed to detect the attack on Target's network?

Here are the answers:

1. The attackers exploited a vulnerability in the Apache Struts web application framework that was not patched promptly.

2. The Cactus ransomware group gained initial access through phishing emails containing malicious attachments, which led to the installation of **Remote Access Trojans (RATs)**.

3. The attackers used ransomware to encrypt critical files and demanded a ransom for decryption.

4. The hackers used a technique known as **Pass-the-Hash** to escalate their privileges within Target's network. **Pass-the-Hash** is an attack method that permits cybercriminals to validate their access to a remote server or service by utilizing the hashed form of a user's password, rather than the actual plaintext password. In essence, if an attacker manages to acquire the password hash, they can impersonate the user and gain entry to systems and resources without needing to know the original password. This method is notably effective in environments that rely on outdated authentication protocols. It underscores the crucial need for strong password management practices and the adoption of modern authentication techniques to mitigate such vulnerabilities.

5. The failure of advanced threat detection systems and inadequate network segmentation allowed the attackers to move laterally within Target's network undetected.

These case studies, along with the questions and answers, provide a comprehensive look into recent cybersecurity threats and attacks. They emphasize the importance of robust security measures, proactive defense strategies, and timely updates to safeguard sensitive data and maintain business resilience.

Conclusion

This chapter explored security concepts and security strategies. We explored technology-based, human, and environmental attacks. The most significant means of counteracting these attacks is employing a combination of effective security policies and procedures with training and education. For example, an **Acceptable Use Policy** (**AUP**) defines proper system usage or the rules of behavior for employees when using the organization's network or information technology systems. The AUP often describes the purpose of computer systems and networks, how users can access them, and the responsibilities of users when they gain access to the network and its resources. Attacks on a network or its users can be incredibly destructive. Organizations should plan procedures to implement security controls. Moreover, there is no point in having plans for countering attacks if security controls are not adequately enforced and plans and consequences for non-compliance are neglected in practice.

In the upcoming chapter, we will understand network hardening techniques and learn how to implement them on a network.

Points to remember

The reader should understand the following:

- Various types of cybersecurity attacks.
- Specific technology-based attacks.
- Strategies to mitigate technology-based attacks.
- Different types of social engineering attacks.
- How social engineering attacks operate.
- How attackers use impersonation and deception to deceive network system users.
- The content of *Chapter 17, Cybersecurity Attacks*, is mapped to *Domain 4, Network Security*. Summarize various types of attacks and their impact to the network.

Key terms

- **Dictionary attack**: In a dictionary attack, the attacker uses a list of words and phrases to try to guess the password. These attacks can also be brute-force. The use of complex passwords with appropriate character length and alpha-numeric, plus symbols, counters these attacks.
- **DNS poisoning**: This is a cyber-attack that modifies or corrupts DNS results. **Domain Name System Security Extensions** (**DNSSEC**) help counteract DNS poisoning. *DNS is used to resolve host names to IP addresses.

- **Dumpster diving**: The practice of searching through trash, looking to gain information from discarded documents. Shredding incineration/burning papers resolves this attack.

- **Evil twin**: In an evil twin cyber-attack, the attacker configures a rogue access point that mimics or duplicates an authentic access point on the network. The attacker uses a jamming or disassociation attack to disconnect users from the legitimate WLAN. When users re-connect to the WLAN, they inadvertently connect to the attacker's rogue access point. Now, the attacker can observe and capture all data transmissions that move through the rogue access point. Consequently, administrators should monitor and be aware of the network devices to identify suspect equipment.

- **IP spoofing**: This is a security attack where the attacker changes the source IP address of a host or device.

- **Jamming**: Transmits noise at the same frequency as a wireless network.

- **MAC spoofing**: This occurs when an attacker changes the source MAC address of a host or device.

- **Phishing**: A widespread social engineering cyber-attack. Phishing happens when an attacker sends out an email that is seemingly legitimate but has a malicious payload. The attacker fashions the email with the objective and aim, and the target will click on a link. The link will either forward the user to a malicious website (that is, a redirector) or download an attachment that contains malware.

- **Personally identifiable information**: Information about individuals that can be used by attackers to trace a person's identity, such as a full name, date of birth, public services number, biometric data, and more.

- **Ransomware**: A form of malware used to steal/extort money from individuals and organizations. Ransomware normally encrypts the user's data and then demands a ransom before decrypting the data.

- **Spear phishing**: A targeted phishing attack. Spear phishing involves the attacker performing research on a specific target (reconnaissance) and producing an e-mail that is geared to that target.

- **Whaling**: This occurs when the CEO of the company or a high-profile director is the target of the attack.

- **Vishing**: A human-based social engineering attack that takes place over a phone. In this attack, the attacker tries to gain confidential information, such as a user's login credentials. These attackers sometimes use emotionally charged strategies to influence or even scare a person into handing over data.

- **Smishing**: A human-based social engineering attack that takes place over a phone using text instead of voice. It is a combination of the words SMS and phishing. Fraudsters use mobile phone text messages to dupe individuals into clicking on and opening a malicious attachment or link.

- **Shoulder surfing**: The practice of looking over someone's shoulder to obtain information, such as on a computer screen. A privacy/screen filter placed over a monitor helps decrease the success of shoulder surfing.

- **Tailgating**: A human-based social engineering attack. It is used to bypass building access control measures, such as security personnel, fobbed doorways, barriers, or badge reader. The attacker attempts to closely follow a legitimate employee or user into the physical building to gain unauthorized access. The action of following closely behind another user without using credentials is also known as **piggybacking**. Mantraps and security guards are effective ways to counter this form of attack.

Questions

1. What is meant by technology-based cyber-attacks? Give examples.
2. Give some examples of human and environmental cyber-attacks.

Join our book's Discord space

Join the book's Discord Workspace for Latest updates, Offers, Tech happenings around the world, New Release and Sessions with the Authors:

https://discord.bpbonline.com

CHAPTER 18

Network Hardening Techniques

There's no silver bullet solution with cybersecurity,
a layered defense is the only viable defense.

- James Scott

Introduction

In *Chapter 16, Security Concepts*, **layering** was defined when discussing **defense in depth** (**DiD**). We now understand that an approach to DiD occurs where there is layering in security practices and where an administrator applies the right technologies in each chosen layer of defense. We have also observed that layering involves employing various security measures to protect the same asset. In other words, DiD or security in depth is the principle, which means that **no single layer is completely effective in securing the assets on its own**. The most secure system or network has many layers of security, and this act of layering eliminates single points of failure and further hardens the network. In short, as articulated in the quote by *James Scott*, there is no *silver bullet* with cybersecurity. As such, network hardening techniques are of prime importance.

Techopedia expands on the definition of hardening by stating that *Protecting* in layers means to protect at the host level, the application level, the operating system level, the user level, the physical level, and all the sublevels in between. Essentially, hardening's goal is to eliminate as many risks and threats to a computer system as necessary.

Structure

This chapter explains the following topics:

- Securing a workstation
- Techniques to secure a network
- Best practices of WLAN attack countermeasures
- Internet of Things security considerations

Objectives

After reading this chapter, you will be able to understand the techniques used to harden a network and apply security measures on end devices, and network hardware and software.

Securing a workstation

Networks are made up of intermediary network devices, security systems, and hosts/ end devices such as networked PCs, VoIP phones, or laptops. Consequently, a network administrator ensures that protection occurs effectively at the host level upwards. Let us concentrate on securing workstations first. Essentially, the strategies used to secure workstations involve the following:

- Educating the user
- Setting up a secure workstation policy
- Implementing the **principle of least privilege (PoLP)**
- Changing the default administrator's user account/password
- Installing virus and spyware protection or using the integrated Windows Defender
- Including an anti-adware tool so that malicious software cannot compromise the computer
- Ensuring anti-malware definitions are kept up to date
- Using timeout/screensaver locks, failed attempts lockout, privacy screens, and filters
- Logging off when the workstation is not in use
- Securing **personally identifiable information (PII)** and passwords

Workstation security can be further enhanced by the following:

- **Users and accounts**
  - o Ensuring the workstations are managed by strong firewall policies and rules.
  - o Implementing port security.

o Keeping security patches and hotfixes relevant and updated.

o Monitoring security bulletins that are pertinent to a workstation's operating system and applications.

o Applying local vs. Microsoft account (users and groups).

- **Passwords/encryption and authentication**

  o Using standard accounts and disabling the guest user account.

  o Applying password best practices (for example, character length and complexity, password expiration requirements, SSO, Multifactor authentication, PIN, and biometrics).

  o Implementing **User Account Control** (**UAC**), BitLocker, BitLocker To Go, **Encrypting File System** (**EFS**), or data-at-rest encryption.

  o Activating **Basic input/output system** (**BIOS**)/ Unified Extensible Firmware Interface (b) passwords.

  o Disabling AutoRun and AutoPlay features.

  o Not allowing file sharing among programs.

  o Maintaining a computer system backup, such as a hard drive.

These strategies are common methods to meet best practices for security. Some common methods for securing mobile and embedded devices align with many practices listed for workstations and additionally include the following:

- Remote wipes, remote backup applications (for example, Google Cloud)
- Mobile screen locks, biometrics, BYOD policies, and profile security best practice

Figure 18.1 illustrates two-factor authentications. The lady shown in the figure is using a combination of the factors *something you know* (as in her login credentials) and *something you have* (as in her smartphone and the input of a code generated by the software). The use of multifactor authentication makes security more robust.

Figure 18.1: Two-factor authentication

Techniques to secure a network

Now that we have looked at workstation security, we will explore some techniques for hardening a network.

Access control lists

As described by *Techopedia*, an **access control list** (**ACL**) refers to the permissions attached to an object that specifies which users are granted access to that object and the operations it is allowed to perform. The object referred to can be a file, process, program, protocol, or a piece of equipment participating in network operations. The term also applies to entry into the physical building or particular areas of an organization. ACLs are commonly implemented on **Domain Name System** (**DNS**) servers, web servers, routers, firewalls, and other devices.

Regarding routers, ACLs are lists of conditions used to assess and test network traffic that tries to travel across a router interface. These ACEs/lists inform the router as to what types of packets to accept (permit) or deny (block). Acceptance and denial can be based on specific conditions or states at entry or exit interfaces. As a result, ACLs enable the secure management of traffic and provide safe access and management of data as it travels in and out of a network.

The syntax and makeup of ACLs are very precise, so much so that ACLs must be defined per protocol, direction, or port basis. An ACL must be specified for each protocol that is active on the interface. ACLs control traffic in one direction at a time on an interface, controlling it on the ingress and egress interface of the router. Thus, two distinct ACLs must be created to validate and control both inbound and outbound traffic. Every router interface can have several protocols and directions defined and aligned to the ACE generated. In short, there would be one ACL created for each protocol, times two for the number of ports, and times two for each direction. There are two types of ACL: *standard* and *extended*.

Figure 18.2 shows how ACLs are implemented on inbound and outbound interfaces:

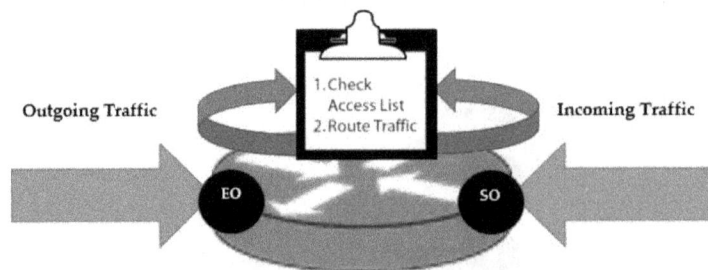

Figure 18.2: ACLs on a router

As traffic reaches the router interface, it is verified against the ACL. If it is permitted, it is routed and then sent to the outbound interface. If a network administrator is intent on applying ACLs on a device, the best practice is to consult the relevant documentation because ACLs will not work if misconfigured, if the syntax is incorrect, or if the order of operations is misunderstood. It is best to do the research first.

The best security strategy when configuring ACLs between the public internet and your LAN or private internetwork is to *deny* any:

- Addresses from your internal networks
- Local host addresses (127.0.0.0/8)
- Reserved private addresses
- Addresses in the IP multicast address range (224.0.0.0/4)

These IP addresses should not be allowed to enter your organization's internetwork. Remember, a threat actor based on the *public* internet may carry out IP spoofing by pretending to be a host in the private network and gain access to the internal internetwork.

Example of ACLs

Some examples of ACLs include the following:

- **Standard Access Control List**: (numbers 1–99 or 1300–1999) as follows:
  `R1(config)#access-list 1 permit 192.168.13.0 0.0.0.255`

  Context: Our router's name is **R1**. The number of the ACL as **1** identifies it as a standard ACL.

  This ACL permits traffic from network 192.168.13.0/24 to travel through the router. The statement is a single permit entry. Even though we are not stating that all other networks are denied (that is, *deny any*), there is an *implicit deny* that occurs on the router. If traffic is not *explicitly allowed* within an access control list, then by default, it is denied.

  > **Note: Standard ACLs filter the packets based only on the source address. When the ACL is created, it is applied to a specific interface.**

  `R1(config)#interface fastEthernet 0/1`
  `R1(config-if)#ip access-group 1 in`
  `Note the number of the ACL in the entry.`

  The ACL is applied to inbound traffic. In this scenario, that is sufficient.

- **Extended range ACLs**: (numbers 1300-1999.)

  Extended ACLs filter packets are based on the following:

  o Protocol type/Protocol number (for example, IP, ICMP, UDP, TCP, FTP, and so on)

  o Source and destination IP addresses

       o   Source and Destination TCP and UDP ports

```
Access-list 102 permit tcp 192.168.13.0 0.0.0.255 any eq 80
```

In the example, **eq** means equal to, as in, equal to port 80. This ACE is applied to a specific interface as with a standard ACL.

ACLs can be numbered or named. Most rules are static and remain the same unless an administrator reviews and changes them manually. However, some ACL rules are dynamic. For example, **intrusion prevention systems (IPSs)** can identify attacks and then modify ACL rules to block traffic from an attacker. In this case, it is the attack that triggers a change in the ACL rules, thus allowing the security device to respond efficiently and dynamically.

Network servers, network firewalls, routers, or security devices can implement port filtering to block traffic per protocol.

Similarly, ACLs can be used to filter traffic based on port numbers as well as IP addresses. Typically, a majority of firewalls default to permitting only the open ports that you specify and blocking all others. This is another version of *implicit deny*, whereby anything not allowed is denied. Network administrators must be aware of the port numbers of all traffic that needs to be allowed through the filtering device in and out of the network. Otherwise, errors will be made, and devices/firewalls will be misconfigured. The advice is to learn the port numbers and know the applications and protocols they are associated with. Moreover, be aware of how important managing a firewall is to network functionality as much as to network hardening techniques.

Router advertisement guard

Routers announce their availability and presence using **Router Advertisement (RA)** messages as part of a legitimate method of IPv6 addressing and provisioning. Nodes that read these RA messages are presented with the necessary information to auto-configure an IPv6 address and may respond to the RA message with a **Router Solicitation (RS)** response. RAs are also used in **Neighbor Discovery Protocol (NDP)**, as routers find out about specific routers in their vicinity, their hop limits, **Maximum Transmission Units (MTU)**, and other information relevant to effective packet transmission. Unfortunately, these RA messages can be forged or spoofed.

The **Internet Engineering Taskforce (IETF)** in RFC 7113 explains that *The IPv6 Router Advertisement Guard (RA-Guard) mechanism is commonly used to mitigate attack vectors, based on forged ICMPv6 Router Advertisement messages. Many existing IPv6 deployments rely on RA-Guard as the first line of defense against the aforementioned attack vectors* (**https:// datatracker.ietf.org/doc/rfc7113/**).

An administrator can configure an IPv6 RA guard to safeguard against rogue RA messages produced by illicit or misconfigured routers connecting to the network segment. RA messages are compared with an RA policy. If the messages comply with the policy, they are forwarded by the router. If the messages are deemed invalid and do not match policy, the packets are dropped.

ARP inspection

ARP spoofing can be used by attackers to perform **denial of service (DoS)** attacks by redirecting communications to bogus or non-existent MAC addresses. Attackers can also capture the traffic in legitimate conversations between two hosts in on-path attacks, intercepting the communication flow.

Many of these MitM attacks are made possible by the attacker polluting the ARP cache of the two victims so that their cache maps each other's IP addresses to the MAC address of the attacker's device. **Dynamic ARP Inspection (DAI)** is a feature that, when set up, uses the DHCP snooping database of IP-to-MAC address mappings to verify the MAC address mappings of each frame going through the switch. In this way, any frames with incorrect or altered mappings are dropped by the switch, thus breaking any attacks depending on these false mappings. Since it uses the DHCP snooping database, the configuration of DHCP snooping is a prerequisite to enabling DAI.

Dynamic ARP Inspection best practice

Packets arriving on trusted interfaces can be configured to bypass all DAI validation checks. Packets arriving on untrusted interfaces must undergo the DAI validation process.

This means that *untrusted* connections to workstations, printers, servers, or other end devices will be rigorously put through some validation checks. Valid bindings stored in the DHCP snooping binding database will be forwarded. Suspect IP-to-MAC address bindings will be dropped by the switch. *Trusted* connections are typical switch ports connected to other switches, configured as trusted.

Figure 18.3 demonstrates how the DHCP binding table operates to verify mappings:

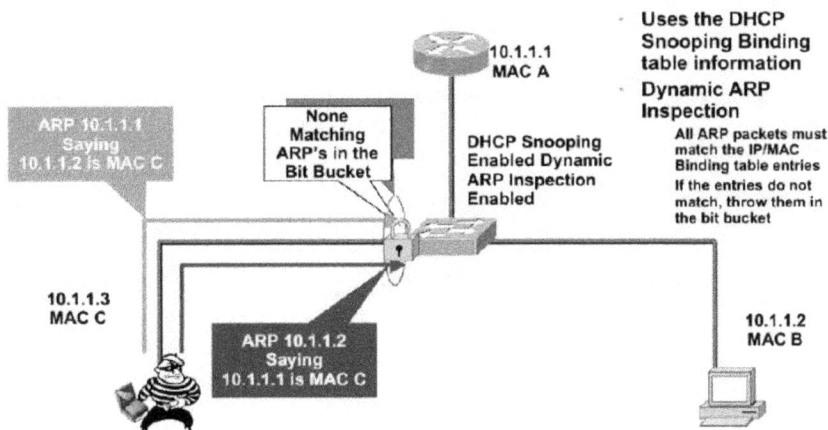

Figure 18.3: *DHCP binding table*

Dynamic ARP inspection uses the DHCP snooping table.

DHCP snooping

DHCP snooping is a layer 2 security technology generally used on **access layer switches** in a network. Note that in *Figure 18.4*, the access layer switches provide connectivity to end devices or hosts:

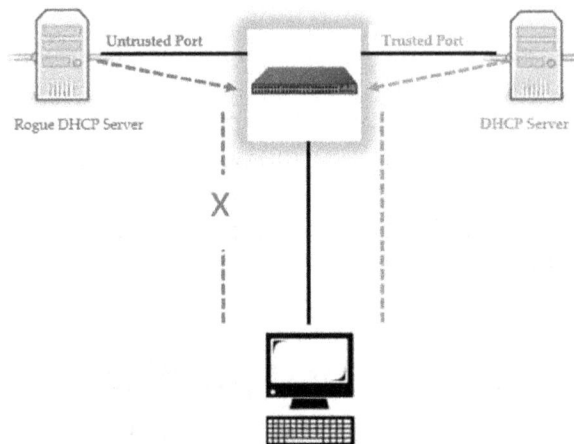

Figure 18.4: DHCP snooping

DHCP snooping prevents your devices from communicating with illegitimate or rogue DHCP servers. With this feature and switch configuration enabled, the switch keeps a DHCP snooping binding table that matches MAC addresses with DHCP messages. It is up to the network administrator to define the trusted switch ports (that is, the ports connected to legitimate DHCP servers). This mitigates against the creation of rogue DHCP servers being used on the network because these rogue servers will not be able to respond to DHCP requests.

Untrusted DHCP messages are regarded as those received from outside the network or firewall. These messages are dropped/discarded by the switch. Messages are also dropped if the source MAC address in the message and the DHCP client MAC address do not match in the DHCP snooping binding table. As noted, this binding table is also used for Dynamic ARP Inspection.

VLAN security considerations

Network administrators need to be aware of security considerations when implementing VLANs in the organization. Though security features and commands are integrated into most VLAN technologies and protocols, it is beneficial for the administrator to be able to identify security features, when met.

At the physical layer, just as with other hardware in the building, switches, routers, and other intermediary devices need to be located in a secure area. Administrators should:

- Strictly control physical access to switches.

- Use VLANs to isolate network traffic.

- Change the default VLAN from VLAN 1 for each role the default has.

- Remove console-port cables and password-protect the console (line con 0) and virtual terminal (VTY) lines.

- Use timeouts and policies for restricted access.

- Create an ACL restricting telnet/SHH access from specific networks and hosts.

- Disable high-risk protocols on any port that does not require them (for example, CDP, DTP, PAgP, LACP, and UDLD).

- Deploy VTP domain and VTP pruning.

- Manage inter-VLAN routing through IP access control lists.

The main focus of the administrator is to pay attention to layers 1 and 2 of the OSI model regarding network hardening techniques. A network is only as strong as its weakest link.

Note: VLAN 1 is the default Data VLAN because all interfaces are initially assigned to this VLAN. It is also the default Native VLAN and Management VLAN. (The management VLAN is used for SSH/Telnet VTY traffic and should not be carried with end-user traffic. This serves as the VLAN that is the SVI for the layer 2 switch.)

Figure 18.5 illustrates how VLANs isolate network traffic, thus hardening the network:

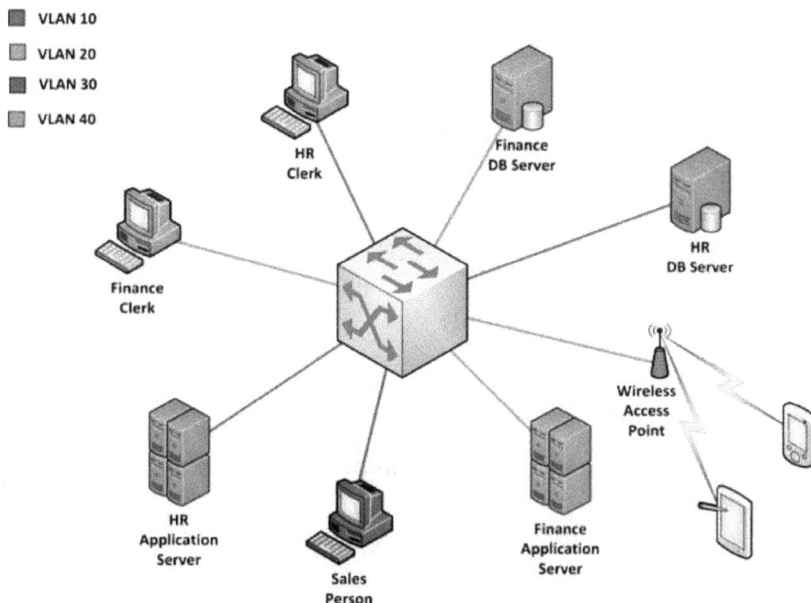

Figure 18.5: VLAN segmentation

Secure SNMP

Simple Network Management Protocol (**SNMP**) is an industry standard used for network management. Unfortunately, hundreds of tools exist to attempt to exploit this protocol. SNMP is present on any decent network equipment. *Figure 18.6* demonstrates how hosts are monitored and managed using SNMP. The key to understanding the process is detailed in the figure:

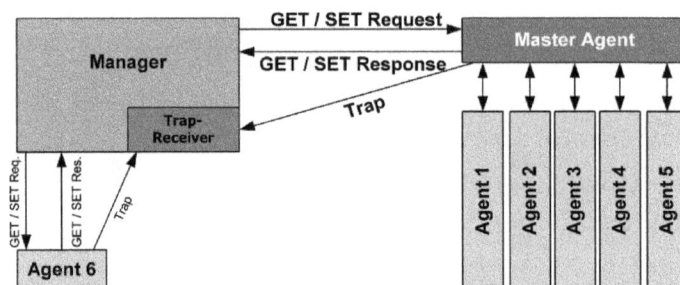

Figure 18.6: The SNMP process
Source: @snmpcenter.com

The terminology used in the illustration (**Key**) is as follows:

Manager (the monitoring client)

Agent (running on the equipment/server)

Basic commands

GET   (manager -> agent)

The query for a value

GET-NEXT   (manager -> agent)

Get the next value (list of values for a table)

GET-RESPONSE   (agent -> manager)

Response to GET/SET, or error

SET   (manager -> agent)

Set a value, or perform an action

TRAP   (agent -> manager)

Spontaneous notification from equipment (line down, temperature above the threshold, and so on).

Note: These are only the basic commands to show how the SNMP Manager (that is, monitoring client) can yield beneficial results from equipment being monitored. Numerous network hardware manufacturers include SNMP with devices to make it simpler for an organization to monitor their network infrastructure. However, as stated, it is not foolproof and has its limitations as a protocol.

There are several versions of SNMP, including the following:

- **SNMPv1**: The Simple Network Management Protocol, a Full Internet Standard, defined in RFC 1157 as the original version of SNMP. SNMPv1, though easy to set up, is only protected by a community string. This community string means a **plain text community string** is sent from devices within a set range of allowed IP addresses.

    o **Security vulnerabilities**: Threat actors can discover this community string, advance to IP Spoofing, and then interact further with the network. Lack of privacy, access control, and authentication.

    o **Countermeasures**: One way to mitigate against this risk is to provide read-only access to SNMP devices. Permit write access only if absolutely necessary.

- **SNMPv2c**: Defined in RFCs 1901 to 1908; uses community-string-based Administrative Framework.

    o **Security vulnerabilities:** This version of SNMP still transmits community strings as clear text with no options for encryption, leaving it susceptible to the same security concerns as SNMPv1. Lack of privacy, access control, and authentication.

    o **Countermeasures**: This provides read-only access to SNMP devices. Permit write access only if absolutely necessary. Additionally, as part of the steps to configure SNMP on a device, an administrator could restrict SNMP access to NMS hosts (SNMP managers) that are permitted by an ACL or define the ACL and then reference it with the `snmp-server community string access-list-number-or-name` command.

- **SNMPv3**: Interoperable standards-based protocol originally defined in RFCs 2273 to 2275; provides secure access to devices by authenticating and encrypting packets over the network. SNMPv3 includes these security features: message integrity to ensure that a packet was not tampered with or modified in transit, authentication to verify that the message is from a valid source, and encryption to counteract the contents of a message from being read by an illicit source.

    o **Security vulnerabilities**: The *discovery mechanism* of SNMPv3 can be targeted to permit an attacker to pick the encryption and authentication keys used by the protocol. In other words, attackers can gain control of the authentication keys and manipulate them. This allows data gathering for IP spoofing, for example, or reconnaissance to occur.

o **Countermeasures (for all versions)**: IPsec, **Transport Security Model (TSM)**, Nmap, pen testing, firmware updates, choose strong community strings, disable SNMP if it is not being used on devices, block ports 161 and 162 in the firewall or monitors the ports carefully if required for SNMP traffic. Set up an ACL for all endpoints and devices with read and/or write SNMP permissions.

Note: All versions of SNMP are prone to vulnerabilities, even version 3, which is the most secure version of the protocol to date. Mitre's website outlines these CVEs, and these vulnerabilities can be viewed at https://cve.mitre.org/cgi-bin/cvekey. cgi?keyword=snmp.

As noted, SNMP is integrated into the operating systems of many network devices, for example, Cisco switches, routers, and **Wireless LAN Controllers (WLC)**. Servers and Windows servers are among the devices with integrated SNMP functionality. *Figure 18.7* shows the setup step in enabling and installing SNMP services on a Windows Server 2019 machine. Observe that the community's name default is set to public.

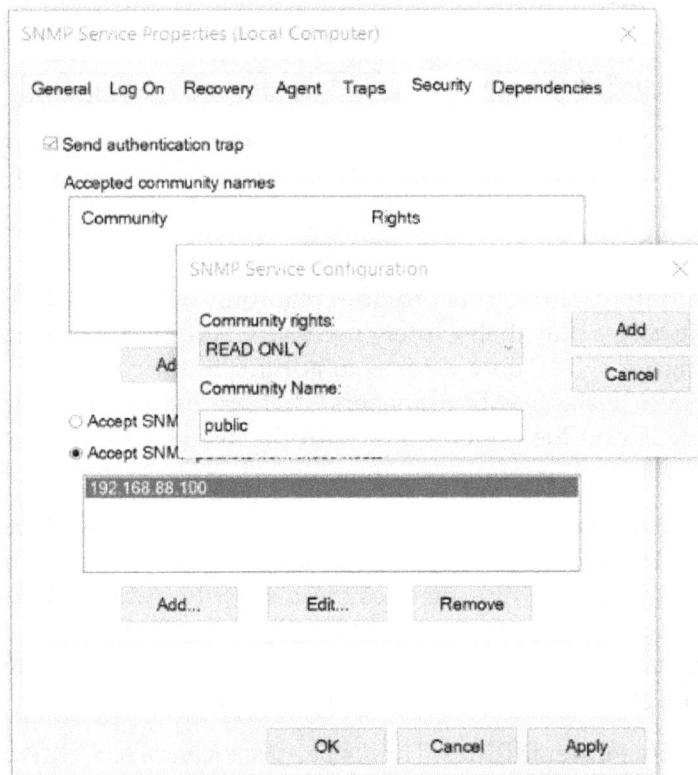

Figure 18.7: SNMP setup, community name

Under **Trap destinations**, we can add a destination server collecting traps, that is, a **Network Monitoring Solution** (**NMS**), as shown in *Figure 18.8*:

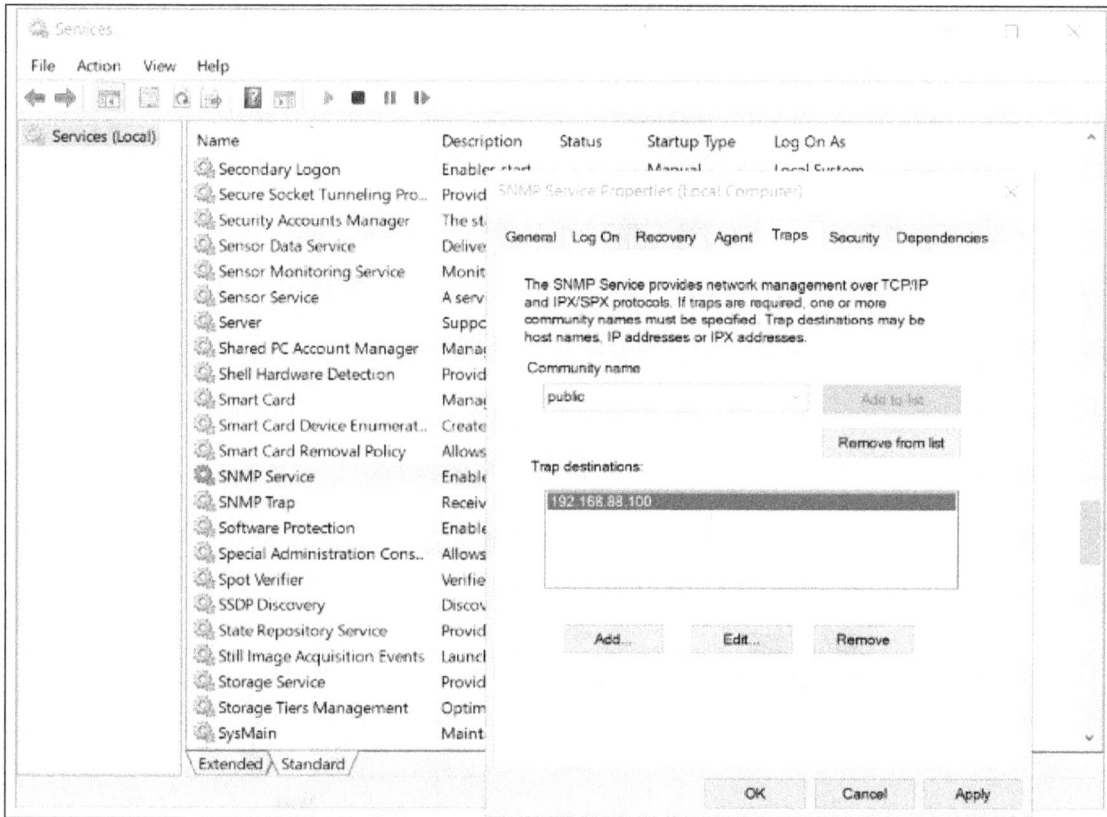

Figure 18.8: SNMP setup, trap destination

In *Figure 18.9*, we see the security best practices implemented across a network, where monitoring and managing networks is regarded as an element of network design:

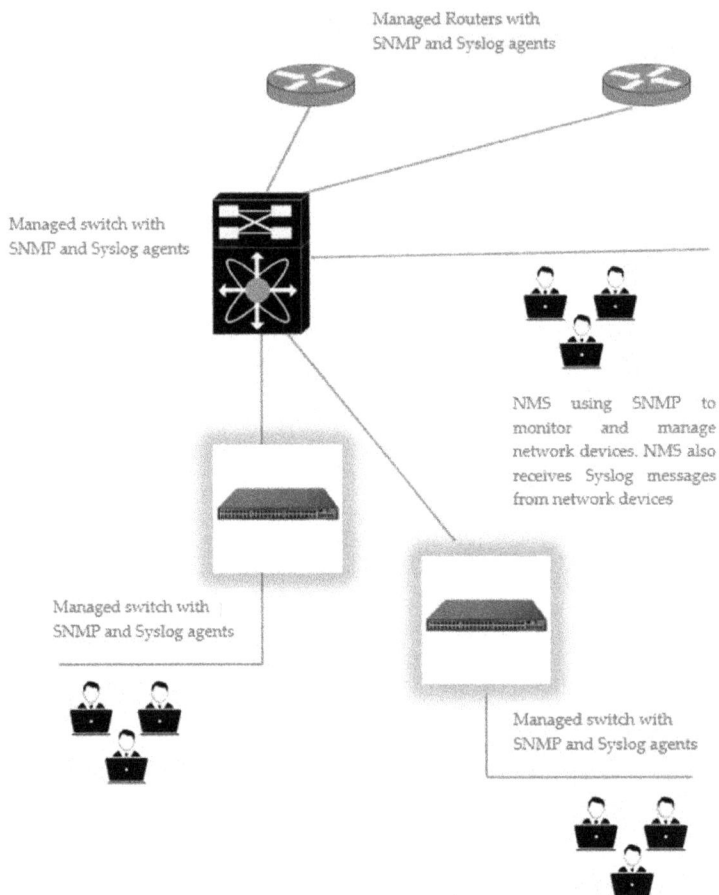

Figure 18.9: Configuring SNMP, security best practices

Note: An NMS is a network management system. Examples are NetFlow, Solar Winds, WhatsUp Gold, and Nagios. AN NMS helps a network administrator keep track of the network's bandwidth, availability, (HA stats) performance, and functionality of hardware.

Wireless security

When we consider that a WLAN is open to anyone within the range of an access point and accessible to anyone holding the appropriate credentials to associate with it, we understand how securing wireless technologies and networks is essential.

Attacks on WLANs can be created by outsiders, discontented employees, *insiders*, and even inadvertently generated by IT-unaware employees. Wireless networks are vulnerable to several threats. Authentication processes can be manipulated and cracked into. Protocols can be snooped on, or packets sniffed. Data and frames can be intercepted or redirected.

Access points are configured with a unique character identifier, which is known as a **service set identifier** (**SSID**), to ensure that each wireless client is communicating with the appropriate wireless network. Each SSID can be set to a maximum of 32 characters. Once a connection to an access point has been established, each packet sent over the network must include the SSID. This guarantees that the data being transmitted over the air arrives at the correct location.

Although an SSID is essential for a secure network, it by no means creates a secure network.

Irrespective of whether you use a default SSID or a unique, personalized SSID, hackers can still get through your Wi-Fi network using brute-force attacks. They achieve this by using password spraying (trying millions of combinations within seconds) to predict your Wi-Fi password. Hackers know the right tools to carry out these attacks, such as Wireshark, Auvik, Windump, or TCPdump. Remember, SSID packets are sent in *plain text*. Some administrators opt to hide the SSID and disable SSID broadcasting on their network APs. However, even this technique alone is not foolproof. It might deter an attacker from further exploring and exploiting the network if they see visible targets. Again, with the right tools, an attacker can easily see and view the stats on hidden networks when they really want to. In wardriving, for example, where an attacker uses a laptop or smartphone to drive around and search for wireless networks to attempt to break into, a hidden network might be a deterrent to carry out further attacks, but it is not a total security solution.

Securing wireless networks involves **layering** in the same way as securing wired networks does. SSIDs are only one example of a wireless technology, standard, or protocol that can be discovered and then attacked. InSSIDer Plus and Wi-Fi Explorer in the wrong hands are equally optimum in the early stages of discovery and reconnaissance.

Wireless encryption protocols

To fortify your Wi-Fi network, it is advised to use strong encryption methods. An *open* network has no security at all. All routers come with default encryption standards to include WEP. WPA, WPA2, and, since 2018, WPA3.

In *Table 18.1*, the details and security features are summarized to capture the evolution of security mechanisms used in wireless networking:

Encryption standard	Details	Security level	Best practice re use
Wired equivalent privacy (WEP) 1997 WEP was the first standard used to protect the data between clients and access points and prevent attacks from hackers.	To comply with US maximum levels, WEP was using 64-bit encryption. After the restrictions were lifted, 128-bit and 256-bit WEP were developed. **Weaknesses**: WEP has a 24-bit **initialization vector (IV)** and weak security. If the RC4 cipher stream for a given IV is found, an attacker can decrypt the following packets that were encrypted with the same IV. Packets can also be forged. This means that an attacker does not need to know the WEP key to decrypt packets if they know what key stream was used to encrypt that packet.	Very low The IV is identified as too small. The **Integrity Check Value (ICV)** or *key checking* algorithm is not appropriate. WEP's use of the RC4 cipher stream is weak. Authentication Messages can be easily counterfeited. *The number one rule of the RC4 application is to never, *ever* reuse a key.	No
Wi-Fi Protected Access (WPA) 2003 Due to WEP's weaknesses, a new protocol was developed. WPA implemented 256-bit WPA-PSK (Pre-Shared Key). Wi-Fi Alliance released WPA as a temporary standard in 2003, while IEEE worked to develop a more advanced and secure long-term replacement for the WEP standard.	**Temporal Key Integrity Protocol (TKIP)** with RC4 Message Integrity Check Longer IVs and 256-bit keys. A pre-shared encryption key helps to ensure that only authorized users connect to the network. Two modes: Enterprise Mode (WPA-EAP) Personal Mode (WPA-PSK) *WPA Enterprise mode (EAP) requires an **Authentication Server.**	Low Stronger authentication strategies with 802.1x and EAP *As with all types of wireless security encryption, the advice is to use complex passwords.	No

Encryption standard	Details	Security level	Best practice re use
Wi-Fi Protected Access 2 (WPA2) 2004 This is the successor to the WPA. WPA2 encryption standard. It was ratified by IEEE in 2004 as 802.11i. Similar to its predecessor, WPA2 also offers enterprise and personal modes.	**Advanced Encryption Standard (AES)**, an encryption mechanism; and Counter Mode with Cipher Block Chaining Message Authentication Code Protocol (CCMP), an authentication mechanism. 128 bits using either 128-, 192- or 256-bit encryption keys. Weakness: The security weakness is in the four-way handshake. An encrypted WPA2 connection starts with a four-way handshake. The third part of the handshake and process can be repeated multiple times, and this creates a pattern that an attacker can exploit. A typical tool used to carry out these attacks is the Aircrack-ng set of tools.	High Key Reinstallation Attack. (KRACK) All routers employing WPA and WPA2 are susceptible to this dictionary brute-force attack. *If feasible, the best defense is to keep routers up to date and for users to only connect to wireless networks using a purchased well-managed, up-to-date **virtual private network (VPN)**.	Yes, If WPA3 is not available.
Wi-Fi Protected Access 3 (WPA3) 2018 Wi-Fi Alliance commenced certification for WPA3. This, to date, is the most recent wireless security standard. It is considered to be the most secure.	**Simultaneous Authentication of Equals (SAE)** SAE replaces the four-way handshake and eliminates the need for the reuse of the encryption keys. Messages are sent as a discrete, one-off transaction initiated by the client or the AP (that is, passive or active). Enterprise mode has optional 192-bit encryption and a 48-bit IV.	Very high Attacks as discussed include *downgrade attacks*, in which an attacker forces a device to return to WPA2 and then carries out a dictionary attack. *Offline-dictionary attacks*— implementing two-sided channels. *The advice given to offset these potentialities is to ensure all software is updated and patched.	Yes

Table 18.1: Wireless encryption protocols

As of July 2020, Wi-Fi Alliance required all devices seeking Wi-Fi certification to support WPA3.

Plan, Plan, Plan

There are many proficient, user-friendly wireless site survey tools available on the market. These tools assist with tasks and actions, such as floor plans and blueprints, signal strength predictions, plus the ongoing analysis and reporting of signal strength. They visualize and assess AP placement noise and interference, channel allocation, data rates, cables required, lengths, cost specifications, and a calculation of the materials needed. The tools typically include WLAN management options, scope the scalability of the wireless network, and display performance indicators.

These tasks can be time-consuming and very intricate, especially in the initial site survey and decision-making stages. Decisions like the positioning of access points and their coverage areas demand clear focus and attention to detail. With some tools using GPS, outdoor surveys can be conducted. Tools commonly have a reporting feature so that documentation and visuals can be printed and saved for accounting purposes.

There are typically three site survey methods given as follows:

- **Passive site surveys**: They are implemented before the access points are installed with the software in listening mode. Passive surveys allow the installer to assess the wireless network prior to permanent access points being mounted and fitted. It also allows them to generate a heat map, measuring the signal's strengths in color-coded visualization modeling techniques. Passive surveys can equally detect rogue access points after APs are in place.

- **Active site surveys**: These mechanisms again measure signal strengths and identify weak spots, barriers, or obstructions. The surveys are carried out after the installation of the access points is finalized. This survey will enable an administrator to fine-tune the network, realign any configurations, or adjust the channel selection if overlaps or inconsistencies have been discovered.

- **Predictive surveys**: These may be carried out remotely or on-site. Similar to how an architect works with frameworks and blueprints, a designer/installer can use existing maps of the building and mark out the locations where access points should be installed. Predictive surveys might be *seemingly* more cost-effective, but in the long term, they may not be as accurate or as strong as the other two types.

When an organization needs to deploy and maintain Wireless LANs, it is beneficial to simultaneously consider the security impacts of AP placement and other security issues. Security is as important as network performance and coverage.

Wireless access point security measures

Some wireless access point security measures are as follows:

- Change the default login credentials. Do this straight out of the box as best practice.

- Change the default SSID and, *if required,* disable SSID broadcast. Note that this configuration has been known to cause some connectivity issues with devices, so be aware. As discussed, it is not a foolproof safeguard against attackers.

- Use WPA3 wherever possible. Otherwise, apply WPA2—AES or WPA2-EAP.

- Enable MAC address filtering. This technique may be unviable due to the time spent on configuration and management. It is suitable for smaller WLANs.

- Grant wireless access to guests using a separate wireless channel with a separate passphrase/password.

- Update the firmware. Test new updates before deployment in case there are bugs and glitches.

- Enable the Wireless Access Point built-in firewall.

- Keep virus definitions up to date.

- Be aware of file-sharing practices. Use a dedicated directory with restricted access and password protection. Avoid sharing in the public realm or on public networks.

- Manipulate the Wi-Fi signal strength to ensure it stays within the building. Test this.

- Where possible, connect using a VPN.

Best practices of WLAN attack countermeasures

Let us now discuss some best practices when it comes to WLAN attack countermeasures.

As previously discussed, enhancing wireless network security can be achieved by implementing robust measures such as enabling WPA3 encryption, using strong and unique passwords, and regularly updating firmware. Furthermore, deploying **wireless intrusion prevention systems** (**WIPS**) can effectively detect and mitigate unauthorized access points and other malicious activities.

Wireless intrusion detection/prevention systems

A **wireless intrusion detection system** (**WIDS**) or WIPS system monitors the radio spectrum used by wireless LANs and instantly alerts a network administrator, notifying them that there is a rogue access point detected on the network. This detection is achieved by comparing the MAC address of the participating wireless devices. A WIPS or WIDS can be implemented via hardware or software. A WIDS will detect and check devices using detection mechanisms such as fingerprinting. However, a WIPS is more proactive as it has both the ability to detect and prevent against the threat automatically. It achieves this by detecting and classifying a threat. WIPS systems comprise three elements: sensors for detection, a server holding the software, and a console with a **user interface** (**UI**) for administration and management. The sensors should be positioned in all areas that present potential security targets.

Figure 18.10 demonstrates how an intrusion detection system can handle the monitoring of a WLAN when it is interconnected to the wired LAN:

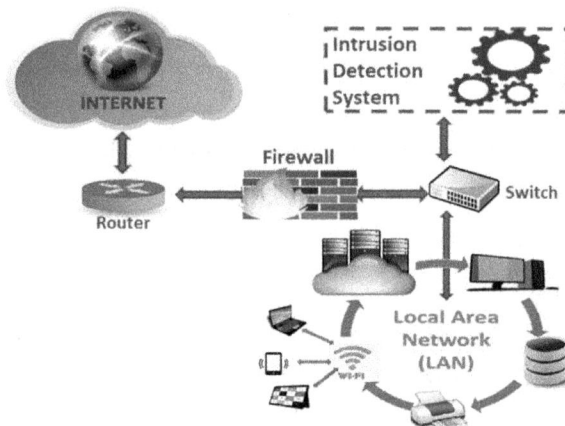

Figure 18.10: Intrusion detection system

It is interesting to note that currently, the Python programming language is one of the most popular development environments for implementing learning-based systems and is used in **anomaly detection** in IDSs. This shows us how scripting, programming, and AI all contribute to security systems and security provisions.

Penetration testing

A wireless penetration test tries to break into the wireless network. If the network has been sufficiently protected, the penetration test will only trigger alarms. The benefits of a pen-test lie in its potential to discover security loopholes that may have gone unnoticed. The pen-test differs from vulnerability testing because it attempts to exploit vulnerabilities rather than merely identify them. As explained by *Techopedia*, *Pen-testing may be conducted to complement background investigations and ensure social engineering and networking safety.* This security assessment is applicable to both wired and wireless networks, including the presence of **Internet of Things** (**IoT**) devices.

Pen-testing is an instrumental process in network hardening techniques. Benefits include the following:

- Minimalizing and reduction of security breaches.
- Identification of CVEs or high-risk weaknesses in network setup, connectivity, or configuration.
- The opportunity for a more reliable network.
- Compliance with governmental or regional legislation.
- Proof of data integrity and HA to market to customers.

Basically, penetration testing is a controlled form of hacking, sometimes referred to as ethical hacking. The reports produced from the penetration testing of the network enable the organization to address and rectify the security flaws discovered.

Vulnerability scanning

Vulnerability scanning is a security technique used to recognize security weaknesses in a wireless network. The overall goal is to identify weaknesses that can be used to compromise the network. Vulnerability testing can and should be run continuously. Weaknesses include poor access control, weak authentication processes, misconfigured software or hardware, poorly patched or unpatched systems, password issues and weaknesses, arbitrary coding, and a lack of overall management and accountability. A vulnerability scanner can probe for a diversity of security weaknesses, so the best practice is to be aware of effective and reliable scanners on the market.

Internet of Things security considerations

In *Chapter 9, Managing Network Devices,* we discussed IoT. We learned that the IoT describes the network of physical objects, that is, things, that use embedded software, technologies, and sensors with the intention of connecting and exchanging data with other devices and systems over the internet. These devices range from ordinary household objects to complex and more sophisticated industrial tools. Examples of IoT devices presented were:

- Smart refrigerators
- Smart speakers
- Smart thermostats
- Smart doorbells
- Smart actuators, gadgets, or machines

The proliferation and demand for these devices have led to a lack of **intentional focus** on security issues and vulnerabilities by some manufacturers. It is analogous to the introduction of WEP and early wireless security encryption protocols when device production possibly exceeded the ability to plan, research, and future-proof access issues and protocols. IoT devices and embedded systems have come into the networking space with a boom. Sometimes, when that happens in marketing and production, security issues concerning data access, IoT data management, and IoT device security may be neglected, poorly prioritized, or simply ill-thought-out.

IoT weaknesses

The following are some examples of IoT security weaknesses:

- Unsecured devices connecting to the internet can be easily accessed.

- Embedded device software and web interfaces are susceptible to buffer overflow and SQL injection attacks.

- PII is sent through or may be stored on these devices.

- Hardcoded or default passwords in use.

- Some IoT network sensors do not support encryption, so data is transmitted and received in plain text.

- Open ports, such as listening and gathering data *continuously*, are the prime functions of a *sensor*.

- In many cases, little or no IoT device updates are released for products as new products are released, and the focus is on the speed of production as opposed to the quality of security of the product over time.

Best security practices of IoT

The **Open Web Application Security Project (OWASP)** is a community-led open-source initiative with members and subscribers worldwide. OWASP identified weaknesses in IoT devices and produced the top 10 IoT challenges and threats.

The OWASP Internet of Things Project commenced in 2014 as a way to help developers, manufacturers, enterprises, and consumers make better decisions regarding the manufacturing, production, and use of IoT systems.

The idea is to keep moving this project forward by ensuring that everything on the list reflects a current threat. The aim is also to get feedback from the community, including input from manufacturers, developers, pen-testers, or part of a security team implementing network hardening techniques. The OWASP forum is inclusive of all stakeholders in IoT, and all contributions are welcome.

Going into 2019, CrowdStrike Intelligence anticipated that **Big Game Hunting (BGH)**—targeted, criminally motivated, enterprise-wide ransomware attacks—was expected to continue at least at the 2018 pace. However, what was observed was not just a continuation but an escalation. Ransom demands grew larger. Tactics became more cutthroat. Established criminal organizations like WIZARD SPIDER expanded operations, and affiliates of the

Ransomware-as-a-Service (RaaS) malware developers adopted BGH attacks. In short, the greedy got greedier, and the rich got richer.

– CROWDSTRIKE — 2020 Global Threat Report

In *Figure 18.11*, typical IoT threats are captured on an infographic:

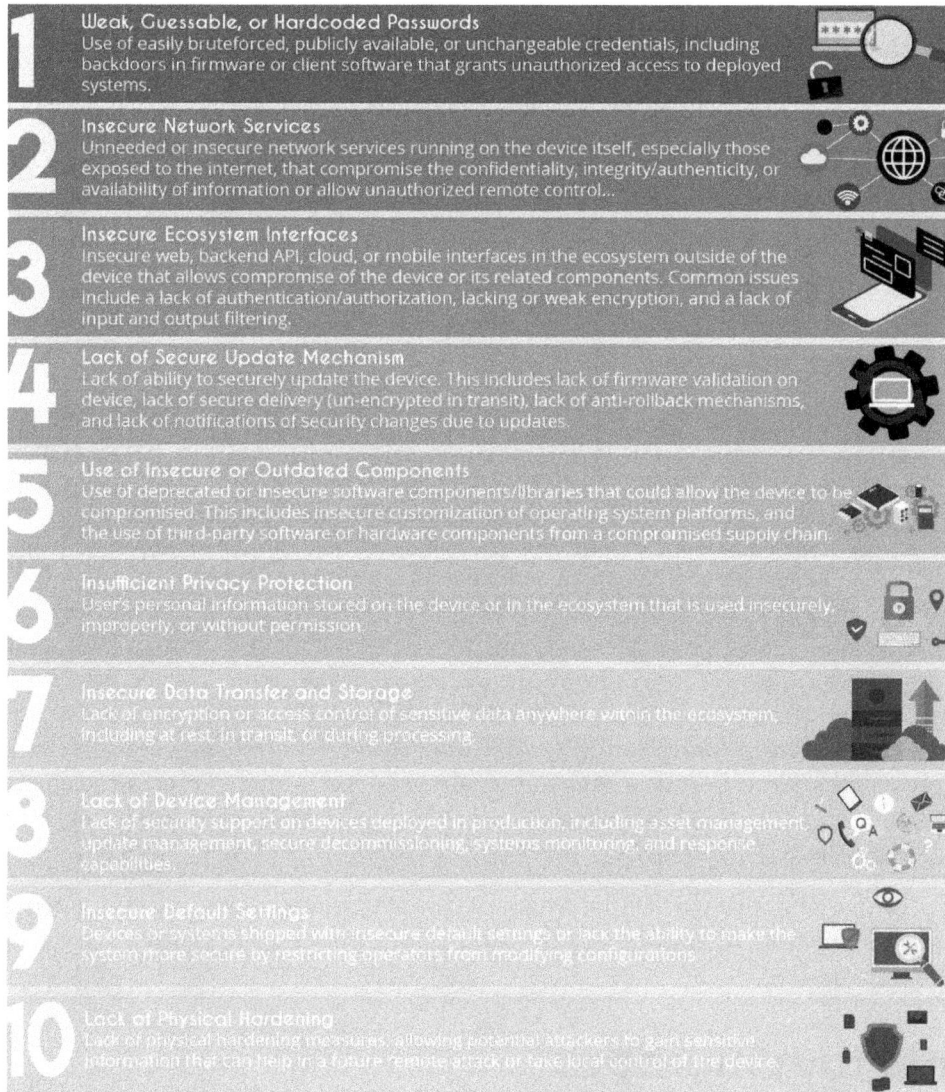

1 Weak, Guessable, or Hardcoded Passwords
Use of easily bruteforced, publicly available, or unchangeable credentials, including backdoors in firmware or client software that grants unauthorized access to deployed systems.

2 Insecure Network Services
Unneeded or insecure network services running on the device itself, especially those exposed to the internet, that compromise the confidentiality, integrity/authenticity, or availability of information or allow unauthorized remote control...

3 Insecure Ecosystem Interfaces
Insecure web, backend API, cloud, or mobile interfaces in the ecosystem outside of the device that allows compromise of the device or its related components. Common issues include a lack of authentication/authorization, lacking or weak encryption, and a lack of input and output filtering.

4 Lack of Secure Update Mechanism
Lack of ability to securely update the device. This includes lack of firmware validation on device, lack of secure delivery (un-encrypted in transit), lack of anti-rollback mechanisms, and lack of notifications of security changes due to updates.

5 Use of Insecure or Outdated Components
Use of deprecated or insecure software components/libraries that could allow the device to be compromised. This includes insecure customization of operating system platforms, and the use of third-party software or hardware components from a compromised supply chain.

6 Insufficient Privacy Protection
User's personal information stored on the device or in the ecosystem that is used insecurely, improperly, or without permission.

7 Insecure Data Transfer and Storage
Lack of encryption or access control of sensitive data anywhere within the ecosystem, including at rest, in transit, or during processing.

8 Lack of Device Management
Lack of security support on devices deployed in production, including asset management, update management, secure decommissioning, systems monitoring, and response capabilities.

9 Insecure Default Settings
Devices or systems shipped with insecure default settings or lack the ability to make the system more secure by restricting operators from modifying configurations.

10 Lack of Physical Hardening
Lack of physical hardening measures, allowing potential attackers to gain sensitive information that can help in a future remote attack or take local control of the device.

Figure 18.11: Top 10 IoT threats

These threats are now being handled by stronger password use, more focus on updates, and more robust integration of security features. As a governing standards body, the US **National Institute of Standards and Technology (NIST)** has released NISTIR 8259A, establishing a cybersecurity feature baseline for scalable IoT devices. In Europe and the UK, the European **Telecommunications Standards Institute** (**ETSI**) has sought to legislate similar prescriptive security features for Consumer IoT. Security features covered are secure boot requirements and secure firmware updates for IoT-embedded devices. Network hardening techniques for IoT and embedded devices are being driven more seriously because it is now a critical element of global networking. In *Figure 18.12*, we can see how IoT devices and embedded systems are prevalent in everyday life:

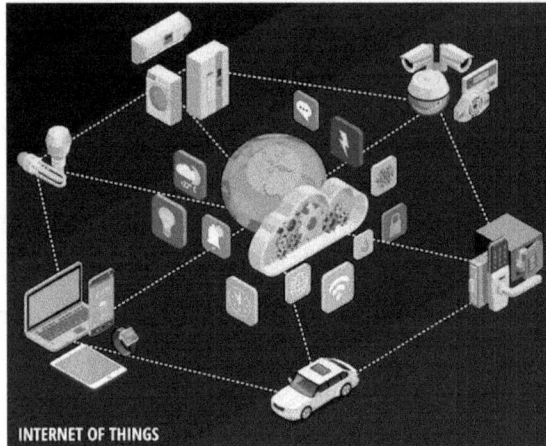

Figure 18.12: The prevalence of IoT devices

Conclusion

This chapter explored network hardening techniques. We explored security issues and hardening techniques across the OSI model, from the host level upwards, including management and network monitoring. We discussed techniques used on wired and wireless networks, including devices exclusively used for security layering strategies such as an IDS, IPS, firewall, or NMS device. As *Silicon Labs* suggests, *security should evolve at the same pace as threats and regulations*.

In the upcoming chapter, we will learn about remote management, such as **Secure Shell** (**SSH**) and VPNs. We will learn about the security implications of remote access and how to handle these issues.

Points to remember

- In order to effectively mitigate against cybersecurity attacks, a network administrator should know:
  - The techniques for hardening a network.
  - How to apply security measures to end devices.
  - How to Implement security measures on network hardware.

o How to implement security measures on network software.

- The content of *Chapter 18* is mapped to *Domain 4, Network Security*. Given a scenario, apply network security features, defense techniques, and solutions.

Key terms

- **Control Plane Policing (CoPP)**: This feature polices traffic going through a router. The control plane is the portion of a network that controls how data is forwarded on the network. In contrast, the data plane is the actual forwarding process.

- **Role-based access**: This access is in operation when a person's role in the organization is mapped to their access rights, permissions, and privileges.

- **Geofencing**: This occurs when a virtual boundary is drawn around a distinct geographical area using GPS. It may be used in security, development, and marketing strategies.

- **Captive portal**: A captive portal is a Web page/interface that is initially reached by users logging on to a network. It provides restricted access initially, and this access must be granted before considering access to the broader network. It is often referred to as a landing or log-in page.

- **Fingerprinting**: In a WIPS system, the concept of fingerprinting is to compare the unique signatures displayed by the signals produced by each wireless device against the known signatures of legitimate and pre-authorized wireless devices.

Questions

1. Explain what is meant by network hardening.
2. Give some examples of hardening techniques in wired and wireless networking.

Join our book's Discord space

Join the book's Discord Workspace for Latest updates, Offers, Tech happenings around the world, New Release and Sessions with the Authors:

https://discord.bpbonline.com

CHAPTER 19

Remote Management

Introduction

With the introduction of the *Hybrid Work Model*, we are seeing substantial changes in the way we work, communicate, and socialize with each other in the work environment. The traditional view of work occurring in a specific place and fixed environment has radically changed with the coming of a hybrid workforce. Regarding technology, IT systems need to be in place to permit mobile workers to access and use corporate network resources. Consequently, client-server (or clientless) models need to incorporate reliable and secure strategies for remote access and connectivity to external locations for users and administrators alike.

So, what does this change mean for IT support? Network administrators and IT professionals are expected to understand the various methods for remote access to the company's network and how access to the network's resources and services is being implemented, tracked, and monitored. The technical support staff will need to be able to configure, troubleshoot, install, or upgrade software irrespective of the client's geographical location. Therefore, awareness of topologies and the organization's infrastructure will need to be fine-tuned.

In general, with this change in traditional work concepts and remote work, organizations are focusing on building long-term, sustainable strategies instead of hasty *band-aid* fixes that do not provide long-term success. Now that IT support and network administrators support networks and digital workspaces with unfixed and mobile boundaries, in workspaces that include connectivity to or through the cloud; having the appropriate **remote management tools** is critical to realize this success.

Structure

This chapter explains the following topics:

- Virtual private network
- Remote desktop connection
- Remote Desktop Gateway
- Virtual network computing
- Authentication and authorization considerations
- In-band vs. out-of-band management

Objectives

By the end of this chapter, we will learn how to compare and contrast the procedures in use to access a host, server, or network device remotely . We will also discuss the security impacts associated with these remote access procedures. You will be able to understand remote access strategies and differentiate between them. You will also be able to appreciate and explain how each remote access strategy and procedure impacts the security of a network.

Virtual private network

A **virtual private network (VPN)** is a type of private network connection that implements encryption to allow IP traffic to travel securely over a TCP/IP public network, such as the Internet. A VPN is principally used to support secure (that is, encrypted) communications over an untrusted network. VPNs use both encryption and tunneling protocols to optimize security strategies. **Tunneling** protocols typically encrypt packet contents and then wrap these encrypted packets in an unencrypted packet—thus the term *tunneling*. As we know, a router will consult the packet's **header** to make decisions about routing to the packet's destination address and then look at its routing table to discover the appropriate exit interface. Routers will consult the data in the *unencrypted* packet headers to make forwarding decisions. All other routers involved in the data transmission do not see or cannot read the encrypted packet contents.

Figure 19.1 compares a packet type using **Encapsulating Security Payload (ESP)**. ESP is a method of authentication that authenticates, encrypts, and secures the payload (that is, data).

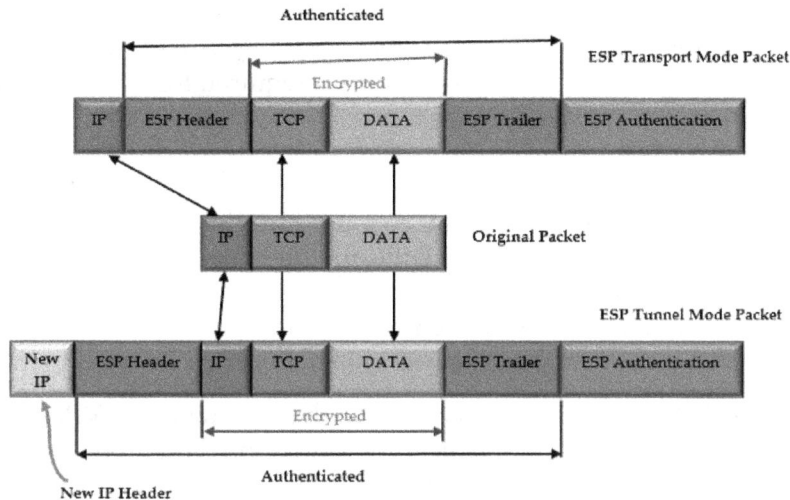

Figure 19.1: ESP Transport vs. Tunnel Mode

Essentially, there are two ESP transport modes: *Transport Mode* and *Tunnel Mode*. Tunnel Mode encrypts the packet, and places that packet into a new packet. This packet is then routed to agreed IP addresses between the **Tunnel Endpoints.** Transport mode also encrypts the packet, but the IPsec header is inserted behind the IP header. This strategy exposes the source address of the data. Consequently, tunnel mode keeps the source IP address secure and is a preferred strategy for data transmission.

Note: In TCP/IP networks, the IP tunnel establishes a virtual link between two endpoints on two different networks, enabling data to be exchanged as if the endpoints were directly connected to the same network. Tunnel endpoints are devices that can encrypt and decrypt IP packets. When you build a VPN, you create a security association between the two tunnel endpoints. These tunnel endpoints create a secure virtual communication channel. Moreover, the destination tunnel endpoint is the only device that can unwrap packets and decrypt the contents of the IP packet or PDU.

VPNs can be implemented in the following ways:

- **Host-to-host**: Hosts typically run IPsec as an encryption method, with hosts using the same authentication key. The two hosts will establish a secure channel and communicate with each other directly. For this to work, both devices must be capable of creating a VPN connection.

- **Remote access VPN**: This enables users who are working remotely to securely access and use applications and data stored on a corporate network/in a data center. In the case of a remote access VPN, a VPN concentrator is configured to receive VPN connections. Consequently, multiple remote networks and clients can connect to a central corporate network. Hosts that are allowed to connect using the VPN connection are granted access to resources on the VPN server or the private network. These concentrators are deployed at the edge of the corporate network. Companies tend to implement VPN concentrators when the number of connections increases or more bandwidth is required for VPN transmissions.

Site-to-site VPN

The purpose of a site-to-site VPN is to connect individual networks to each other. Organizations and businesses typically use this method to connect two or more networks to different geographical locations. A company may establish a VPN to interlink its headquarters with a branch office. Remember, a company's headquarters may be in a totally different state or country than the branch(es) that are connected to it.

With a site-to-site VPN, routers on the edge of each site establish a VPN with the router at the other location. This connection suits an organization with more than one branch or office spread over disparate or large geographical areas. The resources of the company, for example, applications or data, may be housed in the corporate headquarters. All sites connected to the main hub or corporate network can access these resources as if they were housed locally or within their local physical facility. For example, imagine you have a company based in London having several branch offices, one in Paris, one in Spain, and another in Sweden. Let us say, each location has between 30 or more employees. To optimize cost and efficiency, and to secure communications, the company's e-mail system may be housed on the central server. The company may also have a data server that holds important digital and printable marketing collateral and confidential company information. It may have an application server or a database server. Rather than replicating or duplicating these files and having them stored in several places, it is more beneficial to have them securely stored, where access is occurring via a secure connection and duplicates are minimized. File security can be implemented in addition to securing remote access as a security layering and hardening technique.

Figure 19.2 is an example of a site-to-site VPN. In the illustration, there are three branch offices connected to corporate headquarters via a VPN tunnel. Note that each distinct tunnel links a single branch to the corporate network, and there is a separate tunnel per connection.

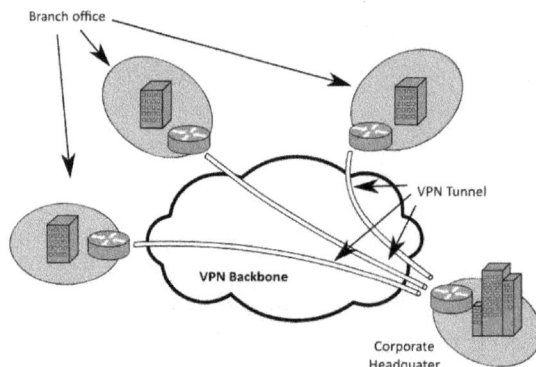

Figure 19.2: Site-to-site VPM

Client-to-site VPN

With a client-to-site VPN configuration, the corporate network is accessed via the cloud/ internet. This connectivity involves authentication with a server. The LAN or corporate network is behind the server. This means that remote access is flexible, but the configuration still maintains the security of the network and its resources. This feature is very useful since it creates a new VPN tunnel that would permit remote users or teleworkers to access the corporate network. This connection is achieved using client software and is implemented with the aim of maintaining connectivity and access while *not* compromising privacy and security. The VPN client running on the client machine connects to the VPN service running on the firewall or a VPN-enabled router.

With this VPN type, data is transmitted from the client machine to a point in the organization's network. The VPN endpoint encrypts the data and sends it through the internet. Another endpoint in the VPN network decrypts the data and sends it to the appropriate internet resource. The targeted resource may be a Web server, a data server, an e-mail server, or even the organization's *intranet*, should they have one.

In short, clients can access their on-premises private network from a client-to-site VPN server directly.

In *Figure 19.3*, we have shown a laptop with VPN client software installed. The client has access to the LAN's resources, such as the web server (**192.168.0.120**).

The security principles of **authentication, authorization, and accounting** (AAA) apply to VPNs. A VPN server administrator must choose at least one **authentication** method and configure it during the VPN server configuration and provisioning. The options for authentication tend to be a client certificate, some added security with a user ID and passcode, or both types of client authentication methods. Administrators will aim to ensure only legitimate users access the network (**authorization**) and that this access is duly monitored and tracked (**accounting**).

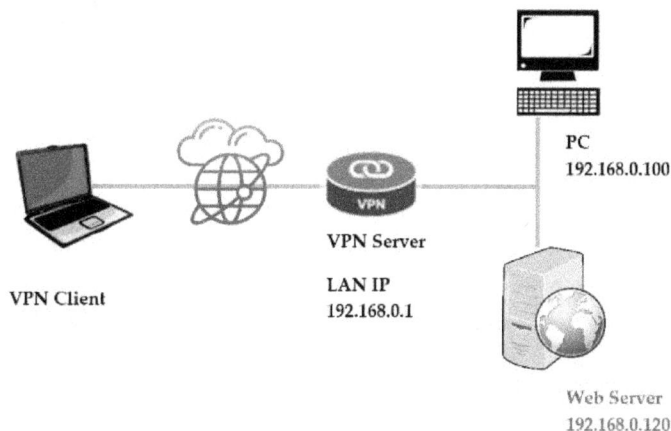

PC
192.168.0.100

VPN Server

LAN IP
192.168.0.1

VPN Client

Web Server
192.168.0.120

Figure 19.3: Client-to-site VPM

Clientless VPN

It is not always necessary to install VPN client software to access services such as file shares, hardware resources, or VPN endpoint devices. For example, when using **Secure Sockets Layer (SSL)** or **IPsecure (IPsec)**, a clientless VPN connection can be established through a Web browser. Using SSL VPN configuration, firewall policies can be implemented to provide restricted access to resources and services rather than allow access to entire systems or networks.

IPsec VPN permits connections between an authorized remote host and any system inside the enterprise boundary or perimeter. In contrast to this, SSL VPN can be configured to permit connections to **specific services** accessible to remote hosts so that *only* particular services are allowed to be reached. Consequently, IPsec is deemed to be preferable for site-to-site VPNs, and SSL is more appropriate for remote access. Since security considerations are different for IPsec VPNs and SSL/TLS VPNs, some enterprises opt to deploy both VPN types since each type has its own vulnerabilities and tailored security solutions to mitigate particular security threats. The best practice is to understand how VPN implementations work, how they should be tested, and the impacts on the network when one or both types of VPNs are chosen.

In *Figure 19.4*, an end user is using **remote access** via a web browser and web app. Note that the clientless VPN user can implement different protocols such as RDP, **Secure Shell (SSH)**, or **Virtual Network Computing (VNC)**. These protocols are just some of the protocols accessible to the end user.

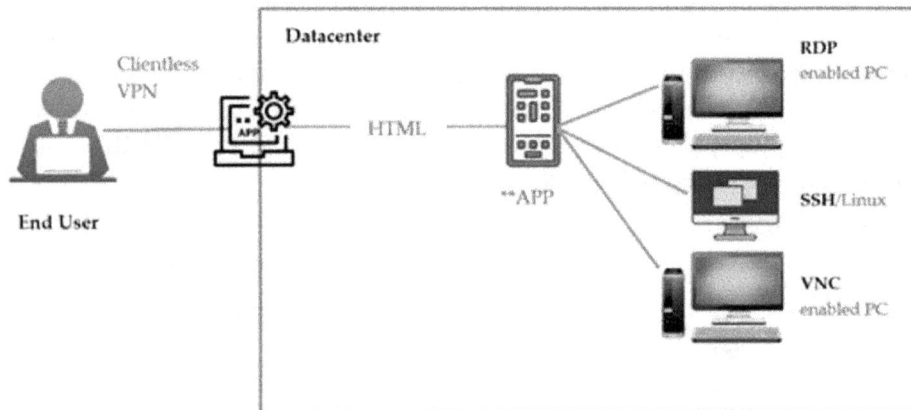

Figure 19.4: *Clientless VPN*

In *Table 19.1*, a site-to-site VPN is compared with a remote access VPN:

Factor	Site-to-site VPN	Remote access VPN
Perspective and approach	This implementation applies to a security method called IPsec to form an encrypted tunnel between the sites. The tunnel goes from one private network to the customer's remote site. The private network is normally a company's headquarters, or it may be an organization's *infrastructure*, resident in a **data cente**r (**DC**).	With remote access VPN connectivity, only individual users connect to corporate/private networks (again, these networks are typically headquarters or DC.)
VPN client software	This VPN client software is not required in this implementation.	Individual users may or may not be required to have their own VPN client software. Remote access VPNs can be client or clientless.
Tunnel generation	Individual users are not expected to *initiate* to set up the VPN tunnel.	Individual remote access users must *initiate* forming the VPN tunnel.
Typical use	This type of VPN suits users in branch offices, these branch offices need to access network resources on servers in headquarters or in the DC.	Hybrid workers, teleworkers, or roaming users/employees who travel while working. This type of VPN suits individuals who aim to securely connect and gain access to corporate network resources/servers.
Encryption/ decryption	With site-to-site VPNs, the VPN gateway is in control of encapsulating and encrypting outbound traffic. Data is encrypted as it traverses the internet. The peer VPN gateway will then decrypt the data at the other side of the tunnel as it is receiving the transmission.	VPN client software encapsulates and encrypts traffic before sending it over the internet to the VPN gateway at the edge of the target network.
Security protocols and technologies supported	IPSEC	IPSEC and SSL
Capacity for multiple users and/or VLAN traffic flow	This type of VPN permits multiple users/VLAN traffic to flow through the VPN tunnel.	This type of VPN does not allow multiple-user traffic to flow through the created VPN Tunnel.

Table 19.1: Site-to-site VPN vs. remote access VPN

Source: *https://ipwithease.com (adapted)*

Split tunnel and full tunnel configuration

A split tunnel configuration is in place when an end user can access a public network while connected to a VPN and access both network connections concurrently. In other words, split tunneling provides a multi-branch networking path and parallel operations. The public network accessed can be any network, such as a LAN, CAN, WAN, or even the internet.

According to *Techopedia*, using split tunneling often depends on the business' needs and helps in securing the data traffic of users working in a remote login environment. Split tunneling can provide a much-needed network speed and performance boost in a multi-network environment.

Split tunneling case use an example

Solutions such as split tunneling were encouraged by many vendors of technology products including Microsoft, especially during large-scale work-from-home events such as in the COVID-19 crisis. As a first-line strategy, Microsoft recommended that the key Microsoft 365 scenarios Microsoft Teams, SharePoint Online, and Exchange Online ought to be routed over a VPN split tunnel configuration. The goal of the recommendation was to mitigate the risk of VPN infrastructure saturation and to improve the performance of the network in its entirety and in remote access to the use of Office365 applications. It was identified that bypassing the VPN tunnel could significantly enhance the user's experience of cloud-based applications. Additionally, recommended configurations remained integral to the **principle of least privilege** (**PoLP**) and could be implemented without exposing the network infrastructure to additional security risks.

Regarding the transmission of multimedia traffic (for example, in Teams), encryption is handled through **Secure Real-Time Transport Protocol** (**SRTP**). SRTP is an extension of **Real-Time Transport Protocol** (**RTP**). SRTP has enhanced security features. It provides confidentiality, authentication, and replay attack protection to RTP traffic. Media traffic is encrypted using SRTP, which uses a session key generated by a secure random number generator and then exchanged using the signaling TLS channel. In addition, media flowing bi-directionally between the Mediation Server and its internal next hop (that is, the closest router) is also encrypted using SRTP. In the case cited, this existing security mechanism became a counter-argument to those who expressed the vulnerabilities introduced by implementing split tunneling strategies.

Irrespective of these contesting opinions and supporting evidence, in times of load stress, split tunneling succeeded in helping the virtual network manage less stressful and lighter traffic. This was achieved with the assistance and support of gateways, servers, and clients. Microsoft's recommended implementations during these years serve as one example of the use and benefits of split tunneling.

Specific network routes are made possible in split tunneling configurations. Routes can be taken directly to the client. If a split tunneling configuration is permitted, security measures will need to be pre-tested and then made robust. Security is importance since there might be potential external attacks from hackers. These potential threats need to be researched, assessed, tested, and analyzed before a specific solution is implemented on the productivity network. As IT technicians, we know the same goes for any new protocol or configuration introduced on our networks.

Figure 19.5 shows the difference in connectivity using a full tunnel as opposed to a split tunnel solution. Note that in the illustration on the left side of the figure, the end user accesses the internet through the VPN. Whereas on the right side, the connection to the Internet is separate, thus easing the stress load on the VPN's resources.

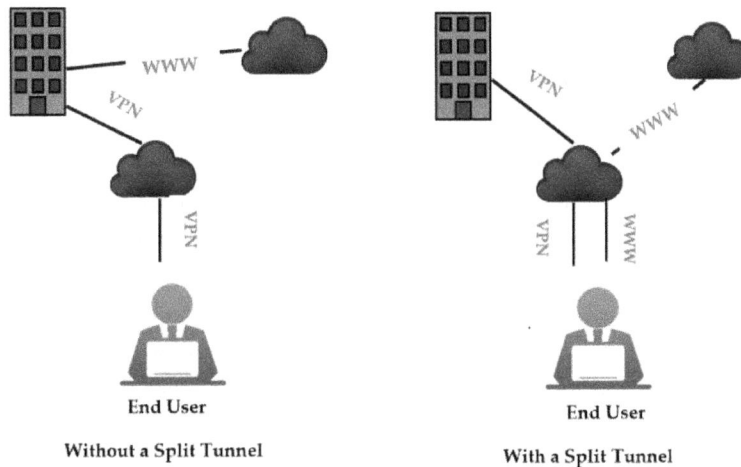

Figure 19.5: Full tunnel vs. split tunnel

Remote desktop connection

If a user wants to connect to a PC or Windows server remotely, they can use the Windows **Remote Desktop Connection** tool. This tool enables remote access via the public internet and through WAN links or through local links on a LAN.

This connection (with full permissions) permits the user access to the programs and software residing on the drive(s) of the remote host or server. When used in Windows, this protocol is known as **Remote Desktop Protocol (RDP)**.

RDP allows Windows PCs and servers to connect to Windows devices. However, only specific versions of Windows operating systems allow RDP connections to take place. The following Windows versions do not support RDP:

- Windows 7 Starter version
- Windows 7 Home edition
- Windows 8 Home edition

- Windows 8.1 Home edition
- Windows 10 Home edition
- Windows 11 Home edition

These Windows versions need to be upgraded to support RDP. Remote desktop is hugely beneficial to IT support staff and network administrators when configuring, managing, monitoring, and troubleshooting client desktops or managing servers. Remote desktop can also be used by remote or mobile employees when they need to access and use corporate network resources or as administrators managing servers.

One of the attractions of Remote Desktop is that the tool displays a **graphical user interface (GUI)** as opposed to a **command line interface (CLI)**. This gives the user full desktop experience and the ability to see and manage apps and issues while navigating the desktop.

The two components required for RDP connections to work are an RDP server and an RDP client. The RDP server is the (remotely accessed) Windows PC or the server that you are connecting to and intend to control. The RDP client is the PC, laptop, or mobile device with the RDP client app installed on it. This client is the device from which you will control the remotely accessed server.

The PC/laptop that sets up the connection (that is, the RDP client computer) can run programs or apps, make configuration changes and modifications, or access data on the remote host computer (that is, the RDP server).

TIP: You cannot make a connection to a PC or server that is asleep or hibernating. Ensure that the settings for sleep and hibernation on the remote PC or server are set to Never. *And remember, Hibernation is not available on all PCs. Users can be selected to remotely access PCs/servers. Members of the Administrators group will automatically have access.

The proprietary protocols are as follows:

- RDP is a Microsoft proprietary protocol. It was established by Microsoft to be used in Microsoft's Remote Desktop Services and Remote Assistance diagnostic and troubleshooting solutions.

  o **Regarding Macintosh® terminal server software**: The provider *Aqua Connect* has licensed RDP and created a version for Mac OS X as a server. At the stage of software development, by accessing Microsoft's RDP's protocol specifications, *Aqua Connect* decreased its software development time. Additionally, there was no need to sacrifice compatibility with RDP devices currently available.

- **Independent Computing Architecture (ICA)** is the Citrix proprietary protocol used in products such as WinFrame and MetaFrame, or XenApp. Citrix is regarded as an excellent solution for remote access, even under low bandwidth conditions. It has been noted that Citrix has stronger embedded security than RDP. Citrix also offers a secure browser service that safeguards the corporate network by separating Web browsing from the corporate network. Network users can access the internet, but the Web browser is still isolated from the corporate network. Needless to say, RDP is the tried and tested protocol and by no means the inferior option. Citrix and RDP are unique and distinct protocols; reliable, efficient, and effective. Like all other business options, choices are made to use products based on cost, reliability, scalability, flexibility, and guaranteed delivery of performance.

- VNC is an open-source protocol. It is typically used on Linux and other OS platforms.

Remote desktop protocol

In *Chapter 5, Ports and Protocols*, RDP was defined. *Table 19.2* reviews this definition:

Protocol	Port number	Description
RDP	3389 TCP, UDP	RDP enables a person to access a host remotely. Providing the user with a GUI, they can interact with the PC/server remotely and engage with the machine as if it were a local connection. RDP supports many different types of network topologies. Services included are keyboard and mouse data encryption, clipboard sharing, running of desktop applications, Printer port, and file redirection. These are some of the services RDP provides.

Table 19.2: Definition of remote desktop protocol

The connection methods supported by the RD client for remote access to company networks include the following:

- Remote Desktop Web Access
- Terminal Server Gateway or Remote Desktop Gateway
- VPN (through iOS built-in VPN options)

In *Figure 19.6*, the Remote Desktop Connection tool is depicted. The **General** tab displays the settings for logging on.

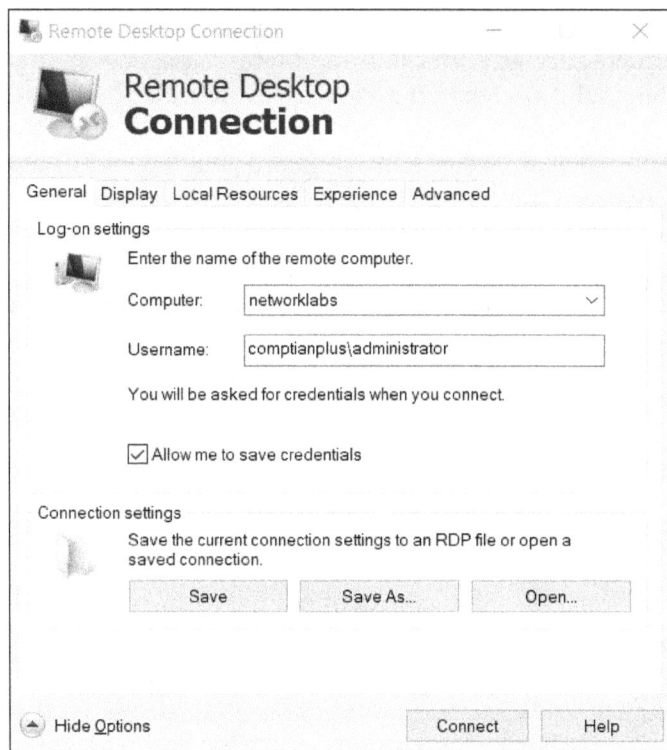

Figure 19.6: RDP log on interface

To connect to a PC/server over the internet:

1. Check that the Windows Firewall is not blocking Remote Desktop.

2. If it is blocked, go to the settings of your firewall and allow an app or feature through Windows Defender Firewall.

3. If you are running a third-party firewall, you may need to temporarily disable this before continuing.

4. Configure your router so that it knows the correct addresses for your computers. This can be achieved by using ipconfig/all in the command prompt for discerning the private addresses (LAN) or typing *whatismyaddress* into a web browser to discover the public (WAN) IP address and other network data required.

5. Enable the Port Forward setting so that it points at Port 3389 (RDP).

RDP: Security considerations

RDP port (port 3389), as a *well-known port,* is regularly scanned for exploits. To ensure the best security practice, follow the given steps:

1. Use an RD Gateway or create a VPN. Avoid using RDP connections over the public Internet without taking security measures.

2. Implement the PoLP. Restrict permissions on all non-administrator accounts for RDP. This restriction mitigates rogue or fraudulent connections.

3. Apply time-outs on passwords and lock out users after several incorrect login attempts.

4. Use complex passwords with a mix of characters to include alphanumeric and symbols.

5. Use **Network Level Authentication (NLA)**.

6. Use the Group Policy Editor to set the encryption level of RDP to the highest available.

Remote Desktop Gateway

Remote Desktop Gateway is a Microsoft Windows Server role that provides a secure encrypted connection to the RDP server. RD gateway encrypts the data using SSL over HTTP. Since port 443 is already allowed through most firewalls, the administrator does not need to configure a separate VPN connection.

RDP gateway policies include the following:

- Connection and Authorization Policy (RD CAP)
- Remote Authorization Policy (RDRAP)

If Active Directory is in use, the RDP Gateway Server must be a domain member. If you have multiple RD Gateway servers in a **load-balanced solution**, you can set up an RD Gateway server farm.

Configuring an RDP Gateway on a Windows server

One of the simplest ways to facilitate remote work from home in a hybrid workforce environment is to set up a Remote Desktop Gateway with a Windows Server system. This setup allows remote workers or mobile users to access a desktop environment to run typical business applications. The setup steps are as follows:

1. Open **Server Manager**. Click on **Manage** | **Select Add Roles and Features**.

2. Select the **Installation type: Role-based or feature-based installation**, as shown in *Figure 19.7*:

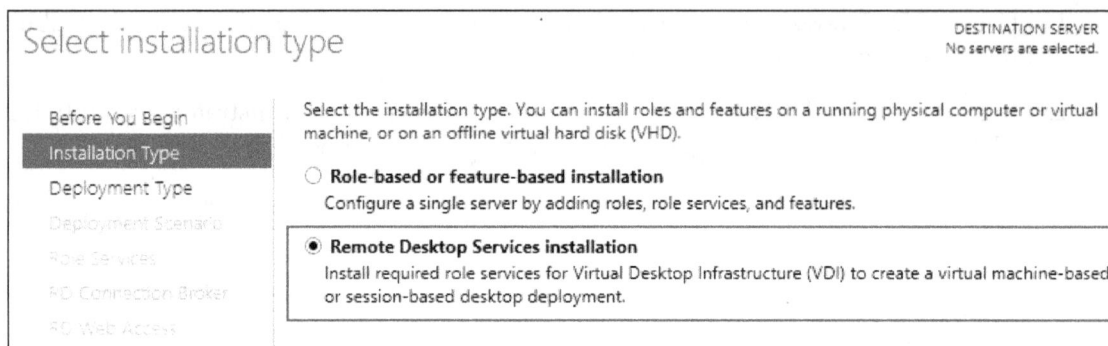

Figure 19.7: Installing RDP Gateway role, step 1

3. Select the destination server from the server pool. Then, click on the RD Gateway icon.

4. Select **Remote Desktop Services** from the server Roles displayed and click **Next**.

5. Select services from Role Services, select all services shown *with the exception of* Remote Desktop Virtualization Host and Remote Desktop Web Access, and then click **Next**.

6. Select **Network Policy Server**, click **Next** and then **Install**.

Note: Wait for the role to install. This will take some minutes.

Configuration of remote desktop gateway

To configure the remote desktop gateway, follow the following steps:

1. Open the **Server Manager**, select **Remote Desktop Services**, and then click on **RD Gateway**, as shown in *Figure 19.8*:

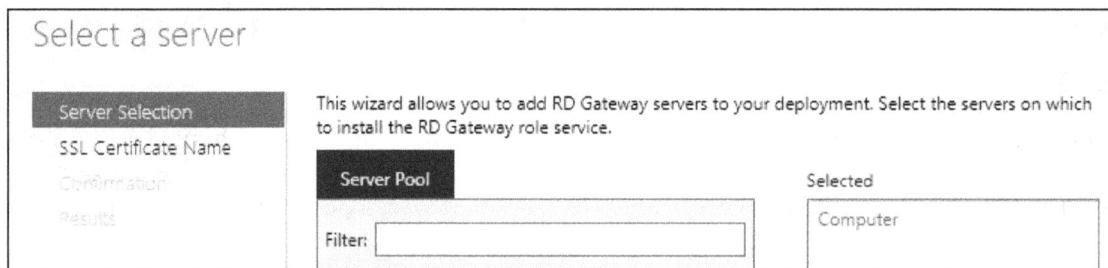

Figure 19.8: Configuring RDP Gateway role, step 2

2. Select the server from the pool.

3. Enter the SSL certificate name. Use the external *Fully Qualified Domain Name* of the RD Gateway server. Click **Next** and start the configuration. (Select the **Import a certificate into the RD Gateway bubble** option, then select **Browse and Import Certificate**.)

   Note: The recommendation is to use a publicly issued certificate. If a private certificate is selected, the certificate's trust chain would need to be configured in advance, and all clients identified beforehand.

4. After installation completes, click on **Configure certificates**. At this point, you should **review** the gateway properties you aim to deploy, as shown in *Figure 19.9*:

Figure 19.9: Configuring RDP Gateway role, step 3

5. Verify RD Gateway certificate, as shown in *Figure 19.10*:

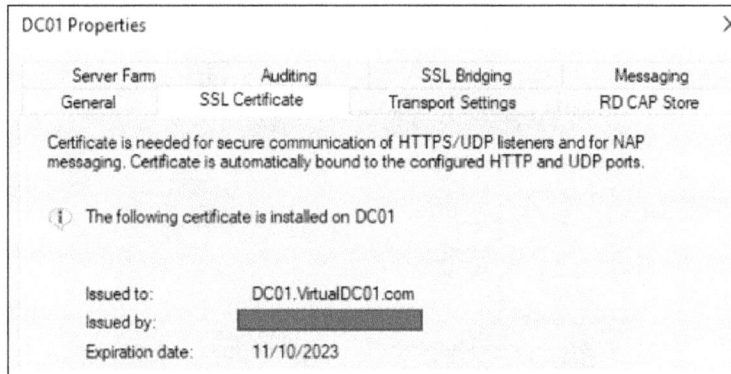

Figure 19.10: Configuring RDP Gateway role, step 4

6. Configure the Remote Desktop Gateway deployment, as shown in *Figure 19.11*:

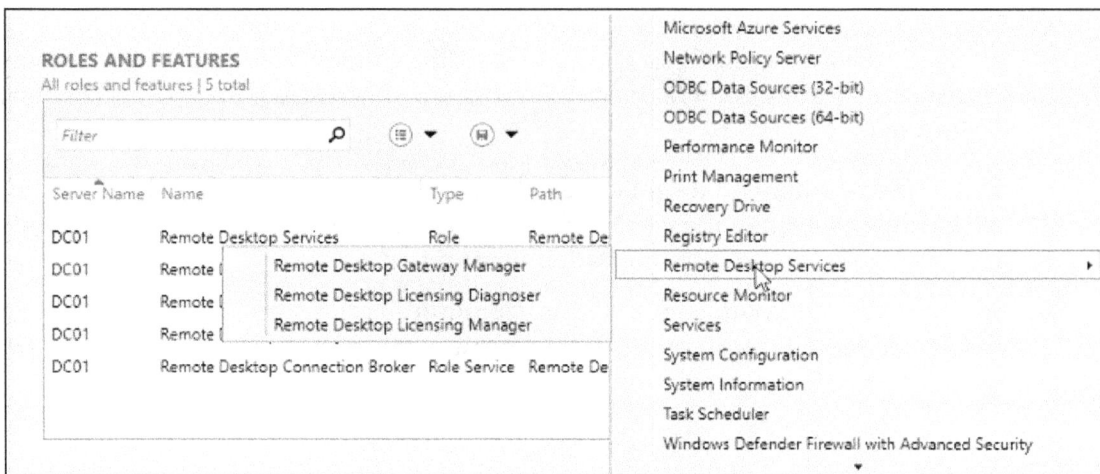

Figure 19.11: Configuring RDP Gateway role, step 5

Configuring remote desktop gateway servers/ settings

To configure the Remote Desktop Gateway settings, follow the given steps:

1. Open the **Server Manager** and select **Servers**. Choose the appropriate server. Right-click on **Server**, and then click on the **Remote Desktop Gateway Manager**, as shown in *Figure 19.12*:

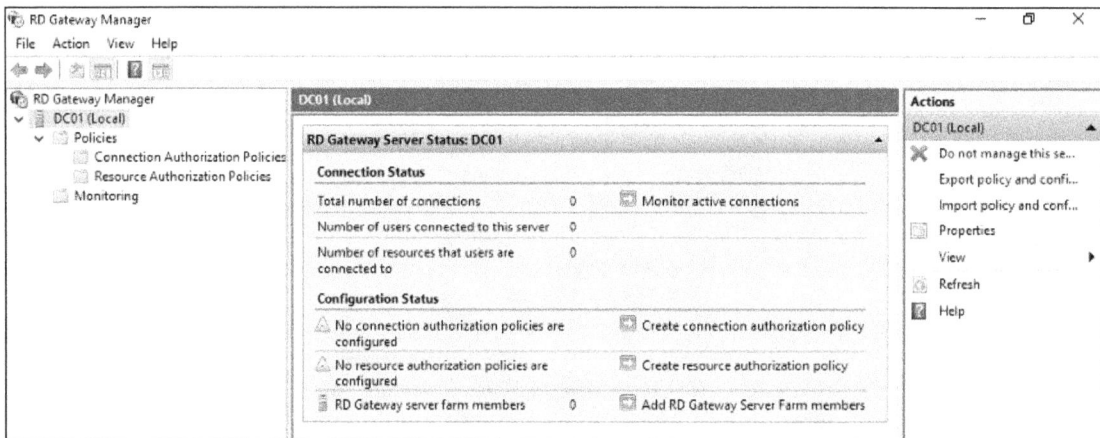

Figure 19.12: Configuring RDP Gateway settings, step 1

2. Go to **Connection Authorization Policies**, as shown in *Figure 19.13:*

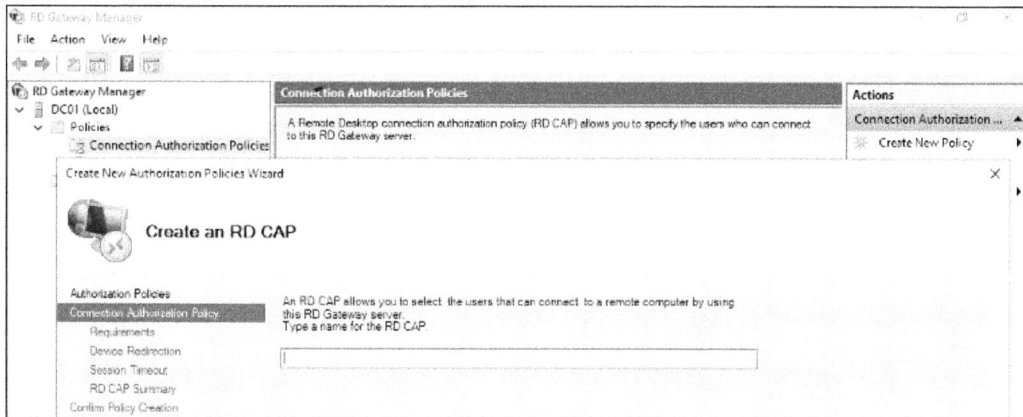

Figure 19.13: *Configuring RDP Gateway settings, step 2*

3. State the policy name. Following this, activate this policy and click **OK**.

4. Choose the authentication method. Select **Password** and then add the user group required for RD Gateway authentication.

5. Select the required session timeouts.

6. Go to **Resource Authorization Policies**.

7. Select the Policy name and enable the policy.

8. Specify the user groups. The members of these user groups will have access to remote computers on the network through the remote desktop gateway, as shown in *Figure 19.14*:

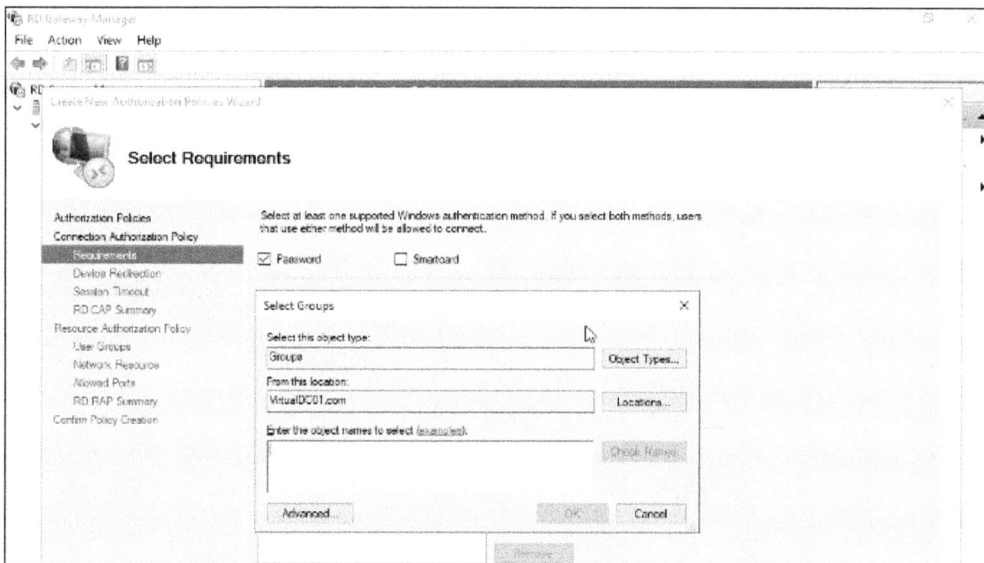

Figure 19.14: *Configuring RDP Gateway settings, step 3*

9. Select the user group/network resources to be accessed. These resources will be accessible via the internet. Users can connect to network resources by using the RD gateway. Network resources can include computers in an Active Directory Domain Services security group or a remote desktop server farm.

Creating computer groups

To create computer groups, follow the given steps:

1. In the right pane, in **Actions**, click on **Manage Local Computers Groups**, as shown in *Figure 19.15*:

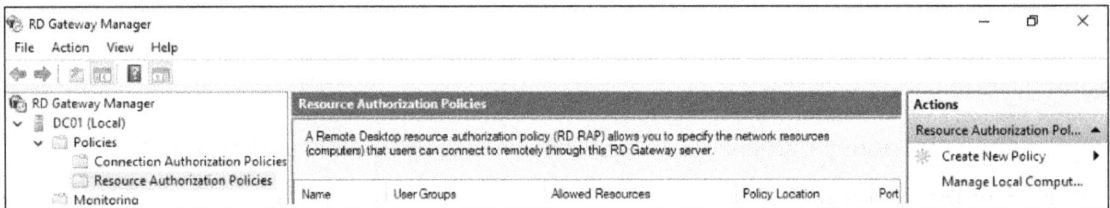

Figure 19.15: Configuring RDP Gateway settings, step 1

2. Create a group, as shown in *Figure 19.16*:

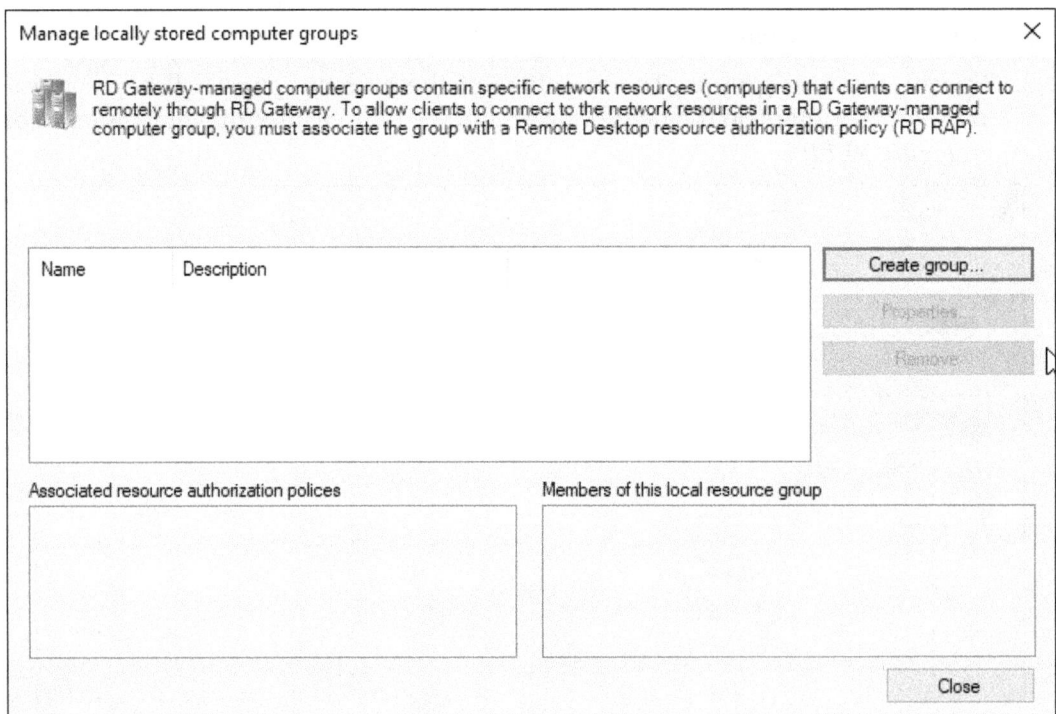

Figure 19.16: Configuring RDP Gateway settings, step 2

3. State the computer Group name and description, as shown in *Figure 19.17:*

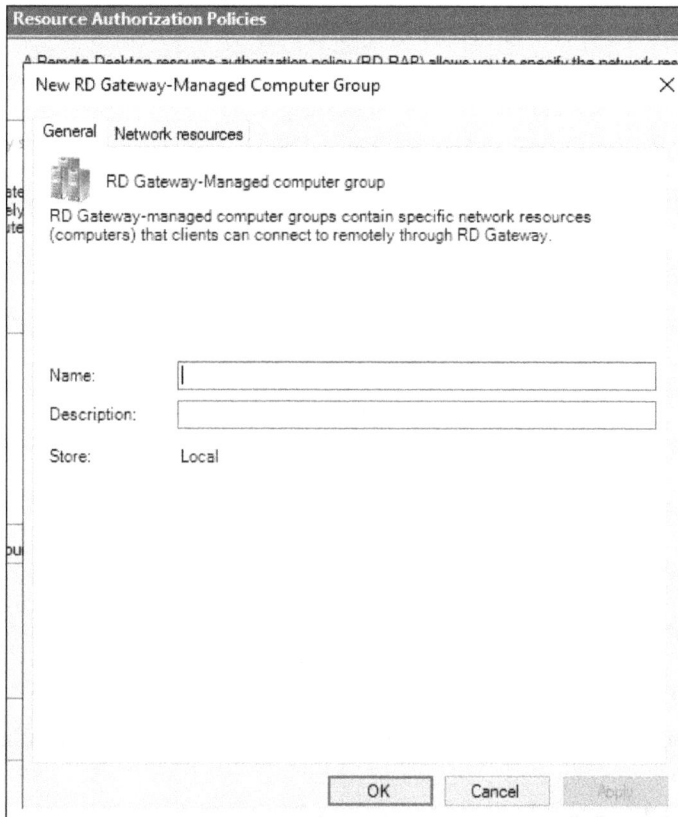

Figure 19.17: *Configuring RDP Gateway settings, step 3*

4. Add the name or IP address of the server. Alternatively, add the details of the Remote Desktop Session Host server farm. This step ensures that the PoLP is implemented as best practice. The administrator is prompted to name each member in the computer group. Members must be specified to maintain the security of remote access and comply with any organizational policies. Refer to *Figure 19.18*:

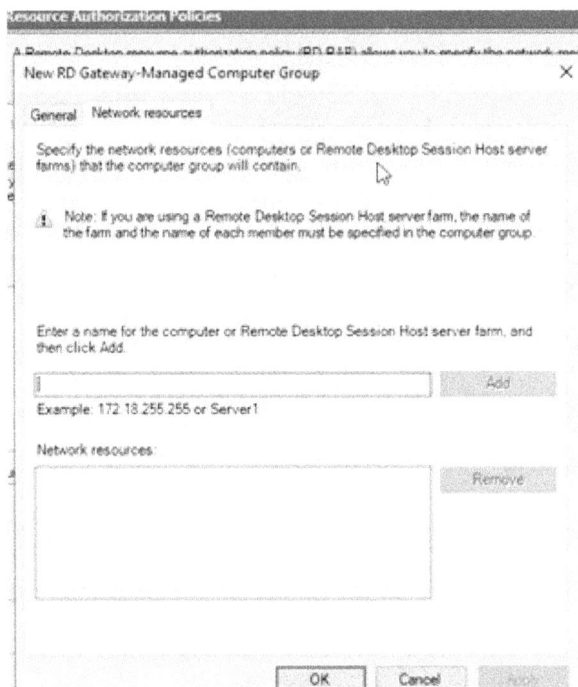

Figure 19.18: Configuring RDP Gateway settings, step 4

To conclude, remote desktops can be accessed securely by using RDP Gateway.

Virtual network computing

VNC is an open-source GUI desktop sharing system. As a vendor-neutral remote desktop solution, it is used for Linux machines and optimized for Windows and macOS. Applications such as RealVNC, TightVNC, UltraVNC, and Vine Server use VNC. VNC can be tunneled over SSH or a VPN connection. A remote frame buffer is the protocol used in VNC connections. RFBP is a free, open-source protocol that works at the framebuffer level, making it viable for Windows, MacOS, and UNIX/Linux clients.

There are also freeware applications that create instant VPN tunnels between computers.

There are many other third-party remote management tools available for download. Apple Remote Desktop extended on the RFB protocol, enhancing its security and tweaking its features. This is Apple's solution for macOS devices. Chrome Remote Desktop was developed by Google to enable remote access between Chrome OS devices.

Virtual desktop

The concept of a virtual desktop is to provide the user with the same look and feel as a physical workstation, even if the desktop image or applications are not installed on the local machine. Thin clients have been used in networking for some time now and are not a new technology. These workstations have connections to server-based computing environments, with the server holding the necessary applications and calculations required to provide the services offered. The thin client would establish a remote connection with the required server, and these devices would be low-cost devices that rely heavily on the server's resources and computing power.

With thin computing, all computing is taking place on the server. A thin client displays the output from the operating system that is resident and running on the server. The user's keyboard and mouse are essentially used to interact with the operating system running on server components. Organizations that need endpoint devices to be more reliable and secure may opt to use thin clients over other architectures.

Applications can be accessed on Chromebooks, PCs, or other mobile devices such as tablets or smartphones. In brief, thin clients are used for their scalability, security, and manageability. With newer implementations of virtual desktops, the desktop images (and applications) are delivered virtually. These applications, which are at times resource-intensive, are running in a VM in the cloud / data center, thus aligning with the newer focus on software-defined networking. This technology is implemented in cloud provisions such as **software as a service (SaaS)** or **infrastructure as a service (IaaS)**.

At times, with a **Virtual Desktop Infrastructure** (**VDI**), the user experience can be more enhanced and effective with optimum performance levels offered, where the user accesses the remote network (or cloud-based) resources with High Availability and quality performance. Some common implementations of remote desktop virtualization involve hosting multiple desktop operating system instances on a server hardware platform running a hypervisor such as VMware or HyperTerminal. This form of virtualized infrastructure offsets the need to provide every user with a dedicated desktop PC or device and is a cost-effective way of centralizing and safeguarding network resources. The benefits for a network administrator include ease of management, centralized administration, and the ability to respond faster to IT issues and problems.

Authentication and authorization considerations

The importance of authentication and authorization was discussed in *Chapter 16, Security Concepts*. In this section, we are focusing on authentication and authorization considerations as they relate to remote access and VPNs.

Remote Authentication Dial-In User Service

Remote Authentication Dial-In User Service (RADIUS) is a networking protocol that allows end users to access corporate networks. Due to the security benefits of RADIUS, combined with the ability of centralized access and supervision in managing and monitoring access and resource use, it is a highly regarded protocol. RADIUS is defined by the **Internet Engineering Task Force (IETF)**, which makes it a standards-based protocol. Additionally, RADIUS aligns with the three principles of AAA, aligning it with security best practices and actions. When RADIUS authenticates the user as a legitimate user on the network, it allows the administrator to specify the rights and permissions a user has. Moreover, it controls what they do (or cannot do) throughout the session.

Since RADIUS uses **User Datagram Protocol (UDP)** as its transport protocol, it is fast and scalable. RADIUS supports large numbers of clients as a connectionless protocol without the overhead controlling sessions and other overheads that **Transmission Control Protocol (TCP)** has. Security of access and authorization is within the features of the protocol itself.

Cloud providers implement RADIUS-as-a-Service to organizations. This cloud solution and delivery model is attractive for many businesses that perceive it as a cost-effective means of handling remote users while passing the cost of management and monitoring to the cloud provider. RADIUS supports Zero Trust Network Access, wireless networks, and VPNs, demonstrating its versatility and adaptability as an authentication strategy.

Figure 19.19 demonstrates how the RADIUS protocol is used to authenticate remote users against a RADIUS server. Access can be accepted or rejected in accordance with the entries and credentials listed in the Remote User Database. We can also visualize the scalability of the model with UDP as the connectionless transport protocol in use. Speed of access is ensured, and tracking and monitoring are integrated into the user experience.

Using RADIUS as a network security system preserves the privacy and security of each individual user in remote access and *over-the-air* transmissions.

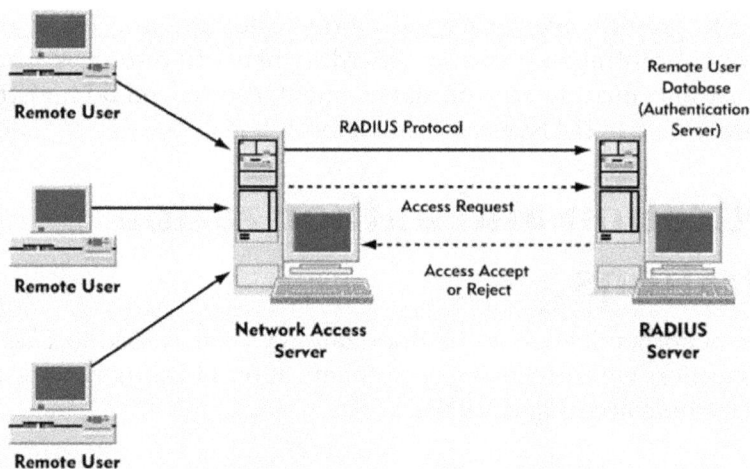

Figure 19.19: RADIUS authentication

Table 19.3 shows how the access point on a WLAN becomes an authenticator when you choose the RADIUS authentication method in the configuration of the router:

802.11 network	Enterprise edge	Enterprise network
Supplicant	Authenticator	Authentication server
Operates on a client	802.1x traffic only Access point acts as an authenticator	EAP plug-in goes into RADIUS server.

Table 19.3: RADIUS in WLAN

This is one configuration strategy for using RADIUS authentication in a wireless network.

While the RADIUS server might have a database of users and passwords, it is more *commonplace* for it to pass the user credentials on to another server to verify/validate them. The RADIUS server can pass the credentials on to a **Lightweight Directory Access Protocol (LDAP)** server as part of the authentication process. In a Microsoft domain, the LDAP server is configured as a Windows domain controller.

Terminal Access Controller Access-Control System Plus

The **Terminal Access Controller Access-Control System Plus (TACACS+)** protocol is an alternative to RADIUS. It is a Cisco proprietary protocol that also uses the AAA method but is not an open standard like RADIUS.

There are also some other major differences between the two protocols. In terms of functionality, RADIUS combines authentication and authorization. TACACS+ separates the two processes. It provides control over the authorization of commands, allowing granular control. Because of this separation, different protocols can be used for each part of AAA, for example, Kerberos. Regarding confidentiality, RADIUS encrypts the password only, whereas TACACS+ encrypts all packets transmitted, therefore, the entire authentication process. In terms of transmission, RADIUS uses UDP as its transport protocol, whereas TACACS+ uses TCP and port 49, making the transaction guaranteed and connection-oriented. The TACACS+ protocol permits administrators access to network servers, routers, and other network computing devices that require remote management. This makes TACACS+ totally suitable for device administration and network access. RADIUS is primarily a network access protocol. Since TACACS+ has additional security features, such as support of command accounting and multiple privilege levels, it is a preferred choice when network administrators want to access the network's intermediary devices remotely.

Diameter is a separate networking protocol that exchanges AAA data between two parties. It was introduced to overcome some of the limitations of RADIUS, as it is sometimes used instead of it.

In *Figure 19.20*, we see how authentication methods are implemented in remote access or VPN scenarios. Enterprise networks contain many infrastructure devices, and each one of these devices must be secured and managed.

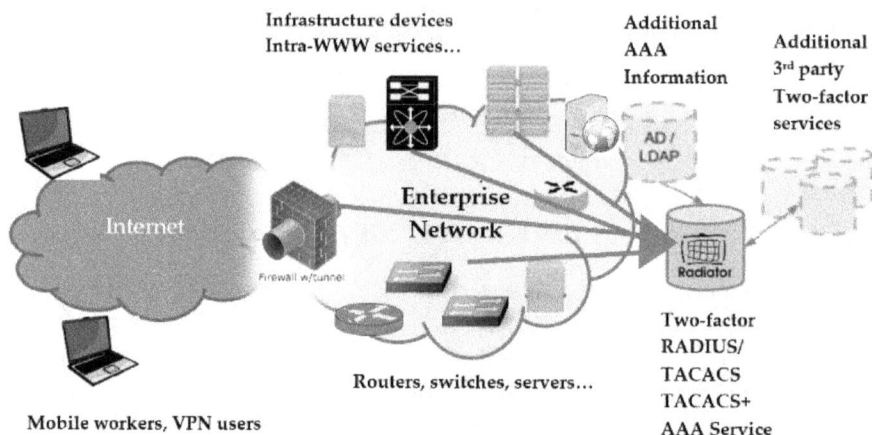

Figure 19.20: Remote management

A network administrator needs to understand the options available to provide users with remote access. They must also understand the critical nature of remote management of users and devices as data transverses the cloud.

In-band vs. out-of-band management

Essentially, there are the following two ways to manage a network:

- In-band management
- **Out-of-band management (OOBM)**

In-band management uses the same primary channel and pathway that data and production are using on the network. It is implemented by using a Telnet/SSH connection to a switch/router or by using SNMP-based tools. In short, an administrator is managing devices *through* the network itself. An example of this strategy is using Telnet/SSH via one of the device's **virtual terminal lines** (**VTY**), such as the SVI management interface on a switch. Despite having the advantage of a secure connection to the network infrastructure and devices, in-band management heavily relies on the production network.

It is best practice for administrators to manage their servers and other network devices remotely. As stated, this is often done over the production network using protocols such as SSH, VNC, and remote desktop.

However, remember that if your network fails, your user traffic will also fail, and inevitably, so will in-band management. Consequently, an administrator should also configure an out-of-band management solution.

In accordance with the definition of OOBM on *Techopedia*, Device management through out-of-band management is still done via a network connection, but this is entirely separate physically from the in-band network connection that the system is serving. This difference can at times cause confusion in understanding or in an ability to differentiate between the two methods of managing networks and devices. *Techopedia* offers an easy-to-understand analogy of OOBM.

Imagine you are entering a restaurant via the public entrance to the building. Once you are inside the restaurant, there will be many other doors or areas that you have access to, for example, an upstairs or extended area or the restrooms. However, there will also be a door(s) throughout the building named *staff only* or *employees only beyond this point*. Think of this door as being on a separate network channel to the door serving the general public, which is permissible to all legitimate users. No unauthorized person should go beyond the door marked *employees only* or equivalent. But it is accessible. There is just no network connection to it from the regular network channel. This configuration makes the separate channel much more secure.

OOBM is commonly done through operating system extensions and using dedicated hardware, which is explicitly designed for OOBM. When an administrator requires an alternate path to devices, for example, if the network is down or inaccessible, they can do so using independent network channels or OOBM tools. **Terminal servers** commonly provide this form of access. Examples include console ports on switches or routers. The terminal server provides access to the console ports of many devices. This or other management ports (that is, an OOBM interface) is usually available even though the network may be down or even if the device is powered down, in sleep or hibernate mode, or basically inaccessible through the operating system. Troubleshooting and diagnostics are now viable. A network administrator using a terminal server is accessing a Windows Server Desktop with all the tools that the server offers.

Regarding access to servers, OOBM uses a *dedicated connection* with greater access to the server's BIOS/**Unified Extensible Firmware Interface (UEFI)** settings, NIC configurations, RAID controllers, and other relevant firmware management tools. Built for use in data center environments or comms rooms, some vendors, such as Dell and Oracle, have created their own out-of-band connectivity standards and tools. The Dell product is called the **Dell Remote Access Controller (DRAC)**. Oracle's solution is known as **Oracle Integrated Lights Out Manager (iLOM)**.

OOBM can use copper and fiber Ethernet network access, a PSTN phone line connected to a modem, which is connected to the console port, a dedicated console server, or by establishing a connection via an independent internet connection over cellular or xDSL, or cable.

Telnet/Secure Shell

Telnet enables a user to virtually access a computer while providing a bi-directional, collaborative, and text-based communication channel between the two machines communicating. The Telnet protocol operates in a client-server TCP/IP model.

Telnet is now regarded as a legacy protocol and, as such, an insecure means of remotely accessing network devices and servers. In contrast to Telnet, SSH encrypts the transmission and is preferred because of its security when handling data in transit.

The reason why Telnet is regarded as an insecure protocol is that it sends data remotely in plain text. In contrast with this insecure transmission, SSH encrypts the traffic as it traverses public networks. Because of this added security, network administrators prefer to use SSH, especially when managing network equipment remotely. FTP also uses SSH when transferring files. Another protocol that is based on SSH is the **Secure Copy Protocol** (**SCP**). This protocol copies encrypted files that are being sent over a network. The Linux command to copy a file is *cp*. Therefore, *scp* is the command for secure copy. SCP uses the same encryption mechanism as SSH to guarantee file integrity and confidentiality.

SSH can also encrypt TCP Wrappers, which is a type of access control list used on Linux systems to filter traffic. This ACL system is used for network access to operating systems on IP servers, such as Linux or **Berkeley Software Distribution** (**BSD**). Note that BSD is now a defunct and disused operating system, though it has formed the basis of use in later system software. Another security feature of SSH is the account lockout feature. **Secure Shell** (**SSH**) can disconnect an attacker if he has not logged on within 60 seconds and limit the number of authentication attempts per session/connection. These settings often prevent brute force attacks against networks and remote protocols and services. As we can see, SSH comes with additional features to address data-in-transit and secure file transfers.

Ports: When SSH encrypts traffic, it uses TCP port 22. Telnet uses port 23.

Conclusion

This chapter explored VPNs, remote access, and remote management tools. We also covered RADIUS and TACACS+ and compared and contrasted how they function. In the upcoming chapter, we will examine physical security measures and discuss how they are implemented.

Points to remember

- Network administrators need to know:
  - Various remote access methods.
  - The security implications of each remote access method.

o   Strategies used to secure remote access.

o   How to optimize remote access for organizations and enterprise networks.

- The content of *Chapter 19* is mapped to *Domain 3, Network Operations*. Compare and contrast network access and management methods.

Key terms

- **Secure Sockets Layer (SSL)**: The predecessor to TLS. SSL is used to encrypt data in transit with the use of certificates.

- **Transport Layer Security**: The replacement for SSL. TLS is used to encrypt data in transit. Like SSL, it uses certificates issued by CAs.

- **VDI/VDE**: A virtual desktop infrastructure or virtual desktop environment. Users access a server hosting virtual desktops and run the desktop operating system from the server.

Questions

1. Explain what is meant by a virtual private network.

2. Give some examples of VPNs and explain where and why they are used.

3. Describe the differences between RADIUS and TACACS+.

4. Describe the differences between Telnet and Secure Shell.

Join our book's Discord space

Join the book's Discord Workspace for Latest updates, Offers, Tech happenings around the world, New Release and Sessions with the Authors:

https://discord.bpbonline.com

CHAPTER 20

Implementing Physical Security

Introduction

There are many models and frameworks that can be used to support the design, development, and implementation of *physical security* in an organization. Some of these security models overlap in concepts but differ slightly in the technical terms or language used: for example, the technical terms used in CIA, AAA, and DiD. The important point is that when further explored as a cybersecurity model, they are all reinforced by the safeguarding of property, people, hardware, software, networks, and data.

One of the security models we have explored in *Chapter 16, Security Concepts,* is called **defense in depth** (**DiD**). The DiD occurs where there is layering in security practices and where an administrator applies the right technologies in each chosen layer of defense. We should now understand that no single layer is completely effective in securing assets on its own, and we should appreciate that the most secure system or network has many layers of security. This act of layering eliminates single points of failure and further hardens the network.

Organizations can implement a wide variety of security controls to reduce security risks. Physical security (that is, physical controls) is one type of security control. As stated, it is essential for all organizations to protect the organization, its employees, hardware, software, data, and all other network resources within its sphere. Physical controls, such as *controls,* are as important as implementing *technical controls,* where the security control uses technology as a means of implementation. They are also as important as *administrative controls*, which use administrative or management methods as a security strategy. These combined controls come back to the concept of layering as it exists in a *DiD* approach, whereby network hardening is the cumulative effect of various security mechanisms and controls.

In short, the objective of physical security is to protect people, information (data), equipment, and assets from damage, compromise, theft, or harm, and to do so through optimized security controls. Therefore, if a step in the layer or sequence fails, the next step should be implemented automatically.

Physical security measures should be planned, designed, developed, assessed, and tested. Security measures should be systematically inspected in a time frame conducive to ongoing best practices.

Structure

The chapter explains the following topics:

- Physical security controls
- Detection methods
- Configuration management
- Prevention methods

Objectives

In this chapter, we will learn how to implement physical security. Upon completing this chapter, you will be able to understand diverse physical security controls and appreciate their best use. You will be able to explain the need for asset disposal and the methods in place to sanitize and dispose of hard drives.

Physical security controls

The best practice in the design and administration of a physical security plan is to create and then apply *layers* of physical security methods and strategies in a multi-layered defense system. Moreover, using various types of security controls within the same layer further enriches security. The DiD model can be broken down into the following four layers:

- Perimeter defense
- Host protection
- Operating systems
- Application protection and data/information protection

Another way to visualize the approach to security is by looking at *The Information Security Triad: CIA* diagram shown in *Figure 20.1*. Here, we can see where physical security sits in the model. It lies at the perimeter of hardware and software but remains an aspect of its protection very much.

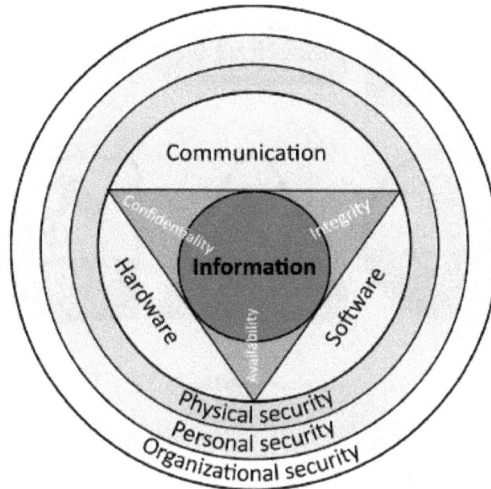

Figure 20.1: *The Information Security Triad CIA*

All organizations should have a security plan that includes the four layers of DiD to include where the physical security of all elements in the organization is safeguarded.

Deter

Deterrence discourages people from carrying out security breaches or dissuades them from attempting to gain unauthorized access to your premises. An organization can implement measures that unauthorized people perceive as too difficult or need special tools and training to defeat. The hope is that they may be encouraged to move on and away from your organization as a target.

Examples of security measures that *deter* intruders include warning signs, brightly lit areas, and perimeter barriers, such as clearly marked perimeter boundaries, fences, natural barriers, and bollards. Other deterrents are the physical presence of security guards, open spaces with good visibility, and, in some cases, guard dogs. Additionally, the controls should deny direct physical access.

Figure 20.2 offers some examples of warning signs that may deter an intruder and initial access attempts:

CCTV SIGN COLLECTION

designed by 🖌 **freepik**

Figure 20.2: CCTV warning signs

Detect

The security controls should enable detection and detect unauthorized access as early as possible. An organization can implement measures to figure out whether an unauthorized action is occurring or has already occurred.

Examples of security measures that *detect* intruders include surveillance systems and security guards controlling access to the building, CCTV systems, IP camera data and PoE networks, motion sensors, alarms on doors, gates, windows, tilt and zoom cameras, and other **Perimeter Intrusion Detection Systems (PIDS)**.

> **Note: When choosing cameras, be mindful of the following characteristics: resolution, focal length, the types of lenses (that is, fixed vs. varifocal), the angles of viewing (for example, pan-tilt-zoom cameras, bullet or dome), and the camera's sensitivity to light. The features of focal length and zoom are extremely important considerations in camera selection.**

Some cameras come with pre-set locations, and the company can select the areas and accurately fit them per area and space to be covered.

The technology of CCTV is forever evolving; there have been significant improvements in the quality and abilities of these surveillance cameras. The intelligence of camera systems and camera solutions has grown over the years, with abilities such as Automated Number Plate Recognition, Remote Access Viewing, and facial recognition.

In *Figure 20.3*, we can see the variety of angles a camera may tilt to:

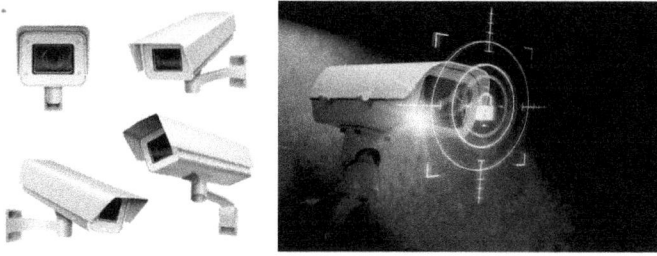

Figure 20.3: *Detection mechanisms*

Figure 20.4 illustrates security controls organizations can use to secure entry and perimeter boundaries. Controls will include fences, gates, walls, sensor systems, and natural barriers such as foliage, trees, or a density of shrubbery or plants.

Figure 20.4: *Motion sensors, barriers, and turnstiles*

Delay

The security controls should *delay* an unauthorized access attempt for as long as possible to allow an effective security response to be activated. The objective is to implement security measures to slow the progress of a harmful event or intrusion. Even in the absence of harmful events or security breaches, people or vehicles can be slowed down, and the procedure to enter and move around the building is made more difficult (that is, access control-related).

Examples of security measures that *delay* intruders include multiple lock types using keys, cards, or codes, ID badges, biometrics, RFID smartcards, turnstiles, and access control vestibules (previously known as mantraps).

RFID cards typically use the 125 kHz frequency to communicate with proximity readers.

The RFID reader is otherwise known as an **interrogating device**. The *object* (tag) communicates with the RFID reader. The objective of RFID technologies is to secure transactions and authenticate the user of the card as a legitimate cardholder.

Passive tags do not have an independent power source, and the energy required is transmitted by the RFID reader. The reader achieves this by emitting an electromagnetic signal to power operations. In contrast, active tags use an independent power source, such as a battery. This method technically means an active tag will have the potential for more processing capabilities, and the tag's transmission and range abilities may also be enhanced.

Figure 20.5 shows an RFID reader and how it is implemented:

Figure 20.5: *RFID reader*

Note that the RFID technology is not foolproof or immune to security vulnerabilities. It is still possible for an intruder, social engineer, or rogue individual to carry an RFID reader and, with the know-how and required distance, access an RFID-enabled card in an attempt to access the card's data. This is another reason why DiD is the best practice.

An **access control vestibule** occurs where one gateway leads to a bounded or enclosed space. This space is protected by another barrier or door. These vestibules are often seen in banks. One of the benefits of these vestibules and turnstiles is the prevention of tailgating, where an unauthorized person piggybacks behind an authorized person and gains access to the building.

In *Figure 20.6*, security delay (and authentication) mechanisms are evident. The organization can fit one of these diverse physical security controls in any area requiring secure entry/exit. Each delay mechanism provides the company with a means to slow down potential intruders.

Security

Access Controlled

Figure 20.6: *Access control vestibule, revolving door, and smart door*

Respond

Organizations should plan for an effective *response to security incidents*. Appropriate responses counteract the predicted activity of an unauthorized person and do so within a time that is suited to the **delay** security controls that are in place. These response measures are planned and implemented to *prevent*, resist, or mitigate the impact of a security breach or incident and should be included in an incident response plan.

Recover

Organizations should take the steps required to *recover* from a security incident. Plans ought to be in place to restore operations to as near normal as possible in a timely manner following any security breach or incident.

Other prevention methods that may be implemented in physical security controls include the following:

- Biometrics
- Locking racks
- Locking cabinets
- Smart lockers
- Employee training

Detection methods

Let us now go over a few detection methods. To further enhance the physical security of IT hardware, it is important to consider various protective measures such as locks, chassis alarms, asset tags, and inventory records.

Asset tags

An asset tag is a tracking tag that can be attached to each piece of equipment to uniquely identify the part.

Asset tags typically include the company name and asset number. Organizations should hold an IT inventory database that records and maintains inventory data for all their end devices, such as PCs, laptops, or VoIP phones, and their network/intermediary devices, like switches or routers, and so on. Cloud assets and other IT infrastructure should also be included in the inventory. This inventory forms part of the company's IT-related documentation and enables network administrators to control and manage the network effectively. Administrators have keen insight into network operations and the whole network infrastructure.

Asset tags can also be used for tracking purposes. They can be used to locate lost or stolen equipment. If there is any change or movement in the location of devices, this movement should also be recorded as a critical part of asset tracking procedures. Remember, from the network administrator's perspective, administrators need to be able to track:

- The physical relocation of device(s)
- Any subsequent IP address change, if required
- All hardware devices removed from the network

- Software installation/upgrading/configuration changes/uninstallation
- Software license expiration (as in end-of-life cycles)

Tamper detection can also be implemented on asset tags. This form of detection sends a notification if the tag is removed. The functions of these tamper-proof labels are as follows: if anyone attempts to remove the label, the word *void* appears on both the device/asset and the label. This evidences that the label has been tampered with and cannot simply be stuck or fixed back together again. These tags are referred to as **tamper-evident tags**.

Alarms

Other alarms can be placed on the actual equipment itself. Chassis intrusion detection can be enabled in the system setup. If the motherboard or chassis is opened, the next time a user accesses the device, a pop-up notification will appear from the system. This notification is illustrated in *Figure 20.7*.

The chassis intrusion sensor or switch sends a high-level signal to this connector if an intrusion occurs. The chassis intrusion event is then generated. This feature may also be enabled/disabled in the BIOS and exists on regular hosts/workstations and on enterprise server boards.

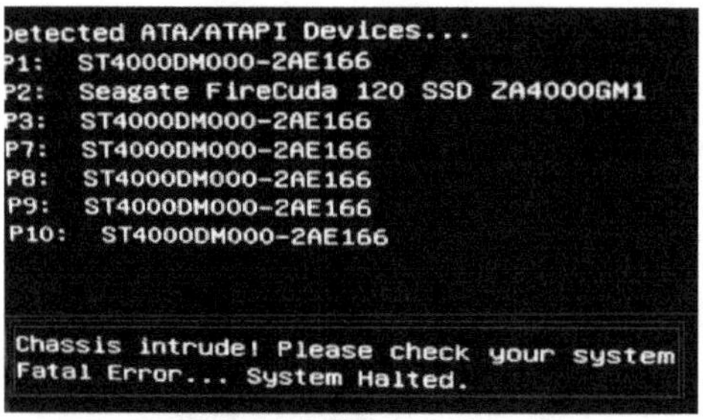

```
Detected ATA/ATAPI Devices...
P1:    ST4000DM000-2AE166
P2:    Seagate FireCuda 120 SSD ZA4000GM1
P3:    ST4000DM000-2AE166
P7:    ST4000DM000-2AE166
P8:    ST4000DM000-2AE166
P9:    ST4000DM000-2AE166
P10:   ST4000DM000-2AE166

Chassis intrude! Please check your system
Fatal Error... System Halted.
```

Figure 20.7: Chassis intrusion alarm

Configuration management

Configuration management (CM) is a process used in IT operations as part of business management. CM aims to identify and document all the components in the network infrastructure and document devices installed at a company's site. Cloud-based assets (for example, SLAs) will also need to be monitored. CM should capture the device/product's lifecycle in all its aspects and stages: that is, its performance, functionality, and physical characteristics with its needs and requirements, its design, and the state and condition of operational information throughout its life. The application of CM provides a network administrator with control and insight into the corporate network.

The *IT Infrastructure Library (ITIL®)* is an internationally acclaimed service delivery model. ITIL provides IT management with a framework and recommended standardized set of best practice processes and actions for provisioning IT services. ITIL is also a certifying body that assesses and validates a person's competence and proficiency in managing IT systems and IT asset management. If an organization decides to implement the ITIL framework, it may request an IT department member to become ITIL certified.

In short, a **configuration management system** (**CMS**) gathers, collates, stores, maintains, and presents information about **configuration items** (**CIs**). This database or group of spreadsheets will form the basis of CM management in an organization. The tools and complexity of the system used relate to the size and capacity of the company's network.

Regarding physical security controls, these asset management tools and database reports should complement the *tangible* asset tags. The location of the asset and its documented presence in the CMS optimally should match up.

Prevention methods

Let us now go over a few prevention methods.

Biometrics

Bio stems from the Greek word *bios*, which relates to the course of human life. In scientific terms, bio is extended to include all organic life. **Metrics** are measures of quantitative calculations based on selected data or criteria. Consequently, **biometrics** are biological body or physical measurements and calculations related to human characteristics with the primary purpose of human identification.

Some examples of biometrics include iris recognition, retina recognition, face recognition, fingerprint recognition, voice recognition, DNA matching, finger geometry recognition, hand geometry recognition, signature recognition, vein patterns recognition, biometric recognition, and ear shape recognition.

In IT and in organizations, biometric authentication permits a user to perform a biometric scan to activate an entry point or access system. The collection of physical characteristics of legitimate users (employees) is stored as a digital data template where cross-checking can be run to authenticate a specific user or permitted personnel.

Role-based access controls permit users to access areas of the building, hardware, or software. It is a great way to implement physical security controls since an individual's role determines their level of access. We have previously discussed the effectiveness of multi-factor authentication, two-factor authentication, and single sign-on, and how these techniques improve the overall security of network resources. Facial recognition, retinal scans, and fingerprints can be further enhanced by MFA methods. These biometrics or inherence factors are combined with MFA, such as using an access card, key fob, or hardware token. Card readers identify users by reading chipped cards that contain authentication certificates. Electronic keyless locks will open only for an authorized combination comprising complex passwords or codes containing a mix of alphanumeric characters or specific gestures or patterns. Each method employed results in network hardening. *Figure 20.8* illustrates the many means of implementing biometrics as a security technique:

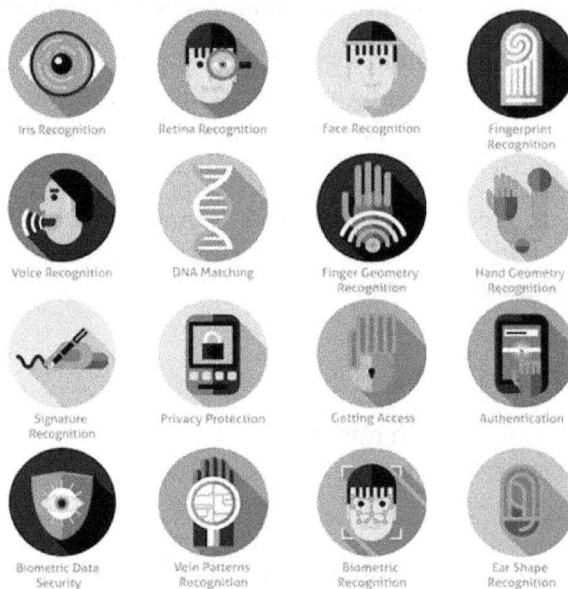

Figure 20.8: Biometrics
Source: @www.freepik.com

In some cases, when using codes, personal security questions may be used alongside time limitations for authentication codes to be input correctly by the user.

Locking racks

There are many ways to secure equipment: smart lockers, cases, cages, locked chassis, secure cabinets, secure brackets or drawers, or locked rack mount systems. *Figure 20.9* illustrates three diverse rack mount systems and displays some examples of how these systems are locked:

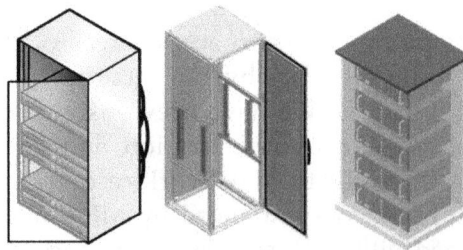

Figure 20.9: Rack mount systems
Source: www.clipartmax.com

Security zones

An organization can divide the building and network into different security zones. Several varied layers of security can exist in these identified zones. An example of a security zone could be the location of the network servers and the backbone switch(es) and router(s). These network devices may be located in a comms or server room, in a designated locked area, or in the case of a data center, in a numbered colocation (colo) center. Many data centers have multiple racks of servers and equipment owned by different organizations, thus the term *colocation*. This means that the racks might be separated and protected by cages so that technicians or administrators of a company are restricted to *only* overseeing their specific company's devices. Data centers will have tailored approaches to this activity and access from external individuals to the company. This mutual arrangement will form part of the agreement between the data center provider and the client.

The purpose of these security zones is to demark boundaries and identify areas that employees have access rights to enter (or not), depending on their roles, contracts, and privileges. At times, access is tied to a person's competencies and certifications. For example, IT employees may be the only people permitted in the IT zone, server room, or comms room. These users will enter the zone with RFID badges, show safety clearances, use biometrics, or meet other forms of authentication and authorization to travel internally in a security zone or move between them.

To summarize, a corporate network can have multiple security zones with security layers in each zone. Aside from the comms room example, other examples of security zones consist of the CEO's office, the Accounting and HR department, or a **demilitarized zone** (**DMZ**) such as the company's private intranet.

Employee training

The importance of employee training cannot be underestimated. Evidence has shown that a high degree of security breaches and incidents occur through human error or with individuals inadvertently enabling a security breach to take place. Usually, this happens because the employee(s) is not cybersecurity aware and lacks training in these matters. The only way to mitigate human error and accidents is by having properly trained staff who are empowered with knowledge of the ways and means by which attacks take place. Employees with IT awareness save a company money in the long term.

The risk of an employee falling victim to a phishing attack by clicking on a link is quite high. Employees are still duped and deceived by a charismatic or convincing social engineer. The area of privacy and compliance has become increasingly important with a hybrid workforce and an expansion of cloud-based activity and network operations. Many cybersecurity companies provide organizations with state-of-the-art, real-world training scenarios and packages where awareness training is key. Phishing simulation packages assess the employees' knowledge of the components of a phishing e-mail and demonstrate how to spot them without clicking the links or being hooked in by the attacker. Employees are also advised to report all phishing attempts to their IT department so the department can decide how to act. Some awareness programs use gamification to bring fun to learning and provide immersive cyber-gaming software to stimulate interest and support knowledge retention. However, irrespective of the strategies used by training providers, the primary objective of the training content is to build a security-aware culture in the organization, a culture that embeds best practices into its everyday business operations.

Other areas in which employees should be trained are in the proper use and storage of passwords and data, mindfulness of tailgating and awareness of how to identify employee authenticity, holding data backups and maintaining data integrity, and in paper shredding and other privacy and compliance techniques. Using these strategies mitigates data theft or corruption. Additionally, they prevent data from being leaked through a physical copy, as does disk shredding or disk incineration.

In *Figure 20.10*, we can see an example of formalized employee training. This training session consists of graphs and data and enables the trainer to quantify such things as security breaches per type of incident and threat.

Figure 20.10: Employee security awareness training
Source: Wei via Adobe Stock

Asset disposal

When devices or systems reach the end of their life, we need to ensure that they do not have any sensitive, confidential, or valuable data on them before disposing of them. The term associated with this activity is called **sanitization**. Organizations should have a template or checklist to ensure personnel follow the procedures for sanitization and proper disposal of obsolete or end-of-life devices.

We need to remember that when data is in use on the network, it has particular characteristics. Data on these devices might be *public* and, therefore, available to everyone. Data might be *confidential* and intended for a selective group of individuals. It might be *proprietary* and owned by a person, group, or company. Otherwise, it might be *private* information about individuals or groups of individuals and should not be disclosed to others. Data may also be of a *sensitive* nature. Ultimately, it may be comprised of more than one of these particular attributes. Even though the data type will differ, the company policy will stipulate the procedures for data destruction and media sanitization.

Sanitize devices for disposal

Disposal activities should be completed by a qualified, licensed destruction service. We must be aware that the deletion of files and formatting of hard drives are not permanent data disposal solutions. Employees should be informed that there are multiple methods for retrieving and recovering lost or deleted files from a hard drive, even after the drive has been formatted.

Organizations should always aim for absolute compliance with data protection laws and additionally, meet safety standards for proper disposal of assets. Sanitization and disposal processes should be time-managed, documented, and time-stamped. The following are some methods of data disposal:

- **Magnetic data storage:**
  - **Degaussing** uses a powerful magnetic force to wipe the data completely from the drive and render the disk useless. This process usually destroys the motors that drive the platters, so the drive cannot be re-used. Ultimately, degaussing causes irreversible damage to the HDD.

  - **Disk-wiping tools** involve writing different patterns of 1s and 0s multiple times until the disk is unreadable. It uses a bit-level overwrite procedure to do this.

  - **Crushing** involves punching a hole into the hard drive with great force. This hole shatters and destroys the platters, making them unusable. Crushing is a cost-effective and reliable means of destroying data. Companies who provide this service offer a chain of custody documentation, a report of serial numbers, asset ID or username, and in some cases, video proof of the disk-crushing process itself.

  - **Shredding** involves slicing the drive into minute pieces. Most companies providing this service offer on-site or off-site destruction with legally compliant certificates of destruction distributed on completion.

- **Solid-state drives (SSDs)**: They require a special process for sanitization. Since they use flash memory instead of magnetic storage platters, standard drive wiping tools are ineffective. Some organizations require their personnel to *physically destroy* SSDs as the only acceptable method of sanitization.

- **Incineration:** It is most effective for paper disposal. Burning completely destroys a hard drive. Pulverizing (for example, with a sledgehammer) might be used for the destruction of optical media.

Factory reset/wipe configuration

There are many examples available of resetting end devices or network intermediary devices back to factory defaults. Smartphones, PCs, laptops, switches, routers, and other network hardware all hold this capacity. A factory reset can be implemented on practically all devices with firmware, ICs, or ROM chips. Operating systems can also be reverted to their factory images as a reset option. *Figure 20.11* illustrates a factory reset option on a Microsoft Windows 10/11 operating system:

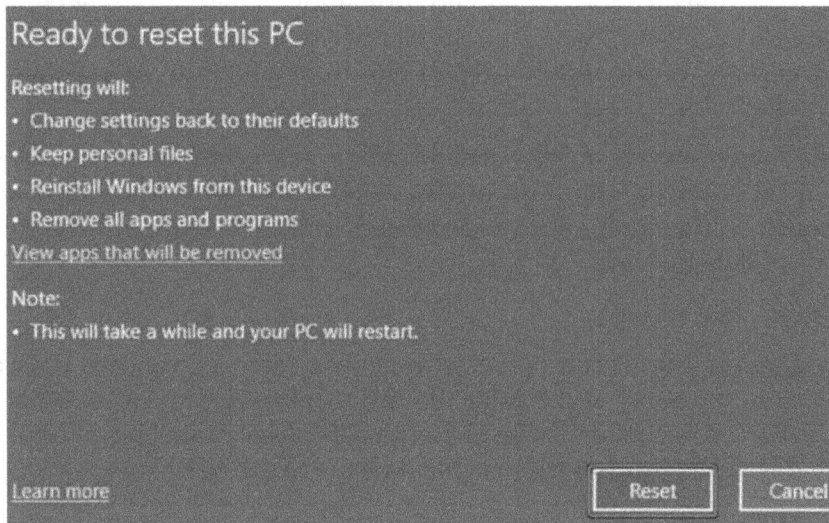

Figure 20.11: Resetting process of the system to factory settings

A user may opt to keep their personal files and remove all apps and programs. After a couple of minutes, Windows will be reinstalled, as captured in *Figure 20.12*. This installation will be followed by a welcome message.

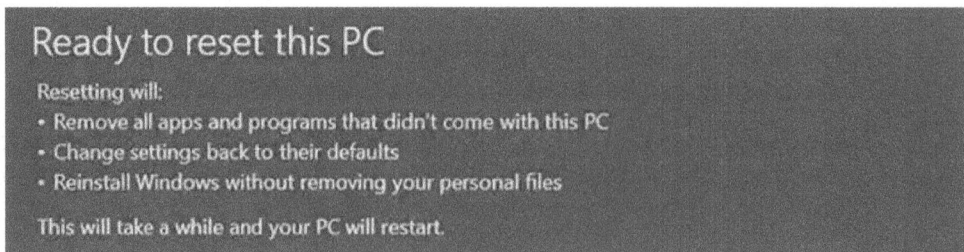

Figure 20.12: Installing Windows: reset option, Windows 10

Figure 20.13 shows the Windows 10 built-in hard drive wiper settings page:

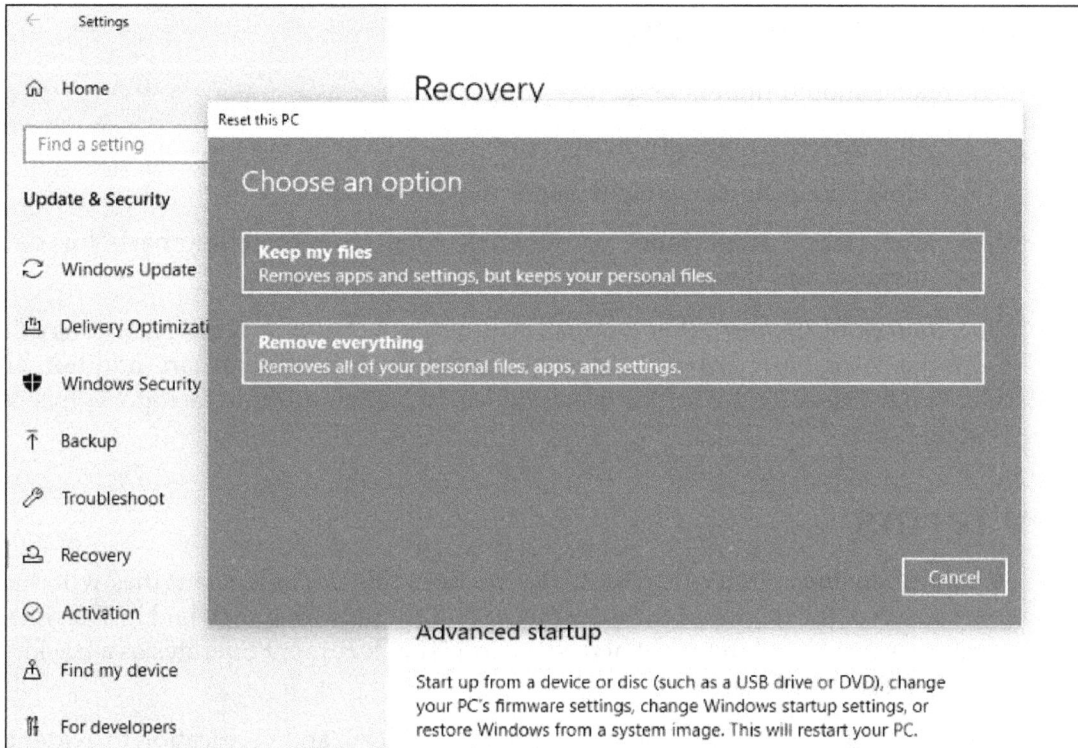

Figure 20.13: Windows 10 built-in hard drive wiper

As can be seen, Windows 10 comes preloaded with its own integrated hard drive eraser tool.

If a device has been lost or stolen, an administrator can perform a **remote wipe** on the device. In this case, the administrator sends a command that deletes data to a computing device or perhaps a work phone or iPad.

An owner of a phone can send a remote wipe signal to the phone to delete all the data on the phone. This action also deletes any cached data, such as cached online banking passwords or other sensitive data. Remote wipe capabilities provide a complete sanitization of the device by removing all valuable data.

Conclusion

In this chapter, we explored physical security controls and how they are applied to protect all the elements in a corporate network or organization. We also discussed asset sanitization, asset disposal techniques, and the options open to businesses.

In the upcoming chapter, we will examine CompTIA's troubleshooting methodology. We will also understand how this model is applied in real-world networking.

Points to remember

- The reader should understand:

  - How to implement physical security controls in an organization.

  - How data is destroyed at the end of its life cycle.

  - The critical importance of adhering to a structured approach for data disposal and destruction.

- The content of *Chapter 20* is mapped to *Domain 4, Network Security*. Explain the importance of basic network security concepts. The contents are additionally mapped to *Domain 2, Network Implementation*. Explain important factors of physical installations.

Key terms

- **Chain of custody**: In terms of data destruction, this document outlines who had possession of the device(s) to be destroyed and for how long they had it. The detail continues right until the point of destruction. The document operates as a tracking and auditing mechanism.

- **Certificate of destruction**: This is the official certificate and verification to evidence the destruction of the device.

- **Low-level format (LLF)**: An LLF erases your hard disk and writes new sectors and tracks to the drive. This type of format is normally done by the manufacturer when the device is first built and newly assembled.

- **High-level format (HLF)**: An HLF uses integrated tools into the operating system. This method of formatting removes the pointers to files. However, the data remains resident on the drive and can be recovered with the correct recovery tools and software. If new data is written to the hard drive from the point of loss/accidental deletion, the old data will be ultimately overwritten.

Questions

1. Describe what is meant by physical security.
2. Give some examples of how an organization can deter intruders.
3. Give some examples of how an organization can prevent security incidents from occurring.
4. List the ways data can be sanitized or disposed of.

CHAPTER 21

Network Troubleshooting

Introduction

One of the main tasks of a network administrator is to troubleshoot and solve problems on the network. In networking environments, problems and issues happen with hardware, software, network operations, and everyday business processes and procedures. Problems can impact every aspect of the corporate network. An administrator demonstrating proficiency must manage and find the correct solutions for expected issues and confront the challenge of the unexpected. To carry out these troubleshooting tasks successfully, the skillset of problem-solving includes logical, innovative, and creative critical thinking. In short, a network administrator must be sharp, intuitive, and highly attentive to detail.

As a certifying body, CompTIA encourages individuals pursuing a career in technology to hold a strong set of problem-solving skills and competencies. Their course objectives include a troubleshooting methodology and framework to enable learners to frame their skills to interpret problems and apply logic to any problem with strategic thinking, flexible mindsets, logical analysis, and planned actions. The model they support is the focus of this chapter.

Structure

In this chapter, we will cover the following topics:

- The stages of troubleshooting
- Working through the stages of troubleshooting

Objectives

In this chapter, we will learn the network troubleshooting model. After reading this chapter, you will be able to understand the stages of troubleshooting and appreciate the best troubleshooting practices. You will be able to apply the techniques and strategies that underpin optimum troubleshooting steps and understand the broad skillset problem-solving skills are comprised of. When applied appropriately, troubleshooting is easier, even when confronted with more complex challenges. Following this model and methodology will equip you with the cognitive awareness required for a job role in administering networks.

Stages of troubleshooting

The stages of the CompTIA (Network) troubleshooting model are as follows:

1. Identify the problem
2. Establish a theory of probable cause
3. Test the theory
4. Establish a plan of action
5. Implement the solution
6. Verify full system functionality
7. Document findings, actions, and outcomes

Each stage and step requires the technician to apply specific skills to achieve the results of that particular step. In *Figure 21.1*, the steps of the CompTIA (Network) troubleshooting model are outlined:

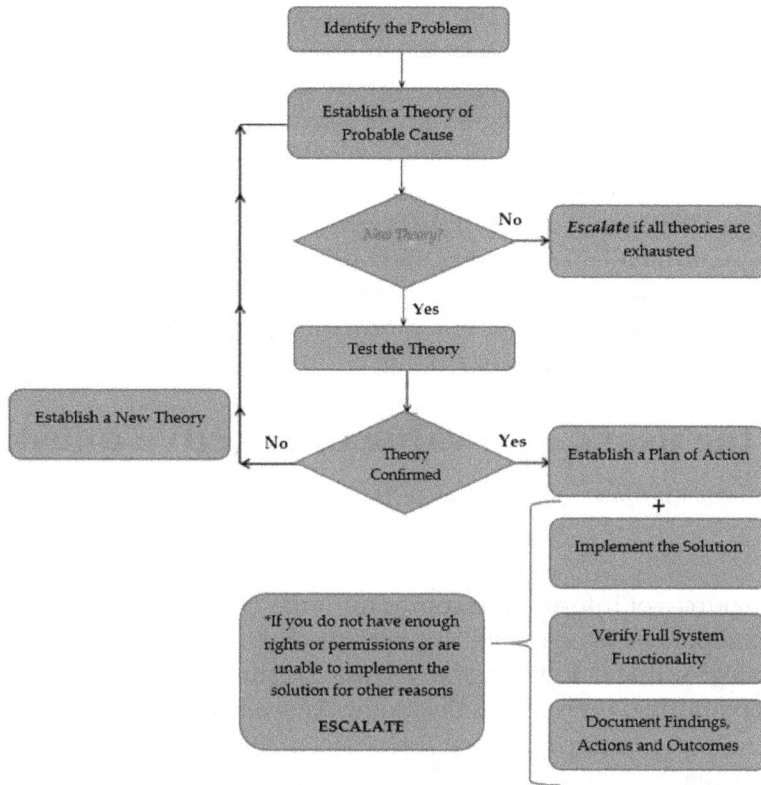

Figure 21.1: *The network troubleshooting model*

First step

Identify the problem

This aspect of problem-solving breaks down into specific factors, which are as follows:

- Gather information about the problem.
- Question the users.
- Identify the symptoms of the problem(s).
- Determine if anything has changed recently (in hardware, software, or application).
- Duplicate (replicate) the problem, where possible.
- Approach multiple problems individually as discrete and separate issues.

Gather information about the problem

Most network administrators will have a *structured* means of accessing user reports of problems on the network. The organization might be using a ticketing system for capturing

IT problems and issues. If this is the case, the generated ticket (software) should encourage and prompt the user to describe the problem clearly and evidence it with screenshots, images, error messages, error codes, or system log entries. The operating system or applications' in-built troubleshooting tools are also an effective means of capturing what is happening or what is *not going as it should be* with the component or software giving trouble. An administrator might run diagnostic tools, consult the BIOS/event viewer, or view system logs. These tools can help determine where the issue is occurring. In terms of reporting issues, in smaller companies, network users might email the IT technician or network administrator to outline the issues they are having. Whatever the system in use is for reporting and logging IT issues, the information gathered is key to this first step and stage to move us further into troubleshooting.

Question the users: The value of effective questioning

You can increase your problem-solving skills by honing your question-asking ability.

— American author: Michael J. Gelb

One of the best sources of information comes from the users themselves because they use the hardware component or software application that is giving them trouble. Effective questioning strategies, that is, knowing how to ask questions and which questions to ask, in other words, good timing, is critical at this point. Answers to meaningful questions posed are invaluable sources of support when a technician is discovering the main symptoms and indicators of the problem at hand. Gathering information effectively requires active and engaged listening skills.

Closed-ended questions

Closed-ended questions have simple, straightforward answers. A few examples of closed-ended questions are as follows:

- When did the problem first begin?
- How often has the problem been happening?
- Has this problem happened before?

The answer to the question, *When did the problem first begin?* enables the user to answer with a specific time/date/period of time. It allows the technician to gather facts. The answer could be *yesterday, last week, this morning when I switched on the power,* and so on. The main point is that the answer is pinned down to a specific time period, which assists the technician/administrator with gathering data and factual information.

Questions such as *How often does this happen?* or *How often has the problem been happening?* let the administrator know the *frequency* of the problem and how often the problem is reoccurring.

Has this problem happened before? gives us a similar result.

What did the error message say? ties us into the specifics of the problem.

Remember, our initial purpose here is to identify the symptoms of the problem. Symptoms are something we see or witness. They are observations and features that point to underlying causes or root issues of problems. As problem-solvers, we form and make our decisions based on the symptoms observed and identified.

Closed-ended questions limit or curtail the responses a user can give. When used wisely, they furnish us with the facts, frequency, and timescale of the problem to be solved.

Open-ended questions

Open-ended questions do not limit or curtail the responses a user can give. They encourage the user to say more and add to their descriptions. The user can give us more detailed, in-depth insights into the issue, and this freedom of expression enables us to gather more information and decipher more comprehensive, valuable data.

Questioning should always be courteous and calm and never accusatory in tone. Our purpose is to glean information and not to provoke or cause anxiety or self-blame in the user. A professional will remember that not all users are IT-aware or advanced in technical terms. Consequently, an IT professional should not use technical jargon or try to impress the user with their *superior* knowledge. A professional will always speak at the appropriate level and aim to match the user's technical understanding and IT capacity. Additionally, every repair opportunity is an opportunity to educate the user to use technology better. So, a technician will also try to foster best practices with friendly discretion and incorporate advice conversationally.

Some examples of open-ended questions are as follows:

- What were you doing when the problem first began?
- Do you know if other users are having this problem?
- Has anything changed recently?

These questions help us to determine if anything has changed recently (in hardware, software, or use of the device/app). Note that we are building the case on as many facts as possible. Plus, we are estimating the extent of the problem and the scale of impact on network users.

Replicating the problem, where possible, is an excellent way of seeing the problem as it occurs in real time. If there is any way to visualize and reproduce the problem, then take the opportunity to do so. This is important as we need to verify the problem exists and be provided with a starting point for troubleshooting. Regarding observation, the user may have a particular way of navigating a piece of software. It is important to view the way they are using the hardware or software because the problem can be tied very closely to a particular detail in their individual means of execution or use. Furthermore, this form of duplication permits us to take screenshots and gather other forms of evidence that support us in formulating theories.

When we establish a theory of probable cause, we need some degree of evidence or even healthy *guesstimation* or approximation. Never be afraid to think outside the box.

If there are multiple problems, approach them separately/individually. We need to differentiate between problems that are related and problems that are unrelated. Take one problem at a time and handle it as a discrete unit. If the user reported multiple problems, let them know that problems are being handled separately and are being tackled in order of priority and severity. Sometimes, a user may request a check on a different issue altogether.

The best practice is to hold integrity to the policies and procedures of the IT department. If a separate issue is preventing the user from doing their job, it would automatically be ticketed as urgent and needing a fast repair. It is human nature for a person to want everything to be fixed at once, but this approach may be to the detriment of best practices and not be aligned with IT policy. Remain integral to the ticketing system.

In short, the information gathered shows signs and indicators that point the administrator in the right direction to solve the underlying issue and find the fundamental source of contention.

Second step

Establish a theory of probable cause

When establishing theories, ensure they are of *probable* cause. Probable means that the theory is likely to be the case and, therefore, must hold some perceivable value. To ensure probability:

- Do not overcomplicate by questioning the obvious.

- Consider multiple methodologies and means of approaching the problem.

- Use an OSI model *top-to-bottom or bottom-to-top approach*, that is, from layers 1–7/ layers 7–1.

- Break the problem down with a *divide-and-conquer* approach. This approach targets a specific layer of the OSI model and then moves in either direction through the relevant layers.

Our objective is to solve a puzzle and, metaphorically speaking, *find the missing piece*. Sometimes in life, we can overcomplicate problems and their solutions. The world of IT is, at times, a complex world. However, the network troubleshooting model incorporates the idea that sometimes, the problem is simple, and simple problems can get overlooked. The way to avoid this is to move from the simple to the more complex theories and avoid assuming that all problems, by their nature, are complex. This might be as straightforward as checking whether cables are secure, and the power is on. How often do we go to assist a person with a display issue, only to discover a loose VGI/HDMI cable is the culprit? How frequently do we locate a loose RJ45 cable or a damaged or broken network point?

Remember, always check for the simpler solution first. This approach can save time and money for clients and employers alike and can make life easier. That is why we ask ourselves what a simpler cause could be.

The OSI model can be used as a framework for problem-solving. Using the breakdown of the model, we can organize our thoughts and ideas by moving them to the bottom-up from layers 1 to 7 or by organizing them in a top-down approach, moving from layers 7 down to 1. By this approach, we analyze the problem or issue in terms of protocols, features, and characteristics that are mapped to a particular layer, moving in a layer-by-layer approach. By using this framework, we are implementing a methodical approach to troubleshooting.

Another tactic is to use the framework of OSI in a **divide-and-conquer** approach. Based on feelings about the *most likely* layer that applies to the problem, aim for the part of the OSI model that works for the case and then continue to work through the model to figure out where the problem is happening. In this strategy, it is acceptable to move up or down the model more freely in whatever direction seems best and in accordance with that initial intuitive feeling and target.

An example of this **divide-and-conquer** approach occurs when an administrator hears a problem that points to dropped packets or data continually being lost in transmission on the network. The administrator might decide to initially check the host PC's NIC with a **ping -t** command on the loopback address, and if nothing is wrong with the physical adapter and other tests prove the protocol stack is functioning, then perhaps remote in to check the behavior of routers on the network. (To verify that the network adapter is able to send and receive frames without errors, you may also use the command **netstat -e**.) In addition, while conceptualizing and collating data, they will be estimating the scope and coverage of the problem to establish more theories. The likelihood is that there will be multiple theories to be worked through with a problem such as this.

During the course of divide-and-conquer troubleshooting, if we can confirm that a layer is operational and performing well, we can more than likely assume that the layers below this layer are working as well. If a layer is not operational at all or it is working sporadically, intermittently, or erroneously, inspect the layer below it straight away, where applicable. If the layer below the current layer is functioning well and fully operational, the source of the problem is in the existing layer. If the layer below is also broken or malfunctioning, we should gather information and symptoms of the problem at that layer. Then, we will work our way through the relevant layers.

Figure 21.2 illustrates the divide-and-conquer troubleshooting approach:

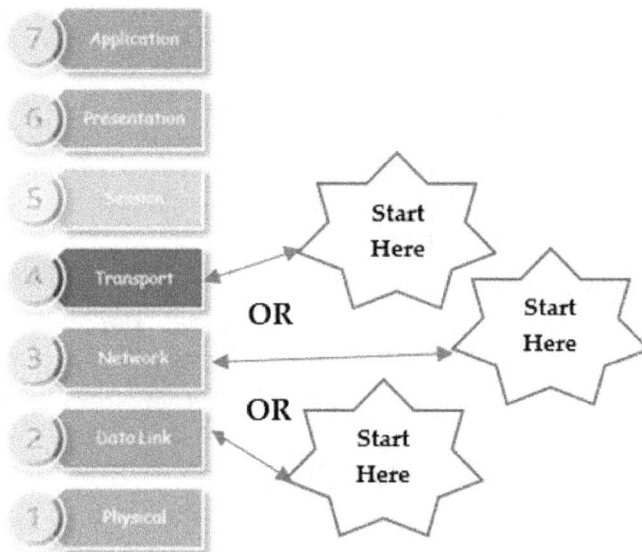

Figure 21.2: *The divide-and-conquer troubleshooting approach*

In this illustration, we see that the investigation did not begin at layer 1 or layer 7 but at a specific layer in the *middle or lower end* of the OSI model.

Third step

Test the theory

Testing a theory is the way we check to see if a theory is correct. Theories can be simple or more complex, depending on the nature of the problem and the area or users impacted.

As part of testing:

- Begin with the simplest theory first.
- If the theory is verified, we determine the next steps required to resolve the problem.
- If the theory is not verified, we re-establish a new theory, review our findings, and test the new theory.
- If we do not have enough rights or permissions or have exhausted all our theories, we **escalate** the problem to a higher level of knowledge/action/expertise.

Escalation is essentially a process of involving someone with more skills, certification, knowledge, privileges, or a higher rank to help remediate a problem. It occurs when:

- More expertise or authority is required to resolve the issue.

- The issue will take additional time and resources than what can be achieved in the time originally allocated.

- The issue is broader, more complicated, *or* is impacting more users than initially perceived, *or* if the problem is more widespread on the network.

Please note that before we escalate, we must document each test that has been attempted so other IT personnel can assess what has been tried already. We might have used testing tools or swapped out parts to try new configurations. Everything we do or use in carrying out the test(s) must be documented.

In *Figure 21.3*, the technician's movement is shown between *Steps 2, 3,* and *4*:

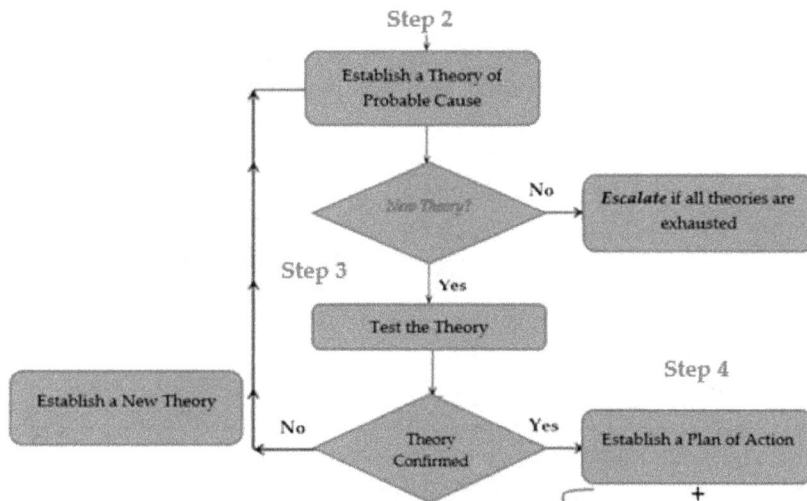

Figure 21.3: Testing the theory

Note: Escalation is a divide-and-conquer approach. The layer that is initially targeted by an administrator will be based on a combination of factors. For example, the specifics and quality of the data gathered, and the theories established will demonstrate and be underpinned by the skills and competencies of the network technician. Consequently, without judgment on abilities and skills, some problems will inevitably be outside the knowledge level or area of networking technology. Other problems may demand other or different expert knowledge.

Fourth step

Establish a plan of action

When we reach this step, we have pinpointed the problem and know how to fix it. However, before we go ahead and apply the fix, we should have a plan of action.

We should also identify the *potential effects* of a repair strategy. For example, with added emphasis on the high availability of network resources, all plans will need to be cognizant of timing and the potential downtime for users. High availability concepts must be respected while repair plans are designed and put into place. The objective here is to reduce or minimize the impact of the solution on users of the network or minimize disruption for clients or customers.

Making a plan can be as simple as a few steps taken over an hour or a number of hours to a complex plan spread over several days. Having a plan of action helps the resolution of the problem run smoother and enables the administrator to identify who needs to be notified about the repair and when.

Having a solid plan helps increase efficiency, builds personal confidence and competence, avoids the urge to steamroll ahead with partially thought-out repairs, and supports a solution-focused goal set in IT outcomes. The solutions we choose will either be to replace, repair, or document and workaround (that is, leave very much alone). Sometimes, the problem can be of very low severity, and working around the issue is better than a costly or unnecessary fix. As network administrators, we must be mindful of **service level agreements** (**SLAs**), licensing, and warranties. At times, we may need to consult or collaborate with other technicians, vendors, or third-party providers. It is essential to know your stakeholders.

Fifth step

Implement the solution

This is the step where we follow and execute the plan. The main tip is to avoid taking shortcuts as they may *come back to bite you* further on in the repair process. The plan is written to be followed comprehensively. Check each step and verify what changes have been made and the impact of each change on the component, system, or device.

The best practice is to have a baseline configuration for the component or system. For example, if we make configuration changes, they should match the organization's policies and agreed-upon network environment. If we discover an inconsistency with policies or non-compliance (for example, installation of unauthorized or personal software), we should revert the system to the company's baseline and log how this could have occurred on the system since this activity also breaches our AUP and other security-related policies.

Sixth step

Verify full system functionality

At this stage, the reported problem should be fixed. On top of this, the entire system should be fully functioning. Never walk away and assume a fix. Always verify and validate. Check that *everything* works. If we do not do this systematically, another ticket will be generated, or new problems will stem from the initial repair. Observe the user carry out the impacted task, where possible, or demonstrate to the user what was done and how the repair has recovered functionality. Whenever possible, *educate the user* if this is mutually beneficial and if their permissions allow them to sort out an issue should it reoccur. This action encourages self-sufficiency with users on the network and inspires confidence and respect for the IT support team. Education in security matters is especially important, and users should be alerted to their behaviors, habits, and methods if a risk or threat has been observed. Get the user/client's agreement that the problem is resolved. Once the user's acceptance is gained and the agreement confirmed, we can close the ticket or state the job as completed. If it is *not* advised to educate the user directly or engage with users, in case they perceive this dialogue as confrontational, this education can be fed into employee training under other catered-for conditions.

After we verify the full system functionality, we can proceed to implement preventive measures. Being proactive and reducing problems is our primary objective here.

If we identify a preventive measure, we should note it down. This measure can be within our direct control or might need a conversation with a colleague, employer, or provider. We should never bypass an opportunity to be proactive and put preventive measures in place. Always aim to eliminate any factors that caused the problem to occur.

Restate the problem. Get agreement on the repair. Confirm the fix. And only then, walk away.

Seventh step

Document findings, actions, and outcomes

In the final step of the network troubleshooting model, we document. Documents are future treasures when similar or even new problems occur. When a technician or network administrator documents their repairs and methodologies well, the pathway is carved for simpler and future navigation through network issues.

We document our findings and what we gleaned from the research and repair stages. Actions and tasks are duly noted and itemized. If there needs to be a fuller description of a more complex action, then it is best practice to include this description. This focus will save time, energy, and potentially money in future troubleshooting activities.

Our documentation should include all lessons learned throughout the troubleshooting process. They should be written clearly and succinctly and offer the reader precise knowledge and facts about the problem, its (suspected) root cause, and the actions involved in resolving the issue. Remember, other people will have to be able to read and interpret what you found and the actions you took to handle the problem. So be aware!

Working through the stages of troubleshooting

Troubleshooting involves the mastery of a skill. It is a skill that we build and perfect with experience and over time. Every time we meet and solve a problem, we enhance and augment our troubleshooting skills, especially when adhering to a framework that is proven and tested. The framework is the scaffolding that holds and molds our skills so that our successes will grow and evolve when we use the framework and model optimally. Ultimately, when using the network troubleshooting model, we learn how and when to combine steps or select steps to reach a solution quickly (as with the divide and conquer approach). The network troubleshooting process is a guideline that is adaptable and flexible to fit our organization's needs. Even when companies have a more customized or tailored approach to troubleshooting, the steps we have outlined will be spotted within the optimum custom build.

Working through the stages of troubleshooting might initially be a slow process, but once the mind is trained in problem-solving strategies, the pace of application becomes faster and more acute. With time and practice, the mastery of the task will come.

Conclusion

In this chapter, we examined CompTIA's network troubleshooting methodology. We discovered how this model is applied in real-world networking and used in ticketing systems.

In the upcoming chapter, we will learn how to troubleshoot common cable connectivity issues and select the appropriate tools to do so.

Points to remember

- In this chapter, we learned:
    - How to implement the stages and steps of troubleshooting
    - The best troubleshooting practices
    - How troubleshooting is made easier, even with complicated challenges
    - The cognitive awareness required for a job role that involves troubleshooting networks.

- The content of *Chapter 21, Network Troubleshooting*, is mapped to *Domain 5, Network Troubleshooting*. Explain the troubleshooting methodology.

Key terms

- **Service level agreement**: An SLA is a contract that outlines the service being given by a service provider that has been agreed upon by a client. The nature and scope of the service are defined as well as the type and quality of service agreed to.

- **System log**: A system log captures the details of events occurring on a device or system. Logs typically document the functionality and processes of the system as they happen in real time.

- **Event Viewer**: This tool is integrated into the Microsoft Windows operating system. Based on specific criteria, for example, applications, security, and systems, it captures information, errors, or warnings about events as they are running in the system.

- **Ticketing system**: A ticketing system is a piece of software package that enables the listing of errors or generated tickets. The software allows for the management and maintenance of problems and issues in a way that prioritizes severity and allocates a time scale suited to their handling/repair.

Questions

1. List the steps of the network troubleshooting model.
2. Give some examples of open and closed-ended questions.
3. Give some examples of when it is appropriate to escalate a problem.
4. Describe some skills that are enhanced by adhering to a framework or model when troubleshooting networks.

Join our book's Discord space

Join the book's Discord Workspace for Latest updates, Offers, Tech happenings around the world, New Release and Sessions with the Authors:

https://discord.bpbonline.com

CHAPTER 22

Troubleshooting Cable Connectivity

Introduction

In *Chapter 3, Cables and Connectors*, we learned that understanding physical network cabling and maintaining compliance with current cabling standards and protocols is essential. We discovered that cabling is the foundational backbone of all networks, and we explored Ethernet, coax, and fiber cabling in terms of its structure and functionality, as well as its specifications and limitations. Additionally, we explored problems and issues inherent in Ethernet cabling, for example, the cable's susceptibility to electromagnetic interference, attenuation, and crosstalk. We noted this susceptibility occurs more so in **unshielded twisted pair** (**UTP**) as opposed to **shielded twisted pair** (**STP**), discussed the impact of this susceptibility, and covered some fixes and workarounds. Furthermore, we assessed the characteristics of coax and fiber cable, analyzing the cable type, function, advantages and disadvantages, and best use practices.

In this chapter, we will look further into troubleshooting cable connectivity and explore the types of tools used for diagnosing and repairing issues when working with different types of cables.

Structure

The chapter explains the following topics:

- Common cable connectivity issues
- Common network tools

Objectives

This chapter focuses on the common cable connectivity issues that are inherent in the cables themselves or produced by errors made by the technician at the time of installation of the cable or when replacing or swapping out cables.

After reading this chapter, you will be able to appreciate how to troubleshoot cable connectivity issues and follow the best troubleshooting practices. You will be able to identify and use the appropriate network tools to diagnose and repair problems with diverse network cable types. This chapter will enable you to enhance your skills while handling cables in Ethernet and fiber networks.

Common cable connectivity issues

Some of the more common physical layer (OSI layer 1) problems include the following:

- A device is not receiving power (either turned off or unplugged)
- Loose network cable connection(s)
- Use of incorrect cable type at installation/replacement
- A faulty network cable
- Wiring issues
- Attenuation
- Interference
- **Decibel (dB)** loss
- Duplexing issues
- Incorrect pinout
- Bad ports
- Open/short
- **Light-emitting diode (LED)** status indicators displaying errors
- Incorrect transceivers
- Transmit and receive (TX/RX) reversed
- Dirty fiber optical cables

Both hardware and software troubleshooting tools may be used to monitor the network infrastructure, including performance issues generated by cabling. However, most of these issues will need to be fixed with a networking hardware tool.

In preliminary tests, a network administrator or technician will ensure that there are no errors showing on any LEDs that display the connectivity status. If the administrator is on-site, they can visually inspect all (suspect) network cabling and reconnect cables to ensure a proper connection. If using wireless, they can verify that the device is operational, and its settings are configured correctly.

Link status troubleshooting

After verifying physical connectivity and confirming secure connections, observing the status of LEDs can support and advance troubleshooting strategies. Network Interface Cards and network devices use various light combinations to indicate the status and activity on the network. These light combinations (via LEDs) are visual clues to the administrator for diagnosing and troubleshooting cable connectivity and gauging the functionality and performance of devices. Network devices have unique built-in light combinations at production, and therefore, their meanings vary in accordance with the make, model, and structure of the device, and also how the manufacturer has used these visual aids to support status interpretation and diagnostics. These light combinations and their meanings are to be found in the device manual or may be located on the manufacturer's website. The number of LEDs on the device and their functionality depends on the device.

Typical status lights are Unlit, Red/Amber, Solid Green (Flashing), Solid Green, and Flashing (Lit) constantly. These lights can relate to the link itself, activity on the link, and point to the presence or absence of collisions with the link or associated device.

Basic common indicators: In terms of a network card, if the LEDs are on, then your system is picking up your network, and a connection is in place. If the LEDs are off, then the NIC is not detecting the network, and no connection is set. This means that there is a connection issue. If the LEDs are flashing, then the NIC is communicating on the network.

Figure 22.1 shows a technician viewing the device and cable configuration. Note how he is visually observing the layout and placement of components and parts:

Figure 22.1: *Analyzing a network*
Source: *Senivpetro on Freepik*

There is a lot to be said about visual observation. Using our sense of sight, we can see cables that are not connected, identify cables connected to the wrong port or ports, note potentially damaged cables and/or connectors, locate loose connections, look at the standard of cable (usually printed on the jacket), and in general, view the state and condition or age of the device and cable. Visual testing is a valuable asset to the person resolving the problem. Never underestimate the usefulness of LEDs in troubleshooting scenarios. Do not just take a quick glance at them; really *look* and then interpret what you see.

Note: Using our senses, such as sight, smell, hearing, taste, and touch can support us in the troubleshooting process. Mechanical problems, electrical issues, power, overheating and even burning in insulation or dust particles in fans can be detected by our sensory perceptions.

Meeting cabling standards

Organizations starting out should always aim for a standards-based cabling structure. This approach will minimize a lot of potential hassle and cost further along in business operations, especially as the network grows. It is not *out of the ordinary* to see a company's network with the look and feel of a *patchwork quilt* of technology due to the way the network has developed, and newer cables and devices added to the existing infrastructure. It has been the gritty task of many, such as a systems administrator or network engineer, to *level out* and update older technologies so that the network is kept current and consistent. Some of this is unavoidable. However, for this and other reasons, following proper standards and procedures at the time of cable installation is critical. Our mindset and focus should be on network growth as we maximize our options on cable and equipment. We should comply with current standards while allowing for future growth and scalability of the network. The **International Electrotechnical Commission (IEC)**, the **International Organization of Standards (ISO)**, and the **Telecommunications Industry Association (TIA)** are some of the certifiers that create standards for electrical, electronic, and other related technologies. Regarding fiber optics, compliance must be checked with IEEE, TIA/EI, and ISO/IEC standards. Companies can invest in cable *certifiers* for both LAN and fiber networks, but these certifiers are expensive and possibly unaffordable for SOHO or **small to medium enterprises (SMEs)**. The value of these tools is that they sometimes combine cable certification with network analysis, enabling more effective network management procedures.

In *Figure 22.2*, we see a rack system in a data center environment. Without a doubt, a data center will need tight reins on cabling, labeling, and tracking all its resources. The logistics of cables and their location in the *colocation* are strictly monitored and tracked. All functionality and performance issues must be logged and noted with diligence. The following figure shows two employees checking out rack-mounted devices, possibly with the option of decommissioning:

Figure 22.2: *Checking rack devices*

Note: Cable testers simply tell you if the cable will function. Cable certifiers run much more complex and sophisticated tests that determine if the cable performs according to the specifications called for in the standard of the cable used.

Basic cable tests

Let us look at a few basic tests we can do when installing or replacing the cable. Above all else, remember to use the network troubleshooting model and always move from the simple checks to the more complex ones. Look at the following tests:

- Ensure the cable meets appropriate wiring standards, distance limitations, and other relevant specifications on installation. (Non-compliance with standards could be a factor in problems arising with the cable connectivity at a later stage, post-installation.) In short, be sure to use the correct type of cable.

- Check UTP cables (straight-through or crossover). Using the wrong type of cable may prevent connectivity.

- Improper cable termination is one of the main problems encountered in networks. Terminate using the T568A or the T568B standard. Avoid untwisting too many of the wire pairs during termination. Crimp connectors on the cable jacket to support the cable and avoid too much strain and stress on the cable's weight.

- Use a cable tester to confirm that the network cable is properly functioning and that the pins are aligned.

- Confirm that the network cable is securely plugged into the workstation/RJ45 or another relevant device.

- Verify the connection to the wall jack and check the LED status indicators on the network switch. The access switch will have the corresponding patch panels for each end device connected. Ensure to check the patch cables on the switch to test if they are secured and check the status lights of the associated port(s).

- Check the link activity light on the network adapter *and* the network switch.

- Verify that all network intermediary devices are powered on and are fully functional.
- Check maximum cable run lengths.
- Verify that the correct port is used between devices.
- Protect cables and connectors from physical damage. Run cable neatly and follow proper cable management procedures.
- Use labeling/tags to identify links. Be sure to maintain consistency with labeling practices.

Cable management

Let us look at some methods for cable management best practices, given as follows:

- Orient the cables so that they feed into the device/rack system without stress or strain.
- Organize the cables with cable ties.
- Use identification cable ties or labels to identify wires/links.
- Optimize cable management with suitable cable management tray systems (vertical or horizontal), rails, baskets, cable clamps, and Velcro or plastic organizers. These items provide an effective means of bundling and grouping cables together.
- Use trunking on walls and fabric cord covers to protect cables under flooring.
- In the event that there are unsightly wires or longer lengths of cable, organize them in loops with Velcro or disguise them in areas alongside equipment (without disrupting airflow or power cooling). Be careful not to exceed the bend radius for specific cable types when grouping or organizing cables together.
- In data centers or telecommunications closets, use a standardized labeling system, for example, the TIA-606B/C labeling system.
- Utilize **Move/Add/Change** (**MAC**) documents wherever applicable, or alternatively, use an Excel spreadsheet. Each organization or company will have its own management system, database, or recommended standards for labeling in place.

In short, tidiness and neatness, systematic labeling, and easy-to-understand documentation are the keys to cable management best practices.

Cable faults

Testing a network cable is called **verification**. This is where the actual cable is checked for errors. When using a cable tester, wiring errors can sometimes be discovered in the cable. The following are some examples of these faults or errors:

- **Open pair**: When one or more of the conductors in the twisted pair are not connected to a pin at one or the other end, this is referred to as an open pair. Effectively, the electrical continuity of the conductor has been stopped. This can happen when a conductor is physically broken or damaged. It also occurs if a user incorrectly uses a punch-down tool and incompletely connects a cable to an IDC connector.

- **Shorted pair**: When the conductors of a twisted wire pair are connected together at any point in the cable, we refer to this as a shorted pair. This connection is usually an unintentional error by the user.

- **Short between pairs**: This happens when the conductors of two wires in different pairs are connected together at any point in the cable.

- **Reversed pair**: This happens when the two wires in a single twisted pair are misaligned to the opposite pins of the pair at the other end of the cable.

- **Crossed pair**: This happens when the two conductors of a one-color pair are connected to the pin positions of a different color pair at the opposite end.

- **Split pairs**: Split pairs occur when the wire from one pair is split away from the other and cross over a wire in an adjacent pair. Since this type of fault requires that the same mistake be made at both ends of the connection, the accidental occurrence of split pairs is relatively rare.

These cable faults are discovered using wire mapping techniques.

Note: Categories of cable above CAT3 need additional testing. Wire mapping techniques are simple tests and, on their own, are only required for voice grade UTP and consequently in locations where Plain Old Telephone Systems (POTS) is in place. Categories of cabling above CAT3 (typically in structured cabling scenarios) will be verified and tested with other tests and potentially via more complex certification tools than a basic wire map.

Figure 22.3 illustrates the following cable faults: short or open and reversed pair in a T568B standard wiring scenario:

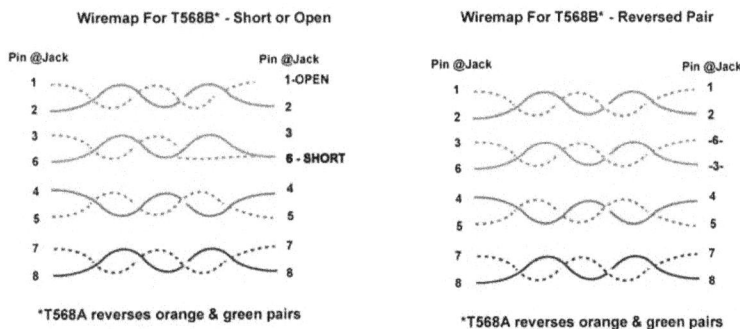

Figure 22.3: *Short or open, reversed pair cable faults*
Source: *The Fiber Optic Association (FOA)*

Figure 22.4 illustrates the following cable faults: crossed pairs and split pairs in a T568B standard wiring scenario:

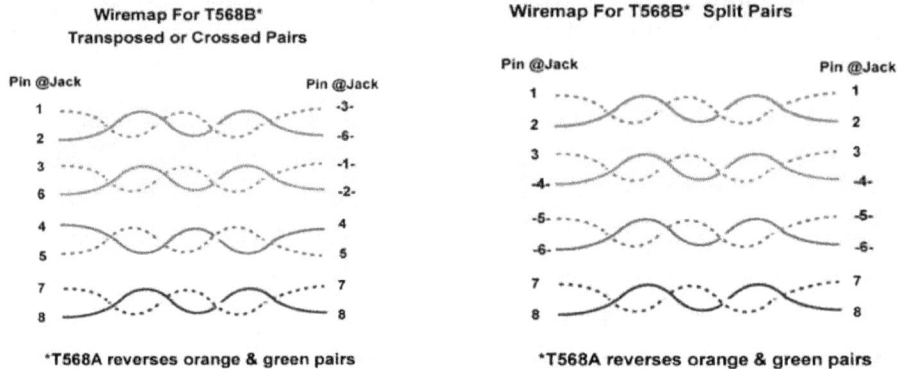

Figure 22.4: *Crossed pairs, split pairs, and cable faults*
Source: *The Fiber Optic Association (FOA)*

Qualification of a cable is an active measurement of the possible speed of transmission of a cable. **Certification** is a test to ensure the cable complies with standards and protocols.

Common network tools

Identifying a problem on a network and resolving it is a huge and rewarding part of network administration. Like any system that is built, issues may arise, and difficulties may take place frequently and as part of daily routines. Creating and maintaining a wired Ethernet or fiber (physical) network requires cables, components, devices, and the technical know-how to monitor and maintain things as they operate and perform. Inevitably, the network infrastructure at the physical and other levels requires hardware *and* software tools to ensure that it runs smoothly. Moreover, even at the core of wireless connectivity, we find hardware and *physical* things that are connected and linked and need ongoing monitoring and handling. For now, we will focus on the hardware tools.

Let us now go over some standard network hardware tools.

Cable crimper

This multi-function crimping tool is hand-powered. It permits the user to crimp, strip, and cut the cable. The tool illustrated in *Figure 22.5* supports RJ45 CAT5E, CAT6, and RJ 11/12 connectors. It has a built-in wire stripper and wire cutter. Blades are replaceable on this and most other similar products.

Essentially, a crimper is used to fix a jack to a patch cord. This tool (or similar) is also used for making *regular runs* of cable and/or replacing broken connectors. Advice and instructions on how to make cables are covered in *Chapter 3, Cables and Connectors*.

RJ11/12 Crimp Cavity
RJ45 Ethernet Crimp

Round Cable Stripper

Flat Cable Stripper

Cable Cutter

Rachet Machanism
With Quick Release

RJ45 CRLMP TOOL

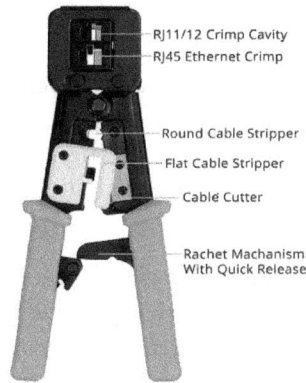

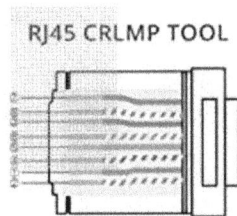

Figure 22.5: *Cable crimper*

Punch down tool

A punch down tool is a hand tool. It is typically used to terminate the Ethernet cables and connect them to a patch panel or to punch down blocks.

- **Method**: The user inserts the cable wires into the **Insulation Displacement Connectors** (**IDC**) using *impact action*, thus the term *punch down*.

  These IDCs are on the punch-down blocks, patch panels, surface mount blocks, or keystone modules.

- **Best practice**: Users should ensure to position the cables in the color-coded terminals in the IDC and check that they are in the appropriate termination order, that is, T568A or T568B. No more than 13 mm of cable should be untwisted to minimize interference. Users should check that the wires are securely connected to the terminal.

Refer to *Figure 22.6*:

Figure 22.6: *Punch down tool*

Tone generator

A tone generator enables the user to find and track cables, use tone and probe, or trace wires within a bundle or a group of cables. The probe detects the signal and follows the cable through conduits, ducts, or through a ceiling to locate its origins. These tasks and traces should be carried out without the user causing damage to the insulation or to the implementation of cabling.

Best practice: Users can locate cables or wires and track them to pinpoint the breakpoint. They can identify the other end of a cable by using the tracker, especially if the cables are in conduits or in large bunches. The tone generator will produce a tone as the user nears the wire at the end of the cable.

Refer to *Figure 22.7*:

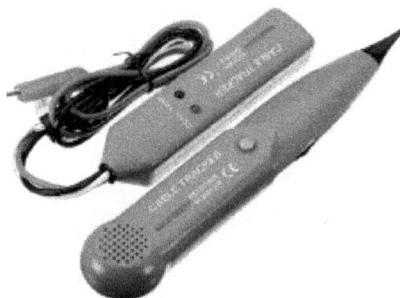

Figure 22.7: *Tone generator*

Loopback adapter

A loopback adapter (Plug) is commonly used in network administration to test ports (and NICs) and check the port's ability to send and receive signals (thus the term loopback). These adapters save the user from carrying around an Ethernet hub or similar device to check the functionality of ports or network cards. Adapters are available for testing in Ethernet or fiber optic environments. The top two images are used for LC and SC fiber connectors in single-mode/multimode test applications.

Method: Typically, a solid link LED displays on detection of a functioning port.

Figure 22.8 shows an Ethernet CAT6 Gigabit RJ45 loopback adapter designed for simple use and transport on a keyring:

Figure 22.8: *Loopback adapter*

Optical Time-Domain Reflectometer

This tool uses a laser source in combination with a detector to see inside fiber links. The output of what is detected and viewed produces a visual real-time graph for analysis, diagnostics, and troubleshooting. When the user processes and analyzes the signal, they can calculate signal loss, reflection, the total length of the link, and attenuation. In essence, the **Optical Time-Domain Reflectometer (OTDR)** detects light loss in a single fiber. By injecting short laser pulses into the fiber core, users can measure the *backscatter level* at all points along the fiber link. A user can also discover the cable's estimated length and attenuation (loss in dB) and the location of faults.

Best practice: Dirty or contaminated fiber connectors are the biggest causes of signal loss. Proper cleaning and inspection of fiber connectors on installation/repair are critical.

Refer to *Figure 22.9*:

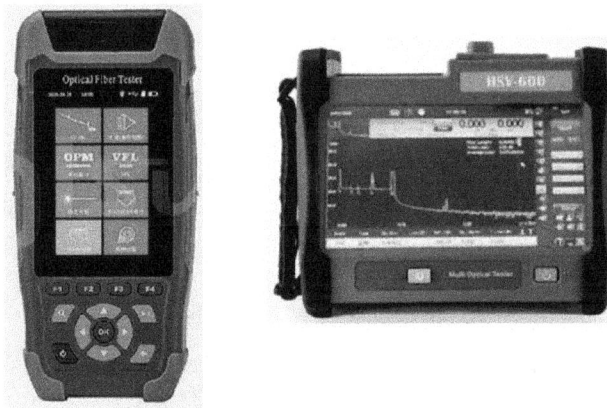

Figure 22.9: Optical Time-Domain Reflectometers

Multimeter

This tool is a hand-held multi-purpose tool. The functions of a multimeter include the measurement of voltage (volts), resistance (ohms), and current (amps) and determining circuit continuity. A multimeter is regarded as a standard tool in the electrical or electronic industry. Displays can be analog or digital, depending on the type purchased. The most important thing to remember about using this tool is your own experience and understanding of electrics. Only measure DC current and never test an AC main unless you are qualified and certified in this area.

Refer to *Figure 22.10*:

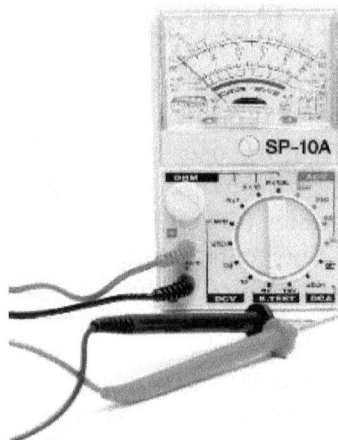

Figure 22.10: *Multimeter*

Cable tester

This tool is used to test a patch cord or Ethernet cable. It is an excellent tool to use for cable installation or diagnostics. If the insulation on an IDC has been damaged or if the wire is not conducting a signal, this is a good indicator of improper installation. The wires in RJ45 jacks or IDCs need to be inserted correctly and secured. The output of the cable tester should show lights activating in the same sequence at either end of the cable, and if this is not the case, the user needs to check where the pins have been terminated.

Cable testers can be used in Ethernet copper or fiber environments. Typical cable faults are open circuits, insulation damage, incorrect wiring (split pairs, crossed wires, and reversed connections), and PoE issues with voltage and current.

Refer to *Figure 22.11*:

Figure 22.11: *Cable testers*

Wire map

To guarantee continuity, the rudimentary requirement for cabling is to ensure the pins on one end are connected to the correct pins on the other end of the cable. This alignment/connectivity is verified during wire map testing. A wire mapper is basically a continuity checker that determines if pins are correctly connected.

Wire mapping tests for opens, shorts, crossed pairs, reversed pairs, and split pairs. All Cable UTP testers verify and validate wire mapping as a fundamental test.

Refer to *Figure 22.12*:

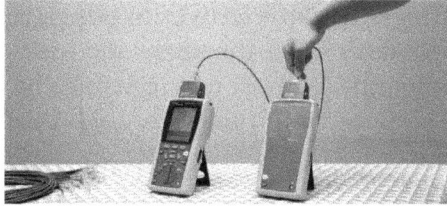

Figure 22.12: Wire map

Network tap

This tool is used to measure, test, or troubleshoot the flow of traffic in Ethernet or fiber networks, thus the term **Traffic/Test Access Point (TAP)**. It is inserted in specific points of a network to test or troubleshoot traffic and allow data capture regarding real-time traffic flow. Consequently, network taps monitor traffic in the infrastructure of the network.

Best practice: As networks scale and develop, users can monitor the network infrastructure. Network Taps can monitor data as it travels around a small to medium network or flows in an enterprise or data center. The idea is to have seamless access to the traffic flow and handle bottlenecks or other issues without disrupting network operations.

Figure 22.13 shows a passive Ethernet RJ45 LAN Tap:

Figure 22.13: Passive Ethernet RJ45 LAN Tap

Figure 22.14 shows a fixed panel passive fiber optic tap solution:

Figure 22.14: Fixed panel passive fiber optic tap solution

Fusion splicers

This tool enables the user to splice two cables together and create one longer cable. Splicing mechanically involves connecting two bare fiber ends directly. The user aligns the two ends and then fastens them together with a cover or adhesive. This cover acts as a more permanent splice. The fusion splicer melts the fibers and fuses them together. This creates a more durable fiber than when the job is done mechanically. The goal of splicing is that light is not reflected back or scattered as it passes through the fiber.

Refer to *Figure 22.15*:

Figure 22.15: Fusion splicer

Spectrum analyzers

This tool is primarily used to analyze the RF spectrum. Some of these spectrum analyzers resemble oscilloscopes, and some products combine the functions of both hardware tools. With this tool, the output is displayed in a graph, which is then interpreted by the user. RF signals and audio are the typical input signals generating the visual output and resulting graphed data. This visualized data occurs in real time, so the user can interpret the readings as they happen dynamically. Frequency and amplitude are two sets of data that can be analyzed with this tool. Additionally, the user can test entire circuits and systems and look for spurious signals, noise, or interference, and determine the strength (or weakness) of signals being generated.

Best practice: The signal spectrum across a range of frequencies is displayed and assessed. Using this tool, the technician can discover the source of interference (or overcrowding) in a wireless network and handle troublesome device(s). Some spectrum analyzers also perform calibration and signal conditioning.

Refer to *Figure 22.16*:

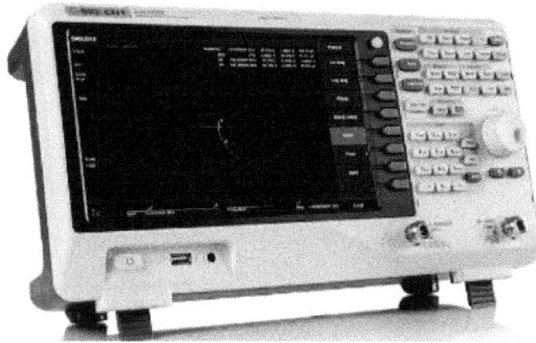

Figure 22.16: Spectrum analyzers

Cable strippers/snips/cutters

This tool is designed to score/nick the outer jacket of cable just enough to allow it to be removed. A user sets the stripper to the correct diameter. Then, they place the cable in the stripper and rotate the tool once or twice. The groove cut into the insulation should now permit the user to remove the section of the jacket. These tools can be purchased for Ethernet or fiber cables. *Figure 22.17* depicts a handheld fiber optic wire stripper:

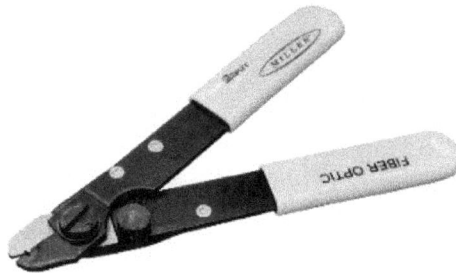

Figure 22.17: Handheld fiber optic wire stripper

Fiber light meter

The light or power meter comes as an integrated function of a fiber optic cable tester. These tools are low-cost methods for certifying fiber cable connectivity. They measure light continuity, light loss, and the strength of the signal of the link. The light source sends light down the length of fiber, and the power meter analyzes and interprets loss, strength, and continuity at the other end of the cable.

Interpreting these outcomes and reading fiber displays requires specialized training. Refer to *Figure 22.18*:

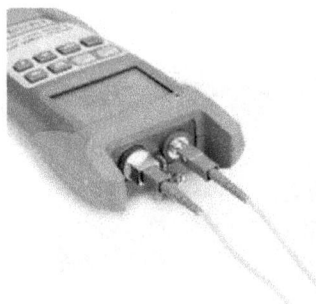

Figure 22.18: Fiber light meter

Conclusion

In this chapter, we explored common cable connectivity issues that occur in networks and how to troubleshoot problems using appropriate tools.

In the upcoming chapter, we will explore the appropriate software networking tools and utilities used in network management.

Points to remember

- Regarding cable installation and related practices, network administrators should:
  - o Integrate the best troubleshooting practices at cable installation and ongoing network maintenance.
  - o Identify and use appropriate network tools to diagnose and repair problems with diverse network cable types.
  - o Enhance their skills while working with cables in Ethernet and fiber networks.
- The content of *Chapter 22, Troubleshooting Cable Connectivity*, is mapped to *Domain 5, Network Troubleshooting*. Given a scenario, troubleshoot common cabling and physical interface issues.

Key terms

- **Attenuation**: Otherwise known as signal degradation, attenuation is the reduction of a signal's strength as it travels along a wire. As the signal is transmitted, it degrades in strength if it is being carried over a long distance, especially when the standards for maximum transmission lengths of cable are not being adhered to.
- **Backscatter levels**: As a pulse moves forward through a fiber link, a small proportion of light can be reflected backward and travel in the opposite or original

direction. This signal loss is referred to as backscatter. An OTDR measures the backscatter level as it occurs in the fiber being measured and analyzed.

- **Interference**: A process or activity that impedes or distorts another process from being carried out optimally. Examples of signal transmission are **electromagnetic interference (EMI)**, crosstalk, and **radio frequency interference (RFI)**.

- **Decibel loss**: A dB is a unit of measurement that is equivalent to one-tenth of a **bel** (**B**). If the signal strength at the end of transmission is less than that of the source, there is said to be a loss in decibels. The calculation is applied in evaluating fiber cables in terms of their power to transmit over distance and the amount of light loss at the receiving end.

- **Duplexing issues**: Data transmits in simplex, half-duplex, or full-duplex modes of operation. Any problems with directional data flow fall into the category of duplexing issues.

- **Oscilloscope**: An oscilloscope displays a graph of the waveform of electronic signals. The graph typically shows the frequency of the signal as it is moving (oscillating). Oscilloscopes measure the voltage as it varies over time. They are used for testing and analyzing more complex electronic or machine controls or systems.

Questions

1. Describe the importance of cabling standards.
2. Give some examples of basic cable tests.
3. Give some examples of network hardware tools and outline their purpose.
4. Describe some skills that are enhanced by adhering to a framework or model when troubleshooting networks.

Join our book's Discord space

Join the book's Discord Workspace for Latest updates, Offers, Tech happenings around the world, New Release and Sessions with the Authors:

https://discord.bpbonline.com

CHAPTER 23

Network Utilities

Introduction

One of the main misperceptions in entering IT support can be the idea that troubleshooting in technology is somehow similar to what a car mechanic does when they are under the hood of a car. We often hear individuals express their interest in a role in technology with an initial expectation of ongoing and continuous engagement with the hardware and components inside the case or device as if they are ready to plunge into the *guts and core* of the physical engine. That concept has changed somewhat over the decades as we focus more and more on the proliferation of software and how software interacts in a computing environment. It has been stated that every organization has seen some form of digital transformation over the last few years. However, the perception of the predominance and focus on a technical role as a hardware role still exists with some new learners.

Hardware goes wrong, and that fact is inevitable and indisputable. The software also goes wrong or has glitches, malware, or bugs, and that fact is equally indisputable and true. However, if we are to measure the time a network administrator spends on monitoring, detecting, and diagnosing issues regarding the overall network infrastructure and its performance, we can see that the time spent with software greatly exceeds the time spent upgrading the hardware parts. Note that this is when considering a typical IT support environment in an organization and not a specific hardware technician role, where duties and tasks focus exclusively on hardware management, maintenance, and repair. Most administrators tend to spend more of their time troubleshooting software and/or using network management tools to support them in troubleshooting hardware.

Staying with this analogy of car mechanics, troubleshooting software is like being *under the hood* of a logical engine. The software controls and runs the system. Consequently, the engine of a device consists of the hardware components and software as they interact and perform. The three typical types of software that interact in computing devices are: system software, application software, and utility software. A network administrator should understand these types of software and know how they interact and the problems that can arise with and among them. Technicians also need to be knowledgeable about network utilities embedded in the operating system to assist in troubleshooting and the availability of third-party utilities, principally designed for managing network systems. They should have the *skills* to use them.

Figure 23.1 shows a professional engaging with software code. Analyzing and interpreting code and scripts, viewing visual outputs, and managing software interfaces require focus, awareness, and acute attention to detail. Viewing the following figure, we perceive this focus. We may also discern the organization it took for the professional to set up and coordinate the workspace and applications that are in use, thus reinforcing focus and deliberation.

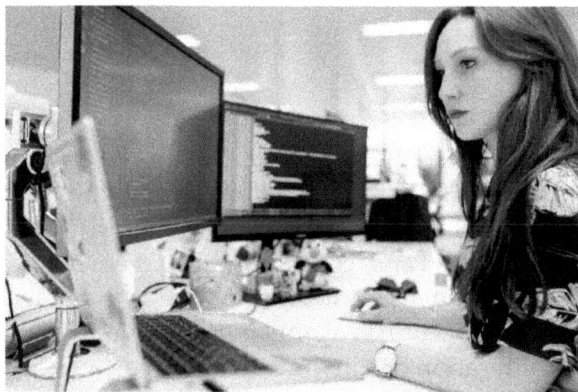

Figure 23.1: Analyzing and interpreting software

Although a network administrator may not necessarily work with multiple monitors or multiple outputs, the skills are the same. Focus, understanding of software, awareness of what we should be viewing, and attention to detail are essential. These skills and competencies are what we, as administrators, bring to the tools. It is *how* we use the tools that make the difference to our degree of expertise.

To conclude, network administrators install, upgrade, configure, and manage network hardware, software, many applications, and network components. Furthermore, much of this time is typically spent working and engaging with software.

Structure

In this chapter, we will cover the following topics:

- Network software tools
- Command line tools
- Basic network platform commands
- Putting commands into action

Objectives

This chapter will explore (third-party) network software tools and network utilities integrated into the operating system. After reading this chapter, you will be able to differentiate between the network software tools available and identify their functionality and purpose. Additionally, you will be able to choose appropriate tools and commands to verify TCP/IP functions on network hosts and confirm connectivity to other intermediary devices, such as switches, routers, and firewalls. Your competence in reading, analyzing, and interpreting command output will be enhanced as your understanding of each tool and command deepens. With practical application, your ability to execute and combine multiple commands while troubleshooting will also be strengthened.

Network software tools

There are diverse software tools available that monitor, analyze, measure, and record all kinds of information relating to the functionality of the network. Tools can tell us the network's speed when it is performing well or poorly. Tools can inform us about how data interacts with protocols or network equipment. With tools, we can get to know our network comprehensively.

The following section describes the network software tools and outlines their uses. By using these tools, a network administrator can keep track of what is happening on the network, optimize processes, and improve overall productivity as an informed analyst.

Let us look at some of the most commonly used network software tools.

Wi-Fi analyzer

One example of a Wi-Fi analyzer is InSSIDer. This tool is used for monitoring and troubleshooting wireless networks. The tool retrieves and displays the performance of **access points (AP)**, WLAN controllers, and clients on the network. A user views the wireless coverage on the dashboard, analyzes the performance metrics, and can identify, diagnose, and resolve wireless issues. APs can be assessed for their range, the existence of potential obstructions to the signal, time delays, channel usage, interference, and attenuation. The user will also see how neighboring wireless networks interact with their network, and these metrics can be visualized and investigated. The user can maximize security on their network and view potential risk factors in the configuration of the wireless LAN. Refer to *Figure 23.2*:

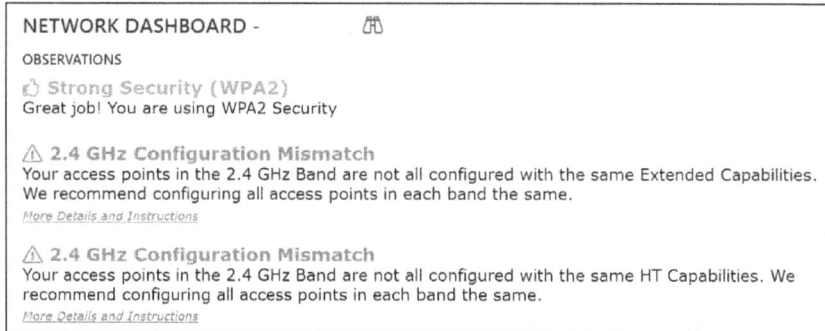

NETWORK DASHBOARD -

OBSERVATIONS

⟳ Strong Security (WPA2)
Great job! You are using WPA2 Security

⚠ 2.4 GHz Configuration Mismatch
Your access points in the 2.4 GHz Band are not all configured with the same Extended Capabilities. We recommend configuring all access points in each band the same.
More Details and Instructions

⚠ 2.4 GHz Configuration Mismatch
Your access points in the 2.4 GHz Band are not all configured with the same HT Capabilities. We recommend configuring all access points in each band the same.
More Details and Instructions

Figure 23.2: inSSIDer view

Best practice: Users will be able to evaluate the location of APs and antennae orientation; if the problems are persistent, review the location of the AP. Other tests will include bandwidth saturation, latency, channel width, signal strength, load and stress on devices, and other factors relevant to wireless communication.

Protocol analyzer/packet capture

One example of a protocol analyzer is Wireshark. This tool has a diverse range of functions and uses. The software captures data packets as they traverse the network and presents the user with a graphical interface and visual of what is transpiring in real time. The data capture is converted into meaningful, itemized protocol sequences and displays network traffic. The communication channel under review can range from activity on a single local host to more complex switching and signaling activities. The key performance indicators are viewed, detected, and analyzed. With the aid of the output, many issues detected can subsequently be resolved. For example, if a particular protocol is in use and consuming network bandwidth, this impact can be further investigated. Or if a protocol is deemed to be a security risk, for example, FTP or TFTP, these data transmissions can be explored to assess what data is being sent or received and by whom. For example, some identified actions may form supporting evidence stating why ports **20** and **21** ought to be blocked on the company firewall or, if protocol use is permissible, why a particular employee may be abusing the privilege. In short, as the administrator assesses the protocols and ports in use on the network, decisions can be made to streamline traffic and curtail actions that are not conducive to business operations or are against the company's acceptable use policy. Refer to *Figure 23.3*:

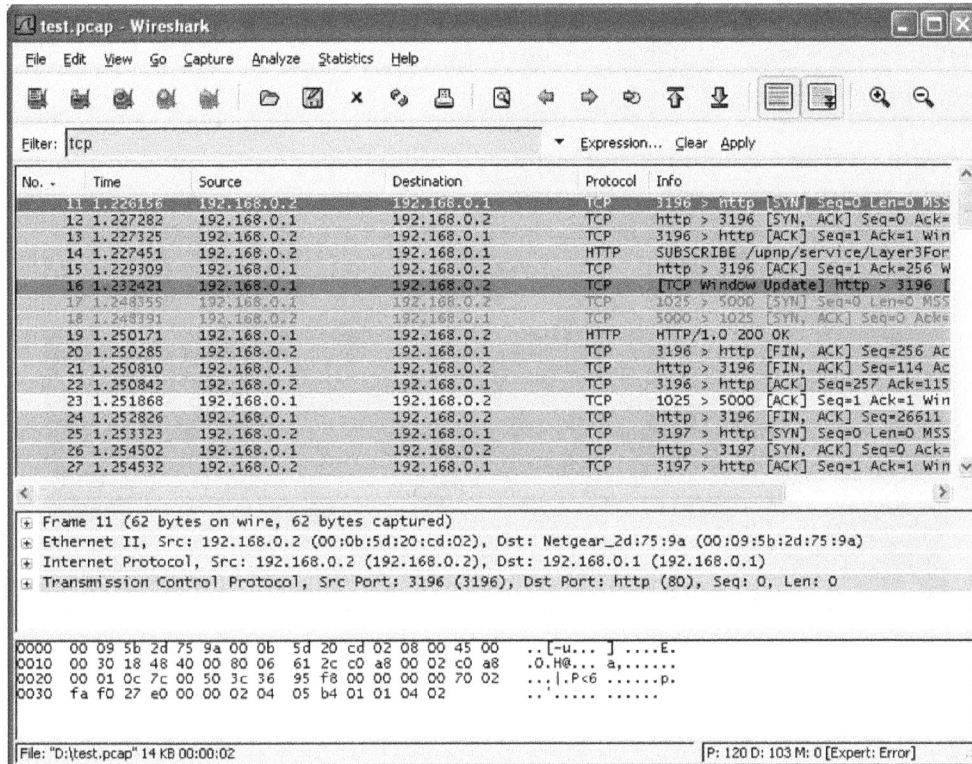

Figure 23.3: Wireshark

Best practice: Protocol analyzers (such as Wireshark) enable users to view live data. Security analysts can use this tool to sort and filter per protocol and detect suspect or actual security breaches. With this tool, a user can analyze ARP spoofing, DHCP flooding, DNS spoofing, Dos/DDoS attacks, and VLAN hopping. The nature of these attacks is covered in *Chapter 17, Cybersecurity Attacks.*

Bandwidth speed tester

One example of a bandwidth speed tester is SpeedTest Master. A bandwidth speed tester is a frequently used tool by general users of networks and the internet, as well as network administrators. This tool calculates the maximum bandwidth of a connection on a network or to the Internet. As *Techopedia* explains, *A bandwidth test operates by sending one or more files of known sizes over the network to the computer. It then measures the time needed for the files to download successfully at the other end. With this, it obtains a figure for representing the data speed between the points.*

This end result is displayed graphically to the user in an easy-to-understand format. The measurements also give the user an idea of how stable the connection or link they are measuring is.

Companies pay for their internet connections to Internet service providers. The upload and download speeds of the connection will largely depend upon the subscribed package/bundle. Using this tool, a network administrator can determine the performance trends and usage of the internet connection in addition to the maximum upload and download speeds being paid for. Administrators can determine if the internet connection suits the needs of the organization. Refer to *Figure 23.4*:

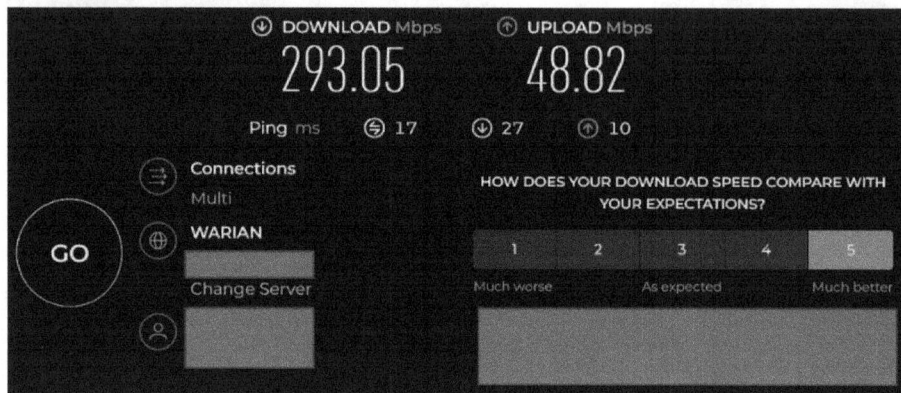

Figure 23.4: Bandwidth speed tester

iPerf

iPerf is a command line tool used to test network bandwidth. It is supported by multiple platforms, such as Windows, Linux, and MacOS. iPerf tests data throughput between two systems, confirms bandwidth usage, and views performance metrics. The tool uses a client-server model to run tests on both devices. One of the hosts acts as a server, and the other acts as a client. For example, a user can install the tool on the *client* and *server* machine and run the software to see how fast the data transmits over the network infrastructure. The data passes through switches and router(s) to be received by the server machine at the end of transmission.

This enables the administrator to gather statistics for **data throughput** and compare this result to the network's **bandwidth** or capacity. The administrator can subsequently carry out tests on network devices that may be lagging or impacting network performance due to age, insufficient system resources, or other flaws in the device's configuration.

In short, iPerf is also used to troubleshoot performance problems with networks and fine-tune TCP and UDP connections. Refer to *Figure 23.5*:

Figure 23.5: iPerf

Port scanner

One example of a port scanner is Nmap. Network ports are software-based. They are used for routing data to a specific application on a designated machine and are aligned with particular services or protocols. These ports are communication endpoints where communication on the network begins and ends. A port scan typically uses the ports identified as well-known ports by the **Internet Assigned Numbers Authority (IANA)**. For example, HTTP uses port 80 (as seen before), and PoP3 uses port **110**.

A port scanning tool scans the machine for open ports. It allows the user to discover the programs and protocols that are running on these ports. Note that when a port is shown as open, this means that it can be accessed remotely. With port scanning tools, a network administrator can determine whether specific ports should be open or closed. In this way, security on the network or on devices can be monitored and verified. As seen in *Figure 23.6*, the columnar data shows the **port**, its **state**, and the associated **service** (protocol). Multiple ports are displayed as open in the command's output.

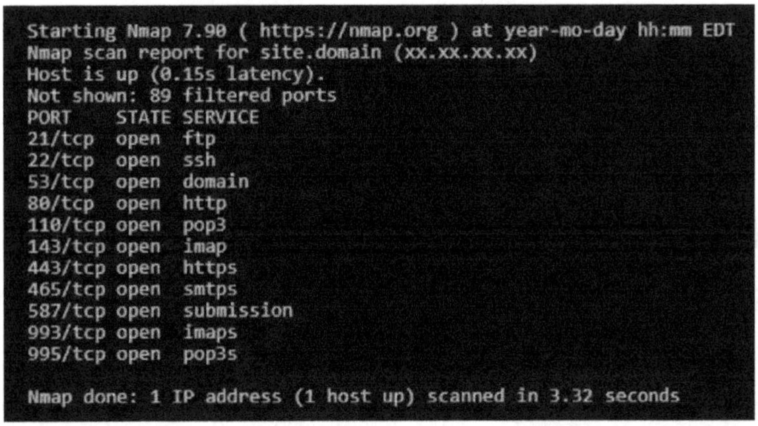

```
Starting Nmap 7.90 ( https://nmap.org ) at year-mo-day hh:mm EDT
Nmap scan report for site.domain (xx.xx.xx.xx)
Host is up (0.15s latency).
Not shown: 89 filtered ports
PORT      STATE SERVICE
21/tcp    open  ftp
22/tcp    open  ssh
53/tcp    open  domain
80/tcp    open  http
110/tcp   open  pop3
143/tcp   open  imap
443/tcp   open  https
465/tcp   open  smtps
587/tcp   open  submission
993/tcp   open  imaps
995/tcp   open  pop3s

Nmap done: 1 IP address (1 host up) scanned in 3.32 seconds
```

Figure 23.6: Port scanner

Best practice: A network administrator can use this tool to examine what traffic is on their network. Since administrators know that hackers search networks for vulnerabilities and loopholes, they should also know that understanding the status of ports on hosts and devices is critical to awareness of a network's security. Port scanners are a security risk in the wrong hands. Open ports can be assessed by hackers and then compromised. The hacker can determine whether a firewall is active or even go as far as carrying out *data theft*. Furthermore, these open ports can be the entry point for a hacker whose intention is to install a Trojan, virus, or botnet client software onto the network. Consequently, open ports are significant network security risks. To mitigate the risk, administrators should detect and disable unwanted ports. They should apply port filtering on the firewall and ensure it is patched and updated. They can also carry out vulnerability assessments and/ or organize for penetration (pen) testing of the network. This pen testing scans the network for vulnerabilities by simulating network attacks and discovering where loopholes exist.

Sometimes, port scanners can be used along with a **vulnerability scanning** tool. One example of a vulnerability scanner is **Nessus**. It is used by security analysts to scan a network for vulnerabilities or weaknesses. Nessus enables security professionals to respond swiftly and recognize and remediate vulnerabilities. As a result, the administrator can resolve software defects, missing security patches, and problems emanating from human error or negligence. On top of this vigilance, administrators should actively manage the *services* associated with these ports.

Nessus scans include the following:

- Malware scans
- Audit
- Audit cloud infrastructure
- Badlock detection (CVEs)
- Mobile Device Managers
- Mobile Device Scan
- Advanced Scan

Nessus products can now be used in the private address space and in commercial environments.

NetFlow analyzers

One example of a NetFlow analyzer is Solar Winds. NetFlow analyzers allow the network administrator to drill down into the statistics on a range of data flows. Users can monitor the use of bandwidth and network resources and calculate the amount of bandwidth used by protocols, applications, and by individual users. The tool is very granular, meaning the administrator can capture and graph usage and data flows with in-depth inspections. These thorough visualizations provide the user with helpful insights and observations that can be acted upon to improve network performance. Refer to *Figure 23.7*:

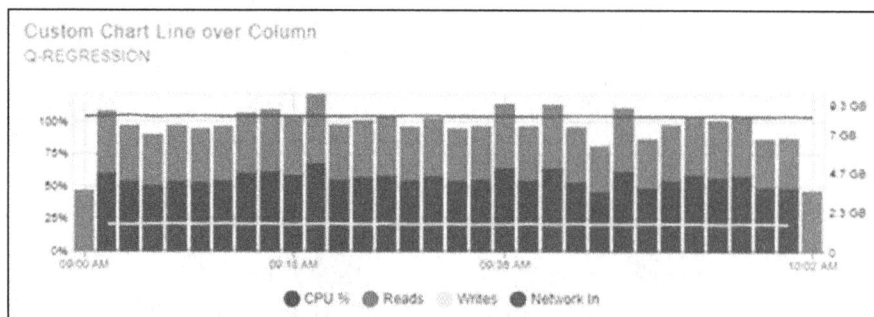

Figure 23.7: *NetFlow analyzers*

Best practice: The tool is ideal for capacity planning and all decision-making relating to the appropriate allocation of an organization's network resources.

Trivial file transfer protocol server

This tool transfers files over the private or local/public network. Users can transfer files between multiple devices. TFTP is practically unused in an Internet or WAN file transfer. The TFTP protocol uses UDP (port **69**) as its transport mechanism. Therefore, it uses fast but connectionless and best-effort delivery.

TFTP is regarded as a *lighter* version of FTP; thus, the term *trivial*. It uses a server-client model, whereby users can push files out to a host or access files from a TFTP server. If it is to be used, administrators should be aware that it is a simple tool that lacks security features such as encryption and, if required, is best used locally. Refer to *Figure 23.8*:

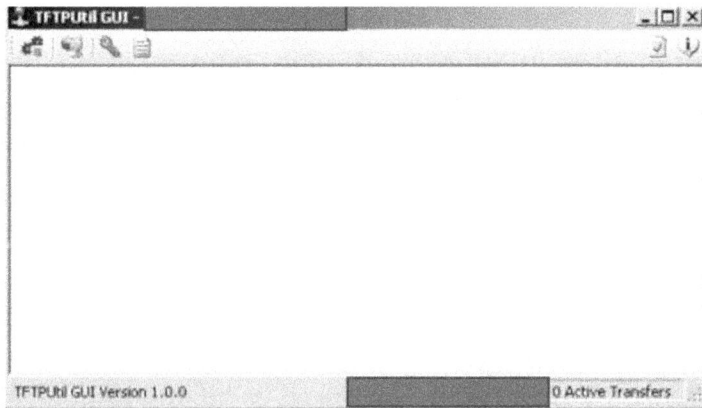

Figure 23.8: TFTP server

Terminal emulator

A terminal emulator such as Putty or Cmder offers the ability to access a host or device via a CLI/GUI to configure or make changes to the device. It is used frequently in networking to configure devices such as Cisco switches and routers. The tool also allows developers and programmers to interface with the operating system at a deeper level (that is, shell access) so they can access files and run applications.

An administrator can use this software to remotely access a device securely using the Secure Shell protocol. Refer to *Figure 23.9*:

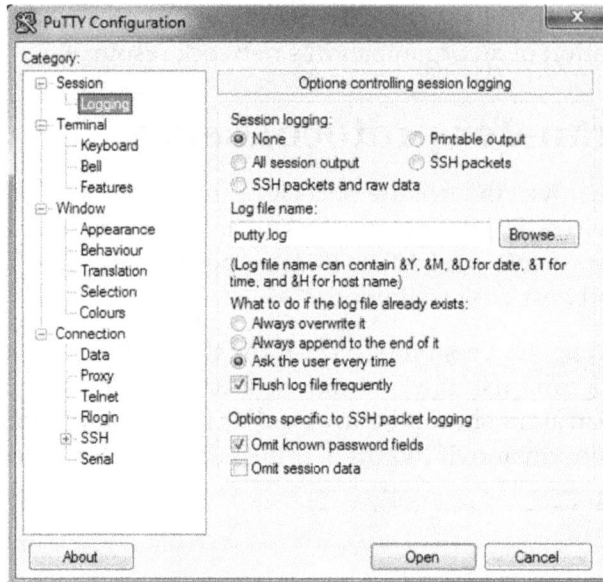

Figure 23.9: Terminal emulator

IP scanner

An IP scanner scans the entire network and displays the IP addresses that are in use on the network. It is an excellent tool for scanning addresses to troubleshoot DHCP, assessing the allocation of static and dynamic addresses, and viewing network devices. Some advanced scanners permit the user to use RDP and switch on or shut off computers remotely. Refer to *Figure 23.10*:

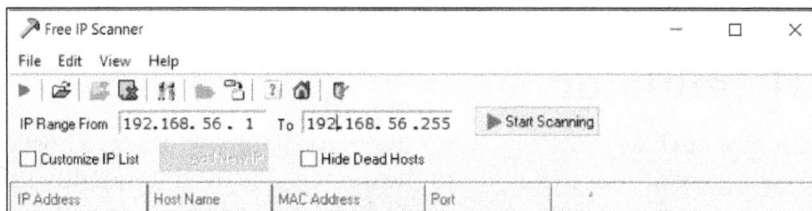

Figure 23.10: IP scanner

Command line tools

One of the main benefits of a **command line interface** (**CLI**) is that it can be faster to launch and run than a GUI alternative. For example, an IT professional or system administrator can quickly run cmd.exe or PowerShell, and as long as they know the commands, they can interact with the system to perform administrative tasks adeptly. The CLI functions much like a professional's toolkit because it is bundled with an immense diversity of tools.

With CLIs, the tools are always on hand for decisive and immediate interaction. This is not to suggest that the utilities are simplistic or limited in their functionality; it is quite the opposite. Command line tools can support network administration with a powerful degree of depth and productivity.

When using a CLI for the first time, a user might feel slightly overwhelmed by the vast range of options for each command engaged with. However, with practice and application, the user will build on their foundational knowledge and feel more confident exploring the parameters of individual commands. Understanding the structure of commands provides the user with precision and control, plus the ability to perform network diagnostics in an organized, timely manner.

The following section describes and guides the reader through the most commonly used commands in the network administrator's armory. Understanding the purposes of these network utilities is a wise decision for a budding or novice administrator. Moreover, even with years of practice, it is never a surprise for users to discover something new entirely or a command or option that had previously gone unnoticed.

Let us have a look at some of these network command line tools.

PING

Ping is a network utility for testing connectivity to a local or remote host. If the connection to the host is successful, the host is said to be *reachable*. This action works like making a phone call. If the expected receiver answers the call when we ring them, we have successfully connected with them, and the person is deemed to be reachable. If the connection times out, we may be disconnected or redirected to voicemail, *or* the phone may simply be offline or broken. We can see that the person is not reachable for various reasons. In the same way, in networking, we may be connected successfully, or there may be alternative, less successful outcomes. Ping helps us to establish the reasons for these outcomes. For example, using ping, *a request time out* showing in the command output has the same outcome as the phone call timing out on us. Connectivity is not fully established with the targeted host, and the *packet* is consequently not responded to with 100% accuracy. Again, where networking issues and configurations are concerned, there may be various reasons for this outcome.

Process

Ping sends an IP **echo request** to a target host (or IP). The utility waits for a reply, also known as an **echo reply**, and measures how long it takes to reach the specified target. The approximate round-trip time taken is measured in milliseconds. The statistics generated by ping include bytes sent and received, packets lost, and **Time to Live** (**TTL**) values. Loss is measured as a percentage of 100%.

Ping is essential for network diagnostics.

Ping is used for troubleshooting the following:

- Network speed
- Network congestion
- Host-to-host connectivity
- Router availability and router resource capacity
- Packet loss and latency issues
- Consistency in a connection
- TCP/IP bindings on a NIC

Output error messages include the following:

- Destination host unreachable
- Request timed out
- Ping request could not find a host
- PING: transmit failed. General failure.

Best practice: Users can implement a timeout, send ping packets to the specified host until they stop, resolve addresses to hostnames, and change the size of the ping packets being transmitted.

These are just some of the uses for ping.

Troubleshooting examples

When troubleshooting, always test connectivity to hosts closest to the machine that the ping is being run from, and then move the connectivity tests incrementally to devices at *further distances*. For example, ping the host itself, then another machine on the same network segment, followed by the default gateway, and where viable, yet another router(s) in the organization's network. After this series of pings, ping a Web address or external domain, and so on. This strategy keeps us in control of our testing, supports the gathering of data, and informs subsequent evaluations of connectivity and configuration problems.

Using the loopback address (**127.0.0.1**), an administrator can test an NIC to ensure it is not faulty or jabbering. A jabbering NIC sends a continuous stream of undesirable signals and may obstruct network performance and communication. Ping combined with –t will test the NIC's ability to send and receive packets over time until the command is stopped. For example, a jabbering NIC on a Web server would be disastrous on a network. Users can type either ping localhost, ping **127.0.0.1**, ping (host IP), or ping (NetBIOS-friendly name).

Administrators can discover router issues using ping. They may have received successful pings to a default gateway on a network but are not successfully reaching any host on the network. This lack of success points to a problematic or offline router.

At times, a router may not be handling traffic well. It may have poor resources or just be too old to handle the amount of traffic passing through its interfaces. Ping, along with pathping and tracert, assists an administrator who suspects a router on the network needs a hardware upgrade, redeployment, or replacement. Sometimes, there can be issues with timing and packet delivery. Troubleshooting with ping can be used to identify lag or latency in the network.

Regarding security, network administrators need to know how hackers can abuse commands by using them for malicious attacks. Hackers can change the size of the ping packet to generate Dos/DDoS attacks, overwhelming the server with ICMP echo requests. They can also carry out ping sweeps to discover hosts on the network. For these reasons, an administrator will block WAN pinging and use the tool internally in an organization's infrastructure. They may decide not to allow pings to be received by any externally facing network device or specific servers in their network.

Sample output

For pinging the localhost with the loopback address:

```
C:\WINDOWS\system32>ping 127.0.0.1
Pinging 127.0.0.1 with 32 bytes of data:
Reply from 127.0.0.1: bytes=32 time<1ms TTL=128
Reply from 127.0.0.1: bytes=32 time<1ms TTL=128
Reply from 127.0.0.1: bytes=32 time<1ms TTL=128
Reply from 127.0.0.1: bytes=32 time<1ms TTL=128

Ping statistics for 127.0.0.1:
    Packets: Sent = 4, Received = 4, Lost = 0 (0% loss),
Approximate round trip times in milli-seconds:
    Minimum = 0ms, Maximum = 0ms, Average = 0ms
```

> **Note: The output confirms the functionality of the NIC and its ability to send and receive data. It also indicates that TCP/IP is properly bound to the network card.**

For pinging the default gateway (the first **usabl** address on the **10.10.0.0/24** network):

```
C:\WINDOWS\system32>ping 10.10.0.1
Pinging 10.10.0.1 with 32 bytes of data:
Reply from 10.10.0.1: bytes=32 time<1ms TTL=64
Reply from 10.10.0.1: bytes=32 time=1ms TTL=64
Reply from 10.10.0.1: bytes=32 time=1ms TTL=64
Reply from 10.10.0.1: bytes=32 time=1ms TTL=64

Ping statistics for 10.10.0.1:
    Packets: Sent = 4, Received = 4, Lost = 0 (0% loss),
Approximate round trip times in milli-seconds:
    Minimum = 0ms, Maximum = 1ms, Average = 0ms
```

Note: The output confirms that the host (10.10.0.18) can successfully reach the default gateway on the network. It also indicates the host is correctly addressed and packets reach the router's (internal/LAN) interface.

For pinging an external public IP address:

```
C:\WINDOWS\system32>ping www.google.com
Pinging www.google.com [172.253.116.105] with 32 bytes of data:
Reply from 172.253.116.105: bytes=32 time=3ms TTL=60
Reply from 172.253.116.105: bytes=32 time=3ms TTL=60
Reply from 172.253.116.105: bytes=32 time=3ms TTL=60
Reply from 172.253.116.105: bytes=32 time=3ms TTL=60

Ping statistics for 172.253.116.105:
    Packets: Sent = 4, Received = 4, Lost = 0 (0% loss),
Approximate round trip times in milli-seconds:
    Minimum = 3ms, Maximum = 3ms, Average = 3ms
```

Note: The output confirms that the host (10.10.0.18) is successfully reaching an external website. It also indicates that WAN connectivity is established, and the router is successfully transmitting packets.

IPCONFIG/IFCONFIG/IP

Ipconfig is a network utility used to show the TCP/IP statistics and configuration of a given host or workstation on a Windows platform. The same function is available on other platforms, but the command on a Linux, macOS, or Unix host is **ifconfig**.

Ipconfig has many options. It can also be used to reset or refresh the network settings on the host with the **/release** or **/renew** parameter implemented. Using these parameters, a user can inform the DHCP server that they no longer wish to use the current IP address (**/release**), and then they can request a new address (**/renew**). Expired IP addresses or other connectivity issues with a computer's current IP address lease are often the reason for network problems. By implementing these parameters, a user can troubleshoot issues with network connectivity.

Best practice: The user can determine if DHCP is functioning, if the DHCP server is online, and whether the DNS server is operational or not. DHCP lease times are displayed so that the administrator immediately knows approximately what stage the host is in, in terms of nearing the DORA process. They can also determine whether the adapter is configured by DHCP, **Automatic Private IP Addressing (APIPA)**, or via an alternate configuration.

Troubleshooting examples

If the IPv4 address is displayed in the range **169.254. 0.1** to **169.254. 255.254**, with a subnet mask of **255.255.0.0.**, the administrator determines that the DHCP server is down, and that the workstation has limited connectivity, just to the local network resources, and has no internet connection. With APIPA running, a client uses the self-configured IP address until a DHCP server becomes available. This APIPA output indicates that the administrator should troubleshoot the DHCP server.

Using ipconfig, the user can identify whether the host is addressed correctly and if it is on the proper network segment. At times, IP addresses and subnet masks can be misconfigured, especially when there are subnets on the network or where the addressing structure is more complex. For example, if a workstation is moved to another part of the building, this simple change can impact the IP structure of the host machine, and when plugged into a new network point, it can be inadvertently taken *off* the network. You may wonder why. It may be the case where the workstation is now on a new network segment/subnet, but still carries the old IP address with an incorrect subnet mask pointing to the wrong gateway. This is where the parameters **/release** and **/renew** become a troubleshooting tool and repair kit to get a new leased address from the DHCP server for the correct network segment.

The **/flushdns** parameter can be used to clear the **Domain Name System** (**DNS**) cache to guarantee future DNS queries use fresh DNS information. Using this parameter, the contents of the cache are purged, and current mappings are removed. This parameter forces hostnames to be resolved again from scratch. At times, the DNS cache holds mappings where changes may have recently occurred on the internet. For example, a domain name may have changed on the Internet, but as of yet, the new record may not have been updated by the host machine as it is still calling on the old mapping (record) from the cache.

A change to a DNS record can take up to 72 hours to propagate worldwide. However, it usually takes a few hours. Even so, this gap in time can impact a host if the DNS cache still holds the old record. By applying this quick fix, an administrator can identify or eliminate this occurrence as the source of a problem.

Sample output

For ipconfig:

```
C:\WINDOWS\system32>ipconfig
Windows IP Configuration

Ethernet adapter Ethernet:

   Media State . . . . . . . . . . . : Media disconnected

   Connection-specific DNS Suffix  . : test.local

Ethernet adapter VirtualBox Host-Only Network:

   Connection-specific DNS Suffix  . :
   Link-local IPv6 Address . . . . . : fe80::6cfa:b5d5:e3f8:fbce%5
   IPv4 Address. . . . . . . . . . . : 192.168.56.1
```

```
Subnet Mask . . . . . . . . . . . : 255.255.255.0
Default Gateway . . . . . . . . . :

Connection-specific DNS Suffix  . :
Link-local IPv6 Address . . . . . : fe80::cfc9:fa48:f4d2:d4ab%20
IPv4 Address. . . . . . . . . . . : 10.10.0.18
Subnet Mask . . . . . . . . . . . : 255.255.255.0
Default Gateway . . . . . . . . . : 10.10.0.1
Connection-specific DNS Suffix  . :
```

Note: The output displays limited detail about the status of adapters on the host. This detail includes the media state (connected or disconnected) and IP addressing statistics. The address of the default gateway is also displayed.

For ipconfig/all:

```
Connection-specific DNS Suffix  . :
Description . . . . . . . . . . . : Intel(R) Dual Band Wireless-AC 8265
Physical Address. . . . . . . . . : DC-FB-48-20-B4-E9
DHCP Enabled. . . . . . . . . . . : Yes
Autoconfiguration Enabled . . . . : Yes
Link-local IPv6 Address . . . . . : fe80::cfc9:fa48:f4d2:d4ab%20
(Preferred)
IPv4 Address. . . . . . . . . . . : 10.10.0.18(Preferred)
Subnet Mask . . . . . . . . . . . : 255.255.255.0
Lease Obtained. . . . . . . . . . : Wednesday 3 May 2023 07:47:44
Lease Expires . . . . . . . . . . : Thursday 4 May 2023 07:47:44
Default Gateway . . . . . . . . . : 10.10.0.1
DHCP Server . . . . . . . . . . . : 10.10.0.1
DHCPv6 IAID . . . . . . . . . . . : 199031624
DHCPv6 Client DUID. . . . . . . . : 00-01-00-01-24-BF-82-39-C4-65-16-2F-
2D-29
DNS Servers . . . . . . . . . . . : 10.10.0.1
NetBIOS over Tcpip. . . . . . . . : Enabled
```

Note: The output displays more in-depth IP statistics with the /all parameter added to the command. I have only selected the adapter that is currently in use to focus on additional detail when full IP configuration is displayed. The manufacturer of the WLAN adapter is shown along with the MAC address. DHCP and DNS information is presented.

For ipconfig parameters (options):

```
Options:
        /?                  Display this help message
        /all                Display full configuration information.
        /release            Release the IPv4 address for the specified adapter.
        /release6           Release the IPv6 address for the specified adapter.
        /renew              Renew the IPv4 address for the specified adapter.
        /renew6             Renew the IPv6 address for the specified adapter.
        /flushdns           Purges the DNS Resolver cache.
        /registerdns        Refreshes all DHCP leases and re-registers DNS names
        /displaydns         Display the contents of the DNS Resolver Cache.
        /showclassid        Displays all the dhcp class IDs allowed for adapter.
        /setclassid         Modifies the dhcp class id.
        /showclassid6       Displays all the IPv6 DHCP class IDs allowed for
adapter.
        /setclassid6        Modifies the IPv6 DHCP class id.
```

Note: The options for the ipconfig command are used to check, test, and refresh IP settings.

NSLOOKUP

nslookup/**dig** is a network utility for querying domain name servers. Using this utility, a user can *look up* a domain name to discover the corresponding IP address for the domain in the DNS record. Alternatively, a user can carry out a reverse lookup and discover the domain name by inputting an IP address.

Troubleshooting examples

When an administrator needs to troubleshoot DNS-related issues, they will use this utility. The utility is also used to troubleshoot server or security issues and cybersecurity investigations.

To test if the DNS server is reachable, an administrator can use the following command:

`nslookup <client name> <server IP address>`

If the DNS resolver returns either **Request to server timed out** or **No response from server**, then the following command can be used to restart the DNS server:

`net start DNS`

If this does not resolve the issue, the administrator can further call on other tools to investigate the DNS server configuration. Sometimes, hackers manipulate domain names to carry out *phishing* attacks or *data theft*. IP addresses or domain names in suspect e-mails can be queried with the **nslookup** utility.

In *cache poisoning* attacks, attackers mislead users by distributing false data, which enters the DNS cache. This misinformation redirects the user to the incorrect website. A **nslookup** query can identify these types of attempts to mislead Web users who are navigating websites.

Sample output

For nslookup:

```
C:\WINDOWS\system32>nslookup www.comptia.org
Non-authoritative answer:
Server:   UnKnown
Address:  10.10.0.1

Name:      www.comptia.org
Addresses:  2606:4700::6812:101d
          2606:4700::6812:111d
          104.18.16.29
          104.18.17.29
```

The syntax for using the **dig** utility is as follows:

```
$ dig <website domain>
```

Linux-based operating systems also accept the **nslookup** command.

Traceroute/Tracert

Tracert is a network utility that displays the route and path a packet takes from a source to a destination IP address or domain. Tracert records how the data moves as it travels from its source to its destination and provides the user with a map of how packets made their journey, router by router by router, along the way.

In terms of timing calculations, this diagnostic tool measures the transit delays as the packet travels from **Hand Off Point (HOP)** to **Hand Off Point (HOP)**. As stated, each HOP is a router on an IP network with common features but unique and diverse capacities, varying resources, tailored configurations, and specific sets of abilities. The tracert utility can measure the transmission of packets up to a maximum of 30 HOPS across individual router interfaces. The **Round-Trip Time (RTT)** taken is measured from HOP to HOP as separate and successive computations of data transmit, whereas *ping* calculation results are the computed *final* round-trip time of data transmission. This facility to measure RTT per HOP enables an administrator to assess the capabilities of routers in and outside their organization and manage their network resources and resource allocation effectively.

Troubleshooting examples

Many routers are configured not to accept online tracert packets or deprioritize them. The command output will be *Request timed out* with an asterisk at one or more HOPs. ICMP traffic is not regarded as essential traffic by some of these routers and is, therefore, deprioritized or disregarded altogether if firewalled or blocked. If an administrator sees the *Request timed out* output at an HOP or over consecutive HOPs, it indicates a possible connection issue on the router at that point or that ICMP is blocked or set at a lower priority. Additionally, the router may be simply offline. Alternatively, it might have an issue with traffic congestion, or it might be under-resourced with RAM or CPU capabilities and is suffering from packet loss. The router may be degraded or near its end of life.

As shown, there are multiple reasons for this timeout output, and the administrator must work their way through and *evaluate these theories of probable cause.* Here is a prime example where the steps of the network troubleshooting model are invaluable to network management. If the router in question belongs to the organization, the administrator can investigate the router further by either implementing SSH or by consoling into the router directly in an **Out of Band Management** (**OOBM**) scenario.

HOP times can be impacted by physical distance. The speed of the link(s) between routers can also be a determining factor in terms of performance and speed. Moreover, the administrator can assess the speed of the links on the organization's router and, if the cables are not handling the traffic well, begin researching an upgrade where viable.

Other factors impacting HOP times include the following:

- The type and speed of the internet connection.
- ISP provision and the quality of the service.
- The type of data being transmitted. For example, whether it is multimedia or VoIP.

With tracert, the administrator can review the company's internet speed and bandwidth and make decisions based on the results of this review. Moreover, this tool can be complemented by carrying out speed tests and using other utilities that capture information about internet connections, user utilization, and overall network performance. This *gathering of data* can lead to other company decisions.

Sample output

For traceroute/tracert:

```
C:\WINDOWS\system32>tracert -d www.google.com
Tracing route to www.google.com [2a00:1450:400b:c02::93]
over a maximum of 30 hops:

  1     4 ms     5 ms     5 ms  2a02:8084:4042:d180:aef8:ccff:fe65:4f37
  2    18 ms    21 ms    18 ms  2a02:8081:0:5f::1
```

3	9 ms	18 ms	11 ms	2a02:8080:4:1::1
4	12 ms	12 ms	15 ms	2001:730:2e00::5474:80f6
5	15 ms	14 ms	11 ms	2001:730:2e00::5474:8022
6	18 ms	13 ms	17 ms	2001:4860:1:1::e70
7	14 ms	16 ms	17 ms	2a00:1450:807c::1
8	14 ms	14 ms	18 ms	2001:4860:0:1::18d6
9	23 ms	25 ms	17 ms	2001:4860:0:d::8
10	14 ms	*	18 ms	2001:4860:0:1::5cc9
11	*	*	*	Request timed out.
12	*	*	*	Request timed out.
13	*	*	*	Request timed out.
14	*	*	*	Request timed out.
15	*	*	*	Request timed out.
16	*	*	*	Request timed out.
17	*	*	*	Request timed out.
18	*	*	*	Request timed out.
19	*	*	*	Request timed out.
20	*	*	*	Request timed out.
21	*	*	*	Request timed out.
22	14 ms	16 ms	16 ms	2a00:1450:400b:c02::93

```
Trace complete.
```

Note: The -d parameter used along with the tracert command means that while capturing the route taken, we request:

-d: Do not resolve addresses to hostnames.

This option can speed up the tracert process but still deliver relevant IPv4/6 information. If we need the fuller detail, we can simply omit the -d parameter.

The first HOP will always be the IP of the default gateway on the LAN. The second will be the IP address allocated by the ISP. After that, the router reached can be any router requested to accept the packet and forward it on.

Address Resolution Protocol

ARP is a network utility used for displaying the ARP cache entry. ARP entries can be static or dynamic. When the command is used with the **–a** parameter, current ARP entries are displayed. The process interrogates the current protocol data. If more than one network interface uses ARP, entries for each ARP table are displayed.

Using the **arp** command, an administrator can delete or manually configure a static ARP cache entry.

Troubleshooting examples

In networking, conflicts can occur between logical or physical addresses, so by viewing the current **arp** table entries for the device in question, a user can evaluate an issue that has arisen or suspected conflict. The command's output will show duplicate IP addresses or duplicate MAC addresses in use on the network in the last few minutes. When an administrator checks, the ARP table is viewed from the gateway device or on the LAN switch, and these conflicts can be immediately observed and verified.

IP address conflicts generate problems that are often sporadic. This intermittent aspect of the issue is because the ARP entry that appears in the table is the address of the host that responded fastest to the last ARP request. Sometimes, one host will respond earlier, and other times, the second host may be the first to respond. Due to their nature, they can be difficult to identify. The **arp** utility supports us in this investigation.

The **arp** command is very useful for troubleshooting problems with IP to Ethernet address translation. Using the following three parameters, an administrator can delete a problem entry and replace the entry with a corrected one:

- **-a** will display all ARP entries in the table.
- **-d** hostname permits an administrator to delete a specified (problem) entry from the ARP table.
- **-s hostname ether-address** permits the administrator to add a new (corrected) entry to the table.

Sample output

For arp:

```
C:\WINDOWS\system32>arp -a
Interface: 192.168.56.1 --- 0x5
  Internet Address        Physical Address      Type
  192.168.56.255          ff-ff-ff-ff-ff-ff     static
  224.0.0.22              01-00-5e-00-00-16     static
  224.0.0.251             01-00-5e-00-00-fb     static
  224.0.0.252             01-00-5e-00-00-fc     static
  239.255.255.250         01-00-5e-7f-ff-fa     static

Interface: 10.10.0.18 --- 0x14
  Internet Address        Physical Address      Type
  10.10.0.1               68-d7-9a-5a-9b-15     dynamic
  10.10.0.255             ff-ff-ff-ff-ff-ff     static
  224.0.0.22              01-00-5e-00-00-16     static
  224.0.0.251             01-00-5e-00-00-fb     static
  224.0.0.252             01-00-5e-00-00-fc     static
```

```
239.255.255.250      01-00-5e-7f-ff-fa      static
255.255.255.255      ff-ff-ff-ff-ff-ff      static
```

Here, **-a** displays the **arp** table.

NETSTAT

NETSTAT is a network utility for displaying network statistics such as TCP/IP protocol-specific network connections, network interface and routing statistics, and port states and connections.

The command generates detailed information about how the host is communicating on the network/internet, and it can show the applications (executable) involved in creating each connection or listening port. Port states can be listening, open, established, or waiting.

Netstat is a cross-platform network utility available in Windows, macOS, and Unix/Linux operating systems. Netstat, on its own, displays simple statistics such as the local IP address (localhost), the foreign IP address (the host/device connected to), their respective randomized or fixed port numbers, as well as the TCP state and protocol.

When used along with available parameters, it is an excellent troubleshooting tool.

Troubleshooting examples

Netstat is regularly used with other command utilities such as ping, tracert, and ipconfig.

Netstat can be used along with Task Manager. Task Manager allows the administrator to observe processes running on a host on the network. These processes will need to have open and established ports assigned to transmit traffic successfully. However, not all processes running on a host are legitimate by nature. In some cases, running processes may be a sign of malware or insecure connections. By viewing the **Process Identifier** (**PID**) in Task Manager, the administrator can observe the network statistics and use NETSTAT to verify the executable running the process and begin to investigate the source application and its location on the system. These two tools, when combined, assist a network administrator in discovering malware, identifying suspect activity, and beginning the steps to manually remove the malware/trojan/rootkit or remediate the host/workstation presenting the problem.

As an added help, the **-f** parameter displays **Fully Qualified Domain Names** (**FQDN**) for foreign addresses. This information is very valuable when troubleshooting network connections and security issues. Administrators can find the source domains and check whether these domain names are legitimate URLs.

Using the **-s** option, an administrator can debug network issues and verify the health of a host/system. This parameter displays summary statistics per protocol. Packers sent, received, discarded, or dropped can be seen as a numerical value. This information helps to assess how well the host is performing.

These are some examples of netstat as a supporting tool in troubleshooting network issues.

Sample output

For netstat:

```
C:\WINDOWS\system32>netstat
```

```
Active Connections
```

Proto	Local Address	Foreign Address	State
TCP	10.10.0.18:49720	20.54.36.229:https	ESTABLISHED
TCP	10.10.0.18:49784	20.54.37.73:https	ESTABLISHED
TCP	10.10.0.18:49833	52.112.238.121:https	ESTABLISHED
TCP	10.10.0.18:49847	52.112.238.121:https	ESTABLISHED

Note: The host machine generates a randomized port number for each connection made (for example, 49720 or 49764). In this case, the foreign address is a web server generating a standardized assigned number—in this case, 443 for the protocol HTTPS.

HOSTNAME

This is a simple but useful command.

hostname prints the name of the current host.

Sample output

For hostname:

```
C:\WINDOWS\system32>hostname
PC18
```

ROUTE

The route command enables the user to manipulate network routing tables. For example, when the command is combined with the **-f** switch, it clears the routing tables of all gateway entries. If this is used in conjunction with one of the commands, the tables are cleared before running the command. This action was done before running the route print.

Sample output

For route:

```
C:\WINDOWS\system32>route print
IPv4 Route Table
===========================================================================
```

```
Active Routes:
Network Destination        Netmask          Gateway       Interface  Metric
          0.0.0.0          0.0.0.0        10.10.0.1      10.10.0.18     35
===========================================================================
Persistent Routes:
  None

IPv6 Route Table
===========================================================================
Active Routes:
  None
Persistent Routes:
  None
```

TELNET

Telnet is a command line tool that provides the user with a client/server connection and interface to another host, usually a remote connection. Originally used to service and manage terminals or servers, it can be used to log on and carry out initial configurations on a switch/router or manage them remotely. Telnet protocol uses port **23**. It has been designated as an unsafe means of remote management as the data is unencrypted and travels across networks in plain text, thus presenting a security risk. Telnet's use has waned significantly, now being replaced for its functions by SSH, which holds much-improved security features and encryption.

Options

The Telnet options are as follows:

- **-a**: Attempt automatic logon. Same as the **-l** option, except it uses the currently logged-on user's name.

- **-e**: Escape character to enter telnet client prompt.

- **-f**: File name for client-side logging.

- **-l**: Specifies the username to log in with on the remote system. It requires that the remote system support the **TELNET ENVIRON** option.

- **-t**: Specifies terminal type. Supported term types are vt100, vt52, ansi, and vtnt only.

- **Host**: Specifies the hostname or IP address of the remote computer to connect to.

- **Port**: Specifies a port number or service name.

Sample output

The following output from Telnet shows failed access to a host device:

```
C:\WINDOWS\system32>telnet 192.168.0.1
Connecting To 192.168.0.1...Could not open connection to the host, on port
23: Connect failed
```

Note: The output confirms a closed/blocked port. The firewall blocks telnet connections to the default gateway address. When permissible, telnet can be secured with login credential requirements. However, this command is insecure and somewhat dated due to the transmission of data in plain text.

TCPDUMP

tcpdump is a packet analyzer that is run from the command prompt. It is a cross-platform utility that displays TCP/IP packets as they travel on the network. In contrast to Wireshark, tcpdump is a CLI-based utility. It captures packets and allows the user to monitor data transmission and assess and evaluate data packets as they travel through a host. This tool has many options and features and, similar to Wireshark, has a variety of uses, especially in the field of security.

Sample output

In tcpdump:

- **-c**: We can restrict the number of packets to capture by using **-c** followed by a number. For example, to stop capturing after ten packets, we would use **-c 10**.

- **-e**: Print the link-level header for each packet. This option is beneficial if we want to view the MAC addresses for Ethernet connections.

- **-n**: By default, **tcpdump** will try to convert IP addresses to host addresses. For example, instead of printing the IP **'8.8.8.8'**, it will display **dns.google**. This translation can slow the operation down. The **-n** option causes **tcpdump** to print IP addresses and port numbers instead of trying to look them up with DNS. Using the **-n** option speeds things up and minimizes lag issues. It is similar to the result of the command **no ip domain-lookup** when implemented on a Cisco switch or router.

NMAP

This tool is covered earlier in the chapter in the section covering network software tools.

To give you an idea of the diversity of uses the command prompt in Windows has, there are approximately 280 commands, each with its own specific purpose in Windows editions. Remember, this quantity is integrated into Windows alone, and this is before we even begin looking at Unix, Linux, or macOS capabilities to quantify their tools and functions. Consequently, the commands cited in the preceding section are primarily used for network troubleshooting, configuration, and diagnostics. The commands, detailed on first inspection, may appear to be a small and limited suite. However, when one looks more closely, the more accurate picture of their uses emerges and becomes clearer. The key to competence in the application is to explore more parameters and learn them as one looks deeper into the tools and utilities, and put them into practice whenever possible.

Basic network platform commands

Managed switches (and routers) can also be configured from a CLI. An administrator can manage a switch or router directly with a console cable or via an **Integrated Lights Out (ILO)** management device. They can also manage and configure the switch by setting up an IP address on a **Switch Virtual Interface** (b) and accessing this interface (that is, Management VLAN) remotely. Routers can be managed directly from the console or via their (virtual) loopback addresses. Users can also connect to other physical interfaces using other mechanisms installed and configured to handle this form of remote access.

For example, Cisco IOS has an extensive range of configuration options. Cisco operates with a hierarchical structure when accessing the network platform. This gradation in privileges is similar to the differing accounts we have in Windows, such as a Guest account, Standard User, Power User, and Administrator, among others. Linux operating system uses the root user as its top privilege. In Cisco IOS, there are three main modes of operation. These modes are **User EXEC**, **Privileged EXEC**, and **Global Configuration** mode. Unlike a Windows setup, where you can log out from one account to another or shift between accounts with varying privileges, navigating a Cisco device differs. Once you log in (with the correct password on a password-protected device), you are immediately at the lowest end of the hierarchy, with the least privileges.

In **User EXEC** mode, a user can view the time, date, and version of the operating system, show system status, and view other less critical displays. However, they are not able to change critical settings, IP addresses, or anything that impacts the device in a meaningful way. This mode is a *read-only* setting. Again, without having to log out, the user can type *enable*. With the correct password, the user is moved up in privileges and can do more with the network device. Now, the user is in **Privileged EXEC** mode. They can navigate the IOS fully and move from mode to mode and into sub-modes to configure interfaces, manage protocols, or work with the VTY lines and configure remote access settings. They can configure switch-related protocols such as **Rapid Spanning Tree Protocol (RSTP)**, EtherChannel, or VLANS and trunking (802.1q). On routers, they can set up routing protocols such as **Open Shortest Pathway First (OSPF)** or **Enhanced Interior Gateway Protocol (EIGRP)**, to name but two popular protocols implemented in large enterprise networks.

Moving into **Global Configuration** mode permits the user to make changes that impact the device, such as giving the device a name or a banner to notify users with a cautionary message so that they do not attempt to breach security. More a deterrent, this message is called **Message of the Day** (**MOTD**) and may cite a legal statement declaring prohibited access to the equipment.

Cisco devices can have multiple passwords enabled, activated at specific navigation points, to secure the network device and keep control of device access. These access rights usually align with the **principle of least privilege** (**PoLP**) among IT department members.

In short, accessing a Cisco device is like arriving at a security barrier. Just because you can get by the security barrier does not mean your rights include entry to the comms room or to the colocation center in a datacenter. The layering of security attests to where you can go *and* what you can do. However, with network access privileges and fully equipped with passwords, you can work with the devices and dexterously move from mode to mode with full administrator privileges and control of the IOS and its commands. The device has its own layering of security in place to control access rights and regulate exactly what a person is allowed to do.

Examples of commands in the IOS

Cisco devices have different modes of operation. Depending on the mode used, an administrator has the ability to run commands and view outputs. In standard user exec mode, options are limited to show commands. In contrast, with privileged exec mode, an administrator has elevated permissions and can carry out configuration commands on the terminal accessed.

Let us now go over some examples of commands in the IOS.

User EXEC mode

show interface: This command displays the status of all interfaces on the device. The information includes the state of the interface as *physically* up, down, administratively down, or disabled. Line protocols or logical configurations will show as up or down. An interface could be up/up. This would mean the link is active and operational physically and that the logical protocol/line protocol configuration is also functional. The status of down/up points to a physical problem with the link. Down/down would signify errors that are both physical and logical in nature. Needless to say, there are many simple and more complex reasons for this particular output.

The output shows details, including the MAC address of the interface, packets sent and received, speed and duplex, input/output errors, and whether packets were undersized (runts) or oversized (jumbo). A user can specify a specific interface to view to reduce the output and focus on a specific link for analysis.

For example:

```
S2>show interface g0/1
GigabitEthernet0/1 is up, line protocol is up (connected)
```

Privileged EXEC mode

show config: This command displays the device's configuration settings. **show config** shows the contents of the **startup-config** file that is saved to NVRAM. This file is used when the system boots up and settings are read and applied.

show running-config shows the **running-config** that is accessed from the router RAM, and the IOS is presently running on it. When the user saves the running-config they are working on, the configuration is transferred from running RAM to NVRAM. This occurs when the command **copy running-config startup-config (copy run start)** is implemented. The next time the device boots up, it will use the newer settings and the amended startup file.

Sample output

Here is a sample output from the show running-config command:

```
S2#show running-config
Building configuration...
!
!
!
!
line con 0
!
line vty 0 4
login
line vty 5 15
login
```

Note that we have purposefully left the interface statistics out to focus on the details about the console cable (line con 0) and virtual terminal lines (line VTY) of S2. There are 16 VTY lines on S2, and none of the lines are password protected. Neither is the console cable on the network device. Obviously, this is not recommended, as an intruder could plug a cable into the console port and compromise the settings or access the switch remotely once connected to the network.

Password-protected line output looks like the following:

```
line con 0
password [C0mp1ex!]
```

```
login
!
line vty 0 4
password [C0mp1ex!]
login
line vty 5 15
login
```

Always ensure security settings are in place on all network platforms.

show IP route: This command is used to display the specified router's routing table. The command generates a list of networks that the router *knows about* (locally connected networks) or *learns* (networks learned by a *currently running* dynamic routing protocol or routes previously added manually by the administrator). The administrator might view the networks, their prefix lengths, and the exit interfaces they are associated with. This is the type of information used by routers to make forwarding decisions about packets they are handling and to send the packets on to the next HOP.

When viewing the routing table, the user is also supported by codes to assist them in interpreting the routing protocols related to the network listed. The following are some codes that display every time the command is run, appearing before the routing table and list of networks:

```
R2#show ip route
Codes: L - local, C - connected, S - static, R - RIP, M - mobile, B - BGP
D - EIGRP, EX - EIGRP external, O - OSPF, IA - OSPF inter area
```

This list has been extracted from the full list of codes in the output. The following is an example of the show route command, listing networks in a subnetted network. Observe the codes in use:

```
10.0.0.0/8 is variably subnetted, 4 subnets, 2 masks
C 10.1.1.0/30 is directly connected, Serial0/0/0
L 10.1.1.2/32 is directly connected, Serial0/0/0
C 10.2.2.0/30 is directly connected, Serial0/0/1
L 10.2.2.2/32 is directly connected, Serial0/0/1
```

These are just some of the commands used on network intermediary devices. Note that this section covered basic commands and offered sample output from network platforms. Configuring networking equipment is a specialized area. However, the administrator who takes on this learning and tackles navigating CLI-based operating systems on switches and routers should find it a stimulating and rewarding journey.

To summarize, the **show** commands, when used in network troubleshooting, are formidable allies when battling issues with cable connectivity, switching, routing, and wireless protocols. They help us to verify and diagnose the functionality and performance of our network device settings.

Putting commands into action

Much of network troubleshooting involves hands-on practical applications. In *Figure 23.11*, we see a field engineer. He is consulting a device, and it looks like he is reading and interpreting the statistics of an application to support his network management. Understanding the software, he is consulting will strengthen his ability to handle the networking equipment he is analyzing.

Figure 23.11: Managing devices

Previously in the chapter, we explored some network software tools. One of these tools was a protocol analyzer named Wireshark. This software provides an opportunity to demonstrate how network administrators can troubleshoot issues on their networks and put the network troubleshooting steps into action.

We will investigate the TCP three-way handshake as an extended example of troubleshooting with software tools.

TCP three-way handshake

Some application layer protocols use TCP when establishing communication sessions. TCP controls the safe delivery of data and ensures the data is intact and in the right order. When application layer protocols such as FTP or HTTP are initiated on a host, TCP carries out the three-way handshake to set up a reliable, connection-oriented session. For example, whenever a user starts a browsing session with HTTP, a three-way handshake is initiated between the user's PC/host machine and the web server. The relationship between the two machines will be that of a client-server. Every time a browsing session begins with a server, this handshake occurs to guarantee and safeguard transmission between the host machine and related websites. When we think of how many tabs (active connections) we have when browsing, it should make sense that multiple TCP sessions can be active simultaneously on a host machine.

Figure 23.12 shows a simplified version of what happens throughout the duration of the three-way handshake. The figure demonstrates the process of communication between the host machine as a client and the corresponding server. The entire process results in an established connection between the two machines.

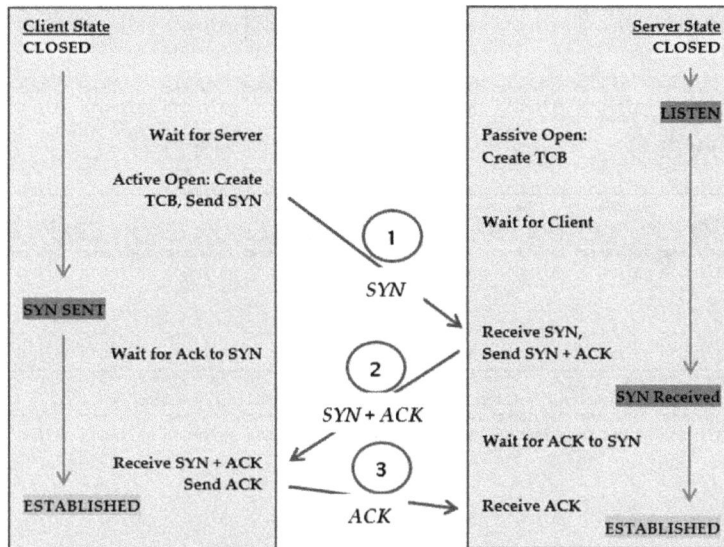

Figure 23.12: TCP three-way handshake

There are the following three steps in a three-way handshake:

1. The connection between the client and server is initiated. The client sends an **SYN** packet to ask if the server is open for any new connections. It also helps the hosts involved in the handshake to synchronize sequence numbers between devices.

2. The server receives the **SYN** packet sent by the client machine and sends an **SYN + ACK** back to the client. This comprises the **SYN** message from the local device and the **ACK** of the earlier packet.

3. The client receives the **SYN+ACK** and responds with an **ACK**. This message is used to verify to the other side that it has received the **SYN**.

Three-way handshake

Let us look at this packet capture in Wireshark.

In *Figure 23.13*, we can see the steps of the process as numbered in the furthest left column. Through our observation of the process, we can verify the process between the source IP and destination IP took place as anticipated:

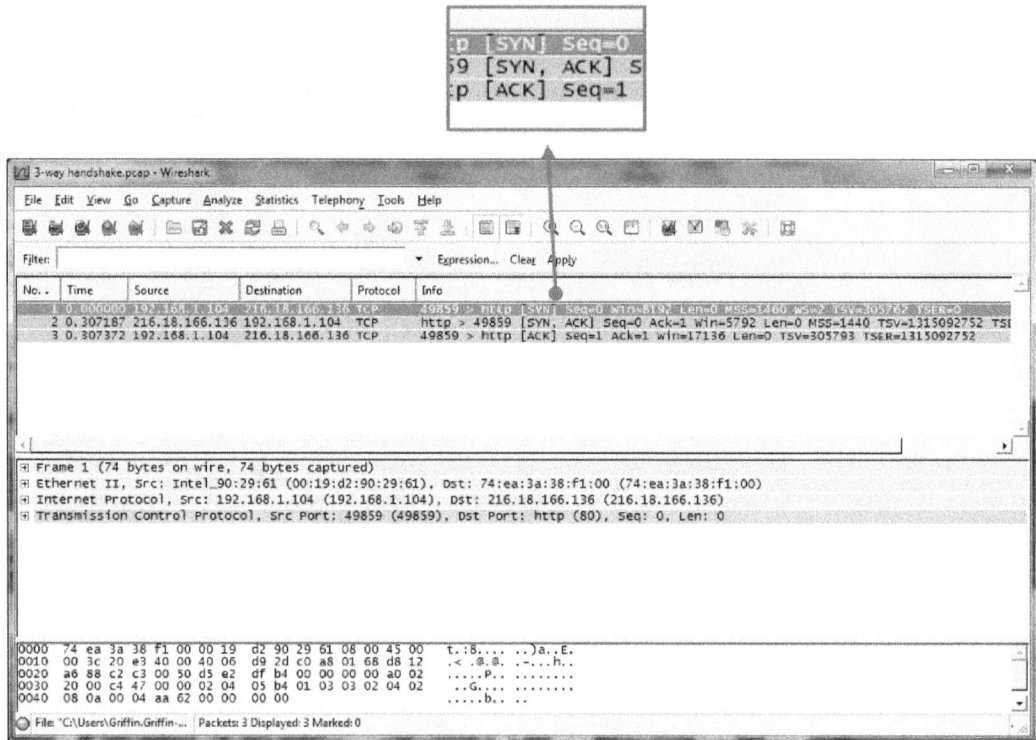

Figure 23.13: Wireshark, TCP three-way handshake

But how does capturing this data help us in real-world troubleshooting?

By using a protocol analyzer, we can check the validity of the IP addresses in transactions and verify the open connections between the two devices communicating. This tool would also show us a security incident called SYN Flooding, otherwise known as a half-open attack. SYN Flooding happens when an attacker continuously sends initial SYN requests to a server. This operates like a DoS/DDoS attack, as the server becomes overloaded and overwhelmed with bogus SYN traffic.

Ultimately, the server denies services and connections to legitimate users and can be brought down or offline as a result. In short, the server is constantly waiting for the third step of the handshake to take place, and this ACK does not arrive from any of the (typically spoofed) IPs. Increasing the backlog queue and creating SYN cookies are ways to mitigate this security threat.

However, Wireshark or another protocol analyzer will let us visualize and verify the attack and even see the spikes in traffic and the rise in TCP packets as the SYNs are sent. This allows the administrator or security analyst to investigate IP addresses or use other tools to attempt to discover the origin and extent of the security breach. For this and many other reasons and uses, protocol analyzers are excellent tools for network administration and security.

Conclusion

In this chapter, we explored network software tools and command-line network utilities. We itemized these tools and utilities and evaluated how they assist administrators in network diagnostics and repair.

In the upcoming chapter, we will learn how to troubleshoot wireless networks and what this troubleshooting involves.

Points to remember

- Managing and monitoring a network entails the ability to:

    o   Differentiate between the network software tools available.

    o   Identify the functionality and purpose of each tool.

    o   Choose appropriate tools and commands to verify TCP/IP functions.

    o   Manage a network more proficiently.

- The content of *Chapter 23, Network Utilities*, is mapped to *Domain 5, Network Troubleshooting*. Given a scenario, use the appropriate tool or protocol to solve networking issues.

Key terms

- **Maximum Transmission Unit (MTU)**: A data payload measured in bytes.
- **Time to live**: (IP–TTL) This is a counter field in the IP header. TTL records the number of hops a packet can make before the packet is dropped (expires).

Questions

1. List examples of common network software tools.
2. Give some examples of their use.
3. Give some examples of command-line network utilities.
4. Describe some skills that are enhanced by using network tools in practical applications.

Join our book's Discord space

Join the book's Discord Workspace for Latest updates, Offers, Tech happenings around the world, New Release and Sessions with the Authors:

https://discord.bpbonline.com

CHAPTER 24

Troubleshooting Wireless Networks

Introduction

I do not think that the wireless waves I have discovered will have any practical application.

- Heinrich Rudolf Hertz,

Physicist and Experimentalist

If the man (*Heinrich Rudolf Hertz*), whose surname is honored with the naming of the unit of frequency (Hertz), could revisit how wireless technology has evolved, he would surely be amazed at the technology's diversity of practical applications. He might also be slightly bemused by its global pervasiveness in our daily lives.

In radio frequency wireless networks, hosts connect wirelessly instead of using cables. This unbounded media makes wireless LANs somewhat invisible to end users, but network administrators must understand its operation as thoroughly as they do Ethernet cables. Wireless networking involves many variables, and connectivity issues require specific strategies and tools, similar to wired networks but with additional environmental factors. Understanding WLAN infrastructure and data transmission methods helps administrators fix connectivity issues and manage other unique problems. Hardware remains crucial for providing network services, so components must be well chosen and suited to the wireless environment.

This chapter focuses on troubleshooting wireless issues. The content is based on topics covered in *Chapter 12, Installing and Configuring Wireless Technologies,* and topics covering network hardware and software tools. The topics covered in the said chapter include wireless standards and specifications, channels and frequency bands, channel bonding, modulation techniques, and wireless deployments. Reviewing that chapter to consolidate the knowledge and skills required to troubleshoot wireless networks would be a good idea.

Structure

The chapter will explain the following topics:

- Wireless deployments
- Standards and limitations
- Common issues and solutions
- Other checks and tests

Objectives

In this chapter, we will consider wireless specifications and identify some limitations of using this technology. Like all technologies, there are rules and guidelines that need to be complied with to maximize performance and uptime. There are also commonly occurring problems associated with wireless networks. After reading this chapter, you will be able to identify the problems and issues in WLANs and follow troubleshooting methods to work through and resolve the issues that arise. By using the understanding from previous chapters, you will build on the skills and select the appropriate hardware and software tools to assist you in problem-solving these issues.

Wireless deployments

The following is a list of hardware components to be found in wireless network infrastructure:

- The NIC and the end device/station itself (STA).
- **Access points** (**APs**) that can hub, switch, bridge, and where applicable, route.
- Wi-Fi extenders, boosters, or repeaters.
- **Autonomous AP**: A single wireless AP operating as a **Basic Service Set** (**BSS**).
- **Ad hoc**: End devices in a peer-to-peer configuration, running as an **Independent BSS** (**IBSS**) without an AP present.

- **Central switching**: One or more basic service sets connected by a **Wireless Distribution System** (**WDS**), running with multiple APs, a main base station, and relay base stations.

Note the number of variables in implementing wireless technology, ranging from simpler to more complex setups and configurations.

An administrator will encounter some, if not all, of this hardware as they troubleshoot WLANs. On top of that, they will encounter the diverse range of software and services underpinning wireless technology and engage with wireless protocols, security mechanisms, and software drivers required for the service's operation. This mixture of hardware and software means that an administrator will need to know how wireless networks work and how hardware and software interact to keep the wireless connection reliable and consistent in a mobile environment.

In *Figure 24.1*, we can observe various wireless configurations. The hardware in the graphic includes APs, routers, a mobile mast station, and an antenna. The activities illustrated are peer-to-peer transmissions, an ad hoc Bluetooth configuration with a wearable device, file uploads, a **Near Field Communication** (**NFC**) data transfer, and other daily communications occurring in a wireless mobile environment.

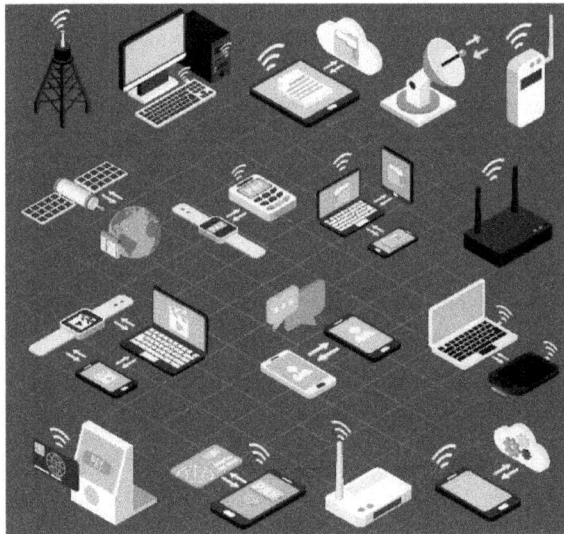

Figure 24.1: *Wireless communication*

Standards and limitations

In *Chapter 12, Installing and Configuring Wireless Technologies*, we explored the various wireless standards and their specifications. The specifications 802.11a, 802.11b, 802.11g, 802.11n, 802.11ac, 802.11ad, and 802.11.ax were defined under the term's frequency, maximum speed, maximum distance, channels, modulation techniques, and compatibility (see *Table 12.2 from Chapter 12, Installing and Configuring Wireless Technologies*). This table gives us insight into the characteristics and recommended standards for each specification. In *Chapter 3, Cables and Connectors*, we defined the following terms: bandwidth, throughput, and goodput. We will review these concepts and discuss them further as they relate to wireless technology:

- **Bandwidth**: This broad term is defined as the bit-rate measure of the transmission capacity over a network communication system. Bandwidth is also described as the carrying capacity or the data transfer speed of a channel. However, it is the capacity of a network. Bandwidth exists in physical or wireless communication networks. In wireless transmission, bandwidth transmission is measured in megabits per second. Remember that bandwidth is not the same as the speed of the internet. Measured in Mbps, it is the *volume* of information that can be sent over the wireless connection in a given amount of time. The transmission speed is faster as a user gets closer to the antenna on the network. In terms of distance, the signal strength increases when the user is relatively near the antenna/AP. For example, 5 GHz is the best-suited band for high-bandwidth devices or internet activities that call on real-time speed with QoS priority, such as multi-media gaming and streaming HDTV. The 5 GHz provides faster speeds and more signal strength over a shorter range when compared with the 2.4GHz band. The nominal link speed is determined by standards in use, for example, Wi-Fi 5 (802.11ac) or Wi-Fi 6 (802.11ax). Wi-Fi 6 supports both frequency bands and has enhanced upgrades to MU-MIMO, battery-saving strategies for IoT, and an improved version of security with WPA3 as a new security protocol. These improvements deliver better speeds and optimum security when compared with earlier generations.

- **Throughput**: This refers to the performance of tasks by a computing service or device over a specific period. It measures the amount of completed work against time consumed and may be used to measure the performance of a processor, memory, and/or network communications. In wireless transmission, throughput is the amount of data successfully transferred through the wireless network.

- **Goodput**: Goodput (a portmanteau of good and throughput) may be seen as *actual* data transmission. In wireless transmission, goodput is the *actual* data transmission. For example, when we look at the concept of Airtime and Airtime Utilization, we can measure channel usage over time. We can view the per-channel Airtime Usage and other statistics using an analyzer. We can determine how much time is free on a specific channel for data transmissions. We can identify clients connected and the airtime used by traffic sent and received. We can also observe peaks in usage when many users connect to the network and when there is an influx of active end devices. Periodic peaks are acceptable and probably unavoidable surges in traffic— once we determine them, they form part of our business operations or trends. An example of a peak in usage would be a video conference where all employees are online at the same time, or when a large group of users are collaborating on a business project. However, we should also note the *baseline* figure for utilization.

If we discover too many APs on the same channel, interference from neighboring networks, or if too many SSIDs are advertised and beaconing, our goodput could be impacted by these issues, as well as the generation of other problems. To counter these issues, the organization may need to review the network design. In short, these measurements and calculations help us to make decisions about the network and inform us about the accurate configuration of our devices. Observing channel utilization can support maximizing goodput on the network. In short, errors due to lost, corrupt, or dropped packets require data retransmission, reducing the goodput of the connection.

Received signal strength indication and dBm

Essentially, received signal strengths can be measured in two ways. We can use **received signal strength indication** (**RSSI**) as a value for interpreting the signal strength, or we can use **decibel-milliwatts** (**dBm**) as a means of measuring the *power level* of the signal.

RSSI

RSSI is a **relative** index and metric. It measures the RF signal strength received by an 802.11 device.

The IEEE 802.11 standard specifies that WLAN chipset manufacturers can set their own maximum value for RSSI. The standard range (measurement parameter) is 0–255. Therefore, vendors can use proprietary ranges, for example, 0–255, 0–100, or 0–60. This explains that RSSI is a relative index of measurement because the manufacturer is measuring signals using the pre-determined range and maximum parameters of their proprietary system.

When displaying the 802.11 device's specifications, a vendor might show both units of measurement. These RSSI metrics are mapped to receive sensitivity thresholds that are conveyed in absolute dBm values.

dBm

dBm is an electrical power unit in decibels as referenced to 1 **milliwatt** (**mW**). It is an **absolute** unit of measurement.

1 mW = 0dBm

1 W is equal to 30 dBm:

1 W = 1,000 mW = 30 dBm

dBm is displayed as a negative number. When the dBm measurement is closer to zero, this indicates the signal strength is better. This value is used to determine if the user will get a good wireless connection and whether the device that they are using is hearing a signal from the AP or wireless router they wish to connect to.

RSSI and **Signal to Noise Ratio (SNR)** can be measured using a Wi-Fi analyzer. This type of software can be installed on a laptop or smartphone. This tool will record statistics for the AP that the client is currently associated with and identify any other APs in the surrounding area. The SNR is a measure of the strength of the desired signal relative to an undesired signal or background noise. This is measured in decibels and has a fixed formula and comparator. Irrespective of the method used to measure this signal, we are looking for a *strong* signal that is not degraded by background noise.

Many third-party tools survey wireless networks and have the ability to measure RSSI and SNR. InSSIDer is another excellent tool used for this purpose.

Table 24.1 describes the quality of signal strengths as measured in dBm:

Signal strength	Quality to expect	Required level for
–30 dBm	Maximum signal strength. The end device is most likely a few feet from the access point or router. This proximity to RF devices is not the usual way for a user to be connected, nor is it a desirable or typical one in real-world network/business operations. Above excellent.	
–50 dBm	Anything down to this level can be regarded as having excellent signal strength.	
–60 dBm	This value is still good and indicates reliable signal strength. Reliable.	
–67 dBm	This value is the minimum signal strength value for all services that require smooth and reliable data traffic—typically, business applications. Very good.	VoIP/VoWi-Fi Video streaming and streaming (Not of the highest quality)
–70 dBm	The signal is not very strong but is adequate for decent packet delivery service. Okay.	Web, e-mail
–80 dBm	This value is not good. It is the minimum value required to make a basic connection. It cannot be counted on for a reliable connection or to provide sufficient signal strength to use services. Not good.	
–90 dBm	It is very unlikely that a device will be able to connect or use any services with this signal strength or power level. Interference may be severely impacting signal strength. Impractical.	

Table 24.1: Signal strength

Note: It is very important to remember that the power level of a device on its own is not necessarily the indicator or measurement of a good wireless experience. This RSSI/dBm measurement is taken from the perspective of the end device. The AP also has to see and hear the end device, so the overall wireless experience is always a two-way thing.

Effective Isotropic Radiated Power/Power settings

Isotropic antennae are intended to distribute power equally in every direction. When the channel is powered in one direction and then calculated, the outcome is known as the **Effective Isotropic Radiated Power** (**EIRP**). The direction will be that with the highest direction gain. We also need to factor in losses in the transmission line. The vendor of the wireless equipment is responsible for setting the EIRP and ensuring they do not exceed maximum standards.

Measuring transmission

EIRP measures the signal we are transmitting. The calculation is given as follows:

$$EIRP = P_T - L_C + G_A,$$

Where,

P_T = Output power of the transmitter in dBm

L_C = Cable loss in dB

G_A = Antenna gain in **decibels over isotropic** (**dBi**)

This calculation is used to measure transmitters and other RF frequency sources.

Increasing the transmit power of an AP is not usually an effective solution to improving wireless coverage. We need to remember that some end devices will have a much weaker power rate. To optimize the data transfer, the client must be able to communicate effectively with the AP. As a rule of thumb, the AP power should be 2nds/3rds of the weakest client power setting. Our aim is to ensure the data rates of both devices will result in packets successfully arriving at their destination, with minimum error and bottlenecks.

Wireless considerations

In *Chapter 12, Installing and Configuring Wireless Technologies, Table 12.4*, we outlined the basic properties of antenna types and their typical usage. The three main types of antennae used in wireless configurations were defined and described. These are omnidirectional, directional, and Yagi. Here, we will focus more on troubleshooting antenna placement and the main types of problems arising from their misplacement or misconfiguration.

Antenna placement

Misplacement of the antenna causes dead spots in the coverage area, low signal strengths, and poor performance, ultimately impacting network access.

Omnidirectional antennas broadcast radio waves in every direction, dispersing the RF wave in an equal 360-degree pattern. The recommended deployments for these antennae are in open office areas, conference rooms, warehouses, manufacturing floors, and outdoor seating areas, plus indoor/outdoor retail environments.

To ensure best practice, we should locate the AP in the middle of the area that needs network access. Generally, when we place APs higher up, this positioning prevents interference problems caused by going through building or structural foundations.

The power of an omnidirectional antenna is measured by the strength and reach of the antenna's signal. This is referred to as **gain**. For the best results indoors, this antenna should be mounted to the ceiling. The coverage area is across one floor because this type of antenna is not suited to covering multiple floors due to the way the antenna radiates the signal.

In outdoor scenarios, an omnidirectional antenna (like all antennae) should be placed as high up as feasible, attached to a wall, roof, or pole, for example. If there is to be an outside antenna mounted, then there should be an appropriate separation between the inside and outside antenna to mitigate against feedback or oscillation. It should be noted that for security and other reasons, businesses and organizations having outside antennae is *not* the norm. Companies will have a secure WLAN with the objective that *no* signal goes beyond the exterior walls or doors of the building. However, it is no harm to mention the correct outside placement of an omnidirectional antenna in a more suitable network environment, such as a home wireless network or a SOHO. Remember, when APs are placed near outside walls, the signal will emanate beyond these walls.

A **directional antenna** creates a narrow, focused signal and focuses the signal to target energy in certain directions. This increases the signal strength and transmission distance. Patch and Yagi antennas are mounted to a wall or mast and provide coverage in a limited-angle pattern. This antenna is very suited to a point-to-point connection and configuration. A directional antenna broadcasts stronger signals than an omnidirectional antenna, largely due to its targeted focus. Ideally, it should be placed on the ceiling; otherwise, it can be placed in a central location mounted to the wall. Typical locations are down a hallway in a hospital or office corridor, a warehouse or manufacturing facility with high steel shelving, or mining shafts and drifts. When properly placed, these antennae provide optimum wireless reception, with the benefit of increased distances.

The amount of directionality, referred to as the **beamwidth**, is measured in degrees. Beamwidth is a physical characteristic of a directional antenna, which can be calculated mathematically. In terms of placement, a pair of 10-degree antennae is very highly directional and will need more precise alignment than if we were to use a pair of 90-degree antennae.

Coverage overlap

When placing APs, we should aim for a good percentage of coverage overlap between APs. When there is a good signal overlap, a device can travel between these signals with slight interruption, and most importantly, there will be no dead spots. A strong target is 15%–20% coverage overlap between the APs. Be aware that too much overlap causes co-channel interference.

Figure 24.2 illustrates an appropriate coverage overlap:

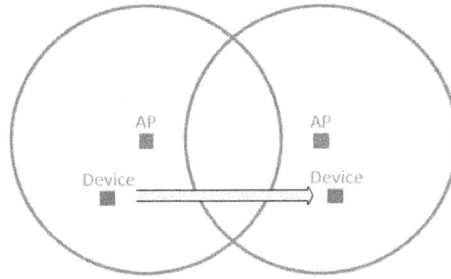

Figure 24.2: *Coverage overlap*

Polarization

A directional antenna is better equipped to handle obstacles, mainly because we can adjust the direction/orientation as required. This process is referred to as **polarization**, which is the orientation of the antenna relative to the surface of the earth. When two antennas are well aligned and have the same polarization, the signal strength will be greater. Conversely, when the antennas are poorly aligned, the signal received will be degraded, if received at all. There are several options available for orienting the antenna. In implementing wireless networks, polarization should be considered as a relative factor in optimizing data transmission. Polarization is important, especially in 5G networking. **Multiple Input/ Multiple Output** (**MIMO**) antenna arrays can attain enhanced data throughput when the use of available spectrum via polarization is applied. This is achieved using an effective arrangement of different signal polarization and spatial diversity (that is, multiplexing) of the antennas in the configuration. This is just one example as to why polarization should always be factored in as an important aspect of wireless networking.

AP association time

AP association time occurs when end devices are associated with an AP. This association can fail if the client is incorrectly configured (for example, incorrect SSID/passphrase, unsupported data types, encryption protocol mismatches, and so on). It can also fail when the client device and AP have incompatibility issues or when a device is roaming between APs and tries to quickly associate before being fully moved out of the first AP's range. Note that a mobile device/station (STA) can be 802.11 authenticated to numerous APs. However, it can only be actively associated and transfer data through a single AP at any given time. Once the STA meets the requirements for the AP, it will be associated, and the device can begin transferring data. If encryption is enabled, the same encryption key must be configured on both the AP and the client.

A network administrator can gather statistics and analyze association times with **Simple Network Protocol Management** (**SNMP**) or track association metrics through the console manager.

Channel utilization

APs share the available network bandwidth between connected devices. As more end devices associate with the AP, there will be a reduction in bandwidth for each individual device. This reduction can cause network performance problems. The solution to this problem is to reduce the number of wireless clients/devices using each channel in the wireless network design.

Site survey

Carrying out a site survey is a critical part of wireless network deployment. Site surveys happen as one of the steps in designing a wireless network. Before this survey even takes place, a lot of preliminary planning and negotiation between the clients and network providers/installers will have occurred. All the stakeholders come together for a briefing on the type of network required, its purpose and function, and the anticipated network performance desired. Estimations will be discussed on the hardware needed for the coverage area, the geographical location of the services, how many devices are to be procured and of what type, and the level of support needed for the services being provided. This stage and time scale is where all the data is gathered to begin designing the wireless network.

The likelihood with these kinds of business projects is that one meeting will not be sufficient to cover all the requirements for the network to be designed and deployed. In these meetings, the network expectations should be clearly documented and defined. Documentation is a key part of every part of this process. As an organization, we will need a clear vision of what the WLAN will look like and how devices will interconnect with the recommended number of clients. This clarity will support us in creating a wireless network that is effective, fully operational, and does what it is intended to do. Most WLAN designers will require a completed **request for information** (**RFI**) form from the business or organization to assist the design process. This RFI form usually holds precise details as to what the organization expects, as well as building diagrams, room layouts, and illustrations.

Wireless network design considerations might include some or all of the following:

- AP types required for point-to-point bridging or roaming.
- The availability of mounting points.
- Use of wireless networks/estimated bandwidth.
- The number of expected network users (overall and per AP).
- Construction materials or other entities that could cause an obstruction to the RF signal.
- Any potential sources of RF interference (for example, neighboring networks and machinery).
- Environmental considerations.

- The types and abilities of the wireless client end devices.
- Existing infrastructure devices in the WLAN network.
- The presence or plan for IoT devices or sensors.
- Site survey.

An initial design document can be drawn based on the building and infrastructure of the area/rooms to be covered. The initial design will cover key areas in wireless network design considerations. This initial design diagram can be validated or edited when the site survey is completed. In a sense, the site survey further *tests* the conceptual blueprint in a real-world scenario.

One strategy for designing wireless networks is by using the WLAN modeling software. An example of this software is WLAN predictive modeling by *Ekahau*. This modeling software enables the user to place virtual APs on a building floor plan and mathematically calculate signal losses by inputting attenuation values into the design. Building infrastructure data can be input, such as the presence of walls, doors, or other obstacles that might cause obstructions to the wireless signal. This modeling means that actions can be proactively taken before the deployment of the WLAN. Other software tools for wireless management and monitoring include AirMagnet and SolarWinds NPM.

In the site survey stage, we can further assess the RF environment. Mounting points, APs, distances between APs, and the ability to reach the wireless controller or central switch can be identified and evaluated. We can ensure that all devices receive appropriate power and that electrical considerations are adhered to. The building infrastructure can be thoroughly explored for obstructions and signal issues such as absorption, reflection, refraction, or scattering. This site survey might reveal more details than the initial design or even deliver more insights than the predictive modeling outcomes. As expressed, it is important to carry it out. A site survey gives us the opportunity to fully test all the hardware in the location it will be installed in, and also use our test kit to test predicted network performance. Equipped with a spectrum analyzer in our kit, we can gather data about neighboring networks, check utilization statistics in both frequency bands, and determine the best ranges and channels for the wireless network. Two of the measurements we can calculate with the spectrum analyzer are as follows:

- **Signal to Noise Ratio (SN/SNR)**
- **Received Signal Level (RSL)**

The RSL indicates the strength of the RF signal. This increases when we are closer to the AP. When the site survey is completed, we should have lists and documents to return to the office and carry out a final plan of action and prepare for deployment and installation.

Note that the network administrators and security personnel from time to time will repeat the site survey to verify the environment has not changed and to discover potential security issues. If changes to the infrastructure have happened or new factors have emerged, the design of the WLAN will be revisited.

Figure 24.3 shows a map of signal strength in a wireless network. This heat map enables a network administrator to discern how to adjust the APs to achieve better coverage:

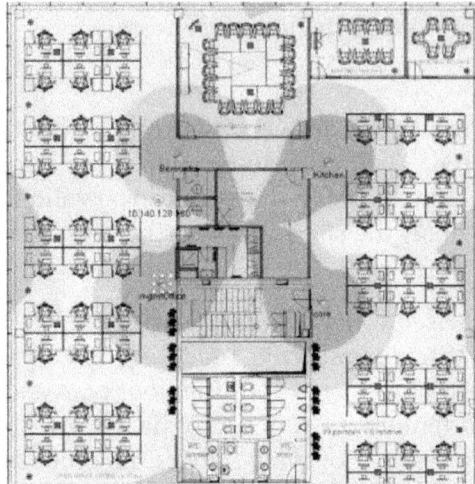

Figure 24.3: *A wireless heat map*
Source: *SolarWinds Worldwide LLC, www.solarwinds.com*

SolarWinds **Network Performance Monitor (NPM)** tests Wi-Fi signals and creates a heat map using its Network Atlas function. The map is superimposed onto the office floor plan.

Common issues and solutions

Let us look at some common issues that occur in wireless network settings. These issues can range from signal interference and weak signal strength to security vulnerabilities and device compatibility problems. Understanding these challenges is crucial for maintaining a reliable and secure wireless network. By addressing these common issues, network administrators can ensure optimal performance and user satisfaction.

Misconfigured devices

The most common issues in wireless networking stem from misconfigured devices and settings. These errors include the following:

- Wrong SSID
- Incorrect passphrase
- Encryption protocol mismatch
- Mismatched wireless standards

The solution to these common issues is to check all settings and ensure they have been entered correctly. Remember, passphrases are case-sensitive, so something as *simple* as this data input error may be the culprit preventing connectivity to the network. Wireless problems happen at the physical and data-link layers of the OSI model. Ensure the wireless NIC in the laptop/device is enabled and power is on. Configure the wireless router with a compatible protocol to match the correct settings for security and data transmission.

Remember to always use the network troubleshooting model and move from the simple to the more complex possibilities. Implement a theory of probable causes. Test the theory and verify full functionality.

Signaling and coverage

These issues include the following:

- Interference
- Channel overlap
- Antenna cable attenuation/signal loss
- RF attenuation/signal loss
- Insufficient wireless coverage

To counteract poor signaling, we can set up multiple routers in bridge mode and place them on different levels of a building to boost the RF signal.

Interference

Unlike wired networks, wireless networks are visible to other wireless networks. This visibility can cause issues like interference between the neighboring networks if they are in close proximity and there is channel overlap, or when both networks use multi-AP configurations. Wireless networks share the *air space*. If the wireless signal is experiencing interference from outside sources, we can change the channels on the wireless network. This will mitigate against channel saturation. As network administrators, we should identify the channels in use around the APs impacted. This is where we can implement our knowledge of wireless tools. Using a spectrum analyzer, we can visualize the channels in use. This tool helps to select the best channel automatically. However, the ideal solution is to make changes manually and check the functionality and performance with each change made or channel selected. By manually testing one channel at a time, we are incorporating troubleshooting steps into our practice (that is, evaluating, testing, and verifying the results).

If there are too many wireless clients connected to the AP, we can add another AP or a repeater to boost/strengthen the signal.

If a client is too far away from the AP and this is a locational issue, we can move the AP and ensure it is centrally located to produce good signaling. Alternatively, if the end device is simply out of wireless range, we can advise the user to move closer to the wireless router/access point.

Other common sources of interference on wireless networks are as follows:

- Cordless telephones operating in the 2.4 GHz range. Interference occurs during the phone's active call time

- PDAs and cellphones

- Wireless video cameras

- Other APs in proximity to the network (for example, neighboring companies might have a wireless network configured to use a similar channel.)

- Microwave ovens or outdoor microwave links.

- Bluetooth devices or Zigbee devices (Zigbee is a personal area network technology that uses Bluetooth)

- Wireless peripherals

- Wireless game controllers

These devices should be identified and noted as to where and when they are in use.

Channel interference or overlap

Check that channel utilization meets the standards when using the 2.4 GHz or 5 GHz bands. The 5 GHz band functions over a larger number of unique channels. Less overlap across these channels means far less radio interference. This factor equals better performance.

The 2.4 GHz frequency range has three non-overlapping channels, and the 5 GHz range has 24 non-overlapping channels. The channels used in 2.4 GHz networks are channel 1, 6, and 11. Refer to *Figure 12.1* of *Chapter 12, Installing and Configuring Wireless Technologies*.

NetSpot is an example of a wireless channel scanner. This tool can support the troubleshooting process in home, office, or enterprise operations. Other tools applicable here are Wi-Fi Explorer, NetStumbler, iPerf, and KisMAC, along with other diagnostic and software tools referred to earlier in the chapter. In *Figure 24.4*, we can see an example of distancing and overlap in neighboring wireless networks:

Figure 24.4: Interference in wireless networks
Source: *favpng.com*

Figure 24.5 shows a graphical illustration of a home in a neighborhood, capturing dead spots and showing color-coded, varying levels of signal strength:

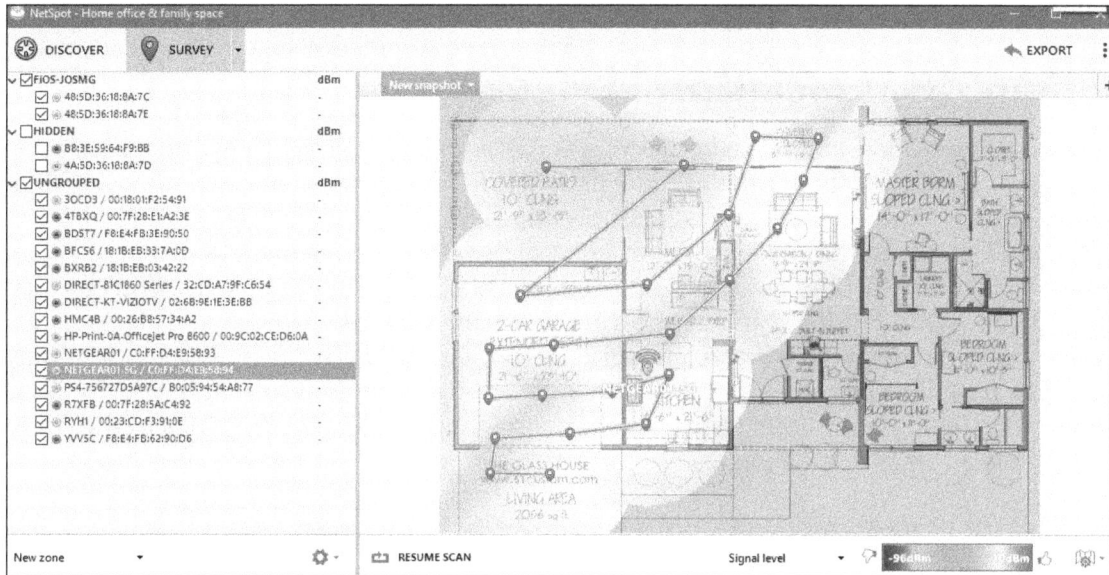

Figure 24.5: *NetSpot: Free edition, home and office image*

Captive portal issues

In wireless networks, captive portals are generally used to present a landing or log-in page to a user who wishes to access the network. These portals require authentication, or in some cases, payment or subscription, before a user is permitted access to network resources or services. These portals can have issues or problems, especially security-related ones. The threats associated with these portals include MAC spoofing, HTTP redirectors, arbitrary DNS traffic, and other point-of-entry attacks. A security check and analysis should verify that all measures have been applied to ensure that this *way in* to the network is firmly protected. Administrators who implement this portal in their WLAN need to be aware of the Web framework, not only to be able to fix issues with the portal itself; they also need to know the broader Web environment to ensure the functionality and consistency of the captive portal's operation. Though there are many benefits to a company having a captive portal, (for example, captured data for marketing, or deeper insights to users) for an administrator, they add an extra weight to managing a wireless network.

On the positive side, an administrator can weed out users who tend to hog the bandwidth. The file size of downloads can be restricted. Since users are prompted to agree to terms before using the network, this necessitates agreeing to personal accountability and responsibility while using the network. This prior agreement serves to remove liability from the owners of the WLAN, should problems or disagreements arise, or litigation occur. When functioning optimally, security will be improved, and performance enhanced as network congestion is reduced. In short, the administrator has more control over the entry route to the network and can manage access and customize the settings to suit the network's purpose.

Client disassociation issues

After authentication happens between an AP and a wireless client, an association message is exchanged between the client and AP to associate the client with the AP. Client disassociation occurs when clients keep disassociating from the network. If this occurs, we should check the device and AP to ensure all settings are correct and that they are compatible. If the AP does not handle connections at all, we will need to check this further. We can do this by using packet-capturing software such as Wireshark. This tool will capture the frames in the session, allowing us to interpret the frame information. It may be a case that the AP is older and cannot handle the transmissions or that the power level of the AP is very poor. While testing, we can also check the timeout settings in the AP to make certain, times and idle times are correct.

Disassociation attack

This attack can take place when an attacker sends a spoofed message to an AP. In normal operation, a wireless client sends a disassociation frame to the AP to terminate the connection. When the AP receives the message, the AP disassociates with the client whose MAC address is mentioned in the message received. Consequently, the client is effectively removed from the wireless network. With the spoofed MAC address, the hacker can send the disassociation frame and the AP will disconnect the client device, forcing the user to re-authenticate. This client is now the victim of a disassociation attack.

Attackers can also carry out a **denial-of-service** (**DoS**) attack on the AP and cause it to deny services to legitimate clients on the network. Wireless networks are also vulnerable to other forms of **Man in the Middle** (**MitM**) attacks if not fully secured. Attackers can carry out these attacks, where they might steal data or eavesdrop on data transmissions for other hostile purposes.

In terms of security, one way to secure a wireless network is to create network zones. These network zones provide separation for networks based on usage. Examples of network architecture zones are guest, wireless (for employees), and ad hoc (for temporary or *as-needed* connections).

There are numerous steps to securing a wireless network, but the critical step is in planning and in implementing a robust security protocol (for example, WPA2-AES or WPA3).

In short, our main objective in troubleshooting and resolving security issues is to aim to reduce attacks against our wireless network and to do so proficiently.

Other checks and tests

As part of troubleshooting practice, an administrator will frequently:

- Ensure the client device is using the correct and latest WLAN driver. BIOS firmware and chipset drivers should also be up to date.

- Check **Power over Ethernet (PoE)** is functioning.

- Ensure all updates and patches are implemented on all network devices.

- Check for time and date synchronization issues. (Errors here can impact real-time applications.)

- Check DHCP and DNS settings.

- Use network utilities such as ping, tracert, pathping, ipconfig, netstat, and nslookup, among others.

- Implement a strong password policy and AUP.

- Implement **multi-factor authentication (MFA)**.

- Educate the user.

Conclusion

In this chapter, we identified and discussed wireless issues and problems. We sought out ways to optimize wireless networking and create a reliable, secure network.

In the upcoming chapter, we will learn how to troubleshoot common network issues as they arise in our networks.

Points to remember

- Relating to wireless technologies and WLANs, it is important that a network administrator is able to:

  o Identify some limitations of using wireless technology compared to a wired network.

  o Detect problems and issues in WLANs.

  o Follow troubleshooting methods to resolve issues in WLANs.

  o Select appropriate hardware and software tools for problem-solving a broad range of wireless issues.

- The content of *Chapter 24, Troubleshooting Wireless Networks,* is mapped to *Domain 5, Network Troubleshooting.* Given a scenario, troubleshoot common performance issues.

Key terms

- **Absorption**: Some materials like walls, wooden doors, windows, and water can absorb the potential energy of RF signals. This absorption reduces signal strength.

  Table 24.2 outlines some absorption figures for common objects:

Material	2.4 GHz	5 GHz
Wooden door	4 dB	7 dB
Concrete wall	20 dB	30 dB
Plain glass window	3 dB	8 dB
Steel door	20 dB	30 dB
Human body	3 dB	5 dB
Trees/Vegetation	0.5 dB/m	1 dB/m

  Table 24.2: *Absorption figures for common objects*

- **Reflection**: When an electromagnetic wave meets a surface or obstacle and bounces back to its source. This reflection causes a decrease and loss of signal. These signal reflections can bounce and travel in any number of directions, interfering with the signal. This is also known as **multi-path fading**.

- **Refraction**: Different materials have their own refractive index. A refractive index is the measure of the bending of a ray of light as it is passing from one medium into another. This phenomenon can cause signal phase shifts or attenuation. As a result, signals may deviate from their intended direction and cause packet loss or poor communication.

- **Scattering**: As signals hit a rough or uneven surface, they can be scattered and diffused. This scattering or dispersal can be caused by dust, smoke, vegetation, or water particles in the air (for example, humidity levels or condensation). This negative phenomenon reduces the overall quality of the signal as it is received.

Questions

1. Explain the terms bandwidth, throughput, and goodput as they relate to wireless networking.

2. Give some examples of wireless considerations when building a wireless network.

3. Give some examples of common problems and issues in wireless networks.

4. Outline the importance of carrying out a site survey.

CHAPTER 25

Troubleshooting General Networking Issues

Introduction

As network technicians, we encounter various common issues when troubleshooting, ranging from simple to complex tasks. Throughout this guide, we focused on the OSI model, learning about its seven layers, functions, processes, and protocols. This foundational knowledge was integrated into practical applications and tools discussed in subsequent chapters. It is fitting to revisit the OSI model in this final chapter, reinforcing its importance in our troubleshooting approach. The OSI model operates like a map. In the complete map, the path of the data is plotted from source to destination as it travels through the seven layers of the OSI model, aligning with the functions and processes of each specific layer along the way. Each layer enables us to visualize the stage of the journey in which the data is and what ought to be happening at this particular phase and layer of the data's journey. The journey holds particular points of reference, where we can check and test things with hardware, software, or settings to support us in resolving a networking issue. In a sense, we can check the waypoints on the map to help us locate the source of the problem that is giving us trouble. At each waypoint, we can test and verify our findings. The map is our guide and expert.

Understanding the map of the OSI model enables us to handle the common issues and issues we meet as network administrators. In this chapter, we will discuss some of those more general problems and issues.

Structure

The chapter explains the following topics:

- General considerations
- Common issues
- Business operations/operational procedures

Objectives

In this chapter, we will explore general troubleshooting problems as they occur on our networks. After reading this chapter, you will be able to identify the common problems and issues met by an administrator and follow the troubleshooting methods to work through and resolve the issues described. Using your understanding from previous chapters, you will build on the understanding, knowledge, and skills and apply the troubleshooting models and methods in a systematic approach as you diagnose and solve the problems.

General considerations

Each layer of the OSI model depends on the proper functionality of the layers below it. If problems exist on the lower layers, they will inevitably impact the layers above and cause issues. This explains why an administrator, meeting a *new* problem, will typically work their way up through the OSI layers from the physical layer upwards, checking functions and protocols, layer by layer. This bottom-up approach is also an excellent strategy and method for building confidence and efficiency in budding technicians and network administrators.

Other considerations that administrators must manage and handle will occur in the planning and design stage of the network and also in situations when the network grows (that is, scalability) or when the network topology is modified or upgraded. As such, **network documentation** is designed and generated to inform us about the network and assist us in our problem-solving practices. Documentation should include physical and logical network maps and designs, a network performance baseline, configuration diagrams outlining VLAN implementation, interface status, VLAN membership, subnet configuration (where applicable), and the maps and tables from all routers in the network. The following is a list of documents required for networking:

- Device type, make and model OS version, and compatibility
- Cabling type and specifications
- Cabling endpoints
- Device configuration review
- Interface status

- VLAN assignment, for example, VLAN IP structures and VLAN names
- Network performance baselines
- Device identifiers
- Interface identifiers and description of links
- Routing tables
- Routing protocols
- Static and dynamic routes
- WAN technologies in use
- Cloud provision (for example, SLAs and licensing)
- Any other cloud/web-based services (for example, VPN or web-based printing)
- Network security considerations

This list will vary as it pertains to individual, organizational structures, and network sizes.

Establishing a network baseline

Baseline metrics measure the ideal performance metrics of a network. They are achieved using hardware and software network tools to manage and monitor the network. Wired and wireless networks have unique characteristics, and as such, an administrator will use specialized tools for measuring the network performance and validating a baseline. Baseline statistics provide us with the normal or expected network performance of devices and networking equipment on our LAN/WLAN and verify our current connection to the internet in relation to anticipated speed, bandwidth, and goodput. Network baseline statistics provide us with an excellent point of reference while troubleshooting common issues. They give us a real-world, real-time vision of what is occurring on our network and how it is performing in comparison to what is expected from its performance. The baseline viewpoint also gives us insights into network trends and patterns as we use the networks, and they are accessible for us to see as our clients are connected to the LAN or WLAN. There are many tools available to support us in baselining, some of which are covered in earlier chapters (for example, SolarWinds, NMS, InSSIDer, and so on).

The main point is that if you do not know what *normal* is, then how do you evaluate an issue or identify that an issue exists in the first place?

Using the OSI model in troubleshooting

Essentially, there are the following three different ways to use the OSI model when troubleshooting:

- **Bottom-up**: Troubleshooting by going from the physical layer up to the application layer.

- **Top-down**: Troubleshooting by going from the application layer down to the physical layer.

- **Divide-and-conquer**: Troubleshooting by focusing on the layer we perceive is most likely the cause of the problem and then moving in whatever direction we feel is the most likely cause of the issue. This method is achieved by moving either up or down the OSI model.

Depending on the severity of the problem, combined with our experience in meeting them, we can apply any of the three troubleshooting methods in our troubleshooting approach. In *Figure 25.1*, we can see some reasons for choosing the appropriate method:

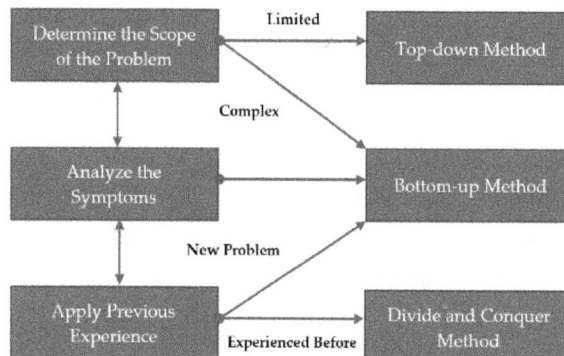

Figure 25.1: Three networking troubleshooting methods

Experienced network administrators will move through the model with an underpinning conceptual understanding of why they are making their choices. Newer administrators prefer to use the bottom-up approach until they gain experience in the divide-and-conquer strategy.

Administrators will also use methods based on educated guesses. As the name suggests, this approach is based on prior knowledge and understanding.

Another troubleshooting method involves *swapping out* components or parts. This involves comparing an operational or fully functioning component with one that is faulty or non-operational. The administrator can locate the troublesome component (or application) and resolve the issue by applying this troubleshooting method. This method tends to be implemented with common hardware issues and with some software glitches or common system settings. Again, the understanding of this method's use is directly related to the administrator's level of knowledge and experience of the problem.

Common issues

Network administrators will experience issues that might arise on the network frequently. Using the OSI model provides us with practical help. Now, we will move through the OSI model from the bottom-up and discuss some of these general issues that are found on networks.

Physical layer

In *Chapter 22, Troubleshooting Cable Connectivity*, we focused on troubleshooting the physical layer of the OSI model. In this specific chapter, we considered and expanded on cabling issues and connectivity diagnostics. We looked at the relevance of the status of the interface(s) in networking and how to interpret the link lights via the light combinations, especially if we have met a hardware and/or connectivity issue. Now, we will continue with our strategy and look at problems as they are associated with the OSI model, its functions, and processes.

The main symptoms to be watched out for in networks are poor network performance, connectivity issues, bottlenecks, and traffic congestion. Devices might be suffering from high use of system resources such as RAM and CPU utilization. If this is the case, an administrator needs to check the hardware and its ability to run the services required. Regarding WLANs, they should also test power levels on access points and ensure all strategies for minimizing attenuation and noise have been applied in the network design.

When troubleshooting errors at this level, an administrator will use cable testing tools, consult compliance documents and standards for configuration, interpret link lights, and swap out parts and components. Remember, network communications depend on interfaces and the cables that connect them. We must ensure they comply with standards and protocols, meet the rules for use, and are configured accordingly.

Data-link layer

Problems that can occur at the data-link layer include duplicate MAC addresses/MAC addressing errors, speed and duplex errors, collisions, **Cyclic Redundancy Check** (**CRC**) frame errors, and problems with **spanning tree protocol** (**STP**). When using Cisco IOS or other switching technologies and models/commands, the methods for detecting if layer 2 errors happen using various show commands. These commands include show interface, show port, and show spanning-tree commands. Irrespective of the make and model of the switch concerned, we want to see how interfaces and ports function.

The presence of **Frame Check Sequence** (**FSC**) errors, single, multiple, and late collisions, incorrect frame sizes, Runts and Giants, and broadcast storms are general ways to determine if layer 2 issues are occurring on the network. To a large degree, to view these events, administrators log in and interact with the interface of the switches (typically via a CLI) on the network and view and evaluate the device's output.

The following is a list of common layers 2 issues:

- Collisions
- Broadcast storm
- Duplicate MAC address
- Encapsulation errors

- Framing errors
- Multicast flooding
- Switching loops
- Incorrect or misconfigured VLANs

MAC address settings are a critical aspect of networking. These layer 2 addresses are used to move the frame within the local network. Though these addresses are pre-burned into the NIC/device at the point of manufacture, MAC addresses can be spoofed or changed and, therefore, must be noted as malleable components of a network.

Layer 2 addresses are used to move the frame within the local network. Additionally, it is the combination of MAC and IP that facilitates the end-to-end communication between source and destination across networks. This means incorrect MAC or IP addressing causes significant problems in communication. This is also why ipconfig, ping, and tracert, among other utilities, are invaluable network tools for testing and verifying addressing statistics and checking to see if they enable devices to be fully operational.

Note: Remember that the ping command can be used to test connectivity to another device on the local network or to a remote website on the internet.

Collisions on Ethernet networks are unavoidable, but they can be managed and reduced by the segmentation of a network. Segmentation at layer 2 occurs when an administrator implements VLANs. This action reduces the broadcast domain. Access methods are used in networking to handle collisions. CSMA/CD and CSMA/CA are discussed in more detail in *Chapter 1, OSI Model*. It is useful to know how they work.

Speed and duplex mismatches can be checked on the physical adapters and network intermediary devices, such as switches and routers. Devices with speed mismatches may not be able to communicate. Devices with duplex mismatches can still communicate, but transmission will not be optimal.

Switching loops

STP is essentially a loop-prevention network protocol that facilitates redundancy (fault tolerance) while creating a loop-free layer 2 topology. Without this protocol enabled, layer 2 loops can form between switches. These loops cause broadcast, multicast, and unknown unicast frames to loop endlessly between interconnected switches, and in the worst-case scenario, they can bring a network down. This happens because, unlike the TTL mechanism that is incorporated into packet switching technology, frames do not have a count-down value for them to decrement and expire on the network. In contrast, a router at layer 3 decrements the TTL value on receipt of a packet in IPv4 systems. The router will also modify the Hop Limit field in every IPv6 packet, bringing the packet closer to expiration. This *HOP limit* mechanism is an effective way to stop packets from traveling from HOP to HOP into an infinite, endless transmission. As stated, switches do not have this mechanism, and that is why STP must be enabled correctly on the switches, as they interconnect. STP uses a loop-free topology, where specific ports are placed in a blocked state and only brought online if a failure occurs on a link. STP creates a very organized, dynamic system in a multi-path switching environment.

Figure 25.2 illustrates a layer 2 loop:

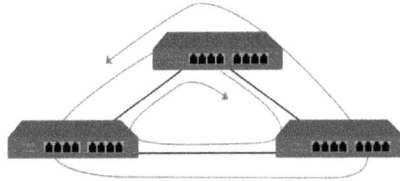

Figure 25.2: *A layer 2 switching loop*

In *Figure 25.3*, we can see a loop-free topology with one of the ports in a blocked state:

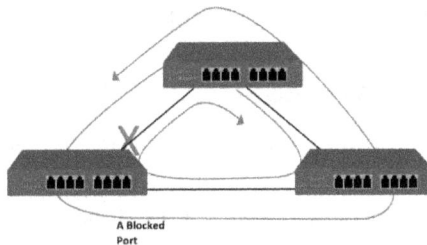

Figure 25.3: *A loop-free topology*

What are the impacts of switching loops? Layer 2 loops can cause high CPU utilization, MAC address instability, broadcast storms, and inaccessibility to the network. This inaccessibility can be perceived as a *denial of service*, where the switch is so overwhelmed and busy caught up managing the traffic in the loop that it denies services to the other hosts and network traffic.

Blocking specific ports will stop the traffic from looping, and frames will be sent between the switches in a more systematic way. The solution provides us with redundancy and is a scalable solution in switching technology. Please note that it is not just the loop we are solving with these measures. These problems are caused by the loop.

The other problems that switching loops may create are as follows:

- **Broadcast storms**: They can consume all the link bandwidth.

- **MAC address instability**: This causes the MAC (CAM) tables of the switches to become unstable, which in turn causes data transmission lags or errors. Depending upon the resources of the switch, it may or may not be able to manage these rapid transitions in its MAC table database and manage the table's mappings.

There are a series of intricate steps and phases involved in creating this loop-free topology. depending on the protocol in use, for example, STP or **Rapid Spanning Tree Protocol**

(RSTP), but the primary objective for troubleshooting loops is to be aware of their existence and the reason loop-avoidance is required. Additionally, we may have to check for cable, port, or transceiver faults or possible administrative misconfigurations.

The reason: STP will not function correctly if there is a cable fault, a fault in a port or transceiver, or if the administrator has inadvertently misconfigured a setting. Therefore, understanding STP operation is important in network communications.

Remote access

The **Switch Virtual Interface** (**SVI**) configuration allows us to remotely manage a switch over a network. This is achieved by giving the SVI interface IP addressing structures. Using this IP address, a network administrator can remote in and configure or manage the switch settings.

Always make sure to use a secure remote access protocol, for example, SSH.

Troubleshooting VLAN assignment issues

Ensure each VLAN is receiving the services for DHCP and DNS. Remember, each VLAN is a discrete entity and, therefore, must be provided with services appropriately. Check the address on the host machines and confirm the DHCP settings regarding the name of the pool, its scope, and available addresses, alongside other configuration checks.

Confirm devices are in the correct VLAN or that the VLAN is not missing. Consult the configuration baseline and check that all VLANs are accurate, and port ranges are appropriately assigned. Verify inter-VLAN routing is configured correctly and that, if need be, VLAN-to-VLAN communication is enabled if this communication is required on the network.

Network layer

The network layer has essentially the following two functions:

- It breaks up data into network packets and reassembles data on the receiving end (that is, incoming packets at the destination).

- Using a layer 3 intermediary device, it routes packets from source to destination by discovering the *best* path from source to destination across the physical network.

To do this correctly, we need to address the systems. Consequently, the problems that can occur at this layer of the OSI model are network addressing issues and routing issues.

The following is a list of common layer 3 issues:

- IP setting issues
- Incorrect IP address

- Incorrect subnet mask
- Incorrect gateway
- Duplicate IP address
- Routing loops
- Asymmetrical routing
- Missing route

These errors can result in connectivity issues, suboptimal performance, and at times, network failure or communications failure in data transmission. This is where our networking utilities become valuable troubleshooting tools and where **ping** is an excellent problem-solving tool for testing connectivity to hosts inside and outside the network. The ping utility is covered comprehensively in *Chapter 23, Network Utilities*. Ipconfig, ping, tracert, nslookup, and other command-line networking tools are also detailed, with troubleshooting examples, scenarios, and solutions referenced. The advice at this point is to review these troubleshooting examples since many of the issues discussed are directly related to the network layer of the OSI model.

On network devices, trace, show IP route, and show IP protocols will assist the administrator in verifying correct addressing and ensuring data transmission is optimal. If a router continuously drops packets, for example, we will discover this on a workstation with pathping, and a router with trace. In this scenario, the administrator might have to review routing protocols or assess the router's resources. For example, the CPU, RAM, and network configuration/performance baseline settings may need to be assessed.

Issues with routing tables

When routers make forwarding decisions, they consult their routing table. This table is like a map to the router to forward the packets to locally connected networks or remote networks. If the map is wrong, then errors in transmission will inevitably occur. An error in a routing table may result in the following:

- Traffic is being forwarded to the wrong (exit) interface.
- Traffic not being forwarded when it ought to have been.
- Packets being dropped or discarded.

If the interface is *up*, routes are created in the table for these directly connected networks. Therefore, the traffic will not be forwarded if the interface is *down*, *administratively down*, or if the link has failed. An administrator should always check the status of the interfaces on the organization's routers and ensure they match the network configuration baselines.

Static and dynamic routes

A network administrator can implement static routes. If packets are not reaching a particular network, the administrator should check these entries in the table.

If a router has a **point-to-point** (**PPP**) link with another router, this entry will also be automatically created, and a default route will be created to the network at the end of that PPP link.

In larger networks and more complex topologies, the routers might be using dynamic routing protocols. These protocols, such as Open Shortest Pathway First, Enhanced Interior Gateway Routing Protocol, and Border Gateway Protocol, are capable of constructing a real-time map of networks based on what they have learned from routers participating in the dynamic routing protocol. These protocols are described in more detail in *Chapter 11, Managing Routing Protocols,* should a reader wish to review them.

Basically, a router builds its table on what it *knows* (as in directly connected networks or manually configured routes) and what it *learns* from other routers. An administrator should be able to read a routing table and identify errors if they exist.

To counteract errors found in routing tables, administrators should verify the routes listed in the routing table and rectify them as required. Inspecting and verifying the routing table is a critical part of layer 3 troubleshooting.

Routing loops

If all routers do not broadcast their routes in a synchronized manner, and the routing update timer is mismatched on the routers, routing loops can occur. This mismatch in timing causes confusion in the reachability of a given network since the update timer is used to propagate networks. This router looping issue is specifically associated with distance-vector routing protocols.

In *Figure 25.4*, a routing loop is depicted:

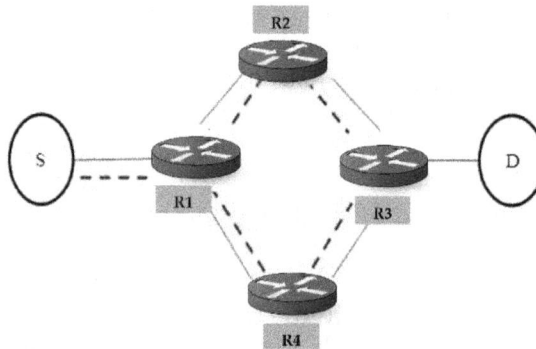

Figure 25.4: A layer 3 routing loop

The solutions for avoiding routing loops are achieved by implementing **Split Horizon**, which stops the router from advertising failed routes, and by applying **hold-down timers**:

- **Hold-down timers**: This function prevents the router from updating within a specified time. As a result, other routers are given some time to reconfigure and prevent a routing loop. The only routing updates about the failed route that will be processed by the router are the ones sent by the same router that originally advertised the failed route. When the hold-down timer and the time period expire, the router will disregard any information given by other routers stating that the route is reachable.

Troubleshooting DNS settings

To test and verify our DNS settings, we should check the DNS server configuration.

We can also use **nslookup** to test the ability of DNS to provide a host machine with reliable records and confirm that names are correctly being resolved to IP addresses.

By doing this, we are effectively testing the DNS IP Configuration Settings.

If problems persist and we cannot resolve the DNS Server name, we can flush the DNS resolver cache on a Windows machine using the following command in the Windows Command Prompt:

```
dnscmd /clearcache
```

Alternatively, in Windows PowerShell, we can run the following **cmdlet**:

```
Clear-DnsServerCache
```

Then, we can re-attempt to lookup the name of the DNS server to get a response:

```
nslookup <name> <IP address of the DNS server>
```

If we are still having issues at this point, we will need to move our focus away from the host machine to begin troubleshooting the DNS server role and configuration.

Transport layer

In the previous chapters, we learned that TCP and UDP function at the transport layer of the OSI model. These protocols use open ports to handle data transmission. Since both protocols depend on the configuration of ports and firewall policies and rules, most issues with these protocols are associated with blocked ports or misconfigured firewall rules and ACLs.

Typical misconfigured ACLs include an error in the order of ACL entries or an error in the implicit deny-all statement. Troubleshooting communication issues at this layer involves checking the firewall rules and ensuring ports that should be open to traffic are permitting traffic, and, alternatively, ports that should be blocking or denying traffic are configured to do so.

If there are issues with QoS settings, network performance for some protocols might be impacted or traffic slowed down. If QoS is enabled, an administrator can temporarily disable it while troubleshooting layer 4 network issues.

Session layer

Possible problems occurring within the session layer include website server misconfigurations. Troubleshooting sessions with external hosts or websites are also reflected at the application layer, as we use application layer protocols.

Possible problems with the presentation layer are associated with encryption, formatting, and conversion. The field of networking expertise and troubleshooting belongs more in the hands of software developers, programmers, and security analysts.

Attacks at layer 6 include **Secure Sockets layer** (**SSL**) hijacking and sniffing, and interception through bad coding practices. In a MitM attack, an attacker might use a proxy as an untrusted certificate authority. If this happens, the browser will trust the wrong certificate authority; from this point, the attacker will be able to read all messages. A network administrator should be 100% clear that it is imperative that the network users' antivirus is up to date and that the organization is doing its utmost to prevent malware from entering the end devices and servers on the network.

Application layer

In troubleshooting problems at the application layer, we will most likely be working with users on the network. This is where our people skills and communication abilities become most prevalent. As humans, we are all prone to err. Handling errors at this level is where technicians (and security analysts) spend much of their troubleshooting time. Data theft, impersonation, malware, application misconfigurations, and corruption all take place in this layer. The surface area of issues at this layer is immensely broad. Errors also include user errors with implementing file formats, codecs, software compatibility issues, and meeting problems from incorrect plugins. Additionally, the list of cybersecurity threats at this layer of the OSI model is equally quite exhaustive. Therefore, troubleshooting issues at this layer involves more than the network administrator to solve them.

Issues at layer 7 include the following:

- A network service or application does not meet the standard expectations of one or more network users. That is, it is when the service performs at an inadequate level.
- Applications do not function as expected.
- Network baselines are being met, *but* users are complaining about slow performance or lag.
- Users require assistance with application errors or software settings.
- Driver or plugin issues for personal devices.
- BYOD configuration settings.

BYOD can bring extra troubleshooting for the network administrator.

Figure 25.5 depicts a technician engaging in troubleshooting a laptop's settings. This could be a network user's personal device.

Figure 25.5: *Troubleshooting device settings*
Source: *freepik.com*

Business operations/operational procedures

This is where business operations relating to policies, procedures, and practices come into play. Consequently, network user concerns are also listed as relevant to human interactions at this top layer. Remember, the application layer is closest to the user. To resolve issues, the network administrator will generally interact with users face-to-face or via remote access technologies. Even when engaging with users remotely, it remains human interaction.

Other issues to be managed to achieve optimum business operations include the following:

- BYOD challenges, especially regarding compliance with the network policies.
- Licensed feature issues, where some features of software, services, protocols, or applications may not be included with the license (or should be).
- Network-user-related cybersecurity awareness.
- Network-user-related IT/technology awareness.
- Access rights, permissions, and privileges.
- Separation of duties.
- Role-based (people) or rule-based (files) management and monitoring compliance
- Compliance with AUP, SLAs, and other legal requirements.
- Safety and health issues relating to the use of the network.
- General interactions with network users, third-party providers, managers, and stakeholders.

There are so many diverse areas where network administrators find themselves in work-related scenarios and discussions. This aspect of the job role is where they might become a much-needed voice in policy and decision-making practice, especially where the corporate network is concerned.

Above all else, as network administrators, we strive to maximize network performance and reach targets. Hence, the experience of using the network is positive, safe, and secure for all parties concerned.

Conclusion

In this chapter, we explored general troubleshooting problems as they occur on our networks.

In the upcoming chapter of this book, there are **two practice exams** with typical questions on areas of study outlined in the CompTIA Network+ course objectives.

Points to remember

Regarding the area of troubleshooting network problems, it is important to know:

- The general issues typically encountered by an administrator.
- Troubleshooting methods to resolve these issues.
- Appropriate troubleshooting methods for specific issues.
- Troubleshooting models.
- The OSI model as a guide and map to solving problems in networking.
- The content of this chapter is mapped to *Domain 5, Network Troubleshooting*. in the context of the OSI model, bringing together theory and application.

Key terms

- **Split Horizon**: This is a method used in distance-vector routing to prevent routing loops. The rule is straightforward: never send routing information back in the direction, that is, to the router, from which the route was learned or received.
- **Acceptable Use Policy (AUP)**: A set of rules and guidelines that outline the acceptable and unacceptable use of organizational resources, such as computers, networks, and internet access. It aims to protect the organization from legal issues and ensure the security and integrity of its systems.
- **Service Level Agreement (SLA)**: A formal contract between a service provider and a customer that specifies the expected level of service, performance metrics, and

responsibilities of both parties. It includes details on service availability, response times, and remedies for service failures.

- **Bring Your Own Device (BYOD)**: A policy that allows employees to use their personal devices, such as smartphones, tablets, and laptops, for work purposes. This approach can increase productivity and flexibility but also introduces security and management challenges.

- **Choose Your Own Device (CYOD)**: A policy where employees can select from a range of company-approved devices for work purposes. This approach balances the flexibility of BYOD with better control over security and device management.

Questions

1. List and describe the three troubleshooting methods. Are there other methods used by administrators? Explain.

2. Give some examples of situations where understanding the OSI model supports troubleshooting practice.

3. Give some examples of common problems and issues in networks.

4. Outline the importance of having a systematic approach to troubleshooting.

Join our book's Discord space

Join the book's Discord Workspace for Latest updates, Offers, Tech happenings around the world, New Release and Sessions with the Authors:

https://discord.bpbonline.com

CHAPTER 26

Network+ Practice Exams

Exam 1

Networking fundamentals

1. How many layers does the OSI model have?

    a. 1

    b. 3

    c. 5

    d. 7

2. Which of the following network devices is a data link layer (layer 2) device designed to forward frames between local area network (LAN) segments?

    a. Switch

    b. Router

    c. Firewall

    d. Gateway

3. Some network switches can also provide additional functions at higher levels of the OSI model and have routing capabilities. What is the name of this network device?

    a. Router

    b. Multilayer switch

    c. Managed switch

    d. Hub

4. A range of IP addresses that a DHCP server can lease out to DHCP clients is called a:

    a. Lease

    b. Reservation

    c. Pool

    d. Scope

5. A network administrator requires a network that provides centralized authentication for its users. Which of the following logical topologies should they implement?

    a. VLANs

    b. Peer-to-peer

    c. Client/Server

    d. Mesh

6. Which of the following network types is described as an ad hoc temporary form of connection in which the link between networked devices uses Bluetooth technology?

    a. **Campus area network (CAN)**

    b. **Wireless local area network (WLAN)**

    c. **Local area network (LAN)**

    d. **Personal area network (PAN)**

7. Which of the following network types uses special hardware to provide high-speed, high-performance access to storage across the network?

    a. Client-server network

    b. Peer-to-peer network

    c. Wide area network

    d. Storage area network

8. You recently created VLANs in your local area network to enhance your network's performance and security. A subnet/VLAN was created for each department, and a management VLAN address on each switch to manage and monitor the switches.

   An employee in sales was able to access a shared file from the marketing department previously, but since the change, he has been unable to do this. The employee can access other resources in the Sales department and can print locally. He is also able to access the Internet successfully.

   Which of the following would be the most likely reason the employee in Sales is no longer able to access files from the marketing department?

   a. His workstation has an invalid IP address

   b. Sales and marketing are no longer on the same subnet

   c. The subnet mask has been misconfigured

   d. His device has an invalid gateway IP address

9. A number of IoT devices are networked together in a small network. Each device connects to each other and acts as a relay for the network signal.

   Which of the following best describes this type of network topology?

   a. Campus area network

   b. Personal area network

   c. Wireless mesh network

   d. Wireless wide area network

10. You have been asked to make a crossover cable. Which of the following is the correct method?

   a. Use the T568B standard on both ends of the cable

   b. Use the T568A standard on both connectors at each end of the cable

   c. Use the T568C standard on one end and the T568A standard on the other end

   d. Use the T568A standard on one connector and the T568B standard on the other connector

11. Which of the following connectors is used with fiber optic cables and requires that you use a twisting motion to connect it?

   a. SC

   b. ST

c. STP

d. LC

12. **Hypertext transfer protocol operates on which layer of the OSI model?**

   a. Application layer

   b. Transport layer

   c. Network layer

   d. Data link layer

13. **Which port number is allocated to Secure Shell?**

   a. 20

   b. 21

   c. 25

   d. 22

14. **How many bits have an IPv6 address?**

   a. 64 bits

   b. 128 bits

   c. 32 bits

   d. 256 bits

15. **What is the name of a networking device that combines multiple transmissions from I/O devices into a single line?**

   a. A hub

   b. A concentrator

   c. A modem

   d. A multiplexor

16. **In cloud computing, when referring to virtualization, which architecture provides the virtual isolation between the several tenants?**

   a. PaaS

   b. Multitenant

   c. Deployment

   d. Client architecture

Networking implementations

1. **Which of the following devices are used to help share connections with wireless access points?**

    a. Cable
    b. Hub
    c. Bridge
    d. Switch
    e. Router

2. **Although security is significant on a network, why do we need to use a wireless AP as a pass-through set-up that permits any server to connect to the wireless network?**

    a. APs prevent unknown users from getting connected to the network.
    b. APs block firewalls from disturbing communications.
    c. APs enable the end devices to exchange data without too much difficulty.
    d. APs will improve fast server access.

3. **Which of the following terms identifies a network based on a given name?**

    a. RFID
    b. ESS
    c. SSID
    d. BSS

4. **Which access method is used in IEEE 802.11 wireless LANs?**

    a. CDMA
    b. CSMA/CA
    c. Divide-and-conquer
    d. CSMA/CD

5. **A _____ operates at layer 3 of the OSI reference model. It interprets the network layer protocol and makes forwarding decisions based on the layer 3 address.**

    a. Switch
    b. Bridge
    c. Router
    d. Hub

6. **Switches that use _____ forwarding start sending a frame immediately after reading the destination MAC address into their buffers.**

   a. Cut-through

   b. Fragment-free

   c. Store-and-forward

   d. Adaptive cut-through forwarding

7. **As layer 2 devices, these switches read the entire frame, no matter how large, into their buffers before frame forwarding. These switches are called:**

   a. Fast-forward

   b. Fragment-free

   c. Store-and-forward

   d. Cut-through

8. **In computer networking, what kind of resolution does the address resolution protocol (ARP) provide?**

   a. IPv6 addresses to IPv4

   b. Domain name to IP address

   c. IP address to MAC address

   d. MAC address to IP address

9. **Which of the following options would permit a network administrator to set up three wireless access points (WAPs) on non-overlapping channels?**

   - 1
   - 5
   - 6
   - 9
   - 11

     a. 1, 5, and 6

     b. 1, 6, and 11

     c. 5, 9, and 11

     d. 1, 5, and 11

10. **Channel bonding refers to a strategy that allows an administrator to combine adjacent wireless channels to increase the amount of available bandwidth on a wireless network.**

    a. True

    b. False

11. **How many usable addresses are there on an IP network with a /30 prefix length?**

    a. 2

    b. 4

    c. 6

    d. 8

12. **What is the correct subnet mask for the 192.168.0.0/21 network?**

    a. 255.255.255.0

    b. 255.255.0.0

    c. 255.255.248.0

    d. 255.255.0.248

13. **Which of the following masks is the BEST mask to use on a point-to-point link between two routers?**

    a. /27

    b. /22

    c. /30

    d. /24

14. **The default mask for class A is:**

    a. 255. 0.0.0

    b. 255. 255.0.0

    c. 255. 255.255.0

    d. 255. 255.255.255

Network operations

1. **A bottleneck is a condition that occurs when a system is unable to keep up with the demands placed on it.**

    a. True

    b. False

2. **Which of the following is the best practice when establishing a baseline?**

   a. Establish baselines within a network or device's first few days of installation

   b. Determine baselines over time by analyzing network traffic and establishing trends

   c. Establish baselines using only specialized network hardware tools

   d. Establish baselines only during the busiest times of the day when network use is highest

3. **Which of the following is a protocol used for network management?**

   a. SMTP

   b. NTP

   c. SNMP

   d. FTP

4. **In SNMP, an agent is running the SNMP process. This process is called the _____ process.**

   a. Server

   b. Client

   c. Both A and B

   d. None of the above

5. **Which of the following company policies would a network user agree to when they bring in a personal tablet to connect to the company's guest wireless network to access the internet?**

   a. NDA

   b. IRP

   c. BYOD

   d. SLA

6. **A network administrator determines that multiple switches on the network need a major update. Which of the following policies should the administrator consult?**

   a. Change management policy

   b. Remote access policy

   c. AUP

   d. MOU

7. **What is the minimum number of disks required to implement RAID 1 mirroring?**

    a. 1

    b. 2

    c. 3

    d. 4

8. **Storage devices include:**

    a. Tape drives

    b. Raid arrays

    c. SSDs

    d. All of the above

9. **A company's network includes VoIP in its infrastructure. Users have sent in tickets reporting an intermittent degradation of sound on their IP phones. What could the administrator do to alleviate the problem?**

    a. Use plenum-grade cables instead of UTP

    b. Implement fault tolerance for the switch on the segment

    c. Configure 802.1q VLAN trunking on the switch

    d. Configure QoS

10. **Which of the following services can a network administrator implement to reduce latency levels and prioritize the flow of real-time data?**

    a. Fault tolerance

    b. Tacacs+

    c. Qos

    d. Load balancing

11. **In addition to preventing switching loops, the Spanning Tree Protocol provides fault tolerance and failover when links fail in multi-switching environments.**

    a. True

    b. False

Network security

1. **Which of the following is a term to denote the name of the wireless network?**

    a. Encryption

    b. DHCP

    c.   Network portion

    d.   SSID

2. **Which of the following security threats involves impersonation?**

    a.   Dumpster diving

    b.   Tailgating

    c.   Social engineering

    d.   Backdoor

3. **AAA stands for:**

    a.   Authentication, administration, and accounting

    b.   Administration, accounting, and authorization

    c.   Authentication, authorization, and accounting

    d.   None of these are correct

4. **Which of the following principles denotes that only authorized users can access the information?**

    a.   Confidentiality

    b.   Integrity

    c.   Availability

    d.   Principle of least privilege

5. **A network administrator has permission to access the company servers and carry out tasks, but there are still some tasks that they are not able to do since tasks are distributed among IT personnel. This strategy is known as:**

    a.   Delegation

    b.   Teamwork

    c.   Separation of duties

    d.   Collaboration

6. **Which of the following mitigation techniques would a network administrator apply to a device to restrict remote access?**

    a.   Disable TELNET

    b.   Enable RDP

    c.   Enable SSH

    d.   Install VNC screen sharing

7. **What is the most secure method to remotely access a Linux server?**

   a. TELNET

   b. SSH

   c. RDP

   d. VNC

8. **Which of the following physical security controls is most likely to be vulnerable to resulting in a false positive?**

   a. Identification card

   b. Fingerprint reader

   c. Proximity reader

   d. CCTV

9. **A network administrator wants to detect unauthorized users entering the comms room. The administrator is advised to use the following detection method:**

   a. Smart card

   b. Biometrics

   c. Retina scanning

   d. Video surveillance

Network troubleshooting

1. **A network user is complaining of sporadic issues with Internet connectivity. The administrator has gathered data from the user and machine, which is the first step in the network troubleshooting model. What should the administrator do next?**

   a. Document findings, actions, and outcomes.

   b. Establish a theory of probable cause.

   c. Establish a plan of action to resolve the problem.

   d. Replicate the problem, if possible.

2. **An open-ended question has a simple yes or no answer.**

   a. True

   b. False

3. **A closed-ended question can be answered with a single word, no.**

   a. True

   b. False

4. **A cable tester is a network hardware tool that verifies if a signal is being transmitted by a cable. You can use this tool to find out whether the cables in your network are functioning properly when investigating cable connectivity issues.**

   a. True

   b. False

5. **A punch-down tool is used to measure fiber optic cables to ensure maximum length compliance.**

   a. True

   b. False

6. **An administrator is testing a local host on a network. He types in ping localhost at the Windows command prompt. What is the administrator diagnosing?**

   a. The CPU utilization

   b. Embedded graphics functionality

   c. The PCIe slot

   d. The physical adapter

7. **We need to discover what ports are open on a Windows machine. What command line network tool do we use?**

   a. net

   b. ping

   c. tracert

   d. netstat

8. **A network administrator recently installed a web proxy server on the organization's network. A few days after this installation, a system administrator replaced the DNS server. At this point, the issue began with users unable to access public websites. Which of the following will the administrator do to solve the issue?**

   a. Update the DNS server with the proxy server information

   b. Implement a split-horizon DNS server

    c.   Restart the DNS server and then reboot the proxy server

    d.   Put the proxy server on the other side of the organization's demarcation

9. **A demarcation (demarc) marks or establishes a boundary.**

    a.   True

    b.   False

10. **After remediating a workstation infected with malware, a network technician establishes that the web browser fails to go to accurate addresses for some websites. Which of the following should the administrator check?**

    a.   Windows server host file

    b.   Subnet mask

    c.   Local hosts file

    d.   Simplex settings

11. **Domain Information Grope is used by Linux machines to lookup DNS resolutions. Effectively, it is the equivalent of the nslookup command on a Windows machine.**

    a.   True

    b.   False

12. **A network technician has observed the presence of routing loops on the network. Which of the following will help the technician prevent these routing loops from occurring?**

    a.   Default gateway

    b.   Routing table

    c.   Convergence

    d.   Split horizon

13. **A network administrator can use an OTDR network hardware tool to troubleshoot optical fiber connections. This tool can measure impedance and calculate the transmission of the fiber being tested.**

    a.   True

    b.   False

14. **A network technician troubleshoots an issue with a network user's laptop. The user is unable to connect to the company LAN or WAN. The network technician**

discovers that the laptop's wireless switch is off and fixes the issue. At which layer of the OSI model did the technician discover and fix the issue?

    a. Layer 1—Physical

    b. Layer 2—Data link

    c. Layer 3—Network

    d. Layer 4—Transport

    e. Layer 7—Application

Exam 2

Networking fundamentals

1. In which service model does the service provider own the equipment, including servers and storage devices, among other hardware?

    a. PaaS

    b. IaaS

    c. SaaS

    d. DaaS

2. The three layers of the data center design are defined as the core, aggregation, and access layers. Which of these layers provides the backplane for all data transmissions flowing in and out of the data center?

    a. Access layer

    b. Core layer

    c. Aggregation layer

    d. All three layers provide this function

3. Which of the following topologies connect each device to a neighboring device?

    a. Mesh

    b. Ring

    c. Bus

    d. Star

4. Which of the following is the most common unshielded twisted pair connector?

    a. RJ-58

    b. RJ-49

    c. RJ-45

    d. RJ-59

5. **A device has the following IP statistics: 192.168.1.253 /24 with a subnet mask of 255.255.255.0.**

   Which of the following best defines which network this device is connected to?

    a. CIDR

    b. Network ID

    c. Subnet mask

    d. Host ID

6. **Which of the following can you create using a virtual LAN?**

    a. Hub

    b. Switch

    c. Router

    d. Wireless access point

7. **Which type of address is the IP address 232.109.255.251?**

    a. Loopback

    b. Private

    c. Unicast

    d. Multicast

8. **Which of the following mail protocols stores email on the mail server and allows users to access messages from multiple devices without downloading the emails to their device?**

    a. SNMP

    b. SMTP

    c. IMAP4

    d. POP3

9. **Which of the following service models provides flexible access to computer hardware plus the ability of the organization to have administrative control of the virtual machines?**

    a. PaaS

    b. IaaS

    c.   SaaS

    d.   All of the above

10. **All twisted-pair cabling types feature wires inside the cable that are grouped into pairs. The wires in each pair are twisted around each other in a ratio that decreases signal interference from an adjacent wire pair since these wires lie parallel to each other. This type of interference is called crosstalk.**

    a.   True

    b.   False

11. **Which of the answers below refer(s) to UTP cabling? (Select all that apply)**

    a.   ☐Twisted-pair copper cabling

    b.   ☐Used in Ethernet networks and telephone systems

    c.   ☐Low cost and ease of installation

    d.   ☐Coaxial cabling used in cable modem

    e.   ☐No options to minimize crosstalk or EMI

    f.   ☐Takes advantage of additional protective cover, decreasing signal interference from outside sources

    g.   ☐Used in point-to-point links

    h.   ☐In wired networks, typically configured with an RJ45 connector

12. **Which of the following answers refers to a recommended minimum requirement for twisted-pair copper cabling in 1000BASE-T networks?**

    a.   Cat 3

    b.   Cat 5

    c.   Cat 5e

    d.   Cat 6

    e.   Cat 6a

13. **What are the characteristic traits of single-mode fiber optics? (Select all that apply)**

    a.   ☐Transmission distances of up to 2 km

    b.   ☐More expensive than multimode fiber optics

    c.   ☐Uses LED as the source of light

    d.   ☐Transmission distances of up to 100 km

e. ☐Uses laser as the source of light

f. ☐Less expensive than multimode fiber optics

14. **The Automatic Private IP Addressing (APIPA) address allows a Windows host to self-configure an IPv4 address and subnet mask when Dynamic Host Configuration Protocol (DHCP) fails or is unavailable. The range of addresses is between 169.254.0.0 and 169.254.255.255. When an APIPA address is assigned to a host on the network, it will have limited connectivity and no internet access.**

a. True

b. False

15. **Which of the following answers refers to a valid IPv6 EUI-64 format address generated from a MAC address of 29:88:68:0B:1B:DE?**

a. 2001:DB8:ABCD:12:2A88:68FF:FE0B:1BDE

b. 2001:DB8:ABCD:12:2B88:68FF:FE0B:1BCDE

c. 2001:DB8:ABCD:12:2C88:68FF:FE0B:1BDE

d. 2001:DB8:ABCD:12:2D88:68FF:FE0B:1BDE

16. **What is the name of a solution that increases the efficiency of IP address space management by allowing network administrators to divide/segment networks into subnets of different sizes?**

a. DNAT

b. VLSM

c. MPLS

d. VLAN

Networking implementations

1. **An access point is a network device that connects wired and wireless networks together and enables data transmission between wireless clients and the wired network. Using several access points increases total system bandwidth and range. Users roam between the access points. They can authenticate with the APs without losing a connection as they move around the building.**

    Wireless clients can be authenticated and associated with all APs in the wireless network at the same time.

a. True

b. False

2. **802.11ac WLANs have the ability to operate up to:**

    a. 11 Mbps

    b. 54 Mbps

    c. 6.77 Gbps

    d. 600 Mbps

3. **Which of the following statements is/are true about wireless access points? Select all that apply.**

    a. ☐Wireless access points cannot be autonomous. They must be installed in groups.

    b. ☐Wireless access points are often referred to as Zigbee devices.

    c. ☐Wireless access points can be connected to two separate Ethernet networks.

    d. ☐Wireless access points connect devices using Bluetooth connectivity and ad hoc configurations.

4. **How can the range of WLANs be increased?**

    a. By adding sensors

    b. By adding access points

    c. By using repeaters

    d. By adding clients

5. **To view the configuration of a port, use the _____ command.**

    a. Display

    b. Interface

    c. Show

    d. Port

6. **Switches provide increased security benefits on networks because unicast traffic is sent directly to its destination, and this traffic is not broadcast to all other stations on the collision domain.**

    a. True

    b. False

7. **A _____ is an intermediary network device that connects two networks.**

    a. Bridge

    b. Hub

    c. Repeater

    d. Gateway

8. **Multiple Input/Multiple Output (MIMO) is a wireless technology that utilizes multiple transmitters and receivers. This technology allows for a significant increase in the amount of data throughput. It achieves this using several antennas and multiple data streams working simultaneously. The technology can only be used when using a Yagi antenna.**

    a. True

    b. False

9. **Automatic routing table update applies to the following form of routing.**

    a. Static routing

    b. Route redistribution

    c. Dynamic routing

    d. Route aggregation

10. **A network technician manually adds a route to the routing table. The type of route created is known as:**

    a. Static route

    b. Dynamic route

    c. Hybrid route

    d. Default route

11. **A network administrator is testing the local host's physical adapter. He suspects that the NIC is faulty and dropping packets at times. Which command is the best option to explore this card further?**

    a. ping

    b. trace

    c. pathping

    d. ping –t

12. **Which of the following is the IPv6 loopback address?**

    a. 127.0.0.1

    b. :1

    c. ::1

    d. FF80

13. **The default mask for class B is:**

   a.   255. 0.0.0

   b.   255. 255.0.0

   c.   255. 255.255.0

   d.   255. 255.255.255

14. **The default mask for class C is:**

   a.   255. 0.0.0

   b.   255. 255.0.0

   c.   255. 255.255.0

   d.   255. 255.255.255

Network operations

1.   **In SNMP, the GetRequest PDU is sent from a source to a destination host. The objective of the PDU is to retrieve variables or a set of variables from the destination host. Transmission takes place from _____ to _____.**

   a.   Network, host

   b.   Client, server

   c.   Server, client

   d.   None of the above

2.   **In SNMP, the response PDU is sent from a source to a destination host. The objective of the PDU is to respond with variables or a set of variables to the requesting machine. Transmission takes place from _____ to _____.**

   a.   Network, host

   b.   Client, server

   c.   Server, client

   d.   None of the above

3.   **What port numbers are used for SNMP data transmission?**

   a.   160, 161

   b.   161, 162

   c.   160,162

   d.   None of the above

4. **What network tool in Windows allows an administrator to look at log files of system errors and alerts?**

   a. Event Viewer

   b. Performance Monitor

   c. Device Manager

   d. Baseline Viewer

5. **A network administrator is inspecting performance issues on the file server. the administrator has gathered the file server's utilization statistics. Which of the following documents should the administrator consult to decide which of the server's statistics are not in the normal range?**

   a. Baseline review

   b. Log files

   c. System life-cycle report

   d. SIEM

6. **An organization has agreed on a contract with an outside vendor. This vendor will perform a service that will provide hardware, software, and procedures in case of a catastrophic failure of the organization's primary data center. This contract does not contain a long-term strategy for extended outages or for maintaining business operations. Which of the following plans should the company's executive complete?**

   a. Disaster recovery plan

   b. Business continuity plan

   c. SLA

   d. Separation of duties

7. **Which of the following RAID types uses striping with dual parity?**

   a. 1

   b. 5

   c. 6

   d. 0

8. **In layer 2 switching, links can be aggregated and formed into wider channels for data transfers. This technology is known as:**

   a. EtherChannel

   b. OSPF

     c. EIGRP

     d. RSTP

9. **Which of the following features would be the *best* to implement, in order to optimize real-time voice and video-conferencing? (Choose two)**

     a. Load balancing

     b. Cache memory

     c. Qos

     d. Traffic shaping

     e. Network monitoring systems

10. **In which of the following topologies could the failure of one workstation/link bring the entire network down?**

     a. Mesh

     b. Token ring

     c. Star

     d. Spanning tree

11. **A customer is looking for a cloud provider with excellent percentage rates for High Availability. Which of the following percentage rates would the customer choose, with corresponding potential downtime cited as 52.60 minutes per year?**

     a. 90% ("one nine")

     b. 99% ("two nines")

     c. 99.9% ("three nines")

     d. 99.99% ("four nines")

Network security

1. **A company needs to apply strong wireless security on their access points. Which of the following security measures is the best measure to apply?**

     a. Wired equivalent privacy

     b. Port-based filtering

     c. WPA 2/3

     d. Longer SSID broadcast intervals

2. **What is the security term used when cybersecurity experts attempt to hack into a network to check for vulnerabilities or security loopholes?**

   a. Defense in depth

   b. Layering

   c. Pen testing

   d. Channel bonding

3. **A network administrator has identified that a wireless network signal from one of the company's access points is available from outside the building. How should the administrator remove this threat?**

   a. Implement WEP encryption on the WLAN

   b. Decrease the signal strength

   c. Change the wireless channels to reduce this overlap

   d. Disable the SSID from broadcasting

4. **Identify the technology whereby information is hidden inside a picture.**

   a. Rootkits

   b. Malware

   c. Steganography

   d. Stenography

5. **Name a specific network tool that can be used in hacking wireless networks.**

   a. Aircrack-ng

   b. Protocol analyzer

   c. Wireshark

   d. Kali

6. **Which of the following strategies is the most secure approach to facilitate remote users accessing a company's internal network resources?**

   a. VPN concentrator

   b. Network-based firewall

   c. DMZ

   d. IPS

7. **Two of the following protocols allowing users to authenticate when remotely accessing private LANS are:**

    a. RADIUS

    b. Policy

    c. Regulation

    d. TACACS

    e. a and c

    f. a and d

    g. d and c

8. **Chassis intrusion detection is enabled or disabled in the BIOS or system settings.**

    a. True

    b. False

9. **Which of the following is classified as a legal form of hacking?**

    a. Black hat

    b. Ethical hacking

    c. Hacktivist

    d. Intrusion detection system

Network troubleshooting

1. **Questioning users and duplicating a problem are two ways a network administrator can apply when gathering data.**

    a. True

    b. False

2. **At times, it is unnecessary to verify the full functionality of a machine when the administrator knows it is fixed.**

    a. True

    b. False

3. **What should a network administrator do after verifying full functionality?**

    a. Document actions and outcomes

    b. Test a theory of probable cause

    c.   Implement a solution

    d.   Duplicate the problem, if possible

4. **A network administrator extended the range for a 2.4-GHz WLAN. However, the users are now stating that the connection is dropping as they roam from one coverage area to another. The administrator identifies the issue stems from insufficient overlap. What percentage of coverage overlap should the administrator have implemented for these adjacent areas?**

    a.   5% to 10%

    b.   15% to 20%

    c.   10% to 15%

    d.   25%

5. **An administrator has detected an issue with a UTP cable connecting a PC to a switch. He replaces the cable with a working cable. The cable he uses is:**

    a.   Straight through

    b.   Crossover

    c.   Coax

    d.   Fiber optic

6. **A network administrator needs to purge the DNS resolver cache on a local machine. Which command does the administrator use?**

    a.   ipconfig / displaydns

    b.   ipconfig / release

    c.   ipconfig / renew

    d.   ipconfig / flushdns

7. **The DHCP server has just gone down and network users are complaining that they have no internet. Is this the correct outcome of this service failing in a Windows environment?**

    a.   Yes. Without this service, network users will only have limited connectivity to local resources. Users' machines will have self-configured APIPA addresses until the problem is resolved.

    b.   No. The DNS service is sufficient on its own for internet access.

8. A network host has been assigned the address 169.254.0.3. This address is an example of which of the following IP address types?

    a. APIPA

    b. MAC

    c. Public

    d. Personal

9. A technician notices that the link light on a physical adapter does not light up and is showing amber. After testing the device on a different RJ-45 port, the device connects successfully, and the light is green. Which of the following is causing this issue?

    a. Bad wiring

    b. Interference

    c. RFI

    d. Impedance

10. After several attempts, the network administrator is unable to get the network's DNS server's record (that is, domain name/IP statistics) from a host machine. Ipconfig also shows an error with the DNS server. This connectivity issue is network-wide. What should the administrator do next?

    a. Check another host

    b. Check the DNS server's settings and role

    c. Wait for the issue to be resolved, as it will, over time

    d. Type in netstat

11. A user has been having issues uploading files to the internal FTP server. The administrator checks the firewall to ensure ports for file transfer are not blocked. What ports will they be checking?

    a. 20 and 21

    b. 22 and 53

    c. 443 and 110

    d. 20 and 22

12. A network administrator is troubleshooting UDP transmissions. Which term correctly describes UDP?

    a. Connection-oriented

    b. Guaranteed

    c. Connectionless

    d. Reliable

13. **A network administrator is troubleshooting TCP transmissions. Which term correctly describes TCP?**

    a. Connection-oriented

    b. Connectionless

    c. Unreliable

    d. Best-effort delivery

14. **An administrator needs to troubleshoot a recently installed network card. Using the command prompt, they begin to ping the local loopback address. Which of the following addresses is the correct IPv4 loopback address?**

    a. 10.0.0.1

    b. 127.0.0.1

    c. 169.254.0.1

    d. 192.168.1.1

Exam 1 answers

Networking fundamentals

1. d
2. a
3. b
4. d
5. c
6. d
7. d
8. b
9. c
10. c
11. b
12. a
13. d
14. b

15. d
16. b

Networking implementations

1. d
2. c
3. c
4. b
5. c
6. a
7. c
8. c
9. b
10. True
11. a
12. c
13. c
14. a

Network operations

1. a
2. b
3. c
4. a
5. c
6. a
7. b
8. d
9. d
10. c
11. a

Network security

1. d
2. c

3. c
4. c
5. c
6. a
7. b
8. c
9. d

Network troubleshooting

1. d
2. b
3. a
4. a
5. b
6. d
7. d
8. d
9. a
10. c
11. a
12. d
13. a
14. a

Exam 2 answers

Networking fundamentals

1. b
2. b
3. b
4. c
5. b
6. b
7. d

8. c

9. b

10. True

11. a, b, c, h

12. c

13. b, d, e

14. True

15. b

16. b

Networking implementations

1. False

2. c

3. d

4. c

5. c

6. a

7. a

8. b

9. c

10. a

11. d

12. c

13. b

14. c

Network operations

1. b

2. c

3. b

4. a

5. a

6. b

7. c

8. a
9. c and d
10. b
11. d

Network security

1. c
2. c
3. b
4. c
5. a
6. a
7. f
8. True
9. b

Network troubleshooting

1. a
2. b
3. a
4. c
5. a
6. d
7. a
8. a
9. a
10. b
11. a
12. c
13. a
14. b

Join our book's Discord space

Join the book's Discord Workspace for Latest updates, Offers, Tech happenings around the world, New Release and Sessions with the Authors:

https://discord.bpbonline.com

APPENDIX

Network+ (N10-009) Certification Exam Objectives

1.0 Networking concepts

1.1 Explain concepts related to the **Open Systems Interconnection** (**OSI**) reference model.

1.2 Compare and contrast networking appliances, applications, and functions.

1.3 Summarize cloud concepts and connectivity options.

1.4 Explain common networking ports, protocols, services, and traffic types.

1.5 Compare and contrast transmission media and transceivers.

1.6 Compare and contrast network topologies, architectures, and types.

1.7 Given a scenario, use appropriate IPv4 network addressing.

1.8 Summarize evolving use cases for modern network environments.

2.0 Network implementation

2.1 Explain characteristics of routing technologies.

2.2 Given a scenario, configure switching technologies and features.

2.3 Given a scenario, select and configure wireless devices and technologies.

2.4 Explain important factors of physical installations.

3.0 Network operations

3.1 Explain the purpose of organizational processes and procedures.

3.2 Given a scenario, use network monitoring technologies.

3.3 Explain **disaster recovery (DR)** concepts.

3.4 Given a scenario, implement IPv4 and IPv6 network services.

3.5 Compare and contrast network access and management methods.

4.0 Network security

4.1 Explain the importance of basic network security concepts.

4.2 Summarize various types of attacks and their impact to the network.

4.3 Given a scenario, apply network security features, defense techniques, and solutions.

5.0 Network troubleshooting

5.1 Explain the troubleshooting methodology.

5.2 Given a scenario, troubleshoot common cabling and physical interface issues.

5.3 Given a scenario, troubleshoot common issues with network services.

5.4 Given a scenario, troubleshoot common performance issues.

5.4 Given a scenario, troubleshoot common performance issues.

5.5 Given a scenario, use the appropriate tool or protocol to solve networking issues.

Join our book's Discord space

Join the book's Discord Workspace for Latest updates, Offers, Tech happenings around the world, New Release and Sessions with the Authors:

https://discord.bpbonline.com

Index

www.ingramcontent.com/pod-product-compliance
Lightning Source LLC
Chambersburg PA
CBHW061737210326

41599CB00034B/6709